P9-ECS-827

CALIFORNIA GUN LAWS

A guide to state and federal firearm regulations

COLDAW
PUBLISHING

COLDAW
PUBLISHING

©2017 Coldaw Publishing - C.D. Michel
All rights reserved

No part of the original content of this book may be reproduced or
transmitted in any form or by any means now known
or which will become known,
without written permission from the publisher.
Permission is granted for reviewers and others to quote
brief passages for use in newspapers, periodicals,
or broadcasts provided credit is given to: California Gun Laws,
published by Coldaw Publishing. For information contact:

COLDAW PUBLISHING
C. D. Michel
180 E. Ocean Blvd., Suite 200
Long Beach, CA 90802
562-216-4444 Office ~ 562-216-4445 Fax
www.CalGunLawsBook.com
www.MichelLawyers.com

Michel & Associates, P.C.
Environmental ~ Land Use ~ Firearms ~ Employment Law
Civil Litigation ~ Criminal Defense

Images Provided Courtesy Of
The National Rifle Association of America, NRA National Firearms Museum,
NRA Firearms Sourcebook, NRA Shooting Illustrated, Defense Distributed,
iStock, Bigstock & Bruce Krell, PhD

Cover Design: Jason O. Crye
Project Manager/Editing/Layout: Grace Wu
ISBN: 978-0-9884602-4-9
Library of Congress Control Number: 2017960166

ATTENTION
Contact the publisher for information on quantity discounts!

Printed and bound in the United States of America
at Color House Graphics, Grand Rapids, Michigan

Fifth Edition

A SUMMARY OF THE PAST YEAR AND WHAT'S NEW IN THE FIFTH EDITION

It's been an odd year for firearm rights advocates. And things just get tougher in California.

In November 2016, on the same day Californians approved Proposition 63 ("Prop. 63"), voters across the nation elected Donald Trump as the 45th president of the United States. In December, we dealt with the deceptively timed regulations for "large-capacity" magazines and "assault weapons." The California Department of Justice ("DOJ") pulled the regulations for "large-capacity" magazines, apparently based on a potential rejection by the California Office of Administrative Law ("OAL"), and these regulations never reared their heads again. But we ended up seeing the "assault weapon" regulations proposed two more times before becoming California law.

We saw Neil Gorsuch nominated and appointed to the United States Supreme Court. While the Supreme Court declined to review our *Peruta* case, Justice Gorsuch joined in a dissent to that decision and signaled an openness for Second Amendment cases to come.

In January, a number of Prop 63 and legislative restrictions went into effect. Most notable were the "assault weapon" restrictions and the problems with registration (or more accurately put, the lack of any registration scheme due to the DOJ's delay in implementing regulations).

July 1st was the deadline for the DOJ to have in place regulations for certain ammunition sellers to get "ammunition vendor licenses" so that they can stay in business after January 1, 2018 (the date when ammunition vendor licenses become required). The DOJ proposed flawed regulations after the July 1st deadline, and representatives from the CRPA and NRA pointed out these flaws in writing and during the public hearing on these regulations. As of the writing of this book, the regulations still have not been submitted to the OAL for final review and publication. It remains to be seen whether the regulations will become law before ammunition vendor licenses are required.

Also in July, Governor Brown signed a bill extending the "assault weapon" registration deadline from December 31, 2017 to June 30, 2018 as a result of the DOJ's failure to get the "assault weapon" regulations straight and the lack of money to implement the registration system sooner. That same bill extended the restriction for firearm possession to those with an outstanding warrant for any felony and misdemeanor firearm restrictions located in Penal Code section 29800 and 29805. And in July, the DOJ received the $2,588,000 it sought for additional employees and services to process new "assault weapon" registrations, along with the $1,368,000 it requested for additional employees to implement the provisions of the 2016 "Ghost Gun" bill (AB 857).

It took the DOJ until the end of July 2017 to get the OAL to approve its proposed regulations for "assault weapon" regulations. Soon after, our office filed a lawsuit on behalf of the NRA, arguing that these regulations violate California's Administrative Procedures Act because they were enacted without appropriate legislative authority and without any input from members of the public.

In the fall of 2017, the legislative session ended and the gun-ban lobby once again pushed a variety of anti-gun bills through the California Legislature. More than a dozen gun-related bills passed and were sent to Governor Jerry Brown for approval. Governor Brown signed all of them except one (SB 464), which he vetoed after gun-rights groups pointed out that it places excessive requirements on firearms dealers. Among the bills that he signed are Assembly Bill ("AB") 7, which extends the restriction on carrying long guns so that it also applies to a public place or a public street in a prohibited area of an unincorporated area of a county and AB 424, which removes the authority of school officials to authorize individuals to possess a firearm in a school zone.

This Fifth Edition will discuss all the gun-related bills that were signed into law in 2017 and explain how they affect you. The laws passed during the 2017 legislative session, along with some other laws that were passed in 2016, take effect on January 1, 2018. These laws are summarized in the "New Laws for 2018" section.

For the Fifth Edition, we have revised, updated, and expanded the Fourth Edition to reflect the new changes the new laws will make over the coming year, particularly the DOJ's new "assault weapon" regulations. The Fifth Edition guides you through the new process for "assault weapon" registration. And, we have added entirely new sections that discuss the legality of gun trusts and "bump stocks."

Contents

TABLES...xxv

ACKNOWLEDGMENTS...xxix

DEDICATION...xxxi

DISCLAIMER...xxxiii

INTRODUCTION...xxxvii

I.   GUN SAFETY IS YOUR RESPONSIBILITY.........................xxxvii

II.   HOW TO USE THIS BOOK xxxviii

      A.   The Materials Posted at www.CalGunLawsBook.com and
           www.crpa.org Complement This Book xxxix

      B.   Symbols Used Throughout This Book.......................................xl

III. HOW TO READ LAWS AND DETERMINE WHETHER
      THEY APPLY..xl

      A.   Federal Laws, State Laws, and Local Laws..............................xl

      B.   Statutory Interpretation Techniques..xli

      C.   Determining Which Statute Controls When There
           Are Duplicate Laws for the Same Crime.................................xli

      D.   How to Read Court Opinions...xliii

IV.   HOW TO JUDGE A LAWYER...xliv

ABBREVIATIONS USED THROUGHOUT THIS BOOK........................xlv

NEW LAWS FOR 2018..xlvii

CHAPTER 1: THE CALIFORNIA REGULATORY ENVIRONMENT.....................1

I.   THE UGLY PROCESS OF GUN LAW POLITICS....................................1

      A.   The Legislative Process...1

      B.   Local Laws...3

      C.   The Initiative Process 3

      D.   The Gun Ban Lobby's "Feel Good" Laws..................................4

      E.   Law Enforcement's Overaggressive Enforcement.....................5

      F.   The Pro-Gun Lobby..5

           1.   The National Rifle Association and The California
                Rifle and Pistol Association..6

      G.   Gun Violence Research 6

II.   THE RIGHT TO KEEP AND BEAR ARMS AND TO
      SELF-DEFENSE... 9

A. The United States and California Constitutions.................................9

B. Primary Issues Being Addressed in Current Second
   Amendment Litigation...10

III. THE PREEMPTION DOCTRINE..12

A. Federal Preemption Doctrine...12

B. California Preemption Doctrine...13

IV. THE CALIFORNIA LEGAL SCHEME...15

A. The Dangerous Weapons Control Act (DWCA)............................15

B. Confusion Runs Rampant...15

C. 2012 Reorganization of the Dangerous Weapons
   Control Act..17

D. "Gray Areas" and Test Cases...18

E. Government Bias in Applying Gun Laws.......................................19

CHAPTER 2: WHAT IS LEGALLY CONSIDERED A "FIREARM"
            AND "AMMUNITION"?...21

I. "FIREARM" DEFINITIONS...21

A. Federal Law "Firearm" Definitions..21

   1. The Gun Control Act 22

   2. The National Firearms Act 22

   3. What Is a Frame or Receiver Under Federal Law? 24

   4. Are Precursor (80%) Receivers "Firearms"?............................25

   5. Are Non-Functioning Firearms "Firearms"?..............................25

B. California Law "Firearm" Definitions 25

   1. History of California's "Firearm" Definition................................26

   2. When Is a Frame or Receiver Considered a
      "Firearm"?...27

   3. What is a Frame or Receiver under California Law? 27

   4. Are Non-functioning Firearms "Firearms"? 28

   5. Are Precursor (80%) Receivers "Firearms"
      Under California Law?...29

II. FIREARM SUBGROUP DEFINITIONS..29

A. "Handguns"...29

   1. Pistols...30

   2. Revolvers...31

B. "Rifles," "Shotguns," and "Long Guns"..32

   1. Rifles...32

   2. Shotguns...33

3. Long Guns...33

C. Other "Firearms"..35

D. Definition of "Weapon"..35

E. "Antique Firearms"...36

    1. Federal Law Definitions......................................36

       a. The Gun Control Act 36

       b. The National Firearms Act 38

    2. California Law Definition.....................................39

F. "Curios or Relics" 39

III. IS THAT THING CONSIDERED A "FIREARM"?.........................40

A. Bang Sticks/Shark Killers..41

B. Coyote Booby Traps...42

C. Potato Guns a.k.a. "Spud Guns"................................42

D. Flare Guns With Metal Inserts....................................43

E. 37mm Flare Launchers 44

F. Explosive-Powered Nail Guns....................................44

G. Items Meeting the "Firearm" Definition, but Expressly Exempted...45

IV. "AMMUNITION"...45

A. Federal Law "Ammunition" Definition..........................45

B. California Law "Ammunition" Definitions......................46

    1. Deactivated Ammunition.....................................47

C. "Ammunition" Parts...48

CHAPTER 3: WHO CAN OWN AND POSSESS FIREARMS AND AMMUNITION?............................51

I. WHAT DOES "POSSESSION" MEAN?......................................52

II. WHAT DOES "OWN" MEAN?..53

III. DETERMINING WHEN FIREARM POSSESSION PROHIBITIONS APPLY DURING FIREARM PURCHASES................................53

IV. CALIFORNIA'S ARMED PROHIBITED PERSON SYSTEM (APPS) AND FIREARM DENIALS REPORTED TO LAW ENFORCEMENT..54

V. FIREARM AND AMMUNITION POSSESSION RESTRICTIONS FOR MINORS (UNDER AGE 18)..56

A. Shotguns and Rifles..56

B. Handguns..56

C. Ammunition 57

D. Exemption to Federal Restriction on Handguns and "Handgun Ammunition"..58

VI. CRIMINAL CONVICTIONS RESULTING IN LOSS OF FIREARM POSSESSION RIGHTS..60

A. Federal Restrictions for Certain State or Federal Convictions..60

B. California Restrictions for Felony Convictions.....................................61

D. California Convictions of Offenses Listed in Penal Code Section 23515(a), (b), and (d), or Two or More Convictions Under Penal Code Section 417(a)(2) Resulting in a Lifetime Restriction.................63

E. California Restrictions for Certain Misdemeanor Convictions..............64

   1. Misdemeanor Convictions Resulting in a Ten-Year Restriction 64

   2. Misdemeanor Convictions Resulting in a Five-Year Restriction...69

F. Federal Restrictions for a Misdemeanor Crime of Domestic Violence (MCDV)...69

   1. California Offenses that May Be a Misdemeanor Crime of Domestic Violence 70

      a. Injuring a Spouse, Cohabitant, Fiancé, Etc.....................70

      b. Battery Against a Spouse, Cohabitant, Fiancé, Etc................71

   2. Other California Crimes That May Be Considered a Misdemeanor Crime of Domestic Violence 73

G. Juvenile Offenses 73

H. Persons on Probation or Parole...75

I. Notice Required..76

J. Unlawful Detainer Actions..77

VII. APPLICATION OF EX POST FACTO PROHIBITIONS ON FIREARM POSSESSION...78

A. The Effect of a California Conviction in Other States 78

VIII. POSSESSING A FIREARM WHILE BEING A "FUGITIVE FROM JUSTICE" AND THE CALIFORNIA RESTRICTION FOR POSSESSING A FIREARM WHILE HAVING AN OUTSTANDING WARRANT FOR CERTAIN OFFENSES.........................79

A. Federal Law for Firearm Prohibitions Based on "Fugitive from Justice" Status...79

B. California Law for Firearm Prohibitions Based on an Outstanding Warrant for a Felony or for Certain Misdemeanors.............................80

IX. DRUG ADDICTION FIREARM POSSESSION PROHIBITIONS................81

A. Federal Restrictions for Drug Addiction and Use..............................81

    B. California Restrictions for Drug Addiction...83

X.   MENTAL HEALTH RELATED FIREARM RESTRICTIONS.......................84

    A. Federal Mental Health Restrictions...85

        1. California Commitments Resulting in Federal Restrictions...........86

    B. Dangerous Inpatients...86

    C. Communicating Threats to a Psychotherapist................................86

    D. Mental Disorders, Illnesses, or Disordered Sex Offenders.................87

    E. Not Guilty by Reason of Insanity..87

    F. Incompetence to Stand Trial...87

    G. Individuals Under Conservatorship 88

    H. Dangerous or Gravely Disabled Persons 88

    I. Those Committed to Intensive Treatment.......................................89

XI.   RESTRAINING ORDERS AND FIREARM POSSESSION
    RESTRICTIONS...90

    A. Federal Domestic Violence Restraining Orders.............................90

    B. California Law Restrictions..91

        1. "Gun Violence Restraining Orders" 92

XII.   EXCEPTIONS FOR PROHIBITED PERSONS POSSESSING
    FIREARMS...95

    A. Self-Defense...95

    B. Momentary Possession..98

    C. Justifiable Possession..98

XIII.   OTHER FEDERAL LAW FIREARM POSSESSION RESTRICTIONS........99

    A. Aliens...99

    B. Dishonorable Discharge From the Armed Forces..........................101

    C. Renouncing United States Citizenship..101

    D. Federal Restrictions Against Indicted Persons Receiving
       Firearms...101

XIV. Dealer's Record of Sale (DROS) Delays...102

XV   ACQUIRING YOUR CRIMINAL RECORDS AND DETERMINING
    YOUR ELIGIBILITY TO POSSESS FIREARMS.....................................104

    A. Obtaining Your Criminal History..104

    B. Determining Your Firearm Eligibility 105

CHAPTER 4: OBTAINING FIREARMS AND AMMUNITION............................**107**

I.   PURCHASING FIREARMS FROM A LICENSED DEALER....................108

    A. Sale Requirements for All Firearms (Both Handguns
       and Long Guns)...108

1. Federal Form 4473 Requirements...108
2. California Dealer's Record of Sale (DROS) Form.......................109
3. Proof of Identity, Age, and Address...110
   a. Federal Identification Requirements......................................110
   b. California Identification Requirements...................................112
   c. Special Circumstances..113
   i. Members of the Military Stationed in California....................113
   ii. Non-Citizens (Aliens)..113
   iii. Dual Residents..114
   d. Dealer Record of Sales Fees...115
4. Background Checks...115
5. Registration at Time of Purchase...116
   a. Voluntary Registration..116
   b. Confusion Regarding the Requirement to
      Register Firearms After January 1, 2014...............................117
6. Waiting Period...117
7. Required Locking Devices and Warnings....................................119
8. Firearm Safety Certificate...120
   a. "Firearm Safety" Certificate Exemptions...............................121
   b. Firearm Safe-Handling Demonstration..................................130
B. Additional Handgun Purchase Requirements 132
   1. Only One Handgun Purchase Every 30 Days............................132
   2. Proof of Residency...133

II. PRIVATE PARTY FIREARM TRANSFERS.....................................137
III. DEALER LICENSE REQUIREMENTS AND SELLING
     YOUR FIREARMS 140
     A. Federal Law..140
     B. California Law...141
        1. Exceptions...142
IV. INTERSTATE FIREARM PURCHASES AND TRANSFERS...................142
     A. Transfers From Out-of-State Dealers..142
     B. Interstate Private Party Transfers..144
        1. Shipping Firearms..145
     C. Exemptions to California's Restriction on Out-of-State Transfers 146
V.   LOANING FIREARMS TO ADULTS..153
VI. TRANSFERRING AND LOANING FIREARMS TO YOUNG PEOPLE.....158
     A. Dealer Sales..158

1. Federal Law..158

2. California Law..158

B. Those Under Age 18...158

VII. EXCEPTIONS TO TRANSFERRING FIREARMS THROUGH A
FEDERAL FIREARMS LICENSEE IN CALIFORNIA...............................160

A. Federal Law..160

B. California Law...161

1. Intra-Family Transactions..161

a. Change in Law for Long Guns...161

2. Transfers Between Spouses or Domestic Partners....................162

a. Firearms and Divorce 163

3. "Operation of Law" Transfers Other than Transfers
Between Spouses Involving Transmutation of Property..............163

4. Gun Trusts..165

a. NFA Trusts..165

b. Non-NFA Gun Trusts in California..166

i. California Firearm Transfer Laws in the Context
of Gun Trusts...166

ii. Relevant Exceptions to Having to Process
Firearm Transfers Through a Licensed Firearms
Dealer, As Applied to Non-NFA Gun Trusts.........................168

Intra-Familial Transfers...168

Transfers of Firearms Between Spouses.............................168

Taking Title by Operation of Law...169

Transfers of Long Guns to Minors by Immediate
Family Members...170

"Antique Firearms"..170

iii. Limitation of Non-NFA Gun Trusts: Firearms
Cannot be Shared Amongst Trustees, So California
Laws on Firearm Loaning Must be Followed if
Trustees Want to "Share" Firearms......................................170

iv. Limitations of Non-NFA Gun Trusts as Applied to
"Assault Weapons"/.50 BMG Rifles and "Large-
Capacity Magazines"...171

"Assault Weapons" and .50 BMG Rifles...............................171

"Large-Capacity Magazines" 171

5. Transfers to Those With an Entertainment Firearm
Permit (EFP)..172

6. Acquiring Antiques and "Curio or Relic" Firearms......................172

a.   Antique Firearms..172

b.   "Curio or Relic" Firearms..172

7.   Nonprofit Auction of Non-Handguns..175

8.   "Gun Buybacks"..176

VIII.   BUILDING YOUR OWN FIREARM..177

A.   Ways to Build Your Own Firearm..178

1.   Creating a Firearm From a Prefabricated Frame or Receiver......178

2.   Creating a Firearm From an 80% Receiver................................178

3.   "Build Parties"...179

4   3D Printing...180

B.   Registration Requirements for Manufacturing or
Assembling Your Own Firearm 181

1.   Obtaining Serial Numbers or Identification Marks
Before Assembling or Manufacturing a Firearm.........................181

2.   Obtaining a Serial Number or Identification Mark for
Firearm Owned After July 1, 2018 That Does Not
Bear a Serial Number Assigned to It..183

3.   Exemptions 183

IX.   COMING INTO CALIFORNIA WITH FIREARMS...........................184

A.   Visiting California..184

B.   Moving Into California...185

X.   FIREARM STORAGE...187

A.   Criminal Storage in the First, Second, and Third Degree
for Loaded Firearms..187

B.   Storage of Handguns and Any Firearm......................................188

C.   Exceptions to Criminal Storage in the First, Second, and
Third Degree and Storage of Handguns or Any Firearms.............188

D.   Residing With a Person Who Is Prohibited from
Possessing, Receiving, Owning, or Purchasing Firearms.............189

E.   Storage of Handgun in Unattended Vehicle................................190

1.   Storage of Lawfully-Obtained "Unsafe" Handgun in
Unattended Vehicle by Certain Law Enforcement
Officers...191

F.   Local Storage Laws 193

G.   Civil Penalties for Community Care Facilities, Residential
Care Facilities, Residential Care Facilities for the Elderly,
Family Care Homes, and Day Care Centers 193

XI.   FALSE REPORTS OF LOST OR STOLEN FIREARMS...............196

XII.   REPORTING LOST OR STOLEN FIREARMS 196

XIII. ACQUIRING AMMUNITION 197

A. Assembly Bill 962 and Similar Ammunition Regulation Efforts...........198

B. Ammunition Sales & Transfers..199

1. Requirement that Ammunition Sales Must Be
Conducted Through a Licensed Ammunition Vendor 199

2. Face-to-Face Transaction Requirement.....................................200

3. Exceptions to the Requirement that Ammunition Sales
Must Be Conducted Through a Licensed Ammunition
Vendor and Face-to-Face Requirement......................................201

4. Recording of Ammunition Purchaser or Transferee
Information 202

5. Authorization to Purchase Ammunition 203

C. Restriction on California Resident's Bringing or
Transporting Ammunition Into California 207

**CHAPTER 5: CARRYING FIREARMS OPENLY,
CONCEALED, AND/OR LOADED..209**

I. WHAT DOES "CARRY" MEAN?..209

II. WHAT DOES "IN A VEHICLE," "ON," OR "UPON THE
PERSON" MEAN? 210

III. CONCEALED CARRY LAW..211

A. Carrying "Concealed" 211

B. What Does "Concealed" Mean?...213

IV. LOADED CARRY LAW...214

A. Loaded Firearm Restrictions 214

B. What Does "Loaded" Mean?...217

1. General Definition of "Loaded"..217

2. "Loaded" While Committing a Felony or in Sensitive Places.......219

3. Fish and Game's Definition of "Loaded" 219

V. OPEN CARRY OF HANDGUNS RESTRICTION...................................220

VI. RESTRICTION ON CARRYING FIREARMS OTHER THAN
HANDGUNS 222

A. "Firearm That Is Not a Handgun"...222

B. Penalties for Unlawful Carry of Non-Handguns............................223

VII. PLACES WHERE CARRY RESTRICTIONS APPLY............................224

A. What Does "Public Place" Mean? 225

B. What Does "Public Street" Mean? 227

**CHAPTER 6: FIREARM CARRY RESTRICTION EXEMPTIONS
          AND TRANSPORTING FIREARMS.......................................229**

I.   HOW TO USE THIS SECTION..229

II.   EXEMPTIONS TO THE GENERAL CARRY RESTRICTIONS
       IN NON-PUBLIC PLACES: RESIDENCES, PRIVATE
       PROPERTY, AND PRIVATE PLACES OF BUSINESS............................230

       A. Exemptions for Carrying Loaded Firearms and Openly
           Carrying Unloaded Handguns..230

       B. Exemptions for Carrying a Concealed Handgun.....................231

       C. Exemptions for Carrying "Firearms That Are Not Handguns"............231

III.   EXEMPTIONS TO THE GENERAL CARRY RESTRICTIONS
       IN PUBLIC PLACES...232

       A. Temporary Residences and Campsites................................232

       B. Business or Other Privately Owned or Possessed
           Property Open to the Public..233

       C. Vehicle or Boat as a Residence...234

       D. Vehicle or Boat as a Place of Business................................235

       E. Motor Vehicles 235

           1. Locked Container Requirement....................................236

           2. "Lawful Purpose" Requirement....................................237

           3. Transporting "Assault Weapons" and .50 BMG Rifles
               in Motor Vehicles..238

       F. Motorcycles and Bicycles..238

       G. Boats...239

       H. Being in "Grave Danger"...239

           1. Protected by a Restraining Order................................239

           2. Not Protected by a Restraining Order.........................240

IV.   CARRYING WHILE HUNTING OR FISHING.......................................240

V.   ADDITIONAL EXEMPTIONS TO THE GENERAL CARRY
       RESTRICTIONS 241

       A. Exemptions for Carrying Concealed Handguns.....................241

           1.   Conditional Exemptions for Carrying Concealed Handguns.......242

           2. "Other Exemptions" for Carrying Concealed Handguns............244

       B. Exemptions for Carrying Loaded Firearms............................244

       C. Exemptions to the Restriction on Openly Carrying
           Handguns in Public 246

       D. Exemptions to Restriction on Carrying "Firearms That Are
           Not Handguns" 248

           1. "Locked Container" or "Encased"................................249

2. Other Exemptions to the Restriction on Carrying
"Firearms That Are Not Handguns" 249

VI. LICENSES TO CARRY A LOADED HANDGUN.......................................253

A. Criteria for Issuance...255

1. "Good Cause"...256

2. "Good Moral Character"..256

3. Residency 257

4. Training Course..257

B. Issuing Authorities' Mandatory Written Policy.........................258

C. Application Process and Fees...258

D. License Revocation and Moving Out of the Jurisdiction.....................260

E. License Restrictions...260

F. Form of Physical License...260

G. License Amendments..261

VII. EXEMPTIONS FOR ACTIVE & RETIRED PEACE OFFICERS..............262

A. Concealed and Loaded Restrictions 262

1. Current Law Enforcement Officers....................................262

a. California Peace Officers..262

b. Current Reserve Peace Officers..................................263

c. Other Current Officers 263

d. Current Federal and Out-of-State Officers..................263

2. Retired Law Enforcement 264

a. Retired California Peace Officers 264

b. Retired Reserve California Peace Officers..................266

c. Retired Federal Peace Officers 267

B. Law Enforcement Officers Safety Act (LEOSA/H.R. 218) 267

1. QLEO Definition and ID Requirements..............................268

2. QRLEO Definition and ID Requirements............................268

3. LEOSA and the California Department of Justice...........................271

4. Limits on LEOSA and the Types of Firearms One May Carry......272

5. LEOSA and Reserve Officers (Active and Retired)....................273

VIII. TRANSPORTATION OF FIREARMS IN PUBLIC
TRANSPORTATION OR ACROSS STATE LINES..............................274

A. Transporting Firearms on Airplanes...274

B. Transporting on a Bus or Other Public Transportation.......................276

C. Transporting Firearms Across State Lines................................276

IX.   SUGGESTIONS ON HOW TO CARRY FIREARMS IN COMPLIANCE WITH CALIFORNIA FIREARMS LAWS.........................278

X.   CARRY EXEMPTIONS TABLE..280

CHAPTER 7:   PLACES WHERE FIREARM POSSESSION IS PROHIBITED AND FIREARM USE IS RESTRICTED...........305

I.   FIREARM POSSESSION IN GOVERNMENT BUILDINGS....................306

    A. Federal Law...306

    B. California Law...306

II.   FIREARM POSSESSION IN "SCHOOL ZONES"................................308

    A. Federal Law...309

    B. California Law 310

    C. California and Federal Discharge Restrictions....................312

III.   AMMUNITION & WEAPON POSSESSION ON "SCHOOL GROUNDS"...313

IV.   FIREARM POSSESSION IN AIRPORTS, ON AIRPLANES, AND ON COMMON CARRIERS..................................314

    A. Possession in Airport "Sterile Areas"........................314

        1. Federal Law..314

        2. California Law..315

    B. Possession on Commercial Airplanes........................316

    C. Possession on Amtrak Trains.................................316

    D. Possession on Greyhound Buses.............................317

    E. Possession on All Other Common Carriers.....................317

    F. Possession in Harbors & Ports...............................317

    G. Possession in "Sterile Area" of Public Transportation Facility 318

V.   FIREARM POSSESSION IN PARKS, FORESTS, AND REFUGES.........319

    A. Federal Lands...319

        1. National Parks and Wildlife Refuges.....................319

        2. National Forests..320

        3. Bureau of Land Management (BLM) and Other Federally Protected Areas.................................321

        4. United States Army Corps of Engineers (USACE) Managed Land..321

    B. California State Lands.......................................322

        1. Other Parks...323

VI.   FIREARM POSSESSION IN UNITED STATES AND INTERNATIONAL WATERS..323

VII. FIREARM POSSESSION AT PROTEST EVENTS..............................325

VIII. FIREARM POSSESSION AND POLITICIANS..326

IX. OTHER RESTRICTED PLACES UNDER CALIFORNIA LAW................326

    A. Gun Shows...326

    B. Polling Places...326

    C. Playgrounds and Youth Centers...327

X. RESTRICTING FIREARM POSSESSION BY PRIVATE
    BUSINESSES 327

XI. GENERAL FIREARM DISCHARGE RESTRICTIONS..........................327

XII. SHOOTING RANGE USE RESTRICTIONS...330

XIII. SUGGESTIONS FOR SHOOTING IN PUBLIC.....................................330

**CHAPTER 8: REGULATION OF "ASSAULT WEAPONS" AND
    .50 BMG RIFLES..333**

I. Roberti-Roos Assault Weapons Control ACT (AWCA) of 1989.............334

    A. Passing the "Assault Weapon" Ban...334

II. THE "ASSAULT WEAPON" BAN'S EVOLUTION..................................338

    A. The Original 1989 AWCA Ban...338

    B. 1991 Amendment...339

    C. SKS With Detachable Magazine...341

    D. *Kasler* and "Category 2 Assault Weapons"..................................343

    E. SB 23: Old Definition of "Category 3 Assault Weapons"................344

    F. SB 23: Expanding Peace Officer Exceptions 344

    G. *Silveira:* Assault Weapons and "Equal Protection".......................345

    H. *Hunt:* Clarifying Vague & Ambiguous Terms Under SB 23..............347

    I. *Harrott* and "Off-List Lower" Receivers..349

    J. The DOJ's Attempts to Attack "Bullet Button" Firearms.................351

    K. AB 2728: Removing the Add-On Provision and Civil
       Compromise for "Assault Weapon" Possession.............................354

    L. Second Amendment Challenges to "Assault Weapons"
       Bans Post-*Heller* 355

    M. Further Attempts by the California Legislature to Classify
       More Firearms as "Assault Weapons" 357

    N. AB 1135 and SB 808: 2017 Change to the Definition of
       "Assault Weapons"..358

III. "ASSAULT WEAPON" DEFINED...359

    A. Category 1 "Assault Weapons"...359

    B. Category 2 "Assault Weapons"...360

C. Category 3 "Assault Weapons"..363

　　1. AB 1135/SB 880 and the DOJ's Regulations for Shotguns
　　　　with Ability to Accept a Detachable Magazine............................364

　　2. Old Category 3 – Rifles..364

　　3. Old Category 3 – Pistols...365

　　4. Old Category 3 – Shotguns..365

　　5. Old Category 3 Definitions for Pre-2017 "Assault Weapons".......366

D. Making Category 3 "Assault Weapons" Comply With the
　　Old Definition of "Assault Weapon"..367

　　1. Troublesome Magazine Locks – Pushing the Law Too Far.........369

E. New Definition of Category 3 "Assault Weapons"..............................370

　　1. Rifles that Are Now Considered "Assault Weapons" as a
　　　　Result of the New Change in Law on January 1, 2017................370

　　2. Pistols that Are Now Considered "Assault Weapons"
　　　　as a Result of the Change in Law on
　　　　January 1, 2017...370

　　3. Shotguns that Are Now Considered "Assault Weapons"
　　　　as a Result of the Change in Law on July 31, 2017...................371

　　4. History Behind the DOJ's New "Assault Weapon"
　　　　Regulations and Analysis of Some of the Definitions
　　　　Set Forth by the Regulations 371

　　　　a. The DOJ's Embattled Attempts to Implement Regulations
　　　　　　for the New Category 3 "Assault Weapons" 371

　　　　b. The New Definitions that the DOJ Added as Part of Its
　　　　　　2017 Regulations for "Assault Weapon" Registration
　　　　　　and Analysis of Some of Them 373

F. Making Newly-Designated Category 3 "Assault Weapons"
　　Compliant With California Law..383

　　1. Aftermarket Parts...383

　　2. Compliant Features...383

G. Possessing the Parts of an "Assault Weapon" 384

IV. .50 BMG RIFLES...385

V. "ASSAULT WEAPON" AND .50 BMG RIFLE USE
　　RESTRICTIONS..386

A. Grace Period for Newly-Designated "Assault Weapons" 387

B. Civil Compromise for Illegally Possessing an "Assault
　　Weapon" or .50 BMG Rifle 388

C. Infraction for First Violation of Possessing an
　　"Assault Weapon"..388

VI. EXCEPTIONS TO "ASSAULT WEAPON" AND .50 BMG
RIFLE LAWS..389

A. Law Enforcement and Other Government Agencies.............................389

B. Peace Officers and Federal Law Enforcement Acquiring
"Assault Weapons" and .50 BMG Rifles..390

C. Carrying "Assault Weapons" Under the Law Enforcement
Officer Safety Act (LEOSA)..391

D. Estate Executor and Inheritance..391

E. Loaning and Returning an "Assault Weapon" or
.50 BMG Rifle...392

F. Nonresident Possession at Match or Competition.............................392

G. California Department of Justice Permits 393

H. "Licensed Gun Dealer" Exceptions...394

   1. Service or Repair...394

   2. Other Special Allowances...395

VII. ACQUIRING NEW "ASSAULT WEAPONS" OR .50
BMG RIFLES...395

A. Registration...395

   1. Firearms that the DOJ Will Not Register as "Assault
Weapons" Under the New Registration Scheme for
Newly-Defined Category 3 "Assault Weapons".............................399

   2. The DOJ's Requirements for Registering Firearms
Manufactured by an Unlicensed Subject (FMBUS)....................399

   3. Age Requirement to Register and Possess "Assault
Weapons"...401

   4. The Requirement to Create a California Firearms
Application Reporting System ("CFARS") Account and
Enter Your Personal Information...401

   5. Joint Registration of Newly-Designated Category 3
"Assault Weapons"...402

   6. Firearm Information and Photographs That Need to
be Submitted for Registration..404

   7. Fees Required for Registration..405

   8. Processing of Applications..406

   9. Post-Registration Modification of "Bullet Buttons" of
Registered Assault Weapons Is Prohibited...............................406

   10. Voluntary Deregistration...407

B. Alternatives to Registration...407

VIII. MOVING INTO CALIFORNIA WITH AN "ASSAULT
WEAPON" OR .50 BMG RIFLE..408

IX. LAWFULLY USING "ASSAULT WEAPONS" AND
.50 BMG RIFLES...408

    A. Transporting Registered "Assault Weapons" and .50
BMG Rifles...409

X. WHAT TO DO IF YOU THINK YOU HAVE AN "ASSAULT
WEAPON" OR .50 BMG RIFLE THAT YOU AREN'T SURE
IS LEGAL..409

    A. Determine if It *Is* an "Assault Weapon" or .50 BMG Rifle..................409

    B. Determine if Your "Assault Weapon" or .50 BMG Rifle
Was Registered or Can be Registered...409

    C. If Your "Assault Weapon" or .50 BMG Rifle Is Unregistered...............410

XI. "ASSAULT WEAPONS" LISTED BY NAME..410

    A. Combined Listing of Category 1 and Category 2
"Assault Weapons"...410

**CHAPTER 9: OTHER HEAVILY REGULATED
FIREARMS AND DEVICES..415**

I. "MACHINEGUNS"...415

    A. Prohibitions...417

    B. California Exceptions to "Machinegun" Restrictions.........................417

        1. Law Enforcement and Military...418

        2. Permits to Possess, Manufacture, and Transport........................418

    C. Licenses to Sell "Machineguns" 419

    D. "Bump Stocks" in the Context of Machinegun Restrictions...............419

        1. Bump Stocks Under Federal Law...420

        2. Bump Stocks Under California Law...420

II. "DESTRUCTIVE DEVICES"...423

    A. Permits..424

    B. Exceptions for Peace Officers, Firefighters, and Military..................438

    C. 37mm Flare Launchers v. 40mm Grenade Launchers and
22mm Grenade Launchers v. Flash Suppressors/Muzzle
Brakes..424

    D. Cannons..425

III. "GENERALLY PROHIBITED WEAPONS"..426

    A. "Cane Gun"..428

    B. "Wallet Gun"..428

    C. "Undetectable Firearm"...429

    D. Firearms Not "Immediately Recognizable" as Firearms....................429

    E. "Camouflaging Firearm Container"..430

    F. "Multiburst Trigger Activator"...430

1. Bump Stocks Should Not be Considered "Multiburst Trigger Activators" Under California Law 431

G. "Short-Barreled Shotguns" and "Short-Barreled Rifles"....................433

    1. "Short-Barreled Shotguns" 433

    2. "Short-Barreled Rifles" 435

    3. Possession of Parts Constituting "Short-Barreled Shotguns/Rifles"....................................437

    4. Pistol Stabilizing Braces 438

H. "Zip Gun"..440

I. "Unconventional Pistol"....................................441

J. "Large-Capacity Magazine" and "Large-Capacity Magazine Conversion Kits"....................................441

    1. Definition..441

    2. Restricted Activity for "Large-Capacity Magazines"....................444

    3. Restricted Activity for "Large-Capacity Magazine Conversion Kits"....................................446

    4. Local Restrictions on "Large-Capacity Magazines"....................448

IV. EXCEPTIONS TO CALIFORNIA LAW FOR "GENERALLY PROHIBITED WEAPONS," "LARGE-CAPACITY MAGAZINE CONVERSION KITS," AND THE BAN ON "LARGE-CAPACITY MAGAZINE" POSSESSION....................................451

A. "Antique Firearms"....................................451

B. "Curios or Relics"....................................451

C. "Any Other Weapons" 452

D. Historical Society, Museum, or Institutional Collection....................452

E. Media or Entertainment Events....................................452

F. People Who Sell Items to Historical Societies, Museums, Institutional Collections, or Entertainment Events....................453

G. Law Enforcement Firearm Purchases and Those Who Sell to Law Enforcement....................................453

H. Transporting Most "Generally Prohibited Weapons" to Law Enforcement....................................453

I. Forensic Laboratory....................................454

V. ADDITIONAL CALIFORNIA LAW EXCEPTIONS FOR "LARGE-CAPACITY MAGAZINE" AND "LARGE-CAPACITY MAGAZINE CONVERSION KIT" RESTRICTIONS....................454

A. Law Enforcement Agencies....................................455

B. Use During a Basic Training Course Prescribed by the Commission on Peace Officer Standards and Training....................455

C. Peace Officers....................................456

1. Federal Law Enforcement 456
2. Honorably Retired Sworn Peace Officers & Federal Law Enforcement Officers..456
D. Dealer Acquisition 457
E. Loans Between Individuals...457
F. Dealer or Gunsmith Loan for Maintenance/Repair............458
G. Importing or Selling Between Out-of-State Clients With a Permit..458
H. Entities Operating An Armored Vehicle Business..............458
I. Manufacturing "Large-Capacity Magazines" by Law Enforcement..459
J. Entertainment Industry Props.....................................459
K. Purchase by Special Weapons Permit Holder..................459
L. Receipt or Disposition by Trustees, Executors, or Administrators...460
M. Finding and Delivering "Large-Capacity Magazines" to Law Enforcement..460
N. Possessing the "Large-Capacity Magazine" Solely for Use with a Firearm that Is Lawfully-Obtained Prior to 2000 that Is Incompatible with Magazines Holding 10 or Fewer Rounds...460
VI. ADDITIONAL EXCEPTIONS TO CALIFORNIA LAW FOR RESTRICTIONS ON "SHORT-BARRELED SHOTGUNS/RIFLES".........461
A. Law Enforcement Agencies...461
B. Permit Authorization...461
VII. "SILENCERS"/"SOUND SUPPRESSORS"................................462
VIII. OBLITERATED OR COVERED SERIAL NUMBERS...................464
IX. "UNSAFE" HANDGUNS 466
A. "Microstamping"...468
1. "Smart Gun" Technology...469
B. Exceptions to the "Unsafe" Handgun Roster Requirement...............470
1. Law Enforcement and Military..................................470
2. Purchase of a State-Issued Handgun to Spouse or Domestic Partner of a Peace Officer Who Died in the Line of Duty 471
3. Private Party, Spousal, Operation of Law, Etc. Transfers...........471
4. Certain Peace Officers from Specified Agencies/ Departments..471
5. Testing and Prototypes...473

6. "Curios or Relics"..473

7. Repairs...473

8. Pistols Used as Props and Loans to Consultant-
Evaluators...473

9. Certain Handguns Exempt From the Roster Requirement..........474

X. AMMUNITION RESTRICTIONS...475

A. Ammunition With "Flechette Darts" and "Explosive Agents".............476

B. Armor-Piercing Handgun Ammunition..................................476

1. The Attempt to Ban "Green Tip" Ammunition...............................478

C. Tracer Ammunition...479

D. Lead-Based Ammunition Used in Certain Hunting
Applications...480

1. The Push to Ban Hunters' Use of Lead-Based Ammunition........481

2. The Future of the Lead-Based Ammunition Debate....................483

3. Phased-in Lead Ammunition Restrictions...................................483

a. Phase 1: Wildlife Areas and Ecological Reserves;
and Nelson Bighorn Sheep...483

b. Phase 2: Additional Restrictions on
Shotgun Shells...484

c. Phase 3: Statewide Lead Ammunition Ban for
All Species 486

d. General Exceptions to the Lead Ammunition
Restrictions 486

i. Possession of Handguns for Self-Defese.............................486

ii. Temporary Exception for "Calibers" that Are
Commercially Unavailable in Non-lead Due to Federal
"Armor Piercing Ammunition" Restrictions............................487

iii. Law Enforcement Engaged in Official Duties Exception.......487

e. Penalties for Violating Restriction on Lead
Ammunition...488

XI. OTHER REGULATED DEVICES...488

A. BB Guns..488

B. Toy Guns a.k.a. "Imitation Firearms".....................................489

C. "Tear Gas," "Less Lethal Weapons," and "Stun Guns".................492

1. "Tear Gas," Pepper Spray, and Mace.......................................492

2. "Less Lethal Weapons"..493

3. "Stun Guns" 494

D. "Blowguns"..495

E. 3D-Printed Guns..495

F. Sniperscopes (Night Vision Scopes) and Laser Scopes
    or Laser Pointers...496

XII. NATIONAL FIREARMS ACT – FIREARM POSSESSION........................497

A. "Any Other Weapon" Defined..498

B. Transferring NFA Firearms 499

XIII. EXPLOSIVES..500

A. "Fireworks" and "Explosives"...500

B. Ambiguity Concerning the Amount of Black Powder a
    Person Can Possess 500

C. Binary Exploding Targets...501

XIV. IGNORANCE OF THE LAW IS NO EXCUSE....................................502

ABOUT THE AUTHOR..503

TABLES

CHAPTER 3: WHO CAN OWN AND POSSESS FIREARMS AND AMMUNITION

Table 3.1   Summary of Restrictions for Minors Possessing Firearms and Ammunition 59

Table 3.2   Violent Crimes Resulting in a Lifetime Restriction in California 62

Table 3.3   Conduct Resulting in a Lifetime Restriction in California 63

Table 3.4   Conduct Resulting in a Ten-Year Restriction in California 64

Table 3.5   Juvenile Offenses 73

Table 3.6   Summary of California Criminal Convictions Resulting in the Loss of Firearm Rights 76

Table 3.7   Summary of Drug Prohibitions 83

Table 3.8   Mental Health Restrictions 89

Table 3.9   Restraining Order Restrictions 95

Table 3.10   A Quick Wrap Up on Other Federal Firearm Possession Restrictions 102

CHAPTER 4: HOW TO OBTAIN FIREARMS AND AMMUNITION

Table 4.1   Identification Requirements 112

Table 4.2   Firearm Safety Certificate Exemptions 121

Table 4.3   Proof of Residency Requirement: An Additional Requirement when Purchasing Handguns in California 135

Table 4.4   Quick Guide: The Process and Required Materials Needed to Purchase a Firearm from a Licensed Firearms Dealer in California 136

Table 4.5   Private Party Transfers 139

Table 4.6   Interstate Firearms Purchases and Transfers 145

Table 4.7   Exemptions to California's Restriction on Out-of-State Transfers 147

Table 4.8   Loan Exemptions 154

Table 4.9   Registration Deadlines for Individuals 186

Table 4.10   California's Firearm Storage Laws...............................194

Table 4.11   Exemptions to California's Ammunition
              Vendor & Face-to-Face Requirements......................201

Table 4.12   Exemptions to California's Ammunition Purchase
              Authorization...204

Table 4.13   Exemptions to California's Restrictions on Brining or
              Transporting Ammunition into California....................208

CHAPTER 5: CARRYING FIREARMS OPENLY, CONCEALED, AND/OR LOADED

Table 5.1   Carrying Concealed Handguns...................................214

Table 5.2   Carrying Loaded Firearms..216

Table 5.3   The Different Ways "Loaded" is Defined in
             California...217

Table 5.4   Openly Carrying Unloaded Handguns........................221

Table 5.5   Carrying "Firearms That Are not Handguns"..............224

CHAPTER 6: FIREARM CARRY RESTRICTION EXEMPTIONS AND TRANSPORTING FIREARMS

Table 6.1   Conditional Exemptions for Carrying Concealed
             Handguns...242

Table 6.2   "Other Exemptions" for Carrying Concealed
             Handguns...244

Table 6.3   Exemptions for Carrying Loaded Firearms.................245

Table 6.4   Exemptions to the Restriction on Openly Carrying
             Handguns in Public..246

Table 6.5   Exemption to Restriction on Openly Carrying
             Handguns on Your Person in Public.............................247

Table 6.6   Other Exemptions to the Restriction on Carrying
             "Firearms That Are not Handguns"..............................250

Table 6.7   Quick Tips for Transporting Your Firearm Using
             Public and Private Transportation...............................277

Table 6.8   Carry Exemptions Table..282

CHAPTER 8: REGULATION OF "ASSAULT WEAPONS" AND .50 BMG RIFLES

Table 8.1   "Assault Weapon" Identification Flowchart................382

Table 8.2   Quick Review of Registration Deadlines for
             Assault Weapons and .50 BMG Rifles...397
Table 8.3   Combined Listing of Category 1 and Category 2
             "Assault Weapons" 411

ACKNOWLEDGMENTS

I would like to extend my gratitude to Joe Silvoso and Grace Wu for their work on this edition. Joe has now provided considerable content and information on all five editions of this book. Grace, by picking up the reigns from Ben Machida, in addition to providing content, piloted this book through the drafting, production, and publication process. I would also like to thank previous contributors to past editions. Ben Machida, Sean Brady, Jessica Hawari, Hillary Green, and Tamara Rider, your contributions on past editions were the foundation on which this Fifth Edition was built.

I also thank all of the Michel & Associates, P.C. staffers, attorneys and law clerks who work or worked for Michel & Associates, P.C., or have contributed to the firm's body of firearms law knowledge and resources over the years. These contributors include Anna Barvir, Tiffany Cheuvront, Matthew Cubeiro, Joshua Dale, Scott Franklin, Margaret Leidy, Thomas Maciejewski, Glenn McRoberts, Clint Monfort, Claudia Nuñez, W. Lee Smith, Haydee Villegas-Aguilar, and many others.

I also owe thanks to the firearm, constitutional, and other lawyers throughout the country who have mentored, counseled, employed, worked for, or worked with me over the years. These include Eric Archer, Jim Baker, Mark Barnes, Chris Chiafullo, Paul Clement, Bruce Colodny, Chris Conte, Jason Davis, John Eastman, Eric Epstein, John Frazer, Steve Halbrook, David Hardy, Irwin Nowick, , Judge Eleanor Hunter, Burt Jacobson, Don Kates, Larry Keane, Don Kilmer, David Kopel, David Lehman, Judge J.D. Lord, John Machtinger, Erin Murphy, Pat O'Malley, Al Peacock, James René, Judge Jesse Rodriguez, and Guy Smith.

I am particularly grateful to civil rights activists and leaders George Barr, Sheriff Tom Bosenko, Tom Boyer, Chris Chang, Clayton Cramer, Paul Dougherty, Jim Erdman, Joel Friedman, Hayden Heal, Steve Helsley, Dwight Van Horn, Ed Hunt, John Lott, Tanya Metaksa, Sam Parades, Paul Payne, Senator H.L. Richardson (ret.), Kim Rhode, Rick Travis, Jerry Upholt, Norm Vroman, Gene Wolberg, Ed Worley, and Sheriff Donny Youngblood for their support and insight over the years. And all the individual plaintiffs in the various lawsuits who volunteered to stand up for all of our self-defense civil rights deserve special thanks.

Activist and Bloomfield Press publisher Alan Korwin and Tiger Lilly Enterprises publishing consultant Penny Callmeyer also deserve special mention for their patience and help in making this book happen.

Cooperation and information has been gratefully received from the California Department of Justice Firearms Bureau, the Bureau of Alcohol, Tobacco, Firearms, and Explosives, Los Angeles District Attorney Steve Cooley (ret.) and the Los Angeles County District Attorney's Office, the Los Angeles County Public Defender's Office, officers with the Long Beach and Sacramento Police Departments, Redondo Beach City Attorney Mike Webb and the Redondo Beach City Attorney's Office, San Francisco Public Defender Jeff Adachi and the San Francisco Public Defender's Office, and Turner's Outdoorsman Vice President of Operations Bill Ortiz.

My wife Sydne and my sons Colton and Dawson have also been particularly patient with me.

Last, but certainly not least, I thank my clients the National Rifle Association and the California Rifle and Pistol Association for the meaningful, challenging, and fulfilling legal work that those associations have allowed me to perform on behalf of NRA and CRPA members over the past twenty years, and for the knowledge base that legal work created, much of which was put to use in writing this book.

DEDICATION

To my father, Carl Robert Michel,
a volunteer NRA Instructor who taught his three sons how to shoot.
And to my mother, Joan Hancock Michel,
who loved us enough to put up with it,
and to occasionally plink a can off the back stoop
with the Crosman 760 herself.

DISCLAIMER

This book is not "the law," and it is not a substitute for "the law." "The law" includes all of the legal obligations imposed on you as a gun owner and involves a much greater volume of work and opinion than the coverage of firearm statutes and regulations contained in this book. No book can cover everything or replace a competent and experienced lawyer's advice. This book is only a guide, designed to provide general information regarding California gun laws and to provide references to seek additional information. It is not intended to be a legal treatise or a summary of the entire body of law covering firearms.

We expressly disclaim any liability for errors or omissions that may be in this book. There are many legal and technical "gray area" questions about firearms law that have not been decided by the courts and may never be. Although we do our best to identify the gray areas of which we are aware and provide *our* analysis and *likely* or *possible* interpretations as to how courts *may* decide certain issues, by no means should our analysis or interpretations be taken as the law. Despite our efforts in researching, collecting, organizing, writing, and preparing this book, we do not make any claims, promises, or guarantees about the absolute accuracy, completeness, or adequacy of the contents of this book. The opinions of other attorneys, and particularly prosecuting attorneys or judges, may be different from ours.

Many people find laws hard to understand, and gathering all the relevant ones, let alone explaining them, is a lot of work. This book helps you with these chores. Again, while great care has been taken to accomplish this with a high degree of accuracy, *no guarantee of accuracy is expressed or implied, and the explanatory sections of this book are not to be considered legal advice or a restatement of law.*

The exact language of the principal state laws controlling gun use in California are generally not reprinted verbatim in this book. Typically only edited pieces of laws are included here. The laws and other regulations are expressed in conversational terms for your convenience and are cross-referenced with statutes or published court cases. In using plain English to explain the general meanings of the laws, differences inevitably arise, so *you must always check the actual laws.*

You are fully accountable under the exact words and current official interpretations of all applicable laws, regulations, court precedents, executive orders, and more when you deal with firearms under any circumstances. You are responsible for researching any federal, state, and/or local law(s) that are applicable to your particular inquiry or circumstance, or for hiring an attorney to advise you on your particular question given your particular circumstances. For guidance on how to find a competent attorney, review the "How to Judge a Lawyer" memorandum published on my website, www.CalGunLawsBook.com.

Even though we are attorneys, we are not providing legal advice nor are we rendering other professional services. The use of this book does *not* create an attorney-client relationship. Please do not send us or our law firm any confidential or sensitive information until you speak with one an attorneys and obtain prior written authorization to send that information to our law office. Guidance on how to communicate with our office so that confidentiality can be preserved is available through our website, www.MichelLawyers.com. Communication of information by, in, to, or through this book and your receipt *or* use of it (1) is *not* provided in the course of and does not create or constitute an attorney-client relationship, (2) is *not* intended as a solicitation, (3) is *not* intended to convey or constitute legal advice, and (4) is *not* a substitute for obtaining legal advice from a qualified attorney. You should not act upon any such information without first seeking qualified professional counsel on your specific matter. The hiring of an attorney is an important decision that should not be based solely upon this book or its promotional materials.

For the most part, local ordinances, rules, regulations, and policies are not covered by this book. This book concerns the general gun laws as they apply to law-abiding private residents in the state of California only. Though this book touches on certain aspects of these topics, it is not intended to and does not describe most situations relating to licensed gun dealers; museums or educational institutions; state or federal military personnel; Native Americans; hunting; foreign nationals; the police or other peace officers; other government employees summoned by a peace officer to help in the performance of official duties; people with special licenses, authorizations or permits; non-residents; bequests or intestate succession; persons under indictment; felons; prisoners; escapees; dangerous or repeat offenders; criminal street gang members; incorrigible juvenile delinquents; or unsupervised juveniles.

While this book discusses possible criminal consequences of improper gun use, it avoids most issues related to deliberate gun crimes, particularly violent ones. This means certain laws are excluded or not explained in the text. Some examples are: 1st degree murder, 2nd degree murder, homicide, manslaughter, gun theft, gun-running, concealment of stolen firearms, enhanced penalties for commission of crimes with firearms (including armed robbery, burglary, theft, kidnapping, drug offenses, assault, and priors), smuggling firearms into public aircraft, threatening flight attendants with firearms, possession of contraband, possession of a firearm in a prison by a prisoner, false application for a firearm, shooting at a building or vehicle, possession of a firearm in association with a criminal street gang, removal of a body after a shooting, drive-by shooting, and retaliation. This is only a partial list.

New laws and regulations may be enacted at any time by federal, state, and local authorities. The authors and publisher make no representation that this book includes all requirements and prohibitions that may exist. Be aware that firearm laws are subject to change anytime. You are strongly urged to consult with a qualified attorney and local authorities to determine the current status and applicability of the law to specific situations you may encounter.

You are accepting this book, and the contents thereof, "as is" without any warranty of any kind, express or implied, including but not limited to the implied warranty of merchantability or fitness for a particular purpose. All liability and/or resulting damages from this book's use are disclaimed. Again, the author and publisher expressly disclaim any liability whatsoever arising out of reliance on information contained in this book. *The Author and the Publisher Shall Not Be Liable for Any Direct, Indirect, Incidental, Special, Exemplary, or Consequential Damages However Caused and on Any Theory of Liability, Whether in Contract, Strict Liability, or Tort, Arising in Any Way out of the Use of this Book.* Damages disclaimed include, but are not limited to, direct, indirect, incidental, compensatory, equitable, exemplary, special, and/or consequential damages, regardless of any cause of action by which the damages may arise.

Again, the information contained in this book is not a substitute for professional advice and does not constitute professional advice, nor is the information contained in this book conveyed or intended to be conveyed as professional advice. Under no circumstances shall you hold the author responsible for any acts you decide to take or not to take. Any decisions you make, and any subsequent consequences, are your own. If you need legal advice or other expert assistance, hire a lawyer familiar with firearms law.

INTRODUCTION

I. GUN SAFETY IS YOUR RESPONSIBILITY

Firearm ownership, possession, and use are individual rights that carry extraordinary responsibilities, both morally and legally. Firearms are deadly. Possessing and using them demands the acceptance of the highest level of responsibility by you. Depending on your individual circumstances, accepting that personal responsibility may require you to do more than the law demands to avoid accidents.

The overwhelming majority of gun owners are extremely responsible. Gun accidents claim far fewer lives than most people are made to think. In the last reporting year, 48 children under age 14 died from gun accidents.[1] With over 90 million adults owning a gun and over 60 million children under age 14 living in the United States, the improper use of guns causes astoundingly few accidental deaths. Meanwhile, thousands more tragically die from car accidents, residential fires, bathtub drownings, accidental poisonings, and household hazards.[2] In fact, homes where gun accidents occur usually are not typical homes. Alcoholism and criminal histories are common, as is a disproportionate involvement in automobile accidents and driver's license suspensions. All of this reflects individual irresponsibility in homes where accidents happen.

If everyone obeyed the NRA's three simple rules of firearm safety, accidents would not happen. The three rules of firearm safety are: (1) always keep the firearm unloaded until it is ready to use – no exceptions; (2) always keep the firearm pointed in a safe direction (e.g., never allow the muzzle of your firearm to point toward anything you do not intend to destroy); and (3) always keep your finger off the

---

[1] To find statistical information on the number of children who died as a result of a gun accident, see *Fatal Injury Reports, 1999-2014, National, Regional, and States (Restricted)*, CENTERS FOR DISEASE CONTROL AND PREVENTION, NAT'L CENTER FOR INJURY (last updated Feb. 19, 2017), https://webappa.cdc.gov/sasweb/ncipc/mortrate.html (last visited July 11, 2017).

[2] For example, in 2010, motor vehicle accidents resulted in 1,302 deaths of children under 14 years old, versus just 50 unintentional firearms related deaths during that same time period. *Fatal Injury Reports, 1999-2014, National, Regional, and States (Restricted)*, CENTERS FOR DISEASE CONTROL AND PREVENTION, NAT'L CENTER FOR INJURY (last updated Feb. 19, 2017), https://webappa.cdc.gov/sasweb/ncipc/mortrate.html (last visited July 11, 2017).

trigger until your sights are aligned with the target and you have made a conscious mental decision to shoot. [3]

The gun-ban lobby typically distorts facts and resists efforts to promote real gun-safety instruction, or offer gun owners more opportunities to learn. They fear that merely mentioning a firearm in an educational context would tacitly endorse the concept that firearms have social utility. But firearms do have social utility both as self-defense tools and for their crime deterrent effect. Firearms are used at least four times more often to prevent a crime than to commit one.[4] Nonetheless, instead of education, gun-ban lobbyists have pushed one-size-fits-all legislation such as mechanical lock and storage mandates that, while potentially one part of an individualized safety system, often are inappropriate or create a false sense of security that can actually increase carelessness and accidents.

Thanks to the efforts of over 40,000 certified gun-safety instructors who teach gun safety to law enforcement and civilians across the country, as well as the award-winning, time-proven, and law enforcement-endorsed safety programs being used nationally, firearm accident rates from 2014 onwards are lower than they have ever been previously recorded.[5] To do your part, you can learn those guidelines, live by them, and teach them to others. Taking classes in firearms handling is an excellent way to do this. Free materials concerning firearm safety are available in almost every gun store and from the National Rifle Association, National Shooting Sports Foundation, and the California Rifle and Pistol Association websites.

II. HOW TO USE THIS BOOK

Along with your responsibility to know and follow safety procedures, you also have increasing legal responsibilities. The goal of this book is to educate you about California's complex firearms laws so that you can avoid inadvertently violating them, as well as to educate those tasked with enforcing those laws so they avoid causing innocent people unnecessary legal problems.

This book discusses how to legally buy, own, transport, and possess firearms, and how to get firearms or firearm ownership rights back if they are taken away. This book also explores, explains, and summarizes the major firearms laws affecting firearm owners in California and particularly warns about legal "traps" that California firearm owners often unintentionally fall into.

---

[3] *See* National Rifle Association of America, Gun Safety Rules (Brochure) (Apr. 2013).

[4] In 2011, the Bureau of Justice reported around 478,400 crimes committed with a firearm, compared to estimates of 2.1-2.5 million defensive gun uses. Gary Kleck & Marc Gertz, *Armed Resistance to Crime: The Prevalence and Nature of Self-Defense with a Gun*, 86 J. CRIM. L. & CRIMINOLOGY 150, 167 (1995); MICHAEL PLANTY & JENNIFER L. TRUMAN, U.S. DEPT. OF JUSTICE, FIREARM VIOLENCE, 1993-2011 1 (2013).

[5] *Fatal Injury Reports, 1999-2014, National, Regional, and States (Restricted)*, CENTERS FOR DISEASE CONTROL AND PREVENTION, NAT'L CENTER FOR INJURY (last updated Feb. 19, 2017), https://webappa.cdc.gov/sasweb/ncipc/mortrate.html (last visited July 11, 2017).

As the Disclaimer makes clear, this book only serves as a general guide. It is not a complete legal treatise of firearms law. Individual circumstances vary and can change any legal analysis. Since firearms laws frequently change, only constant study and legal analysis will keep you informed about their current status and applicability. As always, you are strongly encouraged to seek advice from an attorney experienced in firearms law if you have additional questions or concerns about firearms law and how it applies to your personal circumstances.

While reading this book, keep in mind that the exact language from many code[6] sections and court decisions have been shortened and/or paraphrased to highlight the particular point being made. Please note that all code sections referenced in this book are to the 2017 editions unless otherwise indicated. For exact statutory language, and when analyzing the cited cases, the particular statute, code, and/or specific case(s) can and should be consulted directly. It's fairly easy to find these resources online. The California Legislative Counsel maintains all California codes on its website at www.leginfo.ca.gov. Case opinions of the California Supreme Court and Courts of Appeal are available on the Judicial Branch of California website at www.courts.ca.gov/opinions.

Because this book is intended for a wide audience, including firearm owners, firearm consumers, law enforcement, and lawyers, exact legal "Bluebook" citation format is not used.[7] For example, "*id*" and "*supra*," (terms used by lawyers to denote preceding or subsequent authority), do not appear in this book. But, *general* Bluebook citation format is utilized for consistency. For the exact and proper legal citations, please refer to the specific case, statute, or website in which you are interested.

A. The Materials Posted at www.CalGunLawsBook.com and www.crpa.org Complement This Book

More detailed legal memoranda elaborating on particular subjects covered in each chapter of this book and additional helpful materials are posted at www.CalGunLawsBook.com. This website complements this book, and vice versa.

If you have firearms law questions, or would like to make suggestions for topics to be included in upcoming editions, email gunlawquestion@calgunlaws.com. To receive blog articles and email news bulletins on cutting-edge self-defense issues, civil rights issues, cases, court rulings, and other legal developments, subscribe to receive these bulletins from www.CalGunLawsBook.com and www.crpa.org.

---

[6] "A code is a set of books containing all of the statutes in force in a given jurisdiction, organized by subject matter." THE BLUEBOOK: A UNIFORM SYSTEM OF CITATION 15 (Columbia Law Review Ass'n et al. eds., 19th ed. 2010).

[7] The Bluebook is a style guide for legal citation in the United States that is used by law students, lawyers, scholars, judges and other legal professionals.

B. Symbols Used Throughout This Book

Throughout this book I use the following symbols to bring your attention to certain information:

This "New Law" symbol indicates an important change in the law. Since many new laws will take effect in 2018, it is imperative for you to understand the changes that these new laws make and how they may affect you.

This "Caution" symbol points out notable information and potentially troublesome gray areas that you should pay particular attention to as you are reading this book.

This "California Gun Laws" symbol indicates that a reference has been made to the www.CalGunLawsBook.com website or to the www.crpa.org website, where you can find updates and supplemental materials that complement this book.

III. HOW TO READ LAWS AND DETERMINE WHETHER THEY APPLY

A. Federal Laws, State Laws, and Local Laws

This book covers both federal and state firearms laws. Local laws, however, are mostly beyond the scope of this book. Federal law is made up of the "United States Constitution, federal statutes and regulations, U.S. treatises, and federal [case] law," *i.e.*, court opinions.[8] State law consists of the "state's constitution, statutes, regulations," and state court law cases.[9] Local laws are statutes or ordinances that are applicable to a particular locality rather than the entire state.[10] This book discusses both California and federal law under the main topic or heading, pointing out where most people run into problems with law enforcement. Even though this book does not discuss every local law in California, you are always obligated to comply with federal, state, and also local law.

---

[8] BLACK'S LAW DICTIONARY 645 (8th. ed. 2004).

[9] BLACK'S LAW DICTIONARY 1444 (8th. ed. 2004).

[10] BLACK'S LAW DICTIONARY 957 (8th. ed. 2004).

B. Statutory Interpretation Techniques

Regardless of whether you or a court is examining a federal or state law, the following rules governing statutory interpretation apply.

As the United States Supreme Court explained, "in interpreting a statute a court should always turn first to one, cardinal canon before all others . . . courts must presume that a legislature says in a statute what it means and means in a statute what it says there . . . . When the words of a statute are unambiguous, then, this first canon is also the last: 'judicial inquiry is complete.'"[11] "Congress is presumed to act intentionally and purposely when it includes language in one section but omits it in another."[12]

If a statute's plain language is ambiguous, courts then look to the legislature's intent and give it "a reasonable and common sense interpretation consistent with the apparent purpose, which will result in wise policy rather than mischief and absurdity."[13] If necessary, courts will break down the words of the statute and compare their placement within the statute as a whole. Courts will also consider its context, purpose, evils to be remedied, other legislation, and public policy.[14] For example, in *People v. Squier*, the California Court of Appeal said that "[t]he rule of strict interpretation of penal statutes does not apply in California" and "where two interpretations of a penal statute are possible, that construction which favors the defendant is preferred unless such a construction is contrary to public interest, sound sense, and wise policy."[15] Therefore, according to the rule of lenity, when a statute is susceptible to two reasonable interpretations, the court should prefer the interpretation that most favors a defendant. In reality, the rule rarely works to a defendant's advantage.

Courts are also permitted to review secondary sources like legal treatises and law review articles to see what experts in a particular field say about the statute. These secondary sources are not binding, however, and serve merely as persuasive authority.

C. Determining Which Statute Controls When There Are Duplicate Laws for the Same Crime

Although it does not happen often, sometimes duplicate laws are passed that criminalize the same conduct. For example, in 2016, the California Legislature passed Assembly Bill (AB) 1695, making it a crime to falsely report that a firearm has been

---

[11] *Conn. Nat'l Bank v. Germain*, 503 U.S. 249, 253-54 (1992) (internal citations omitted).
[12] *Estate of Bell v. Comm'r*, 928 F.2d 901, 904 (9th Cir. 1991).
[13] 7 B.E. WITKIN, SUMMARY OF CAL. LAW, CONST. LAW § 115 (10th ed. 2012).
[14] *See* 7 B.E. WITKIN, SUMMARY OF CAL. LAW, CONST. LAW § 115 (10th ed. 2012).
[15] *People v. Squier*, 15 Cal. App. 4th 235, 241 (1993).

lost or stolen to a law enforcement agency.[16] Yet, that same year the voters passed Proposition (Prop.) 63, which also made it a crime to falsely report that a firearm has been lost or stolen to a law enforcement agency.[17] Interestingly, instead of simply amending or adding the same Penal Code statutes, AB 1695 amended P.C. section 148.5, making it a misdemeanor to falsely report the theft or loss of a firearm, and Prop. 63 added P.C. section 25275 to the Penal Code, making it an infraction to falsely report the theft or loss of a firearm.

Currently, case law is silent as to whether two statutes condemning the same crime can coexist. But, dicta[18] from some cases suggests that they can, and their duplication is merely a "housekeeping" issue for the Legislature to eventually clean-up by removing one of the duplicate statutes.[19] For example, the Legislature did this with Penal Code (P.C.) section 29805 by using AB 785 to reconcile the two different versions of P.C. section 29805 implemented by Prop. 63 and the Legislature.

That being said, just because two duplicative criminal statutes may be able to coexist together, it does not mean that a person can be punished under both statutes. For instance, notice that while both AB 1695 and Prop. 63 prohibit the same type of conduct, the punishments between these statutes are different: one treats the crime as a misdemeanor, while the other treats it as an infraction.

Although nothing expressly prevents a person from being charged and convicted of the same crime under two different statutes, California law does prohibit multiple punishment for a single physical act that violates different provisions of law.[20] In fact, P.C. section 654 provides in relevant part:

An act or omission that is punishable in different ways by different provisions of law shall be punished under the provision that provides for the longest term of imprisonment, but in no case shall the act or omission be punished under more than one provision.[21]

In other words, although a person can be charged with and convicted of a violation of both P.C. section 148.5 and P.C. section 25275 for falsely reporting that a firearm has been lost or stolen, they can only be punished under the statute that

---

[16] AB 1695, 2015-2016 Leg., Reg. Sess (Cal. 2016), *available at* https://leginfo.legislature.ca.gov/faces/billNavClient. xhtml?bill_id=201520160AB1695 (last visited July 11, 2017).

[17] FULL TEXT OF PROPOSITION 63, CALIFORNIA ATTORNEY GENERAL, *available at* https://www.oag.ca.gov/system/ files/initiatives/pdfs/15-0098%20(Firearms)_0.pdf (last visited July 11, 2017).

[18] Dictum (the single form of dicta) is "[a] statement of opinion or belief considered authoritative because of the dignity of the person making it." BLACK'S LAW DICTIONARY 485 (8th ed. 2004). Dicta is merely persuasive and not binding authority.

[19] *See Weiner v. City of San Diego*, 229 Cal. App. 3d 1203, 1208 n. 3 (1991), *superseded by statute on other grounds by Morgan v. Beaumont Police Department*, 246 Cal. App. 4th 144, 159 (2016) (stating "[a]lthough the Legislature by enacting those two identical sections in 1987 may have added more to the Vehicle Code than intended, it is an accepted maxim of jurisprudence 'superfluity does not vitiate.'"); *see also Landeros v. Flood*, 17 Cal. 3d 399, 407, 414 (1976) (stating "[t]here is nothing to prevent the Legislature from imposing a reporting requirement on physicians in two separate statutes, even if their coverage apparently overlaps.").

[20] P.C. § 654.

[21] P.C. § 654.

carries the harsher sentence, which in this case would be the misdemeanor under P.C. section 148.5.

D. How to Read Court Opinions

When a dispute results in a lawsuit, the court's rulings will usually be issued through an "opinion." These court opinions can be issued by either trial or appellate court judges.[22]

When reading a court opinion, the first thing to look at is the case name or caption. This will identify the parties to the case. The party bringing the lawsuit is the plaintiff. The one defending against the lawsuit is the defendant. If the case is a criminal case, the state or federal prosecutor will bring a lawsuit on behalf of the government. The plaintiff in a criminal case is typically the "United States" or the "People of the State of California."

After the case name you will see a legal "citation." This tells you where you can locate the actual opinion of the case. Many court opinions are now available for free online. The case citation can tell you which court rendered the decision and when the opinion was rendered. For example, *District of Columbia v. Heller*, the 2008 United States Supreme Court case that determined there is an individual right to keep and bear arms for self-defense, is cited as *District of Columbia v. Heller*, 554 U.S. 570 (2008). The citation of "554" is the volume of the United States Reports, "U.S." is the abbreviation of the United States Reports, and "570" is the page number where this opinion begins. The final "2008" represents the year in which the opinion was rendered.

Under the case name there is a courthouse case number, dates indicating when the lawsuit was filed and when it was decided, and the names of the attorneys who represented the parties (if any). The judge who rendered the opinion will also be identified.

In most opinions the judge first discusses the facts of the case, then the procedural history of the case (*i.e.*, how the case has progressed through the court system), and then the ultimate legal or factual issue(s) the judge had to resolve.

After discussing the governing law and doing a statutory analysis, if the meaning of a law is subject to dispute (as it often is), the judge will discuss how the law applies to the facts. By weaving the governing laws into the facts of the case, the judge will reach an ultimate ruling, a decision or opinion that is also referred to as the court's "holding," on the issue(s) of the case.

Reading court opinions helps determine how laws will be interpreted and applied to different sets of facts. The United States has a "common law" system where-

---

[22] For a more substantive analysis on how to read court opinions, see Orin S. Kerr, *How to Read a Legal Opinion: A Guide for New Law Students*, 11 GREEN BAG 2D 51 (2007), *available at* http://www.volokh.com/files/howtoreadv2.pdf (last visited Jun. 30, 2017).

by, in addition to state and federal laws, courts look to previously decided cases to aid in making their judgments. Under this "common law" system, some court decisions are considered binding legal "precedent," which means that lower courts must defer to the higher courts' prior interpretation of the law.

Since not all cases are factually the same, lawyers either try to distinguish their facts from the facts that formed the basis of any earlier adverse court opinion(s) so the court does not adopt that opinion as its rationale, or the lawyers try to show why the earlier court opinion(s) should be legal "precedent" that the court should follow and adopt. This can be a difficult task. It is one of the things lawyers really earn their money doing.

IV. HOW TO JUDGE A LAWYER

If you ever need a lawyer, regardless of whether it is an attorney with experience in firearms law or an attorney in another practice area, it is important that you properly evaluate the attorney before you retain him or her for your case. There are a lot of bad lawyers out there. Meaningful factors to consider when evaluating an attorney are years of experience, cases actually tried to a jury, practice area(s), specializations, and competence in the particular area in which you need assistance.

There is a lot of helpful information about lawyers on the internet. But do not be fooled by slick internet marketing techniques, inflated website "ratings," and meaningless "awards." These days, a lawyer's reputation can be manipulated online. Just because the attorney claims to be "the best attorney" in a particular area or shows up first on a Google or Yahoo! search or has a high rating on some forums does not necessarily mean that attorney is the right or best one for you. There are ways attorneys can manipulate their marketing profiles and endorsements to appear accomplished in a particular field when, in actuality, they either refer those cases to other attorneys or are themselves novice attorneys.

For more guidance on how to evaluate and select an attorney who is right for you, see the "How to Judge a Lawyer" memorandum on the www.CalGunLawsBook.com website.

ABBREVIATIONS USED
THROUGHOUT THIS BOOK

Numerous laws from various sources are discussed, quoted, or paraphrased throughout this book. Additionally, common firearm language is discussed as well. Important laws or language will be fully listed when discussed for the first time in each chapter but then will be subsequently abbreviated. Below is a list of commonly used terms and their corresponding abbreviations that are consistently used throughout the book:

Armed Prohibited Persons System..APPS

Assault Weapon Identification Guide..AWIG

Assault Weapons Control Act...AWCA

Assembly Bill...AB

Attorney General...AG

Automated Firearms System...AFS

Bureau of Alcohol, Tobacco, Firearms, and Explosives......................ATF

Bureau of Land Management..BLM

California Business and Professions Code..............................Cal. Bus. & Prof. Code

California Civil Code..Cal. Civ. Code

California Code of Civil Procedure...Cal. Civ. Proc. Code

California Code of Regulations..Cal. Code Regs.

California Department of Justice..DOJ

California Elections Code..Cal. Elections Code

California Family Code..Cal. Fam. Code

California Fish and Game Code..Cal. Fish & Game Code

California Government Code...Cal. Gov't Code

California Health and Safety Code..Cal. Health & Saf. Code

California Law Revision Commission...CLRC

California Penal Code...P.C.

California Rifle and Pistol Association..CRPA

California Vehicle Code...Cal. Veh. Code

California Welfare and Institutions Code...............................Cal. Welf. & Inst. Code

Carry Concealed Weapon...CCW

Certificate of Eligibility...COE

Code of Federal Regulations..C.F.R.

Code of Public Resources..C. Pub. Res.

Dangerous Weapons Control Act...DWCA

Dealer's Record of Sale...DROS
Entertainment Firearms Permit..EFP
Environmental Protection Agency...EPA
Exclusive Economic Zone...EEZ
Federal Aviation Administration..FAA
Federal Bureau of Investigation...FBI
Federal Firearms Licensee...FFL
Firearm Owners' Protection Act..FOPA
Firearm Safety Certificate..FSC
Gun Control Act..GCA
Handgun Safety Certificate...HSC
Immigration and Nationality Act...INA
Law Enforcement Gun Release..LEGR
Law Enforcement Gun Release - Firearms Eligibility
    Clearance Letter...LEGR Letter
Law Enforcement Officer Safety Act......................................LEOSA
Misdemeanor Crime of Domestic Violence...........................MCDV
National Firearms Act..NFA
National Instant Criminal Background Check System...........NICS
National Rifle Association..NRA
National Shooting Sports Foundation......................................NSSF
The Office of Administrative Law...OAL
Peace Officer Standards and Training.....................................POST
Personal Firearms Eligibility Check Application....................PFEC
Post-Traumatic Stress Disorder...PTSD
Private Party Transfer...PPT
Qualified Law Enforcement Officer...QLEO
Qualified Retired Law Enforcement Officer.........................QRLEO
Senate Bill..SB
Transportation Security Administration....................................TSA
United Nations Convention on the Law of the Sea............UNCLOS
United States...U.S.
United States Code...U.S.C.
United States Department of Justice.....................................U.S. DOJ

NEW LAWS FOR 2018

All of the new and amended laws below will take effect on January 1, 2018, unless otherwise noted. Some of these laws were passed in 2016 and go into effect in 2018 or 2019.

AB: Assembly Bill

SB: Senate Bill

AB 7: Open Carry   Chapter 5
Amends P.C. § 26400 and the headings of Chapter 7 and Article 1 of Part 6, Title 4, Division 5 of the P.C.

Extends the restriction on carrying long guns so that it also applies to a public place or a public street in a prohibited area of an unincorporated area of a county.

AB 97: 2017 Budget Act of 2017   Intro., Chapter 8

This Budget Bill set a $125 billion state budget by making appropriations for the support of the California state government for the 2017-2018 fiscal year, including giving the DOJ the $2,588,000 it requested for additional employees and services to process new "assault weapon" registrations and the $1,368,000 it requested for additional employees to implement the provisions of the 2016 "Ghost Gun" bill (AB 857).

Effective July 1, 2017

AB 103: Omnibus Public Safety   Chapters 4 and 8
Amends Cal. Code Civ. Proc. §§ 384, 1010.6; Cal. Gov. Code §§ 11040, 11041, 11042, 11045, 24000, 69580, 69592, 69594, 69600; Cal. Pen. Code §§ 1170.18, 1370, 1370.6, 1372, 1463.007, 1464, 1557, 2801, 2808, 3453, 5075, 6031, 6031.1, 29800, 29805, 30680, 30900; Cal. Veh. Code §§ 3365, 13365.2, 40509, 40509.5; Cal. Welf. & Inst. Code §§ 209, 1982, 4100, 4358.5, 7228, 7234
Adds Cal. Gov. Code §§ 7310, 7311, 12532, 15007, 15820.948, 27770, 27771, 27772, 68514, 69614.4, 70500-70508; Cal. Military and Veterans Code § 329; Cal. Pen. Code §§ 1170.127, 4032; Cal. Pub. Contract Code § 10340.1
Repeals Cal. Gov. Code § 11043; Cal. Pen. Code §§ 1203.6, 1464.2, and 1203.5 (repeal and add); Cal. Welf. & Inst. Code §§ 270, 271 (repeal and add)

This bill makes statutory changes necessary to enact the public safety provisions of the Budget Act of 2017. It includes a provision that extended the "assault weapon" registration deadline from December 31, 2017 to June 30, 2018 and a provision that extends the restriction for firearm possession to those with an outstanding warrant for felonies and certain misdemeanors listed in Penal Code sections 29800 and 29805, respectively.

Effective June 27, 2017

AB 424: Possession in School Zone   Chapter 7
Amends P.C. §§ 626.9, 26370, 26405

Removes the authority of school officials to authorize individuals to possess a firearm in a school zone but adds two new exceptions to the Gun-Free School Zone restrictions: (1) the possession of unloaded firearms as part of a state-certified hunter education program pursuant to Fish and Game Code § 3051, as long as participants do not possess live ammunition in a school building and (2) the possession of firearms as part of a program involving shooting sports or activities (including, but not limited to, trap shooting, skeet shooting, sporting clays, and pistol shooting) that is sanctioned by a school, school district, college, university, or other governing body of the institution, and that occurs on the grounds of a public or private school or university or college campus.

AB 693: Exemptions for Law Enforcement   Chapters 4 and 9
Cadets
Amends P.C. § 30312
Adds P.C. §§ 26625, 27970, 32455

Exempts a firearm loan from the requirement that the transaction be conducted through or by a dealer, if the loan is made to a person enrolled in the course of basic training prescribed by the Commission on Peace Officer Standards and Training, or in any other course certified by the Commission, for purposes of participation in the course. Also exempts from the prohibition on large-capacity magazines (1) the sale, gift, or loan of large-capacity magazines to persons enrolled in such a course, and (2) the possession of, or purchase by such person, for purposes of participation in the course during his or her period of enrollment. Further exempts from the new ammunition purchasing requirements (1) a person in such a course or in the basic training academy for peace officers, (2) an instructor of the academy or course, (3) or a staff member of the academy or entity providing the course, provided that they are purchasing the ammunition for the purpose of participation or use in the course.

AB 785: Possession by Convicted Persons   Chapter 3
Amends P.C. § 29805

Reorganizes P.C. section 29805 as a matter of housekeeping and also imposes a ten-year firearm prohibition against any person convicted of a misdemeanor of (1) using force or threat of force to interfere with another person's free exercise of constitutional right or privilege because of the other person's actual or perceived race, religion, national origin, disability, gender, or sexual orientation or (2) knowingly defacing, damaging, or destroying the property of another person, for the purpose of intimidating or interfering with the exercise of any constitutional right or privilege

AB 857 (2016): Firearms Identifying Information Chapter 4
Amends P.C. §§ 11106, 16520, 23910 & 30105
Adds P.C. §§ 29180-29184

Requires a person, beginning July 1, 2018, to apply and obtain from the California Department of Justice a unique serial number or other identification mark prior to manufacturing or assembling a firearm. This bill also requires that any person who owns a firearm as of July 1, 2018, that does not have a serial number assigned to it to obtain a unique serial number or other mark of identification before January 1, 2019. Further, the bill prohibits the sale or transfer of ownership of a firearm that was manufactured or assembled pursuant to the bill's requirements.

This bill also makes it a misdemeanor to aid another person who is prohibited from possessing a firearm in manufacturing or assembling a firearm.

Date a Person Must Seek Permission and Identifying Information Prior to Manufacturing or Assembling a Firearm	*July 1, 2018*
Last Day to Obtain a Serial Number or Other Identifying Mark and Register the Firearm for Any Firearms Possessed After July 1, 2018 that Do Not Bear a Serial Number	*December 31, 2018*

AB 1516: Maintenance of Codes
Makes various revisions to a number of California Codes, include some relating to firearm laws

Makes numerous non-substantive, technical changes to California statutes.

AB 1525: Firearms Warning Chapter 4
Amends P.C. §§ 26340, 26835, 31630, 31640, 31645

Starting on January 1, 2018, requires specific warnings regarding the risks of firearms and the laws regulating firearms to be included on the packaging of firearms and descriptive materials that accompany firearms. Also, starting January 1, 2019, requires additional specified warnings to be included at the premises of a licensed firearms dealer and to be given to a person taking the firearms safety certificate examination.

Date Dealers Must Include New Warnings on the Packaging/ Materials Included with Firearms	*January 1, 2018*
Date Firearm Dealers Must Include Specified Warnings on Premises and Date FSC Testing Materials Must be Updated with Specified Warnings	*January 1, 2019*

SB 393: Sealing Arrest Records   Chapter 3
Amends P.C. §§ 851.87, 851.90, 1000.4, 1001.9, 11105
Adds P.C. §§ 851.91, 851.92

Allows certain persons suffering an arrest with no conviction to petition the court to have the arrest sealed. States that the arrest shall be sealed as a matter of right unless the person has been charged with certain crimes. Also, even though the sealing of the arrest will result in a court order stating that the arrest is deemed not to have occurred, the sealing of the arrest does not affect the petitioner's authorization to own, possess, or have in his or her custody or control any firearm—or the petitioner's susceptibility to a firearm-prohibiting offense—if the arrest would otherwise affect that authorization or susceptibility.

SB 497: Firearm Storage in Vehicle   Chapter 4
Amends P.C. § 25140

Allows peace officers to lock a handgun out of plain view within the center utility console of an unattended motor vehicle not equipped with a trunk, provided that he or she cannot lock the handgun in a locked container and place the container out of plain view and cannot lock the handgun in a locked container that is permanently affixed to the vehicle's interior and not in plain view. Also defines "trunk" and "plain view" for purposes of leaving handguns in an unattended vehicle.

SB 536: Info for Firearm Violence Research   Chapter 1
Adds P.C. § 14231.5

Requires the DOJ to provide information about gun violence restraining orders to the University of California's Firearm Violence Research Center, or, at the DOJ's discretion, to any other entity that is concerned with the study and prevention of violence, provided that information identifying specific individuals is not revealed or used for anything other than research or statistical activities and will not be reported in publications.

SB 620: Crime Enhancements
Amends P.C. §§ 12022.5, 12022.53

Allows courts to strike or dismiss enhancements pertaining to the use of firearms in the commission of a felony.

SB 1235 (2016): Ammunition | Chapter 4

Amends P.C. §§ 16150, 17315, 30000 & 30306
Adds P.C. §§ 30355-30357 & 30360-30370

Requires the California Department of Justice (DOJ) to record ammunition vender and ammunition purchaser information. Also requires individuals to undergo a background check when purchasing ammunition from an ammunition vendor, and requires individuals and businesses obtain a license to sell ammunition.

Date the DOJ Was Required to Start Issuing Ammunition Vendor Licenses (but, as of the date of the book's completion, this process is still not available)	*July 1, 2017*
Date a Person and/or Business Must Have an Ammunition Vendor License to Sell Ammunition (but due to the DOJ's delays, we do not know if this system will be in place)	*January 1, 2018*
Date Ban on Importation of Ammunition by California Resident Goes Into Effect	*January 1, 2018*
Date Face-to-Face Requirement for Ammunition Transfers Goes Into Effect	*January 1, 2018*
Date Ammunition Vendors Must Record and Submit Purchaser Information to the DOJ, and Date the DOJ Will Begin to Conduct Background Checks	*July 1, 2019*

SCR 62: Proclamation of Asking Saves Kids Day

Proclaims June 21, 2017 as "Asking Saves Kids" day to prompt people to ask children about the presence of firearms in home out of fear that gun violence is plaguing children.

Effective September 7, 2017

CHAPTER 1:
THE CALIFORNIA REGULATORY ENVIRONMENT

This book provides a practical guide to California and federal laws regulating firearms. But that area of law is evolving fast because of two Supreme Court decisions that addressed the meaning and application of the Second Amendment to the United States Constitution. This chapter addresses some of the recent developments in Second Amendment jurisprudence and provides a constitutional context for reading the laws discussed in this book. This chapter also addresses some of the other legal doctrines that limit the expansion of laws that restrict your right to self-defense.

So if you just want to get a question answered about whether a law applies to a situation, you can skip this chapter. But if you are interested in how the Second Amendment may change the legal playing field in the future and how your life, your children's lives, notions of freedom, and perhaps the very way our government interacts with citizens may be changed by the way the Second Amendment is interpreted and applied by courts in the future, read on.

As a society, we are at a turning point. The country is diametrically divided ideologically to perhaps a greater extent than almost any other time in our history, except during the Civil War. So it is an understatement to say that the issue is important to us all.

I. THE UGLY PROCESS OF GUN LAW POLITICS

A. The Legislative Process

The California State Legislature is currently controlled by a liberal-Democratic majority and has been for years. Control is unlikely to shift in the foreseeable future. As the party in control, the Democrats shape the agenda and will not allow anything to pass that might make Republicans look good.

Although technically any legislator can author a bill on any subject, when it comes to gun control laws there are certain Democrat legislators who lead the gun ban movement amongst their colleagues. Depending on the demographics of a legislator's district, gun control can translate to press coverage, and press coverage translates to name recognition. Having name recognition is critical to getting elected or reelected. When a group like the National Rifle Association (NRA) is pulled into the debate, it can actually serve the purposes of an anti-gun legislator because it increases the level of conflict for the media to cover as was seen in 2016 when Lieutenant Governor Gavin Newsom and Senate President Pro Tem De León feuded over their competing gun-control measures.[1]

A comprehensive treatment of the California legislative process, and just how corrupt it is, is beyond the scope of this book. But for the purposes of this chapter, suffice it to say that legislators often vote for or against a bill for reasons having nothing to do with its merits and frequently do not read the bills they are voting on. For more information on California's legislative process, refer to "California's Legislature" published by the Legislative Counsel of California, available at www.leginfo.ca.gov/califleg.html.

Over the years, I have had a number of private conversations with anti-gun politicians who were candid enough to admit that their agenda was to ban all civilian gun ownership, or at least civilian ownership of handguns. This undisclosed agenda makes it tough to debate the merits of specific gun laws. I once lobbied a Los Angeles City Councilman to vote against a ban on affordable self-defense handguns that anti-gun politicians demonized by calling "Saturday Night Specials." I pointed out that by the way the proposed ordinance defined that term, the Glock handguns used by the LAPD would be deemed "junk guns." The politician replied that it did not matter since all they really wanted to do was take another step toward banning all handguns. At a luncheon with another anti-gun politician, I established that a ban on .50 caliber target rifles was unnecessary since these rifles were never used in crime. The politician, who had not known this, justified her position by arguing that it was important to "make people *feel* safe." That one floored me. Do we really want our legislators to make us *feel* safe? Particularly, do we want to be fooled into *feeling* safe if we are not *actually* safe? This strikes me as a patronizing approach to governing, one that keeps placated citizens blissfully ignorant of reality while politicians get credit for passing complicated "feel good" laws that actually do nothing – except, too often, turn good people into accidental criminals.

Unfortunately, the reality is that firearm laws are rarely based on technical knowledge, rational principle, or a genuine need for regulation. Rather, politics drives the process, not logic. A retired California Department of Justice (DOJ) official has explained that when he has met with the authors of significant gun legislation, they have displayed a level of ignorance about firearms which shows they

---

[1] Jeremy B. White, *Newsom Camp Calls de León Gun Change 'Shockingly, Sickeningly Cynical,'* THE SACRAMENTO BEE (June 24, 2016), *available at* http://www.sacbee.com/news/politics-government/capitol-alert/article85899487.html (last visited July 11, 2017).

do not even understand what their proposed laws do. For example, the legislator who authored the "Unsafe Handgun Act" had to ask the DOJ official, "Where is the barrel?"

For an eye-opening account from a retired Sacramento politician about how laws are created and made, read "What Makes You Think We Read the Bills?" by California State Senator H.L. Richardson (ret.). Senator Richardson deserves special recognition because he founded Gun Owners of California and sponsored California's preemption statute, which prohibits local governments from over-regulating firearms.

B. Local Laws

Despite being prohibited from over-regulating firearms, local governments across the state have nonetheless been swayed by local anti-gun groups into passing their own firearms regulations. Cities that are notoriously anti-gun, such as Los Angeles, San Francisco, Oakland, and Sunnyvale have all passed local ordinances that either expand on or are similar to state law. For instance, all of these localities have adopted firearm storage laws that regulate how gun owners must store their firearms when at home and have banned the possession of so-called "large-capacity magazines." And these cities are not alone.

As explained in the Introduction, we will not cover local firearm regulations in detail in this book. It is important to realize the gun ban lobby has focused many of their efforts on convincing certain city governments, especially those that are predominantly liberal, to further restrict firearms and pass anti-gun legislation.

The NRA and CRPA, through its Local Advocacy Program (LAP), has worked to stem the creeping tide of local gun control ordinances in California. Over the years, the NRA and CRPA have actively monitored and opposed attempts to restrict Second Amendment rights at the city and county level. But, the NRA and CRPA cannot be everywhere. With over 58 counties and 482 municipalities in California, the NRA and CRPA need your help. Whenever you hear that a gun control proposal is coming to your town, please notify the NRA or the CRPA immediately.

C. The Initiative Process

Shamelessly exploiting the San Bernardino terror attack to further his own political career, Governor Gavin Newsom collected signatures to get his own gun control initiative on the November 2016 election ballot. Deceptively entitled "The Safety for All Act," Newsom's ballot initiative was full of measures that do nothing to stop criminals from acquiring firearms. Still, this did not stop Newsom from peddling his ill-conceived gun-control initiative to voters as a way to stop gun violence. He was able to collect the necessary signatures to get the initiative on the 2016 election ballot as Proposition 63 (Prop. 63).

After announcing this initiative, the NRA, CRPA, and other gun rights groups avidly fought to defeat these measures. Despite the efforts of hundreds of thousands of gun owners who showed up to vote on election day, Prop. 63 was passed by the voters.

D. The Gun Ban Lobby's "Feel Good" Laws

Anti-gun groups spend millions of dollars on public relations consultants and efforts to demonize guns, exaggerate their dangers, make it politically incorrect to choose to own one, and "spin" pending legislation to appeal to legislators and unsophisticated constituents.[2] Common platitudes include "talk concept, not content," meaning do not get into a debate about the actual language of a bill or what it actually does. Bills often do much more than their emotionally appealing title would reveal. But gun ban lobbyists focus on the seemingly benign concepts of a bill, like some notion of public safety, often "for the children." If they can be pulled into a discussion of what the specific language of a bill actually does, they argue, "don't let the perfect be the enemy of the good." This, to me, is another way of saying "close enough for government work."

Regardless, the gun ban lobby has been quite successful in getting most of their anti-gun-owner agenda passed in California, and they have not stopped pushing for more restrictive laws. But despite their efforts, polls show an increasing recognition and appreciation of the right to choose to own a gun to defend yourself or your loved ones.

Perhaps in recognition of this trend and what appears to be a disturbing new approach, the gun ban lobby has been pushing laws that actually compel otherwise law-abiding gun owners to report themselves to the police, which forces gun owners into a position where they should decline to cooperate.

For example, several cities passed ordinances that require gun owners to report the theft or loss of their firearms within 48 hours[3] and Prop. 63 enacted this on a statewide level. The gun ban lobby claims these laws help prevent unlawful "straw sales," and stop persons engaged in illegal firearm transfers from falsely claiming that a "crime gun" traced to the owner is "stolen" or "lost" when in fact the firearm was supplied to a criminal. But they often further victimize crime victims and *frustrate* police investigations. For example, if you do not report the loss or theft of a gun and you are then contacted by police who have recovered the gun at a crime scene, you face possible criminal prosecution for failing to report the missing gun. Most gun owners would ordinarily be happy to assist the police with their investigation, but the misdirection of police focus in this situation ultimately delays the police in getting the information they need to investigate the crime.

---

[2] A story concerning this issue and a link to the "anti-gun playbook," entitled "Preventing Gun Violence Through Effective Messaging," can be found at www.NRAILA.org and www.CalGunLawsBook.com.

[3] A state-wide version of this law, SB 299 (authored by Senator Mark DeSaulnier), was proposed in 2013, only to be vetoed by Governor Brown.

Ronald Reagan was right when he said, "There are two things the public should never watch being made, sausage and laws." Lawmaking in this state is not pretty. Gun-law-making is especially ugly.

E. Law Enforcement's Overaggressive Enforcement

Aside from indecipherable laws and laws making criminals out of crime victims, federal, state, and local law enforcement authorities are continuing their stepped-up efforts to conduct "stings" at gun shows (inside and outside of California) and against licensed gun dealers, particularly throughout California and in neighboring states. Rare or "almost legal" guns are sometimes offered at "too good to be true" prices in order to seduce the "stingee." The Police also monitor internet message boards, *Shotgun News*, Gun List USA, Gunbroker.com, and other trade magazines, and even run fake ads themselves. Suspects who fall for these "stings" typically have their businesses and residences searched and all of their firearms seized. Meanwhile, DOJ continues to aggressively enforce the "Armed Prohibited Persons System" (APPS) program by going after, in some cases, non-violent felons and misdemeanants whose only conviction was years in the past and who are often unaware that they are prohibited from possessing firearms.

While many of the efforts of these agencies are laudable, far too often the people being arrested are not violent felons. They typically have no prior criminal record and are solid citizens who did not know they were violating the law. Some police agencies simply go for the "easy meat" to bolster their prosecution and gun seizure statistics, regardless of whether violent crime actually gets reduced in the process.

Every violation of the law, however inadvertent, is politicized and ultimately used by the gun ban lobby to advance its cultural and political war against civilian firearm ownership in general, and to urge closure of gun stores or an end to gun shows in particular. Sadly, caution must increasingly be exercised before cooperating with authorities. Your attempt at cooperation could easily lead to making an incriminating admission that results in criminal charges for an inadvertent violation. If you are approached about a possibly illegal transaction, remember: do not equivocate – refuse to participate!

F. The Pro-Gun Lobby

There are a number of pro-Second Amendment groups working in Sacramento, including the NRA, CRPA, National Shooting Sports Foundation, and Gun Owners of California. The NRA, the CRPA, and the Gun Owners of California have full-time lobbyists in the California Capital.

The NRA and CRPA deserve special mention because I have had the privilege of representing them for many years.

1. The National Rifle Association and The California Rifle and Pistol Association

Dismayed by the lack of marksmanship shown by their troops, Union veterans Col. William C. Church and Gen. George Wingate formed the NRA in 1871. That makes it the oldest civil rights organization in the country. In response to repeated attacks on Second Amendment rights, the NRA formed the Legislative Affairs Division in 1934. While the NRA did not lobby directly at first, it did mail out legislative facts and analyses to members whereby they could take action on their own. In 1975, recognizing the critical need for political defense of the Second Amendment, the NRA formed the Institute for Legislative Action (ILA). Meanwhile, the NRA continued its commitment to training, education, and marksmanship.

While widely recognized today as a major political force and as America's foremost defender of Second Amendment rights, the NRA has, since its inception, been the premier firearms education organization in the world. But the NRA's successes would not be possible without the tireless efforts and countless hours of service the NRA's nearly four million members give to champion Second Amendment rights and support NRA programs. As former Clinton spokesman George Stephanopoulos said, "Let me make one small vote for the NRA. They're good citizens. They call their congressmen. They write. They vote. They contribute. And they get what they want over time."[4]

As mentioned, the NRA employs a much needed lobbyist in Sacramento. But given California's politics, the NRA's power in Washington, D.C., does not translate to the same extent in Sacramento.

Founded in 1875, the CRPA is the official state affiliate of the NRA. The CRPA is dedicated to protecting firearm freedoms and promoting shooting sports solely in California. CRPA's full-time lobbyist in Sacramento also fights adverse firearm legislation and works to promote laws that protect your right to choose to own a gun to protect yourself or your family. CRPA Foundation is the 501(c)(3) sibling of the CRPA and funds some of the Second Amendment litigation and other litigation in which I am often involved.

As you read this book, I hope becoming educated about some of the problems with California's gun laws will cause you to consider getting involved in California's political process, which means joining these associations and staying informed about efforts to restrict your right to choose to own a gun for sport or to defend yourself and your family.

G. Gun Violence Research

In 2016, the California Legislature passed Assembly Bill (AB) 1602, which, among other things, establishes a center for research on gun violence that will be adminis-

---

[4] *About Us*, NATIONAL RIFLE ASSOCIATION (NRA), http://www.nra.org/aboutus.aspx (last visited Oct. 14, 2017).

tered by the University of California, Davis. In 2017, the Legislature passed Senate Bill (SB) 536, which requires DOJ to give information about gun violence restraining orders to this research center.[5] This center is tasked with studying the effectiveness of existing laws and policies intended to reduce firearm violence.[6] Although in theory politically neutral research would be helpful in determining what kind of laws could encourage the safe and responsible use of firearms and reduce the number of firearm related deaths, history has shown that government-funded research into gun violence tends to be politically biased.

A long time ago, Congress used to fund research into gun violence through the Center for Disease Control and Prevention's (CDC). During the late '80s and early '90s, the CDC was not shy about their bias towards gun ownership and that their intentions in publishing these studies was to convince citizens that firearms should be banned altogether. In a 1989 issue of the Journal of the American Medical Association, Dr. Patrick O'Carroll, the acting section head of the Division on Injury Control at the CDC, was quoted as saying, "We're going . . . to systematically build a case that owning firearms causes deaths. [] . . . We're doing the most we can do, given the political realities."[7] Dr. O'Carroll later contended that he was misquoted in the journal. But, his predecessor Dr. Mark Rosenberg reiterated this sentiment in the Washington Post when he explained that, "We need to revolutionize the way we look at guns, like what we did with cigarettes. It used to be that smoking was a glamour symbol – cool, sexy, macho. Now it is dirty, deadly – and banned."[8]

By the early '90s, the CDC's plan to convince people through science that firearm ownership should be banned was well underway. In 1993, the New England Journal of Medicine released a study by Dr. Arthur Kellermann – an epidemiologist, physician, outspoken gun-control advocate, and recipient of 1.7 million dollars in grant money from the CDC – entitled *Gun Ownership as a Risk Factor for Homicide in the Home*.[9] In this study, Dr. Kellermann concluded that people who kept guns in their homes were 2.7 times more likely to be victims of a homicide as people who don't keep firearms in their homes.[10] This statistic is still cited by gun

---

[5] DOJ can even give information identifying specific individuals to this research center, provided that information identifying specific individuals is not revealed or used for anything other than research or statistical activities and will not be reported in publications. SB 536, 2016-2017, Leg. Counsel's Digest (Cal. 2017), *available at* https://leginfo.legislature.ca.gov/faces/billNavClient.xhtml?bill_id=201720180SB536 (last visited Oct. 14, 2017). Nothing in this bill prevents the researchers from skewing or misapplying the information to forward their cause.

[6] *See* AB 1602, 2015-2016, Leg. Counsel's Digest (Cal. 2016), *available at* http://leginfo.legislature.ca.gov/faces/billNavClient.xhtml?bill_id=201520160AB1602 (last visited July 11, 2017).

[7] Marsha F. Goldsmith, Epidemiologist Aim at New Target: Health Risk of Handgun Proliferation, 261(5) J. OF THE AMERICAN MED. ASSOC. 675, 676 (1989).

[8] William Raspberry, *Sick People With Guns*, WASHINGTON POST (Oct. 19, 1994), *available at* https://www.washingtonpost.com/archive/opinions/1994/10/19/sick-people-with-guns/6c7f2bd2-fa57-4d69-b927-5ceb4fa43cf4/ (July 11, 2017).

[9] Arthur K. Kellermann, et al., *Gun Ownership as a Risk Factor for Homicide in the Home*, 329 NEW ENGLAND J. OF MED. 1084 (1993), *available at* http://www.nejm.org/doi/full/10.1056/NEJM199310073291506#t=article (July 11, 2017).

[10] Arthur K. Kellermann, et al., *Gun Ownership as a Risk Factor for Homicide in the Home*, 329 NEW ENGLAND J. OF MED. 1084 (1993), *available at* http://www.nejm.org/doi/full/10.1056/NEJM199310073291506#t=article (July 11, 2017).

control activists to this day, despite the fact that multiple studies have proven that the research methods of this study were flawed.[11]

In fact, subsequent studies have shown quite different results than those found by Dr. Kellerman and other publicly funded studies through the CDC. For example, research conducted by Dr. Gary Kleck, a Florida State University criminologist; Professor Gary Mauser, an urban studies expert at Simon Fraser University; Professors James D. Wright and Peter H. Rossi, sociologists at University of Massachusetts, and Dr. John Lott, who formerly taught at the University of Chicago, raised serious questions about the results of Dr. Kellermann's work and generally affirmed the social utility of firearms.[12]

Because of the clear bias against gun ownership, Congress decided to defund these programs. In 1996, it passed the 1996 Omnibus Consolidated Appropriations Bill. This bill included language that prevented the CDC from using tax-payer money to fund advocacy science, specifically stating that "none of the funds made available for injury prevention and control at the [CDC} may be used to advocate or promote gun control."[13]

Despite this defunding, the gun-ban lobby has continued to fund a number of studies to further gun control. For example, there have been a number of studies conducted by Doctor Garen Wintemute of the University of California, Davis. Dr. Wintemute has been a long-time advocate of restricting the right to keep and bear arms, and has received thousands of dollars from the gun-control movements financier, the Joyce Foundation. His studies often argue that more gun-control would lead to less crime and gun violence.

Having received thousands of dollars from anti-gun groups to conduct his research, Dr. Wintemute is far from being an impartial researcher. Nonetheless, the University of California has chosen him to lead up the University of California Firearm Violence Research Center at Davis.[14]

Hopefully, this new center for research at the University of California will not have these same issues or produce advocacy science like the CDC did in the 90's.

---

[11] See Don B Kates, et al., *Public Health Pot Shots: How the CDC Succumbed to the Gun Epidemic,* REASON (Apr. 2007), *available at* http://reason.com/archives/1997/04/01/public-health-pot-shots (last visited Oct. 15, 2017).

[12] Gary Kleck, *What Are the Risks and Benefits of Keeping a Gun in the Home?* JAMA (Aug. 5, 1998), *available at* http://www.guncite.com/kleckjama01.html (last visited Oct. 15, 2017); Gary Mauser and Don B Kates, *Would Banning Firearms Reduce Murder and Suicide? A Review of International and Some Domestic Evidence,* 30(2) HARV. J. LAW & POLICY 649 (2007), *available at* http://www.law.harvard.edu/students/orgs/jlpp/Vol30_No2_KatesMauseronline.pdf. (last visited Oct. 15, 2017); James D. Wright and Peter Rossi, *Gun Control Research- Wright and Rossi Department of Justice Study: Deterrent Effect of Armed Citizens upon Criminal Behavior?* http://www.leg. state.co.us/clics/clics2012a/commsumm.nsf/b4a3962433b52fa787256e5f00670a71/5de089825c00843e872579b80 079912d/%24FILE/SenState0305AttachB.pdf (last visited Oct. 15, 2017); John R Lott, MORE GUNS, LESS CRIME: UNDERSTANDING CRIME AND GUN CONTROL LAW (3d ed. 2010).

[13] Pub. L. No. 104-208, 110 Stat. 3009 (1996), *available at* https://www.gpo.gov/fdsys/pkg/PLAW-104publ208/pdf/PLAW-104publ208.pdf (last visited Oct. 16, 2017).

[14] Zusha Elinson, *Doctor to Run New Gun-Violence Research Center in California,* THE WALL STREET JOURNAL (Aug. 21, 2016), *available at* http://www.wsj.com/articles/doctor-to-run-new-gun-violence-research-center-in-california-1472667927 (last visited July 11, 2017).

But given Dr. Wintemute's instatement as the head of the research center, I wouldn't hold my breath.

II. THE RIGHT TO KEEP AND BEAR ARMS AND TO SELF-DEFENSE

A. The United States and California Constitutions

The Second Amendment provides, "A well regulated Militia, being necessary to the security of a free State, the right of the people to keep and bear Arms, shall not be infringed."[15]

In 2008, the U.S. Supreme Court confirmed in *District of Columbia v. Heller* that the Second Amendment protects an *individual's* right to keep and bear arms for self-defense – contrary to gun control advocates' claims for decades that the Second Amendment only provides collective rights for state militias.[16]

In 2010, in *McDonald v. Chicago*,[17] the Supreme Court confirmed that an *individual's* right to keep and bear arms is fundamental and is thus "incorporated" into the Bill of Rights through the 14th Amendment. This means that federal, state, and local governments cannot infringe upon your Second Amendment right to keep and bear arms and to self-defense.

After these decisions came down, hundreds of cases raised the Second Amendment as an issue, and hundreds of courts have addressed the scope of the Second Amendment's protections. Unfortunately the issue was most often raised as a defense in criminal cases, where the chances of success are decreased by court overcrowding and by lawyers who are insufficiently prepared to properly present such novel and complicated issues to the court.

Even in the few civil cases challenging firearms regulations, or that would serve as precedent to challenge some of California's ill-conceived laws, the lawyers bringing the claims are often inexperienced and lack the resources needed to do the job competently. The NRA and the CRPA, along with several other Second Amendment advocacy groups, have brought a few dozen cases, with mixed success. Those cases, and others that have yet to be filed, are making their way inexorably toward the Supreme Court.

Since the *Heller* and *McDonald* decisions, several petitions have been filed with the Supreme Court asking them to address cases raising Second Amendment related issues. Though the high court has expressed some heightened interest in hearing a Second Amendment case, it has so far rejected all Second Amendment related petitions.

---

[15] U.S. CONST. amend. II.

[16] *Dist. of Columbia v. Heller*, 554 U.S. 570, 592-93 (2008).

[17] *McDonald v. Chicago*, 561 U.S. 742 (2010).

The high court will inevitably have to address the foundational issues that have been raised regarding the scope and application of *Heller* and *McDonald,* and then subsequently address the additional issues that will inevitably arise in cases brought thereafter. But this will be a dynamic and rapidly changing legal landscape.

Most states have their own version of the Second Amendment right to keep and bear arms in their respective constitutions.[18] California, however, does not.

It has been argued though that one provision of the California constitution *does* implicate the right to self-defense: "All people are by nature free and independent and have inalienable rights. Among these are enjoying and defending life and liberty, acquiring, possessing, and protecting property, and pursuing and obtaining safety, happiness, and privacy."[19] Unfortunately, the California Supreme Court has rejected this notion.[20]

B. Primary Issues Being Addressed in Current Second Amendment Litigation

Laws regulating firearms typically fall into one of three categories: (1) laws that regulate where and how firearms can be possessed, (2) laws regulating how to acquire firearms and which types of firearms or firearm accessories can be acquired and possessed, and (3) laws regulating whether certain people can possess firearms.

In a Second Amendment case, the judge must first decide whether the individual conduct being legislatively restricted implicates the Second Amendment at all. In some cases, this initial inquiry should be relatively simple.

For instance, a case regarding the possession of a handgun in the home for self-defense clearly concerns conduct protected by the Second Amendment. Such was the very conduct at issue in *District of Columbia v. Heller*, and the Supreme Court ruled 5-4 that Mr. Heller did have a Second Amendment right to own a handgun for self-defense.

But how about possessing a rifle or shotgun in the home for self-defense? What about air guns? Knives, clubs, swords, or bows? Electronic devices such as tasers? Or chemical self-defense sprays? Is carrying a handgun outside the home for self-defense within the scope of the right? What about possession in gun-free zones? What rights do we have to possess a firearm for things other than self-defense, like target shooting, hunting, or collecting? What kinds of people can have their Second Amendment rights taken away and for how long? Felons? Yes. Forever? Not so clear. What about people with misdemeanor convictions? Which convictions should be prohibiting? For how long? Some would say that a person with any type of criminal conviction should be prohibited from possessing firearms forever.

---

[18] *See* Eugene Volokh, *State Constitutional Right to Keep and Bear Arms,* 11 TEX. REV. L. & POL. 191-952 (2006).

[19] CAL. CONST. art. I, § 1.

[20] *Kasler v. Lockyer*, 23 Cal. 4th 472, 481 (2000) ("If plaintiffs are implying that a right to bear arms is one of the rights recognized in the California Constitution's declaration of rights, they are simply wrong.").

Each of these questions regarding the scope of the Second Amendment remain unanswered. But cases raising these questions are making their way through the various federal circuit courts, and the Supreme Court will eventually and inevitably be compelled to consider them. Stay current on these developments through www.crpa.org.

Once an activity is acknowledged as being within the scope of a constitutional right, does that mean that any restrictions on the right are invalid? Definitely not. Courts use various tests, or "standards of review," to determine if a law is unconstitutional. The three most commonly used of these tests are "strict scrutiny,"[21] "intermediate scrutiny,"[22] and "rational basis review."[23] As its name suggests, strict scrutiny is the most rigorous of the three standards, and most laws subjected to it will be struck down. Rational basis, at the other end of the spectrum, is the least rigorous. Under it, only the most egregious laws will be invalidated because the government can posit almost any reasonable justification for the law. Because constitutional rights are so important, rational basis is rarely used when a law infringes on them. Intermediate scrutiny lies somewhere in the middle, giving the courts great discretion to either uphold or overturn a law. Which test a court utilizes depends on various factors, including the nature of the right at issue. The important question currently before the courts is which test should be applied in Second Amendment rights cases.

Before *Heller* acknowledged the importance of the rights protected by the Second Amendment, many courts upheld all firearm laws because they believed that the Second Amendment did not protect ordinary citizens. Under rational basis review, even a firearm ban would be upheld because the government could posit a "rational" belief that preventing ordinary citizens from having firearms would reduce firearm misuse.

After *Heller*, lower courts have struggled to determine exactly what standard to apply when reviewing laws that impact Second Amendment rights. Aside from explicitly rejecting the before-mentioned rational basis review, the *Heller* Court did not formally declare which standard of review should apply. So lower courts have been crafting their own analyses by drawing inferences from *Heller's* reasoning. Of course, many judges have taken very different approaches.

Most courts will review the law to see if the conduct being challenged is within the scope of the Second Amendment right, as that right was understood when the Bill of Rights was drafted. If the conduct being challenged does affect that right,

---

[21] Strict scrutiny requires that a law "be narrowly tailored to promote a compelling Government interest, and if a less restrictive alternative would serve the Government's purpose, the legislature must use that alternative." *See U.S. v. Playboy Entertainment Group, Inc.* 529 U.S. 803, 804 (2000).

[22] Intermediate scrutiny requires that the law be "substantially related" to an "important government interest." *Clark v. Jeter,* 486 U.S. 456, 461 (1988).

[23] Rational basis review requires that the law be "rationally related" to a "legitimate government interest" offered as its justification. *City of New Orleans v. Dukes,* 427 U.S. 297, 303 (1976).

courts will then determine which level of heightened scrutiny[24] to apply based on a number of factors.[25] Many courts, for instance, look to (1) whether a restriction touches upon conduct at the "core" of the Second Amendment and (2) how severely it burdens that conduct. This analysis has often led courts to select intermediate scrutiny—despite the Second Amendment being considered a fundamental right.

In addition, some courts have found that when a statute or regulation causes Second Amendment rights to be *destroyed*, rather than merely burdened, it is appropriate to strike the law down without determining which level of heightened scrutiny to apply.[26] That is the approach *Heller* took in striking down a total denial of the ordinary citizen's right to keep arms.[27]

The scope of the Second Amendment's protection and the means the courts will apply in upholding the right are, and will likely continue to be, defined through litigation. Certain cases and examples are therefore highlighted throughout this book to help you understand the different ways firearms laws are being interpreted and applied. These lawsuits encompass a variety of issues, ranging from what types of firearms are constitutionally protected to defining what constitutes a "sensitive place" where firearms may lawfully be prohibited.

Again, to stay updated on the status of Second Amendment litigation and other firearm-related litigation and issues, sign up for free alerts at www.crpa.org.

III. THE PREEMPTION DOCTRINE

A. Federal Preemption Doctrine

Setting California's constitution and politicians aside, it is helpful to address federal and state law preemption before diving into California's firearms laws and their various nuances.

The concept of federal preemption is found in the Supremacy Clause of the United States Constitution:

> This Constitution, and the Laws of the United States which shall be made in Pursuance thereof; and all Treaties made, or which shall be made, under the Authority of the United States, shall be the supreme Law of the Land;

---

[24] The U.S. Supreme Court expressly explicitly rejected the rational basis standard for evaluating Second Amendment claims. "If all that was required to overcome the right to keep and bear arms was a rational basis, the Second Amendment would be redundant with the separate constitutional prohibitions on irrational laws, and would have no effect." *District of Columbia v. Heller*, 554 U.S. 570, 629 n. 27 (2008).

[25] *See, e.g., United States v. Chovan*, 735 F.3d 1127, 1138 (9th Cir. 2013); *see, e.g., Ezell v. City of Chicago*, 651 F.3d 684, 703 (7th Cir. 2011).

[26] *See, e.g., Wrenn v. District of Columbia*, 864 F.3d 650, 664-66 (D.C. Cir. 2017); *see, e.g., Peruta v. County of San Diego*, 742 F.3d 1144, 1175 (9th Cir. 2014); *see, e.g., Moore v. Madigan*, 702 F.3d 933, 941-42 (7th Cir. 2012); *see, e.g., Palmer v. District of Columbia*, 59 F. Supp. 3d 173, 182-83 (D.C. Cir. 2014).

[27] *District of Columbia v. Heller*, 554 U.S. 570, 628-29 (2008).

and the Judges in every State shall be bound thereby, any Thing in the Constitution or Laws of any State to the Contrary notwithstanding.[28]

The Supremacy Clause means that if a conflict exists between state and federal law, "the federal law controls and the state law is invalidated because federal law is supreme."[29]

Because federal law can preempt California law in many ways, this book addresses both state and federal firearms laws, though the emphasis is on California law.

B. California Preemption Doctrine

Just as federal law can supersede (or preempt) conflicting state laws, state laws can likewise preempt conflicting local (*i.e.*, city and county) laws.

The California Constitution explicitly notes that a county or city must take care not to fall "in conflict with general laws."[30] Courts have long interpreted this as a limitation on local government's ability to interfere with the proper operation of state law through local legislation. In doing so, courts have looked into whether a local ordinance "*duplicates, contradicts, or enters an area fully occupied* by general law, either expressly or by legislative implication."[31]

Often, California's statutory scheme preempts local firearms laws by fully occupying the field, either expressly or implicitly,[32] or as is the case with Prop 63, they can expressly provide that local governments are not preempted from enacting further measures.[33] Where state laws expressly preempt local laws, the preemptive effect is generally clear. But, sometimes the law does not expressly state whether local laws are preempted, or the scope of the preemptive effect is unclear. In these circumstances, California's implied preemption doctrine may be implicated. This doctrine allows for a law to be preempted if the state demonstrates an intent to preempt local regulation. The state's intent can be ascertained by considering whether:

(1) the subject matter has been so fully and completely covered by general law as to clearly indicate that it has become exclusively a matter of state concern; (2) the subject matter has been partially covered by general law

---

[28] U.S. CONST. art. VI, cl. 2.

[29] ERWIN CHEMERINSKY, CONSTITUTIONAL LAW PRINCIPLES AND POLICIES 376 (Erwin Chemerinsky et al. eds., 2d ed. 2002). *See also Gade v. Nat'l Solid Wastes Mgmt. Ass'n*, 505 U.S. 88, 108 (1992) (stating "any state law, however clearly within a State's acknowledged power, which interferes with or is contrary to federal law, must yield") (citation and internal quotation marks omitted).

[30] CAL. CONST. art. XI, § 7.

[31] *Sherwin-Williams Co. v. City of Los Angeles*, 4 Cal. 4th 893, 897 (1993) (emphasis added)(citation and internal quotation marks omitted).

[32] For example, in *Fiscal v. City and County of San Francisco*, the California Court of Appeal held that a San Francisco ordinance which totally prohibited the possession and sale of handguns within the city was preempted by state law. *See Fiscal v. City and County of San Francisco*, 158 Cal. App. 4th 895 (2008); *see also* FULL TEXT OF PROPOSITION 63, OFFICE OF THE ATTORNEY GENERAL, *available at* https://www.oag.ca.gov/system/files/initiatives/pdfs/15-0098%20(Firearms)_0.pdf (last visited July 11, 2017).

[33] *See Viva! Intern. Voice for Animals v. Adidas Promotional Retail Operations, Inc.*, 41 Cal. 4th 929 (2007).

couched in such terms as to indicate clearly that a paramount state concern will not tolerate further or additional local action; or (3) the subject matter has been partially covered by general law, and the subject is of such a nature that the adverse effect of a local ordinance on the transient citizens of the state outweighs the possible benefit to the locality.[34]

What local laws are preempted by California's legal scheme is unclear. But it is clear that localities cannot ban firearms outright, require their registration, or require licenses to own them.

The gun ban lobby has tried to limit the preemption doctrine as it applies to regulating firearms. For example, in 2013, the gun ban lobby pushed legislation that would have created an exception to California's preemption of firearms laws for the City of Oakland, and would have permitted Oakland to enact laws concerning firearms that are more restrictive than state laws. Thankfully, Governor Brown vetoed the legislation, commenting, "[t]he State of California has among the strictest gun laws in the country. Allowing individual cities to enact their own more restrictive firearms regulations will sow confusion and uncertainty."[35]

Governor Brown is absolutely right. Residents of the city would have had to stay updated with any new city ordinances in addition to state law. The legislation was proposed under the guise that it would help to reduce gun violence in the city, but the city is already ill-equipped to enforce state gun laws and local laws. Had the legislation been signed into law, law enforcement efforts would have likely been diverted to implement and maintain further licensing and registration databases to track law-abiding gun owners. And this legislation would have opened the door for other localities to request special exemptions from preemption for firearms laws leading to a patchwork of local laws governing firearms throughout the state.

For years, the preemption doctrine prevented local governments from creating firearm laws that were more restrictive than state laws.[36] But, in 2013, an ill-conceived lawsuit brought the effect of the preemption doctrine into question.[37] Since then, the gun-ban lobby has shifted gears and is now using new tactics to limit the preemption doctrine and get their anti-gun agenda passed in California. For instance, the gun-ban lobby has begun to take pieces of anti-gun legislation that failed to pass out of the California Legislature and push them in cities that are highly sympathetic to their cause, such as Sunnyvale, San Francisco, and Los Angeles.

Although the question of whether these local ordinances violate the preemption doctrine is outside of the scope of this book, it should be noted that the firearms

---

[34] *In re Hubbard*, 62 Cal. 2d 119, 128 (1964), *overruled in other part by Bishop v. City of San Jose*, 1 Cal.3d 56 (1969).

[35] Letter from Edmund G. Brown, Governor of California, to the Members of the California State Assembly (Oct. 11, 2013), *available at* http://gov.ca.gov/docs/AB_180_2013_Veto_Message.pdf (last visited July 11, 2017).

[36] For example, in *Fiscal v. City and County of San Francisco*, the California Court of Appeal held that the state law preempted a San Francisco ordinance that prohibited the possession and sale of handguns within the city. *See Fiscal v. City and Cnty of San Francisco*, 158 Cal. App. 4th 895 (2008).

[37] *See Calguns Foundation, Inc. v. Cnty of San Mateo*, 218 Cal. App. 4th 661 (2013).

laws passed in Sunnyvale, San Francisco, and Los Angeles[38] have created a mine-field for gun owners who reside in or are traveling through these cities. Because each of these local laws are more restrictive than state law, any gun owner traveling through or residing in these cities must ensure that they know, understand, and comply with the cities' firearms laws.

For a more in-depth analysis of California's preemption doctrine, see the law review article I co-authored: *Local Gun Bans in California: A Futile Exercise*.[39]

IV. THE CALIFORNIA LEGAL SCHEME

A. The Dangerous Weapons Control Act (DWCA)

California's Penal Code (P.C.) sections 16000 *et seq*. are collectively referred to as the Dangerous Weapons Control Act (DWCA), the reorganization of which is further discussed below. These Penal Code sections are home to most of California's firearms laws. But some firearms laws are also found in the California Fish and Game Code (Cal. Fish & Game Code), California Welfare and Institutions Code (Cal. Welf. & Inst. Code), California Vehicle Code (Cal. Veh. Code), California Business and Professions Code (Cal. Bus. & Prof. Code), California Health and Safety Code (Cal. Health & Saf. Code), California Government Code (Cal. Gov't Code), California Code of Regulations (Cal. Code Regs.), and other parts of the Penal Code. California is somewhat unique in that some municipal governments have also passed extensive local gun control ordinances.

Of course, federal firearms laws also apply in California and are contained in federal statutes and regulations.

B. Confusion Runs Rampant

There are hundreds of federal laws and regulations covering firearms. California state statutes regulating the manufacture, distribution, sale, possession, and use of firearms now number over 800! That does not include administrative regulations, local ordinances, or the California DOJ "Bureau of Firearms" written and unwritten policies. As former California Attorney General Dan Lungren once noted, thanks to politicians, California firearms laws are now as complex as the state's byzantine environmental and tax laws. And the politicians are not backing off. Unfortunately, unlike corporations with lawyers on retainer to answer legal questions and ensure compliance with the environmental and tax laws, gun owners don't typically have

---

[38] Sunnyvale, San Francisco, and Los Angeles have all enacted ordinances that prohibit the possession of "large-capacity magazines" within their respective city limits. See Chapter 9. As of the date of publication, it remains to be seen whether the new restrictions on "large-capacity magazines" that were enacted by Prop. 63 and Senate Bill 1446 preempt these local ordinances. San Francisco also has enacted ordinances that require residents to keep their handguns in locked containers or use trigger locks when storing the firearm inside their homes. See Chapter 4.

[39] Don B. Kates & C.D. Michel, *Local Gun Bans in California: A Futile Exercise*, 41 U.S.F. L. Rev. 333 (2007).

expert lawyers on retainer to advise them on what the increasingly complex gun laws require.

Unsurprisingly, all of the overlapping and constantly changing rules have led to rampant confusion among California gun owners. As a result, inadvertent gun law violations by well-intentioned good people have become increasingly common. And in the politicized environment of California firearms laws, the consequences of even an inadvertent violation can be severe.

Because firearms are so extensively regulated, even those tasked with enforcing them are oftentimes confused about what the laws require. This confusion also commonly extends to those who choose to own a gun for work, hunting, sport, or defense of themselves and their families.

In commenting on a proposed anti-gun bill in September of 2004, Governor Arnold Schwarzenegger acknowledged:

> Such ambiguity in the law invites arbitrary enforcement and judicial review . . . . Before a government exercises its power to take away one's liberty, it should be clear to every person what actions will cause them to forfeit their freedom. Instead of adding to the lengthy and complex area of firearm laws, a reorganization of the current laws should be undertaken to ensure that statutes that impose criminal penalties are easily understandable.[40]

Judges are equally confused. California Court of Appeal Justice William Bedsworth, writing about firearms law said it best: "At first blush, the statutes seem impenetrable. Reading them is hard, writing about them arduous, reading about them probably downright painful. The [complexity] makes for tough sledding. As Alfred North Whitehead wrote of rationalism, the effort is, itself, 'an adventure in the clarification of thought.'"[41]

The California Assault Weapons Control Act (AWCA) is perhaps the most complicated of all California firearms laws, and the consequences for violation are severe. Not only do ordinary citizens find it difficult – if not impossible – to determine whether a semiautomatic firearm should be considered an "assault weapon," trained law enforcement officers, prosecutors, and judges have a similar difficulty.

The author of the legislation requiring the Attorney General to produce the Assault Weapon Identification Guide (AWIG) recognized this difficulty:

> I am writing to request your signature on SB 2444 which would enable law enforcement personnel in the field the means to be able to recognize what actually is or is not an "assault weapon," as defined under state law . . . . Un-

---

[40] Letter from Arnold Schwarzenegger, Governor of California, to the Members of the California State Senate (Sept. 20, 2014), *available at* ftp://leginfo.public.ca.gov/pub/03-04/bill/sen/sb_1101-1150/sb_1140_vt_20040920.html (last visited July 11, 2017).

[41] *Rash v. Lungen*, 59 Cal. App. 4th 1233, 1235 (1997) (quoting Whitehead, Process and Reality (1929) pt. I, ch. 1, § 3).

fortunately, a great many law enforcement officers who deal directly with the public are not experts in specific firearms identification . . . . There are numerous makes and models of civilian military-looking semi-automatic firearms which are not listed by California as "assault weapons" but which are very similar in external appearance. This situation sets the stage for honest law-enforcement mistakes resulting in unjustified confiscations of non-assault weapon firearms. Such mistakes, although innocently made, could easily result in unnecessary, time consuming, and costly legal actions both for law enforcement and for the lawful firearms owners affected.[42]

C. 2012 Reorganization of the Dangerous Weapons Control Act

To improve the California Penal Code's organization and understandability, and in recognition of the tremendous confusion surrounding the interpretation and enforcement of California firearms laws, the Dangerous Weapons Recodification Act of 2010 was adopted. Under this recodification, the California Law Revision Commission (CLRC) completely renumbered the DWCA, as well as parts of some other California codes, to "improve the organization and accessibility of the deadly weapons statutes, without making any change to criminal liability under those statutes."[43]

The Dangerous Weapons Recodification Act was adopted pursuant to Assembly Concurrent Resolution 73 in 2006,[44] which directed the CLRC, a neutral body of legal experts, to study, report on, and prepare recommended legislation to simplify and reorganize the portions of the Penal Code relating to the control of deadly weapons, without making any substantive change to the scope of criminal liability under those provisions.

The author of ACR 73 said:

In addition to the criminal storage laws, *many other provisions of the Penal Code are very confusing. In particular, the laws relating to the transfers of firearms are lengthy, with numerous cross-references, highly fact-specific exemptions, and complex provisions.* For example, Penal Code Section 12078 is 5,880 words long and occupies eleven pages if printed in a 12-point font with conventional margins. The section has cross-references to many scattered sections of other firearms provisions, some of them hundreds of sections away. *The firearms laws occupy over 100 pages of an unannotated ver-*

---

[42] *See Harrott v. Cnty. of Kings*, 25 Cal. 4th 1138, 1147 n.4 (2001) (citing Letter from Don Rogers, United States Senator, to George Deukmejian, Governor of California (Aug. 23, 1990)).

[43] *Nonsubstantive Reorganization of Deadly Weapons Statutes*, 38 CAL. L. REVISION COMM'N REPORTS 217, 219 (2009) (citing letter from Pamela L. Hemminger, Chairwoman, California Law Revision Commission, to Arnold Schwarzenegger, Governor of California), *available at* http://clrc.ca.gov/pub/Printed-Reports/Pub233.pdf (last visited July 11, 2017).

[44] *See* 2006 Cal. Stat. 7397-98.

sion of the Penal Code when printed in dual column in tiny print. These areas of the law are not for legal experts only. Firearms owners, licensed dealers, and law enforcement need to be able to interpret these provisions in order to comply with the law and avoid criminal liability. Ambiguity and confusion do not promote the public policy goals that those laws were designated to accomplish.[45]

The CLRC completed their task on time in 2009, and the Dangerous Weapons Recodification Act was adopted in 2010. It took effect on January 1, 2012.

To assist persons using those laws, I have posted a disposition table on www.CalGunLawsBook.com showing where each provision was relocated. Visit the site for that and additional information on the reorganization.

D. "Gray Areas" and Test Cases

Despite my best efforts to explain the firearms laws in California, there are some unanswered questions, as is the case with most any legal scheme as convoluted as California's. I may have my own personal beliefs as to how law enforcement would likely interpret these laws. My purpose in addressing these legal "gray areas" is not to provide my position on what the law actually is or should be, nor to persuade or dissuade you from deciding to engage in activities falling in a "gray area" category. But, as an attorney, I believe part of my obligation is to make you aware of the uncertainty about what some of the laws allow and that there are potential risks associated with certain activities. I will let you decide what makes sense for your personal situation. When these legal "gray areas" arise in the book, I have tried to indicate them as such and remind the reader of the admonition in this chapter.

Some people choose to push the legal "envelope" by engaging in activities that would fall in these legal "gray areas." And some even insist that certain activities are not "gray" at all, but are clearly legal, and that their interpretation precludes law enforcement from causing you any legal problems. This overly academic mindset is driven by wishful thinking, a misunderstanding of the context of California firearms law, and the practically oriented judicial system in which they are typically applied. When in doubt, if possible, ask a qualified attorney before engaging in legally questionable activity.

And be very careful about relying on the opinions of internet-pseudo-lawyers for answers to your firearms law-related questions. As one court elegantly explained:

> Beware of the dangers of the Internet. It makes semiautomatic assault
> weapon kits available at the click of a mouse. Furthermore, it would appear
> to provide guidance on assembling the weapon, as well as suggestions for

---

[45] *Analysis of ACR 73*, CAL. SEN. RULES COMM., OFFICE OF SENATE FLOOR ANALYSES (S. 2004-2005 Reg. Sess.), ftp://www.leginfo.ca.gov/pub/05-06/bill/asm/ab_0051-0100/acr_73_cfa_20060822_195816_sen_floor.html (last visited July 11, 2017) (emphasis added).

avoiding criminal convictions arising out of the possession of the parts, their assembly, and even the possession of the completed weapons. But woe betides the consumer who trusts every schematic espoused on the Internet.[46]

E. Government Bias in Applying Gun Laws

People just cannot count on logic or reasonableness alone in deciphering California's firearms laws in a way that protects them. If that were the case, there would be little need for this book; at least, it would be much shorter.

In my many years of handling thousands of criminal and civil matters involving firearms, it is my experience that some law enforcement officers, many prosecutors, and most California courts are unsympathetic toward civilian firearm ownership. They have repeatedly gone, and likely will continue to go, out of their way to interpret a questionable practice as unlawful. This is the case even if a technical reading of a statute or regulation suggests the practice is legal. Once your defense depends on parsing the language of statutes and/or explaining technical discrepancies, you are fighting an uphill battle. And the cost of taking that proverbial "hill" can often be significant. I do not need to warn you that lawyers cost money.

A prime example of the troublesome nature of interpreting firearms laws is the fact that the preeminent case from the U.S. Supreme Court interpreting the Second Amendment right to keep and bear arms as an individual right, *District of Columbia v. Heller*, was decided by a vote of 5-4. That means four justices in the country's highest court disagree that there is even an individual right to firearm possession. The same vote count was repeated in the following Supreme Court ruling on whether the Second Amendment applied to the states and local governments in *McDonald v. Chicago*. And despite this promise from the Supreme Court's *Heller* and *McDonald* decisions, many courts and politicians still remain opposed to fundamental Second Amendment rights and resistant to the Supreme Court's pronouncements.

Unfortunately, *what the law says and what authorities and courts do are not always an exact match*. You must remember that each legal case is different and may lack prior court precedents. A decision to prosecute a case and what charges are brought may involve a degree of discretion from the authorities involved. Sometimes, there is not a plain or clear-cut answer you can rely upon. Abuses, ignorance, carelessness, human frailties, and plain fate subject you to legal risks, which can be exacerbated when firearms are involved. Take nothing for granted, recognize that legal risk is attached to everything you do with a firearm, and unless you are ready to be a test case or have a life and death need, my recommendation is that you err on the side of compliance.

---

[46] *People v. Nguyen*, 212 Cal. App. 4th 1311, 1315 (2013).

My law firm has been fighting and will continue to fight bad gun laws in courthouses every day, and we have no shortage of test cases and unfortunate gun owners.

CHAPTER 2:
WHAT IS LEGALLY CONSIDERED A "FIREARM" AND "AMMUNITION"?

What is a firearm? What is ammunition? These may seem like dumb questions because you may already have an idea of what a "firearm" and what "ammunition" is. But for regulatory purposes, the legal definitions of a "firearm" and "ammunition" can be tricky to apply. Under the law, the term "firearm" includes more than just what we informally call "guns." For example, under California law, flare *guns* might be considered "firearms," while BB *guns* may not. And sometimes only *part* of a firearm is enough to constitute a "firearm" under the law. There are also differences between federal and state law definitions of "firearm" and "ammunition," and even different definitions of those terms *within* those federal and state laws. Misconstruing these definitions causes legal trouble for firearm owners. And in the highly politicized legal environment of gun control laws, the consequences of even an innocent mistake can be severe.

Understanding these legal terms will help you avoid problems with things like flare guns, tear gas guns, certain air and BB guns, and other types of "guns" that might be regulated as "firearms." Knowing how these definitions apply will also help you understand this book's later discussion about restrictions on firearm and ammunition possession and provide you the information you need to lawfully acquire "firearms" and "ammunition."

I. "FIREARM" DEFINITIONS

A. Federal Law "Firearm" Definitions

Federal law defines the term "firearm" in both the federal Gun Control Act (GCA)[1] and the National Firearms Act (NFA),[2] the two Acts that are most relevant to gun owners.

---

[1] Gun Control Act of 1968, 18 U.S.C. §§ 921-931.
[2] National Firearms Act, 26 U.S.C. §§ 5801-5872.

On the one hand, the GCA regulates "firearms" generally with respect to transfers and restricts who can possess them. On the other hand, the NFA defines the term "firearm" by specifically listing highly restricted items in one category (some of which are not "guns"), making it easier to explain the detailed requirements to lawfully possess, import, and transfer those items.

1. The Gun Control Act

The GCA defines a "firearm" as:

(1) Any weapon (including a starter gun) which will or is designed to or may readily be converted to expel a projectile by the action of an explosive; *or*

(2) The frame or receiver of any such weapon;[3] *or*

(3) Any firearm muffler or firearm silencer;[4] *or*

(4) Any destructive device.[5]

An "antique firearm" is not considered a "firearm" for purposes of the GCA.[6] The definition of an "antique firearm" is discussed later in this chapter.

2. The National Firearms Act

Under the NFA, the term "firearm" means:

(1) A shotgun with a barrel or barrels of less than 18 inches in length; *or*

(2) A weapon made from a shotgun if such weapon as modified has an overall length of less than 26 inches or a barrel or barrels of less than 18 inches in length; *or*

(3) A rifle with a barrel or barrels of less than 16 inches in length; *or*

(4) A weapon made from a rifle if such weapon as modified, has an overall length of less than 26 inches or a barrel or barrels of less than 16 inches in length; *or*

(5) "Any other weapon" as defined in subsection (e) of 26 U.S.C. section 5845; *or*

(6) A machinegun;[7] *or*

(7) A silencer as defined in 18 U.S.C. section 921; *or*

(8) A destructive device.[8]

---

[3] See Section I(A)(3) in this Chapter.

[4] The definitions for "silencer" and "destructive device" are the same under the GCA and the NFA. *See* 18 U.S.C. § 921; 26 U.S.C. § 5845(a), (f). Although "firearm muffler" is not defined in the NFA, the Code of Federal Regulations provides a definition for "muffler," which is the same as the GCA's definition. 27 C.F.R. 479.11. These definitions are discussed in Chapter 9.

[5] 18 U.S.C. § 921(a)(3). See Chapter 9.

[6] 18 U.S.C. § 921(a)(3).

[7] Discussed in Chapter 9.

[8] 26 U.S.C. § 5845(a). The definitions and restrictions on "short-barreled shotguns," "short-barreled rifles," "any other weapons," "machineguns," "silencers," and "destructive devices" are discussed in further detail in Chapter 9.

Similar to the GCA, the NFA's definition of "firearm" also excludes "antique firearms." But, the NFA's definition for "antique firearm" is slightly different than the GCA's definition (explained below).

As the GCA and the NFA are two separate acts, you should keep in mind that although your firearm may fit within the definition of an "antique firearm" under the GCA, it might not be considered one under the NFA because its definition encompasses fewer firearms.[9]

Also, keep in mind that the "firearms" located in the NFA are considered "firearms" under the GCA. Not all "firearms" under the GCA are considered to be "firearms" under the NFA, however. Consequently, the requirements for the GCA apply to NFA "firearms," in addition to all of the other restrictions and requirements located in the NFA.

Moreover, the definition of a "firearm" under the NFA excludes any device (other than a machinegun or destructive device) that the Secretary of Treasury finds is "primarily a collector's item" and thus unlikely to be used as a weapon.[10]

As mentioned, the NFA's definition of "firearm" simply lists several highly restricted items. These restrictions came about as a result of the NFA's passage in the 1930's when the government sought to curtail gangland violence by restricting weapons generally associated with gangs in that era, like fully automatic "Tommy guns" and grenades. Though the government wanted a comprehensive legal scheme to deal with these items, it did not ban them at the time because it believed doing so would violate the Second Amendment.[11] Instead, the government heavily taxed possession and transfer of these items and required that they be registered to assure the tax was paid if they were ever transferred again.[12] Paying a $200 tax was highly cost-prohibitive in the 1930's, but nowadays, that amount is small in comparison to the high costs of the firearms and devices covered in the NFA. The specific characteristics of these "firearms," along with their respective restrictions, are further discussed in Chapter 9.

The Bureau of Alcohol, Tobacco, Firearms, and Explosives (ATF) opines that an item may lose its "firearm" status under the NFA if it is modified in a way that permanently removes the characteristics that make it an NFA firearm or that completely destroys the item.[13]

---

[9] *See* 18 U.S.C. § 921(a)(16); 26 U.S.C. § 5845(g).

[10] 26 U.S.C. § 5845(a).

[11] *See generally, National Firearms Act of (1934)-Further Readings,* http://law.jrank.org/pages/8725/National-Firearms-Act-1934.html (last visited Oct. 13, 2017).

[12] *Firearms-National Firearms Act (NFA),* U.S. Dept. of Justice, Bureau of Alcohol, Tobacco, Firearms and Explosives, https://www.atf.gov/content/firearms/firearms-industry/national-firearms-act (last visited July 11, 2017).

[13] *See* U.S. Dept. of Justice, Bureau of Alcohol, Tobacco, Firearms, and Explosives, ATF National Firearms Act Handbook 21-22 (rev. Apr. 2009), *available at* http://www.atf.gov/files/publications/download/p/atf-p-5320-8/atf-p-5320-8.pdf (last visited July 11, 2017).

3. What is a Frame or Receiver Under Federal Law?

Unfortunately, the terms "frame" and "receiver" are not defined within the federal code. They are defined in the Code of Federal Regulations[14] (C.F.R.). Specifically, for purposes of the GCA and the NFA, a "firearm frame or receiver" is defined as "[t]hat part of a firearm which provides the housing for the hammer, bolt or breechblock, and firing mechanism, and which is usually threaded at its forward position to receive the barrel."[15]

Notice that it is unclear which part of a two-part receiver (*i.e.*, those made of an upper and lower receiver) would be considered the firearm's "frame or receiver" for purposes of federal law. Take for example a receiver for an AR15 semiautomatic rifle, which is made up of both an upper and a lower receiver. Although the upper receiver contains the housing for the bolt and is threaded at its forward position to receive a barrel, it is not considered the "firearm"; the lower receiver is. But according to the definition mentioned above, an AR15 lower receiver should not be considered a "receiver" for purposes of federal law because it does not house *all* of the components mentioned in the federal definition.

Recognizing this ambiguity, the ATF attempts to clarify which part of a two-part receiver is considered to be the "receiver" for certain firearms. But, these classifications are very arbitrary and they seem to be made without any rhyme or reason. For example, despite the fact that an AR15 lower receiver clearly does not fit within the definition of a "firearm frame or receiver" for purposes of federal law, the ATF still considers it to be the "receiver" of the firearm. In contrast, the ATF considers the upper receiver of an FN FNC, FN FAL, and FN SCAR to be "receivers" for purposes of federal law.[16]

Similar to the two-part receivers, some semiautomatic firearms and machineguns incorporate a "split" or "hinged" design so that the main portion of the weapon can be separated into upper and lower sections. For purposes of these firearms, the ATF has also attempted to classify which part (*i.e.*, the upper or lower section) is considered to be the "receiver" for purposes of the NFA.[17] But once again, there is no rhyme or reason as to how the ATF made these decisions. For example, the ATF considers the right side plate of a Browning M1917 to be the "receiver" of the firearm, but considers the upper section of an Armalite AR10 to be the 80% "receiver."

---

[14] The Code of Federal Regulations is a compilation of rules adopted by federal agencies in furtherance of implementing federal laws enacted by Congress.

[15] 27 C.F.R. § 478.11 (relating to the regulations for the GCA); 27 C.F.R. § 479.11 (relating to the regulations for the NFA).

[16] *See* ATF Rul. 2008-1.

[17] For a list of specific models that incorporate the "split" or "hinged" design, and what portion of those "machineguns" are considered to be the "receiver," see the National Firearms Handbook at https://www.atf.gov/file/58196/download.

4. Are Precursor (80%) Receivers "Firearms"?

Incomplete receivers, which are commonly but inaccurately referred to as "80%[18] receivers" or "80% side plates," are generally not considered to be "firearms" because they have not yet been machined into complete functional receivers.

Although there are no laws or regulations that explain when a precursor receiver is complete enough to be considered a "firearm," the ATF has issued letters to 80% receiver manufactures explaining what features cannot be present on a precursor receiver in order for it to not be considered a "firearm." For "80% AR receivers," ATF takes the position that no work can be done to the "fire control cavity" and trigger, no drilling into the receiver for the hammer and trigger pins, and no drilling for the safety.[19] Once work has been started in those areas, then the ATF considers the receiver to be a "firearm" for purposes of federal law.

5. Are Non-Functioning Firearms "Firearms"?

Some "paperweights" (i.e., firearms that no longer function) may be considered "fire- arms" under federal law. For instance, machineguns that appear to have been destroyed so that they are essentially "paperweight firearms" may still be considered "machineguns"[20] if they can be "readily restored to shoot" automatically. In other words, if you possess a machinegun that was poorly "demilled" (i.e., rendered non-operational) or was not destroyed in accordance with an ATF-approved method of destruction,[21] it may still be considered a "machinegun" under federal law. Or, you may be in possession of a broken firearm, but the receiver is intact. As discussed before, frames/receivers can be considered "firearms" by themselves.

B. California Law "Firearm" Definitions

California Penal Code (P.C.) section 16520(a) generally defines the term "firearm" as it is used within other California statutes: "'[F]irearm' means any device, designed to be used as a weapon, from which is expelled through a barrel, a projectile

---

[18] In 2014, the ATF went even further with its position on "80% AR receivers" stating that 80% receivers that have material that extends "past the exterior walls of the casting, indicating the approximate location of the holes to be drilled for the selector, hammer, and trigger pins" were considered to be "firearms" for purposes of federal law. Moreover, the ATF has also taken the position that 80% receivers that have so-called "indexing" (i.e., different colored material that outlines where to drill the fire control cavity) are "firearms" for purposes of federal law. A company tried to challenge ATF's stance on when an 80% receiver is considered a "firearm," but it was ultimately unsuccessful. *See Lycurgan, Inc. dba Ares Armor v. B. Todd Jones*, No. 14-CV-0548-JLS-BGS (Complaint filed Mar. 3, 2014).

[19] The "80%" denotes how close the firearm is to being a complete firearm, though this is more of an estimate since it is impossible to say what percentage of work remains for a given firearm, which can vary based on experience, available tools, etc.

[20] For the definitions of a "machinegun," see Chapter 9.

[21] To learn more about the ATF-approved method to destroy a "machinegun," see ATF Rul. 2003-1, ATF Rul. 2003-2, ATF Rul. 2003-3, ATF Rule 2003-4, and the *ATF Guidebook-Importation & Verification of Firearms, Ammunition, and Implements of War*, BUREAU OF ALCOHOL, TOBACCO, FIREARMS, AND EXPLOSIVES, *available at* https://www.atf.gov/file/61771/download (last visited July 28, 2017).

by the force of an explosion or other form of combustion."

This definition of "firearm," from Penal Code section 16520(*a*), does not include a bare frame or receiver. But the definition of "firearm" in P.C. section 16520(b), which is applicable only to certain code sections,[22] does include the frame or receiver. This means that when the P.C. section 16520(b) definition applies, the frame or receiver is considered a "firearm" all by itself, even though it cannot function as a firearm without additional parts.

Example of a receiver from a pistol

1. History of California's "Firearm" Definition

To understand the reasoning behind P.C. section 16520 and why some code sections treat frames and receivers as "firearms" while others do not, you need to understand the definition's history and how it developed from former P.C. section 12001.

Before 1969, P.C. section 12001 defined a "firearm" as a "'pistol,' 'revolver,' and 'firearm capable of being concealed upon the person' . . . [including] any device, designed to be used as a weapon, from which is expelled a projectile by the force of any explosion, or other form of combustion, and which has a barrel less than 12 inches in length."[23] Believe it or not, rifles and shotguns were not regulated as "firearms" for purposes of firearm transfers or for the restrictions on prohibited persons at the time.

In 1968, a California court said that if a firearm was unable to fire because its firing pin was broken and another firing pin was unavailable to make the firearm work, the other parts alone were insufficient to be considered a "firearm."[24] In other words, a firearm missing a piece of equipment necessary to make it fire (like a firing pin) was *not* considered a "firearm" until the missing piece was replaced.[25] This meant that if someone did not technically possess a functioning "firearm," he or she could not be convicted of feloniously possessing a firearm.

To avoid this result, a broader "firearm" definition was subsequently added to the Penal Code in 1969, but it only applied to certain statutes.[26] This broader definition of "firearm" included frames and receivers – which are not functional firearms by themselves.

---

[22] See Section I(B)(2) of this chapter, for a more detailed discussion on when the definition of "firearm" that includes frames and receivers applies.

[23] *See People v. Thompson*, 72 Cal. App. 3d 1, 4 (1977) (quoting P.C. § 12001 (1968)).

[24] *People v. Jackson*, 266 Cal. App. 2d 341, 349 (1968), *superseded by statute/rule as stated in People v. Nelums*, 31 Cal. 3d 355 (1982).

[25] *People v. Jackson*, 266 Cal. App. 2d 341, 349 (1968), *superseded by statute/rule as stated in People v. Nelums*, 31 Cal. 3d 355 (1982).

[26] *See* P.C. § 12001(1970).

2. When Is a Frame or Receiver Considered a "Firearm"?

The definition of a "firearm" is codified in P.C. section 16520. Although P.C. section 16520(b) sets forth a broader "firearm" definition, which includes frames and receivers, that definition should only apply in certain contexts, usually relating to transfers and illegal possession.[27]

The rationale behind certain firearm *parts* being considered "firearms" themselves is to prevent "prohibited persons"[28] from having access to the operating parts of a firearm, which could be put together to make a functional firearm. By defining "firearm" to include frames or receivers and regulating them as functional firearms, California law ensures that no one can lawfully sell or transfer these essential parts to those prohibited people.[29] It also closes a loophole for prohibited persons who might try to avoid criminal liability by keeping their firearms disassembled.

3. What is a Frame or Receiver under California Law?

Similar to federal law, the terms "frame" and "receiver" are also not defined in the Penal Code. The new "bullet button assault weapon" regulations that the DOJ adopted in July 2017, however, defines them for purposes of "assault weapon" registration. These regulations define "receiver" as "the basic unit of a firearm which houses the firing and breech mechanisms and to which the barrel and stock are assembled."[30] Courts have also provided some guidance as to what the definition of the term "receiver" is. Courts have defined a "receiver" as "the metal frame in

---

[27] P.C. § 16520(b). This definition applies to the following provisions: P.C. sections 16550 (Firearm transaction records); 16730 ("Infrequent" firearm transactions); 16960 ("Operation of law" transfers); 16990 (Taking firearm title or possession by "operation of law"); 17070 (Definition of "responsible adult"); 17310 (Definition of "used firearm"); 26500-26588 (License requirements to sell, lease, or transfer and exceptions; sales, leases, or transfers of firearms by licensees; loans of firearms by licensees to specific persons; sales, delivers, and transfers of firearms by licensees to certain persons within and outside the state); 26600-27140 (Exceptions for sale, lease, or transfer to law enforcement; license to sell, lease, or transfer firearms at retail; grounds for forfeiture of license, exception extending waiting period for delivery of a firearm; exceptions for law enforcement for sale, delivery, transfer, or loan of firearm; other exceptions); 27400-28000 (Exceptions for law enforcement at gun shows or events, and crimes relating to firearm transfer); 28100 (Electronic and telephonic transfer register or record); 28400-28415 (Exceptions for law enforcement record keeping, background checks, and fees for firearm sale, lease, or transfer); 29010-29150 (License requirements for firearm manufacturer, licensing process, and prohibitions and requirements applicable to licensed manufacturers); 29610-29750 (Illegal firearm and ammunition possession by minors and exemptions from those restrictions; also punishments for minors violating those restrictions); 29800-29905 (Firearm access prohibitions; exemptions from prohibitions and petitions for relief; and persons convicted of violent offense); 30150-30165 (Exceptions for law enforcement firearm eligibility checks); 31615 (Handgun Safety Certificate requirement); 31705-31830 (Exceptions for sale, delivery, or transfer from the Firearm Safety Certificate requirement); 34355-34370 (Exceptions for the sale, delivery or transfer to authorized law enforcement representatives for ballistics identification system); and California Welfare and Institutions Code (Cal. Welf. & Inst. Code) sections 8100, 8101, 8103 (Mental health restriction prohibitions). *See* P.C. § 16520.

[28] "Prohibited persons" are individuals who are prohibited from possessing firearms. This is further discussed in Chapter 3.

[29] *See* P.C. §§ 26500-26588, 26700.

[30] CAL. CODE REGS. tit. 11, § 5471(aa).

which the action[31] of a firearm is fitted and to which the breech end of the barrel is attached."[32]

Although not defined by statute or court, the term "frame" is defined by the DOJ's new "assault weapon" regulations as "the receiver of a pistol" for purposes of "assault weapon" registration.[33] Also, it is defined within California's unofficial jury instructions (CALJIC). Under these jury instructions, the term "frame" is defined as "the basic unit of a handgun which serves as a mounting for the barrel and operating parts for the gun."[34] Although these jury instructions are not binding on the courts and are merely persuasive authority, they nonetheless provide some guidance on what the term "frame" may mean for purposes of California law.

4. Are Non-functioning Firearms "Firearms"?

Under California law, "paperweights" may be considered "firearms" under most "use" of firearm offenses[35] and sentencing enhancements,[36] as long as the paperweight still looks like or appears to be a functioning firearm.[37] This is because these statutes focus on the effect that a firearm (whether functional or not) can have on the victim of the crime. As explained by the California Court of Appeal:

> The victim [of crime like robbery, burglary, assault, or rape] is placed in fear and cannot be expected to inquire into the condition of the gun [when being threatened]. The danger remains that the reaction by the victim or some third person to the appearance of the gun will cause harm to befall someone . . . . [the "use" of firearm offenses in P.C. section 12022.5] appl[y] even if the evidence conclusively proves that the firearm was inoperable, so long as there is evidence of a gun designed to shoot and which gives the appearance of shooting capability.[38]

In other words, as long as the "paperweight" was once designed to shoot and reasonably appears that it can still shoot, then, even if it can't shoot, it may still be considered a "firearm" under certain California Penal Code sections.

---

[31] An "action" is defined in the DOJ's new regulations for as "the working mechanism of a semiautomatic firearm, which is the combination of the receiver or frame and breech bolt together with the other parts of the mechanism by which a firearm is loaded fired and unloaded." Cal. Code Regs. tit. 11, § 5471(b).

[32] *People v. Arnold*, 145 Cal. App. 4th 1408, 1414 (2006) (citing *Harrott v. Cnty. of Kings*, 25 Cal. 4th 1138, 1147 n. 6 (2001)).

[33] Cal. Code Regs. tit. 11, § 5471(u).

[34] CALJIC No. 12.48.

[35] *See* P.C. § 12022.5.

[36] *See* P.C. § 12022.53.

[37] *See People v. Nelums*, 31 Cal. 3d 355, 359 (1982) (In Bank). The term "paperweight" would also include any antique firearms that no longer function.

[38] *People v. Jackson*, 92 Cal. App. 3d 899, 903 (1979) (internal quotes and citations omitted); *People v. Nelums*, 31 Cal. 3d 355, 359 (1982) (en banc).

As stated above, remember that, under California law, machineguns that appear to have been destroyed so that they are essentially "paperweight firearms" may still be considered "machineguns."[39] California has not taken a position as to the extent a machinegun must be "de-milled," although it may be assumed that the DOJ or law enforcement may turn to the ATF analysis and federal regulations for guidance.

5. Are Precursor (80%) Receivers "Firearms" Under California Law?

California takes no position on when a precursor receiver becomes a firearm. But California law enforcement will likely turn to the ATF's position for guidance (see above). For firearm manufacturing (P.C. sections 29010-29150), however, the term "firearm" includes "the unfinished frame or receiver of a weapon that can be readily converted to the functional condition of a finished frame or receiver."[40]

There are a number of pending and current requirements under California law that must be met before you can lawfully complete a precursor receiver and turn it into a functional receiver. To learn more about these requirements, see Chapter 4.

II. FIREARM SUBGROUP DEFINITIONS

Certain items meeting the general "firearm" definition are further classified into groups based on their characteristics and have more specific definitions under California law, the GCA, and the NFA. The most common of these groups are handguns, rifles, and shotguns. But even these groups are further divided into subgroups with more specific definitions, as explained in Chapters 8 and 9. Knowing which classification a firearm belongs within is crucial to understanding which regulations apply to it. It can mean the difference between conduct being perfectly legal or a crime.

A. "Handguns"

Under the GCA a "handgun" is:

(1) A firearm which has a short stock and is designed to be held and fired by the use of a single hand; *and*

(2) Any combination of parts from which such a "firearm" as described in (1) can be assembled.[41]

---

[39] For the definitions of a "machinegun," see Chapter 9.

[40] P.C. § 16520(g).

[41] 18 U.S.C. § 921(a)(29). The NFA does not define "handgun." *See* 26 U.S.C. § 5845. But the NFA regulations do define "pistol" and "revolver." A "pistol" is defined as "[a] weapon originally designed, made, and intended to fire a projectile (bullet) from one or more barrels when held in one hand, and having (a) a chamber(s) as an integral part(s) of, or permanently aligned with, the bore(s); and (b) a short stock designed to be gripped by one hand and at an angle to and extending below the line of the bore(s)." 27 C.F.R. § 479.11. And a "rifle" is defined as "[a]

The federal Code of Regulations defines "handgun" as:

(1) Any firearm which has a short stock and is designed to be held and fired by the use of a single hand; *and*

(2) Any combination of parts from which a firearm described in paragraph (a) can be assembled.[42]

Under California law, a "handgun" is "any pistol, revolver, or firearm capable of being concealed upon the person."[43] The terms "firearm capable of being concealed upon the person," "pistol," and "revolver" are further defined as:

[A]ny device designed to be used as a weapon, from which is expelled a projectile by the force of any explosion, or other form of combustion, and that has a barrel less than 16 inches in length. These terms also include any device that has a barrel 16 inches or more in length which is designed to be interchanged with a barrel less than 16 inches in length.[44]

1. Pistols

Under federal law, both the GCA and the NFA do not define the term "pistol." The Code of Federal Regulations does, however. Specifically, the Code of Federal Regulations defines the term "pistol" as "[a] weapon originally designed, made, and intended to fire a projectile (bullet) from one or more barrels when held in one hand, and having (a) a chamber(s) as an integral part(s) of, or permanently aligned with, the bore(s); and (b) a short stock designed to be gripped by one hand and at an angle to and extending below the line of the bore(s)."[45] This definition is applicable to the regulations for the GCA and NFA.[46]

Glock 9 mm Semiautomatic Pistol

Under California law, a "pistol" means the following for purposes of "assault weapon" registration.

any device designed to be used as a weapon, from which a projectile is expelled by the force of any explosion, or other form of combustion, and that

---

weapon designed or redesigned, made or remade, and intended to be fired from the shoulder and designed or redesigned and made or remade to use the energy of the explosive in a fixed cartridge to fire only a single projectile through a rifled bore for each single pull of the trigger, and shall include any such weapon which may be readily restored to fire a fixed cartridge." 27 C.F.R. § 479.11.

[42] 27 C.F.R. § 478.11.

[43] P.C. § 16640(a).

[44] P.C. § 16530(a).

[45] 27 C.F.R. §§ 478.11, 479.11.

[46] 27 C.F.R. §§ 478.11, 479.11.

has a barrel less than 16 inches in length. This definition includes AR-15 style pistols with pistol buffer tubes attached. Pistol buffer tubes typically have smooth metal with no guide on the bottom for rifle stocks to be attached, and they sometimes have a foam pad on the end of the tube farthest from the receiver.[47]

A "semiautomatic pistol" is "a pistol with an operating mode that uses the energy of the explosive in a fixed cartridge to extract a fired cartridge and chamber a fresh cartridge with each single pull of the trigger."[48] But, this definition is only applicable to the "unsafe handgun" and "handgun testing laws" under P.C. sections 16900 and 31910.

Oddly, the "unsafe handgun" and "handgun testing" laws also regulate other varieties of "pistols" and "revolvers," but these terms are not defined in the Penal Code. The California Code of Regulations (Cal. Code Regs.), however, does define "pistol" as "a handgun in which the chamber is part of the barrel. A pistol can either be semiautomatic or non-semiautomatic, but not fully automatic."[49] This definition also only applies to the "unsafe handgun" and "handgun testing" laws.

2. Revolvers

Neither the GCA nor the NFA define the term "revolver." The Code of Federal Regulations does. Specifically, the Code of Federal Regulations defines the term "revolver" as "[a] projectile weapon, of the pistol type, having a breechloading chambered cylinder so arranged that the cocking of the hammer or movement of the trigger rotates it and brings the next cartridge in line with the barrel for firing."[50] This definition is applicable to the regulations for both the GCA and the NFA.[51]

Ruger & Co.
Speed Six Revolver

While the California Penal Code does not provide a general definition for "revolver," it is defined in the California Code of Regulations as "a handgun with a cylinder having several chambers so arranged as to rotate around an axis and be discharged successively by the same firing mechanism through a common barrel."[52] This definition of "revolver" applies to the "unsafe handgun" and "handgun testing" laws.[53]

---

[47] CAL. CODE REGS. tit. 11, § 5471(y).

[48] P.C. § 17140.

[49] CAL. CODE REGS. tit. 11, § 4049(p).

[50] 27 C.F.R. §§ 478.11, 479.11.

[51] 27 C.F.R. §§ 478.11, 479.11.

[52] CAL. CODE REGS. tit. 11, § 4049(t).

[53] See Chapter 9.

B. "Rifles," "Shotguns,"[54] and "Long Guns"[55]

1. Rifles

The GCA's and NFA's definitions for "rifle" are practically identical. Under the GCA, a "rifle" is defined as "a weapon designed or redesigned, made or remade, and intended to be fired from the shoulder and designed or redesigned and made or remade to use the energy of an explosive to fire only a single projectile through a rifled bore for each single pull of the trigger."[56]

On the other hand, the NFA and the Code of Federal Regulations defines a "rifle" as "a weapon designed or redesigned, made or remade, and intended to be fired from the shoulder and designed or redesigned and made or remade to use the energy of the explosive *in a fixed cartridge* to fire only a single projectile through a rifled bore for each single pull of the trigger, and shall include any such weapon which may be readily restored to fire a *fixed cartridge*."[57] Notice that the difference between the NFA and the GCA's definition of a "rifle" is that the NFA's definition contains the "in a fixed cartridge" qualifier, but the GCA does not.[58]

Unlike federal law, California law does not provide a general definition for the term "rifle." It does define the term "rifle" in the context of "short-barreled rifles" as being "a weapon designed or redesigned, made or remade, and intended to be fired from the shoulder and designed or redesigned and made or remade to use the energy of the explosive in a fixed cartridge to fire only a single projectile through a rifled bore for each single pull of the trigger."[59]

Also, California law provides a definition for "rifle" in the context of the new "bullet button assault weapon" registration scheme. The DOJ's new regulations state that:

> "Rifle" means a weapon designed or redesigned, made or remade, and intended to be fired from the shoulder and designed or redesigned and made or remade to use the energy of the explosive in a fixed cartridge to fire only a single projectile through a rifled bore for each single pull of the trigger.[60]

---

[54] Shotguns and rifles are commonly referred to collectively as "long guns," and will be referred to in this way throughout this book when the distinction is not relevant.

[55] When the phrase "long guns" is used in this book, unless it is with respect to the Firearm Safety Certificate (discussed further in Chapter 4), it means "long guns" in general and not as specifically defined in P.C. section 16865.

[56] 18 U.S.C. § 921(a)(7).

[57] 26 U.S.C. § 5845(c) (emphasis added); 27 C.F.R. § 479.11.

[58] *See* 18 U.S.C. § 921(a)(7); 26 U.S.C. § 5845(c). But, 27 C.F.R. section 478.11 does use the language "in a fixed metallic cartridge" in its definition of "rifle." But this definition is only applicable to the Code of Federal Regulations.

[59] P.C. § 17090.

[60] CAL. CODE REGS. tit. 11, § 5471(ee).

2. Shotguns

Again, the GCA's and NFA's "shotgun" definitions are practically identical. The GCA defines a "shotgun" as "a weapon designed or redesigned, made or remade, and intended to be fired from the shoulder and designed or redesigned and made or remade to use the energy of an explosive to fire through a smooth bore either a number of ball shot or a single projectile for each single pull of the trigger."[61]

On the other hand, the NFA and the Code of Federal Regulations defines a "shotgun" as "a weapon designed or redesigned, made or remade, and intended to be fired from the shoulder and designed or redesigned and made or remade to use the energy of the explosive in a *fixed shotgun shell* to fire through a smooth bore either a number of projectiles (ball shot) or a single projectile for each pull of the trigger, and shall include any such weapon which may be readily restored to fire a *fixed shotgun shell*."[62] Notice that similar to its definition for the term "rifle," the NFA's definition of a "shotgun" contains the "in a fixed shotgun shell" qualifier, while the GCA does not.[63]

California law also does not provide a general definition for "shotgun." It does, however, define "shotgun" in the context of "short-barreled shotguns" as being "a weapon designed or redesigned, made or remade, and intended to be fired from the shoulder and designed or redesigned and made or remade to use the energy of the explosive in a fixed shotgun shell to fire through a smooth bore either a number of projectiles (ball shot) or a single projectile for each pull of the trigger."[64]

3. Long Guns

The Penal Code defines a "long gun" as "any firearm that is not a handgun or machinegun."[65] All "rifles" and "shotguns" are encompassed under the "long gun" definition.

---

[61] 18 U.S.C. § 921(a)(5).

[62] 26 U.S.C. § 5845(d) (emphasis added); 27 C.F.R. § 479.11.

[63] *See* 18 U.S.C. § 921(a)(5); 26 U.S.C. § 5845(d). But, 27 C.F.R. section 478.11 does define shotgun using the phrase "in a fixed shotgun shell." But once again, this definition is only applicable to the Code of Federal Regulations and not the GCA.

[64] P.C. § 17190.

[65] P.C. § 16865.

Examples of "Long Guns"

Example of a Semi-Automatic Shotgun

Example of a Pump Action Shotgun

Example of a Lever Action Rifle

Example of a Bolt Action Rifle

Example of a Semi-Automatic Rifle

C. Other "Firearms"

Like receivers, certain other items do not fit neatly into the "handgun," "rifle," or "shotgun" categories but still meet the legal definition of, and are treated as, "firearms." For example, a stockless firearm of legal length that shoots shotgun shells (like the Mossberg 500) is not a "shotgun" because it does not have a stock, and therefore it cannot be fired from the shoulder. It is also not a "short-barreled shotgun" because of its length. Nevertheless, it would still be considered a "firearm" because it is a "device, designed to be used as a weapon, from which is expelled through a barrel, a projectile by the force of an explosion or other form of combustion."[66]

"Machineguns" and the NFA's "any other weapon" categories are also firearm subgroups with specific definitions, which are further discussed in Chapter 9. Moreover, modifying a "handgun," "rifle," or "shotgun" may cause it to move from one category to another, or fall outside of one of these categories.

There are sometimes issues regarding whether an item actually meets the applicable "firearm" definition, which is important in determining whether the item is regulated under California and/or federal law, as discussed below.

D. Definition of "Weapon"

An element included in all the above "firearm" definitions is that, in order for something to be a "firearm," it must first be considered a "weapon." Unfortunately, the term "weapon"[67] is not actually defined in the California Penal Code or federal code. Nonetheless, courts have provided some guidance on what a "weapon" is.

Federal courts have defined a "weapon" as "an instrument of offense or defense."[68] Similarly, California courts have instructed that the term "weapon" can "be broadly defined as an instrument of offensive or defensive combat."[69]

Certain items, such as standard firearms, dirks, and daggers, unquestionably meet the definition of a "weapon" and are considered to be "weapons per se."[70] But when an item's uses for "combat" are uncertain or untraditional, such as pen guns (discussed in Section III), it is not always clear as to whether these items actually meet the definition of a "weapon."

In order for an item to be considered a "weapon," California courts have held that the person who possessed the item must have known that the object was a

---

[66] P.C. § 16520(a).

[67] This issue rears its head again in Chapter 9 concerning "destructive devices." In order to be a "destructive device," an item must be a "weapon." P.C. § 16460.

[68] STEPHEN P. HALBROOK, FIREARMS LAW DESKBOOK 601 (West 2013-2014 ed. 2013) (italics added). *See also United States v. Dalpiaz*, 527 F.2d 548, 551 (6th Cir. 1975) (holding that a "ground burst projectile simulator" that was designed for military training purposes was not a "destructive device" because it was meant to be used for training troops, not for use as a "weapon.").

[69] 63 CAL. JUR. 3d *Weapons* § 1 (citing Am. Jur. 2d, Weapons and Firearms § 1).

[70] The phrase "per se" means "[o]n, in , or by itself; standing alone, without reference to additional facts." Per Se, BLACK'S LAW DICTIONARY (10th ed. 2014).

"weapon," may be used as a weapon, or they must have possessed the object "as a weapon." The prosecution can prove that a person had knowledge of an item's uses through circumstantial evidence.[71]

When an item is not a "weapon per se," but an instrument of ordinary innocent uses, the prosecution must prove that the person actually possessed the item as a weapon in order for the item to be considered a "weapon."[72] In other words, the prosecution must show that the person "would use the object for a dangerous, not harmless, purpose."[73]

In short, although no set legal definition for "weapon" exists, there are items, such as certain standard firearms, that are likely to be considered "weapons per se." Items that do not fall within the "weapons per se" category are characterized by considering the person's knowledge of the item's uses or the person's actual or intended use of the item as a weapon to determine whether the item is legally considered a "weapon."[74]

E. "Antique Firearms"

Because items meeting the definition of "antique firearm" are not regulated as "firearms" for most purposes, understanding the federal and California definitions for "antique firearm" is useful.

1. Federal Law Definitions

a. The Gun Control Act

As mentioned above, the GCA's "firearm" definition does not include "antique firearms."[75] An "antique firearm" under the GCA is defined as:

(1) Any firearm (including any firearm with a matchlock, flintlock, percussion cap, or similar type of ignition system) manufactured in or before 1898; *or*

(2) Any replica of any firearm described in (1) if such replica:

---

[71] The prosecution does not need to prove that the defendant knew there was a law against possessing the item, nor that the defendant intended to break or violate the law; it must prove that the defendant knew of the item's uses. *People v. King*, 38 Cal. 4th 617, 627 (2006). Evidence is circumstantial when it is "based on inference and not on personal knowledge or observation." EVIDENCE, BLACK'S LAW DICTIONARY (10th ed. 2014).

[72] *People v. Fannin*, 91 Cal. App. 4th 1399, 1400 (2001). In *Fannin*, the California Court of Appeal considered whether a bicycle chain with a lock at the end was a "slungshot," which is a prohibited weapon under the Penal Code. The court held that "if the object is not a weapon per se, but an instrument with ordinary innocent uses, the prosecution must prove that the object was possessed as a weapon." *People v. Fannin*, 91 Cal. App. 4th 1399, 1404 (2001); *see also People v. Grubb*, 63 Cal. 2d 614, 621 (1965) (possession of modified baseball bat).

[73] *People v. Fannin*, 91 Cal. App. 4th 1399, 1403 (2001).

[74] See discussion on pen guns, coyote catchers, and potato guns in Section III of this Chapter for application of this rule.

[75] 18 U.S.C. § 921(a)(3).

(a) Is not designed or redesigned for using rimfire or conventional centerfire fixed ammunition; *or*

b) Uses rimfire or conventional centerfire fixed ammunition which is no longer manufactured in the United States and which is not readily available in the ordinary channels of commercial trade;[76] *or*

(3) Any muzzle-loading rifle, muzzle-loading shotgun, or muzzle-loading pistol, which is designed to use black powder, or a black powder substitute, and which cannot use fixed ammunition, but does not include any weapon which incorporates a firearm frame or receiver, any firearm which is converted into a muzzle-loading weapon, or any muzzle-loading weapon which can be readily converted to fire fixed ammunition by replacing the barrel, bolt, breechblock, or any combination thereof.[77]

Items not meeting any of these definitions are regulated as "firearms" under the GCA.[78]

Since "antique firearms" are excluded from the GCA's "firearm" definition, the GCA requirements and restrictions (discussed in Chapters 3 and 4) do not apply to those items meeting the "antique firearm" definition.

---

[76] With almost anything available on the internet, previously rare rimfire and centerfire cartridges have become more easily available. So the question of what ammunition is "not readily available" in subsection (3) becomes obscured. For further analysis of this issue, *see* C.D. Michel, *Gun Ammo Googling: Does Internet Access to Rare Ammunition Calibers Limit the Availability of "Replicas" to Qualify as "Antique Firearms?,"* available at http://www. calgunlaws.com/wp-content/uploads/2012/07/Gun-Anno-Googling.pdf (last visited July 11, 2017). The ATF also discusses this issue in the NFA Handbook: "[c]oncerning ammunition availability, it is important to note that a specific type of fixed ammunition that has been out of production for many years may again become available due to increasing interest in older firearms. Therefore, the classification of a specific NFA firearm as an antique can change if ammunition for the weapon becomes readily available in the ordinary channels of commercial trade." U.S. DEPT. OF JUSTICE, BUREAU OF ALCOHOL, TOBACCO, FIREARMS, AND EXPLOSIVES, ATF NATIONAL FIREARMS ACT HANDBOOK 20 (rev. Apr. 2009), *available at* http://www.atf.gov/files/publications/download/p/atf-p-5320-8/ atf-p-5320-8.pdf (last visited July 11, 2017).

[77] 18 U.S.C. § 921(a)(16).

[78] Additionally the ATF maintains a list – which it warns is *not* exhaustive and frequently changes – of certain weapons that load from the muzzle that it considers to be "firearms" under the GCA, which includes:

(1) Savage Model 10ML (early, 1st version).

(2) Mossberg 500 shotgun with muzzle loading barrel.

(3) Remington 870 shotgun with muzzle loading barrel.

(4) Mauser 98 rifle with muzzle loading barrel.

(5) SKS rifle with muzzle loading barrel.

(6) RPB sM10 pistol with muzzle loading barrel.

(7) H&R/New England Firearm Huntsman.

(8) Thompson Center Encore/Contender.

(9) Rossi .50 muzzle loading rifle.

Top 10 Frequently Asked Questions and Answers, U.S. DEPT. OF JUSTICE, BUREAU OF ALCOHOL TOBACCO, FIRE-ARMS, AND EXPLOSIVES, https://www.atf.gov/file/61721/download (last visited July 11, 2017).

The above GCA "antique firearm" definition does not apply to California's "firearm" restrictions for prohibited persons, meaning an "antique firearm" is considered a "firearm" for purposes of California's restrictions for prohibited persons. Consequently, a person prohibited from possessing firearms under California law cannot possess "antique firearms" either.[79] But, the above GCA "antique firearm" definition does apply to California's firearm transfer laws (discussed in Chapters 3 and 4).[80]

b. The National Firearms Act

The NFA has a slightly different definition for "antique firearms" than the GCA, which includes:

> [A]ny firearm not designed or redesigned for using rim fire or conventional center fire ignition with fixed ammunition and manufactured in or before 1898 (including any matchlock, flintlock, percussion cap, or similar type of ignition system or replica thereof, whether actually manufactured before or after the year 1898) and also any firearm using fixed ammunition manufactured in or before 1898, for which ammunition is no longer manufactured in the United States and is not readily available in the ordinary channels of commercial trade.[81]

The main difference between the GCA's and the NFA's definitions is that the NFA does not expressly include muzzle-loading firearms that use black powder and that cannot use fixed ammunition, although these firearms appear to fall within the

---

[79] *See* P.C. § 16520.

[80] Sec 18 U.S.C. § 921(a)(3), (16); P.C. § 16170(b). As used in the following California provisions, the term "firearm" does not include an unloaded "antique firearm": P.C. sections 16550 (Firearm transaction records); 16730(a), (c) ("Infrequent" firearm transactions); 16960 (Operation of law transfers); 17310 ("Used Firearm"); 26350-26391 (Open carry of unloaded handgun laws and exemptions); 26400-26405 (Open carry of unloaded "firearm that is not a handgun" laws and exemptions); 26500-26588 (License requirements to sell, lease, transfer, or loan firearms and exemptions); 26700-26915 (License to sell, lease, or transfer firearms at retail and grounds for forfeiture of license); 27510 (Sale, supply, delivery, or giving possession of handgun by licensed person to minor or young adult); 27530 (Sale or transfer of handgun requirements); 27540 (Delivery of firearm by dealer requirements); 27545 (Sale, loan, or transfer of firearm through licensed firearms dealer); 27555-27570 (Sale, delivery, or transfer of firearm by licensee, verification number required; review of centralized lists of firearm dealers, licensees, and manufacturers; bringing a handgun, firearm, or curio or relic into the state and requirements; and punishments, statutes of limitations, and exceptions); 29010-29150 (Licensing requirements for manufacturing firearms; issuance, forfeiture, and conditions of license to manufacture firearms); 25135 (Requirements for storing firearms when living with a prohibited person). P.C. § 16520(d). NOTE: Outside of these provisions, an "antique firearm" is still considered to be a "firearm" under California law.

[81] 26 U.S.C. § 5845(g).

definition regardless. A similar analysis applies to silencers that attach to muzzle-loading rifles. We discuss why this is important in Chapter 9.

2. California Law Definition

"Antique firearm" is defined in different contexts under California law. For firearm transactions, "antique firearm" means the same as it does in the federal GCA, provided in the next section above.[82]

For "generally prohibited weapons,"[83] "antique firearm" means:

(1) Any firearm not designed or redesigned for using rimfire or conventional centerfire ignition with fixed ammunition and manufactured in or before 1898. This includes any matchlock, flintlock, percussion cap, or similar type of ignition system; *or*

(2) Replicas of any of the firearms discussed above, whether actually manufactured before or after the year 1898; *or*

(3) Any firearm using fixed ammunition manufactured in or before 1898, for which ammunition is no longer manufactured in the United States and is not readily available in the ordinary channels of commercial trade.[84]

Example of a Matchlock Musket   *Example of a Percussion Cap Rifle*

Finally, as it relates to "assault weapons" and .50 BMG rifles, the term "antique firearm" means "any firearm manufactured before January 1, 1899."[85]

F. "Curios or Relics"

"Curios or relics" are defined in the Code of Federal Regulations as firearms "of special interest to collectors by reason of some quality other than is associated with

---

[82] *See* 18 U.S.C. § 921(a)(16) (stating the GCA's definition of "antique firearm"); P.C. § 16170(b). See also Chapter 4 for "antique firearm" transactions.

[83] Discussed in Chapter 9.

[84] P.C. § 16170(c).

[85] P.C. § 16170(a). See also Chapter 8.

firearms intended for sporting use or as offensive or defensive weapons."[86] To be "curios or relics," firearms must either be:

(1) Manufactured at least 50 years before the current date, but not including replicas thereof; *or*

(2) Certified by the curator of a municipal, State, or Federal museum which exhibits firearms to be curios or relics of museum interest; *or*

(3) A firearm which derives a substantial part of their monetary value from the fact that they are novel, rare, bizarre, or because of their association with some historical figure, period, or event. Proof of qualification of a particular firearm under this category may be established by evidence of present value and evidence that like firearms are not available except as collector's items, or that the value of like firearms available in ordinary commercial channels is substantially less.[87]

This definition is the same under both California and federal law.[88]

The ATF has opined that a "receiver" is not a "curio or relic" item, and that a firearm must be in its original configuration to qualify as a "curio or relic." But, minor alterations to a "curio or relic" firearm, such as adding scope mounts or sling swivels, are not likely to change its "curio or relic" status.[89]

Example of a "Curo or Relic":
An M1 Carbine

III. IS THAT THING CONSIDERED A "FIREARM"?

Due Process requires each element of the pertinent "firearm" definition to be proven beyond a reasonable doubt to a jury for a person to be convicted of a "firearm" violation.[90] Whether an item meets the applicable "firearm" definition is sometimes unclear. For example, toy guns, pellet guns, and BB guns are not considered "fire-

---

[86] 27 C.F.R. § 478.11.

[87] 27 C.F.R. § 478.11.

[88] P.C. § 17705(a); 27 C.F.R. § 478.11.

[89] ATF Rul. 85-10 (1985); *see Firearms Curios or Relics List*, U.S. DEPT. OF JUSTICE, BUREAU OF ALCOHOL TOBACCO, FIREARMS, AND EXPLOSIVES 52 (rev. Dec. 2007), *available at* https://www.atf.gov/firearms/docs/guide/firearms-curios-or-relics-list-1972-2007-atf-p-530011/download (last visited July 11, 2017).

[90] *See Medley v. Runnels*, 506 F.3d 857, 863-64 (9th Cir. 2007).

arms" "because, instead of explosion or other combustion, they use the force of air pressure, gas pressure, or spring action to expel a projectile."[91]

The "projectile" does not need to be traditional ammunition either. One court found a crude device made by a prison inmate – consisting of a tube sealed at one end packed with around 30 match heads with a hole to light them – to be a "firearm" even though no projectiles were found with it.[92] An officer testified that such devices are often used to shoot melted or broken plastic and tinfoil balls.[93] Another court found taser "barbs" that make contact with the target to be "projectiles" within the "firearm" definition.[94] That same court, in holding that a taser *is* a "firearm,"[95] also found the plastic, squared chambers holding the barbs to be "barrels" because "there appears no reason logically or semantically to insist that a gun's barrel must be made of metal or that it be cylindrical."[96]

In another example, a defendant was charged with unlawfully possessing an "unconventional pistol," which, as explained in Chapter 9, is an illegal "firearm." The defendant had a tear gas pen gun designed for launching flares or tear gas canisters – not firing ammunition – though it was shown that ammunition *could be* fired from it (with a likelihood of explosion and causing injury to the shooter). Because ammunition *could* be fired from it, there was an issue about whether it was actually "*designed* to be used as a weapon." The state needed to prove that the pen gun was "designed" to be used as a weapon in order to prove it was a "firearm" and that the owner *knew* it could be used in this way.

There was also an issue as to whether the tear gas pen gun even had a "barrel" through which a projectile was expelled because the tear gas canisters and flares were designed to screw on to the end of it.[97]

A. Bang Sticks/Shark Killers

Sometimes an item that would not generally be referred to as a firearm still meets the legal definition of one. A relatively common example is a "bang stick" – a shaft or pole carried by divers with a "power head" (a device containing a cartridge that has a fixed firing pin) attached at the end that discharges the cartridge when thrust forcefully in a linear motion, usually toward a shark. No trigger or sophisticated mechanics are involved, and it looks more like a boat antenna than a typical firearm.

---

[91] *People v. Law*, 195 Cal. App. 4th 976, 983 (2011) (citing *People v. Monjaras*, 164 Cal. App. 4th 1432, 1435 (2008)).

[92] *People v. Talkington*, 140 Cal. App. 3d 557 (1983).

[93] *People v. Talkington*, 140 Cal. App. 3d 557, 562 (1983).

[94] *People v. Heffner*, 70 Cal. App. 3d 643, 652 (1977).

[95] *People v. Heffner*, 70 Cal. App. 3d 643, 652 (1977). As an aside, older model tasers used primers to launch the barbs while modern tasers use compressed air, and thus are not considered "firearms."

[96] *People v. Heffner*, 70 Cal. App. 3d 643, 648-49 (1977) (noting that the taser in question discharged the barbs using combustion).

[97] I litigated this case in Ventura County and ultimately obtained a dismissal of charges for the defendant, but that does not mean the same result is guaranteed for everyone.

But since it is a device designed to be a weapon (albeit against sharks and although blanks can be used just as effectively), and its projectile is still expelled by explosive force, the only real question is whether the "power head" where the cartridge is contained constitutes a "barrel." Though it is unclear, it is arguably a barrel because the cartridge is fully contained and even set back from the opening of the "power head" – especially since a court has considered tasers to have a barrel – likely making a "bang stick" a "firearm" under California law and subject to all applicable restrictions.

B. Coyote Booby Traps

Sometimes, even when the item may technically meet the "firearm" definition, courts will conclude the item is *not* one. For example, a Colorado court decided a "coyote getter" – a device with a hollow tube of light metal, crimped at one end and a spring-loaded firing pin that propels cyanide into a coyote's mouth when it pulls on the bait – was not a "firearm" under the NFA because it lacked practical use as a weapon and because the ATF's expert refused to fire one using live ammunition.[98]

C. Potato Guns a.k.a. "Spud Guns"

A potato gun or "spud gun" is a device that, as its name implies, shoots potatoes, typically using some form of flammable aerosol or liquid. The flammable material is stored in the device that is attached to the barrel, and the potato (or piece of potato) is crammed into the barrel. A well-built potato gun can shoot a potato 100 yards or more.

Since a potato gun is a device that expels a projectile through a barrel by combustive force, the question of whether it is a "firearm" turns on whether it is a "weapon." As explained above, no exact legal definition exists for the term "weapon." But, given the above "weapon" definition and its subsequent analysis, it seems unlikely that a potato gun would be considered a "weapon" unless it was intentionally used as one. An argument could be made, however, that a person need only know that it *could* be used to injure or kill for it to be considered a "weapon."

If potato guns *are* considered "weapons," a question also exists as to whether these devices are illegal "destructive devices" under state and/or federal law (see Chapter 9).

In California, these devices may be considered a launching device for a bomb, grenade, explosive missile, or similar device – though they usually cannot shoot

---

[98] *United States v. Brady,* 710 F. Supp. 290, 292-93 (D. Colo. 1989). In *Brady,* the court noted that the expert would not fire the coyote getter using live ammunition because it was possible that the getter would explode. *United States v. Brady,* 710 F. Supp. 290, 292 (D. Colo. 1989). The court concluded that the getter was not considered "any other weapon" under the federal law definition of a firearm because "[r]esearch ha[d] found no cases in which a court or administrative agency found that a device which was likely to explode if used with normal ammunition was any other weapon." *United States v. Brady,* 710 F. Supp. 290, 293 (D. Colo. 1989).

anything as dense as a bomb or grenade. And some designs or building materials are so flimsy that launching anything heavier than a potato may result in catastrophic failure. Nevertheless, criminal cases have been and will continue to be filed alleging potato guns are "firearms," "destructive devices," or "zip guns" (see Chapter 9).

Under federal law, a potato gun can be considered an illegal "destructive device" that expels a projectile by explosive force with a barrel diameter of more than half an inch. And even if it is not considered a "firearm," it may still meet the definition of some other prohibited item.

It is strongly advised you proceed cautiously before deciding to make a potato gun because of the confusion about their legality.

D. Flare Guns With Metal Inserts

Flare guns, or signal launchers, may be considered "firearms" depending on their construction. Certain flare guns are 12-gauge and fire flares that are specifically designed for these guns. These flare guns are often made of plastic and cannot withstand the pressure of standard ammunition being discharged from them (and certainly not a 12-gauge shotgun shell). For most purposes, these flare guns do not meet the definition of a "firearm" under state or federal law because they are considered signaling devices, not "weapons."[99]

Example of a 12-Gauge Flare Gun

But, there are metal inserts available to the general public that can be used to modify flare guns to discharge certain calibers of conventional ammunition, thereby potentially turning them into "firearms." These metal inserts are typically

Examples of Metal Flare Launcher Inserts

25MM .38 INSERT

12 GA ADAPTER

12 GA .38 INSERT

designed to allow shotguns of varying gauges to fire conventional ammunition (including smaller gauge shotgun shells), but they can also be used to modify flare guns. In a shotgun, the metal insert is slid into the shotgun barrel through the breech with a round of ammunition inserted within it. The breech is closed and the shotgun can fire the single cartridge. To reload, the shooter reopens the breech and removes the insert and the expended ammunition case from the insert. The shooter then reloads another round into the insert and the entire insert is placed back inside the shotgun.

---

[99] For very limited purposes, California laws treat rockets, rocket propelled projectile launchers, and similar devices containing an explosive or incendiary material as "firearms" whether or not the device is designed for emergency or stress signaling purposes. P.C. § 16520(c). This is mostly a concern relating to carrying a concealed handgun or a loaded firearm, as discussed in Chapter 5.

The same metal insert can usually be inserted into a 12-gauge flare gun with only minor modification to the flare gun required. The metal insert, in theory, reinforces the flimsy plastic flare gun and allows it to discharge certain calibers of conventional ammunition, including shotgun shells. When the metal insert is placed inside the flare gun, the flare gun becomes a "weapon" and is therefore considered a "firearm" under California and federal law.[100]

Under federal law, the ATF opines[101] that these metal inserts are considered part of the "any other weapons"[102] category when inserted into or possessed with flare guns.[103] The ATF also notes that four out of the four flare guns they tested using these metal inserts suffered "catastrophic failure" as a result.[104]

E. 37mm Flare Launchers

37mm flare launchers may be considered "weapons" under federal law, depending on whether you possess certain kinds of ammunition with the flare launcher. Generally, a 37mm flare launcher by itself is not considered to be a "weapon" because it is not an instrument of offensive or defensive combat.

There are certain types of "anti-personnel" ammunition that contain materials like wood pellets, rubber pellets or balls, or beanbags that can be used in 37mm flare launchers. And the ATF has opined that, when a person possesses both this "anti-personnel" ammunition and a 37mm flare launcher at the same time, then the 37mm flare launcher becomes a "weapon" because it can be used for offensive or defensive combat and would therefore be regulated under federal law as "destructive devices" (see Chapter 9).[105]

In the past, certain California law enforcement agencies tried to classify all 37mm flare launchers as "destructive devices" under California law because somewhere there exists a 37mm grenade that can be launched from the launcher.

---

[100] *See* 18 U.S.C. § 921(a)(3)(A). See also P.C. section 16520(a) and possibly subdivision (c) as well.

[101] *Flare Insert – Any Other Weapon*, U.S. Dept. of Justice, Bureau of Alcohol, Tobacco, Firearms and Explosives (May 4, 2006), http://www.atf.gov/press/releases/2006/05/050406-openletter-nfa-flare-inserts.html (last visited July 11, 2017).

[102] "Any other weapon" "means any weapon or device capable of being concealed on the person from which a shot can be discharged through the energy of an explosive, a pistol or revolver having a barrel with a smooth bore designed or redesigned to fire a fixed shotgun shell, weapons with combination shotgun and rifle barrels 12 inches or more, less than 18 inches in length, from which only a single discharge can be made from either barrel without manual reloading, and shall include any such weapon which may be readily restored to fire. Such term shall not include a pistol or a revolver having a rifled bore, or rifled bores, or weapons designed, made, or intended to be fired from the shoulder and not capable of firing fixed ammunition." 26 U.S.C. § 5845(e). These are discussed in Chapter 9.

[103] Consequently, metal inserts inserted into or possessed with flare guns must be registered as required by federal law to avoid violating 26 U.S.C. section 5861(d).

[104] *Flare Insert – Any Other Weapon*, U.S. Dept. of Justice, Bureau of Alcohol, Tobacco, Firearms and Explosives (May 4, 2006), http://www.atf.gov/press/releases/2006/05/050406-openletter-nfa-flare-inserts.html (last visited July 11, 2017).

[105] ATF Rul. 95-3 (1995). *See also* 18 U.S.C. § 921(a)(4); 26 U.S.C. § 5845(f)(2).

F. Explosive-Powered Nail Guns

Not all devices that use a combustive force to operate are considered "firearms." Certain nail guns, often referred to as "powder-actuated nail guns," use powder as an explosive charge to drive nails into hard surfaces like stone, concrete, or steel. These devices are commonly available at hardware stores and over the internet.

Because nail guns are not instruments of offensive or defensive combat, they are not considered "weapons" and are therefore not regulated by California or federal law.

G. Items Meeting the "Firearm" Definition, but Expressly Exempted

Even if something you possess is considered contraband by law enforcement because they claim it is a "firearm," it may still be exempt from certain restrictions based on the *type* of "firearm" it is. For example, as explained above, "antique firearms" are usually exempt from certain restrictions, and firearms considered "curios or relics" may be as well.

You are responsible for knowing whether the device you own is a "firearm" and which restrictions do and do not apply to it. The examples listed are just some of the considerations courts make in determining whether something is a "firearm."

IV. "AMMUNITION"

A. Federal Law "Ammunition" Definition

For purposes of the GCA, "ammunition" is "ammunition or cartridge cases, primers, bullets, or propellent powder designed for use in any firearm."[106] Also, the Code of Federal Regulations defines "ammunition" as "[a]mmunition or cartridge cases, primers, bullets, or propellant powder designed for use in any firearm other than an antique firearm. The term [does] not include (a) any shotgun shot or pellet not

Assorted Calibers of Ammunition

designed for use as the single, complete projectile load for one shotgun hull or casing, nor (b) any unloaded, non-metallic shotgun hull or casing not having a primer."[107]

---

[106] 18 U.S.C. § 921(a)(17)(A). This definition also applies to those federally prohibited from possessing firearms and ammunition as discussed in Chapter 3.

[107] 27 C.F.R. § 478.11.

Although the NFA does not provide a definition for "ammunition," the Code of Federal Regulations does provide a definition for "fixed ammunition" as "[t]hat self-contained unit consisting of the case, primer, propellant charge, and projectile or projectiles."[108]

Interestingly, for purpose of the restrictions on juveniles, the GCA expressly restricts juveniles from possessing "ammunition that is suitable for use only in a handgun."[109] The GCA and the Code of Federal Regulations do not provide a definition for this phrase, however.

B. California Law "Ammunition" Definitions

The word "ammunition" is undefined throughout most of the Penal Code, but it is given a specific definition in certain sections.[110] Pay close attention because these specific definitions often include items you would not commonly consider "ammunition."

For those prohibited from possessing firearms and "ammunition" (see Chapter 3) and the restrictions on ammunition purchases by and on behalf of a prohibited person created by Proposition 63 and Senate Bill (SB) 1235, "ammunition" includes, but is not limited to, "any bullet, cartridge, magazine, clip, speed loader, autoloader, or projectile capable of being fired from a firearm with a deadly consequence. 'Ammunition' does not include blanks."[111] In other words, mere components of ammunition like bullets and ammunition-feeding devices like magazines are themselves considered "ammunition" in this context.

Now you may be wondering why the legislature chose to include both the terms "bullet" and "cartridge" within the above definition of "ammunition." The legislature likely did one of two things in writing this definition. Either they meant to prohibit the possession of the projectile and complete "live" cartridges (*i.e.*, the bullet, powder, primer, and case), which would explain the use of the terms "bullet," "cartridge," and "*projectile* capable of being fired from a firearm with a deadly consequence." Or, they didn't realize that a "bullet" and "cartridge" are not synonymous terms and inadvertently included a single part of a cartridge (the bullet) in the definition while meaning a complete round. Given my past experience with the legislature and their general understanding of firearm parlance, I would say that the latter is probably what happened.

In any event, I strongly caution against possessing ammunition (live or otherwise) or any component of ammunition if you are prohibited from possessing ammunition.

---

[108] 27 C.F.R. § 478.11.
[109] 18 U.S.C. § 922(x)(2)(B).
[110] *See* P.C. § 16150.
[111] P.C. § 16150(b).

The term "ammunition" is also defined for purposes of the restrictions on ammunition vendors and all of the restrictions relating to acquiring ammunition from an ammunition vendor, face-to-face requirements, and importation of ammunition contained in Proposition 63 and SB 1235 (see Chapter 4). The term "ammunition" will be defined for purposes of these restrictions as "one or more loaded cartridges consisting of a primer case, propellant, and with one or more projectiles. 'Ammunition' does not include blanks."[112] This does not include the mere components of ammunition like the projectile, primer, case, or powder when we are talking about the restrictions and requirements for "ammunition" transferred through an ammunition vendor. Therefore, it is important to always be mindful what definition applies to you.

The Penal Code also provides a definition for the term "handgun ammunition." "Handgun ammunition" means ammunition principally for use in handguns, even if it can be used in some rifles.[113] "Handgun ammunition" does *not* include ammunition for "antique firearms" or blanks.[114]

1. Deactivated Ammunition

Although California law regulates certain types of ammunition (see Chapter 9) and who can possess ammunition generally (see Chapter 3), it does not prohibit the possession, importation, sale, attempted sale, or transportation of any deactivated ammunition, *i.e.*, ammunition for which the propellant has been removed and the primer has been permanently deactivated.[115]

Because California does not prohibit the possession of deactivated ammunition, a person who is prohibited from possessing firearms and ammunition under California law can possess deactivated ammunition. But if you are prohibited from possessing firearms and ammunition, you should be cautious in choosing to possess these items. When law enforcement officers stumble across a piece of deactivated ammunition, like a deactivated artillery shell, they often arrest the person for possessing "ammunition" or classify these objects as "destructive devices," despite the fact they no longer carry propellant and the primer has been otherwise made permanently deactivated. Although they are likely wrong on this matter, it may be

---

[112] P.C. § 16150(a).

[113] P.C. § 16650(a), *held unconstitutionally vague by Parker v. State of California*, 221 Cal. App. 4th 340 (2013). The standard "principally for use in a handgun" has been found in at least one context to be unconstitutionally vague because it is impossible to know whether any given cartridge is used more often in a handgun or a rifle, and for this reason, most ammunition venders ask the purchaser what type of firearm ammunition will be used in to meet this standard. *See Parker v. State of California*, 221 Cal. App. 4th 340 (2013). I litigated this case. In December 2016, the California Supreme Court dismissed its review of a Court of Appeal opinion affirming the trial court's order on the finding of vagueness. The Court of Appeal's decision is now the final opinion in the case, and Plaintiffs are seeking their attorneys' fees against the State. You can keep up to date on this case by visiting www.crpa.org.

[114] P.C. § 16650(b)(1)-(2), *held unconstitutionally vague by Parker v. State of California*, 221 Cal. App. 4th 340 (2013).

[115] P.C. § 30335.

safer to not possess deactivated ammunition if you are prohibited from possessing firearms and ammunition under either California or federal law.

C. "Ammunition" Parts

California does not generally regulate the possession of ammunition parts,[116] other than for those persons prohibited from possessing firearms and ammunition. But it does regulate possessing ammunition *powder*. So reloaders beware.

Even though smokeless powder does not technically explode, it is still considered an "explosive" in California because an "explosive" includes, but is not limited to, the following:

(1) "[A]ny substance, or combination of substances, the primary or common purpose of which is detonation or rapid combustion, and which is capable of a relatively instantaneous or rapid release of gas and heat, or any substance, the primary purpose of which, when combined with others, is to form a substance capable of a relatively instantaneous or rapid release of gas and heat"; *or*

(2) Any "explosive" as defined in 18 U.S.C. section 841 and published per 27 Code Fed. Regs. section 555.23; *or*

(3) "Dynamite, nitroglycerine, picric acid, lead azide, fulminate of mercury, *black powder, smokeless powder*, propellant explosives, detonating primers, blasting caps, or commercial boosters";[117] *or*

(4) Certain substances classified by the Department of Transportation;[118] *or*

(5) Any material designated by the Fire Marshal pursuant to regulations in accordance with Department of Transportation standards.[119]

The term "explosive" does "not include any destructive device, [or] ammunition or small arms primers manufactured for use in shotguns, rifles, and pistols."[120]

No one may possess an "explosive" without a permit.[121] You can, however, possess black powder in quantities of five pounds or less and smokeless powder in quantities of 20 pounds or less without a permit.[122]

---

[116] But note that California does regulate the possession of certain prohibited ammunition parts. For example, it would likely be illegal to possess the parts of tracer ammunition because tracer ammunition is considered to be a "destructive device" under California law. *See* P.C. § 18720. To learn more about destructive devices, see Chapter 9.

[117] P.C. § 16510(a) (emphasis added).

[118] P.C. § 16510(b)-(c).

[119] P.C. § 16510(d).

[120] P.C. § 16510(f). "Destructive devices" are discussed in Chapter 9.

[121] CAL. HEALTH & SAF. CODE § 12101(a)(3).

[122] CAL. HEALTH & SAF. CODE § 12001(f)(1).

Examples of Ammunition Parts

Cutaway of Center Fire Shell

bevel

case rim

extracting groove

cartridge case wall

"boat-tailed" base

propellant

bullet

crimp

cannelure

primer cup/pocket

meplat

primer

head

case body

shoulder

neck of cartridge case

case mouth

core

point filler

jacket

cartridge case

Cutaway of Rimfire Shell

rim

crimp

cannelure

priming compound

propellant

bullet

Cutaway of Shotgun Shell

metal head

base wad

case or hull

shot

crimp

primer

powder charge

combination over-powder wad,
filler wad and shot wrapper

star crimp

roll crimp

CHAPTER 3:
WHO CAN OWN AND POSSESS FIREARMS AND AMMUNITION?

Both California and federal law restrict certain classes of people from owning and/or possessing firearms and ammunition.[1] Aside from age restrictions, there are several situations where your right to own and/or possess firearms can be restricted, either temporarily or permanently. For example, you may be prohibited from owning or possessing a firearm because of a criminal conviction, restraining order, or mental health commitment.

How long you may be prohibited, depends on which class you are in, the specific situation, and the applicable state and/or federal law. It is possible, for example, for you to be restricted under *both* state and federal law, or under only one of them. The restriction may also be temporary under one set of laws, but last a lifetime under the other.

One general distinction between California and federal firearm restrictions is that California law bars prohibited persons[2] from owning firearms,[3] while federal law does not ban firearm *ownership* but rather *possession* (and certain other activities).[4] As explained below, this distinction can significantly impact the activities in which a prohibited person may lawfully participate.

---

[1] What constitutes a "firearm" or "ammunition" is different under California and federal law (see Chapter 2). All firearm restrictions listed in this chapter also include "ammunition" unless specifically stated otherwise.

[2] "Prohibited person" as used in this book means an individual who is subject to one or more legal restrictions relating to the person's legal ability to own and/or possess firearms and ammunition. But, if a corporation gets convicted of a crime, it too can be prohibited. This is especially problematic if the corporation has a federal contract to manufacture firearms.

[3] The California firearm and ammunition prohibition generally restricts owning, purchasing, receiving, and possessing firearms, or having firearms under your custody or control. *See* P.C. §§ 29800, 29805, 29815, 29820, 29825, 29900, 30305; CAL. WELF. & INST. CODE §§ 8100, 8103. A person with California firearm and ammunition prohibitions is precluded from all of these activities. In the interests of brevity, this book only mentions the prohibition on "possessing" firearms, but remember that all of these activities are also precluded for a person prohibited from "possessing" firearms *and ammunition*. And remember that "ammunition" includes clips and magazines as well, as discussed in Chapter 2.

[4] 18 U.S.C. section 922(g) makes it illegal for those with a firearm restriction "to ship or transport in interstate or foreign commerce, or possess in or affecting commerce, any firearm or ammunition; or to receive any firearm or ammunition which has been shipped or transported in interstate or foreign commerce." See 18 U.S.C. section

I. WHAT DOES "POSSESSION" MEAN?

Most state and federal violations occur when a prohibited person is found in "possession" of a firearm. Determining whether you "possess" a firearm, however, is not always easy. There are two kinds of legal possession: "actual possession" and "constructive possession."

"Actual possession" means that you knowingly have direct physical control of an object.[5] For example, you may have "actual possession" of an object in your hands, clothes, purse, bag, or other container. Knowingly having the object for even a limited time and purpose can constitute "actual possession."[6]

"Constructive possession" means that you knowingly have control of, or have *the right to* control the object, either directly or through another person.[7] More than one person can possess the same object at the same time.[8] Whether you can direct the object's movement and whether it would be reasonable to think you have such control are factors in determining if you have "constructive possession."[9] But you must also, in fact, *know* that you have this control over the object to be legally considered to constructively "possess" it.[10]

The idea of "possession" can be problematic if you live with someone who owns firearms (*e.g.*, a family member or roommate) or if you transfer your firearms to someone with who you live. For instance, although your spouse can legally keep their firearms inside the home during your probationary period (provided that you do not have any access to them), doing so can still be very problematic because it is very easy for a prosecutor to claim that you had access to firearms that are kept inside your home – especially, if you still have a key or know the combination to the gun safe where your firearm is kept. Because of this risk, you should strongly consider removing any firearms in your residence while you are prohibited from possessing them. And if you live with someone who refuses to remove their firearms and ammunition from your home, then you may want to consider living at a different place until you are no longer prohibited. Although this may sound extreme, it is the best way to ensure that you are not found to be in "possession" of any firearms or ammunition.

922(n) for restrictions on shipment, transportation, and acquisition, discussed at the end of this chapter. Once again, in the interest of brevity, this book only mentions the prohibition on "possessing" firearms, but remember all of these activities are precluded under federal law for a person prohibited from "possessing" firearms *and ammunition.*

[5] *People v. Scott*, 45 Cal. 4th 743, 748 (2009) (citing CALJIC No. 1.24).

[6] *People v. Neese*, 272 Cal. App. 2d 235, 244-45 (1969).

[7] *See Henderson v. United States*, 135 S. Ct. 1780, 1784 (2015); *see also People v. Neese*, 272 Cal. App. 2d 235, 244-47 (1969); *see also People v. Rogers*, 5 Cal. 3d 129, 134 (1971).

[8] *See People v. Azevedo*, 161 Cal. App. 3d 235, 243 (1984), *overruled on other grounds by People v. King*, 38 Cal. 4th 617 (2006) (holding knowledge of a weapon's prohibited character is a necessary element that the prosecution must prove); *see also* CALCRIM No. 2510.

[9] *Armstrong v. Superior Court*, 217 Cal. App. 3d 535, 539 (1990); *see also People v. Scott*, 45 Cal. 4th 743, 757 (2009).

[10] CALJIC No. 1.24.

If you have police or probation officers coming to your residence for any reason, you should seriously consider whether you are in "possession" of any firearms or ammunition. And if you are prohibited and still have firearms inside your home that belong to you, then you should call an attorney experienced in firearms law to discuss how to dispose of them.

II. WHAT DOES "OWN" MEAN?

While the California Penal Code (P.C.) doesn't define what it means to "own" a firearm, the California Civil Code (Cal. Civ. Code) states that "ownership of a thing is the right of one or more persons to possess and use it to the exclusion of others."[11] The California Civil Code also states that all inanimate things, such as property, "which are capable of appropriation or of manual delivery," can be owned.[12]

Since firearms are personal property that can be appropriated or manually delivered, they may be "owned." Therefore, to "own" a firearm, you only need to have *the right to* possess or use it.[13] You don't necessarily need to be in possession of it.

III. DETERMINING WHEN FIREARM POSSESSION PROHIBITIONS APPLY DURING FIREARM PURCHASES

California is a "point of contact" state, meaning the California Department of Justice (DOJ) conducts the background check to determine your eligibility to purchase or receive firearms when you try to buy a firearm, rather than the Federal Bureau of Investigation (FBI). When conducting background checks, the DOJ looks for criminal convictions, restraining orders, and mental health records. They access the Federal National Instant Criminal Background Check System (NICS) in addition to other state databases.[14] If your background information doesn't meet any of the firearm restriction criteria explained below, your name is not "flagged." On the other hand, if you have a criminal conviction, are subject to a restraining order, or had a mental health commitment, the DOJ will investigate further to determine if you are subject to a firearm restriction.[15]

---

[11] CAL. CIV. CODE § 654.

[12] CAL. CIV. CODE § 655.

[13] *See, e.g., People v. Kozlowski*, 96 Cal. App. 4th 853, 866 (2002) (explaining that "[t]he right to own property implies the right to possess or use a thing to the exclusion of others.").

[14] The DOJ also accesses the California Department of Motor Vehicles database, the Automated Firearm System, the Automated Criminal History System, the Wanted Persons System, Mental Health Firearms Prohibition System, and the California Restraining and Protective Orders System.

[15] For example, convictions for felonies, offenses designated as "violent" under P.C. section 29905, and misdemeanor crimes of domestic violence will prohibit you from possessing a firearm for life. Other offenses, such as those misdemeanor convictions listed within P.C. section 29805, will prohibit you from possessing firearms for a ten-year period.

It isn't unusual for the DOJ to determine that a person is subject to a firearm restriction, despite the fact that they may have allowed the person to purchase firearms in the past without incident. Although nothing may have changed since your last firearm purchase (*i.e.*, you have not been convicted of a crime, committed to a mental institution, and are not subject to a restraining order), the DOJ may have discovered some information that has caused them to believe you are subject to a firearm restriction. If the DOJ believes that you are subject to a firearm restriction, you should consider yourself to be prohibited from owning and possessing firearms until you resolve the issue.[16]

This would also apply to ammunition. Beginning July 1, 2019, unless an exception applies, ammunition vendors can only transfer or sell ammunition to a person if the DOJ verifies that he or she is authorized to purchase ammunition.[17] If the purchaser is prohibited from possessing firearms, then DOJ will consider the purchaser to be prohibited from acquiring or possessing ammunition.[18] Similarly, if DOJ finds that a person is prohibited from acquiring ammunition, then DOJ would probably consider him or her to be prohibited from possessing firearms. We do not know yet what DOJ will do if it cannot figure out for certain whether or not a person is prohibited. There is no guidance, as of yet, for that situation. So, DOJ's *belief* that you may be prohibited from owning firearms will also soon have wider implications.

IV. CALIFORNIA'S ARMED PROHIBITED PERSON SYSTEM (APPS) AND FIREARM DENIALS REPORTED TO LAW ENFORCEMENT

As of 2006, if you fall under one of the categories of persons prohibited from possessing firearms under California or federal law, your name is entered into the Automated Criminal History System. Once that happens, the DOJ is required to check if you possess or own any firearms, including registered "assault weapons" or .50 BMG rifles.[19] If it is discovered that you have firearms, your name and information will be placed on a list accessible to law enforcement via the Armed Prohibited Persons System (APPS).[20] The DOJ is required to perform an initial review of any

---

[16] To find out more about how to resolve the issue, or if you want to know what can be done if you are incorrectly considered prohibited from purchasing or owning firearm by the DOJ, read *Gun Owner's Guide to Restoring Your Rights* (tentative title), a book by Coldaw Publishing that will be available for purchase on Amazon in mid-2018.

[17] P.C. §30352(c)-(d). Until July 1, 2019, ammunition vendors can transfer ammunition without a background check, so long as (1) the person is of age and (2) the ammunition vendor knows, or should know, that the person is not prohibited from possessing ammunition. P.C. § 30306.

[18] P.C. § 30370(b).

[19] P.C. § 30005(a).

[20] The funding for this program is discussed in Chapter 4. Details regarding the program and how law enforcement utilizes it will be discussed in the upcoming book by Coldaw Publishing, which will center on firearms seizure, surrender, and return. This book will be available on Amazon by mid-2018.

person who is added to this list within seven days of the person being added to the APPS list.[21]

Since 2012, money collected from Dealer's Record of Sale (DROS) fees can be used to pay for the APPS program, allowing law enforcement to go after more people on the APPS list.[22] In 2013, the California Legislature passed Senate Bill (SB) 140, which authorized the DOJ to *raid all monies* in the "DROS Account" to further fund the APPS program.[23] Consequently, there has been a rise in law enforcement visiting and arresting people who have firearms registered in their name and have a record of a potentially prohibiting event.

Not content on just raiding the DROS Account to fund a failed program, in 2016, the California Legislature passed another bill (SB 826) to further fund the APPS program. This time, however, the California Legislature decided to take 5 million dollars from the Firearm Safety and Enforcement Special Fund and give it to the DOJ so that they can contract with local law enforcement agencies to reduce the backlog of individuals who are in APPS.[24]

If you are prohibited from possessing firearms and ammunition but still possess or have firearms registered in your name, you should speak with an attorney experienced in firearms law and transfer them as soon as possible, as discussed in the following section. If you are prohibited and no longer possess firearms or ammunition, but nonetheless still have firearms registered in your name, you may be able to remove your name from the APPS system by submitting a "Notice of No Longer in Possession" form with the DOJ. You can obtain a copy of this form at: http://oag.ca.gov/sites/all/files/agweb/pdfs/firearms/forms/BOF4546NLIP0209.pdf. DOJ currently requires proof that you no longer possess the firearm before removing the registration.

If you are denied a firearm through a firearm purchase or transfer, the DOJ is required to report the denial to local law enforcement.[25] Increased enforcement of prohibited person laws may prompt law enforcement to look into the matter further to determine if the denied purchaser possesses other firearms or whether to file criminal charges for lying on the DROS form.[26]

---

[21] P.C. § 30020. In addition to having a strict time frame to investigate individuals who have been added to this list, the DOJ will also be required to periodically reassess whether they can complete review of APPS matches more efficiently. P.C. § 30020.

[22] P.C. § 28225.

[23] The NRA is currently challenging the appropriation of these funds as an invalid tax in *Gentry v. Harris*. Updates on this case can be found at www.crpa.org.

[24] AB 826, 2015-2016 Leg., Reg. Sess. (Cal. 2016), *available at* https://leginfo.legislature.ca.gov/faces/billNavClient.xhtml?bill_id=201520160SB826 (last visited July 11, 2017).

[25] P.C. § 28220(b).

[26] Providing false information either on the DROS form or the federal 4473 form is illegal. If you think you may be prohibited from owning or possessing firearms under state or federal law, you should fill out a Personal Firearms Eligibility Check (PFEC) form (discussed at the end of this chapter) instead of attempting to purchase a firearm to determine your eligibility.

V. FIREARM AND AMMUNITION POSSESSION RESTRICTIONS FOR MINORS (UNDER AGE 18)

A. Shotguns and Rifles

Neither California nor federal law regulates minors[27] *possessing* rifles and shotguns, but under California law it is illegal to *give possession of* any firearm (handgun or long gun) to a minor without the parent or legal guardian's express permission.[28]

B. Handguns

Under federal law, juveniles are prohibited from *possessing* handguns unless they meet an exception (see below). Federal law also prohibits the transfer of handguns to minors except in certain situations.[29]

In California, individuals under age 18 may not generally *possess* handguns[30] unless they are actively engaged in, or are going directly to or from, a "lawful activity"[31] that involves using a handgun, and are either:

(1) With their parent or legal guardian; *or*

(2) With a "responsible adult"[32] and have prior *written* consent from their parent or legal guardian; *or*

(3) At least age 16 with prior *written* consent from their parent or legal guardian; *or*

(4) On lands owned or lawfully possessed by their parent or legal guardian and possess the parent or legal guardian's prior *written* consent.[33]

This handgun restriction also applies to "antique" handguns because "antique firearms" are still considered "firearms" for purposes of minors' possession of firearms.[34] So minors must satisfy one of the above exceptions when possessing an "antique" handgun.

---

[27] Although the Penal Code uses the term "juveniles" for those persons under the age of 18, we will refer to them as "minors" throughout the book.

[28] Transferring (meaning giving ownership to) rifles or shotguns to minors is limited to either the parents or grandparents giving the child these firearms. P.C. § 27945(a)-(b). But, there are laws that may prevent the transfer of a long gun to a minor. See discussion in Chapter 4. In addition, note that there are additional restrictions and exemptions on loaning firearms to minors. See Chapter 4.

[29] For more information relating to the laws for transferring firearms to minors see Chapter 4.

[30] P.C. § 29610.

[31] *I.e.,* "a lawful recreational sport, including, but not limited to, competitive shooting, or agricultural, ranching, or hunting activity, or a motion picture, television, or video production, or entertainment of theatrical event" P.C. § 29615.

[32] "Responsible adult" means someone "at least age 21 who is not prohibited by state or federal law from possessing, receiving, owning, or purchasing a firearm." P.C. § 17070.

[33] P.C. §§ 29610, 29615.

[34] Under the definition of "firearms," "antique firearms" are not considered firearms for the following listed Penal Code sections: 16130, 16370(a), (c), 16400, 16550, 16620, 16810, 16960, 17110, 17310, 26500-26588 (inclusive),

C. Ammunition

Under federal law, minors are generally prohibited from *possessing* ammunition that can only be used in a handgun,[35] unless they meet an exception (see below).

Under California law, minors are generally prohibited from possessing any kind of live ammunition, unless the following conditions are met:

(1) The minor has *written* consent from his or her parent or legal guardian; *or*

(2) The minor is with his or her parent or legal guardian; *or*

(3) The minor is "actively engaged in, or [is] going to or from, a lawful, recreational sport, including, but not limited to, competitive shooting, or agricultural, ranching, or hunting activity, the nature of which involves the use of a firearm."[36]

Minors who violate this provision can be charged with a crime.[37] When giving written permission to a minor to possess firearms, don't forget to mention that the minor can possess both firearms *and ammunition*. Also, make sure that the minor knows that they must retain that permission on their person while they possess the firearm.

Because of these ammunition restrictions for minors, ammunition sellers often ask to see identification to determine a purchaser's age, regardless of how old the individual appears.

D. Exemption to Federal Restriction on Handguns and "Handgun Ammunition"

Although minors are generally prohibited from possessing handguns and from possessing ammunition that can only be used in a handgun, both those restrictions do not apply if the *handgun* and/or *ammunition is possessed temporarily* and *all* of the following are satisfied:

(1) The handgun is only possessed while engaged in the following activities (including transportation directly between the point of transfer to the place where these activities take place so long as the handgun is unloaded and in a locked container):

    (a) In the course of employment; *or*

26700-26915 (inclusive), 27510, 27540, 27545, 28100, and 31615. But the Code section prohibiting minors from possessing handguns is not one of these.

[35] 18 U.S.C. § 922(x)(2). Enforcement of this law is very difficult because there really is no such thing as ammunition "suitable for use only in a handgun." Some non-handguns can safely discharge virtually any cartridge in existence. Regardless, this is a non-issue in California as minors are generally prohibited from possessing any kind of ammunition, unless certain criteria are met as explained below.

[36] P.C. § 29655.

[37] P.C. § 29700.

    (b) In the course of ranching or farming related to activities at the juvenile's residence (or on property used for ranching or farming at which the juvenile, with the permission of the property owner or lessee, is performing activities related to the operation of the farm or ranch); *or*

    (c) Target practice; *or*

    (d) Hunting; *or*

    (e) A course of instruction in the safe and lawful use of a handgun;

AND

(2) The minor's parent or guardian is not prohibited from possessing firearms by federal, state, or local law and the parent provides prior *written* consent (however, a minor with a prohibited parent or guardian may use a handgun for the ranching or farming related activities discussed above so long as he or she obtains *written* permission and is under the direction of an adult who is not prohibited by federal, state or local law from possessing a firearm);

AND

(3) The minor has the prior written consent of his or her parent or guardian and such written consent is in the minor's possession at all times the handgun is possessed by the minor;

AND

(4) All state and local laws are complied with.[38]

The federal handgun and ammunition restrictions mentioned above also do not apply to minors in the following situations:

(1) The minor is a member of the Armed Forces of the United States or the National Guard who possesses or is armed with a handgun in the line of duty; *or*

(2) Transfer by inheritance of title (but not possession) of a handgun and/or ammunition to a minor[39]; *or*

(3) The minor takes possession of the handgun and/or ammunition in defense of himself or herself, or other persons, against an intruder into the residence of the minor or a residence in which the minor is an invited guest.[40]

---

[38] 18 U.S.C. § 922(x)(3).

[39] Meanwhile, as stated above, California law generally restricts minors from possessing handguns and/or ammunition (see P.C. sections 29650, 29610, 29615, 29655). So, it appears that, in California, minors can inherit ownership of a handgun but are restricted when it comes to possession of a handgun. But with California's restrictions on transferring handguns to minors (see Chapter 4 and P.C. section 27505), it is uncertain how all of this would work.

[40] 18 U.S.C. § 922(x)(3).

Table 3.1

SUMMARY OF RESTRICTIONS FOR MINORS POSSESSING FIREARMS & AMMUNITION		
TYPE OF FIREARM	CALIFORNIA LAW	FEDERAL LAW
Shotguns & Rifles	California law does not regulate the possession of rifles or shotguns by minors.	Federal law does not regulate the possession of rifles or shotguns by minors, unless they meet one of the other firearm prohibitions explained in the sections below.
Handguns	Handgun possession is allowed if the minor is actively engaged in, or is going directly to or from, a lawful activity that involves using a handgun, and the minor has met the requirements enumerated in Section (V)(B).	Handgun possession is allowed if the minor possesses the handgun temporarily and has met the requirements enumerated in Section (V)(B).
Ammunition	Minors cannot possess any kind of live ammunition unless the conditions enumerated in Section (V)(C) are met.	Minors are prohibited from possessing ammunition that can *only* be used in handguns, unless the ammunition is possessed temporarily and all the requirements enumerated in Section (V)(C) are met.

VI. CRIMINAL CONVICTIONS RESULTING IN LOSS OF FIREARM POSSESSION RIGHTS

Felony and certain misdemeanor convictions cause most firearm restrictions. You can also be prohibited from possessing firearms under certain probation terms. California and federal law sometimes differ as to which convictions trigger restrictions, and to what extent. It is crucial that you and your attorney know what restrictions, if any, apply to any criminal conviction you receive so that you know how to comply with them.

Generally, California restrictions based on criminal convictions are set out in P.C. sections 29800-29875, and 29900-29905.[43] The federal prohibitions are listed in 18 U.S.C. section 922(g). If you are facing criminal charges that may result in firearm restrictions and you currently own firearms, know that some courts have held that a person "has been convicted of a felony" when a verdict is entered or a plea bargain is entered into, while others have required that a final sentence be entered.[44]

A. Federal Restrictions for Certain State or Federal Convictions

In California, anyone who has been convicted of a felony under California law, federal

While California firearm restrictions focus on the *type* of offense you were convicted of, federal law for the most part focuses on the type of *sentence* you *could* have received with your conviction (except when it comes to "misdemeanor crimes of domestic violence" (MCDV), see Section VI(F)).

Specifically, if your conviction under either state or federal law was for a crime *punishable* by imprisonment for more than one year, federal law prohibits you from possessing any firearm or ammunition for life.[45] Whether you have been convicted of a "crime punishable by imprisonment for a term exceeding one year" is determined according to the jurisdiction where you were prosecuted,[46] but does not include any:

(1) Federal or state offenses pertaining to antitrust violations, unfair trade practices, restraints of trade, or other similar offenses relating to the regulation of business practices; *or*

(2) State offenses classified by the laws of the State as a misdemeanor and punishable by a term of imprisonment of two years or less; *or*

(3) Convictions that have been expunged, set aside or for which you have been pardoned or had your civil rights restored unless the pardon, expungement, or restoration of civil rights expressly provided for firearm restrictions.[47]

Because the maximum sentence for any California *felony* conviction always exceeds one year, you are prohibited from owning and possessing firearms under

---

[41] For a list of state prohibiting charges and situations: see *Firearms Prohibiting Categories*, CAL. DEPT. OF JUSTICE, BUREAU OF FIREARMS, http://oag.ca.gov/sites/all/files/pdfs/firearms/forms/prohibcatmisd.pdf (last visited July 11, 2017). The Bureau of Alcohol, Tobacco, Firearms, and Explosives (ATF) also lists persons who are federally prohibited from shipping, transporting, receiving, or possessing firearms online. *Identify Prohibited Persons*, U.S. DEPT. OF JUSTICE, BUREAU OF ALCOHOL, TOBACCO, FIREARMS AND EXPLOSIVES, https://www.atf.gov/firearms/identify-prohibited-persons (last visited July 11, 2017).

[44] *People v. Rogers*, 57 Cal. 4th 296, 345 (2013) (stating, "for the purpose of determining if the defendant had acquired the status of a person convicted of a felony, one is 'convicted' when a verdict is entered").

[45] 18 U.S.C. § 922(g)(1). It is not necessary that you actually receive such a sentence.

[46] *United States v. Marks*, 379 379 F.3d 1114, 1117 (9th Cir. 2004).

[47] 18 U.S.C. § 921(a)(20).

federal law for *any* California felony conviction. But because a California *misdemeanor* conviction is only punishable by a year or less in jail, you are not federally prohibited for any such conviction[48] unless it is for an MCDV (discussed below). Federal firearm prohibitions extend to all 50 states and territories.[49]

B. California Restrictions for Felony Convictions

In California, anyone who has been convicted of a felony under California law, federal law, or another state or country's law,[50] may not own, purchase, receive, or possess firearms or ammunition.[51]

This California prohibition does *not* apply to felony convictions under federal law *unless*:

(1) The conviction was for an offense that would only result in felony punishment under California law; *or*

(2) You were sentenced to a federal correctional facility for more than 30 days and/or were fined more than $1,000.[52]

C. California Restrictions for Certain "Violent Crimes"

California also restricts firearm possession for certain "violent crime" convictions regardless of whether the conviction is a misdemeanor or felony.[53] These "violent crimes" include, but are not limited to, murder, attempted murder, mayhem, rape, and assault with a deadly weapon or force likely to produce great bodily injury.[54] Though most "violent crimes" are felonies – convictions which would carry a firearm prohibition anyway – some can be charged as misdemeanors.[55] Being convicted of any of these "violent crimes," whether a felony or misdemeanor and whether the conviction was inside or outside of California, will result in a lifetime firearm prohibition in California.[56]

---

[48] P.C. § 19.2

[49] *See* 18 U.S.C. § 922(g)(9). There is a limited exception to the firearm and ammunition restrictions under federal law. Except for persons prohibited from possessing firearms for an MCDV, the federal restrictions do "not apply with respect to the transportation, shipment, receipt, possession, or importation of any firearm or ammunition imported for, sold or shipped to, or issued for the use of, the United States or any department or agency thereof or any State or any department, agency, or political subdivision thereof." 18 U.S.C. § 925(a)(1).

[50] Other countries do not possess the same Due Process rights as the U.S. So, under California law you can be prohibited from possessing firearms and ammunition if you are convicted of a felony in a court in another country that does not provide you with similar Due Process rights.

[51] *See* P.C. § 29800(a)(1).

[52] P.C. § 29800(c)(2).

[53] *See* P.C. §§ 29900, 29905.

[54] A full list of "violent crimes" is given in P.C. section 29905 and below.

[55] *People v. Sanchez*, 211 Cal. App. 3d 477, 483 (1989) (the defendant's conviction for a "violent offense" prohibited him from possessing firearms without regard to the misdemeanor status of the conviction). So, both felonies and misdemeanor convictions can be prohibiting offenses under P.C. section 29900.

[56] *People v. Jaffe*, 19 Cal. Rptr. 3d 689, 698-99 (2004), *rev. granted and opinion superseded*, 105 P.3d 115 (Cal. 2005).

If you were convicted of one of these "violent crimes," you may be prosecuted for a felony if you possess a firearm thereafter.[57] And even if probation was granted, or the imposition or execution of your sentence was suspended, you are still likely to be sentenced to a minimum of six months in jail for possessing a firearm.[58]

Being convicted of any of the following "violent crimes" results in a lifetime restriction in California[59]:

Table 3.2

PENALCODESECTION	VIOLENT CRIMES RESULTING IN A LIFETIME FIREARMS RESTRICTION IN CALIFORNIA
P.C. § 29905(a)(1)	Murder or voluntary manslaughter
P.C. § 29905(a)(2)	Mayhem
P.C. § 29905(a)(3)	Rape
P.C. § 29905(a)(4)	Sodomy by force, violence, duress, menace, or threat of bodily harm
P.C. § 29905(a)(5)	Oral copulation by force, violence, duress, menace, or threat of great bodily harm
P.C. § 29905(a)(6)	Lewd acts on a child under the age of 14 years
P.C. § 29905(a)(7)	Any felony punishable by death or imprisonment in the state prison for life
P.C. § 29905(a)(8)	Any other felony in which the defendant inflicts great bodily injury on any person, other than an accomplice, that has been charged and proven, or any felony in which the defendant uses a firearm which use has been charged and proven
P.C. § 29905(a)(9)	Attempted murder
P.C. § 29905(a)(10)	Assault with intent to commit rape or robbery
P.C. § 29905(a)(11)	Assault with a deadly weapon or instrument on a peace officer
P.C. § 29905(a)(12)	Assault by a life prisoner on a non-inmate
P.C. § 29905(a)(13)	Assault with a deadly weapon by an inmate
P.C. § 29905(a)(14)	Arson
P.C. § 29905(a)(15)	Exploding a destructive device or any explosive with intent to injure
P.C. § 29905(a)(16)	Exploding a destructive device or any explosive causing great bodily injury
P.C. § 29905(a)(17)	Exploding a destructive device or any explosive with intent to murder
P.C. § 29905(a)(18)	Robbery
P.C. § 29905(a)(19)	Kidnapping
P.C. § 29905(a)(20)	Taking of a hostage by an inmate of a state prison

---

[57] See P.C. § 29900(a)(1).
[58] P.C. § 29900(a)(3).
[59] See P.C. § 29900(a)(1).

PenalCodeSection	Violent Crimes Resulting in a Lifetime Firearms Restriction in California
P.C. § 29905(a)(21)	Attempt to commit a felony punishable by death or imprisonment in the state prison for life
P.C. § 29905(a)(23)	Escape from a state prison by use of force or violence
P.C. § 29905(a)(24)	Assault with a deadly weapon or force likely to produce great bodily injury
P.C. § 29905(a)(27)	Carjacking
P.C. § 29905(b)	Any attempt to commit a crime listed above other than an assault

D. California Convictions of Offenses Listed in Penal Code Section 23515(a), (b), and (d), or Two or More Convictions Under Penal Code Section 417(a)(2) Resulting in a Lifetime Restriction

As outlined in the chart below, individuals who are convicted of an offense listed in P.C. section 23515(a), (b), or (d); or who have two or more convictions under Penal Code section 417(a)(2) are subject to a lifetime restriction on owning, purchasing, receiving, and possessing any firearm.[60] A violation of this restriction is a felony.[61] A conviction for any one of the following offenses (misdemeanor or felony) results in a lifetime restriction from possessing firearms[62]:

Table 3.3

PenalCodeSection	Conduct Resulting in a Lifetime Firearms Restriction in California
P.C. § 23515(a)	A violation of P.C. section 245(a)(2)-(3) (assault with a firearm or machinegun) or P.C. section 245(d) (assault with a firearm on a peace officer or firefighter)
P.C. § 23515(b)	A violation of P.C. section 246 (maliciously and willfully discharging a firearm at an inhabited dwelling house, occupied building, occupied motor vehicle, occupied aircraft, inhabited housecar, or inhabited camper)
P.C. § 23515(c)	A violation of P.C. section 417(c) (brandishing a firearm in the presence of a peace officer)
P.C. § 23515(d)	Two or more convictions of P.C. section 417(a)(2) (brandishing a firearm)

---

[60] P.C. § 29800.

[61] P.C. § 29800.

[62] P.C. §§ 23515(a), (b), (d); 29800.

E. California Restrictions for Certain Misdemeanor Convictions

If a California misdemeanor conviction results in a firearm restriction, it *usually* lasts ten years, but some have lifetime prohibitions as discussed above. For your reference, comprehensive lists of the types of misdemeanor convictions that result in firearm restrictions are included below.

1. Misdemeanor Convictions Resulting in a Ten-Year Restriction

Individuals owning, purchasing, receiving, or possessing any firearm within ten years of being convicted of any of the below listed misdemeanors may be prosecuted for a public offense, punishable by imprisonment in a county jail not exceeding one year, or in the state prison, punishable by a fine not exceeding one thousand dollars ($1,000), or by both imprisonment and fine.[63]

A conviction for any one of the following misdemeanors will result in a ten-year restriction[64]:

Table 3.4

STATUTE	CONDUCT RESULTING IN A TEN-YEAR FIREARMS RESTRICTION IN CALIFORNIA
P.C. § 71	Threatening officers or employees of a public or private school, or any public officer or employee
P.C. § 76	Threatening certain public officers, appointees, judges, staff, or their families, with the intent and apparent ability to carry out the threat
P.C. § 136.1	Intimidating witnesses or victims
P.C. § 136.5	Possessing a deadly weapon with the intent to intimidate a witness
P.C. § 140	Threatening witnesses, victims, or informants
P.C. § 148(d)	Attempting to remove or take a firearm from the person or immediate presence of a public or peace officer
P.C. § 148.5(f)	Falsely reporting that a firearm has been lost or stolen
P.C. § 171b	Unauthorized possession of a weapon in a courtroom, courthouse, or court building, or at a public meeting
P.C. § 171c(a)(1)	Bringing or possessing loaded firearms in the State Capitol, legislative offices, any office of the Governor or other constitutional officer, or any hearing room in which any committee of the Senate or Assembly is conducting a hearing or upon the State Capitol grounds

---

[63] P.C. § 29805.
[64] *See* P.C. § 29805.

Statute	Conduct Resulting in a Ten-Year Firearms Restriction in California
P.C. § 171d	Bringing or possessing loaded firearms in the Governor's Mansion or residence of other constitutional officers
P.C. § 186.28	Supplying, selling or giving firearm possession to anyone to participate in criminal street gangs
P.C. §§ 240, 241	Assault
P.C. §§ 242, 243	Battery
P.C. § 243.4	Sexual battery
P.C. § 244.5	Assault with a stun gun or taser
P.C. § 245	Assault with a deadly weapon other than a firearm, or with force likely to produce great bodily injury
P.C. § 245.5	Assault with a deadly weapon or instrument by any means likely to produce great bodily injury, or with a stun gun or taser, on school employees engaged in performing their duties
P.C. § 246.3	Discharging a firearm in a grossly negligent manner
P.C. § 247	Shooting at an unoccupied aircraft, motor vehicle, or uninhabited building or dwelling house
P.C. § 273.5	Inflicting corporal injury on a spouse or significant other
P.C. § 273.6	Willfully violating a domestic restraining order
P.C. § 417	Drawing, exhibiting, or using a deadly weapon other than a firearm
P.C. § 417.6	Inflicting serious bodily injury as a result of brandishing
P.C. § 422	Threatening to commit a crime that will result in death or great bodily injury to another person
P.C. § 422.6	Using force or threat of force to interfere with victim's civil rights because of victim's characteristics (e.g., race, religion, etc.) or knowingly defacing, damaging, or destroying victim's property for purposes of intimidating or interfering with victim's civil rights
P.C. § 490.2	Petty theft of a firearm (only if convicted between November 5, 2014 and November 9, 2016)[65]
P.C. § 626.9	Bringing or possessing firearms in or upon public schools or grounds
P.C. § 646.9	Stalking
P.C. § 830.95	Wearing of peace officer uniform while picketing or at other informational activities
P.C. § 17500	Possessing a deadly weapon to intentionally commit an assault

NEW
LAW

Statute	Conduct Resulting in a Ten-Year Firearms Restriction in California
P.C. § 17510	Carrying a firearm or deadly weapon while engaged in labor-related picketing
P.C. § 25300	Carrying a firearm in a public place or street while masked
P.C. § 25800	Armed criminal action
P.C. § 26100(b) or (d)	Driver of any vehicle who knowingly allows another person to discharge a firearm from the vehicle, or anyone who willfully and maliciously discharges a firearm from a motor vehicle themselves
P.C. § 27510	Firearms dealer who sells, transfers, or gives firearm possession to a minor or a handgun to anyone under age 21, or a person or corporation who sells any concealable firearm to a minor
P.C. § 27590(c)	Various violations involving the sale and transfer of firearms
P.C. § 30315	Possessing ammunition designed to penetrate metal or armor
P.C. § 32625	Unauthorized machinegun possession/transportation
Cal. Welf. & Inst. Code § 871.5	Bringing or sending contraband into or possession within juvenile hall (The contraband must be a firearm this restriction)
Cal. Welf. & Inst. Code § 1001.5	Bringing or sending contraband into a youth authority institution (The contraband must be a firearm for purposes of this restriction)
Cal. Welf. & Inst. Code § 8100	Purchasing, possessing, or receiving a firearm or deadly weapon while receiving in-patient treatment for a mental disorder, or by someone who has threatened serious physical violence to a licensed psychotherapist against an identifiable victim
Cal. Welf. & Inst. Code § 8101	Providing a firearm or deadly weapon to someone described in California Welfare and Institutions Code (Cal. Welf. & Inst. Code) sections 8100 or 8103
Cal. Welf. & Inst. Code § 8103	Purchasing, possessing, or receiving a firearm or deadly weapon by someone adjudicated a mentally disordered sex offender, incompetent to stand trial, not guilty by reason of insanity, or placed under conservatorship, and those prohibited from possessing firearms following Cal. Welf. & Inst. Code sections 5150, 5250, 5260, or 5270 commitments

Despite the very specific code sections listed above, one California court ruled that certain related code sections also carry a firearm restriction upon conviction.

---

[65] Currently, P.C. section 490.2 (petty theft) does not cover firearms. The section specifically says, "[t]his section shall not apply to theft of a firearm." This was added as a result of Prop. 63. Between November 5, 2014 (the date that P.C. section 490.2 was added to the Penal Code by Prop. 47) and November 9, 2016 (the date when Prop. 63 laws became effective), the theft of a firearm valuing less than $950 (i.e., petty theft of a firearm) was considered to be a misdemeanor. Before that time, the theft of a firearm was a felony (and of course a firearm prohibiting of-

In one case, a minor was convicted of P.C. section 243.6 (battery on a school official), and the court decided that because the *definition* of battery (P.C. section 242) and the *offense* of battery (P.C. section 243) were prohibiting offenses, a conviction for P.C. section 243.6 should also be a prohibiting offense even though it is not on the list.[66] Therefore, the minor was considered prohibited.

There is also some ambiguity as to whether a misdemeanor conviction for assault with a deadly weapon *other than* a firearm (P.C. section 245(a)(1)) would result in either a ten-year or lifetime prohibition. The uncertainty of which prohibition would apply in this context was created by dicta[67] written by the California Court of Appeal in *Rash v. Lungren*.[68]

In *Rash*, the California Court of Appeal was faced with the question of whether a person with a prior conviction under P.C. section 245(a)(2) (assault with a *firearm*) fell under the lifetime or ten-year prohibitions under former P.C. sections 12021 (currently codified at P.C. section 29800) (lifetime prohibitions) and 12021.1 (currently codified at P.C. section 29805).[69] While the court quickly concluded that any conviction (felony or misdemeanor) under any of the P.C. section 245 offenses involving the use of a firearm would result in a permanent prohibition, it also ruled that the ten-year prohibition "is reserved for those with misdemeanor convictions under section 245, subdivision (a)(1) (assaults with deadly weapons *other than* firearms) . . . ."[70]

The court continued to distinguish the two prohibitions and explained that the lifetime prohibition is only applicable to those who are convicted of either a felony or misdemeanor assault *with* a firearm, while the ten-year prohibition is only applicable to those who have a misdemeanor conviction of assault with a weapon *other than* a firearm under P.C. section 245(a)(1).[71] So, the court seemed to suggest that if you have a prior conviction under P.C. section 245(a)(1), you would only be subject to the ten-year prohibition.

---

fense). But because the Legislature wanted to make the theft of a firearm a prohibiting offense, it added the misdemeanor petty theft of a firearm to offenses listed in P.C. section 29805 that carry a 10-year restriction. But Prop. 63 modified P.C. section 490.2 and made it so that a person could not be convicted of petty theft for stealing a firearm. And Prop. 63 failed to change section 29805. Therefore, a person could have only been convicted for petty theft by stealing a firearm between November 5, 2014 and November 9, 2016. Currently, the theft of a firearm is considered grand theft (P.C. section 487) and punishable as a felony (P.C. section 489(a).)

[66] *In re David S.,* 133 Cal. App. 4th 1160, 1163-68 (2005).

[67] Dictum (the single form of dicta) is "[a] statement of opinion or belief considered authoritative because of the dignity of the person making it." BLACK'S LAW DICTIONARY 485 (8th ed. 2004). Dicta is merely persuasive and not binding authority.

[68] *Rash v. Lungren,* 59 Cal. App. 4th 1233 (1997).

[69] *Rash v. Lungren,* 59 Cal. App. 4th 1233, 1234 (1997).

[70] *Rash v. Lungren,* 59 Cal. App. 4th 1233, 1238-39 (1997).

[71] *See Rash v. Lungren,* 59 Cal. App. 4th 1233 n.8 (1997) ("The Legislature has, thus, chosen to differentiate between convictions involving the use, or lack of use, of a firearm – at least in cases involving assaults with deadly weapons . . . . In view of the expressed legislative concern about increasing violent gun use, the distinction drawn . . . between offenses meriting a permanent prohibition as opposed to a ten-year restriction is certainly one that they were entitled to draw.").

This distinction, however, is odd given that P.C. section 29905, which lists the "violent crimes" that are subject to lifetime prohibitions under P.C. section 29900, specifically lists assault with a deadly weapon as a "violent crime."[72] This would arguably include any of the offenses listed in P.C. section 245, including subdivision (a)(1). Therefore, it seems that if you received a misdemeanor conviction for assault with a deadly weapon other than a firearm under P.C. section 245(a)(1), you would still be subject to the lifetime prohibition on owning, purchasing, receiving, or possessing firearms because it would still be considered a "violent crime."[73] But given the court's decision in *Rash*, there is clearly uncertainty as to which prohibition would apply.

 Beware: the California Legislature periodically attempts to expand the list of misdemeanor convictions that result in firearm restrictions. In 2016, the California Legislature expanded the list when it passed AB 1695. In 2017, the California Legislature expanded the list again when it passed AB 785 and added P.C. section 422.6 (interference with another person's civil rights) to the list. While you may not currently be prohibited form possessing firearms due to a misdemeanor conviction, the laws can change.

Your period of prohibition could start years after your conviction. For example, those who were convicted of misdemeanor violations of P.C. section 422.6 will be prohibited from possessing firearms as of January 1, 2018. The length of the prohibition will be 10 years from the date of the convictions. So, a person who was convicted on January 1, 2010 of a misdemeanor violation of P.C. section 422.6 will be prohibited from possessing firearms pursuant to P.C. section 29805 on January 1, 2018, and the prohibition will end on January 1, 2020. There is no mechanism to provide notice to persons who will be prohibited from possessing firearms to let them know that they will be prohibited as of January 1, 2018.

There is a mechanism to restore firearm rights for people who become prohibited from possessing firearms after their date of conviction because the Legislature added their offenses to the list of misdemeanor convictions resulting in ten-year restriction. This mechanism will be discussed in detail in an upcoming book by Coldaw Publishing, tentatively titled *Gun Owner's Guide to Restoring Your Gun Rights*.

2. Misdemeanor Conviction Resulting in a Five-Year Restriction

Any person who has been convicted of a misdemeanor under P.C. section 18205 (possessing a firearm while a "gun violence restraining order" is in effect) will be prohibited from having in his or her custody or control, owning, purchasing, pos-

---

[72] P.C. §§ 29900; 29905(24).

[73] *See* P.C. §§ 29900; 29905(24).

sessing, or receiving, or attempting to purchase or receive, a firearm or ammunition for five years, beginning the date the gun violence restraining order expires.[74]

F. Federal Restrictions for a Misdemeanor Crime of Domestic Violence (MCDV)

An MCDV occurs when someone is convicted of an offense that has, as an element,[75] the use or attempted use of physical force or the threatened use of a deadly weapon, and the accused either:

(1) Is "a current or former spouse, parent, or guardian of the victim"; *or*

(2) "[S]hares a child in common" with the victim; *or*

(3) Is living, or has lived, "with the victim as a spouse, parent, or guardian"; *or*

(4) Is "similarly situated to a spouse, parent, or guardian of the victim."[76]

An MCDV is a misdemeanor offense under federal, state, and tribal law,[77] but it triggers a lifetime ban under federal law.[78] You are not considered to be "convicted" of an MCDV unless you: (1) were represented by counsel or waived your right to be represented by counsel, *and* (2) if entitled to a jury trial, you either tried the case, waived your right to have the case tried by a jury by entering a guilty plea, or waived your right to a jury trial by some other way.[79] That being said, it is highly unlikely that a California judge would allow your guilty or no contest plea without attorney representation or a jury trial, unless you properly waived your rights to both first.

Determining whether an offense under California law meets the definition of an MCDV usually boils down to three issues: (1) the type of offense that was committed, (2) the nature of the relationship between the defendant and the victim, and (3) whether the conviction was legally removed from the defendant's record in order to restore firearm rights.

---

[74] P.C. § 18205.

[75] *See United States v. Hayes*, 555 U.S. 415, 422 (2009) (defining an element as "[a] constituent part of a claim that must be proved for the claim to succeed"). For example, one of the elements of speeding is that the prosecutor must prove that the defendant was going faster than the speed limit. The requirement that the offense has, as an element, the use or attempted use of physical force is discussed below.

[76] 18 U.S.C. § 921(a)(33)(A)(ii). *See also United States v. Hayes*, 555 U.S. 415 (2009). Although a crime must have, as an element, the use or attempted use of force or the threatened use of deadly weapon in order to fall under the definition of an MCDV, the relationship status of the victim does not have to be a defining element of the predicate offense. *United States v. Hayes*, 555 U.S. 415, 429 (2009).

[77] 18 U.S.C. § 921(a)(33)(A)(i).

[78] *See* 18 U.S.C. § 922(g)(9).

[79] 18 U.S.C. § 921(a)(33)(B)(i).

1. California Offenses that May Be a Misdemeanor Crime of Domestic Violence

Two Penal Code sections are typically considered "domestic violence" statutes: P.C. sections 273.5 and 243(e).[80] But, as discussed below, other California crimes can be considered "domestic violence" crimes to which the federal MCDV lifetime firearm restriction applies.[81]

a. Injuring a Spouse, Cohabitant, Fiancé, Etc.

A violation of P.C. section 273.5 – injuring a former or current spouse or cohabitant, the father or mother of one's child, or a fiancé or someone with whom a person has or had an engagement or dating relationship[82] – may meet the definition of an MCDV under federal law. The DOJ (which does the background checks on firearm purchases) considers a P.C. section 273.5 conviction to be an MCDV automatically. But the DOJ may be wrong, especially if the conviction occurred after January 1, 2014.[83] A P.C. section 273.5 violation can *only* be committed against a spouse or former spouse, cohabitant,[84] mother or father of one's child, or a fiancé or someone with whom a person has or had an engagement or dating relationship. But, some of these relationships might not be the type of relationship that triggers an MCDV firearm restriction under federal law (see section above).

P.C. section 273.5 can only be violated when there is a corporal injury resulting in a "traumatic condition."[85] A "traumatic condition" means a condition of the body, such as a wound, or external or internal injury, including, but not limited to, injury as a result of strangulation or suffocation, whether of a minor or serious nature, caused by a *physical force*. For purposes of this definition, "strangulation" and "suffocation" include impeding the normal breathing or circulation of the blood of a person by applying pressure on the throat or neck.[86] While a P.C. section 273.5 violation rests on the type of injury the victim received, an MCDV only requires that a certain level of force is met. A P.C. section 273.5 violation has been deter-

---

[80] Remember, almost all of the Penal Code sections (with the exception of P.C. section 415) discussed here carry a ten-year firearm restriction under California law. You should be mindful of this while reading this section, as well as the possibility that the conviction may also result in a federal firearm restriction.

[81] 18 U.S.C. § 922(g)(9). Under P.C. section 29805, a P.C. section 273.5 or section 243 misdemeanor conviction results in a ten-year California firearm restriction.

[82] "'Dating relationship' means frequent, intimate associations primarily characterized by the expectation of affectional or sexual involvement independent of financial considerations." P.C. § 243(f)(10).

[83] In 2014, the categories of relationships under P.C. section 273.5 were expanded to include former fiancés, as well as current and former dating relationships. AB 16, 2013-2014 Leg. Reg. Sess. (Cal. 2013). These relationships might not be the type of relationship that meets the definition of an MCDV.

[84] *See People v. Holifield*, 205 Cal. App. 3d 993, 999-1000 (1999) (providing that for purposes of P.C. section 273.5, the term "cohabiting" means "something more than a platonic, rooming-house arrangement . . . [it] means an unrelated man and woman living together in a substantial relationship – one manifested, minimally, by permanence and sexual or amorous intimacy").

[85] P.C. § 273.5(a).

[86] P.C. § 273.5(c). "Traumatic condition" includes bruising. *United States v. Hall*, 419 F.3d 980, 986 (9th Cir. 2005); *People v. Beasley*, 105 Cal. App. 4th 1078, 1085-86 (2003).

mined to involve the "use, attempted use, or threatened use of physical force against the person of another" by a federal court trying to determine whether it is a "crime of violence" under federal sentencing enhancements.[87] Under the court's analysis, a P.C. section 273.5 violation was considered to require physical force because it requires the use of force resulting in a "traumatic condition." This same analysis can be extended to whether a P.C. section 273.5 conviction is an MCDV, and it is very likely that this analysis would be used by a court.

b. Battery Against a Spouse, Cohabitant, Fiancé, Etc.

A conviction under P.C. section 243(e) does not necessarily result in a federal MCDV firearm restriction, but it may. You can be charged under P.C. section 243(e) if you commit a battery and the victim is a spouse, someone you are cohabiting with, someone who is the parent of your child, a former spouse, fiancé, or someone you are or were dating.[88]

Note that a fiancé or someone you are or were dating or engaged to be married does not necessarily meet the definition of a victim under the federal MCDV statute.[89] This means that if you are convicted of a P.C. section 243(e) battery where the victim is one of these individuals, you may not have a federal lifetime firearm restriction under 18 U.S.C. section 922(g)(9) because it may not be considered an MCDV. The facts of your relationship need to be further analyzed to determine if the "victim" in your case meets the definition of a person that triggers the restriction.

In 2014, the United States Supreme Court held in *United States v. Castleman* that the element of "physical force" is satisfied by the degree of force that supports a common-law battery conviction – namely, offensive touching.[90] In other words, both P.C. section 243(e) and P.C. section 242 have as an element the "use of physical force" because both crimes require an amount of force either greater than or equal to an offensive touching.

Prior to 2014, there was some ambiguity as to whether a conviction under P.C. section 243(e) or P.C. section 242 qualified as an MCDV because courts were split as to whether an offense that could be violated by a simple touching (such as P.C. section 242) met the required "physical force" element to be an MCDV. For instance, in 2013, the California Court of Appeal held in *Shirey v. Los Angeles County Civil Service Commission* that a person convicted of battery is not automatically considered prohibited from possessing firearms under federal law for an MCDV.[91] As the court explained, under P.C. section 242, a battery can be committed by sim-

---

[87] *United States v. Laurico-Yeno*, 590 F.3d 818 (9th Cir. 2010).

[88] P.C. § 243(e).

[89] *See* 18 U.S.C. § 921(a)(33)(A).

[90] *United States v. Castleman*, 134 S. Ct. 1405, 1413 (2014).

[91] *Shirey v. Los Angeles Cnty. Civil Serv. Comn'n*, 216 Cal. App. 4th 1 (2013). It was undisputed that the relationship between the defendant and the victim in *Shirey* met the relationship requirement of an MCDV.

ply touching the victim. Therefore, when the law requires the "use of physical force" as an element, some type of *force* must be used. Simple touching is not enough. As a result, the court concluded that a battery conviction does not automatically result in a federal firearm restriction.

But, shortly after the decision in *Shirey* was published, another California Court of Appeal reached an opposite conclusion. In *James v. State*, the court determined that a misdemeanor P.C. section 242 conviction *does* meet the definition of an MCDV (provided that the relationship between the defendant an the victim is one falling under the requirement for an MCDV).[92] The court concluded that a P.C. section 242 violation, regardless of the amount of force actually used in the underlying offense, is considered an MCDV.

James was ultimately appealed to the California Supreme Court. But, because the U.S. Supreme Court had granted certiorari in *Castleman*, the California Supreme Court deferred review. After the U.S. Supreme Court issued its opinion on March 26, 2014, the California Supreme Court transferred the case back down to the California Court of Appeal with directions to vacate the decision and reconsider the case in light of the decision in *Castleman*. But, on review, the California Court of Appeal again concluded that a misdemeanor P.C. section 242 conviction does meet the definition of an MCDV because P.C. section 242 has, as an element, the "use of physical force."[93]

Although neither *James* nor *Castleman* expressly overturned the decision in *Shirey*, given both the U.S. Supreme Court's decision in *Castleman* and the California Court of Appeal's subsequent decision in *James*, it seems to be a forgone conclusion that a conviction under P.C. section 242 categorically meets the "physical force" requirement needed to be an MCDV.

2. Other California Crimes That May Be Considered a Misdemeanor Crime of Domestic Violence

Other California crimes that may be considered an MCDV include assault (P.C. section 240); battery (P.C. section 242); assault with a deadly weapon or force likely to produce great bodily injury (P.C. section 245); and fighting, noise, and offensive words (P.C. section 415).

To determine whether a misdemeanor conviction qualifies as an MCDV under federal law, the DOJ will first consider the initial charges. If necessary, the DOJ will review the court file or plea form for additional facts to determine the nature of the relationship between the convicted person and the victim. Defense attorneys will often try to "plea down" a domestic violence charge to something milder than a P.C. section 273.5 conviction (such as a P.C. section 242, 243(e), or 415(1)). But beware

---

[92] *James v. State*, No. F065003 (Cal Ct. App. Sept. 24, 2013), *available at* http://caselaw.findlaw.com/ca-court-of-appeal/1645252.html (last visited July 11, 2017).

[93] *James v. State*, 229 Cal. App. 4th 130, 141 (2014).

before doing this because the DOJ will look at the initial charge of P.C. section 273.5, and if you have pled to a P.C. section 242 or P.C. section 415, the DOJ may still believe that you were automatically convicted of an MCDV. This is because the DOJ will assume that, if the person was originally charged with a P.C. section 273.5, there are sufficient facts to believe the person had a relationship with the victim that satisfies the relationship requirement for an MCDV. This assumption may not be accurate or the DOJ may lack the information to determine that the person is prohibited from possessing firearms for an MCDV restriction. Nevertheless, the DOJ may declare that the person is prohibited from receiving firearms until he or she can prove otherwise to their satisfaction.

If you are facing criminal charges, be sure to discuss all of the possible ramifications of a conviction with your attorney. If your attorney cannot give you answers, or you are concerned that your attorney does not know these answers, you should seek assistance from other counsel.

G. Juvenile Offenses

Certain juvenile offenses may lead to firearm restrictions that prohibit possession of firearms until the age of 30. In order for a juvenile offense to lead to those restrictions, the juvenile must have been:

(1) Alleged to have committed an offense listed in the table on the next page; *and*

(2) "[S]ubsequently adjudged a ward of the juvenile court" because the juvenile committed that offense.[94]

A violation of this firearm restriction is punishable by imprisonment in a county jail or state prison not exceeding one year, by a fine not exceeding one thousand dollars ($1,000), or by both that imprisonment and fine. The following juvenile offenses may lead to these firearm restrictions[95]:

Table 3.5

STATUTE	JUVENILE OFFENSE
CAL. WELF. & INST. CODE § 707(b)(1)	Murder
CAL. WELF. & INST. CODE § 707(b)(2)	Arson as provided in P.C. section 451(a) or (b)
CAL. WELF. & INST. CODE § 707(b)(3)	Robbery
CAL. WELF. & INST. CODE § 707(b)(4)	Rape with force, violence, or threat of great bodily harm

---

[94] P.C. § 29820(a).

[95] *See* P.C. § 29820.

STATUTE	JUVENILE OFFENSE
CAL. WELF. & INST. CODE § 707(b)(5)	Sodomy by force, violence, duress, menace, or threat of great bodily harm
CAL. WELF. & INST. CODE § 707(b)(6)	A lewd or lascivious act as provided in P.C. section 288(b)
CAL. WELF. & INST. CODE § 707(b)(7)	Oral copulation by force, violence, duress, menace, or threat of great bodily harm
CAL. WELF. & INST. CODE § 707(b)(8)	An act of sexual penetration when the act is accomplished against the victim's will by means of force, violence, duress, menace, or fear of immediate and unlawful bodily injury on the victim or another person
CAL. WELF. & INST. CODE § 707(b)(9)	Kidnapping for ransom
CAL. WELF. & INST. CODE § 707(b)(10)	Kidnapping for purposes of robbery
CAL. WELF. & INST. CODE § 707(b)(11)	Kidnapping with bodily harm
CAL. WELF. & INST. CODE § 707(b)(12)	Attempted murder
CAL. WELF. & INST. CODE § 707(b)(13)	Assault with a firearm or destructive device
CAL. WELF. & INST. CODE § 707(b)(14)	Assault by any means of force likely to produce great bodily injury
CAL. WELF. & INST. CODE § 707(b)(15)	Discharge of a firearm into an inhabited or occupied building
CAL. WELF. & INST. CODE § 707(b)(16)	An offense described in P.C. section 1203.09
CAL. WELF. & INST. CODE § 707(b)(17)	An offense described in P.C. section 12022.5 or 12022.53
CAL. WELF. & INST. CODE § 707(b)(18)	A felony offense in which the minor personally used a weapon described in any provision listed in P.C. section 16590
CAL. WELF. & INST. CODE § 707(b)(19)	A felony offense described in P.C. section 136.1 or 137
CAL. WELF. & INST. CODE § 707(b)(20)	Manufacturing, compounding, or selling one-half ounce or more of a salt or solution of a controlled substance specified in Cal. Health & Saf. Code section 11055(e)
CAL. WELF. & INST. CODE § 707(b)(21)	A violent felony, as defined in P.C. section 667.5(c), which also would constitute a felony violation of P.C. section 186.22(b)
CAL. WELF. & INST. CODE § 707(b)(22)	Escape, by the use of force or violence, from a county juvenile hall, home, ranch, camp, or forestry camp in violation of P.C. section 871(b) if great bodily injury is intentionally inflicted upon an employee of the juvenile facility during the commission of the escape

STATUTE	JUVENILE OFFENSE
CAL. WELF. & INST. CODE § 707(b)(23)	Torture as described in P.C. sections 206 and 206.1
CAL. WELF. & INST. CODE § 707(b)(24)	Aggravated mayhem, as described in P.C. section 205
CAL. WELF. & INST. CODE § 707(b)(25)	Carjacking, as described in P.C. section 215, while armed with a dangerous or deadly weapon
CAL. WELF. & INST. CODE § 707(b)(26)	Kidnapping for purposes of sexual assault, as punishable in P.C. section 209(b)
CAL. WELF. & INST. CODE § 707(b)(27)	Kidnapping as punishable in P.C. section 209.5
CAL. WELF. & INST. CODE § 707(b)(28)	Willfully and maliciously discharging a firearm from a motor vehicle at another person other than an occupant of a motor vehicle
CAL. WELF. & INST. CODE § 707(b)(29)	Igniting or exploding destructive device or explosive with intent to commit murder
CAL. WELF. & INST. CODE § 707(b)(30)	Voluntary manslaughter, as described in P.C. Section 192(a)
P.C. § 25400	Carrying a concealed firearm
P.C. § 29805	Any offense enumerated in P.C. section 29805 (see Table 3.4)
P.C. § 25850	Carrying a loaded firearm in public
P.C. § 25400	Carrying a concealed firearm
P.C. § 26100	Permitting loaded firearm in motor vehicle
P.C. § 1203.073	Felony convictions for controlled substances violations involving cocaine, cocaine base, methamphetamine, phencyclidine, or heroin

H. Persons on Probation or Parole

In some cases, courts may prohibit someone convicted of a crime from owning and possessing firearms or "deadly or dangerous weapons"[96] even if the law itself does not require it (commonly referred to as "weapons conditions"). This generally occurs when a firearm restriction is created as a probation condition.[97] This type of restriction may last for the entire length of the probation period. Those who violate their probation condition, in addition to being charged with the crime of a prohibited person in possession of a firearm and with a violation of a court order (which a probation condition is), will have to deal with a probation or parole violation reopening their previous case and exposing them to an additional sentence on the original charges.[98]

---

[96] Probation conditions prohibiting a person from possessing "dangerous or deadly weapons" or from possessing a "replica firearm" are not unconstitutionally vague. *People v. Hall*, 236 Cal. App. 4th 1124 (2015); *People v. Forrest*, 237 Cal. App. 4th 1074 (2015).

[97] P.C. § 29815.

[98] *See* P.C. § 1203.2(c).

Under the Full Faith and Credit Clause of the U.S. Constitution, these probation conditions, like orders issued in restraining orders, travel across state lines.[99]

Table 3.6

SUMMARY OF CALIFORNIA CRIMINAL CONVICTIONS RESULTING IN THE LOSS OF FIREARMS RIGHTS[100]	
CALIFORNIA LAW	FEDERAL LAW
FELONY Felony convictions will result in a lifetime restriction on owning, purchasing, receiving, and possessing firearms.	Conviction of a crime (with some exceptions) that is punishable by imprisonment for more than one year will result in a lifetime restriction on receiving or possessing firearms.
MISDEMEANOR Convictions of any of the crimes listed in Tables 3.2 and 3.3 will result in a lifetime restriction on owning, purchasing, receiving, and possessing firearms. Convictions of any of the misdemeanors listed in Table 3.4 will result in a ten-year restriction on owning, purchasing, receiving, and possessing firearms.	Conviction of a Misdemeanor Crime of Domestic Violence (MCDV) will result in a lifetime restriction on purchasing, receiving, or possessing firearms.
JUVENILE Firearm possession is prohibited until age 30 if the juvenile is alleged to have committed any offense listed in Table 3.5 and is declared "a ward of the juvenile court" because the juvenile committed that offense.	There are no additional restrictions than those explained in Section VII.

I. Notice Required

In order to ensure that individuals who have been convicted of an offense listed in P.C. section 29800 or 29805 understand that they are prohibited from owning and possessing firearms, California law requires courts to notify these individuals

---

[99] JUD. COUNCIL OF CAL., ADMIN. OFFICE OF THE COURTS, JUDGES GUIDE TO DOMESTIC VIOLENCE CASES: FIREARMS AND FULL FAITH AND CREDIT (rev. 2014), *available at* http://www2.courtinfo.ca.gov/protem/pubs/firearms.pdf (last visited July 11, 2017).

[100] Even after being convicted, you may be restricted from possessing and owning firearms and other "deadly or dangerous weapons" because of a condition of your parole or probation.

of their firearm prohibition. As explained in detail below, California law currently only requires courts to notify individuals of their firearm prohibition and provide forms to help facilitate the transfer of firearms. These procedures will be repealed by Prop. 63 on January 1, 2018, and will be replaced by a new process by which courts will be required to notify these individuals of their firearm prohibition, provide a specific form to help facilitate the relinquishment of firearms, and assign the case to a probation officer who will check whether the individual owns and possess firearms and then report to the court whether the individual properly relinquished all firearms.[101]

Currently, if you are subject to a firearm prohibition listed in P.C. sections 29800 or 29805, courts must notify you at the time judgment imposed that you are prohibited from owning, purchasing, receiving, possessing, or having custody or control of any firearm. The notice must include a form to facilitate the transfer of any firearms you may have.[102] More information about the process of relinquishing the firearms pursuant to this process can be found in Chapter 10. A court's failure to provide this notice is not a defense to subsequently being prosecuted for possessing firearms while prohibited.[103] There are probably thousands of people in California who possess firearms that are unaware they are prohibited as a result of a criminal conviction.

J. Unlawful Detainer Actions

In 2014, the California Legislature passed an urgency bill, AB 2310, to reenact provisions that allow city attorneys and city prosecutors in Los Angeles, Long Beach, Sacramento, and Oakland to initiate eviction proceedings against tenants for committing nuisance violations involving "unlawful weapons and ammunition purpose."[104] The original law ended on January 1, 2014. This bill became effective immediately upon it being signed by Governor Brown on September 15, 2014. This law will remain in effect until January 1, 2019.[105]

For purposes of this law, a nuisance violation involving "unlawful weapons and ammunition purpose" is defined as the illegal use, manufacturing, causing to be manufactured, importation, possession, possession for sale, sale, furnishing, or the giving away of any:

(1) Firearm;[106] *or*

---

[101] P.C. § 29810(a)(2) (effective Jan. 1, 2018); CALIFORNIA ATTORNEY GENERAL, FULL TEXT OF PROPOSITION 63, *available at* http://www.oag.ca.gov/system/files/initiatives/pdfs/15-0098%20%28Firearms%29_0.pdf (last visited July 11, 2017).

[102] P.C. § 29810(a).

[103] P.C. § 29810(b). Courts often failed to give this notice, although they are getting better at providing it.

[104] CAL. CIV. CODE § 3485; AB 2310, 2013-2014, Leg. Counsel's Digest (Cal. 2014) *available at* http://leginfo.legislature.ca.gov/faces/billNavClient.xhtml?bill_id=201320140AB2310# (last visited July 11, 2017).

[105] CAL. CIV. CODE § 3485.

[106] As defined in P.C. section 16520(a).

(2) Ammunition;[107] *or*

(3) "Assault Weapon";[108] *or*

(4) .50 BMG Rifle;[109] *or*

(5) Tear gas weapon.[110]

Anytime a person is arrested for any of the above violations, the city attorney or prosecutor is allowed to bring an unlawful detainer proceeding to evict the person from his or her residence, even if the person has not been convicted of the offense.

VII. APPLICATION OF EX POST FACTO PROHIBITIONS ON FIREARM POSSESSION

The list of crimes carrying firearm restrictions has changed over time, with new crimes being added to the list. As a result, many people have been convicted of crimes that did not result in firearm restrictions at the time of conviction, but California and federal courts have permitted the legislature to retroactively apply firearm restrictions to convictions that originally did not carry those restrictions.[111]

In other words, it does not matter if you were convicted of an offense *before* the legislature added a firearm restriction to it because you are *now* in a class of persons the legislature has decided to prohibit from possessing firearms. Therefore, you can be prosecuted for possessing a firearm based on your previous conviction[112] even though the conviction occurred before the restriction was added to the code.

A. The Effect of a California Conviction in Other States

Generally, firearm restrictions under California law resulting from California convictions only apply while you are in California. That means that you may be able to lawfully possess firearms in another state, despite the fact that you are subject to a California restriction.[113] But be careful. Although you may not be subject to a California firearm restriction in another state, you may still be prohibited from possessing firearms because the state may treat your California conviction as if it occurred within the state, thereby subjecting you to a firearm prohibition under that state's laws. Or, you might discover that you are subject to a federal restriction. Because of this potential danger, you should always check the state's laws to deter-

---

[107] As defined in P.C. sections 16150(b), 16650, 16660.

[108] As defined in P.C. sections 30510, 30515.

[109] As defined in P.C. section 30530.

[110] P.C. § 3485. Tear gas weapons are defined in P.C. section 17250.

[111] *United States v. Wilhelm*, 65 Fed. App'x. 619, 620 (9th Cir. 2003); *People v. Mesce*, 52 Cal. App. 4th 618, 622-26 (1997); *Helmer v. Miller*, 19 Cal. App. 4th 1565, 1570-71 (1993).

[112] *United States v. Collins*, 61 F.3d 1379, 1382-83 (9th Cir. 1995).

[113] *People v. Laino*, 32 Cal. 4th 878, 889 (2004); *Williams v. North Carolina*, 317 U.S. 287, 296 (1942).

mine whether your conviction restricts you there *before* possessing any firearms within that state.[114]

Some states have their own procedures for restoring firearm rights that were restricted due to offenses that occurred in a different state, while other states require that the conviction be addressed in the state where it occurred. Contacting an attorney in your new state is best to determine if the conviction can be addressed there. But, if nothing can be done there, you should discuss what can be done to restore your firearms rights with a California attorney. But, as discussed below, California has limited options for vacating convictions or restoring firearm rights under federal law.

To be clear, California felony convictions prohibit firearm possession in all 50 states under federal law (because a California felony is punishable by more than one year in state prison). This means that California felony convictions prohibit firearm possession under federal law no matter where the person resides.[115] Similarly, an MCDV conviction carries a lifetime prohibition under federal law.[116]

VIII. POSSESSING A FIREARM WHILE BEING A "FUGITIVE FROM JUSTICE" AND THE CALIFORNIA RESTRICTION FOR POSSESSING A FIREARM WHILE HAVING AN OUTSTANDING WARRANT FOR CERTAIN OFFENSES

A. Federal Law for Firearm Prohibitions Based on "Fugitive from Justice" Status

Federal law prohibits a "fugitive from justice" from possessing firearms.[117] A "fugitive from justice" is someone who (1) has fled the state; (2) has done so to avoid prosecution for a crime or to avoid giving testimony in a criminal proceeding, and (3) is subject to a current or imminent criminal prosecution or testimonial obligation.[118] In addition, many courts have held that, in order to be a "fugitive from

---

[114] Whether you are prohibited from possessing firearms in any state may be unclear from a plain reading of the law. If you have been convicted of a misdemeanor anywhere, it is a good idea to check with an attorney practicing in the state where you plan to travel while possessing a firearm to find out whether your conviction means you are restricted from possessing or owning firearms in that state.

[115] 18 U.S.C. § 922(g)(1).

[116] 18 U.S.C. § 922(g)(9).

[117] 18 U.S.C. §§ 921 (a)(15), 922(g)(2).

[118] 27 C.F.R. § 478.11; *see also* 18 U.S.C. 921(a)(15); *see also* Letter from Robin A. Start-Nutter, Section Chief, NICS Section of the Federal Bureau of Investigation, to CJIS Systems Officer and State Points of Contact (Feb. 15, 2017), *available at* https://www.documentcloud.org/documents/3493269-Fugitive-From-Justice-Guidance-State.html (last visited Oct. 19, 2017).

justice," a person must *"purposefully"* flee the state when *"knowing* that charges are pending."[119]

Hence, individuals charged with being a "fugitive from justice" in possession of a firearm can defend themselves in court (preferably with the help of an experienced criminal defense attorney) by showing that they were unaware of the charges pending against them.[120] Along the same lines, they can argue that they did not intend to flee for purposes of avoiding prosecution or an appearance in court.

B. California Law for Firearm Prohibitions Based on an Outstanding Warrant for a Felony or for Certain Misdemeanors

The passage of AB 103 into law on June 27, 2017 caused California's firearm prohibitions to also attach when a person merely has an "outstanding warrant" for a felony or for those certain misdemeanors in P.C. sections 29800 and 29805; criminal proceedings need not reach the point of conviction for the firearm prohibition to attach.[121] Presumably, the California Legislature wanted to make a law to mirror the federal restriction against "fugitives from justice," which, as stated in the previous section, prohibits fugitives from justice from receiving and possessing firearms.[122] They failed horribly.

California lawmakers apparently thought that certain persons who simply have an outstanding warrant against them are "fugitives" who should be prohibited from possessing firearms under federal law. But whereas the federal "fugitive from justice" *knows* that he or she is fleeing the state because of criminal proceedings, his California counterpart has no idea that there is an outstanding warrant issued for his arrest, because law enforcement can obtain an arrest warrant from a judge without giving any notice to the person to be arrested. Many Californians don't know that there is an outstanding warrant issued against them, much less that this means that they are now prohibited from owning and/or possessing firearms and ammunition.

It is possible that their due process rights have been violated, depending on the circumstances, as they are forced to defend themselves in court (and paying thousands of dollars in attorneys' fees).

Some members of the California Legislature realized the injustice generated by AB 103's warrant restriction. Through SB 112, they created an affirmative defense for those who are prosecuted because of AB 103's warrant restriction. SB 112 added Penal Code section 29581, which states that P.C. "Sections 29800 and 29805 shall

---

[119] *See United States v. Spillane,* 913 F.2d 1079 (4th Cir. 1990) (emphasis added); *see also United States v. Durcan United States v. Spillane,* 539 F.2d 29 (9th Cir.1976).

[120] *See United States v. Spillane,* 913 F.2d 1079 (4th Cir. 1990); *see also United States v. Durcan United States v. Spillane,* 539 F.2d 29 (9th Cir.1976).

[121] P.C. §§ 29800, 29805; AB 103, 2017-2018 Leg., Reg. Sess. (Cal. 2017), *available at* https://leginfo.legislature. ca.gov/faces/billCompareClient.xhtml?bill_id=201720180AB103 (last visited Oct. 13, 2017).

[122] 18 U.S.C. § 921 (a)(15), 922(g)(2).

not apply to or affect a person who otherwise violates those sections if the person did not have knowledge of the outstanding warrant."[123]

So, a defendant, who is charged for the crime of possessing a firearm as someone who is prohibited from doing so because of an outstanding warrant, can get his or her criminal case dismissed if it is proven that he or she did not have knowledge about the outstanding warrant. Even if the case is dismissed, the defendant will have suffered the stressful experience of being pulled into the criminal justice system, defending himself, and paying thousands of dollars in attorney's fees to hire a criminal defense attorney who will make the affirmative defense for him. SB 112 is not a perfect cure to the "notice" problems generated by AB 103. Depending on the facts and circumstances of a case, it might be possible to file a due process violation claim against the government

IX.   DRUG ADDICTION FIREARM POSSESSION PROHIBITIONS

Illegal drug use may also result in firearm restrictions under federal and California law.[124] The rationale for these restrictions is that individuals who are addicted to narcotics "present a clear and present danger to society" because addicts are often forced to purchase drugs through criminal acts or corruption.[125]

A. Federal Restrictions for Drug Addiction and Use

Anyone who is considered to be an "unlawful user" of any "controlled substance"[126] is prohibited under federal law from possessing firearms. The "controlled substances" that fall under this prohibition do not just include narcotics, but also marijuana.[127]

The ATF has defined an "unlawful user" or an addict of a "controlled substance" as:

> A person who uses a controlled substance and has lost the power of self-control with reference to the use of controlled substance; and any person who is a current user of a controlled substance in a manner other than as prescribed by a licensed physician.[128]

---

[123] P.C. § 295815; SB 112, 2017-2018 Leg., Reg. Sess. (Cal. 2017), *available at* https://leginfo.legislature.ca.gov/faces/billHistoryClient.xhtml?bill_id=201720180SB112 (last visited Oct. 13, 2017).

[124] Although these drug addiction prohibitions rarely arise, the government might begin to prohibit people who have had prior drug convictions on their records under these restrictions because the Charleston Church Shooting suspect was purportedly addicted to a narcotic known as Suboxone.

[125] *People v. Washington*, 237 Cal. App. 2d 59, 66 (1965).

[126] The term "controlled substance" is defined in 21 U.S.C. section 802(6).

[127] 18 U.S.C. § 922(g)(3).

[128] 27 C.F.R. § 478.11.

Although it seems like this definition of "unlawful user" would exclude users of medical marijuana if it was prescribed to them by a licensed physician, the ATF has expressly stated that users of medical marijuana are still considered to be "unlawful users of or addicted to controlled substances.[129] On September 21, 2011, the ATF issued an "Open Letter to All Federal Firearms Licensees" stating:

[A]ny person who uses or is addicted to marijuana, regardless of whether his or her State has passed legislation authorizing marijuana use for medicinal purposes, is an unlawful user of or addicted to a controlled substance, and is prohibited by Federal law from possessing firearms or ammunition. Such persons should answer "yes" to question 11.e. on ATF Form 4473 . . . and you may not transfer firearms or ammunition to them. Further, if you are aware that the potential transferee is in possession of a card authorizing the possession and use of marijuana under State law, then you have "reasonable cause to believe" that the person is an unlawful user of a controlled substance. As such, you may not transfer firearms or ammunition to the person, even if the person answered "no" to question 11.e. on ATF Form 4473.[130]

Title 27 of the Code of Federal Regulations (C.F.R.) section 478.11 also guides the determination of whether someone is an "unlawful user" of a "controlled substance." Some courts have held that the government must show a defendant's "pattern, and recency, of drug use . . . or that the . . . use was sufficiently consistent, prolonged and close in time to . . . possession" of a firearm.[131] This can be as simple as using drugs while possessing a firearm.[132]

Although the Open Letter does not carry the force of the law, several courts have supported this view and the letter itself is indicative of how the government would prosecute these cases.[133] As such, users of medical marijuana should be aware that they are likely prohibited under federal law and that a federal firearms licensee cannot sell a firearm to an individual if they know or have reason to believe that they use medical marijuana. We have heard a number of stories where individuals have used a medical marijuana card as a second form of identification when attempting to purchases a firearm. These individuals are often upset when the dealer refuses

---

[129] *Open Letter to All Federal Firearms Licensees,* U.S. DEPT. OF JUSTICE, BUREAU OF ALCOHOL, TOBACCO, FIREARMS AND EXPLOSIVES, http://www.atf.gov/files/press/releases/2011/09/092611-atf-open-letter-to-all-ffls-marijuana-for-medicinal-purposes.pdf (last visited July 11, 2017).

[130] *Open Letter to All Federal Firearms Licensees,* U.S. DEPT. OF JUSTICE, BUREAU OF ALCOHOL, TOBACCO, FIREARMS AND EXPLOSIVES, http://www.atf.gov/files/press/releases/2011/09/092611-atf-open-letter-to-all-ffls-marijuana-for-medicinal-purposes.pdf (last visited July 11, 2017).

[131] *United States v. Williams,* 216 F. Supp. 2d 568, 575 (E.D. Va. 2002) (internal quotations omitted).

[132] *United States v. Oleson,* 310 F.3d 1085, 1089-90 (8th Cir. 2002); *United States v. Herrera,* 313 F.3d 882, 885 (5th Cir. 2002).

[133] *See, e.g., Wilson v. Lynch,* No. 14-15700 (9th Cir. July 21, 2016) (holding that banning gun sales to people who hold medical marijuana cards does not violate their Second Amendment rights); *see also United States v. Harvey,* 794 F. Supp. 2d 1103, 1105-06 (S.D. Cal. 2011) (providing that Schedule I drugs like marijuana cannot be lawfully prescribed because other federally defined prescription drug "schedules" intentionally omit Schedule I drugs). Several U.S. Supreme Court and California cases purportedly support this position.

to transfer or sell any firearms to them. But, as explained above, any person who uses marijuana for medical purposes is still prohibited for purposes of federal law.

Because of its sharp stance on medical marijuana users, it is also likely that the ATF would also consider any person who uses marijuana for recreational purposes as an "unlawful user" or an "addict" of a "controlled substance." This is especially important to note given the recent passage of Proposition 64 (i.e., the "Control, Regulate and Tax Adult Use of Marijuana Act"). Prop. 64, which was passed during the November 2016 election, legalizes the recreational use of marijuana in California for individuals who are twenty-one -years old or older.[134] Any person who uses marijuana, even if they are doing so legally under Prop. 64, will still be considered an "unlawful user" or "addicted" to a "controlled substance" and will be prohibited from possessing firearms and ammunition under federal law.

B. California Restrictions for Drug Addiction

If you are considered to be addicted to narcotic drugs, you are also prohibited from possessing firearms under California law.[135] Narcotic drugs are specifically defined under the Cal. Health & Saf. Code and include opium and cocaine.[136] Marijuana is not included in the California law definition of narcotic drugs. Users, and even marijuana addicts, are thus not per se prohibited from owning or receiving firearms under California law.

Table 3.7

SUMMARY OF DRUG PROHIBITIONS	
CALIFORNIA LAW	FEDERAL LAW
If you are considered to be addicted to narcotic drugs, you are prohibited from possessing firearms. This does not include marijuana use.	If you are an "unlawful user" or "addict" of any "controlled substance," including marijuana, you are prohibited from possessing firearms.

---

[134] Full Text of Proposition 64, Office of the Attorney General, *available at* https://www.oag.ca.gov/system/files/initiatives/pdfs/15-0103%20(Marijuana)_1.pdf (last visited July 11, 2017). DOJ appears to be denying firearm purchases for people with recent drug-related convictions. It remains to be seen how DOJ knows a person is currently "addicted" to narcotics based on a past conviction. This is a recent development we are currently keeping an eye on for purposes of potential challenges.

[135] P.C. § 29800(a). It is illegal under California law to be in possession of a loaded, operable firearm and in possession of any amount of a substance "containing cocaine base, a substance containing cocaine, a substance containing heroin, a substance containing methamphetamine, a crystalline substance containing phencyclidine, a liquid substance containing phencyclidine, plant material containing phencyclidine, or a hand-rolled cigarette treated with phencyclidine . . . ." Cal. Health & Saf. Code § 11370.1(a). It is also illegal to be under the influence of certain controlled substances and be in the immediate personal possession of a loaded, operable firearm. Cal. Health & Saf. Code § 11550(e). For purposes of Cal. Health & Saf. Code section 11370.1(a), the firearm need only be "available for immediate offensive or defensive use." For section 11550(e), immediate personal possession includes the interior passenger compartment of a motor vehicle.

[136] Cal. Health & Saf. Code § 11019.

X. MENTAL HEALTH RELATED FIREARM RESTRICTIONS

Under California law, if a person is found to suffer from certain mental health conditions, they are also prohibited from owning and possessing firearms and deadly weapons.[137] "Deadly weapon," as used here and in Cal. Welf. & Inst. Code sections 8101, 8102, and 8103, means possessing or carrying any concealed weapon that is prohibited by P.C. section 16590 (*i.e.*, "generally prohibited weapons").[138] Law enforcement officers often believe the term "deadly weapon" includes all weapons (*e.g.*, bows, BB guns, knives) and ammunition, and incorrectly confiscate or charge the individual for violating the law as a result.

The availability of relief from mental health firearm restrictions depends on the nature of the mental health restriction. For example, individuals are prohibited from owning and possessing firearms and deadly weapons while they are admitted (either with or without their consent) to a facility to receive inpatient treatment and are deemed by the health professional primarily responsible for the patient's treatment as a danger to themselves or others, as specified in Cal. Welf. & Inst. Code sections 5150, 5250, or 5300.[139] There is no "inpatient" prohibition once they are discharged from the facility, but they may still be prohibited for any of the reasons below.[140]

My office continues to have an increased number of calls concerning mental health restrictions. These calls typically had to do with one of three issues: (1) post traumatic stress disorder (commonly referred to as "PTSD"), (2) individuals voluntarily seeking, or sought in the past, the help of psychiatrists for issues like depression or anxiety, and (3) prescription medication to deal with a mental health issue like depression, anxiety, etc.

Unless you meet one of the criteria set forth below, you should *not* be considered prohibited from owning and possessing firearms under California or federal law for a mental health restriction. If you still do not know for certain whether you may lawfully own and possess firearms after you read the information below, you should file a "Personal Firearms Eligibility Check" (PFEC), which is discussed at the end of this chapter.

There are a lot of rumors and bad information surrounding mental health restrictions. Most of these are based on misstatements of the law, bad reporting and/or investigation by the media, and internet rumors or the like. Make certain that you obtain information from reputable sources, not just what "some guy" heard at his local firearm dealer's store.

---

[137] CAL. WELF. & INST. CODE §§ 8100, 8103.

[138] CAL. WELF. & INST. CODE § 8100(e). "Generally prohibited weapons" are listed and discussed in Chapter 9.

[139] CAL. WELF. & INST. CODE § 8100(a). "Danger to self," as used in subdivision (a), means one who has made a serious threat of, or attempted, suicide with the use of a firearm or other deadly weapon. CAL. WELF. & INST. CODE § 8100(f).

[140] CAL. WELF. & INST. CODE § 8100(a).

A. Federal Mental Health Restrictions

Federal law prohibits those "adjudicated as a mental defective or who ha[ve] been committed to a mental institution" from owning or possessing firearms for life.[141] In order to determine whether these prohibitions apply to you, you must first understand the meaning of "adjudicated as a mental defective" and "committed to a mental institution."

No federal statute defines "adjudicated as a mental defective" or "committed to a mental institution." Meanwhile, the Code of Federal Regulations provides that an individual is adjudicated as a mental defective if a court, board, commission, or other lawful authority determines that, as a result of marked subnormal intelligence, mental illness, incompetency, condition, or disease, the individual is either a danger to him or herself or to others or lacks the mental capacity to contract or manage his or her own affairs.

The Code of Federal Regulations definition also includes individuals found insane by a court in a criminal case as well as individuals found incompetent to stand trial or found not guilty by reason of lack of mental responsibility under articles 50a and 72b of the Uniform Code of Military Justice, 10 U.S.C. sections 850a, 876b.[142]

The Code of Federal Regulations defines "committed to a mental institution" as:

A formal commitment of a person to a mental institution by a court, board, commission, or other lawful authority. The term includes a commitment to a mental institution involuntarily. The term includes commitment for mental defectiveness or mental illness. It also includes commitments for other reasons, such as for drug use. The term does not include a person in a mental institution for observation or a voluntary admission to a mental institution.[143]

---

[141] 18 U.S.C. § 922(g)(4).

[142] 27 C.F.R. § 478.11. In 2015, ATF proposed a new regulation that expands the scope of the statutory term "adjudicated as a mental defective." This regulation expands the language relating to findings of insanity by a court and persons incompetent to stand trial to include those persons found not guilty by reason of insanity, mental disease or defect, or lack of mental responsibility by a court in a criminal case; those found guilty but mentally ill by a court in a criminal case in a jurisdiction that provides for such a finding; and those persons found incompetent to stand trial by a court in a criminal case. The term does not include any person adjudicated by a department or agency of the Federal Government, if any of the conditions of section 101(c)(1) of the NICS Improvement Amendments Act of 2007 apply; or any person who has been adjudicated and subsequently received relief under 18 U.S.C. section 925(c) or under a program authorized by 18 U.S.C. section 101(c)(2) or section 105(a) of the NICS Improvement Amendments Act of 2007. See Amended Definition of "Adjudicated as a Mental Defective" and "Committed to a Mental Institution," 79 Fed. Reg. 774 (proposed Jan. 3, 2014) (to be codified at 27 C.F.R. pt. 478). As of the date of publication, the ATF has yet to finalize this regulation. To keep up to date with information on this regulation, visit www.crpa.org..

[143] 27 C.F.R. § 478.11. This definition is subject to change just like "adjudicated as a mental defective." The proposed definition states: a formal commitment of a person to a mental institution by a court, board, commission, or other lawful authority. The term includes an involuntary commitment to a mental institution for inpatient or outpatient treatment. The term includes an involuntary commitment for mental defectiveness, i.e., mental illness, to a mental institution. It also includes a commitment to a mental institution for other reasons, such as for drug use. The term does not include a person in a mental institution solely for observation or evaluation, a voluntary admission to a mental institution, or voluntary outpatient treatment. The term shall not include any person so committed by a department or agency of the Federal Government, if any of the conditions of section 101(c)(1) of the NICS Im-

1. California Commitments Resulting In Federal Restrictions

Under federal law, someone who has been committed to a mental health institution for mental defectiveness, illness, or drug use, is prohibited for life from owning and possessing firearms. Whether someone has been "committed to a mental health institution" is a question of federal law and it is often guided by state law.[144] A commitment under Cal. Welf. & Inst. Code section 5150 will not result in a federal firearm restriction, but according to the DOJ and the FBI, a Cal. Welf. & Inst. Code section 5250 commitment does. While California allows a one-time application with the court to restore firearm rights for an intensive treatment commitment,[145] this has no effect on the *federal* restriction.

B. Dangerous Inpatients

Individuals who are admitted to a facility and are receiving inpatient treatment and, in the opinion of the attending health professional who is primarily responsible for their treatment of a mental disorder, who are a danger to themselves or to others, as specified by Cal. Welf. & Inst. Code section 5150, 5250, or 5300, are prohibited from possessing, having under their control, purchasing, receiving, or attempting to purchase or receive any firearms or deadly weapons, even though they have consented to the treatment.[146] But, they are not subject to *this* prohibition after they have been discharged from the facility.[147] They may still be prohibited for another reason (discussed below).

C. Communicating Threats to a Psychotherapist

If an individual communicates "a serious threat of physical violence against a reasonably identifiable victim or victims" to a licensed psychotherapist, they are prohibited form possessing firearms and deadly weapons for a period of five years starting from the date the psychotherapist reports the threat to a local law enforcement agency.[148]

The DOJ is required to mail a notice of the restriction to the restricted person who may thereafter request a hearing to restore his or her firearm rights during the restriction period.[149] Upon petition to the court, the state has the burden of show-

---

provement Act of 2007 apply, or any person who has received relief from disabilities under a program authorized by section 101(c)(2) or section 105(a) of that Act or under 18 U.S.C. section 925(c). But, as of the date of publication, the ATF has yet to finalize this regulation.

[144] *United States v. Whiton*, 48 F.3d 356, 358 (8th Cir. 1995).

[145] CAL. WELF. & INST. CODE § 8103(g)(4).

[146] CAL. WELF. & INST. CODE § 8100(a).

[147] CAL. WELF. & INST. CODE § 8100(a).

[148] CAL. WELF. & INST. CODE § 8100(b)(1).

[149] CAL. WELF. & INST. CODE § 8100(b)(2).

ing that the person would not be likely to use firearms in a safe and lawful manner. If the state fails to make such a showing, the five-year prohibition will not apply.[150]

D. Mental Disorders, Illnesses, or Disordered Sex Offenders

Individuals who "ha[ve] been adjudicated by a court of any state . . . to be a danger to others . . . [because] of a mental disorder or mental illness, or who ha[ve] been adjudicated to be a mentally disordered sex offender" are prohibited from possessing, purchasing, or attempting to purchase or receive, or having in his or her possession firearms or deadly weapons.[151] Firearm rights may be restored, however, if the same court that adjudicated the mental illness or disorder issues a certificate, either at or after that person's release from treatment, stating the person is now safe to possess a firearm or any other deadly weapon.[152]

This rights restoration mechanism is only available as long as the person has not been adjudicated (again) to be a danger to others as a result of a mental disorder or illness before asking for this certificate.[153]

E. Not Guilty by Reason of Insanity

Individuals found not guilty of any crime by reason of insanity[154] cannot purchase or receive, or attempt to purchase or receive, or have under their control any firearm or other deadly weapon.[155] Certain serious offenses have a lifetime firearm restriction without any available relief.[156] For all other less serious convictions where individuals are found not guilty by reason of insanity, firearm rights may be restored if the court finds they have recovered their sanity.[157]

F. Incompetence to Stand Trial

Individuals found to be mentally incompetent to stand trial[158] are likewise prohibited from purchasing or possessing firearms unless their competence to stand trial is restored by the committing court.[159]

---

[150] CAL. WELF. & INST. CODE § 8100(b)(3).

[151] CAL. WELF. & INST. CODE § 8103(a)(1).

[152] CAL. WELF. & INST. CODE § 8103(a)(1).

[153] CAL. WELF. & INST. CODE § 8103(a)(1).

[154] Pursuant to P.C. section 1026 or any other state or the U.S.

[155] CAL. WELF. & INST. CODE § 8103(b)-(c); see also P.C. § 1026.

[156] CAL. WELF. & INST. CODE § 8103(b)(1). Refer directly to Cal. Welf. & Inst. Code section 8103(b)(1) for a list of offenses.

[157] CAL. WELF. & INST. CODE § 8103(c)(1). See P.C. section 1026.2 for recovering sanity.

[158] Pursuant to P.C. section 1370 or 1370.1 or the law of any other state or the U.S.

[159] CAL. WELF. & INST. CODE § 8103(d)(1).

G. Individuals Under Conservatorship

Individuals placed under conservatorship because they are gravely disabled by a mental disorder or chronic alcoholism cannot possess a firearm or deadly weapon while under the conservatorship if, at the time the conservatorship was ordered, the court found that possession of a firearm or deadly weapon by the individual would present a danger to the individual or others.

In this situation, courts must notify the individual placed under conservatorship of the firearm restriction. The firearm restriction can last the duration of the conservatorship or be lifted by the court if it finds that the individual no longer presents a danger to the individual or others.[160]

H. Dangerous or Gravely Disabled Persons

Individuals taken into custody under Cal. Welf. & Inst. Code section 5150 because they are a danger to themselves or others, assessed under Cal. Welf. & Inst. Code section 5151, are admitted to a designated facility and may not possess a firearm or deadly weapon for five years after they are released from the facility.[161] A "5150 commitment" usually occurs after a peace officer or medical health care professional determines the individual is a danger to themselves or others. Often, calls to a suicide hotline or calls by concerned family members prompt law enforcement to investigate and bring individuals in on a "5150 commitment."

Before or at the time of discharge, the facility is required to notify the individual that he or she is "prohibited from owning, possessing, controlling, receiving, or purchasing any firearm for a period of five years."[162] Failure by the facility, however, to provide notice will not necessarily prevent prosecution of the individual for possessing firearms.

Individuals must also be notified of their right to request a hearing to restore their firearm rights.[163]

Failure to request a hearing upon discharge does not preclude the individual from requesting one later. People often think they have a limited time to request a hearing to restore firearm rights. But, the law specifically states that a person prohibited under this restriction may make a "single request for a hearing *at any time* during the five-year period."[164]

---

[160] CAL. WELF. & INST. CODE § 8103(e).

[161] CAL. WELF. & INST. CODE § 8103(f)(1).

[162] CAL. WELF. & INST. CODE § 8103(f)(3).

[163] CAL. WELF. & INST. CODE § 8103(f)(3). The procedure for restoring firearm rights after a 5150 commitment is governed by Cal. Welf. & Inst. Code section 8103(f)(4)-(9).

[164] CAL. WELF. & INST. CODE § 8103(f)(4) (emphasis added).

I. Those Committed to Intensive Treatment

Individuals that undergo intensive treatment under Cal. Welf. & Inst. Code sections 5250, 5260, or 5270.15 cannot possess any firearm or deadly weapon for five years.[165] Lifting this state restriction is similar to restoring firearm rights for someone with a 5150 commitment. But, unlike a 5150 commitment where the government has the legal burden, these restrictions require the *individual* to prove that the firearm(s) will be used in a safe and lawful manner.[166]

Table 3.8

MENTAL HEALTH RESTRICTIONS		
	FIVE-YEAR RESTRICTION	RESTRICTION UNTIL RIGHTS ARE RESTORED BY THE COURT
CALIFORNIA LAW	Under California law, an individual is prohibited from purchasing and possessing firearms and dangerous weapons for a five-year period under any of the following situations: (1) The individual communicates "a serious threat of physical violence against a reasonably identifiable" victim(s) to a licensed psychotherapist; *or* (2) The individual is detained under Cal. Welf. & Inst. Code 5150, receives a mental evaluation, and is admitted to a designated facility. The five-year prohibition starts after the individual is released from such facility; *or* (3) The individual undergoes intensive treatment under Cal. Welf. & Inst. Code sections 5250, 5260, or 5270.5.	Under California law, an individual is prohibited from purchasing and possessing firearms and dangerous weapons until his or her rights are restored by a court under any of the following situations: (1) The individual is adjudicated by a court to be a danger to others because of a mental disorder or illness, or if the individual is adjudicated a mentally disordered sex offender; *or* (2) The individual is found not guilty of any crime by reason of insanity for certain offenses; *or* (3) The individual is found mentally incompetent to stand trial; *or* (4) The individual is placed under conservatorship because he or she is gravely disabled by a mental disorder or chronic alcoholism and the court took his or her firearm rights away when placed under conservatorship.

---

[165] CAL. WELF. & INST. CODE § 8103(g)(1). Restoring rights for state restrictions is governed by Cal. Welf. & Inst. Code section 8103(g)(3)-(4). You are also subject to a federal lifetime ban.

[166] CAL. WELF. & INST. CODE § 8103(g)(4).

[167] As explained above, while federal law allows individuals to have their firearm rights restored by a court, currently this option unavailable in California.

XI. RESTRAINING ORDERS AND FIREARM POSSESSION RESTRICTIONS

A. Federal Domestic Violence Restraining Orders

Unlike the broad California firearm restrictions for restraining orders, discussed below, the federal restrictions are very narrow. Under federal law, individuals are prohibited from receiving and possessing firearms if they are subject to a court order that:

(1) Was issued after a hearing where they received actual notice, and had an opportunity to participate; *and*

(2) Restrains them from harassing, stalking, or threatening an intimate partner or child of such intimate partner or person, or engaging in other conduct that would put an intimate partner in reasonable fear of bodily injury to the partner or the child; *and*

(3) Either includes a finding that they represent a credible threat to the physical safety of an intimate partner or child; or by its terms specifically prohibits the use, attempted use, *or* threatened use of physical force that would reasonably be expected to cause bodily injury against the intimate partner or child.[168]

This means that, unlike California's restraining order restrictions that can take effect without notice of the hearing (*i.e.*, a temporary restraining order or emergency protective order), the federal restriction requires notice and an opportunity to participate.[169] Also, to trigger the federal restriction the specific type of conduct in (2) must be prohibited.

A court has discretion in issuing a restraining order to determine which types of conduct the restrained person should not do. The court can order a person not to contact or come within (for example) 100 yards of the protected individual and their residence. This narrow type of order should not result in a federal restriction. But, in a lot of cases, especially those relating to domestic violence, courts "rubber stamp" probation terms that result in a federal firearm restriction.

---

[168] 18 U.S.C. § 922(g)(8).

[169] 18 U.S.C. § 922(g)(8)(A). For example, a protective order signed without either notice of a hearing and the ability to present evidence is not considered one where the defendant received actual notice. Accordingly, it is not within the scope of 18 U.S.C. section 922(g)(8). *United States v. Spruill*, 292 F.3d 207, 215-20 (5th Cir. 2002). Because the defendant must "receive actual notice," some temporary restraining order issued under California law would not result in a federal restriction if they are issued ex parte, *i.e.*, they can be issued without giving the defendant notice or a hearing. *See, e.g.*, CAL. CIV. PROC. CODE § 527.6 (civil harassment protective orders), 527.8 (workplace violence protective orders), 527.85 (private postsecondary educational institution protective orders); CAL. PENAL CODE § 646.91 (emergency protective orders obtained ex parte enjoining specified behavior); CAL. FAM. CODE § 6218(c) (domestic violence protective orders); CAL. WELF. & INST. CODE § 15657.03(c) (elder and dependent adult abuse protective orders).

B. California Law Restrictions

Under California law, if you are subject to a restraining order, temporary restraining order, or court order under any of the following code sections, you are prohibited from owning, purchasing, receiving, possessing, or attempting to purchase and receive firearms:

(1) California Code of Civil Procedure (Cal. Civ. Proc. Code) section 527.6 (civil harassment temporary restraining order or injunction);[170] *or*

(2) Cal. Civ. Proc. Code section 527.8 (employers seeking a temporary restraining order or an injunction for an employee who has suffered unlawful violence or credible threat of violence); *or*

(3) Cal. Civ. Proc. Code section 527.85 (schools seeking temporary restraining orders or injunctions for students who have suffered off-campus credible threats of violence); *or*

(4) California Family Code (Cal. Fam. Code) section 6218 (protective orders issued in accordance with Cal. Fam. Code sections 6320, 6321, and 6322); *or*

(5) P.C. sections 136.2[171] and 646.91 (court orders against victim and/or witness intimidation and orders protecting against stalking); *or*

(6) Cal. Welf. & Inst. Code section 15657.03 (protective order in response to elder or dependent adult abuse);[172] *or*

(7) Cal. Welf. & Inst. Code section 213.5, 304, 362.4, and 726.5 (juvenile protective orders);[173] *or*

---

[170] When a court issues a temporary civil harassment restraining order, the court may also issue, on a showing of good cause, a restraining order instructing the restrained person to stay away and refrain from taking or harming an animal owned, possessed, leased, kept, held by, or that resides in the house of the person protected by the restraining order. CAL. CIV. PROC. CODE § 527.6 Any person subject to this order is prohibited from owning and possessing firearms and ammunition. CAL. CIV. PROC. CODE § 527.6.

[171] Under P.C. section 136.2, a court must consider issuing a protective order, which can last for up to ten years, in any case in which a criminal defendant has been convicted of a crime involving "domestic violence" as defined in P.C. section 13700 or in Cal. Fam. Code 6211; a violation of P.C. sections 261, 261.5, or 262; or any other crime that requires the defendant register under P.C. section 290(c). "Domestic violence," for the purposes of this code section, has two different meanings "abuse committed against an adult or minor who is a spouse, former spouse, cohabitant, former cohabitant, or person with whom the suspect had a child or is having or has had a dating or engagement relationship" or "abuse perpetuated against . . . a spouse or former spouse; a cohabitant or former cohabitant, as defined in [Cal Fam. Code section 6209]; a person with home the respondent has had a child, where the presumption applies that the mate is the father of the child of the female parent under the Uniform Parentage Act (Part 3 (commencing with Section 7600) of Division 12); a child of a party or a child who is subject to an action under the Uniform Parentage Act, where the presumption applies that the male parent is the father of the child to be protected; [and] any other person related by consanguinity or affinity within the second degree. P.C. § 13700; CAL. FAM. CODE § 6211.

[172] P.C. § 29825(a)-(b).

[173] There seems to be some ambiguity as to whether a juvenile protective order issued under Cal. Welf. & Inst. Code section 213.5 results in a firearm prohibition. This is because Cal. Welf. & Inst. Code section 213.5 does not explicitly provide that a person who is subject to a restraining order under that code section is prohibited from owning and possessing firearms. *See* CAL. WELF. & INST. CODE § 213.5. Despite this ambiguity, however, the Judicial Council form for juvenile protective orders issued under section 215.3 still contains boiler plate language that states that any person subject to a juvenile protective order – even those issued under section 213.5 – is prohibited

(8) P.C. section 18205 ("gun violence restraining orders").

In instances where a temporary restraining order is issued, and regardless of whether the court ultimately issues a permanent restraining order, you are prohibited from possessing firearms until the temporary order ends or expires. You are also prohibited from possessing ammunition clips, magazines, and the like (as discussed in this Chapter). If you knowingly violate this term of the restraining order, you can be held criminally liable.[174]

Individuals served with a restraining order are required to sell their firearms and ammunition or store them with an FFL, or turn them in to law enforcement.[175] Generally, this must be done within 24 hours of being served with the restraining order[176] (or it must be done *immediately* if requested by law enforcement after service of a restraining order under Cal. Fam. Code section 6218 or a temporary "gun violence restraining order").[177] Regardless of which option the restrained person chooses to surrender the firearm, he or she must file a receipt with the court within 48 hours of being served with the restraining order that proves the firearms and ammunition were either surrendered, sold, or transferred to an FFL for storage.[178] This proof of surrender must also be filed within 48 hours with the law enforcement agency that served the restraining order if a "gun violence restraining order" is at issue.[179]

In addition, note that in certain cases, the court may grant exemptions from the relinquishment requirement of most of the previously-mentioned restraining orders,[180] for a particular firearm. The mechanism to obtain these exemptions is explained in Coldaw Publishing's next book, which will be on firearm surrender, seizure, and return.

1. "Gun Violence Restraining Orders"[181]

If you are subject to a "gun violence restraining order," you are prohibited from having in your custody or control, possessing, receiving, or attempting to purchase

---

from owning and possessing firearms. *See* Restraining Order-Juvenile (Form JV-255), *available at* http://www.courts.ca.gov/documents/jv255.pdf (last visited July 11, 2017). As such, if you receive a juvenile protective order, you should play it on the safe side and consider yourself to be prohibited for the duration of the protective order.

[174] P.C. §§ 29825(a)-(b), 18205.

[175] P.C. § 29825(d). These requirements and their exceptions are specifically discussed in Coldaw Publishing's next book, which will be on firearm surrender, seizure and return. This book will be available on Amazon by mid-2018.

[176] *See* CAL. CIV. PROC. CODE § 527.9(a); *see also* CAL. FAM. CODE § 6389(c)(2); *see also* P.C. §§ 18120(b)(2), 29825(d).

[177] *See* CAL. FAM. CODE § 6389(c)(2); *see also* P.C. § 18120(b)(2).

[178] CAL. CIV. PROC. CODE § 527.9(b); CAL. FAM. CODE § 6389(c)(2); P.C. §§ 18120(b)(2), 29825(d).

[179] P.C. § 18120(b)(2).

[180] CAL. CIV. PROC. CODE § 527.9(f); CAL. FAM. CODE § 6389(h). This exemption does not exist for "gun violence restraining orders."

[181] This section will only cover the "gun violence restraining order" insofar as it relates to firearm restrictions. For a more detailed analysis of "gun violence restraining orders," please visit www.CalGunLawsBook.com.

or receive, firearms[182] or ammunition[183] while the restraining order is in effect.[184] "Gun violence restraining orders" were created by AB 1014,[185] which was passed by the California Legislature in 2014 in response to the Isla Vista shootings in Santa Barbara, California. Law enforcement officers and "immediate family members" are allowed to seek a temporary or permanent "gun violence restraining order" to prevent a person, whom they believe is a danger to themselves or another, from owning and possessing firearms and ammunition. If granted, a "gun violence restraining order" can last for up to 21 days and can be extended for up to a year after notice and a hearing.[186]

Although the language of this bill would lead most people to believe that only an "immediate family member," such as a spouse, parent, or child, could request a "gun violence restraining order," the definition of the phrase is actually much more expansive. An "immediate family member" is defined as "any spouse, whether by marriage or not, domestic partner, parent, child, any person related by consanguinity or affinity within the second degree, or any other person who regularly resides in the household, or who, within the prior six months, regularly resided in the household."[187]

Under this definition, not only could your spouse, parents, or children request a "gun violence restraining order," but also your roommates, long-term house guests, and even your in-laws.

As a practical matter, allowing all of these people to seek a "gun violence restraining order" leaves the process open to rampant abuse. For example, a disgruntled roommate could seek a "gun violence restraining order" against you as a form of retaliation, or an ex-wife could potentially request the order to gain an advantage in another lawsuit.

---

[182] The term "firearm" for purposes of "gun violence restraining orders" means "a device, designed to be used as a weapon, from which is expelled through a barrel, a projectile by the force of an explosion or other form of combustion." P.C. § 16520(a). The term does not seem to include frames or receives. *See* P.C. § 16520(b). But, this was likely an oversight by the California Legislature. If you are subject to a "gun violence restraining order," you should err on the side of caution and remove any frames or receivers from your immediate possession and control until you are no longer subject to the restraining order.

[183] For the purposes of "gun violence restraining orders," the term "ammunition" is not defined. *See* P.C. §§ 16150, 18120. Therefore, it is hard to tell whether the term "ammunition" would also include bullets, cartridges, magazines, clips, speed loaders, autoloaders. But, if you are subject to a "gun violence restraining order," I strongly suggest you err on the side of caution and also remove all of these items from your immediate possession and control until you are no longer subject to the restraining order.

[184] P.C. § 18120(a). There are two different paths to obtain a "gun violence restraining order." There is a "temporary emergency gun violence restraining order," which only law enforcement officers can apply for; and an "ex parte gun violence restraining order," which both law enforcement officers and "immediate family members" can apply for and obtain. *See* P.C. §§ 18125, 18150. But note that the titles of these two orders can be somewhat misleading in that a "temporary" order may be issued ex parte, and an "ex parte" order is temporary."

[185] *See* AB 1014, 2013-2014, Leg. Counsel's Digest (Cal. 2014) *available at* https://leginfo.legislature.ca.gov/faces/billNavClient.xhtml?bill_id=201320140AB1014# (last visited July 11, 2017).

[186] Note that a "temporary emergency gun violence restraining order" can only last for 21 days as there is no procedure to extend the order or make it "permanent."

[187] P.C. § 422.4(b)(3).

The potential for abuse is exacerbated by the fact that the evidentiary standard for obtaining a temporary "gun violence restraining order" is very low.[188] In fact, under this law, a court can issue an emergency "gun violence restraining order" to a law enforcement officer if it simply finds that there is a reasonable cause to believe that an individual will cause personal injury to himself, herself, or to another, and that there are no other less restrictive alternatives available.[189] Similarly, a court can also issue a temporary "gun violence restraining order" to an "immediate family member" if it finds that there is a *substantial likelihood*[190] that the individual will cause personal injury to himself, herself, or to another, and that there are no other less restrictive alternatives available.[191]

To make matters worse, a court can issue a temporary "gun violence restraining order" without providing prior notice or a hearing to the individual, and without providing them with a mental health or medical evaluation to ensure that he or she is actually a danger to himself or herself, or to another.

Given these issues, the "gun violence restraining order" process can easily be abused by both law enforcement officers and "immediate family members" to temporarily deprive a person of the right to own and possess firearms and ammunition.

That being said, AB 1014 does make it illegal to file a frivolous request for a "gun violence restraining order." Specifically, under this bill, it is a misdemeanor for a person to file a petition for a "gun violence restraining order" knowing that the information in the petition is false, or if the petition was filed with the intent to harass.[192] If you believe that someone has frivolously requested a "gun violence restraining order" against you, you should immediately contact an attorney experienced in firearms law.[193]

---

[188] *See* P.C. §§ 18125(a), 18150(b), 18155(b), 18175(a)-(b).

[189] P.C. § 18125(a).

[190] The evidentiary standard for a "substantial likelihood" is never defined, which makes it unclear as to what exactly this standard would be.

[191] P.C. § 18150(b).

[192] P.C. § 18200(b).

[193] If you would like to learn more about "gun violence restraining orders," you can purchase an informational booklet on the topic from the California Rifle & Pistol Association at www.crpa.org.

Table 3.9

RESTRAINING ORDER RESTRICTIONS
FEDERAL LAW
If you are subject to a court order that meets the requirements listed in subsection (A) above, you are prohibited from receiving and possessing firearms for the duration of the order.
CALIFORNIA LAW
If you are subject to a restraining order, temporary restraining order, or court order under any of the code sections listed in subsection (B) above, you are prohibited from owning, purchasing, receiving, or possessing firearms while you are subject to the restraining order.
Remember: If you are served with a restraining order, you are required to sell or store your firearms with an FFL, or turn them into law enforcement.

XII. EXCEPTIONS FOR PROHIBITED PERSONS POSSESSING FIREARMS

A. Self-Defense

If you are subject to one of the prohibitions discussed above, you may be able to possess a firearm for self-defense or defense of others under very limited circumstances. Specifically, if you are subject to a prohibition under federal law (or a prohibition that falls under both California and federal law), then you may be able to possess a firearm without violating 18 U.S.C. section 922(g) if you are:

(1) Are under an unlawful and present threat of death or serious bodily injury; *and*

(2) Did not recklessly place yourself in a situation where you would be forced to engage in criminal conduct; *and*

(3) Had no reasonable legal alterative to possessing the firearm or avoiding the threatened harm; *and*

(4) Can show that there was a direct causal relationship between the criminal action and the avoidance of the threatened harm.[194]

On the other hand, if you are subject to a prohibition under California law, you may be able to possess a firearm in self-defense or defense of others without violating P.C. section 29800 when:

---

[194] *See United States v. Mooney*, 497 F.3d 397, 406 (4th Cir. 2007); *see also United States v. Leahy*, 437 F.3d 401, 409 (1st Cir. 2007) (*citing Dixon v. United States*, 548 U.S. 1, 4 n.2 (2006)); *United States v. Deleveaux*, 205 F.3d 1292, 1297 (11th Cir. 2000); *United States v. Gomez*, 92 F.3d 770, 774-75 (9th Cir. 1996); *United States v. Paolello*, 951 F.2d 537, 540–41 (3d Cir. 1991), *holding modified by Government of Virgin Islands v. Lewis*, 54 V.I. 882, 620 F.3d 359 (3d Cir. 2010); *United States v. Vigil*, 743 F.2d 751, 756 (10th Cir. 1984); *United States v. Panter*, 688 F.2d 268, 271 (5th Cir. 1982); *United States. v. Agard*, 605 F.2d 665, 667 (2d Cir. 1979).

(1) You "reasonably believe" you or someone else was "in *imminent* danger of suffering great bodily injury"; *and*

(2) You reasonably believe that the imminent use of force was necessary to defend against that danger; *and*

(3) *A firearm must have become available to you without planning or preparation on your part*; *and*

(4) You only possesses the firearm temporarily, meaning no longer than what was necessary or reasonably appeared to be necessary for self-defense; *and*

(5) There are no other means of avoiding the danger or injury; *and*

(6) Using the firearm was reasonable under the circumstances.[195]

The California Supreme Court created this limited defense to P.C. section 29800 in *People v. King*. In that case, Mr. King, a person prohibited from possessing firearms, was attending a birthday party when a fight broke out between an uninvited guest and another person at the party.[196] As the two men fought outside the apartment, several of the uninvited guest's friends swarmed the balcony to break up the fight. Their efforts were unsuccessful.[197] As the fighting raged on, the apartment owner shut the balcony door so that the remaining people inside the apartment would be somewhat safe.[198] Angered by the fact that they were locked out of the apartment, the people on the balcony began beating on the door and threatening to break it open.[199] Then, one of the men on the balcony grabbed a double hibachi grill and threw it through a window into the dining area of the apartment where Mr. King and his paraplegic friend were seated.[200] The grill struck Mr. King and showered glass over him and his paraplegic friend, and shards of the glass got stuck in Mr. King's eye.[201]

After washing the glass out of his eyes, Mr. King noticed that his disabled friend was having difficulty fleeing the area because the wheels of his wheelchair had locked up.[202] So, Mr. King helped wheel his friend into a neighboring bedroom where many of the partygoers were hiding and attempting to call the police.[203] Mr. King then went outside to confront the men.[204]

---

[195] *See* CALCRIM No. 2514 (emphasis added).

[196] *People v. King*, 22 Cal. 3d 12, 16 (1978).

[197] *People v. King*, 22 Cal. 3d 12, 16-17 (1978).

[198] *People v. King*, 22 Cal. 3d 12, 16-17 (1978).

[199] *People v. King*, 22 Cal. 3d 12, 16-17 (1978).

[200] *People v. King*, 22 Cal. 3d 12, 18 (1978).

[201] *People v. King*, 22 Cal. 3d 12, 18 (1978).

[202] *People v. King*, 22 Cal. 3d 12, 18 (1978).

[203] *People v. King*, 22 Cal. 3d 12, 18 (1978).

[204] *People v. King*, 22 Cal. 3d 12, 18 (1978).

As Mr. King was stepping outside, one of the partygoers hiding inside the apartment pulled out a handgun from her purse and handed to Mr. King.[205] He then stepped outside and fired several shots into the air to disperse the crowd.[206] Although the men fighting outside initially retreated, they then regrouped and again began to run toward the apartment door.[207] Mr. King then fired shots over their heads, wounding one of the men out on the balcony.[208] After the police arrived, Mr. King was arrested and charged with two counts of assault with a deadly weapon, as well as being a felon in possession of a firearm.[209]

In analyzing Mr. King's case, the California Supreme Court noted that the legislature did not intend to deny prohibited persons the right to use a firearm to defend themselves or others in emergency situations.[210] As the Court explained, the laws governing self-defense date back to 1872 (the year the Penal Code was first enacted), and the code sections for justifiable homicide can be traced back to 1850[211] (the year California became the 31st state). The court identified that there was a conflict between the laws for self-defense and the laws that prohibit a person from possessing handguns.[212]

In resolving this conflict, the Court recognized that "the prohibition of [P.C.] section 12021 [now P.C. sections 29800-29825] was . . . intended only to prohibit members of the affected classes from arming themselves with concealable firearms or having such weapons in their custody or control in circumstances other than those in which the right to use deadly force in self-defense exists or reasonably appears to exist."[213]

This means that when prohibited persons are, or believe themselves or others to be, in immediate danger of great bodily harm, and as long as the firearm was made available to them without their preconceived intent or participation, they may temporarily possess a firearm for no longer than necessary to use it in self-defense without violating P.C. section 29800.

Finally, as in all cases where deadly force is used or threatened in self-defense, using a firearm must be reasonable under the circumstances and may be resorted to only if no other alternative means are available. In the case of felons defending themselves, such alternatives may include having to retreat in situations that non-prohibited persons would not be required to do so.[214]

---

[205] *People v. King*, 22 Cal. 3d 12, 18 (1978).

[206] *People v. King*, 22 Cal. 3d 12, 18 (1978).

[207] *People v. King*, 22 Cal. 3d 12, 18 (1978).

[208] *People v. King*, 22 Cal. 3d 12, 18 (1978).

[209] *People v. King*, 22 Cal. 3d 12, 18-19 (1978).

[210] *People v. King*, 22 Cal. 3d 12, 15 (1978).

[211] *People v. King*, 22 Cal. 3d 12, 22-23 (1978). Indeed, the laws governing self-defense are some of the oldest on the books.

[212] *People v. King*, 22 Cal. 3d 12, 23 (1978). The firearm restriction for felons was only limited to handguns at the time of the *King* case.

[213] *People v. King*, 22 Cal. 3d 12, 24 (1978).

[214] *People v. King*, 22 Cal. 3d 12, 23 (1978).

B. Momentary Possession

Prohibited persons may also be able to momentarily possess a firearm under California law in order to abandon, dispose of, or destroy it as long as the prohibited person only if they:

(1) Possessed the firearm for a momentary or transitory period; *and*

(2) Possessed the firearm in order to abandon, dispose of, or destroy it; *and*

(3) Did not intend to prevent law enforcement officials from seizing the firearm.[215]

But, note that this exception is very limited. For example, in *People v. Hurtado*, a felon, who was prohibited from possessing firearms, was given a loaded firearm that his girlfriend's eleven-year-old son had found outside on the ground.[216] Even though the felon intended to eventually dispose of the gun, he still had it in his possession three days later when the police stopped him for a traffic violation.[217]

On appeal, the California Court of Appeal held that the "momentary possession" defense extended to situations where a felon possess a firearm to abandon, dispose of, or destroy the firearm.[218] As the court explained, "Firearms . . . are admittedly dangerous items; [but] it is the retention of these items, rather than the brief possession for disposal . . . which poses the danger which is criminalized by the relevant statutes."[219] But, because the felon possessed the firearm for at least two full days, during which it was loaded and free to use in any way he saw fit, the court held that his possession was not momentary or temporary in any sense.[220] Therefore, the felon was not entitled to a "momentary possession" defense.

Nonetheless, a prohibited person can momentarily possess a firearm to abandon, dispose of, or destroy it as long as they are not doing so to prevent law enforcement from seizing the firearm.

C. Justifiable Possession

A prohibited person may also be able to possess a firearm under California law if he or she can prove that their possession was justified. In order to prove that their possession was justified, he or she must be able to show that they:

(1) Found the firearm or took it from a person who was committing a crime against them; *and*

---

[215] CALCRIM No. 2510; *People v. Hurtado*, 47 Cal. App. 4th 805, 813-14 (1996).

[216] *People v. Hurtado*, 47 Cal. App. 4th 805, 808-9 (1996).

[217] *People v. Hurtado*, 47 Cal. App. 4th 805, 808-9 (1996).

[218] *People v. Hurtado*, 47 Cal. App. 4th 805, 814 (1996).

[219] *People v. Hurtado*, 47 Cal. App. 4th 805, 813 (1996).

[220] *People v. Hurtado*, 47 Cal. App. 4th 805, 814 (1996).

(2) Possessed the firearm no longer than was necessary to deliver or transport the firearm to a law enforcement agency so that the agency can dispose of the weapon or to a licensed firearms dealer for storage pursuant to P.C. section 29830.[221]

Moreover, if the prohibited person plans on transporting the firearm to a law enforcement agency or licensed firearms dealer, they must give prior notice to the agency or dealer that they will be transporting the firearm to them for disposal or storage.[222]

XIII. OTHER FEDERAL LAW FIREARM POSSESSION RESTRICTIONS

A. Aliens

Unless an exception is met, federal law also prohibits "aliens" who are in the U.S. illegally or who have been admitted to the U.S. under a nonimmigrant visa[223] from receiving and possessing firearms.[224] An "alien" is anyone who is not a U.S. citizen or national;[225] however, the phrase "alien[s] illegally or unlawfully in the United States" refers to "[a]liens who are unlawfully in the United States [and] are not in valid immigrant, nonimmigrant, or parole status."[226] The term includes any alien:

(1) Who unlawfully entered the U.S. without inspection and authorization by an immigration officer and who have not been paroled into the U.S. under section 212(d)(5) of the Immigration and Nationality Act (INA); *or*

(2) Who are nonimmigrants and whose authorized period of stay has expired or who have violated the terms of the nonimmigrant category in which they were admitted; *or*

(3) Paroled under INA section 212(d)(5) whose authorized parole period has expired or whose parole status has been terminated; *or*

(4) Under an order of deportation, exclusion, or removal, or under an order to depart the U.S. voluntarily, whether or not they have left the U.S.[227]

---

[221] P.C. § 29850; CALCRIM No. 2510.

[222] P.C. § 29850; CALCRIM No. 2510.

[223] As defined in the Immigration and Nationality Act, 8 U.S.C. section 1011(a)(26).

[224] 18 U.S.C. § 922(g)(5)(B). In 2015, the Seventh Circuit Court of Appeals held that "aliens" may receive Second Amendment protections if they can show that they have come within the territory of the United States and developed a substantial connection with the country. *United States v. Meza-Rodriguez*, No. 14-3271, 2015 WL 4939943, at *7 (7th Cir. Aug. 20, 2015). This case makes it clear that the "Second-Amendment right to bear arms is no second-class entitlement," and even those who are not lawfully in the United States may still receive Second Amendment protections under certain circumstances. *United States v. Meza-Rodriguez*, No. 14-3271, 2015 WL 4939943, at *7 (7th Cir. Aug. 20, 2015).

[225] 18 U.S.C. § 922(y)(1)(A); 8 U.S.C. § 1101(a)(3).

[226] 27 C.F.R. § 478.11.

[227] 27 C.F.R. § 478.11.

Certain aliens lawfully admitted to the U.S. and who hold a nonimmigrant visa[228] may be exempt from this general federal prohibition if they are:

(1) Admitted to the U.S. for lawful hunting or sporting purposes or in possession of a hunting license or permit lawfully issued in the U.S.; *or*

(2) An official representative of a foreign government who is either:

    (a) Accredited to the U.S. Government or the Government's mission to an international organization having its headquarters in the U.S.; *or*

    (b) En route to or from another country to which that alien is accredited; *or*

(3) An official of a foreign government or distinguished foreign visitor who has been so designated by the Department of State; *or*

(4) A foreign law enforcement officer of a friendly foreign government entering the U.S. on official law enforcement business.[229]

An exemption is also extended to those aliens admitted to the U.S. holding a nonimmigrant visa if they have been issued a waiver to possess firearms.[230]

Even if a person has been admitted to the U.S. *without* a nonimmigrant visa, that person might still be eligible to possess firearms. On July 9, 2012, the ATF enacted a change to the Code of Federal Regulations allowing certain aliens without visas to lawfully possess and acquire firearms.[231] This change occurred because the U.S. allows citizens of a number of other countries entry into the U.S. without a visa, and these individuals were considered prohibited from possessing firearms because they did not possess a visa.[232] For instance, it was common for Canadian visitors who entered the U.S. to hunt, and because these visitors were permitted entry without a visa, their possession of firearms within the U.S. prior to this change in the interpretation of the law was illegal.

---

[228] 27 C.F.R. § 478.11 (a nonimmigrant visa is a "visa properly issued to an alien as an eligible nonimmigrant by a competent officer as provided in the Immigration and Nationality Act, 8 U.S.C. section 1101 et seq.").

[229] 18 U.S.C. § 922(y)(2). A lawfully issued hunting license or permit includes those issued by a state, local government, or Indian tribe federally recognized by the Bureau of Indian Affairs. *See Questions and Answers - Revised ATF F4473* (Apr. 2012 ed.), U.S. Dept. of Justice, Bureau of Alcohol, Tobacco, Firearms and Explosives, https://www.atf.gov/file/61841/download (last visited July 11, 2017).

[230] 18 U.S.C. § 922(y)(3).

[231] Firearms Disabilities for Certain Nonimmigrant Aliens, 77 Fed. Reg. 33625-01 (June 7, 2012) (effective July 9, 2012 and codified as 27 C.F.R. §§ 478.32, 478.44, 478.45, 478.99, 478.120, and 478.124). The ATF's previous position was that only aliens holding nonimmigrant visas who met an exception to the firearm restriction could possess and acquire firearms. See Implementation of Public Law 105-277, Omnibus Consolidated and Emergency Supplemental Appropriations Act, 1999, Relating to Firearms Disabilities for Nonimmigrant Aliens, and Requirement for Import Permit for Nonimmigrant Aliens Bringing Firearms and Ammunition Into the United States, 67 Fed. Reg. 5422 (Feb. 5, 2002).

[232] Citizens of 36 participating countries may enter the United States under the Visa Waiver Program. Visa Waiver Program (VWP), U.S. Dept. of State, https://travel.state.gov/content/visas/en/visit/visa-waiver-program.html (last visited July 11, 2017). Certain residents of Canada and Bermuda may also enter the United States without a visa, but under a different exception. Citizens of Canada and Bermuda, U.S. Dept. of State, http://travel.state.gov/content/visas/english/visit/canada-bermuda.html (last visited July 11, 2017).

Now "[n]onimmigrant aliens lawfully admitted to the U.S. without a visa, pursuant either to the Visa Waiver Program or other exemptions from visa requirements, will not be prohibited from shipping, transporting, receiving, or possessing firearms or ammunition. The regulations will also no longer proscribe the sale or other disposition of firearms or ammunition to such nonimmigrant aliens."[233]

B. Dishonorable Discharge From the Armed Forces

Individuals who have been dishonorably discharged or dismissed by a general court martial from the armed forces are likewise prohibited from possessing and receiving firearms.[234] Those who are merely "separated" from service in the armed forces because of any other discharge are not prohibited (*e.g.*, a "bad conduct" discharge does not qualify).[235] But, the "separation" from the armed forces may stem from a criminal conviction. In that case, the restrictions on firearms for criminal convictions may apply.

C. Renouncing United States Citizenship

If you renounce your U.S. citizenship, you are also prohibited from receiving and possessing firearms.[236] To be prohibited under this law, you must have renounced your U.S. citizenship before either:

(1) A diplomatic or consular officer of the U.S. in a foreign state under 8 U.S.C. section 1481(a)(5); *or*

(2) An officer designated by the U.S. Attorney General when the U.S. is in a state of war under 8 U.S.C. section 1481(a)(6).[237]

Your citizenship has not been renounced if the renunciation has been reversed by an administrative or judicial appeal.[238]

D. Federal Restrictions Against Indicted Persons Receiving Firearms

If you are "under indictment for a crime punishable by imprisonment for a term . . . [of more than] one year[239] . . . [you cannot] ship or transport in interstate or for-

---

[233] Firearms Disabilities for Certain Nonimmigrant Aliens, 77 Fed. Reg. 33625-01, 33627 (June 7, 2012) (effective July 9, 2012 and codified as 27 C.F.R. §§ 478.32, 478.44, 478.45, 478.99, 478.120, and 478.124).

[234] 18 U.S.C. § 922(g)(6); see also 27 C.F.R. § 478.11.

[235] *See* 27 C.F.R. § 478.11.

[236] 18 U.S.C. § 922(g)(7).

[237] 27 C.F.R. § 478.11.

[238] 27 C.F.R. § 478.11.

[239] This does not include any federal or state offenses regarding antitrust violations, unfair trade practices, restraints of trade, or similar offenses relating to business practices regulation, and any state misdemeanors punishable by imprisonment for two or less years. 18 U.S.C. § 921(a)(20).

eign commerce any firearm or ammunition or receive any firearm or ammunition which has been shipped or transported in interstate or foreign commerce."[240]

Federal law, however, does not prohibit *possessing* firearms or ammunition during this time; you simply cannot acquire new firearms or remove ones you already own from the state.

Table 3.10

A QUICK WRAP UP ON OTHER FEDERAL FIREARM POSSESSION RESTRICTIONS
The following individuals are prohibited from *receiving* and *possessing* firearms or ammunition under federal law: ✓ Fugitives from justice (as stated previously in the Chapter) ✓ Aliens who are illegally or unlawfully in the U.S. ✓ Aliens who have been admitted to the U.S. under a nonimmigrant visa, unless they meet an exemption listed in 18 U.S.C. section 922(y)(2) ✓ Individuals who have been dishonorably discharged or dismissed by a general court martial from the armed forces ✓ Individuals who have renounced their U.S. citizenship The following individuals are prohibited only from *receiving* firearms or ammunition under federal law: ✓ Individuals who are under indictment for a crime punishable by imprisonment for a term of more than one year

XIV. DEALER'S RECORD OF SALE (DROS) DELAYS

Despite the fact that an arrest should not stop a person from acquiring a firearm, beginning in early 2012, there were instances of firearm transaction *delays* for individuals with arrests and rejected and/or dismissed cases. Further, as a result of (what appears to be) a change in policy at the DOJ, individuals with felony arrests and cases were denied firearms in some instances. If a person has an arrest, criminal case, or conviction on his or her record and attempts to purchase a firearm, the DOJ analyst conducting the background check investigates to determine whether the case resulted in a conviction, and if so, whether the conviction is prohibiting.

In the past, DOJ analysts were giving "approved" responses for firearm transactions where there might have been an arrest or criminal case but there was no confirmation of a prohibiting conviction. Now, DOJ analysts have been giving a "delay" response when they cannot find conclusive proof that an arrest or charge is not firearm prohibiting. This may happen, for example, if a person has a criminal

---

[240] 18 U.S.C. § 922(n).

arrest from 1976 for grand theft auto and the case was later rejected by the District Attorney's office and not filed. Nevertheless, the arrest remains on the person's record. Consequently, when that person attempts to purchase a firearm, he or she gets a "delayed" response because often the reason for the rejection was never recorded (in this case, the decision not to prosecute). In some cases, firearm transactions for individuals whose cases were dismissed were delayed because the dismissal was not entered into the criminal history - the history simply reflects an arrest, a (sometimes felony) criminal charge, and nothing else.

This problem became a pandemic, and countless individuals who previously were able to acquire firearms found themselves "delayed." This problem was compounded by the fact that once the DOJ found a possible prohibiting event with no disposition, they threw their arms in the air and allowed the individual to remain delayed indefinitely. The DOJ, that is when they could be reached, often informed individuals that it is their responsibility to track down their own criminal records and prove that they are not prohibited in order for the DOJ to release their firearm(s).

As with the example above, in many cases the individual's records are 20-30 years old and often no longer exist. It is not unusual for law enforcement agencies to destroy records five years after the case is adjudicated and for courts (depending on the jurisdiction) to destroy closed case files. The delayed individual is often left with no option other than to prove to the DOJ that he or she is not prohibited.

This problem prompted the Legislature to take action. As discussed in Chapter 4, these DROS delays should last no more than 30 days, and if the DOJ cannot make a determination concerning a person's eligibility at the end of this period, the firearm dealer may release the firearm.[241]

But, this "fix" may prove to have some downside. For example, if you have an arrest from years ago and cannot show a favorable result in the case, you may see a 30-day delay every time you try to purchase or transfer a firearm. While this is better than no firearm being released at all, it is still unacceptable.

The Legislature's current stance is to tacitly approve this unacceptable delay. In October 2017, the Legislature passed SB 393, which allows certain individuals, who are suffering an arrest that did not result in a conviction, to petition the court to have their arrests sealed.[242] Sealing the arrest records would mean that the arrest is deemed not to have occurred and that, outside of a few exceptions, the petitioner is released from all penalties and disabilities resulting from the arrest.[243] But, buried in this law is the statement that the sealing of the arrest "does *not* affect the petitioner's authorization to own, possess, or have in his or her custody or control any

---

[241] *See* P.C. § 28220.

[242] SB 393, 2016-2017 Leg., Reg. Sess. (Cal. 2017), *available at* https://leginfo.legislature.ca.gov/faces/billTextClient.xhtml?bill_id=201720180SB393 (last visited Oct. 13, 2017); *see* P.C. §§ 851.91, 851.92 (both effective Jan. 1, 2018)..

[243] *See* P.C. § 851.92 (effective Jan. 1, 2018).

firearm . . . if the arrest would otherwise affect this authorization[.]"[244] But arrests currently *do* "otherwise affect [a person's] authorization" to own, possess, or have firearms because DOJ uses arrests to delay the release of a firearm if DOJ cannot determine how the case ended. DOJ does this even though, under California law, arrests do not result in firearm restrictions; convictions do. So, the sealing of an arrest, not to mention any arrest by itself, will still continue to affect (i.e., delay) a person's authorization to own, possess, or have firearms. It seems the Legislature carved out a special exception to allow DOJ to keep doing what it has been doing in delaying people due to arrests alone. DOJ still persists in using arrests for DROS delays.

XV. ACQUIRING YOUR CRIMINAL RECORDS AND DETERMINING YOUR ELIGIBILITY TO POSSESS FIREARMS

A. Obtaining Your Criminal History

If you have problems acquiring a firearm, you should request a copy of your criminal history from the DOJ or the FBI to confirm its accuracy as these are usually the records the DOJ uses to deny or delay your firearm transaction. Your criminal history can be obtained from the Attorney General's Office by completing the instructions at the Attorney General's website at: http://oag. ca.gov/fingerprints/security.

Once you receive a copy of your criminal history and believe it to be inaccurate or incomplete (which is fairly common), the DOJ provides a form to request that the DOJ correct your criminal record. On this form, you should provide any and all information that you are able to obtain about the inaccuracy or incompleteness of the record, including court records for your case, if accessible. You should also attempt to track down the records from any prior criminal cases and use them as support in your request to correct your record.

You may likewise request your criminal history summary from the FBI, which is strongly recommended if you are currently living outside of California or have a past arrest or criminal case outside of California. The instructions for how you may request your criminal history from the FBI are located at: http://www.fbi.gov/about-us/cjis/criminal-history-summary-checkscrim-inal-history-summary-checks. This website also provides links for how you can challenge the accuracy of your criminal history summary.

---

[244] P.C. § 851.91(e)(2)(B)(iii) (effective Jan. 1, 2018) (emphasis added).

B. Determining Your Firearm Eligibility

If you don't know whether you can legally possess or purchase firearms in California, *do not attempt to purchase a firearm.* If you reside in California, you should instead submit a PFEC to the DOJ. This form can be downloaded at: http://ag.ca.gov/firearms/forms/pdf/pfecapp.pdf. The DOJ will let you know whether you are eligible to possess firearms. If you are ineligible, you can contact them to find out why.

If you think you may be restricted or you find yourself restricted from owning or possessing firearms, you will need to check both California and federal law and obtain copies of specific court and/or medical records relating to your situation to determine the specific nature of your restriction and whether there is a way to restore your rights.[245]

---

[245] Detailed explanations on how to obtain the needed records, how to determine your firearm eligibility, and (if applicable) how to determine the nature of your restriction and restore your firearm rights can be found in the tentatively-titled book *Gun Owner's Guide to Restoring Your Gun Rights*. This book will be published by Coldaw Publishing and made available for purchase on Amazon in mid-2018.

CHAPTER 4:
OBTAINING FIREARMS AND AMMUNITION

The information in this chapter assumes you are eligible to own, possess, and receive firearms under state and federal law. Questions about possessing firearms and ammunition by minors and those with rights restrictions are covered in Chapter 3.

In California, *almost all* firearm ownership transfers, whether money is exchanged or not, must be processed through a licensed firearms dealer. A dealer is commonly referred to as a Federal Firearms Licensee (FFL).[1] As the name suggests, a federal firearms license is required to be a lawful firearms dealer.

The easiest, and in most cases the *only*, way to lawfully obtain a firearm in California is through a properly licensed FFL with a California firearms dealer's license. Most FFLs operate from a retail storefront, but it is not unlawful (unless prohibited by local zoning laws) for FFLs to operate in a non-retail setting like their home. These individuals are sometimes called "kitchen-table" FFLs. Although they are legal under federal and state law, if you decide to obtain a firearm through a "kitchen-table" FFL, make sure that the person you are purchasing from is actually an FFL[2] (if the transaction requires one) and that you are complying with all applicable laws. With the exception of antique firearms,[3] the absence of paperwork is a serious red flag about the legality of the transfer and the operations of the seller.

---

[1] Federal licenses are required for those engaged in business as a firearms dealer (gunsmithing), manufacturer, or importer. There is a separate license for "curio or relic" *collectors*. For purposes of this book, FFL will mean firearm "dealers" (unless specified otherwise) who possess both a Federal Firearms License to engage in the business of dealing in firearms (a Type 01 license) and a California firearms dealer's license. "FFL," in general parlance, is often used to refer to both the licensee and the license. In other words, a person must have an "FFL" in order to be an "FFL."

[2] Under California law, when neither party to the transaction is a licensed firearms dealer, they are required to complete the sale, loan, or transfer of the firearm through an FFL, unless they meet one of the exceptions outlined later in this Chapter. P.C. § 27545. If neither party to the transaction is a licensed firearms dealer, both the seller/transferor and the buyer/transferee can be prosecuted if they complete the firearm transaction without going through an FFL. P.C. § 27590; see also Opinion No. 10-504, 93 Ops. Cal. Atty. Gen. 54 (2013), *available at* https://oag.ca.gov/system/files/opinions/pdfs/10-504.pdf (last visited July 11, 2017). This is true even if the seller/transferor or buyer/transferee didn't know that the other person was unlicensed. *See People v. Vaughn*, 230 Cal. App. 4th 332, 333 (2014). So, always make sure to ask whether the person you plan on purchasing, selling, or transferring a firearm to is an FFL or that an exception to this requirement actually applies.

[3] Discussed later in this Chapter.

The California Penal Code (P.C.) refers to a dealer in firearms as a "licensee" or a "dealer." In order to qualify as a licensee or dealer in California, certain additional state-issued (and sometimes even local government) permits and licenses are required.

To legally operate as a firearms dealer under California law, a "dealer" must *minimally* have *all* of the following[4]:

(1) A valid Federal Firearms License; *and*

(2) A valid Seller's Permit issued by the State Board of Equalization; *and*

(3) A Certificate of Eligibility (COE) issued by the California Department of Justice (DOJ); *and*

(4) Any regulatory business license(s) required by local government;[5] *and*

(5) If required by the local authority, a local firearms license (or if no such license is required, a letter from the city or county confirming no such license is required);[6] *and*

(6) Be listed in the DOJ's Centralized List of Firearms Dealers.[7]

I. PURCHASING FIREARMS FROM A LICENSED DEALER

A. Sale Requirements for All Firearms (Both Handguns and Long Guns)

1. Federal Form 4473 Requirements

Federal law requires you to fill out a federal form, Form 4473, for any firearm (as defined under the Gun Control Act (GCA)) *transferred* to you by an FFL.[8] In most cases, only a single Form 4473 is required regardless of how many firearms are included in the transaction.[9]

---

[4] *See* P.C. § 26700.

[5] Local regulation of FFLs has become increasingly popular among California cities and counties. For example, in 2013, the city of Pleasant Hill caused a stir when it passed a slate of regulations requiring, among other things, that local firearm businesses obtain a local firearm business permit, carry minimum liability insurance, and implement various security measures. Pleasant Hill's law also severely limited the number of locations where a new firearm business may open and operate.

[6] P.C. § 26705(c)(3).

[7] P.C. § 26700.

[8] 27 C.F.R. § 478.124(a). This does not apply to certain loans from an FFL or the return of firearms after repairs by the FFL.

[9] If more than one semiautomatic rifle with a caliber greater than .22 (including .223/5.56) capable of accepting a "detachable magazine" is transferred to the same person within a five-day period, the FFL must additionally complete Form 3310.4. *See ATF E-Form* 3310.12, U.S. DEPT. OF JUSTICE, BUREAU OF ALCOHOL, TOBACCO, FIRE-ARMS, AND EXPLOSIVES, http://www.atf.gov/files/forms/download/atf-f-3310-4.pdf (last visited July 11, 2017). For firearm transaction reporting purposes, a "detachable magazine" includes a rifle with a "bullet button" (discussed in Chapter 8). *See Q&As for the Report of Multiple Sate or Other Disposition of Certain Rifles*, U.S. DEPT.

On Form 4473, you must provide information such as your name, gender, address, birth date, place of birth, height, weight, ethnicity, state of residence, and any factors affecting your eligibility to possess firearms.[10] The FFL will fill out information about the specific firearm(s) being purchased and identify the store (if applicable) and his or her FFL number.[11] FFLs are legally required to maintain all 4473 forms on their premises for 20 years.[12] Those forms must be made available for inspection for law enforcement and legal compliance purposes.[13]

Beware: it is generally illegal to provide false information on a Form 4473.[14] So, always make sure that you provide correct information on the form. If you have any questions about how to properly fill out or answer any questions on a Form 4473, contact an attorney who is experienced in firearms law. Do not rely on any "advice" from the dealer when you are trying to decide how to fill out the form. Dealers are not trained attorneys, and their advice may open you to criminal prosecution.

Full-time paid peace officers[15] are not required to fill out Form 4473 if they certify, on agency letter-head with an authorized signature, that they will use the firearm for official duties and a record check shows they have no misdemeanor crime of domestic violence (MCDV) convictions.[16]

2. California Dealer's Record of Sale (DROS) Form

In addition to the federal form, California requires a dealer to fill out a Dealer's Record of Sale (DROS) form electronically. Your personal information is obtained by the FFL by swiping your driver license or ID card though the dealer's magnetic strip reader.[17] The information required on the DROS form includes firearm type (*i.e.*, the make, model, serial number, etc.); transaction type (*i.e.*, dealer sale, private party transfer (PPT), pawn/consignment, or loan); waiting period requirement exemptions, if any (see below); and your name, address, birth date, etc.

Always check to make sure that the information on the form is correct and accurate before submitting it. It is a crime under California law to provide false

---

OF JUSTICE, BUREAU OF ALCOHOL, TOBACCO, FIREARMS, AND EXPLOSIVES, https://www.atf.gov/files/firearms/industry/080911-qa-multiple-rifles.pdf (last visited July 11, 2017). Likewise, if the transaction involves more than one handgun to the same person within a five-day period, the FFL must additionally complete Form 3310.4. 27 C.F.R. § 478.126a. This is generally not a concern for California FFLs, unless the customer is exempt from the "one handgun per month" rule or the FFL is facilitating a transfer of multiple handguns between two private parties. As an aside, the District Court for the District of Columbia upheld the ATF's multiple-firearm reporting requirement. *See Nat'l Shooting Sports Found., Inc. v. Jones*, 840 F. Supp. 2d 310 (D.D.C. 2012).

[10] ATF E-Form 3310.4, U.S. DEPT. OF JUSTICE, BUREAU OF ALCOHOL, TOBACCO, FIREARMS, AND EXPLOSIVES, https://www.atf.gov/file/61426/download (last visited July 11, 2017).

[11] For further details about the transferee and FFL's obligations regarding Form 4473, see 27 C.F.R. sections 478.11 and 478.124(c).

[12] 27 C.F.R. § 478.129(b).

[13] 18 U.S.C. § 923(g).

[14] 18 U.S.C. §§ 922(a)(6); 924(a)(1)(A).

[15] As defined in P.C. sections 830-832.9.

[16] 27 C.F.R. § 478.134. Because no Form 4473 is filled out, dealers who conduct this transaction must keep the letter for their records and note in their books how this firearm was transferred. 27 C.F.R. § 478.134(c).

[17] P.C. § 28180.

information on a DROS form.[18] If you are unsure as to whether you are eligible to possess firearms, you should run a Personal Firearms Eligibility Check (see Chapter 3) or contact an attorney experienced with firearms law *before* you attempt to obtain a firearm through an FFL.

After filling out the information on a DROS form, the FFL must take your thumbprint unless you qualify for an exception.[19] The FFL is required to keep a copy of the DROS form on file for at least three years and make it available for peace officer, DOJ, or ATF inspection.[20]

The FFL is also required to give you a copy of your DROS form at the time of delivery of the firearm.[21] Although you are not required to keep your copy of the DROS it is strongly suggested you retain a copy for your records in the event your firearm is lost, stolen, or proof of ownership is requested.

Unlike federal law, where you can just fill out one 4473 Form for all firearms purchased at the same time, a separate DROS form is required for each firearm transferred.[22] Formerly, this requirement applied only to handguns, and the transfer of multiple long guns required only a single DROS form.[23] But, California law now requires the submission of a separate form for every firearm transfer, even in a single transaction, for both handguns and long guns.[24]

3. Proof of Identity, Age, and Address

Under both California and federal law, an FFL is prohibited from delivering a *handgun* to anyone under age 21 or any firearm to anyone under age 18.[25] So you must present clear evidence of your identity and age to the FFL before he or she can release a firearm to you.[26]

---

[18] P.C. § 28250.

[19] P.C. § 28160(b). The requirements for handguns apply to all firearms.

[20] P.C. § 28215(c).

[21] P.C. §§ 28210(e), 28215(e). This new requirement was created by AB 538 (2013).

[22] P.C. § 28170(d).

[23] P.C. § 28160 (2013).

[24] P.C. § 28170(d).

[25] You should be aware that even though California law does not prohibit the transfer of any long gun to a person between the ages of 18 and 21 (P.C. § 27510), federal law prohibits dealers from selling a firearm that is neither a "rifle" nor a "shotgun" (*e.g.*, a frame/receiver) to anyone under age 21 (18 U.S.C. § 922(b)(1), (x)). See Chapter 2 for definitions and examples. It is not unusual for persons reaching the age of 18 to attempt to purchase a receiver to build their own rifle. Under federal law, a dealer is required to deny such a purchase.

[26] 18 U.S.C. §§ 922(t)(1)(C), 1028(d)(3); 27 C.F.R. §§ 478.11, 478.124(c)(3)(i); P.C. §§ 26815(c), 27540(c).

a. Federal Identification Requirements

In most situations a California driver license or California ID card will suffice for the identification requirements under federal law.[27] But federal law requires that you present a valid government-issued "identification document" that has your name, picture, date of birth, and residence address.[28] The address on your ID is important because a dealer can only transfer a firearm to someone residing in the same state as the dealer's place of business.[29] This requirement (and consequently, the address requirement), however, shall not apply to the sale or delivery of any *rifle* or *shotgun* to a resident residing in another state than the one which the dealer's place of business is located if (1) the person receiving the gun meets in person with the person transferring the gun to accomplish the transfer, and (2) the sale, delivery, and receipt fully comply with the legal conditions of sale in both such states.[30]

It is not unusual for a person to move and for his or her driver license to reflect their *old* address, or for a person to use a P.O. Box or police station address on their ID rather than a residential address. The address on your ID is important because a dealer can only transfer a firearm to someone residing in the same state as the dealer's place of business.[31]

But beware: failing to provide the address where you reside is a violation of federal law. Under federal law, not only must you complete a 4473 form (discussed further below), but you must also do so truthfully.

According to the Bureau of Alcohol, Tobacco, Firearms, and Explosives (ATF), federal law allows a purchaser to use a combination of *government-issued* documents[32] to satisfy the federal identification requirement.[33] So you could still acquire a firearm if, for example, you have your valid California driver license (to satisfy the California identification requirement) with a P.O. Box listed as your address and a voter registration card with your actual residence address (to satisfy the federal identification requirement).

For those who have a confidential or hidden address, you can obtain a government-issued document that contains your actual residence address by requesting a full ten-year driving record report from the California Department of Motor Vehicles (DMV). In order to obtain your ten-year driving record, you will need to

---

[27] Federal law makes it illegal in most cases for an FFL to transfer a firearm directly to a person who does not reside in the FFL's state of residence. 18 U.S.C. § 922(a)(2).

[28] 27 C.F.R. §§ 478.11; 478.124.

[29] 18 U.S.C. § 922(b)(3).

[30] 18 U.S.C. § 922(b)(3).

[31] 18 U.S.C. § 922(b)(3).

[32] Documents include those which are "made or issued by or under the authority of the United States Government, a State, political subdivision of a State, a foreign government, political subdivision of a foreign government, an international governmental or an international quasi-governmental organization which, when completed with information concerning a particular individual, is of a type intended or commonly accepted for the purpose of identification of individuals." 27 C.F.R. § 478.11.

[33] ATF Rul. 2001-5 (Dec. 31, 2001) ("Examples of documents that may be accepted to supplement information on a driver license or other identification document include a vehicle registration, a recreation identification card, a fishing or hunting license, a voter identification card, or a tax bill. However, the document in question must be valid and must have been issued by a government agency.").

go in person to the DMV and request your record. This report should reflect your confidential address, which you can use as proof of residency to satisfy the federal identification requirement.

b. California Identification Requirements

Under California law, clear evidence of your identity and age must be shown with either a valid California driver license or a valid California identification (ID) card issued by the DMV.[34] If your license has expired or is suspended, your firearm transaction will not be approved. There are additional identification and proof of residence requirements imposed when purchasing a handgun. These are discussed later in this chapter.

Table 4.1

IDENTIFICATION REQUIREMENTS[35]
FEDERAL LAW
You must present a government-issued document (such as a California driver license or ID). The government-issued identification document must contain the following: (1) Your name; *and* (2) Your current residence address; *and* (3) Your date of birth; *and* (4) A photograph of you. In order to meet this identification requirement, federal law allows you to use a *combination* of government-issued documents. Therefore, if your current government-issued identification does not contain your current address, you may present another government-issued document (like a voter registration card) that contains your current address.
CALIFORNIA LAW
You must have clear evidence of your identity and age in order to purchase a firearm. This means you must present a *valid* California driver license or *valid* California ID, issued by the California DMV. If you are a member of the military stationed in California, your Military Identification and permanent duty station orders will satisfy the California ID requirement.

---

[34] P.C. § 16400. California requires additional documentation to show "proof of residency" for the purchase of handguns (discussed in Subsection (B)(2) below). Although the California identification requirement requires that you have a valid California driver license or California ID card, they do not need to reflect your current address. In fact, the information required on the Dealer's Record of Sale (DROS) form is your "local address," and if your current address is temporary, then you need to provide your permanent address. You do not need to provide additional documentation to prove your permanent address. P.C. § 28160. California law does not define these terms "temporary" or "permanent." Federal law, however, does require you to provide documentation to prove your place of residence.

[35] All of the tables within this book are paraphrases of the law and are not a complete summary of each subject area. Please review the corresponding sections within this chapter for a more in-depth discussion of each topic and for the applicable statutes and/or case law that is paraphrased within the tables.

c.   Special Circumstances

i.   Members of the Military Stationed in California

Although California law limits the accepted forms of identification (*i.e.*, California driver licenses and DMV identification cards), the DOJ also accepts military identification and permanent duty station orders as proof of identification.[36]

These same documents satisfy the ID and proof of residency requirements under federal law as well. Section 921(b) of the GCA provides that "a member of the Armed Forces on active duty is a resident of the State in which his permanent duty station is located."[37] The purchaser's official orders showing that his or her permanent duty station is within the state where the FFL's premises are located suffice to establish the purchaser's residence for GCA purposes. "In combination with a military identification card, such orders will satisfy the Brady Act's requirement for an identification document, even though the purchaser may actually reside in a home that is not located on the military base."[38]

ii.   Non-Citizens (Aliens)

As explained in Chapter 3, federal law generally prohibits aliens who are unlawfully in the U.S., as well as those who are lawfully in the country via a "nonimmigrant visa" or who are not required to have a visa, from possessing and, of course, acquiring firearms. There are exceptions, however.[39]

For those aliens who may lawfully acquire a firearm in the U.S., state and federal laws relating to the acquisition of firearms still apply. The alien must therefore possess a California driver license or ID[40] to meet the state requirements. In addition, the individual must "reside" in a state to meet the federal requirement because, though there are a few exceptions, federal law generally restricts people from receiving firearms outside of the state in which they reside (this is discussed in much more detail in the next subsection).[41]

Previously, there was a 90-day residency requirement before aliens could acquire firearms; however, the U.S. DOJ amended the law to remove this require-

---

[36] *Frequently Asked Questions*, CAL. DEPT. OF JUSTICE, OFFICE OF THE ATTORNEY GENERAL, http://oag.ca.gov/firearms/pubfaqs (last visited July 11, 2017) (The answer to question 3 states, "[a]s part of the DROS process, the buyer must present 'clear evidence of identity and age' which is defined as a valid, non-expired California driver license or ID card issued by the Department of Motor Vehicles. A military identification accompanied by permanent duty station orders indicating a posting in California is also acceptable.").

[37] 18 U.S.C. § 921(b).

[38] ATF Rul. 2001-5 (Dec. 31, 2001).

[39] 18 U.S.C. § 922(g)(5)(A),(B). See Chapter 3 for a detailed discussion on who is an "alien" and when an alien is prohibited from possessing and receiving firearms. An alien who is not prohibited may purchase a firearm provided he or she can meet the requirements in this chapter. Often aliens "just visiting" the United States will not possess the proper identification required under federal or California law.

[40] P.C. §§ 26815(c), 27540(c).

[41] 18 U.S.C. § 922(a)(3).

ment. Aliens, when acquiring firearms, must also provide their alien number or admission number on the 4473 form.[42]

iii. Dual Residency

Federal law recognizes "dual residency," *i.e.*, when a person maintains a home in two states and resides in one or the other for certain periods of the year.[43] This means that if you are a resident of California and can establish residency in another state, you can purchase firearms in the other state during the time you reside there, presumably even if the firearms would be illegal in California.

For example, what if you live in California but also have a home in Arkansas where you spend your summers, and you want to purchase a firearm in Arkansas? First, you must determine where you actually "reside" under the law. According to federal law, an individual resides in a state if he or she is present in a state with the intention of making a home in that state.[44] The ATF determines residency by looking at where the individual resides, so if the individual has multiple homes in multiple states, he or she will be considered a resident of each state, respectively, for the portion of the year he or she resides there.[45]

In most instances, you must be a resident of the state in which you are acquiring a firearm.[46] To prove residency, you need to provide valid ID as required by federal law and the laws of that state concerning firearm transactions (if the state has any). For example, if you want to purchase a firearm in Arkansas directly from an FFL licensed in that state, you need to be an Arkansas resident.[47] If you aren't, you need to have the firearm sent to an FFL in the state you reside.[48] But, subject to a few very limited and narrow exceptions, you cannot send or bring firearms into California that are illegal to possess here, even if you obtained them legally in another state.

Moreover, you cannot send or bring a firearm that you lawfully purchased or otherwise obtained on or after January 1, 2015, from another state into California, unless the firearm is first delivered to an FFL in California, or you meet one of the few exceptions (discussed in Section IV(C) of this Chapter).[49] This means that all the pertinent California requirements (*i.e.*, ten-day wait, DROS, etc.) must be satisfied before you can lawfully receive the firearm in California.

---

[42] 27 C.F.R. § 478.124(c)(1).

[43] 27 C.F.R. § 478.11 (see definition for "state of residence"). For example, if you maintain a home in state X and then travel to state Y on a hunting trip, you do not become a state Y resident because of such trip. On the other hand, if you maintain a home in state X and a home in state Y and reside in state X during the week and summer months and state Y for weekends and the rest of the year, you are a state X resident when you are in state X, and you are a state Y resident when you are in state Y.

[44] 27 C.F.R. § 478.11.

[45] 27 C.F.R. § 478.11.

[46] 18 U.S.C. § 922(a)(3), (b)(3).

[47] This requirement is subject to a federal exemption for rifles and shotguns (discussed below) that does not apply to a person who only resides in California.

[48] 18 U.S.C. § 922(a)(3), (b)(3).

[49] P.C. § 27560(a).

d. Dealer Record of Sales Fees

Only one DROS fee can be charged for a single transaction, regardless of whether the second or subsequent firearms are transferred.[50] The current DROS processing fee is $19,[51] but you also need to pay a $1 Firearm Safety Fee and a $5 Firearm Safety and Enforcement Fee.[52] If you purchase a firearm and the dealer completes the transaction, there is no way for a dealer to add another firearm onto the completed DROS form if you change your mind and want to purchase another firearm in the same transaction.[53] Similarly, if the dealer errs by sending an incomplete DROS form, a second fee is charged to the dealer (and potentially passed on to the buyer).

4. Background Checks

The information collected on Federal Form 4473 and the DROS form is used to check your background and eligibility to possess, own, and receive firearms. Both California and federal law require FFLs to perform background checks for all firearm transfers.[54] Recall from Chapter 3 that California is a "point of contact" state, meaning that the California DOJ conducts the background checks for all firearm purchases in California and determines whether a person is eligible to possess firearms.[55]

---

[50] P.C. § 28240(b). "[T]he DROS fee is $19 for one or more firearms (handguns, rifles, shotguns) transferred at the same time to the same transferee." CAL. CODE REGS. tit. 11, § 4001.

[51] In August of 2011, I filed a federal lawsuit on behalf of the NRA against the DOJ, claiming the DOJ's use of monies collected from the DROS fee violate the Second Amendment. *See Bauer v. Harris,* No. 1:11-at-00526 (E.D.Cal. filed on Aug. 25, 2011). On March 2, 2015, the district court ruled that the use of DROS fees to fund APPS did not violate the Second Amendment. On June 1, 2017, the Ninth Circuit affirmed the district court opinion. And on July 12, it denied Plaintiffs' request for an "en banc" hearing. As of the date of publication, Plaintiffs are planning to file a petition for review to the United States Supreme Court. In addition, in 2013, I filed a second lawsuit in state court on behalf of other parties, claiming a subsequent amendment to the DROS fee scheme allowing the fee to fund the DOJ's regulation of the "possession" of firearms is an illegal tax under California law, and the $24 million the legislature appropriated from DROS fee monies to the DOJ for such regulation is illegal. *See Gentry v. Harris,* (Sup. Ct. Cal. filed on Sept. 24, 2013). On August 9, 2017, the district court issued a ruling prohibiting the DOJ from using DROS fees to fund unrelated law enforcement efforts and requiring DOJ to perform its statutorily required review of the current $19 fee to determine whether it is "not more than necessary to fund" the DOJ's costs for processing DROS transactions. A bench trial on Plaintiffs remaining claims has been set for March 16, 2018.

[52] P.C. §§ 23690, 28225, 28240, 28300; CAL. CODE REGS. tit. 11, § 4001. In 2016, the California Legislature passed Senate Bill (SB) 843, giving the DOJ the authority to increase the $1 Firearm Safety Testing fee and the $5 Safety and Enforcement fee at a rate not to exceed any increase in the California Consumer Price Index and the reasonable costs of regulation to the DOJ. But, as of the date of publication, the DOJ has yet to promulgate any regulations to increase these fees.

[53] CAL. CODE REGS. tit. 11, § 4210(a)(4).

[54] 27 C.F.R. § 478.124; P.C. § 28215. Eligibility requirements are discussed in Chapter 3, and procedures for appealing the DOJ's denial of allowing your firearm transfer to proceed will be discussed in an upcoming publication by Coldaw Publishing tentatively titled *Gun Owner's Guide to Restoring Your Gun Rights.* This publication will be available for purchase on Amazon in mid-2018.

[55] Although the DOJ has been tasked with performing all background checks for firearm purchases, it has consistently dropped the ball on performing background checks and has had numerous problems properly identifying people who are prohibited from owning and possessing firearms. In 2015, the California State Auditor released a report that chastised the DOJ for failing to fully implement certain recommendations that the State Auditor made in 2013 when it discovered that the Armed Prohibited Person System (APPS) had trouble identifying individuals who should be prohibited from possessing firearms due to a mental health commitment because the DOJ had not taken any steps to ensure that mental health facilities and courts were properly reporting these incidents. *See* California State Auditor, *Follow-up—California Department of Justice: Delays in Fully Implementing Recommendations*

5. Registration at Time of Purchase

Before January 1, 2014, only handgun transfers were registered, and California law prohibited the DOJ from keeping records relating to transfers of long guns from a dealer.[56] As of January 1, 2014, all firearms acquired from a licensed firearms dealer in California are registered to the transferee.[57] The DOJ takes the information collected by the mandatory DROS form, which includes the purchaser's personal identifying information and the firearm's make, model, serial number, etc., and enters that information into its Automated Firearm System (AFS), thereby registering the firearm in the purchaser's name.[58]

Because of the amount of paperwork and information gathered, it is not unusual for those who went through the DROS process to believe their long gun was registered prior to January 1, 2014. But, aside from documents kept by the dealer and the purchaser, no transaction records on long gun transfers were kept by the government. A disturbingly large number of Californians also mistakenly believe that the DROS process was the same one required to register "assault weapons." But that is also not the case. Because they filled out the long gun purchase paperwork, people are still discovering that firearms they thought were registered as "assault weapons" are not registered as such, and in the case of long guns purchased before January 1, 2014, they are not, in fact, registered at all.

a. Voluntary Registration

You may, however, voluntarily register any lawfully owned firearm by submitting a "Firearm Ownership Record" form to the DOJ.[59] This form is available on the DOJ Bureau of Firearms' website. Though not legally required, having this record on file with the DOJ may help your firearm be returned to you if it is ever seized, lost, or stolen.[60] Registration can also safeguard against a felony. For example, an individual charged for carrying a handgun illegally concealed or loaded that is registered would not result in a felony, because a *registered* firearm carried illegally is, in most situations, only a misdemeanor (discussed in Chapter 5).

Prevent it From Accurately and Promptly Identifying All Armed Persons with Mental Illness, Resulting in Continued Risk to Public Safety (July 2015), *available at* https://www.auditor.ca.gov/pdfs/reports/2015-504.pdf (last visited July 11, 2017). The State Auditor also reported that the DOJ had incorrectly found that certain individuals were prohibited from possessing firearms because the APPS unit did not review all pertinent information when processing background checks, and that the DOJ has not been (and will not be) able to review the backlog cases where a person might be a prohibited person in possession of a firearm. *See* California State Auditor, *Follow-up—California Department of Justice: Delays in Fully Implementing Recommendations Prevent it From Accurately and Promptly Identifying All Armed Per-sons with Mental Illness, Resulting in Continued Risk to Public Safety* (July 2015), *available at* https://www.auditor.ca.gov/pdfs/reports/2015-504.pdf (last visited July 11, 2017).

[56] P.C. §§ 11106(a)-(b), 28210(c)(3) (2013).

[57] P.C. § 11106(b).

[58] P.C. §§ 28155, 28160, 28215(d).

[59] The processing fee for filing a Firearm Ownership Record form is $19. CAL. CODE REGS. tit. 11, § 4002.

[60] *Frequently Asked Questions*, CAL. DEPT. OF JUSTICE, OFFICE OF THE ATTORNEY GENERAL, http://oag.ca.gov/firearms/pubfaqs#26 (last visited July 11, 2017).

Contrary to advice proffered by a number of websites a few years ago, the use of the voluntary registration form is not a way to bypass the requirement that most transactions of firearms must be done through an FFL.

Despite the fact that handguns acquired in California from a licensed firearm dealer should be recorded as registered to the purchaser, this is often not the case. The AFS has holes you can pilot the U.S.S. Missouri through. Individuals who have large collections may find it amusing to request a list of firearms registered to them.[61] These lists are often filled with inaccuracies, including firearms that were transferred years ago through a dealer, firearms the individual never purchased, as well as incorrect serial numbers and/or make/model designations.

b. Confusion Regarding the Requirement to Register Firearms After January 1, 2014

There was some confusion relating to the change in California law that occurred on January 1, 2014. The law did not create a requirement to register firearms acquired/ purchased before January 1, 2014. Rather, the new law only affects firearms transferred through an FFL and firearms you either import into this state as a "personal firearm importer" or received without going through a dealer[62] *after* January 1, 2014. Firearms you transferred (via an exemption to the dealer requirement where the recipient didn't need to register the acquisition of the firearm) or imported (prior to January 1, 2014, the general registration of firearms brought into the state only applied to handguns and "personal *handgun* importers") prior to January 1, 2014, that did not need to be registered, still do not need to be registered.

6. Waiting Period

Under California law, you must wait ten days (ten 24-hour periods) from when your DROS form is submitted until you may lawfully receive any firearm transferred through an FFL.[63] If you clear the background check (assuming all other requirements are satisfied), the FFL may transfer the firearm to you after the ten days.[64]

The following people and transfers are exempt from this ten-day waiting period:

---

[61] You can request a list of firearms registered in your name by filling out and submitting an "Automated Firearms System (AFS) Request for Firearms Records" form. You may download the form at: http://oag.ca.gov/sites/all/files/pdfs/firearms/forms/AFSPrivateCitizen.pdf. The form will need to be notarized and include a photocopy of a valid identification card (driver license, military ID, etc.).

[62] This transfer must have been made pursuant to an exception to the requirement that all private party transfers (PPTs) be conducted through a dealer (see below for the requirement and exceptions to that requirement).

[63] P.C. § 26815(a). A lawsuit was filed to challenge the 10-day wait as applied to current gun owners. In December 2016, the 9th Circuit issued its decision upholding the 10-day wait as applied to current gun owners. *Silvester v. Harris*, 843 F.3d 816 (9th Cir. 2016). Plaintiffs petitioned the Ninth Circuit to rehear the case, but that petition was denied on April 4, 2017. Plaintiffs have petitioned the United States Supreme Court for review and, as of the writing of this book, are now waiting for a decision from the Supreme Court on whether it will review the case.

[64] P.C. § 26815(a).

(1) Properly identified full-time paid peace officers authorized by their employer to carry firearms for their confirmed duties;[65] *and*

(2) Firearm deliveries, sales, or transfers to DOJ-issued special weapons permit holders;[66] *and*

(3) Persons with ATF-issued "curio or relic" collector's licenses who have a valid DOJ-issued COE when purchasing "curio or relic" firearms;[67] *and*

(4) FFLs delivering firearms to another FFL, or an FFL transferring a firearm from store inventory to the FFL's personal collection (subject to additional ATF and California requirements).[68]

Additionally, you have 30 days from the date your DROS was submitted to pick up your firearm from the FFL. Otherwise, federal law voids your background check, and you will be required to go through the entire process again, fees and everything.[69]

Also, your firearm transaction could be delayed up to 30 days if the FFL sends your information to the DOJ and one of the following occur:

(1) You were taken into custody and placed in a facility for mental health treatment or evaluation and may be a person described in section 8100 or 8103 of the California Welfare and Institutions Code (Cal. Welf. & Inst. Code), and the DOJ cannot actually determine whether you are prohibited; *or*

(2) You were arrested for, or charged with, a crime that would make you, if convicted, a person who is prohibited by state or federal law from possessing firearms, and the DOJ is unable to determine whether you were convicted of that offense; *or*

(3) You may be a person who has purchased a handgun in the last 30 days, and the DOJ is unable to determine whether you are or not.[70]

If the DOJ cannot figure out whether or not you are prohibited based on the foregoing, it is required to notify the dealer (presumably before the end of the ten-day wait)[71] and let the dealer know there is a delay in the transaction. The dealer is then required to provide you with information for contacting the DOJ regarding the delay. The DOJ is also required to send you notice by mail regarding the delay

---

[65] P.C. §§ 26950, 27650.

[66] P.C. §§ 26965, 27665. The permits include those issued per P.C. sections 33300 (short-barreled rifle and shotgun permittees), 32650 (machinegun, "assault weapons," and .50 BMG permits), 32700 (permits to sell machineguns), and 18900 (permits for destructive devices).

[67] P.C. §§ 26970, 27670, 27820. Acquiring antique and "curio or relic" firearms is discussed later in this chapter. "Curio or relic" firearms are defined in Chapter 2.

[68] P.C. §§ 26960, 27660.

[69] *See* 27 C.F.R. § 478.102(c).

[70] P.C. § 28220(f)(1)(A).

[71] A regulation that was implemented in now prohibits a dealer from releasing a firearm unless the dealer receives an "Approved" from the DOJ. Under these regulations, if the DOJ had no response, even after the end of the 10-day wait, arguably the dealer could not release the firearm. CAL. CODE REGS tit. 11, § 4230.

and the process for obtaining the criminal or mental health information the DOJ has on file.[72] If during the 30-day delay the DOJ is able to determine your eligibility, they are required to notify the dealer accordingly.[73] If at the end of the 30 days the DOJ is unable to determine your eligibility, they are required to notify the dealer and the dealer *may* immediately transfer the firearm to you.[74] Make a special note of the word "may," because this is not a requirement. A dealer may release the firearm, but doesn't have to.

This legislative change appears to be in response to problems with the processing of a number of firearm transactions. As discussed in Chapter 3, some firearm transactions were taking longer than ten days when the DOJ could not determine whether a person was prohibited. These cases often involved individuals who had an arrest or criminal charge on their record with no disposition of the case available to the DOJ. In some cases, the delay became indefinite. As a result, the legislature implemented the 30-day delay limit.

7. Required Locking Devices and Warnings

Federal law also requires licensed importers, manufacturers, and dealers to provide a "secure gun storage or safety device"[75] when delivering a *handgun* to anyone who is not another FFL or otherwise exempt.[76]

California requires all firearms transferred by an FFL, including Private Party Transfers (PPTs) (discussed in Section II below) or those manufactured in California, be accompanied by an approved "firearm safety device"[77] and warning language or labels upon delivery.[78] The safety device must be one of those listed on the "Roster of Firearm Safety Devices Certified for Sale" and identified as appropriate for the specific firearm.[79]

---

[72] P.C. § 28220(f)(1)(B).

[73] P.C. § 28220(f)(3)(A)-(B).

[74] P.C. § 28220(f)(4).

[75] Defined in 18 U.S.C. section 921(a)(34) as either a device that is designed to prevent the firearm from being operated without first deactivating the device; a device incorporated into the firearm's design to prevent the firearm from being operated by anyone without access to the device; or a safe, gun safe, gun case, lock box, or other device designed to be, or that can be, used to store a firearm and that is designed to only be unlocked with a key, combination, etc.

[76] 18 U.S.C. § 922(z)(1)-(2). Exceptions include: transfer to or by the U.S., a state, its departments, agencies, or subdivisions, or law enforcement officers employed by any of these entities; transfer to a rail police officer for law enforcement purposes; transfer of a "curio or relic" to a licensed collector; and transfer whereby the secure gun storage device is unavailable due to theft, casualty, loss, consumer sales, back orders, etc., beyond FFL control, and where the FFL delivers a secure gun storage or safety device within ten days after the transfer.

[77] P.C. § 23635(a). A "firearm safety device" means a device other than a gun safe that locks and is designed to prevent children and unauthorized users from firing a firearm. The device may be installed on a firearm, incorporated into the design of the firearm, or prevent access to the firearm. P.C. § 16540.

[78] P.C. § 23640. When a firearm is sold or transferred within California, the packaging and any descriptive material must bear a warning label (in both English and Spanish) that states that firearms should be handled responsibly and be securely stored to prevent access by children and other unauthorized users, that information on firearm laws can be found at the California Attorney General's website, and that a firearm owner may face criminal prosecution for failing to abide by California's firearm laws.

[79] P.C. § 23635(a). The entire Roster is found on the DOJ's website. *Roster of Firearm Safety Devices Certified for Sale*, CAL. DEPT. OF JUSTICE, OFFICE OF THE ATTORNEY GENERAL, http://oag.ca.gov/firearms/fsdcertlist (last

This safety device requirement does not apply if:

(1) You own a gun safe that meets certain standards[80] and you present an original receipt for it or proof of owning the gun safe as authorized by the AG;[81] *or*

(2) You purchase an approved safety device no more than 30 days before you take possession of the firearm; you present the approved safety device to the FFL when picking up the firearm; you present an original receipt to the FFL showing the safety device's purchase date, name, and the model number;[82] *or*

(3) You buy an "antique firearm";[83] *or*

(4) You are employed as a salaried full-time peace officer.[84]

Examples of "Firearm Safety Devices"

Example of a trigger lock on a shotgun

Example of a cable lock

Note that federal safety device requirement (see above) is different than California's in both its scope and exceptions because, unlike California law, the federal requirement only applies to handguns. FFLs should be careful to make sure a locking device meets both state and federal requirements. For the general public, however, the most important distinction is that federal law does not recognize California's gun-safe affidavit exception when the transfer involves *handguns*. So, despite California law, a gun-safe affidavit is only valid when the transfer involves a *long gun*.

8. Firearm Safety Certificate

Anyone purchasing a firearm (handgun or long gun) must present a valid Firearm Safety Certificate (FSC) to the licensed firearms dealer to show that he or she

---

visited July 11, 2017).

[80] P.C. § 23650(a)(3).

[81] P.C. § 23635(b)(2). But, this safe-affidavit exception is not recognized for *handgun* transfers under federal law.

[82] P.C. § 23635(c).

[83] P.C. § 23630. Discussed in Chapter 2.

[84] P.C. § 23630.

has passed a written "Firearm Safety" test, unless they fall under an exception (see subsection below). The FSC requirement replaced the former Handgun Safety Certificate (HSC) requirement that was in place prior to January 1, 2015. Under that requirement, handgun purchasers were required to show an HSC to the dealer, showing that he or she passed a written "Handgun Safety" test. In 2013, however, the California Legislature passed a bill Senate Bill (SB) 683, which expanded these requirements and its exemptions to apply to all firearm purchases.

To obtain an FSC, the individual wishing to purchase the firearm must pass a written "Firearm Safety" test administered by a DOJ Certified Instructor. Most FFLs or their employees are FSC Certified Instructors who can administer the written test in their store, even on the same day as your purchase. The test includes thirty multiple-choice questions, and costs up to $25 ($15 of which goes to the DOJ, and the rest goes to the instructor).[85] You must correctly answer at least 75% of the questions in order to get the FSC. That means that you must answer, at least, twenty-three of the thirty questions correctly to pass the "Firearm Safety" test.[86]

After passing the test, the FSC is only good for five years.[87] If you lose or completely destroy your FSC, you can get a duplicate certificate by asking the instructor who issued the test to you for one, proving your identity, and paying up to $15.[88] To be clear, an FSC is only necessary to receive a firearm (handgun or long gun). It is not necessary, however, to *possess* one.

a. "Firearm Safety" Certificate Exemptions

The following people, property, and transactions are exempt from the FSC requirement:

Table 4.2

PENAL CODE SECTION	EXEMPTION
P.C. § 226840	Any person purchasing a handgun who still has a valid HSC may purchase the handgun using his or her HSC
P.C. § 31700(a)(1)	Active or honorably retired peace officers as defined in Chapter 4.5 of Title 3 of Part 2 of the Penal Code (commencing with P.C. section 830)
P.C. § 31700(a)(2)	Active or honorably retired federal officers or law enforcement agents

---

[85] P.C. § 31650(b).

[86] P.C. § 31645(a). Do not be concerned about passing this test. It is relatively straightforward, and the FFL has materials to review before taking it. The dealer should have copies or you can study up online at: http://oag.ca.gov/sites/all/files/agweb/pdfs/firearms/forms/hscsg.pdf (last visited July 11, 2017). If English is not your first language, you are entitled to a translator if you need one. P.C. § 31640(b). But the translator cannot help you answer the questions.

[87] *Frequently Asked Questions*, CAL. DEPT. OF JUSTICE, OFFICE OF THE ATTORNEY GENERAL, http://oag.ca.gov/firearms/hscfaqs#a10 (last visited July 29, 2017).

[88] P.C. § 31660.

Penal Code Section	Exemption
P.C. § 31700(a)(3)	Reserve peace officers as defined in P.C. section 832.6
P.C. § 31700(a)(4)	Anyone who has successfully completed the peace officer training course in P.C. section 832
P.C. § 31700(a)(5)	California FFLs acting in the scope of their duties as an FFL
P.C. § 31700(a)(6)	Licensed collectors who are acquiring or being loaned a firearm that is a "curio or relic" and who have a COE issued by the DOJ under P.C. section 26710
P.C. § 31700(a)(7)	Firearm owners who are having their firearms returned to them
P.C. § 31700(a)(8)	Family members of peace officers or deputy sheriffs killed in the line of duty who receive a firearm under Cal. Gov't Code section 50081
P.C. § 31700(a)(9)	Anyone with a valid carry license (i.e., a license issued under P.C. section 26150 and 26155)
P.C. § 31700(a)(10)	Active or honorably retired members of the U.S. Armed Forces, National Guard, Air National Guard, or the U.S. active reserve
P.C. § 31700(a)(11)	Anyone authorized to carry loaded firearms in the scope of their employment under P.C. section 26025 and 26030(a)-(c); such as patrol special police, animal control officers, zookeepers, harbor police officers, guards, messengers, private investigators, and private patrol officers; and DOJ-issued special weapons permit holders
P.C. § 31700(a)(12)	Anyone who holds a special weapons permit issued under P.C. sections 32650 (for machinegun manufacturing) or 33300 (for short-barreled rifle/shotguns), 18900 through 18910 (for destructive devices), or 32700 through 32720 (for machinegun sales)
P.C. § 31700(b)(1)-(6)	Those who take possession of firearms by operation of law in a representative capacity, such as an executor or administrator of an estate, a secured creditor or employee who possesses it as collateral, a levying officer, a receiver, a bankruptcy trustee, or an assignee for the benefit of creditors
P.C. § 31700(c)	Any person who has been issued a valid hunting license that is unexpired or that was issued for the hunting season immediately preceding the calendar year in which the person is takes title or possession of the long gun. This exception does not apply to handgun purchases

---

[89] "Proper written authorization is defined as verifiable written certification from the head of the agency by which the purchaser or transferee is employed, identifying the employee as an individual authorized to conduct the transaction, and authorizing the transaction to the exclusive use of the agency by which that person is employed." P.C. § 31705(b).

PENAL CODE SECTION	EXEMPTION
P.C. § 31705	The sale, delivery, or transfer of firearms made to an authorized law enforcement representative of any city, county, city and county, or state, or of the federal government, for exclusive use by the governmental agency if, prior to the sale, delivery, or transfer of these firearms, written authorization[89] from the head of the agency authorizing the transaction is presented to the person from whom the purchase, delivery, or transfer is being made
P.C. § 31740	The sale, delivery, or transfer of firearms between or to importers and licensed firearm manufacturers
P.C. § 31830	The loan of an unloaded firearm to a consultant-evaluator by a person licensed under P.C. sections 26700-36915 (i.e., a California-licensed firearms dealer), if the loan does not exceed 45 days from the date of delivery
P.C. § 31710	Loans of firearms by law enforcement agencies to peace officers if the following conditions are satisfied: (1) The loan is made by an authorized law enforcement representative of a city, county, or city and county, or of the state or federal government; *and* (2) The loan is made to a peace officer employed by that agency and authorized to carry a firearm; *and* (3) The loan is made for the carrying and use of that firearm by that peace officer in the course and scope of the officer's duties
P.C. § 31715	The sale, delivery, or transfer of a firearm by a law enforcement agency to a peace officer pursuant to Cal. Pub. Contract Code section 10334
P.C. § 31720	The sale, delivery, or transfer of a firearm by a law enforcement agency to a retiring peace officer who is authorized to carry a firearm under Chapter 5 (commencing with P.C. section 26300) of Division 5
P.C. § 31725	The sale, delivery or transfer of a firearm if both of the following are satisfied: (1) The sale, delivery, or transfer is to an authorized representative of a city, city and county, county, or state government, or of the federal government, and is for the governmental entity; *and* (2) The entity is acquiring the weapon as part of an authorized, voluntary program in which the entity is buying or receiving weapons from private individuals

Table 4.2

Penal Code Section	Exemption
P.C. § 31730	The sale, delivery, loan, or transfer of a firearm by an authorized law enforcement representative of a city, county, city and county, or state, or of the federal government, to any public or private nonprofit historical society, museum, or institutional collection, or the purchase or receipt of that firearm by that public or private nonprofit historical society, museum, or institutional collection, if: (1) The entity receiving the firearm is open to the public; *and* (2) The firearm prior to delivery is deactivated or rendered inoperable; *and* (3) The firearm is not subject to P.C. sections 18000, 18005, 34000, 34005, 34010, or Division 4 (commencing with P.C. section 18250) of Title 2 (governing firearm surrender or forfeiture because it was used in a crime and/or not claimed by law enforcement); *and* (4) The firearm is not prohibited by other provisions of law from being sold, delivered, or transferred to the public at large
P.C. § 31745	The sale, delivery, or transfer of a handgun to an FFL, where the FFL is receiving the handgun in the course and scope of his or her activities as a person licensed under P.C. sections 26700-26915
P.C. § 31735	The sale, delivery, loan, or transfer of a firearm made by a person other than a representative of an authorized law enforcement agency to any public or private nonprofit historical society, museum, or institutional collection, if all of the following conditions are met: (1) The entity receiving the firearm is open to the public; *and* (2) The firearm is deactivated or rendered inoperable prior to delivery; *and* (3) The firearm is not a type prohibited from being sold, delivered, or transferred to the public; *and* (4) Prior to delivery, the entity receiving the firearm submits a written statement to the person selling, loaning, or transferring the firearm stating that the firearm will not be restored to operating condition, and will either remain with that entity, or if subsequently disposed of, will be transferred in accordance with the applicable provisions listed in P.C. section 16575 and, if applicable, with P.C. section 31615

Penal Code Section	Exemption
P.C. § 31750	The loan of a firearm if the following conditions are met: (1) The person loaning the firearm is at all times within the presence of the person being loaned the firearm; *and* (2) The loan is for a lawful purpose; *and* (3) The loan does not exceed three days in duration; *and* (4) The individual receiving the firearm is not prohibited by state or federal law from possessing, receiving, owning, or purchasing a firearm; *and* (5) The person loaning the firearm is 18 years of age or older; *and* (6) The person receiving the firearm is 18 years of age or older
P.C. § 31755	The delivery of a firearm to a gunsmith for service or repair, or to the return of the firearm to its owner by the gunsmith, or to the delivery of a firearm by a gunsmith to a person licensed under Chapter 44 (commencing P.C. section 921) of Title 18 of the United States Code (i.e., a firearms manufacturer, importer, or dealer licensed under federal law) for service or repair and the return of the firearm to the gunsmith
P.C. § 31760	The sale, delivery, or transfer of firearms if all the following requirements are satisfied: (1) The sale, delivery, or transfer is made by a person who resides in California; *and* (2) The sale, delivery, or transfer is made to a person who resides outside this state is an FFL; *and* (3) The sale, delivery, or transfer is in accordance with Chapter 44 (commencing P.C. section 921) of Title 18 of the United States Code and the regulations thereto (i.e., the requirements for firearms trasnsfer under federal law)
P.C. § 31765	The loan of a firearm to a person 18 years of age or older for the purpose of target shooting at targets if the loan occurs on the premises of a target facility that holds a business or regulatory license, or on the premises of any club or organization organized for the purpose of practice shooting at targets upon established ranges, whether public or private, if the firearm is at all times kept within the premises of the target range or on the premises of the club or organization

Table 4.2

PENAL CODE SECTION	EXEMPTION
P.C. § 31770	The delivery, transfer, or return of firearms made pursuant to any of the following: (1) P.C. sections 18000 and 18005 (stating the manner a weapon or instrument should be confiscated and destroyed); *and* (2) Division 4 (commencing with Section 18250) of Title 2 (governing seizure of firearm or other deadly weapon at scene of domestic violence); *and* (3) Chapter 2 (commencing with Section 33850) of Division 11 (governing the return or transfer of firearm in custody or control of a court or law enforcement agency); *and* (4) P.C. sections 34005 (providing alternatives to destruction of firearms) and 34010 (requiring law enforcement retaining custody of, or destroying, a firearm to notify the DOJ of the retention or destruction)
P.C. § 31780	The sale, delivery, transfer of unloaded firearms by an FFL to an FFL outside of California
P.C. § 31785	The sale, delivery, or transfer of unloaded firearms to a wholesaler if the firearms are being returned to the wholesaler and are intended as merchandise in the wholesaler's business
P.C. § 31790	The sale, delivery, or transfer of a firearm if all the following are met: (1) The firearms are unloaded; *and* (2) The sale, delivery, or transfer is made by one FFL to another FFL, upon proof of compliance with the requirements of P.C. section 27555 (which governs the California Firearms Licensee Check System); *and* (3) The firearms are intended as merchandise in the receiving FFL's business

PENAL CODE SECTION	EXEMPTION
P.C. § 31800	The loan of an unloaded firearm by an FFL who also operates a target facility that holds a business or regulatory license on the premises of the building designated in the license or whose building designated in the license is on the premises of any club or organization organized for the purposes of practicing shooting at targets upon established ranges, whether public or private, to a person at that target facility or that club or organization, if the firearm is at all times kept within the premises of the target range or on the premises of the club or organization
P.C. § 31805	The sale, delivery, or transfer of unloaded firearms to a wholesaler as merchandise in the wholesaler's business by a manufacturer or importer licensed to engage in that business under federal law, or by another wholesaler, if the sale, delivery, or transfer is made in accordance with federal law
P.C. § 31815	The loan of a firearm if all of the following requirements are satisfied: (4) The loan is "infrequent";[90] *and* (5) The firearm is unloaded; *and* (6) The loan is made by a person who is neither a dealer nor an FFL; *and* (7) The loan is made to a person 18 years of age or older; *and* (8) The loan is for use solely as a prop in a motion picture, television, video, theatrical, or other entertainment production event

---

[90] For purposes of this code section, "infrequent" means [f]or handguns, less than six transactions per calendar year." And "[f]or firearms other than handguns, occasional and without regularity." P.C. § 16730.

Table 4.2

Penal Code Section	Exemption
P.C. § 31835	The delivery, sale, or transfer of a firearm when made by authorized law enforcement representatives for cities, counties, cities and counties, or of the state or federal government, if all of the following conditions are met: (1) The sale, delivery, or transfer is made to one of the persons or entities identified in P.C. section 26620(a); *and* (2) The sale, delivery, or transfer is not subject to the procedures set forth in P.C. sections 18000 (surrendering weapons to authorities), 18005 (offer of surrendered weapons for sale at public auction, stolen weapons, weapons used in manner constituting nuisance without knowledge of owner, destruction of surrendered weapons), 34000 (firearms no longer needed as exhibits in criminal actions or proceedings, firearms that are unclaimed or abandoned property, sale or destruction), or 34005 (alternatives to destruction of firearms); *and* (3) The sale, delivery, or transfer of the firearm follows the procedures set forth in P.C. section 26620 (i.e., the receiving agency registers the firearm in the Automated Firearms System).

PENAL CODE SECTION	EXEMPTION

P.C. § 31810	The FSC requirement does not apply to or affect the following:
	
	(1) The loan of a firearm to a minor by the minor's parent or legal guardian, provided that both of the following conditions are met:
	
	  (a) The minor is being loaned the firearm for the purpose of engaging in a lawful, recreational sport, including but not limited to, competitive shooting, or agricultural, ranching, or hunting activity or hunting education, or a motion picture, television, or video production, or entertainment or theatrical event, the nature of which involves the use of a firearm; *and*
	
	  (b) The duration of the loan does not exceed the amount of time that is reasonably necessary to engage in the activity.
	
	(2) The loan of a firearm to a minor by a person who is not the minor's parent or legal guardian, provided all the following conditions are met:
	
	  (a) The minor is accompanied by the minor's parent or legal guardian when the loan is made, or the minor has the written consent of his or her parent or legal guardian, which is presented at the time of the loan, or earlier; *and*
	
	  (b) The minor is being loaned the firearm for a lawful, recreational sport, including, but not limited to, competitive shooting, or agricultural, ranching, or hunting activity or hunting education, or a motion picture, television, or video production, or entertainment or theatrical event, the nature of which involves the use of a firearm; *and*
	
	  (c) The duration of the loan does not exceed the time that is reasonably necessary to engage in the activity; *and*
	
	  (d) The duration of the loan does not, in any event, exceed ten days.

PENAL CODE SECTION	EXEMPTION
P.C. § 31820	The loan of a firearm if all the following requirements are satisfied: (1) The firearm is unloaded; *and* (2) The loan is made by a person who is not a dealer but is an FFL; *and* (3) The loan is made to a person who possesses a valid entertainment firearms permit issued under Chapter 2 (commencing with Section 29500) of Division 8; *and* (4) The firearm is loaned solely as a prop in a motion picture, television, video, theatrical, or other entertainment production event; *and* (5) The person loaned the firearm retains a photocopy of the entertainment firearms permit as proof of compliance with these requirements
P.C. § 31825	The loan of the a firearm if all the following requirements are satisfied: (1) The firearm is unloaded; *and* (2) The loan is made by a dealer; *and* (3) The loan is made to a person who possesses a valid firearms permit issued in accordance with Chapter 2 (commencing with P.C. section 29500) of Division 8; *and* (4) The firearm is loaned solely for use as a prop in a motion picture, television, video, theatrical, or other entertainment event; *and* (5) The dealer must retains a copy of the entertainment firearms permit as proof of compliance with this requirement

b. Firearm Safe-Handling Demonstration

Anyone acquiring a firearm (long gun or handgun) must perform a safe-handling demonstration in front of a DOJ Certified Instructor (*i.e.*, the firearm vendor) before receiving the firearm.[91] For example, if you are receiving a pump action long gun, you must demonstrate, among other things, that you can safely open the ejection port, visually and physically inspect the chamber to ensure the firearm is unloaded, that you can remove the firearm safety device, and engage the safety.[92] The

---

[91] P.C. §§ 26850, 26860.

[92] *Firearm Safety Certificate, Manual*, CAL. DEPT. OF JUSTICE, OFFICE OF THE ATTORNEY GENERAL (Jan. 2015), *available at* https://oag.ca.gov/sites/all/files/agweb/pdfs/firearms/forms/hscman.pdf (last visited July 11, 2017).

dealer may assist you during the demonstration if needed. Anyone who is exempt from the FSC requirement is also exempt from the safe-handling demonstration (see subsection above).

As many gun owners may remember, prior to January 1, 2015, only those who were purchasing handguns were required to perform a safe-handling demonstration. But, this all changed when the California Legislature passed Assembly Bill (AB) 683.[93]

Under this bill, the DOJ was required to adopt regulations before January 1, 2015, that establish FSC regulations and a long gun safe-handling demonstration requirement that included, at a minimum, the loading and unloading of the long gun.[94] When January 1, 2015, rolled around, the DOJ had not promulgated or established any kind of regulations for the long gun safe-handling demonstration, despite the fact that they were required to do so under the law. Instead, the DOJ attempted to underhandedly create an FSC and safe-handling program by sending a letter to firearm dealers outlining the new procedures that added additional requirements on DOJ Certified Instructors that did not exist before. For example, under the temporary regulations Certified Instructors are required to obtain a COE, have access to a personal computer, printer, and email; and only allow Instructors to accept payments from major credit cards. As a result, the California Rifle & Pistol Association, FFLGuard, and several individual gun owners and firearm instructors sued the DOJ in *Belemjian v. Harris*.[95]

Ultimately, this lawsuit pushed the DOJ to promulgate temporary emergency regulations for the FSC and safe-handling demonstration requirement. As a result, the lawsuit was dismissed.[96] But, the DOJ was still required to create an adopt permanent regulations for the FSC and safe-handling demonstration program.

After promulgating permanent regulations, pro-gun groups and concerned citizens submitted public comments to voice their opinions about some of the burdensome and unworkable requirements contained in the FSC regulations. But, the DOJ ignored the hundreds of public comments it received and chose not to change anything about its regulations. On March 23, 2016, the Office of Administrative finally approved the DOJ's permanent regulations. These regulations can now be found at Cal. Code Regs. tit. 11, sections 4250-4259.

---

[93] *See* AB 683, 2013-2014, Leg. Counsel's Digest (Cal. 2014), *available at* http://leginfo.legislature.ca.gov/faces/billNavClient.xhtml?bill_id=201320140SB683 (last visited July 11, 2017).

[94] P.C. § 26860(b).

[95] *See* Verified Complaint for Declaratory and Injunctive Relief and Petition for Writ of Mandate, *Belemjian v. Harris*, No. 15 CECG00029 (Cal. Super. Ct. Jan. 6, 2015), *available at* http://michellawyers.com/wp-content/uploads/2015/01/Complaint.pdf (last visited July 11, 2017).

[96] *See* Judgement of Dismissal, *Belemjian v. Harris*, No. 15 CECG 00029 (Cal. Super. Ct. Jan. 6, 2015), *available at* http://michellawyers.com/wp-content/uploads/2015/01/Belemjian_Judgment-of-Dismissal-After-Sustaining-of-Demurrer-to-Firsts-Amended-Complaint-Without-Leave-to-Amend.pdf (last visited July 11, 2017).

B. Additional Handgun Purchase Requirements[97]

1. Only One Handgun Purchase Every 30 Days

You are not allowed to purchase, or even apply to purchase, more than one handgun within any 30-day period.[98]

First-time violators who apply to purchase more than one handgun within any 30-day period may be fined up to $50.[99] A second violation can be punished with a fine up to $100, and a third violation is a misdemeanor.[100]

There are exceptions to this restriction. Specifically, the following people, agencies, and facilities are exempt from the one handgun every 30-day restriction:

(1) Any law enforcement agency; and

(2) Any agency duly authorized to perform law enforcement duties; *and*

(3) Any state or local correctional facility; *and*

(4) Any private security company licensed to do business in California; *and*

(5) Any person who is properly identified as a full-time paid peace officer,[101] who is authorized to, and does, carry a firearm during the course and scope of his or her employment as a peace officer; *and*

(6) Any motion picture, television, or video production company or entertainment or theatrical company whose production by its nature involves the use of a firearm; *and*

(7) Any person who may claim an exemption to the waiting period under P.C. section 27600-27620 (exceptions relating to law enforcement), P.C. section 27650-27670 (exceptions only to waiting period), or P.C. section 27700-27750 (exceptions to the restrictions on delivery of a firearm); *and*

(8) Any transaction conducted through a licensed firearm dealer under P.C. section 28050-28070 (private party transfers); *and*

---

[97] See Chapter 8 and 9 for restrictions on which handguns an FFL can lawfully sell in California.

[98] P.C. § 27535(a). In 2015, the D.C. Circuit Court of Appeals ruled that the District of Columbia's one-pistol-per-month rule, among other things, was unconstitutional under the Second Amendment. *Heller v. District of Columbia (Heller III)*, 801 F.3d 264 (D.C. Cir. 2015). Although as of the date of publication, this decision is not yet final (as the request for en banc hearing has been denied but the case has yet to be appealed to the Supreme Court), it may have strong implications for California's one-handgun-per-month rule if it is upheld. This is especially true given the fact that the DOJ has been requiring people who attempt to purchase more than handgun within thirty days to wait an additional thirty days (*starting from the date they unsuccessfully attempted to purchase the second handgun*) before they can lawfully purchase another handgun. Clearly, it would be hard to show that this additional wait, let alone the initial wait, promotes a substantial government interest if the decision in *Heller III* stands. To keep up-to-date on *Heller III*, visit www.crpa.org.

[99] P.C. § 27590(e)(1).

[100] P.C. § 27590(e).

[101] As defined in P.C. sections 830-832.9.

(9) Any person who is licensed as a collected under 18 U.S.C. 921-931 and the regulations issued pursuant thereto, and who has a current COE issued by the DOJ under P.C. section 26700-26725; *and*

(10) The exchange of a handgun where the dealer purchased the firearm from the person seeking the exchange within the 30-day period immediately preceding the date of exchange or replacement; *and*

(11) The replacement of a handgun when the person's handgun was lost or stolen, and the person reported that firearm lost or stolen prior to the completion of the application to purchase to any local law enforcement agency of the city, county, or city and county, in which the person resides; *and*

(12) The return of any handgun to its owner; *and*

(13) A community college that is certified by the Commission on Peace Officer Standards and Training (POST) to present the law enforcement academy basic course or other commission-certified law enforcement training.[102]

This restriction does *not* apply to intra-familial transfers or transfers due to the operation of law, and it does not apply to PPTs (discussed below).

2. Proof of Residency

In addition to providing proof of your identification and age to obtain a *handgun*, under California law you must also provide documentation that you are a California resident.[103] The address that is considered your "residence" is not explained in the Penal Code. But, California Government Code (Cal. Gov't Code) section 244 sheds some light on what may be considered your place of "residence" in California.

In determining your place of residence, the following criteria apply:

(1) It is the place where one remains when not called elsewhere for labor or other special or temporary purpose, and to which he or she returns in seasons of repose.

(2) There can only be one residence.

(3) A residence cannot be lost until another is gained.

(4) The residence of the parent with whom an unmarried minor child maintains his or her place of abode is the residence of such unmarried minor child.

(5) The residence of an unmarried minor who has a parent living cannot be changed by his or her own act.

(6) The residence can be changed only by the union of act and intent.

---

[102] P.C. § 27535(b).
[103] P.C. § 26845.

(7) A married person shall have the right to retain his or her legal residence in the State of California notwithstanding the legal residence or domicile of his or her spouse.[104]

Under California law you can prove residency by using one of the documents listed in Table 4.3, such as

(1) A utility bill from the last three months; *or*

(2) A residential lease; *or*

(3) A property deed; *or*

(4) Military permanent duty station orders showing assignment within this state, or other residency evidence allowed by the DOJ.[105]

Each of these documents, except for military permanent duty station orders,[106] must meet certain requirements under the California Code of Regulations (Cal. Code Regs.) before they can be accepted.[107]

Issues have occurred with people being unable to make this documentary showing; for example, those living at a place where their name is not on any deed, lease, or utility bill. If you find yourself in this situation, contact a lawyer with experience in firearms law.

---

[104] Cal. Gov't Code § 244.

[105] Cal. Code Regs. tit. 11, § 4045; P.C. § 26845.

[106] Although the California Code of Regulations outlines the requirements for utility bills, residential leases, and property deeds, they do not outline requirements for when a person's military permanent duty station orders can be accepted as proof of residency in California. *See* Cal. Code Regs. tit. 11, § 4045. Therefore, it is unclear as to when a person's military permanent duty station orders would be sufficient to prove residency. For example, is there a specific date or time frame that the permanent duty station orders must have been issued in order for it to be acceptable? This question remain unanswered by the Penal Code and the California Code of Regulations. But, it would appear military permanent duty station orders showing assignment in California are sufficient to meet the residency requirement, regardless of when they were issued.

[107] A list of acceptable forms for "Proof of Residency" can be found at: https://oag.ca.gov/firearms/dlrfaqs#13G (last visited July 11, 2017).

Table 4.3

PROOF OF RESIDENCY REQUIREMENT
AN ADDITIONAL REQUIREMENT WHEN PURCHASING HANDGUNS IN CALIFORNIA

In addition to providing proof of your identity, you must also provide documentation that you are a California resident if you are attempting to purchase a handgun in California. Any of the following documents will be accepted to show proof of residency[108]:

Utility Bill: A utility bill is a statement of charges for providing direct services to your residence. This includes either a physical connection (*i.e.*, a landline telephone, water, gas connection, etc.) or a telemetric connection (*i.e.*, satellite TV, or radio broadcast service bill) to a non-mobile, fixed antenna reception device. The utility bill must state the following in order to fulfill the proof of residency requirements:

(1) A date that is within three months of the current date; *and*

(2) Either your current residential address as declared on the DROS form or your address (or change of address) as it appears on (or attached to) your California driver license or California ID.

Residential Lease: A Residential Lease is either a signed and dated contract by which a tenant agrees to pay some amount or provides other consideration for the right to occupy a residence for a specified period of time, or a rental agreement signed and dated, in which the tenant agrees to pay some amount or provide other consideration at fixed intervals for the right to occupy a residence. The lease must state the following:

(1) Your name; *and*

(2) Either your current residential address as declared on the DROS form or your address (or change of address) as it appears on (or attached to) your California driver license or California ID.

Property Deed: A property deed is a valid deed of trust for your current residence that identifies you as the grantee of trust, or a valid Certificate of Title issued by a licensed title insurance company that identifies you as a title holder to your property of current residence. The property deed must state the following:

(1) Your name; *and*

(2) Either your current residential address as declared on the DROS form or your address (or change of address) as it appears on (or attached to) your California driver license or California ID.

Other Evidence of Residency: The DOJ may accept other forms of proof of residence. This includes a valid peace officer credential issued by a California law enforcement agency to an active, reserve, or retired peace officer. This other proof of residency also includes a current government-issued license, permit, or registration (other than a California driver license or ID) that has a specific expiration date or period of validity. The license, permit, or registration must include the following:

(1) Your name; *and*

(2) Either your current residential address as declared on the DROS form or your address (or change of address) as it appears on (or attached to) your California driver license or California ID.

---

[108] *See* CAL. CODE REGS. tit. 11, § 4045.

Table 4.4

QUICK GUIDE: THE PROCESS AND REQUIRED MATERIALS TO PURCHASE A FIREARM FROM A LICENSED FIREARMS DEALER IN CALIFORNIA & CONDUCT PRIVATE PARTY TRANSFERS

PURCHASING FIREARMS (HANDGUNS & LONG GUNS)

The following is a quick checklist of the process and sale requirements that must be met before you can purchase a firearm (handgun or long gun) from a licensed dealer in California (see above for the specific requirements of each):

BEWARE!

Federal law requires that you bring a valid *government-issued* "identification document" that has your name, picture, date of birth, and *current* home address.

If your identification, such as your California driver license, does not reflect your current home address, then it will not meet the identification requirement and an additional government-issued document is required.

Remember, not providing your current home address and providing a false address is a violation of federal law.

✓ **Identification, Age, and Address**: In order to purchase a firearm, you must have some form of valid identification that presents clear evidence of your identity, age, and address. This requires you to have a California driver license or California identification card. Military identification accompanied by permanent duty station orders indicating a posting in California will suffice.

✓ **Complete Federal Form 4473**: This form is required when any firearm is *transferred* to you by an FFL. If you are a *full-time paid peace officer*, however, then you are not required to fill out this form if you certify, on agency letterhead with an authorized signature, that a records check shows you do not have a misdemeanor domestic violence conviction and will use the firearm for official duties. A single form can be used for all firearms purchased at the same time.

✓ **Complete a Dealer's Record of Sales (DROS) Form**: California law also requires a completed DROS form. As of January 1, 2014, the information required on the form for all firearms includes (1) firearm type; (2) transaction type; (3) waiting period requirement exemptions; (4) and your name, address, birth date, etc. Your thumbprint must also be taken and, as of January 1, 2014, the FFL is required to give you a copy of the DROS form at the time the firearm is delivered to you.[109] A separate DROS form is required for each firearm transferred.

✓ **Ten-Day Waiting Period**: You must wait ten days (meaning ten 24-hour periods) from when your DROS form is submitted until you may lawfully receive any firearm transferred from an FFL. But, certain people are exempt from the ten-day waiting period. See Section I(A)(6) of this Chapter for a list of people who are exempt.

✓ **Receive Required Lock Device and Warnings**: California law requires that all firearms transferred by an FFL be accompanied by an approved "firearm safety device" (with certain exceptions). Federal law requires a safety device for handguns delivered by a dealer. California law also requires warning language or labels upon delivery.

✓ **Firearm Safety Requirement**: Anyone purchasing a firearm must present a Firearm Safety Certificate (FSC) to the dealer, and anyone acquiring a firearm must perform a safe handling demonstration before receiving a firearm from a licensed firearm dealer.[110] There are exceptions to this requirement.

✓ **Firearm Safe Handling Demonstration**: Before receiving your firearm, California law requires you to perform a safe handling demonstration in front of a DOJ Certified Instructor. If you are physically unable to perform the demonstration, you may be exempt from the demonstration requirement if you have a letter from your physician stating you are physically unable to perform it.

---

[109] P.C. §§ 28210(e), 28215(e).
[110] P.C. §§ 26840, 26860, 31615.

QUICK GUIDE: THE PROCESS AND REQUIRED MATERIALS TO PURCHASE A FIREARM FROM A LICENSED FIREARMS DEALER IN CALIFORNIA & CONDUCT PRIVATE PARTY TRANSFERS

ADDITIONAL REQUIREMENTS FOR PURCHASING HANDGUNS

There are additional requirements that you must meet if you intend on purchasing a handgun from a licensed firearms dealer in California:

✓ **Proof of Residency**: In addition to providing proof of your identification and age, you must also provide documentation that you are a California resident. See Section I(B)(2) of this Chapter for information on how to determine where "your place of residence" is located.

BEWARE!

You are not allowed to purchase, or even apply to purchase, more than one handgun from a dealer within a **30-day waiting period** in California. First-time violators who apply to purchase more than one handgun within this waiting period may be fined up to $50, a second violation may result in a fine up to $100, and a third violation is a misdemeanor.

There are exceptions to this restriction, however. See Section (I)(B)(2) of this Chapter for the specific exceptions.

II. PRIVATE PARTY FIREARM TRANSFERS

A PPT occurs when firearms are transferred between two private parties, neither of whom is a California-licensed firearms dealer.[111] Both California and federal law have different requirements for *interstate* and *intrastate* PPTs and for handguns versus long guns. With few exceptions, PPTs must be processed by an FFL.[112] Not using an FFL for a PPT is a misdemeanor, and you can be prosecuted for a felony if the firearm is a handgun.[113] FFLs are *required* to process PPTs upon request unless the FFL does *not* sell, transfer, or keep a handgun inventory.[114] In other words, an FFL can choose not to process PPTs involving handguns if they do not actually sell handguns. But, an FFL must process non-handgun PPTs.

Most of the same requirements for FFL transfers to individual buyers also apply to a PPT. A 4473 and DROS forms are still required, but the DROS form must include both the transferee's *and* the transferor's information.[115] Also, a FSC and safe handling demonstration will be required as discussed above.[116] If the firearm is a handgun, the transferee must also show proof of California residency. The handgun must also have a locking device when the FFL delivers it to the transferee, or

---

[111] You should be aware that an FFL that is *not* licensed *in California* pursuant to P.C. section 26700 is treated like a normal person and not a "dealer" for the purpose of these transfers.

[112] Under California law, years ago transfers by individuals did not need to go through a licensed firearms dealer and no record of the transaction needed to be retained. Through 1990, handguns could still be transferred between two individuals who resided in California, provided that the individuals personally knew each other, and long guns could be freely transferred between residents of California. Provided that the firearm is not illegal for you to possess currently, there is no requirement that you register your firearm or go back through a licensed firearms dealer.

[113] P.C. §§ 27545, 27590(c)(5).

[114] P.C. § 28065.

[115] *See* P.C. § 28060(c). The transferor's information is required in case the transferee is prohibited from acquiring firearms. The DOJ can conduct a background check on the transferor to determine if returning the firearm is legal.

[116] P.C. § 26860.

the transferee must meet one of the exceptions to the locking device requirement (discussed above).

Finally, PPTs are exempt from the "one handgun per month" limitation.[117] This means you can *buy* as many handguns as you want in a month if you do so through a PPT. But, this does *not* mean you can *transfer* as many handguns or firearms as you want in a month. If you are not an FFL, you may not make "frequent" transactions or engage in the business" of dealing firearms. This is explained in detail below.

In addition to the DROS and other transfer fees, an FFL may charge a fee to process a PPT, but it cannot be more than $10 per firearm.[118]

If during the ten-day waiting period it is discovered you are prohibited from possessing firearms, the FFL can return the firearm to the transferor before the waiting period expires, unless the FFL determines the transferor is also prohibited. If this happens, the FFL must deliver the firearm to the sheriff or police chief who will dispose of the firearm accordingly.[119] Recently, however, law enforcement agencies refused to accept these firearms, not realizing that state law requires the FFL to surrender the firearms when this happens.

Lastly, the FFL is required to provide the seller and purchaser in the PPT a copy of the DROS form with the personal information of the other party redacted (*i.e.*, blacked out or removed).[120]

---

[117] P.C. § 27535(b).
[118] P.C. § 28055.
[119] P.C. § 28050(d).
[120] P.C. §§ 28210(e)-(f), 28215(e)-(f).

Table 4.5

PRIVATE PARTY FIREARM TRANSFERS

WHAT IS A PRIVATE PARTY TRANSFER?

A private party transfer (PPT) occurs when firearms are transferred between two *private* individuals, neither of whom is a licensed California firearms dealer.

CHECKLIST FOR A PRIVATE PARTY TRANSFER

✓ **Almost All PPTs Must Be Conducted Through a Federal Firearms Licensee (FFL):** Under California law a PPT must be conducted through an FFL. The seller or transferor of the firearm must deliver the firearm to the FFL who will retain the firearm for the duration of the transfer. After the transaction is complete and the ten-day waiting period has passed, the FFL will deliver the firearm to the buyer or transferee.

> **REMEMBER**
>
> PPTs are exempt from the "one handgun per month" limitation. This means you can *buy* as many handguns as you want if done through a PPT. But, you cannot *transfer or sell* as many handguns or firearms as you want, as there are limits under California and federal law.

✓ **DROS Form:** Under California law both the *seller or transferor* and the *buyer or transferee* of a PPT must provide their information in the DROS form (in contrast, with non-PPTs, the seller/transferor need not provide information). As of January 1, 2014, the dealer is required to provide the seller or transferor and the buyer or transferee this form (with the other parties' personal information redacted) when the firearm is delivered.

✓ **Federal Form 4473:** The transferee or buyer must also complete a federal Form 4473 with all the necessary information.

✓ **Handgun and Firearm Safety Certificates:** If you are purchasing a handgun, or one is being transferred to you, then you must have an FSC.

✓ **Perform Safe Handling Demonstration**: Unless you meet an exception to the requirement you must perform a safe handling demonstration.

✓ **Ten-Day Waiting Period:** You must wait ten days (meaning ten 24-hour periods) from when your DROS Form is submitted until you may lawfully receive any firearm transferred from a PPT.

✓ **Locking Device and Warnings:** When the FFL delivers to the purchaser or transferee a handgun, the handgun must be accompanied by a locking device and warning language or labels. As for other firearms, they need to be accompanied by a locking device or other exception to the lock requirement when the FFL delivers them to you. For more information, see Section I of this Chapter.

✓ **Additional Proof of Residency (Handguns Only):** If you have purchased a handgun or it is being transferred to you in a PPT, you are still required to show proof to the FFL that you are a resident of the state.

III. DEALER LICENSE REQUIREMENTS AND SELLING YOUR FIREARMS

A. Federal Law

Federal law has a different definition of what it means to be a dealer of firearms. Under federal law, it is unlawful for any person[121] "except a licensed importer, licensed manufacturer, or licensed *dealer*, to *engage in the business* of importing, manufacturing, or dealing in firearms, or in the course of such business to ship, transport, or receive any firearm in interstate or foreign commerce."[122]

Both the GCA and the Code of Federal Regulations (C.F.R.) define a "dealer" as:

(1) Any person *engaged in the business* of selling firearms at *wholesale or retail*; *or*

(2) Any person engaged in the business of repairing firearms or of making or fitting special barrels, stocks, or trigger mechanisms to firearms; *or*

(3) Any person who is a pawnbroker.[123]

The Code of Federal Regulations defines a person "engaged in the business" as:

[A] person who devotes time, attention, and labor to dealing in firearms as a regular course of trade or business *with the principal objective of livelihood and profit* through the repetitive purchase and resale of firearms, but such term shall not include a person who makes occasional sales, exchanges, or purchases of firearms for the enhancement of a personal collection or for a hobby, or who sells all or part of his personal collection of firearms.[124]

The phrase "with the principal objective of livelihood and profit" means that the underlying intent of the sale or disposition of firearms is predominantly one of obtaining livelihood and pecuniary gain, as opposed to other reasons, such as improving or liquidating a personal firearms collection. The Code of Federal Regulations notes that proof of profit is not required for anyone engaged in the "regular and repetitive purchase and disposition of firearms for criminal purposes or

---

[121] Under the GCA, the term "person" includes "any individual, corporation, company, association, firm, partnership, society, or joint stock company." 18 U.S.C. § 921(a)(1).

[122] 18 U.S.C. § 922(a)(1)(A) (emphasis added). "The term 'interstate or foreign commerce' includes commerce between any place in a State and any place outside of that State, or within any possession of the United States (not including the Canal Zone) or the District of Columbia, but such term does not include commerce between places within the same State but through any place outside of that State. The term 'State' includes the District of Columbia, the Commonwealth of Puerto Rico, and the possessions of the United States (not including the Canal Zone)." 18 U.S.C. § 921(a)(2).

[123] 18 U.S.C. § 921(a)(11); 27 C.F.R. § 478.11. 18 U.S.C. section 921(a)(11) also defines a "licensed dealer" as anyone licensed under the provisions of 18 U.S.C. section 921.

[124] 18 U.S.C. § 921(a)(21)(C) (emphasis added).

terrorism."[125] Additionally, the Code of Federal Regulations states that you may be considered a dealer even if you engage in these activities on a part-time basis.

It is not unusual for people to believe they are fully complying with the law when they comply only with California's dealer's license requirements. But you must comply with both state and federal laws! Buying and selling *a few* firearms over the course of a year (while complying with both state and federal transfer requirements) might be legal under state and federal law. But conducting multiple transactions, buying and selling a number of firearms, and/or buying and immedi- ately selling a recently purchased firearm may be an indication that you are *dealing* in firearms under federal law. *Dealing* in firearms without the proper licenses has some serious consequences.[126]

If you decide you do not want to possess a firearm anymore, there are some things to consider. Remember you must abide by the requirements discussed in the book relating to PPTs, interstate sales, transfers that don't need to go through a dealer, and laws relating to prohibited persons. The simplest option may be selling your firearm to a licensed firearms dealer.

B. California Law

In most cases, firearm transfers by anyone without an FFL must be "infrequent," even when the transfers are all processed through an FFL.[127] For handguns, "in- frequent" under California law means making no more than five transactions in a "calendar year." A "transaction" in this context means a single transfer of any number of handguns.[128] This means that, under California law, you could sell 100 handguns or more, all at once, without violating the law, as long as you do not do this more than four additional times that same "calendar year."[129]

A "calendar year" begins January 1 and ends December 31.[130] By ending in De- cember rather than being *any* twelve-month period, use of the term "calendar year" in this context is significant. It means you can lawfully make all five of your hand- gun transactions for the year in December and still make up to another five the fol- lowing January, only a month later, so long as you do not make any other transfers until the following January. Again, the ATF may be very interested in your activities

---

[125] 18 U.S.C. § 921(a)(22).

[126] For example, in 2015, former Sacramento County Sheriff's Deputy Ryan McGowan was found guilty of engaging in the business of dealing in firearms without a license when he used his position as a sheriff's deputy to purchase "off-roster" handguns (see Chapter 9) and resold them at inflated prices to private individuals in California. *See Jury Returns Guilty Verdict for Former Sacramento County Sheriff's Deputy and Federal Firearms Licensee in Firearm Straw-Buyer Scheme,* Dep't of Justice, U.S. ATTORNEY'S OFFICE, EASTERN DISTRICT OF CALIFORNIA (June 11, 2015), *available at* https://www.atf.gov/news/pr/jury-returns-guilty-verdicts-former-sacramento-county- sheriff%E2%80%99s-deputy-and-federal-firearms (last visit July 11, 2017).

[127] P.C. §§ 26500, 26520.

[128] P.C. § 16730.

[129] Of course, if you are transferring firearms in the hundreds, the ATF might want to ask you a couple of questions about dealing firearms without a license. This was discussed in the previous section.

[130] BLACK'S LAW DICTIONARY 217 (8th ed. 2004).

in this situation and may want to ask you a few questions to determine whether you were dealing in firearms.

For *non*-handguns, "infrequent" means transfers that are "occasional and without regularity."[131] Because this is a vague standard, it is unclear how often you can lawfully transfer non-handguns. Also, the term "transaction" is not defined for non-handguns as it is for handguns. Presumably, "transaction" means the same thing for both handguns and non-handguns, meaning you can transfer as many non-handguns as you want as long as it is done in a single transaction with the same person.

1. Exceptions

You can transfer as many unloaded "antique firearms" as often as you want without violating the law. Just make sure they are actually "antique firearms" (see Chapter 2). A "Gun Show Trader"[132] may transfer up to 75 used[133] non-handguns in a *calendar* year spanning a total of 12 total gun shows (or similar events). And no more than 15 can be transferred during any given event.[134] But be mindful of federal requirements, law enforcement from both state and federal agencies attend gun shows in undercover capacities and try to entice gun owner to forego the California and federal requirements for gun sales (see Chapter 1).

IV. INTERSTATE FIREARM PURCHASES AND TRANSFERS

A. Transfers From Out-of-State Dealers

California residents can purchase firearms from out-of-state FFLs as long as the transfer would be lawful in California (*e.g.*, the firearm cannot be an "assault weapon" or an "unsafe handgun").[135] But, there are certain restrictions.

Under federal law, an FFL may transfer *rifles or shotguns* over the counter to an out-of-state resident if both states' laws and requirements are satisfied.[136] Yet, given California's mandatory ten-day wait on all firearm transactions and the DROS process, an out-of-state dealer cannot abide by California's stringent transfer requirements. Therefore, barring limited exception to the federal requirement or dual residency, almost all firearms a California resident acquires from outside of California must be passed through a California FFL.

---

[131] P.C. § 16730(a)(2).

[132] A non-California FFL with a COE.

[133] "Used" means the firearm has been previously sold at retail and is more than three years old. P.C. § 17310.

[134] P.C. §§ 26500(a), 26525(a).

[135] 18 U.S.C. § 922(b)(2); 27 C.F.R. § 478.99(b). Firearms that are illegal to possess or have restrictions on transfer in California are discussed in Chapters 8 and 9.

[136] 18 U.S.C. § 922(b)(3).

In addition, given California's requirement that all firearms purchasers have a valid California DMV-issued ID (see above), it is also difficult for out-of-state residents to purchase long guns in California, even though it is legal for them to do so under federal law.

Your "state of residence" is the state where you are present and where you also intend to make your home, and that you can be a "resident" of more than one state.[137] The ATF has explained that:

> An individual resides in a State if he or she is present in a State with the intention of making a home in that State. Ownership of a home or land within a given State is not sufficient, by itself, to establish a State of residence. However, ownership of a home or land within a particular State is not required to establish presence and intent to make a home in that State. Furthermore, temporary travel, such as short term stays, vacations, or other transient acts in a State are not sufficient to establish a State of residence because the individual demonstrates no intention of making a home in that State.[138]

Under federal law, an out-of-state FFL cannot transfer a firearm directly to you if the firearm you are purchasing is *not a rifle or a shotgun* (*i.e.,* a lawful handgun or other non-long gun). Instead, to lawfully transfer the firearm to you, the out-of-state FFL must ship the firearm to an FFL in California, who must then process the transfer in accordance with California law (*i.e.,* the ten-day wait, DROS, etc.) before the firearm can finally be delivered to you.[139]

California law also provides that an out-of-state FFL cannot transfer a firearm directly to you, unless an exception applies.[140] Unlike the federal restriction, the California restriction applies to all firearm purchases (*i.e.,* handguns *and* long guns).[141] That means, in order to lawfully transfer a firearm to you under California law, an out-of-state FFL must ship the firearm to an FFL in California, who must then process the transfer in accordance with California law before the firearm can be transferred to you.

Never assume that because you are in compliance with California law, your concerns are over. You must also comply with *federal law* (and vice versa). For example, a number of the exceptions to the California law allow you to acquire firearms pursuant to a permit, or because they are specific firearms regulated by certain statutes. But, under federal law, you are still required to transfer the firearm

---

[137] 27 C.F.R. § 478.11.

[138] ATF Rul. 2010-6 (Nov. 10, 2010).

[139] 18 U.S.C. §§ 922(a)(3), 922(b)(3). In 2015, this requirement was ruled unconstitutional under the Second Amendment by a federal court in Texas. *See Mance v. Holder*, 4:25-cv-539-O (N.D. Tx. Feb. 11, 2015) (final judgment). The U.S. DOJ appealed this decision to the 5th Circuit. But, as of the date of publication, an opinion has yet to be released. To keep up-to-date on the progress of this case, visit www.CalGunLaws.com.

[140] P.C. § 27585.

[141] P.C. § 27585.

through a dealer, and, in certain situations relating to NFA "firearms," seek ATF approval before receiving the firearm in California.

Also remember that, "dual residents," *i.e.,* those who can establish residency in more than one state, are residents of the state that they are currently "residing" in (see Section I(A)(3)(c)(iii) of this Chapter).

B. Interstate Private Party Transfers

Federal law requires PPTs between residents of different states to take place through an FFL in the *recipient's* home state.[142] Regardless of whether an out-of-state transfer is from an FFL or an individual, the California FFL can charge a service fee for any amount they want, so determine what your FFL charges ahead of time. Bear in mind that this federal restriction includes transfers between family members, so a father living in Missouri cannot give a son living in California a firearm without the transfer going through an FFL in California.

There are some exceptions to this requirement. For instance, a non-licensee can transport into or receive in their state of residence, any firearm that they obtained through bequest or intestate succession.[143] In other words, if you inherit a firearm from a resident of another state by bequest or intestate succession (regardless of whether you are a family member of the person who passed away), federal law allows you to take that firearm in the other state and transport it back into California without using an FFL.[144] But note, under California law, you can only bypass the need for an FFL if you inherit the firearm from an immediate family member.[145] This assumes that the firearm is lawful for you to possess in California in the first place and there are also exceptions for firearms transferred to government and military agencies.[146] Restrictions (or lack thereof) on interstate ammunition sales are discussed below.

Under the new DROS Entry System (DES), California appears to allow PPTs from an individual who doesn't reside in California to a Californian. Previously, under the old DROS system (prior to January 1, 2014), FFLs were only able to input information on California residents into the DROS system. Currently, the DES accepts identification from individuals who reside outside the state of California as transferors in a PPT. If, as discussed above, a transaction in a PPT is denied because the recipient is prohibited from receiving and possessing firearms, California law requires the immediate return of the firearm to the transferor.[147] Presumably, this return would require the California FFL to send the firearm to an FFL in the transferor's home state, who would then return the firearm. Despite this DOJ still prohibits PPTs from an out-of-state individual even when that person is physically

---

[142] 18 U.S.C. § 922(g)(3), (b)(3).

[143] 18 U.S.C. § 922(a)(3), 27 C.F.R. §§ 478.29; 478.30.

[144] 18 U.S.C. § 922(a)(3); 27 C.F.R. § 478.30(a).

[145] P.C. § 27875. Discussed below.

[146] *See* 18 U.S.C. § 925(a).

[147] P.C. § 28050(d).

in California and at the FFL. Dealers are required to treat this transaction as if the dealer purchased the firearm and is selling it to the PPT recipient (therefore restrictions like "unsafe handgun," discussed in Chapter 9, apply).

Table 4.6

INTERSTATE FIREARMS PURCHASES AND TRANSFERS
TRANSFERS FROM OUT-OF-STATE DEALERS
General Rule: A California resident can purchase a firearm from an out-of-state FFL as long as the transfer would be lawful in California (*e.g.*, the firearm cannot be an "assault weapon" or "unsafe handgun").
Restrictions: There are certain restrictions on purchasing firearms from out-of-state dealers.
✓ **Restrictions on Firearms That Are Not Rifles or Shotguns**: Under federal law, an out-of-state FFL cannot transfer a firearm that is not a rifle or a shotgun directly to you. Instead, the firearm must be shipped to a California FFL who will then process the transfer according to California law. This means all pertinent California regulation requirements will be applied to the transfer (see Table 4.4 for these requirements).
✓ **Restrictions on Rifles or Shotguns**: An out-of-state FFL could transfer California-legal rifles or shotguns to you if *both* states' laws are complied with. Because an out-of-state FFL cannot comply with California's requirements, this exception does not apply to California residents.
INTERSTATE PRIVATE PARTY TRANSFERS (PPTs)
Federal Rules: Federal law requires PPTs between residents of different states to take place through an FFL in the *recipient's* home state. For information on the federal laws concerning the shipping or mailing of firearms, read this section.
California Rules: California law appears to require both parties to be present at a PPT. But, this requirement remains contested. DOJ will require the dealer to treat this transfer as a dealer sale to the recipient of the firearm.

1. Shipping Firearms

There are federal laws governing the shipment of firearms that you must comply with when shipping firearms. Long guns may be mailed through the USPS or a private carrier, as long as they are unloaded and comply with any other rules of the carrier.[148] Of course, you should not send firearms into a state where their possession and/or importation is illegal unless there is an exception that applies to you and/or the recipient.

For handguns, the laws differ depending on who is shipping the firearm. If you are not a licensed manufacturer of firearms, an FFL, or an authorized agent of the

---

[148] *Mailability Requirements for Firearms*, USPS, http://pe.usps.com/text/pub52/pub52c4_009.htm#ep308518 (last visited July 11, 2017); *Shipping Firearms*, UPS, http://www.ups.com/content/us/en/resources/ship/packaging/guidelines/firearms.html (last visited July 11, 2017). There are special requirements for shipping most NFA firearms (defined in Chapter 9) across state lines that are not addressed here.

federal or state government, you can only ship handguns via a common or contract carrier[149] (such as FedEx or UPS). Additionally, you can only send handguns to:

(1) Yourself in another state where you intend to hunt or engage in any other lawful activity, so long as the package is sent in the care of another person in the state, and upon reaching its destination, persons other than the owner do not open the package or take possession of the firearm;[150] *or*

(2) An FFL for repair or any other lawful purpose (and the FFL may return it to you without transferring through an FFL in your state of residence).[151]

Finally, federal law requires a non-licensee to provide *written* notice to the common carrier that the package contains a firearm.[152] If you have a federal firearm license, handguns may be shipped via USPS so long as you comply with their procedures.[153] Be sure to confirm the policies and procedures for shipping firearms with the private carrier, since they may change unexpectedly.

C. Exemptions to California's Restriction on Out-of-State Transfers

As explained above, California law generally prohibits individuals from importing, bringing, or transporting into California, any firearms that he or she purchased after January 1, 2015, from outside of the state, unless the firearm is first transferred through an FFL.[154] But, there are a limited number of exceptions to this restriction (note that the federal restrictions still apply). Specifically, the following people, firearms, and transactions are exempt from this restriction:

---

[149] *See* 18 U.S.C. § 1715 (prohibiting handguns from being sent using the USPS).

[150] *Top 10 Frequently Asked Firearms Questions and Answers*, U.S. DEPT. OF JUSTICE, BUREAU OF ALCOHOL, TOBACCO, FIREARMS AND EXPLOSIVES, https://www.atf.gov/files/firearms/industry/0501-firearms-top-10-qas.pdf (last visited July 11, 2017).

[151] 18 U.S.C. § 922(a).

[152] 18 U.S.C. § 922(e).

[153] See the USPS website or your local post office for a list of requirements. *Mailability Requirements for Firearms*, USPS, http://pe.usps.com/text/pub52/pub52c4_009.htm#ep308518 (last visited July 11, 2017).

[154] P.C. § 27585.

Table 4.7

Penal Code Section	Exemption
P.C. § 27585(b)(1)	A licensed collector who is subject to and complies with P.C. Section 27565[155]
P.C. § 27585(b)(2)	A dealer, if the dealer is acting in the course and scope of his or her activities as a dealer
P.C. § 27585(b)(3)	A wholesaler, if the wholesaler is acting in the course and scope of his or her activities as a wholesaler
P.C. § 27585(b)(8)	A person who is on the centralized list of exempted federal firearms licensees (FFLs) under P.C. section 28450 if the person is acting within the course and scope of his or her activities as a licensee
P.C. § 27585(b)(4)	A person licensed as an importer of firearms or ammunition or licensed as a manufacturer of firearms or ammunition, in accordance with 18 U.S.C. sections 921-931 and their regulations, if the importer or manufacturer is acting in the course and scope of his or her activities as a licensed importer or manufacturer.
P.C. § 27585(b)(5)	A "personal firearms importer"[156] who is subject to and complies with P.C. section 27560.

---

[155] Relating to the registration of curio or relic firearm(s) when a curio or relic collector brings these firearm(s) acquired outside of the state into California, which is discussed in this chapter.

[156] "Personal firearm importers" are defined and discussed later in this chapter.

Table 4.7

Penal Code Section	Exemption
P.C. §§ 27585(b)(6), 27875(b)	A person who complies with P.C. section 27875(b),[157] provided the following criteria are met: (1) The person acquires ownership of the firearm from an immediate family member by bequest or intestate succession; *and* (2) The person has obtained a valid FSC, except that in the case of a handgun, a valid unexpired HSC may be used; *and* (3) The receipt of any firearm by the individual by bequest or intestate succession is infrequent as defined in P.C. section 16730; *and* (4) Within 30 days of that person taking possession of the firearm and importing, bringing, or transporting it into the state, the person must submit a report to the DOJ, in a manner prescribed by the department, that includes information concerning the individual taking possession of the firearm, how title was obtained and from whom, and a description of the firearm in question.
P.C. § 27585(b)(12)	A firearm regulated pursuant to Article 2 (commencing with Section 33300) of Chapter 8 of Division 10 acquired by a person who holds a permit issued pursuant to Section 33300,[158] if that person is acting within the course and scope of his or her activities as a licensee and in accordance with the terms and conditions of the permit.
P.C. § 27585(b)(10)	A firearm regulated pursuant to Chapter 2 (commencing with P.C. section 30500) of Division 10 acquired by a person who holds a permit issued pursuant to Section 31005,[159] if that person is acting within the course and scope of his or her activities as a licensee and in accordance with the terms and conditions of the permit.

---

[157] As amended by AB 1609. AB 1609, 2013-2014, Leg. Counsel's Digest (Cal. 2014), *available at* https://leginfo.legislature.ca.gov/faces/billNavClient.xhtml?bill_id=201320140AB1609 (last visited July 28, 2017).

[158] Referring to "short-barreled rifles" and "short-barreled shotguns" and the permits required to possess them.

[159] Referring to "assault weapons" and .50 BMG rifles and the permits a person may acquire to lawfully possess, import, make, transport and/or sell these devices under California law, discussed in Chapter 8.

PENAL CODE SECTION	EXEMPTION
P.C. §§ 27585(b)(7), 27920(d)	A person who imports the firearm into this country pursuant to the provisions of 18 U.S.C. section 925(a)(4),[160] and meets the following criteria: (1) The person is not subject to the requirements of P.C. section 27560(imposing requirements on a personal firearm importer upon bringing a firearm into the state); *and* (2) The firearm is not a firearm that is prohibited by any provision listed in P.C. section 16590 (*i.e.*, a "generally prohibited weapon"); *and* (3) The firearm is not an "assault weapon"; *and* (4) The firearm is not a machinegun; *and* (5) The firearm is not a .50 BMG rifle; *and* (6) The firearm is not a "destructive device"; *and* (7) The person is 18 years of age or older; *and* (8) Within 30 days of taking possession of the firearm and importing, bringing, or transporting it into this state, the person must submit a report to the DOJ, in a manner described by the department, that includes information concerning the individual taking possession of the firearm, how title was obtained and from whom, and a description of the firearm in question[161]
P.C. § 27585(b)(11)	A firearm regulated pursuant to Chapter 6 (commencing with Section 32610) of Division 10 acquired by a person who holds a permit issued pursuant to Section 32650,[162] if that person is acting within the course and scope of his or her activities as a licensee and in accordance with the terms and conditions of the permit
P.C. § 27585(b)(9)	A firearm regulated pursuant to Chapter 1 (commencing with Section 18710) of Division 5 of Title 2 acquired by a person who holds a permit issued pursuant to Article 3 (commencing with Section 18900) of Chapter 1 of Division 5 of Title 2,[163] if that person is acting within the course and scope of his or her activities as a licensee and in accordance with the terms and conditions of the permit

---

[160] This provision of federal law allows certain members of the United States Armed Forces to bring certain firearms into the United States.

[161] This requirement appears to be at odds with the rule governing military members who are active law enforcement and bring their own firearms into the state. Under P.C. section 17000, members of the Armed Forces do not need to register their personal firearms until they are discharged from active service in California. This new law requires active military members to register their firearms acquired from overseas using this rather obscure federal law.

[162] Referring to "machineguns" and the permits required for possession, manufacture, or transportation of "machineguns" under California law. "Machineguns" are discussed in Chapter 9.

[163] Referring to "destructive devices" and permits issued allowing a person to lawfully possess, manufacture, transport, import, and/or sell a destructive device under California law, as discussed in Chapter 9.

PENAL CODE SECTION	EXEMPTION
P.C. §§ 27585(b)(7), 27920(c)	A person who acquired ownership of the firearm by bequest or intestate succession as a surviving spouse or as the surviving registered domestic partner of the decedent who owned that firearm, and meets the following criteria: (1) If acquisition of the firearm has occurred within California, the receipt of the firearm by the surviving spouse or registered domestic partner would be exempt from the provisions of P.C. section 27545 (i.e., requiring the sale, loan, or transfer of firearm to be completed through a licensed dealer) by virtue of P.C. section 16990 (i.e., taking title or possession of a firearm by operation of law); *and* (2) Within 30 days of taking possession of the firearm and importing, bringing, or transporting it into this state, the person must submit a report to the DOJ, in a manner described by the department, that includes information concerning the individual taking possession of the firearm, how title was obtained and from whom, and a description of the firearm in question; *and* (3) The person obtained a valid FSC, except that in case of a handgun, a valid unexpired HSC may be used

PENAL CODE SECTION	EXEMPTION
P.C. §§ 27585(b)(7), 27920(b)	A person who acquired ownership of a firearm as an executor or administer of an estate, and he or she meets the following criteria: (1) If the firearm has been acquired in California, the receipt of the firearm by the executor or administrator would be exempt from the provisions of P.C. section 27545 (i.e., requiring the sale, loan, or transfer of firearm to be completed through a licensed dealer); *and* (2) Within 30 days of taking possession of the firearm and importing, bringing, or transporting it into California, the executor or administer must submit a report to the DOJ, in a manner proscribed by the department, that includes information concerning himself or herself, *i.e.,* the individual taking possession of the firearm, how title was obtained and from whom, and a description of the firearm in question; *and* (3) If the executor or administrator subsequently acquires ownership of that firearm in an individual capacity, prior to transferring ownership to himself or herself, he or she shall obtain a valid FSC, except that in the case of a handgun, a valid unexpired HSC may be used; *and* (4) The executor or administrator is 18 years of age or older

PENAL CODE SECTION	EXEMPTION
P.C. § 27585(b)(13)	The importation of a firearm into the state, bringing a firearm into the state, or transportation of a firearm into the state, that is regulated by any of the following statutes, if the acquisition of that firearm occurred outside of California and is conducted in accordance with the applicable provisions of the following statutes: (1) Chapter 1 (commencing with P.C. section 18710) of Division 5 of Title 2, relating to "destructive devices" and explosives; *and* (2) P.C. section 24410, relating to cane guns; *and* (3) P.C. section 24510, relating to "firearms that are not immediately recognizable as firearms;" *and* (4) P.C. sections 24610 and 24680, relating to "undetectable firearms;" *and* (5) P.C. section 24710, relating to wallet guns; *and* (6) Chapter 2 (commencing with P.C. section 30500) of Division 10, relating to "assault weapons;"[164] *and* (7) P.C. section 31500, relating to unconventional pistols; *and* (8) P.C. sections 33215 and 33225, inclusive, relating to "short-barreled rifles" and "short-barreled shotguns"; *and* (9) Chapter 6 (commencing with P.C. section 32160) of Division 10, relating to machineguns; *and* (10) P.C. section 33600, relating to zip guns and the exemption in Chapter 1 (commencing with P.C. section 17700) of Division 2 of Title 2, as they relate to zip guns.

---

[164] Oddly, .50 BMG rifles are not mentioned here despite the fact that they are regulated in this Chapter of the Penal Code.

V. LOANING FIREARMS TO ADULTS

Under federal law, you may temporarily loan or rent a firearm to an out-of-state resident who is not prohibited from possessing firearms[165] for lawful sporting purposes if you do not know, or have reasonable cause to believe, that the person is prohibited from receiving or possessing firearms.[166]

California law prior to 2017 stated that a firearm may be *infrequently*[167] loaned between two people who are personally known to each other, as long as the loan does not exceed 30 days (with few exceptions).[168]

For years, gun owners have primarily relied on this old exception when loaning firearms to other individuals because the language of the exception was broad. In 2016, however, the California Legislature amended this exception when it passed Assembly Bill (AB) 1511 and narrowed the scope of who a person can loan a firearm to under this exception. Beginning January 1, 2017, a firearm can only be *infrequently* loaned between any of the following individuals, as long as the loan does not exceed 30 days (with few exceptions):

(1) Spouses or registered domestic partners; *or*

(2) Any parent, child, siblings, grandparent, or grandchild, whether related by consanguinity, adoption, or step relation.[169]

Under this new exception, the person being loaned the firearm must have a valid FSC.[170] If the firearm being loaned in a handgun, then the person being loaned the firearm can also use an unexpired HSC.[171] In addition, if the firearm being loaned is a handgun, it must be registered to the person making the loan as provided in P.C. section 11106.[172]

Since AB 1511 was passed, California gun owners have expressed a lot of concern over whether they can loan firearms in specific situations given that the "personally known" language was removed from the infrequently loan exception. But, keep in mind that there are a number of different exceptions to the dealer requirement that gun owners can still use to loan a firearm to another person without having to go through a licensed firearms dealer. These exceptions include:

---

[165] *See* Chapter 3.

[166] 18 U.S.C. § 922(b)(3).

[167] P.C. § 16730(a).

[168] P.C. § 16730(a).

[169] P.C. § 27880.

[170] P.C. § 27880(e).

[171] P.C. § 27880(e).

[172] P.C. § 27880(f).

Table 4.8

PENAL CODE SECTION	EXEMPTION
P.C. §§ 26625, 27970 *(effective Jan. 1, 2018)*	An individual can loan a firearm to another person without going through a licensed firearms dealer if both of the following conditions are met: (1) The person receiving the firearm is enrolled in the course of basic training prescribed by the Commission on Peace Officer Standards and Training, or in any other course certified by the Commission; *and* (2) The loan is for purposes of participation in the course.
P.C. § 27885	An individual who is 18 years of age or older can loan a firearm to another person who is 18 years of age or older without going through a licensed firearms dealer provided the following conditions are met: (1) The person loaning the firearm is at all times within the presence of the person being loaned the firearm; *and* (2) The loan is for a lawful purpose; *and* (3) The loan does not exceed three days in duration; *and* (4) The individual receiving the firearm is not prohibited by state or federal law from possessing, receiving, owning, or purchasing a firearm.
P.C. §§ 27910, 31765	An individual can loan a firearm to a person 18 years of age or older for the purposes of target shooting without going through a licensed firearms dealer, as long as: (1) The loan occurs on the premises of a target facility that holds a business or regulatory license; or on the premises of any club or organization organized for the purposes of practicing shooting at targets upon established ranges, whether public or private; *and* (2) The firearm is at all times kept within the premises of the target range or on the premises of the club or organization.
P.C. § 27950	An individual can loan a long gun to a licensed hunter without going through a licensed firearms dealer, as long as the loan does not exceed the duration of the hunting season for which the firearm is to be used.

PENAL CODE SECTION	EXEMPTION
P.C. § 27955	An individual can loan a firearm to another person 18 years of age or older without going through a licensed firearms dealer, provided all the following are satisfied: (1) The loan is "infrequent"; *and* (2) The firearm is unloaded; *and* (3) The loan is made by a person who is neither a dealer nor a federal firearms licensee pursuant to Chapter 44 (commencing with 18 U.S.C. section 921) of Title 18 of the United States Code; *and* (4) The loan is for use solely as a prop in a motion picture, television, video, theatrical, or other entertainment production or event.
P.C. § 27955	A federal firearms licensee can loan a firearm to a person who possess a valid entertainment firearms permit issued under Chapter 2 (commencing with P.C. section 29500) of Division 8 of the Penal Code without going through a licensed firearms dealer, as long as the following conditions are met: (1) The firearm is unloaded; *and* (2) The firearm is loaned for use solely as a prop in a motion picture, television, video, theatrical, or other entertainment production or event; *and* (3) The person loaning the firearm retains a photocopy of the entertainment firearm permit as proof of compliance with this requirement.
P.C. § 27966	An individual can loan, sell, or transfer a firearm to a collector licensed under Chapter 44 of Title 18 of the United States Code, and the regulations issued thereto without going through a licensed firearms dealer provided that: (1) The loan, sale, or transfer is "infrequent;" *and* (2) The firearm is not a handgun; *and* (3) The firearm is a curio or relic; *and* (4) The person receiving the firearm has a current certificate of eligibility issued in accordance with P.C. section 267410; *and* (5) Within 30 days of taking possession of the firearm, the person to whom it is transferred must forward by prepaid mail, or deliver in person to the Department of Justice, a report that includes information concerning the individual taking possession of the firearm, how title was obtained and form whom, and a description of the firearm in question.

In addition to the exceptions above, there are also a exceptions for loans to historical societies. Specifically, an authorized law enforcement representative of a city, county, city and county, or state, or the federal government can sell, deliver, loan, or transfer a firearm to any public or private nonprofit historical society, museum, or institutional collection without going through a licensed firearms dealer if all the following conditions are met:

(1) The entity receiving the firearm is open to the public; *and*

(2) The firearm is deactivated or rendered inoperable prior to delivery; *and*

(3) The firearm is not subject to any of the following:

   (a) P.C. section 18000 (dealing with the surrender of nuisance weapon to law enforcement) or P.C. section 18005 (offering surrendered weapons for sale at public auction, return of stolen weapons and weapons used in a manner constituting a nuisance without knowledge of owner, destruction of surrendered weapons); *or*

   (b) P.C. section 18250-18275 (firearms seized at a domestic violence incident); *or*

   (c) P.C. section 34000 (Sale or destruction of firearms no longer needed as exhibits in criminal actions or proceedings, and firearms that are unclaimed or abandoned); *or*

   (d) P.C. section 34005 (alternatives to destruction of firearms and parts) or P.C. section 30410 (notice of retention or destruction of firearms); *or*

(4) The firearm is not prohibited by other provisions of law from being sold, delivered, or transferred; *and*

(5) Prior to delivery, the entity receiving the firearm submits a written statement to the law enforcement representative stating that the firearm will not be restored to operating condition, and will either remain with that entity, or if subsequently disposed of, will be transferred in accordance with the applicable provisions listed in P.C. section 16575 (referencing the 2012 renumbering of firearm Code sections and how the new sections are continuations of these sections) and, if applicable with P.C. section 31615 (prohibition on purchase or receipt of, or sale, delivery, loan, or transfer of a firearm to a person lacking a valid safety certificate); *and*

(6) Within ten days of the date the firearm is sold, loaned, delivered, or transferred to that entity, all of the following information is reported to the DOJ:

   (a) The name of the government entity delivering the firearm; *and*

   (b) The make, model, serial number, and other identifying characteristics of the firearm; *and*

(c) The name of the person authorized by the entity to take possession of the firearm.[173]

Any person other than a representative of an authorized law enforcement agency may also sell, deliver, loan, or transfer a firearm to any public or private nonprofit historical society, museum, or institutional collection without going through a licensed firearms dealer if all the following conditions are met:

(1) The entity receiving the firearm is open to the public; *and*

(2) The firearm is deactivated or rendered inoperable prior to delivery; *and*

(3) The firearm is not a type of prohibited from being sold, delivered, or transferred to the public; *and*

(4) Prior to delivery, the entity receiving the firearm submits a written statement to the person selling, loaning, or transferring the firearm stating that the firearm will not be restored to operating condition, and will either remain with that entity, or if subsequently disposed of, will be transferred in accordance with the applicable provisions listed in P.C. section 16575 and, if applicable, with P.C. section 31615; *and*

(5) If title to the firearm is being transferred to the public or private nonprofit historical society, museum, or institutional collection, then the designated representative of that entity shall, within 30 days of taking possession of that firearm, forward by prepaid mail or deliver in person to the DOJ, a single report signed by both parties to the transaction, which include all of the following information:

(a) Information identifying the person representing the public or private historical society, museum, or institutional collection; *and*

(b) Information on how title was obtained and from whom; *and*

(c) A description of the firearm in question; *and*

(d) A copy of the written statement referred to in (4), above.[174]

---

[173] P.C. § 27855.
[174] P.C. § 27860.

VI. TRANSFERRING AND LOANING FIREARMS TO YOUNG PEOPLE

A. Dealer Sales

1. Federal Law

Federal law prohibits firearm dealers from selling firearms to anyone under the age of 18, and handguns may only be sold to those who are who are 21 or over.[175] And federal law only allows the sale of rifles and shotguns to those between ages 18 and 21.[176]

Although federal law allow a person to buy "complete" rifles and shotguns from an FFL once he or she turns 18, frames and receivers (see Chapter 2) cannot be purchased until the purchaser reaches age 21. Federal law specifies that only "rifles" and "shotguns" can be purchased by 18 to 21-year-olds, and the ATF interprets this rule to mean "complete" firearms.[177]

1. California Law

California law also prohibits the sale of firearms to anyone under the age of 18 and the sale of a handgun to an individual under 21 years of age.[178] Once a person reaches 18 years of age, however, California law allows the person to purchase long guns and "antique" handguns from an FFL.[179] California allows "immediate family" (defined below) to give a handgun to someone between 18 and 21 years of age via an intra-family transfer.[180] Once a person reaches 21 years of age, that person becomes eligible to purchase handguns and other non-long guns.[181]

B. Those Under Age 18

With the exception of "assault weapons" and .50 BMG rifles, neither California nor federal law regulates rifle or shotgun *possession* by minors specifically. But, firearm *transfers* to a minor are heavily regulated. This includes loaning firearms without the parent or legal guardian's express permission.

---

[175] *See* 18 U.S.C. § 922(b)(1).

[176] 18 U.S.C. § 922(b)(1), (x)(1).

[177] *Open Letter to All Federal Firearms Licensees*, U.S. DEPT. OF JUSTICE, BUREAU OF ALCOHOL, TOBACCO, FIREARMS AND EXPLOSIVES (Jul. 7, 2009), *available at* http://www.atf.gov/files/press/releases/2009/07/070709-openletter-ffl-gca.pdf (last visited July 11, 2017); *see* 18 U.S.C. § 922(b)(1); *see also ATF Form 4473 - Firearm Transaction Record*, U.S. DEPT. OF JUSTICE, BUREAU OF ALCOHOL, TOBACCO, FIREARMS AND EXPLOSIVES, http://www.atf.gov/files/forms/download/atf-f-4473-1.pdf (last visited July 11, 2017).

[178] P.C. § 27505(a).

[179] P.C. § 27505(a)-(b)(1).

[180] P.C. § 27875.

[181] P.C. § 27505(a).

Under federal law, it is unlawful for anyone to knowingly transfer a handgun or "ammunition that is suitable for use only in a handgun"[182] to a minor. But it is legal to *temporarily* loan a handgun or such ammunition to a minor if:

(1) The handgun and ammunition are possessed and used by the minor in the course of employment, ranching, farming (with consent of the rancher or farmer), target practice, hunting, or in a firearm training course; *and*

(2) The minor's parent, who is not a prohibited person, provides written consent for the minor to possess the handgun or ammunition (subject to transportation and farming exceptions); *and*

(3) The minor keeps the written consent at all times while possessing the handgun or ammunition; *and*

(4) The minor's use is in accordance with State and local law.[183]

A minor may also inherit *title* to a handgun or ammunition, but *not* possession.[184]

Under California law, parents or legal guardians may *loan or transfer* a non-handgun to their minor children. Grandparents may as well, but only with the parent or legal guardian's express permission. This exception appears to run afoul of the requirements of an intra-familial transfer (discussed in Section VII(B)(1) of this Chapter). All others may *only loan* non-handguns to a minor with the express permission of the minor's parent or guardian for no longer than 30 days and only for a "lawful purpose."[185]

If the firearm is a *handgun* and you are not the minor's parent or legal guardian, you may still *loan* it to the minor if *all* of the following conditions are met:

(1) The minor has written consent from his or her parent or legal guardian before or at the time of the loan, or is accompanied by his or her parent or legal guardian at the time the loan is made; *and*

(2) The loan is for a lawful, recreational sport, the nature of which involves the use of a firearm. This includes, but is not limited to, competitive shooting or agricultural, ranching, or hunting activities; motion picture, television, video production, entertainment or theatrical event; *and*

(3) The loan does not last longer than reasonably necessary to engage in those activities listed in subsection (2) above; *and*

(4) The loan does not, in any event, exceed ten days.[186]

[182] 18 U.S.C. § 922(x)(1).
[183] For exact wording of this statute, refer to 18 U.S.C. section 922(x)(3) and/or Chapter 3.
[184] 18 U.S.C. § 922(x)(3)(C).
[185] P.C. § 27505(b)(4).
[186] P.C. § 27505(b)(6).

If you are the minor's parent or legal guardian, you may *loan* the minor a handgun to engage in the activities listed in subsection (2) above as long as the loan does not last longer than reasonably necessary to engage in those activities.[187]

The loan of a firearm (handgun or long gun) in accordance with the California and federal requirements above is exempt from the FSC requirement.

"Antique firearms" are generally not considered "firearms" for purposes of firearm loans and transfers, even though they are considered firearms for purposes of minors possessing handguns.[188] What this means is that a crime will be committed the moment a minor takes *unlawful* possession of a handgun from you (e.g., when the minor doesn't have parental or guardian permission), even though California says that no crime was committed by the act of loaning an "antique" handgun to the minor.

That being said, keep in mind that the exceptions above only apply to the *loan or transfer* of a firearm to a minor; it does not exempt the minor from the restrictions on the *possession* of firearms. In other words, in order for the minor to lawfully possess a firearm that is loaned or transferred to them, they must meet one of the exceptions outlined in Chapter 3.

VII. EXCEPTIONS TO TRANSFERRING FIREARMS THROUGH A FEDERAL FIREARMS LICENSEE IN CALIFORNIA

A. Federal Law

Federal law does not generally regulate firearm transfers between two individuals who reside in the same state. But, federal law does prohibited you from transferring a firearm to a person that you know or have reasonable cause to believe is prohibited from possessing firearms.[189] And remember that if you are not an FFL, you may only transfer firearms "infrequently" under California and cannot "engage in the business" of dealing firearms under federal law (see Section III).

---

[187] P.C. § 27505(b)(5)(B).

[188] *See* P.C. §§ 16170(b), 27505(b)(1), 27510.

[189] 18 U.S.C. § 922(d).

B. California Law

1. Intra-Family Transactions

Under California law, using an FFL is *not* required for *infrequent*[190] transfers of firearms that are generally lawful to possess in California to an "immediate family" member, whether transferred by gift, bequest, intestate succession (*i.e.*, inheritance from someone who passed away without a will), or other means.

"Immediate family" is a parent-child and/or grandparent-grandchild relationship.[191] This means that siblings, aunts, cousins, etc., are not allowed to directly transfer firearms to each other without using an FFL.

To transfer firearms through an intra-family transaction, the transferring party does not need to do anything, but the receiving party must:

(1) Give the DOJ a completed "Report of Operation of Law or Intra-Familial Firearm Transaction" form within 30 days of receiving the firearm; *and*

(2) Have an FSC; *and*

(3) Be at least age 18.[192]

After January 1, 2015, if the transfer only involves one or more handguns, the transferee may take possession of the handgun(s) with a valid HSC or FSC; in all other situations (meaning transfers involving handguns and long guns or just long guns), the recipient must possess an FSC.[193]

a. Change in Law for Long Guns

Before January 1, 2014, an intra-family transfer involving a long gun that was otherwise legal to transfer in California[194] didn't require any paperwork.[195] The only restriction was that the recipient be lawfully eligible to possess firearms. There was no minimum age requirement for the recipient when long guns were transferred

---

[190] P.C. § 16730(a).

[191] P.C. § 16720.

[192] P.C. § 27875.

[193] P.C. § 27875(a)(4). Subject to the person being exempt from this requirement.

[194] If you inherit an "assault weapon" or .50 BMG rifle, and the firearm wasn't otherwise registered to you separately as an "assault weapon" or .50 BMG rifle as discussed in Chapter 9, you have 90 days for "assault weapons" or 180 days for .50 BMG rifles to make the weapon permanently inoperable, sell it to an approved FFL, get a Dangerous Weapons Permit from the DOJ, or remove the firearm from California. P.C. §§ 30925 ("assault weapons"); 30930, 30935 (.50 BMG rifles); 27875 (inheritance of firearms). California law is unclear on what you should do if you inherit machineguns, destructive devices, or other highly regulated firearms (although such inheritance is highly unlikely to happen in California). It is strongly advised you contact an attorney experienced in firearms law to assist you.

[195] P.C. § 27870 (2013). Per AB 809, starting in 2014, long gun transfers between immediate family members will also need to be registered like handguns. See below.

from a parent, but if a grandparent was transferring a gun to a minor, then the minor's parent or guardian must have given express permission.[196]

As of January 1, 2014, immediate family members may still transfer non-handguns if the party taking possession registers the long gun using the "Report of Operation of Law or Intra-Familial Firearm Transaction" form and the person receiving the firearm is over the age of 18.[197]

On January 1, 2014, however, a conflict in the law arose with regard to transferring non-handguns to minors. While the Penal Code allows for the transfer of a non-handgun to a minor by a parent/guardian or grandparent with the parent/guardian's permission,[198] P.C. section 27875 requires that the recipient of a transfer of non-handguns between immediate family members be over the age of 18. The requirements of section 27875 would apply to parent-to-child and grandparent-to-grandchild transfers. It is not clear how this conflict should be resolved. This being said, if a transfer was done prior to January 1, 2014, no documentation or registration needed to be generated. After January 1, 2015, transfers of all firearms will both need to be reported to the DOJ and the transferee will need to possess an FSC.[199] An FSC cannot be issued to anyone under the age of 18.[200]

2. Transfers Between Spouses or Domestic Partners

Under California law, firearm transfers between spouses and domestic partners must go through an FFL unless the transferring spouse "transmutes" his or her interest in the firearm to the recipient spouse or domestic partner.[201] A "transmutation" occurs when, during marriage, a spouse shows an express intent, in a signed writing, to change ownership of his or her property.[202] This means that one spouse's separate property can be transmuted (change classification) into the community property of both spouses or into the separate property of the other spouse.[203]

To "transmute" a firearm, the spouse should create a document stating that he or she wishes to make the firearm transfer or that the transferring spouse is releasing his or her separate or community property interest in the firearm, and that the receiving spouse is taking the property as his or her sole and separate property. Both parties should sign and date the document and keep a copy. Additionally, all of the above requirements for "intra-familial transfers" also apply to transmutations of firearms between spouses. This means that the recipient spouse must register the

---

[196] P.C. § 27505(b)(2)-(3).

[197] A $19 processing fee will be charged for filing this form. CAL. CODE REGS. tit. 11, § 4002.

[198] *See* P.C. § 27505(b)(2)-(3).

[199] P.C. § 27875.

[200] P.C. § 31625(b) (2015).

[201] P.C. § 27920(b).

[202] CAL. FAM. CODE § 852(a).

[203] CAL. FAM. CODE § 850.

firearms, with the DOJ and possess an HSC if the transfer involves a handgun.[204] After January 1, 2015, the spouse receiving the firearm must possess an FSC unless the transfer only involves handguns, in which case a valid HSC will suffice.[205]

a. Firearms and Divorce

California uses the community property method to divide marital possessions at divorce or termination of a registered domestic partnership.[206] Generally speaking, when property (such as a firearm) is acquired by either spouse during the marriage, it is considered community property (*i.e.*, the property belonging to the spouses jointly, barring some other exception).[207] When a marriage is dissolved, the community property is usually divided equally between the spouses.[208] If any firearms are considered community property at divorce, a court may give the firearms to one spouse and compensate the other spouse with other similarly valued community assets to accomplish an equal division of the community estate.[209] Alternatively, a court could order a sale of all community property that cannot be divided and distribute the proceeds equally between the spouses.[210]

As discussed above, when handguns are acquired from a firearms dealer, they are registered to the individual who purchases them. Long guns purchased after January 1, 2014, are likewise registered to the purchaser when acquired from a firearms dealer. Currently, under California law, there is no way to jointly register firearms[211] with the exception of "assault weapons" and .50 BMG rifles that were registered to the possessor(s) as required by California law (see discussion in Chapter 8). Consequently, if firearms were purchased by one spouse and were awarded to the other spouse after a divorce, the firearms would technically need to be transferred in the manner discussed above. When going through a divorce, your family law attorney should consult an attorney familiar with firearms law because dividing community property that involves firearms is often not a simple task.

3. "Operation of Law" Transfers Other Than Transfers Between Spouses Involving Transmutation of Property

The requirement to use a dealer to facilitate firearm transfers does not apply to a person who takes title or possession of a firearm by "operation of law," provided

---

[204] P.C. § 27920(b).

[205] P.C. § 27920(b)(2).

[206] CAL. FAM. CODE § 297.5(a).

[207] CAL. FAM. CODE § 760. Property acquired by a spouse either before or during marriage by "gift, bequest, devise or descent" is the separate property of that spouse, not community property. CAL. FAM. CODE § 770(a).

[208] CAL. FAM. CODE § 2550.

[209] CAL. FAM. CODE §§ 2550-2552.

[210] *In re Marriage of Cream*, 13 Cal. App. 4th 81 (1993).

[211] The California Legislature attempted to change this in 2016 when it passed SB 1332. SB 1332, 2015-2016 Leg., Reg. Sess (2016), *available at* https://leginfo.legislature.ca.gov/faces/billNavClient.xhtml?bill_id=201520160SB1332 (last visited July 11, 2017). But, Governor Brown vetoed the bill.

that the person is not prohibited by state or federal law from possessing, receiving, owning, or purchasing a firearm.[212] "[T]he phrase 'a person taking title or possession of a firearm by operation of law' includes, but is not limited to, any one of the following instances in which an individual receives title to, or possession of, a firearm"[213]:

(1) The executor or administrator of an estate, if the estate includes a firearm; *and*

(2) A secured creditor or an agent or employee of a secured creditor when a firearm is possessed as collateral for, or as a result of, a default under a security agreement under the Commercial Code; *and*

(3) A levying officer;[214] *and*

(4) A receiver performing the functions of a receiver, if the receivership estate includes a firearm; *and*

(5) A trustee in a bankruptcy performing the duties of a trustee, if the bankruptcy estate includes a firearm; *and*

(6) An assignee for the benefit of creditors performing the functions of an assignee, if the assignment includes a firearm; *and*

(7) A transmutation of property between spouses; [215]*and*

(8) The transfer of a firearm by a law enforcement agency to the person who found the firearm where the delivery is to the person as the finder of the firearm;[216] *and*

(9) A firearm received by a family of a police officer or deputy sheriff from a local agency.[217]

Additionally, the dealer-processing requirement does not apply to operation of law transfers when the person who takes possession of a firearm in a representative capacity subsequently transfers ownership of the firearm to themselves in an individual capacity, so long as they possess a valid Firearm Safety Certificate, or in the case of a handgun, a valid Handgun Safety Certificate.[218]

Further, depending on which "operation of law" transfer is at issue, there are some other criteria that must be met before the transaction can be exempt from California's requirement to transfer firearms through a federal firearms licensee, For instance, if the person taking title or possession is an executor or administrator of an estate, a secured creditor or agent/employee of a secured creditor when the firearm

---

[212] P.C. § 27920(a).

[213] P.C. §16990.

[214] As defined in California Code of Civil Procedure sections 481.140, 511.060, or 680.260.

[215] As provided in California Family Code section 850.

[216] As provided in California Article 1 (commencing with Section 2080) of Chapter 4 of Title 6 of Part 4 of Division 3 of the California Civil Code.

[217] As provided in Government Code section 50081.

[218] P.C. § 27925.

is possessed as collateral, a receiver, a trustee in bankruptcy, or an assignee for the benefit of creditors, then he or she must, within 30 days, report the transfer to DOJ by using a *Report of Law or Intra-Familial Firearm Transaction* form.[219]

If the person taking title or possession of the firearm is receiving the firearm pursuant to a transmutation of property under Family Code section 850 or is receiving the firearm as a surviving spouse pursuant to Probate Code sections 13500 through 13506, then the person must:

(1) Within 30 days, report the transfer to DOJ by using a *Report of Law or Intra-Familial Firearm Transaction* form; *and*

(3) Possess a valid firearm safety certificate or, in the case of a handgun, a valid handgun safety certificate.[220]

Where the person receiving title or possession of the firearm is receiving the firearm from a law enforcement agency as the finder of the firearm (i.e., the firearm is delivered pursuant to Civil Code sections 2080 through 2080.10), then that person must present proof to the law enforcement agency that he or she possess a valid firearm safety certificate or, in the case of a handgun, a valid handgun safety certificate.

4. Gun Trusts

A "gun trust" is a legal trust that is specifically created to acquire, hold ownership to, and facilitate the transfer of firearms. A legal "trust" is any arrangement by which property is transferred by a person (i.e., the "settlor") with the intention that it be held and administered by another person (i.e., the "trustee") for the benefit of a third party (i.e., the "beneficiary"). In other words, a trust is basically just a legal relationship that holds assets for the benefit of another. Trusts are generally considered advantageous because they can help people avoid certain estate taxes and avoid the public forum of a probate court.

When people speak of "gun trusts" in California, they usually mean one of two things: (1) trusts that are specifically created to hold ownership to and acquire firearms regulated by the National Firearms Act of 1934 (NFA), or (2) trusts that are created to hold ownership to and facilitate the transfer of other types of firearms (e.g., legal to own handguns and long guns) that are lawful to possess in California.

a. NFA Trusts

As stated in more detail in Chapter 9, the NFA[221] regulates the manufacture, importation, possession, and transfer of certain highly restricted firearms, including "ma-

---

[219] P.C. § 27920(a)(1). The *Report of Law or Intra-Familial Firearm Transaction* form can be accessed at https://oag. ca.gov/sites/all/files/agweb/pdfs/firearms/forms/oplaw.pdf. You can also submit this form to the DOJ through CRIS, which can be accessed at https://cfars.doj.ca.gov/login.do;jsessionid=ZiceNrwzku1-gSNUEdlUWvXW. cfars_worker01.

[220] P.C. § 27920(a)(2).

[221] 26 U.S.C. §§ 5801-5872.

chineguns," "short-barreled rifles," "short-barreled shotguns," "silencers," destructive devices, "and "any other weapons." These items are often referred to as "NFA firearms," and they are subject to strict federal registration, transfer, and tax requirements.

NFA trusts are increasingly popular in some states because they allow multiple individuals to possess the same NFA firearms and they make it easier for future trustees and beneficiaries to deal with an estate containing NFA firearms. But, despite their popularity in other states, NFA trusts are practically irrelevant to most California gun owners. This is because it is generally illegal under California law for individuals to purchase and possess NFA firearms, unless the individual has obtained a "dangerous weapons" permit—something that is virtually impossible to obtain unless, in most cases, the individual can demonstrate that he or she already has a law enforcement customer, military, or entertainment industry base and is obtaining the permit to sell NFA firearms to these entities.[222]

Because most Californians cannot possess NFA firearms in California, NFA trusts will not be discussed in further detail in this book. Readers are warned: be careful when selecting attorneys who profess that they are experienced with gun trusts, especially the attorneys who do not reside in California and who offer a way for you and your family to keep regulated firearms in California for years to come without registration. While these attorneys may be apt in using gun trusts to acquire NFA firearms, that does not mean that they understand the complexities of California law. Often, attorneys who encourage gun owners to establish gun trusts in California misstate California law or do not fully understand it.

b. Non-NFA Gun Trusts in California

Before placing a legally-owned firearm into trust, you must understand that the California and federal law heavily regulating the possession and transfer of firearms, as violation of any of these laws can result in criminal liability.

i. California Firearm Transfer Laws in the Context of Gun Trusts

Understand that when a firearm is placed in trust, ownership over that firearm must be transferred to a trustee and, eventually, to the beneficiary(ies) of the trust.[223] And California law prevents one firearm from being transferred to more than one person; DROS forms and laws covering firearm transfers refer to only a single recipient.[224]

Also, each time ownership over the firearm is transferred to another person, the transfer itself must be conducted in accordance with California and federal law.

---

[222] *See* P.C. § 32650.

[223] Although the settlor can be the trustee of a trust, the settlor cannot be the beneficiary of a trust.

[224] *See* P.C. §§ 27500-27590, 28050-28070, 28100, 28160; *see also* CAL. CODE REGS., tit. 11, § 4210; *see also Dealer's Record of Sales (DROS) Worksheet*, BOF 929, CALIFORNIA DEPARTMENT OF JUSTICE, BUREAU OF FIREARMS (2014), *available at* https://des.doj.ca.gov/forms/DROS_Worksheet_BOF-929.pdf (last visited Oct. 29, 2017).

So, assuming that the trustee is not also the settlor (in which case no transfer would occur because ownership over the firearm is not being given to a third party), then the firearm must be lawfully transferred from the settlor to the trustee. Assuming that the trustee and/or settlor are not licensed firearms dealers, then this transfer would likely be considered a private party transfer (PPT) under California law.[225] Analogously, if the trust documents state that the firearms are to be distributed to the beneficiary at a certain time and if neither the settlor nor the beneficiary are licensed firearm dealers, the firearm must once again be lawfully transferred from the trustee to the beneficiary pursuant to the laws governing PPTs. All PPTs in California (regardless of whether money is exchanged) must be processed through a licensed firearms dealer, unless the transfer meets one of the few exceptions.[226] A violation of this rule is a crime, punishable as a misdemeanor or a felony depending on the type of firearm involved in the transfer.[227]

There is an argument that the "operation of law" exception to the dealer requirement applies here to allow trustees to take possession of a firearm without having to go through a dealer (see the more detailed discussion in the "Taking Title by Operation of Law" subsection below). This is because the definition of "operation of law" has the phrase "including, but not limited to" before its list of examples of "operation of law" transfers. But, this argument has never been tested or litigated to our knowledge.

When the settlor and trustee reside in different states and a transfer through a dealer must occur, remember that federal law requires firearms to be transferred through an FFL in the recipient's home state.[228] While there is an exception for bequest and intestate succession, it is likely that a trust does not fall within that exception.

California law seems to state that both parties in a PPT must appear before the licensed firearms dealer. Given that most current gun owners (*i.e.*, the settlors) will likely want to retain ownership over their firearms while they are still alive,[229] this requirement can cause some difficulty because the original owners cannot appear before a licensed firearm dealer in order to have the firearm transferred after they have died. It is unclear as to whether a PPT can still be conducted after the settlor dies. Because of this ambiguity, it may be best to ensure that each transfer of the firearm (*e.g.*, from settlor to transferee, transferee to successive transferee, and transferee to beneficiary) is done via PPT or meets one of the exceptions explained below or that it occurs before the original gun owner is deceased.

---

[225] See Section II of this Chapter for a more in-depth discussion on private party transfers.

[226] *See* P.C. §§ 16730, 27545.

[227] P.C. § 127545, 27590(c)(5).

[228] 18. U.S.C. § 922(a)(5).

[229] Current owners can retain ownership over their firearms by naming themselves as the initial trustee or by creating a trust that does not come into effect until after the settler dies.

ii. Relevant Exceptions to Having to Process Firearm Transfers Through a Licensed Firearms Dealer, As Applied to Non-NFA Gun Trusts

Intra-Familial Transfers

As stated previously in this Chapter, *"infrequent"*[230] transfers of firearms between members of the same "immediate family"[231]— whether transferred by gift, bequest, intestate succession (i.e., inheritance from someone who passed away without a will), or by other means from one individual to another —do not need to be processed through a licensed firearms dealer.[232]

Transfers of Firearms Between Spouses

The California Penal Code is silent as to whether spouses or domestic partners can jointly register a firearm. Currently, when a firearm is purchased from a licensed firearms dealer, the firearm is registered to the individual who purchased the firearm, meaning that only one spouse or domestic partner can be the registered owner of the firearm.

Despite the fact that the California Penal Code does not state that spouses or domestic partners can jointly register a firearm, California law allows spouses and domestic partners to transfer firearms between each other without using a licensed firearms dealer if the transferring spouse "transmutes" his or her separate interest in the firearm to the receipt spouse or domestic partner (i.e., to community property or to the recipient's separate property).[233] A "transmutation" occurs when, during a marriage, a spouse or domestic partner shows an express intent, in a signed writing, to change ownership of his or her property.[234] In other words, one spouses or domestic partner's separate party can be changed into the community property of both spouses or vice versa.[235]

Under California law, a transmutation is considered an "operation of law" transfer.[236] And, as explained below in further detail, "operation of law" transfers can be conducted without using licensed firearms dealer as long certain conditions are met. Therefore, a spouse may be able to transfer a firearm that was purchased as separate property without using a licensed firearms dealer if he or she transmutes it into community property or into the separate property of the receiving spouse. In

---

[230] "Infrequently" means "[f]or handguns, less than six transactions per calendar year" and "[f]or firearms other than handguns, occasional and without regularity." P.C. § 16730.

[231] "Immediate family" means a parent-child and/or grandparent-grandchild relationship. P.C. § 16720. Hence, under California law, siblings, aunts, uncles, cousins, and other distant family members are not allowed to directly transfer firearms to each other without going through a firearms dealer.

[232] P.C. § 27875.

[233] P.C. § 27920(b).

[234] CAL. FAM. CODE § 852(a).

[235] CAL. FAM. CODE § 850.

[236] P.C. § 16990.

theory, this means that spouses should be able to jointly register a firearm, but this theory has been untested.

Taking Title by Operation of Law

As explained above in the subsection discussing "operation of law" transfers, a firearm can be transferred to an individual without going through a licensed firearms dealer if the person receiving the firearm is taking possession of the firearm by "operation of law," so long as the person is not prohibited by state or federal law from possessing, receiving, owning, or purchasing a firearm. For this exemption to apply when the beneficiary is receiving the firearm pursuant to a transmutation of property under California Family Code section 850[237] (e.g., when spouses sign a trust in which they agree that the firearm is the settlor's separate property and that it shall be transmuted to the other spouse's separate property), then the beneficiary must:

(1) File the *Report of Law or Intra-Familial Firearm Transaction* form within 30 days, *and*

(2) Possess a valid firearm safety certificate or, in the case of a handgun, a valid handgun safety certificate.[238]

For the "operation of law" exemption to apply to other circumstances involving gun trusts is a bit trickier. Recall that the term "operation of law" also includes "[t]he executor or administrator of an estate, if the estate includes a firearm."[239] This would seem to be pertinent when firearms are transferred from the settlor to the trustee, as the trustee seems to be taking possession of the firearm by "operation of law" and in a representative capacity on behalf of the trust. But note that the term "operation of law" does not specifically state that transfers to a trustee (other than one for a bankruptcy proceeding) are included within the term. But, there is likely a strong argument that a firearm transfer to a trustee would also fall within the term "operation of law." This is because California Penal Code section 16960 states that the term "operation of law" is not limited to the types of transfers explicitly listed in section 16960 (i.e., "operation of law" "includes but it not limited to" those examples). And transfers to a trustee would seem to fit within the spirit of those transfers.[240]

That said, given it is still unclear as to whether a transfer from a settlor to a trustee would fit within this exception, it may be prudent for those considering whether to place firearms in a trust to transfer the firearm to the trustee during their lifetime through a licensed firearms dealer via a private party transfer.

---

[237] *I.e.,* transmuting community property to separate property of spouse, transmuting separate property of spouse to community property, or transmuting separate property of one spouse to separate property of the other spouse.

[238] P.C. § 27920(a)(2).

[239] P.C. § 16960.

[240] If this argument prevails, then the trustee, as the person taking title or possession of the firearm as an executor or administrator trust, must, within 30 days, report the transfer to DOJ by using a *Report of Law or Intra-Familial Firearm Transaction* form. P.C. §§ 16990(a), 27920(a)(1). The *Report of Law or Intra-Familial Firearm Transaction* form can be accessed at https://oag.ca.gov/sites/all/files/agweb/pdfs/firearms/forms/oplaw.pdf. You can also submit this form to the DOJ through CRIS, which can be accessed at https://cfars.doj.ca.gov/login.do;jsessionid=ZiceNrwzku1-gSNUEdlUWvXW.cfars_worker01.

Transfers of Long Guns to Minors by Immediate Family Members

Another exception to the dealer processing requirement that is likely applicable to certain estate transfers is the transfer of firearms, other than handguns, to a minor by the minor's parent or legal guardian, or by the minor's grandparent with the permission of the minor's parent or legal guardian (discussed previously in this Chapter).[241]

Keep in mind that minors are still generally prohibited under California law from possessing live ammunition[242] and from possessing a pistol, revolver, or other firearm capable of being concealed upon the person.[243] There are a number of exceptions to this restriction, but they generally require the presence or permission of the minor's parents during a lawful activity, and only if such activities involve the use of a firearm.[244]

So, if the firearm being transferred is a handgun, only title of the firearm can be transferred through a trust to a minor.[245] The parent or legal guardian will be required to maintain possession of the handgun until the minor reaches eighteen years of age.

"Antique Firearms"

As stated in sections III and VI above, "antique firearms" can be transferred between private parties without having to go through a licensed firearms dealer, provided that the recipient is eligible under California law and the "antique" is not illegal to possess.

iii. Limitation of Non-NFA Gun Trusts: Firearms Cannot be Shared Amongst Trustees, So California Laws on Firearm Loaning Must be Followed if Trustees Want to "Share" Firearms

While NFA trusts allow the trustees to possess and use the NFA firearms that have been acquired by, or placed in, the trust, this benefit does not exist when a settlor transfers ordinary firearms into a trust in California. This is because the firearm must be transferred to a specific trustee, not to the trust as a legal entity.

Because the firearm must be registered to a specific trustee, the only way to share a firearm amongst other trustees (or any other person who is not prohibited from possessing firearms for that matter) would be to loan or transfer the firearm. But, there are only certain situations where a firearm can be lawfully loaned, and they are explained in sections V and VI above.

---

[241] P.C. § 27945(a)-(b).

[242] P.C. § 29650.

[243] P.C. § 29610.

[244] P.C. §§ 29615, 29655.

[245] This is because the federal handgun and ammunition restrictions do not apply when a minor inherits title of a handgun and/or ammunition. 18 U.S.C. § 922(x)(3). Meanwhile, as stated above, California law generally restricts minors from possessing handguns and/or ammunition (see P.C. sections 29650, 29610, 29615, 29655). So, it appears that, in California, minors can inherit ownership of a handgun but are restricted when it comes to possession of a handgun. But with California's restrictions on transferring handguns to minors (see P.C. section 27505), it is uncertain how all of this would work.

iv. Limitations of Non-NFA Gun Trusts as Applied to "Assault Weapons"/.50 BMG Rifles and "Large-Capacity Magazines"

Along with complying with California's strict transfer requirements, individuals who intend on placing any lawfully owned "assault weapons" or "large-capacity magazines" in trust need to understand and comply with California's restrictions on the transfer and possession of those devices.

"Assault Weapons" and .50 BMG Rifles

Some individuals have marketed gun trusts as a way to possess, hand down, or transfer "assault weapons" to other individuals or family members in California. What these marketers fail to mention, or mention later in fine print, is that California law does not allow a person inheriting an "assault weapon" to keep it in California, unless the firearm is already registered to him or her.[246] In other words, unless the "assault weapon" is jointly registered to you and the other people in your family, the "assault weapon" cannot be transferred through a gun trust (or any other process) to other people in California and still be possessed within the state.

If the person inheriting the "assault weapon" is not a registered owner, then the person in possession of the "assault weapon" and the registered owner can be charged with a crime for illegally transferring an "assault weapon" (unless another exception applies). Consequently, a person acquiring a firearm meeting the definition of an "assault weapon" (in its "assault weapon" configuration) through a gun trust or any other type of transfer will not be able to possess the firearm in California.

In this respect, a "gun trust" only acts as an inheritance vehicle requiring the new owner to take and possess the "assault weapon" outside of California. But this is nothing novel. Nothing under California law prohibits the inheritance of an "assault weapon" by bequest or intestate succession (we discuss inheritance of "assault weapons" in Chapter 8). As a result, the benefits of a gun trust are dubious when it comes to "assault weapons."

"Large-Capacity Magazines"

Under California law, it is generally illegal to manufacture or cause to be manufactured, import, keep for sale, offer or expose for sale, give, lend, buy, or receive a "large-capacity magazine."[247] Therefore, "large-capacity magazines" cannot be placed in trust without violating California law because the magazine would need to be transferred to a trustee or beneficiary at some point in time. And the potential ban on the possession of "large-capacity magazines" makes this even more problematic.

---

[246] *See* P.C. § 30915. Joint registration of "assault weapons" and .50 BMG rifles, and ways to modify an "assault weapon," are discussed in Chapter 8.

[247] P.C. § 32310.

5. Transfers to Those With an Entertainment Firearm Permit (EFP)

Under California and federal law, people who possess an Entertainment Firearm Permit (EFP) are exempt from several firearm transfer requirements for up to one year from the time they were issued the EFP, including the federal background check and the DROS.[248] Authorized EFP holders may possess firearms for props in motion picture, television, video, theatrical, or other entertainment productions.[249]

6. Acquiring Antiques and "Curio or Relic" Firearms

California laws about "antiques" and "curio or relic" firearms are complex. These are two different classes of firearms, and they accordingly have different state and federal requirements.

a. Antique Firearms

As discussed in Chapter 2, "antique firearms" are not generally considered "firearms"[250] for the state and federal laws governing firearm transfers.[251] This means that "antique firearms" can be bought outside of your state of residence, purchased from an FFL or any retailer without filling out a federal Form 4473 or DROS, or transferred between private parties without going through an FFL.

But, as discussed in Chapter 3, because someone prohibited from possessing firearms in California is also prohibited from possessing "antique firearms," it is illegal to give one to someone knowing he or she is prohibited from possessing firearms.[252] Likewise, it is unlawful to transfer an "antique firearm" that is a "handgun" to a minor.[253]

b. "Curio or Relic" Firearms

Since both California and the ATF define a "curio or relic" firearm the same way (see Chapter 2), if the ATF considers a firearm a "curio or relic," then so does California. The regulations of "curio or relic" transfers, however, differ between California and federal law.

---

[248] P.C. §§ 27960, 29530. The National Instant Criminal Background Check System (NICS) exemption provided by the California Entertainment Firearms Permit (EFP) is a qualifying alternative to the background check requirements for up to one year from the issue date. To check the status of the EFP as an acceptable alternative to NICS, see *Permanent Brady Permit Chart*, U.S. DEPT. OF JUSTICE, BUREAU OF ALCOHOL, TOBACCO, FIREARMS AND EXPLOSIVES, https://www.atf.gov/rules-and-regulations/permanent-brady-permit-chart (last visited July 11, 2017).

[249] P.C. § 27960(a)(4). For other exemptions provided to EFP holders see P.C. sections 27960(a), 27810(a)(3), 31820(a); see also *Entertainment Firearms Permit Application*, CAL. DEPT. OF JUSTICE, OFFICE OF THE ATTORNEY GENERAL, http://oag.ca.gov/sites/all/files/pdfs/firearms/forms/efpapp.pdf (last visited July 11, 2017).

[250] P.C. § 16170(b); 18 U.S.C. § 921(a)(3).

[251] For example, "antique firearms" are not "firearms" for dealer licensing requirements, sales or loans between private parties, firearm safety device requirements, or HSCs. *See* P.C. §§ 16620; 16730(a), (c); 16960; 17310; 26500-26588 (inclusive); 16130; 16400; 16550; 16810; 17110; 26700-26915 (inclusive); 27510; 27540; 27545; 28100; 31615.

[252] P.C. § 27500(a).

[253] P.C. § 27505(a)-(b)(1).

"Curio or relic" firearms are associated with a Type 03 FFL, which is commonly known as a "collector's license."[254] The federal privileges conferred by this license extend *only* to transactions involving weapons classified as "curio or relic" firearms for personal collection purposes. This means a person with a collector's license is still subject to general federal firearm transfer regulations when purchasing non-"curio or relic" firearms and cannot be "engaged in the business"[255] of selling even "curio or relic" firearms without a separate *dealer's* license (*i.e.*, Type 01 FFL).[256] Additionally, Type 03 FFLs must still comply with state laws, meaning they are not exempt from transfer or possession restrictions on certain firearms, even "curio or relic" firearms, if not allowed under state law.[257]

The general advantages of a collector's license are that it exempts you from the federal background check requirement[258] and allows you to purchase "curio or relic" firearms from FFLs from other states.[259] Individuals who do *not* possess a collector's license may acquire "curio or relic" *long guns* in a state where they are not a resident as long as:

(1) The rifle/shotgun is acquired from a federally licensed importer, manufacturer, dealer, or collector; *and*

(2) The purchaser meets with the licensee at the licensee's premises to accomplish the transfer, sale, and delivery; *and*

(3) A background check is conducted and a federal Form 4473 is filled out when the firearm is transferred by the importer, manufacturer, or dealer; *and*

(4) The *conditions of sale in both parties' states* are satisfied.[260]

The option to acquire "curio or relic" long guns out of state is effectively not available to a California-only resident. This is because the out-of-state seller cannot comply with California's transfer requirements. Prior to January 1, 2014, there was an exception that could have applied if the out-of-state seller was a collector and *not* a Type 01 FFL. This is because the transfer of some "curio or relic" long guns (those over 50 years old) *from* a collector did not have to go through a Type 01 FFL if transferred in California. Therefore, they were not subject to California's general transfer requirements (whereas they would be if the seller were a Type 01 FFL). So such a transfer satisfied federal law requirements that both states' laws are complied with (assuming that is also the case for the other state).

---

254 18 U.S.C. § 921(a)(13); 27 C.F.R. § 478.41(c)-(d).

255 18 U.S.C. § 921(a)(21).

256 18 U.S.C. §§ 922(a), 923(b); 27 C.F.R. §§ 478.41(c)-(d), 478.93. To obtain a collector's license, submit ATF Form 7CR, Application for License (Collector of Curios or Relics). 27 C.F.R. § 478.47.

257 18 U.S.C. § 922(b)(2); 27 C.F.R. § 478.99(b)(2).

258 18 U.S.C. § 922(t)(1). This does not mean that you may possess a "curio or relic" firearm if you are prohibited from possessing firearms in general, just that you do not have to undergo a background check to get one. Likewise, it does not allow you to transfer "curio or relic" firearms to prohibited persons. 27 C.F.R. § 478.32(d).

259 18 U.S.C. § 922(a)(2); 27 C.F.R. § 478.41(c)-(d).

260 27 C.F.R. § 478.96(c)(1).

There are additional federal requirements and restrictions for those with a collector's license, including record-keeping requirements of their "curio or relic" transactions, which are beyond the scope of this book but which you need to be aware of before you engage in such transactions.[261]

Before January 1, 2014, a California resident could transfer or buy a "curio or relic" *long gun* from another California resident without going through an FFL as long as the rifle or shotgun was 50 years or older.[262] After January 1, 2014, this type of transfer was no longer possible for the general public. Today, a Type 03 FFL with a COE can infrequently *acquire* "curio or relic" long guns from regular citizens provided the Type 03 FFL holder registers the firearm with the DOJ.[263] "Curio or relic" handguns must be transferred through an FFL just like modern ones, even if the purchaser is a Type 03 FFL.

An FFL must transfer any "curio or relic" firearm the same way as a non-"curio or relic" modern firearm even if it is being transferred to a Type 03 FFL. There are a few exceptions, however.

Specifically, in California, a Type 03 FFL who holds a COE is exempt from California's ten-day waiting period when buying a "curio or relic" firearm, even if it's *less than* 50 years old.[264] And, as explained above, these FFLs are also exempt from California's general requirements for handgun transfers, such as transferees having an FSC, the need to perform the safe-handling demonstration, and the one handgun per month restriction if the handgun is a "curio or relic."[265] Additionally, firearms listed as "curio or relic" handguns need not pass the safety and functionality tests required to be on the DOJ's Roster of handguns that FFLs can sell in California.[266]

Although the Penal Code clearly exempts Type 03 FFLs who hold a COE from the one-handgun-per-30-calendar-day restriction when acquiring even modern handguns (*i.e.,* non-"curios or relics"),[267] the DOJ has nevertheless taken the position that they are only exempt when acquiring "curio or relic" handguns.[268] The DOJ's position was challenged in state court.[269] In 2016, however, a California trial

---

[261] For general information on "curio or relic" licenses, related federal laws, and the list of "curio or relic" firearms, see *Firearms Curios or Relics List*, U.S. DEPT. OF JUSTICE, BUREAU OF ALCOHOL, TOBACCO, FIREARMS AND EXPLOSIVES, http://www.atf.gov/publications/firearms/curios-relics/index.html (last visited July 11, 2017).

[262] *Information Bulletin No. 98-24-BCIA Curio and Relic Long Guns and 30-day Firearms Delivery Requirements*, CAL. DEPT. OF JUSTICE, OFFICE OF THE ATTORNEY GENERAL, http://oag.ca.gov/sites/all/files/pdfs/firearms/infobuls/9824.pdf (last visited July 11, 2017). If you cannot confirm the rifle or shotgun is at least 50 years old, do not purchase it without going through an FFL. As discussed above, you cannot engage in the business of dealing firearms without a license and you must be eligible to possess firearms. P.C. § 27965.

[263] P.C. § 27966(c).

[264] P.C. §§ 26970(a), 27670(a).

[265] P.C. §§ 27535(b)(9), 26970(a), 27670(a).

[266] P.C. § 32000(b)(3). Discussed in Chapter 9.

[267] P.C. § 27535(b)(9).

[268] *Frequently Asked Questions*, CAL. DEPT. OF JUSTICE, OFFICE OF THE ATTORNEY GENERAL, http://oag.ca.gov/firearms/pubfaqs#24 (last visited July 11, 2017).

[269] *See Doe v. Harris*, No. 34-2014-00163821 (Cal. Sup. Ct. March 21, 2016).

court upheld the DOJ's regulation and ruled that Type 03 FFLs are exempt from the one-handgun-per-30-calendar-day restriction *only* when acquiring "curio or relic" handguns.[270] The decisions has been appealed. As of the date of publication, the case is currently being briefed before the California Court of Appeals. Oral arguments are expected to take place late 2017.

When a Type 03 FFL obtains *any firearm* from out of state,[271] it must register it with the DOJ within five days of transporting the firearm into California.[272] This requirement previously only applied to handguns.

Certain firearms meeting the "curio or relic" definition may still have possession and transfer restrictions (*e.g.*, "machineguns" or destructive devices). Make sure the firearm is legal to possess federally and in California, and then, no matter what the firearm's age, consult the ATF "Firearms Curio and Relic List." Also consult California's firearms laws and regulations to make sure the firearm does not fall under California's "assault weapons" ban. While that ban does not include certain "antique firearms,"[273] it can include "curio or relic" firearms, even popular ones like some M1A1 carbines. "Curio or relic" firearms are, however, exempt from California's ban on .50 BMG rifles that are not already "assault weapons."[274]

7. Nonprofit Auction of Non-Handguns

Infrequent[275] PPTs of non-handguns at an auction or similar event by a nonprofit corporation do not need to be processed through an FFL. Likewise, donating a non-handgun through a PPT to a nonprofit for sale at such an auction does not need to go through an FFL if delivered to the nonprofit immediately before or during the auction.[276]

The term "infrequent" does not prohibit different local chapters of the same nonprofit corporation from conducting auctions with such transfers. This means that each *individual* chapter enjoys this exception and can have such transfers at their auctions regardless of the activity of other chapters, as long as each one does so "infrequently"[277] and/or does not "engage in the business" of dealing firearms.

---

[270] *Doe v. Harris*, No. 34-2014-00163821 (Cal. Sup. Ct. March 21, 2016).

[271] Type 03 FFLs from California can obtain a "curio or relic" handgun while outside of the state and bring it back, provided they comply with the California registration requirements for "curio or relic" collectors. 18 U.S.C. § 922(a)(3); P.C. § 27565.

[272] P.C. § 27565(b). Use Form FD 4100A, which is available on the DOJ website, and pay a $19 processing fee per handgun. CAL. CODE REGS. tit. 11, § 4002. Before January 1, 2014, this requirement only applied to "curio or relic" handguns.

[273] The exception to the "assault weapon" ban for antique firearms only applies to firearms manufactured before January 1, 1899. P.C. § 16170(a).

[274] P.C. § 30530(b). Definition of "curio or relic" is located in Chapter 2.

[275] P.C. § 16730(a)-(b).

[276] P.C. §§ 27900(a), 27905.

[277] P.C. § 16730(b).

8. "Gun Buybacks"

A number of the restrictions on transferring firearms are suspended if you transfer your firearms to a state, local, or federal government entity, so long as the transfer is for the governmental entity, and the entity is acquiring the firearm "as part of an authorized, voluntary program in which the entity is buying or receiving weapons from private individuals."[278] These events are known as "gun buybacks."

At a gun buyback, government entities will often exchange money (for example, a prepaid credit or gift card) for firearms. The buyback events are often advertised as "no questions asked" opportunities where the public can turn in their firearms. With the hopes that a large number of firearms will be taken in, the promoters of these events usually claim that the firearms turned in will not be investigated and that no background check will be run on them. Herein lies one huge problem with these types of events. The "no questions asked" policy gives criminals the opportunity to turn in firearms either used in crimes (like homicides) or stolen from lawful owners. Not only can criminals get rid of the evidence of a crime, but they also get paid for it. The lawful firearm owner who had his or her firearm stolen will *never* see that firearm again.

Another problem with gun buyback events is that people usually do not realize that turning their firearms over does not *unregister* the firearm. This can cause huge problems for people down the road, especially if they later become prohibited from possessing firearms and are flagged in the Armed Prohibited Person System (APPS) or are required to surrender their firearms because they still have a firearm registered in their name. And because these gun buyback programs are "no questions asked," it can be very difficult to prove to law enforcement that you are no longer in possession of the firearm because you will likely not be given a receipt showing that you turned the firearm into a government agency. Therefore, it may be nearly impossible to prove that you no longer possess the firearm.

For legitimate firearm owners who turn in their firearms, gun buybacks provide a different concern. For instance, in some cases, the money the gun buyback agency is offering for the firearm is less than what the firearm is worth. Gun buybacks treat junk guns and valuable antiques equally. People often do not know the true value of their firearms, and there are often more cost-effective ways to lawfully dispose of your firearms if you no longer want or need them. For example, firearms dealers and certain nonprofit organizations may be willing to accept your firearm (and potentially provide you more money for the firearm than the buyback will).

I strongly suggest contacting a local gun shop to see if they are interested in buying the firearm or offering your firearm to a nonprofit for a potential tax write-off before giving a firearm to a gun buyback.

---

[278] P.C. §§ 27850, 31725.

VIII. BUILDING YOUR OWN FIREARM

Another way to obtain a firearm is by making one or assembling one from parts. This practice can be lawful under both California and federal law.

Federal law prohibits the "manufacturing" of firearms without a licenses, but only considers those who are "engaged in the business" of making firearms (*i.e.*, those who devote time, attention, and labor to doing so as a regular course of business) to be "manufacturers" who need a license.[279] This means that making a firearm for personal use does not require a license under federal or California law as long as you do not build an item that is prohibited to possess or make under California or federal law (see Chapters 8 and 9).[280]

Exempting licensed manufacturers with government permission and those fixing lawfully acquired firearms,[281] federal law prohibits assembling a semiautomatic rifle or any shotgun using more than ten "imported parts"[282] if the assembled firearm is prohibited from being imported[283] on the basis that it is not "particularly suitable for or readily adaptable to sporting purposes."[284]

Also, unless you make a "firearm" as defined under the National Firearm Act (NFA), which would require a tax payment and ATF approval,[285] there isn't a federal requirement that you register a firearm assembled for personal use.

The 3D printed parts of "The Liberator"

Prior to 2016, California did not require people to register a firearm assembled for personal use. This all changed on July 22, 2016, though, when Governor Brown signed Assembly Bill (AB) 857 into law. This bill requires individuals who plan on assembling or manufacturing a firearm after July 1, 2018 to obtain a serial number or identification mark from the DOJ before actually assembling or manufacturing the firearm.[286] This bill also requires any person who owns a firearm that does not bear a serial number assigned to it after July 1, 2018 to apply for and obtain a serial number before

---

[279] 18 U.S.C. §§ 921(a)(10), (21), 923(a)(1).

[280] Though there are other prohibited items, the main concern is to avoid inadvertently building an "assault weapon" (Chapter 8).

[281] 27 C.F.R. § 478.39(b).

[282] 27 C.F.R. § 478.39(a). "Imported parts" are: (1) frames, receivers, receiver castings, forgings, or stampings; (2) barrels; (3) barrel extensions; (4) mounting blocks (trunions); (5) muzzle attachments; (6) bolts; (7) bolt carriers; (8) operating rods; (9) gas pistons; (10) trigger housings; (11) triggers; (12) hammers; (13) sears; (14) disconnectors; (15) buttstocks; (16) pistol grips; (17) forearms, handguards; (18) magazine bodies; (19) followers; and (20) floor plates. 27 C.F.R. § 478.39(c).

[283] 18 U.S.C. § 925(d)(3); 26 U.S.C. § 5845(a).

[284] 18 U.S.C. §§ 922(r), 925(d)(3); 27 C.F.R. § 478.39(a).

[285] *See* 26 U.S.C. § 5822.

[286] AB 857, 2015-2016, Leg., Reg. Sess. (Cal. 2016), *available at* https://leginfo.legislature.ca.gov/faces/billNavClient.xhtml?bill_id=201520160AB857 (last visited July 11, 2017). *See* P.C. § 29180-29183.

January 1, 2019.[287] This bill and the new requirements will be explained in further detail below.

But, before delving into these requirements, let's first discuss some of the ways that people have built personal firearms.

"The Liberator," a 3D-printed single shot handgun.

A. Ways to Build Your Own Firearm

1. Creating a Firearm From a Prefabricated Frame or Receiver

First, you can purchase a finished "frame" or "receiver"[288] and then assemble it with additional parts to complete the firearm. Laws generally do not prohibit acquiring firearm parts, but because federal and California laws consider a "frame" or a "receiver" to be a "firearm,"[289] you have to get the frame or receiver through an FFL just like any other firearm or meet one of the exceptions. As mentioned above, you also must be at least age 21 to purchase a receiver.

This process is not covered under the "ghost gun"[290] bill requirements discussed below.

2. Creating a Firearm From an 80% Receiver

The second way is to machine a firearm either from completely raw materials or partially finished materials. Making a firearm from partially finished materials is more popular, as it takes less skill. Generally, you start with an incomplete receiver commonly referred to as an "80% receiver" or "80% side plate."

The "80%" denotes how close the receiver is to being a complete firearm – though this is more of an estimate since it is impossible to say what percentage of work remains for a given firearm, which can vary based on experience, available tools, etc.

The ATF has issued letters to 80% receiver manufactures explaining what features cannot be present on an 80% receiver in order for it to not be considered a "firearm." For "80% AR receivers," the ATF has taken the position that no work can be done to the "fire control cavity" and trigger, no drilling into the receiver for

---

[287] *See* P.C. § 29180.

[288] A "receiver" is "[t]he basic unit of a firearm which houses the firing mechanism and to which the barrel and stock are assembled. In revolvers, pistols and break-open firearms, it is called the frame." NAT'L SHOOTING SPORTS FOUND., THE WRITER'S GUIDE TO FIREARMS & AMMUNITION 15 (Jan. 2012 ed.), *available at* http://www.nssf.org/share/pdf/writers_guide.pdf (last visited July 11, 2017).

[289] 18 U.S.C. § 921(a)(3)(B); P.C. § 16520(b). *See* Chapter 2.

[290] The term "ghost gun" is a made up term that generally refers to a firearm that does not have a serial number or a homemade gun, like one created using a 3D printer.

the hammer and trigger pins, and no drilling for the safety.[291] Once work has been started in those areas, the ATF considers the receiver to be a "firearm" for purposes of federal law.

3. "Build Parties"

A number of firearm enthusiasts are participating in activities called "build parties." There are two different types of activities associated with this term.

The first are get-togethers organized around finishing an 80% firearm frame or receiver. Usually the machines needed for these jobs (typically a drill press or manual mill) are expensive and not something found in every garage. Consequently, groups of firearm enthusiasts form "build parties" where they convene at the machine owner's home and finish their 80% receivers together, usually under the oversight of someone experienced in finishing the receiver. Provided nothing created is illegal to own and no money changes hands, there should be nothing troubling about this practice under state or federal law.

"Build party" is also used to describe a type of activity that is more problematic. This activity usually involves a situation where either money exchanges hands for assistance with completing the 80% receiver, machinery is rented, and/or a computer numerical control machine (CNC machine) is used. A CNC machine is an automatic machine that will perform milling based on instructions from a programmable code. Once programed, the machine can perform its program over and over again (for example, finishing 80% receivers). Some companies and organizations have offered to sell 80% receivers and an opportunity to finish the purchased 80% receiver with their machinery. Other businesses are offering an opportunity for people to use their CNC machine for the purpose of finishing 80% receivers.

These practices are problematic, and the ATF has determined that any businesses/individuals engaging in these practices are engaged in the business of manufacturing firearms under federal law.[292] Engaging in the business of manufacturing requires a license, bookkeeping, special engraving, and all of the other requirements associated with manufacturing and transferring firearms.

---

[291] In 2014, the ATF went even further with its position on the "80% AR receiver" stating that 80% receivers that have material that extends "past the exterior walls of the casting, indicating the approximate location of the holes to be drilled for the selector, hammer, and trigger pins" were considered to be "firearms" for purposes of federal law. Moreover, the ATF has also taken the position that 80% receivers that have so-called "indexing," *i.e.,* different colored material that outlines where to drill the fire control cavity, are "firearms" for purposes of federal law. The ATF's stance on when an 80% receiver is considered be a "firearm" is being challenged in court. *See Lycurgan, Inc. dba Ares Armor v. B. Todd Jones,* no. 14-CV-0548-JLS-BGS (Complaint filed Mar. 3, 2014). Although the plaintiff's lost at the trial court level, this case is currently being appealed to the Ninth Circuit. *Lycurgan, Inc. dba Ares Armor v. B. Todd Jones,* No. 16-55341 (Opening Brief filed Sep. 23, 2016). But, as of the date of publication, the Court has yet to decide the case.

[292] ATF Rul. 2015-1 (2015). Manufacturing a firearm without a valid license is a violation of 18 U.S.C. section 922(a)(1)(A).

4   3D Printing

In May 2013, there was a lot of press about 3D-printed handguns. In August 2013, there were reports of a 3D-printed .22 caliber rifle, and in November 2013 a company created a 3D-printed 1911 handgun.[293] While the process of making a firearm for personal use is generally lawful, 3D-printed firearms do have some additional concerns.

There are many processes that can be classified as "3D printing." The general concept is usually the same. An object or device is either designed or scanned in three dimensions, and the data is fed into a computer. The data from the computer is then sent to the 3D printer. Similar to how a computer tells a conventional printer to print out a document, the computer tells the 3D printer how to construct the three-dimensional object.

The 3D printer adds layer upon layer of the material to create the object. The material used depends on the machine and process. Currently, there is no process to create a single object that has moving parts, but existing technology allows the printer to create all of the individual parts of an object comprised of moving parts. While the process cannot make a whole firearm, it can make each of the parts for a firearm, which can then be assembled. For instance, now available for purchase is a computer-numerically-controlled (or CNC) mill that can complete an 80% receiver for you. Most 3D printers use some form of plastic or polymer, though there are more expensive 3D printers that work with metal, such as the one used to create a metal 1911 handgun. To make a firearm, the material must be strong enough to stand up to the stress of being fired. If made solely from plastic or polymer, a "printed" firearm could theoretically be undetectable to airport metal detectors.

Part of the concern when 3D-printed firearms were first discussed was that they might not be able to be detected by airport security. Since these firearms may be considered an "undetectable firearm,"[294] "zip gun"[295] or "an unconventional pistol,"[296] exercise caution in possessing them as these types of firearms are illegal under federal and California law. The legality of 3D-printed firearms is discussed in greater detail in Chapter 9.

---

[293] Solid Concepts Manufactures First 3D-Printed Metal Pistol, Gizmag (Nov. 8, 2013), http://www.gizmag.com/worlds-first-3d-printed-gun/29702/ (last visited July 11, 2017).

[294] 18 U.S.C. § 922(p); P.C. §§ 24610, 17280.

[295] P.C. §§ 17360, 33600.

[296] P.C. §§ 17270, 31500 (this depends on whether or not the barrel is rifled).

B. Registration Requirements for Manufacturing or Assembling Your Own Firearm

Although Governor Jerry Brown vetoed Senate President Pro Tem Kevin de León's infamous "ghost gun" bill in 2014,[297] Governor Brown gave in to Senator de León's repeated attempt to pass his "ghost gun" legislation and signed AB 857 on July 22, 2016. As explained in detail below, AB 857 requires individuals to obtain a serial number or identification mark for certain firearms that do not have identifying marks that they currently own or plan to create after July 1, 2018.

Interestingly, this legislation is nearly identical to Senator de León's "ghost gun" bill that was vetoed in 2014. Yet, Governor Brown signed it anyway. Why Governor Brown chose to sign this bill and veto the other is a mystery. But what is clear is that this legislation will still do nothing to advance public safety.

1. Obtaining Serial Numbers or Identification Marks Before Assembling or Manufacturing a Firearm

Beginning July 1, 2018, unless you meet an exception, you will be required to do all of the following before assembling or manufacturing[298] a firearm:

(1) Apply for a unique serial number or identification mark from the DOJ; *and*

(2) Engrave or permanently affix to the firearm the unique serial number or identification mark in a manner that meets or exceeds the requirements imposed on licensed importers or licensed manufactures of firearms as provided in 18 U.S.C. section 923(i) (requiring licensed manufactures and importers to identify firearms by engraving or casting a serial number on the receiver of the weapon as provided in 27 C.F.R. section 478.92), and the regulations issued thereto, within 10 days of actually manufacturing or assembling the firearm; *and*

(3) If the firearm is manufactured or assembled from polymer plastic, 3.7 ounces of material type 17-4 PH stainless steel must be embedded within the plastic upon fabrication or construction with the unique serial number engraved or otherwise permanently affixed in a manner that meets the requirements imposed on licensed importers and licensed manufactures under 18 U.S.C. section 923(i) and the regulations issued pursuant thereto;[299] *and*

(4) Notify the DOJ (at a time to be determined by the DOJ) that you have engraved or permanently affixed the serial number on the firearm with "sufficient information to identify the owner of the firearm, the unique

---

[297] *See* SB 808, 2013-2014 Leg., Reg. Sess. (Cal. 2014), *available at* https://leginfo.legislature.ca.gov/faces/billNavClient.xhtml?bill_id=201320140SB808 (last visited July 11, 2017).

[298] The terms "manufacture" and "assemble" mean "to fabricate or construct a firearm, or to fit together the component parts of a firearm to construct a firearm." P.C. § 29180(a).

[299] It is unclear whether serial number must be engraved or permanently attached to the piece of steel that must be embedded into the polymer plastic, or whether the serial number can be engraved into or permanently attached to the polymer plastic.

serial number or mark of identification provided by the department, and the firearm."[300]

As of the date of publication, the DOJ has not circulated any regulations with regards to how a person can apply for and obtain a serial number or identification mark.[301] Yet, the law states that the DOJ can only grant an application for a serial number or identification mark if all of the following are completed:

(1) For each transaction, the applicant must complete a Personal Firearms Eligibility Check (PFEC)[302] demonstrating that the applicant is not prohibited by state or federal law from possessing receiving, owning, or purchasing a firearm; *and*

(2) The applicant must present proof of age and identity as provided in P.C. section 16400 (*i.e.*, a valid California driver's license or identification card). The applicant must be at least 18 years old to obtain a unique serial number or identification mark for a firearm that is not a handgun, and at least 21 years old to obtain a serial number or identification mark for a handgun; *and*

(3) Provides a description of the firearm that he or she owns or intends to manufacture or assemble; *and*

(4) The applicant must have a valid FSC or unexpired HSC.[303]

The DOJ can charge a fee for each distinguishing number or mark it issues in the amount sufficient to reimburse it for the actual costs associated with assigning the number and for conducting the PFEC.[304] The specifics of this fee will also be determined by regulations.

Any person who manufactures or assembles a handgun without first obtaining a serial number or identification mark after July 1, 2018 is guilty of a misdemeanor, punishable by up to one year in county jail, $1000 fine, or both.[305] Any person who manufactures or assembles any a firearm, other than a handgun, without obtaining a serial number or identification mark after July 1, 2018 is also guilty of a misdemeanor, punishable by up to six months in a county jail, $1000 fine, or both.[306]

It is also a crime to sell or transfer any firearms manufactured or assembled after July 1, 2018.[307]

---

[300] P.C. § 29180. California law does not state what is sufficient enough information to is to identify the firearm. But, presumably, this would mean the type, caliber, barrel length, etc.

[301] Given DOJ's present problems promulgating regulations on a timely basis, do not expect these regulations to be on time. We will be monitoring this situation as the deadline gets close. And given DOJ's recent penchant for requiring pictures with registration (see Chapter 8 for "assault weapon" registration), expect DOJ to require pictures of your firearm at one point or another.

[302] *See* Chapter 3.

[303] P.C. § 29182.

[304] P.C. § 29183.

[305] P.C. § 29180(f).

[306] P.C. § 29180(f).

[307] P.C. § 29180.

2. Obtaining a Serial Number or Identification Mark for Firearm Owned After July 1, 2018 That Does Not Bear a Serial Number Assigned to It

Anyone who owns a firearm that does not bear a serial number assigned to it on or after July 1, 2018, must do all of the following before January 1, 2019:

(1) Apply to the DOJ for a unique serial number or other identification mark (see subsection above); *and*

(2) Engrave or permanently affix to the firearm the unique serial number or identification mark in a manner that meets or exceeds the requirements imposed on licensed importers or licensed manufactures of firearms as provided in 18 U.S.C. section 923(i) (requiring licensed manufactures and importers to identify firearms by engraving or casting a serial number on the receiver of the weapon as provided in 27 C.F.R. section 478.92), and the regulations issued thereto, within ten days of receiving the serial number; *and*

(3) Notify the DOJ (at a time to be determined by the DOJ) that you have engraved or permanently affixed the serial number on the firearm with "sufficient information to identify the owner of the firearm, the unique serial number or mark of identification provided by the department, and the firearm."[308]

Any person who continues to possess a handgun that does not bear a serial number assigned to it is guilty of a misdemeanor, punishable by up to one year in county jail, $1000 fine, or both.[309] Any person who possess a firearm, other than a handgun, that does not bear serial number assigned to it after July 1, 2016 is also guilty of a misdemeanor, punishable by up to six months in a county jail, $1000 fine, or both.[310]

3. Exemptions

If you own or plan on assembling or manufacturing any of the following firearms after July 1, 2018, you do not have to obtain a serial number or other identification mark:

(1) A firearm that has a serial number assigned to it under P.C. section 23910 (assignment of new firearm identification number or mark when original number or mark is missing or obliterated) or 18 U.S.C. sections 921-931 (assignment of serial number on each firearm imported or manufactured by a licensed importer or manufacturer); *or*

(2) A firearm made or assembled prior to December 16, 1968, that is not a handgun; *or*

---

[308] P.C. § 29180.
[309] P.C. § 29180(f).
[310] P.C. § 29180(f).

(3) A firearm which was entered into the centralized registry set forth in P.C. section 11106 prior to July 1, 2018, as being owned by a specific individual or entity if a distinguishing number or identification mark has been assigned to that firearm by virtue of the DOJ accepting entry of the firearm into the centralized registry; *or*

(4) A firearm that has a serial number assigned to it under the NFA and the regulations issued pursuant thereto; *or*

(5) A firearm that is a "curio or relic" or an antique firearm as those terms are defined in 27 C.F.R. section 479.11.[311]

Theoretically, a person would fit in this exception (meaning that a person would not need to apply for and obtain a serial number before assembling or manufacturing a firearm after July 1, 2018) if he or she stamped their own number or identifying mark on their firearm as provided in P.C. section 23915 and voluntarily register that number or identifying mark with the DOJ in accordance with P.C. section 28000 before July 1, 2018.[312] This is because once the firearm has been voluntarily registered under P.C. section 28000, it will (or at least should) be entered into the centralized registry set forth in P.C. section 11106, meaning that the person would be exempt from this new requirement through subsection (3) in the list above.[313]

IX. COMING INTO CALIFORNIA WITH FIREARMS

A. Visiting California

If you are coming into California to visit or establish residency and are bringing firearms, ammunition, or magazines, your first order of business is to determine if these items are legal for you to possess or import into California. You can do this by reviewing Chapters 8 and 9 of this book and the DOJ Bureau of Firearms' website. If you lawfully possess items out of state that are illegal to possess in California, you will need to get the applicable permits or licenses or meet one of the exceptions mentioned in the corresponding chapters *before* bringing them into California. Also, make sure that you familiarize yourself with California's transportation and storage requirements before you bring your firearms into the state.

It is legal to bring an "off-Roster" handgun on your visit to California.[314]

---

[311] P.C. § 29181.

[312] You can voluntarily register a firearm under P.C. section 28000 by filling out an filing a Voluntary Registration Form with the DOJ. This form can be accessed at: https://oag.ca.gov/sites/all/files/agweb/pdfs/firearms/forms/volreg.pdf (last visited July 11, 2017).

[313] *See* P.C. §§ 11106(a)(2)(D); 16585(a)(10).

[314] California law prohibits the importation of an "unsafe handgun" for sale. P.C. § 32000. "Unsafe handguns" and the DOJ's Roster of Handguns Certified for Sale (Roster) in California are discussed in more detail in Chapter 9.

B. Moving Into California

In addition to the restrictions when just visiting California, if you come to the state intending to make it your permanent residence and you meet the definition of a "personal firearm importer," you will have to register your firearms[315] with the DOJ or sell or transfer them within 60 days of bringing them into California.[316]

You are considered a "personal firearm importer" if you are over 18 years of age, own a firearm, and meet all of the following:

(1) You are not licensed pursuant to P.C. sections 26700 to 26915, inclusive (i.e., you are not a California-licensed firearms dealer); *and*

(2) You are not a licensed firearms manufacturer or importer;[317] *and*

(3) You own the firearm; *and*

(4) You acquired the firearm outside of California; *and*

(5) For handguns, you moved into this state on or after January 1, 1998, and for all firearms, you moved into California on or after January 1, 2014, as a resident[318] of this state; *and*

(6) You intend to possess the handgun within this state on or after January 1, 1998, or firearm within this state on or after January 1, 2014; *and*

(7) The firearm was delivered to you by a person who is not licensed as a California firearms dealer;[319] *and*

(8) While a California resident, you did not previously report ownership of that firearm to the DOJ with information about you and a description of the firearm; *and*

(9) The firearm is not prohibited by any of P.C. section 16590's provisions (i.e., it is not a "generally prohibited weapon"); *and*

(10) The firearm is not an "assault weapon," .50 BMG rifle, destructive device, or "machine gun."[320]

People are often concerned that they have not properly registered their firearm after the 60-day requirement has lapsed. In the past, the DOJ has allowed late handgun registration, but this could change in the future.

---

[315] Before January 1, 2014, this requirement only related to handguns and most of the requirements above for "personal firearm importers" applied to these "personal handgun importers."

[316] P.C. § 27560. In order to register your firearm you must fill out a "New Resident Report of Firearm Ownership" form (BF 4010A) and pay the requisite $19 processing fee. Cal. Code Regs. tit. 11, § 4002.

[317] 18 U.S.C. § 921.

[318] You are a resident of California if California is your true, fixed, and permanent home and principal residence to which you intend to return whenever you are absent. P.C. § 17000(b)(1); Cal. Veh. Code § 12505. For military members, residency is established when you are discharged from active service in California. P.C. § 17000(b)(2).

[319] The person must be licensed per P.C. sections 26700 to 26915, inclusive i.e,. the person is a California-licensed firearms dealer), and must have delivered the firearm as set forth in P.C. sections 27540 and P.C. sections 26700-26915, inclusive (governing dealers' requirements in delivery of firearm, such as abiding by the 10-day wait, and dealers' licensing requirements).

[320] P.C. § 17000.

Table 4.9

REGISTRATION DEADLINES FOR INDIVIDUALS	
TYPE OF TRANSFER	REGISTRATION DEADLINE
Transfers through a licensed firearms dealer, including Private Party Transfers (P.C. § 28155, 28160, 28215(d))	Since the 1990s, handguns transferred through a licensed dealer are required to be registered once the DROS is filed. Effective January 1, 2014, any firearm transferred through a licensed dealer is registered once the DROS is filed.
Individuals bringing a handgun into the state who are considered "personal handgun importers" (P.C. §§ 17000, 27560)	Effective January 1, 1989, must be registered with the DOJ within 60 days of bringing a handgun into the state.
Individuals bringing any firearm into the state who are considered a "personal firearm importer" (P.C. § 27560)	Effective January 1, 2014, must be registered with the DOJ within 60 days of bringing any firearm into the state.
Transfers of any firearms by gift, bequest, intestate succession between members of the same immediate family who both reside in the state of California (P.C. § 27875)	Effective January 1, 1995, must be registered with the DOJ within 30 days of taking possession.
Transfer of a firearm from one spouse to another via transmutation who both reside in California (P.C. §§ 16990(g), 27920)	Effective January 1, 1993, must be registered with the DOJ within 30 days of taking possession.
Transfer, or importation into California, of "curio or relic" *long guns* to a licensed collector of "curio or relic" firearms with a COE (P.C. § 27966)	Effective January 1, 2014, must be registered with the DOJ within 30 days of taking possession.
Transfer of "curio or relic" handguns from out of state to a licensed collector of "curios or relics" (P.C. §§ 27590, 27565(b))	Effective January 1, 1998 , must be registered within five days of transporting a firearm into California.

X. FIREARM STORAGE

Although both California and federal law require that a "safety device" accompany your firearm purchase in certain circumstances, neither set of laws requires that you actually use one while storing it. In fact, there is no general California or federal law specifically requiring you to store firearms in any particular manner, although some cities have local firearm-storage requirements.

Despite this, you may nonetheless be prosecuted for criminally storing a firearm in certain situations.

A. Criminal Storage in the First, Second, and Third Degree for Loaded Firearms

Historically, you could only be criminally prosecuted in situations where children gained access to your firearms. But, with the passage of SB 363 in 2013, criminal liability has been expanded to cover situations where others gain possession of your firearms. Specifically, you may be prosecuted if you store a firearm in a place under your custody or control in a way a person prohibited from possessing firearms under state or federal law may gain access to it and cause tragic results (as discussed below).[321] This would be considered "criminal storage of a firearm" in the first degree or second degree.[322]

You can be charged with "criminal storage of a firearm" in the first degree if you keep a loaded firearm anywhere under your custody or control where you know, or reasonably should know, a child or a person prohibited from possessing firearms under state or federal law is likely to gain unpermitted access to it, a child or prohibited person does get access to it, and death or great bodily injury occurs as a result.[323]

Though it is a lesser offense, you may also be prosecuted if a child or prohibited person who accesses your firearm either injures, "brandishes" it or carries it to a public place.[324] This is "criminal storage of a firearm" in the second degree.

You may be prosecuted for a misdemeanor if you negligently store or leave a loaded firearm in a location where you know, or reasonably should know, that a child is likely to gain access to the firearm. This is considered "criminal storage of a firearm" in the third degree.[325] To violate this law, there is no requirement that the child harm someone or take the firearm to a public place. It is important to note that this crime may be committed even if the child does not actually gain possession of the firearm.

---

[321] P.C. § 25100.
[322] P.C. § 25100(a)-(b).
[323] P.C. § 25100(a).
[324] P.C. § 25100(b)(3).
[325] P.C. § 25100(c).

You are not liable under these laws if you took reasonable action to secure the firearm against access by the child, or your conduct falls under any of the exceptions discussed below.

One important criticism of this law, and something that you should be vigilant of, is the fact that the law seems to leave open a large amount of discretion for law enforcement to determine what constitutes negligent storage. Where the person who allegedly stored a firearm in violation of P.C. section 25100 is the parent or guardian of a child injured or killed, California law gives prosecutors express discretion to bring or not bring charges. It suggests charges should only be brought where the parent acted in a grossly negligent manner or where other "egregious circumstances" exist. But it is best to avoid tragedy and reliance on a prosecutor's mercy by properly storing your firearms whenever children are present.

B. Storage of Handguns and Any Firearm

You can also be prosecuted for a misdemeanor if you keep a handgun, whether loaded or unloaded, anywhere under your custody or control and know, or reasonably should know, that a child or prohibited person is likely to gain unpermitted access to it, and a child or prohibited person does gain access to it and thereafter carries it off-premises.[326] It is also a misdemeanor, with a possible steeper maximum fine ($5,000 vs. $1,000), if the child or prohibited person takes any firearm to a preschool, elementary, middle, or high school, or to any school-sponsored event, activity, or performance, whether it occurs on school grounds or not.[327]

C. Exceptions to Criminal Storage in the First, Second, and Third Degree and Storage of Handguns or Any Firearms

You should not be prosecuted under the laws discussed above for criminally storing a loaded firearm or if a child or prohibited person carries a handgun off-premises if:

(1) The child obtained the firearm as a result of an illegal entry to your premises by any person; *or*

(2) The firearm is kept in a locked container or place a reasonable person would believe is secure; *or*

(3) The firearm is carried on you or is so close in proximity to you that you can easily obtain and use it as if it were actually carried on you; *or*

---

[326] P.C. § 25200(a).
[327] P.C. § 25200(b).

(4) The firearm has a locking device that has made the firearm inoperable; *or*

(5) You are a peace officer or National Guard or military member, and the child obtains the firearm during, or incidental to, the performance of your duties; *or*

(6) The child obtains, or obtains and discharges, the firearm in self-defense or in defense of another person; *or*

(7) Based on objective facts and circumstances, it would be unreasonable to expect a child to be present on your premises.[328]

D. Residing With a Person Who Is Prohibited from Possessing, Receiving, Owning, or Purchasing Firearms

There are restrictions on firearm storage if you reside with someone who is prohibited from possessing, receiving, owning, or purchasing firearms under state or federal law.[329] If you live with such a person, you cannot keep a firearm in the residence[330] unless the firearm:

(1) Kept within a locked container, locked gun safe, or locked trunk, or it is locked with a locking device; *or*

(2) Disabled by a firearm safety device; *or*

(3) Carried on you or is so close in proximity to you that you can easily obtain and use it as if it were actually carried on you.[331]

Disturbingly, this law requires that you keep your firearms locked up if you live with *anyone* who cannot purchase a firearm. As discussed above, minors cannot purchase firearms, so it seems that your firearms must be secured as described above if you live with a minor.

These restrictions do apply to ammunition. Remember that a person with a California firearm prohibition is prohibited from "possessing" firearms and ammunition. And remember that "ammunition" includes clips, magazines, and speed loaders as well, as discussed in Chapter 2.

There have also been attempts in California to enact laws requiring firearms to be locked at all times when the owner is not home, even if they are in a locked home where no one is present. These attempts have so far been unsuccessful. Firearm-storage laws represent an evolving area of firearms law with some localities

---

[328] P.C. §§ 25105, 25205.

[329] P.C. § 25135.

[330] For purposes of this restriction, a "residence" is "any structure intended or used for human habitation, including, but not limited to, houses, condominiums, rooms, motels, time-shares, and recreational or other vehicles where human habitation occurs." P.C. § 17060.

[331] P.C. § 25135.

attempting to place further restrictions on their residents regarding firearms storage.[332]

E. Storage of Handgun in Unattended Vehicle

In response to a string of incidents where individuals stole firearms from unattended law enforcement vehicles and used them to commit heinous crimes, the legislature passed laws in 2016 and 2017 that govern the storage of handguns in unattended vehicles (i.e., SB 869 and SB 497).[333] Under these bills, any person (including any peace officer or honorably retired peace officer) who leaves a handgun in an unattended "vehicle"[334] must:

(1) Lock the handgun in the vehicle's trunk; *or*

(2) Lock the handgun in a "locked container"[335] and place the container out of plain view; *or*

(3) Lock the handgun in a "locked container" that is permanently affixed to the vehicle's interior and not in plain view.[336]

Beginning in 2018, a peace officer[337] will be permitted to lock a handgun out of plain view within the center utility console of an unattended motor vehicle if (1)

---

[332] The City and County of San Francisco, for example, maintains one of the most restrictive firearm-storage laws in the country. San Francisco Police Code section 4512 requires handguns to be kept in a locked container or disabled with a trigger lock *at all times* when not under the control of a peace officer or on the person of an adult over 18. I challenged San Francisco's requirement on behalf of the NRA in *Jackson v. City and County of San Francisco*, No. C09-cv-02143 (N.D. Cal. filed May 15, 2009). In that lawsuit, we argued that the San Francisco's firearm storage laws infringed on the Second Amendment. After the Ninth Circuit Court of Appeals upheld the constitutionality of San Francisco's storage laws, we petitioned the United States Supreme for a writ of certiorari. Although the Supreme Court ultimately denied cert, two Supreme Court Justices, Justice Thomas and Justice Scalia, dissented from the denial of certiorari arguing that the court should have granted review as "San Francisco's law burdens the core of the Second Amendment right." *Jackson v. City and Cnty. of San Francisco*, 134 S. Ct. 2799, 2801 (2015). In 2015, the Los Angeles City Council also approved a measure that may require residents to lock up or disable their handguns with trigger locks when the handgun is not being carried or within arm's reach inside their home. *See* Emily Alpert Reyes, *L.A. to Require that Stored Handguns be Locked up or Disabled*, L.A. Times (Oct. 27, 2015), *available at* http://www.latimes.com/local/lanow/la-me-ln-gun-storage-20151027-story.html (last visited July 11, 2017). In addition, San Jose is pursuing a similar mandatory locked-storage ordinance. A draft ordinance is expected to be introduced to the City Council in late 2017.

[333] SB 869, 2015-2016 Leg., Reg. Sess. (Cal. 2016), *available at* https://leginfo.legislature.ca.gov/faces/billNavClient.xhtml?bill_id=201520160SB869 (last visited July 11, 2017); SB 497, 2016-2017 Leg., Reg. Sess. (Cal. 2017), *available at* https://leginfo.legislature.ca.gov/faces/billTextClient.xhtml?bill_id=201720180SB497 (last visited Oct. 13, 2017).

[334] "Vehicle" is defined as "a device by which any person or property may be propelled, moved, or drawn upon a highway, excepting a device moved exclusively by human power or used exclusively upon stationary rails or tracks." CAL. VEH. CODE § 670.

[335] "Locked container" means a secure container that is fully enclosed and locked by a padlock, keylock, combination lock, or similar locking device. The term "locked container" does not include the utility or glove compartment of a motor vehicle. P.C. § 25140(d)(1)(A) (effective Jan. 1, 2018).

[336] P.C. §§ 25140(a); 25452.

[337] "Peace officer" means a sworn officer described in Chapter 4.5 (commencing with Section 830) of Title 3 of Part 2, or a sworn federal law enforcement officer, who is authorized to carry a firearm in the course and scope of that officer's duties, while that officer is on duty or off duty. P.C. § 25140(d)(1(B) (effective Jan. 1, 2018).

that vehicle is not equipped with a trunk and (2) he or she is unable to otherwise comply with the requirements listed above.[338]

Failing to abide by these requirements for storing handguns in an unattended vehicle is an infraction, punishable be a fine not to exceed one thousand dollars.[339]

For purposes of this restriction, a vehicle is considered to be "unattended" when "a person who is lawfully carrying or transporting a handgun in a vehicle is not within close enough proximity to the vehicle to reasonably prevent unauthorized access to the vehicle or its contents."[340] Also for purposes of this restriction, "plain view" includes any area of the vehicle that is visible by peering through the windows of the vehicle with or without illumination and regardless of whether the windows are tinted.[341]

This general restriction does not apply to any "peace officer during circumstances requiring immediate aid or action that are within the course and scope of his or her official duties," or to "the transportation of unloaded firearms by a person operating a licensed common carrier or an authorized agent or employee thereof when the firearms are transported in conformance with applicable or federal laws."[342]

1. Storage of Lawfully-Obtained "Unsafe" Handgun in Unattended Vehicle by Certain Law Enforcement Officers

As explained more fully in Chapter 9, "unsafe" handguns are handguns that are not listed on DOJ's Roster of Handguns Certified for Sale (Roster). Generally, California residents cannot acquire "unsafe" handguns unless they meet one of the exceptions listed in P.C. section 32000 (and discussed in detail in Chapter 9).[343] Individuals that meet one of those exceptions can lawfully obtain an "unsafe" handgun. One of those exceptions is located in P.C. section 32000(b)(6), and it applies to the purchase of an "unsafe" handgun by sworn members of certain law enforce-

---

[338] P.C. § 25140(b) (effective Jan. 1, 2018).

[339] P.C. § 25140(b); *see* P.C. § 25140(c) (effective Jan. 1, 2018).

[340] P.C. § 25140(b)(3); *see* P.C. § 25140(d)(2) (effective Jan. 1, 2018).

[341] P.C. § 25140(d)(3) (effective Jan. 1, 2018)

[342] P.C. §§ 25140(d) (2017), 25645; *see* P.C. § 25140(e) (effective Jan. 1, 2018).

[343] P.C. § 32000.

ment entities[344] who have satisfactorily completed the firearms portion of a training course prescribed by the Commission on Peace Officer Standards and Training.[345]

If an individual obtained an "unsafe" handgun pursuant to the specific exception stated in P.C. section 32000(b)(6), he or she must do one of the following when leaving their "unsafe" handgun unattended[346] in a vehicle[347]:

(1) Lock the "unsafe handgun" in the vehicle's trunk, *or*

(2) Lock the "unsafe handgun" in a "locked container"[348] and place the container out of plain view, *or*

(3) Lock the "unsafe handgun" in a "locked container" that is permanently affixed to the vehicle's interior and not in plain view.[349]

This restriction does not apply to a peace officer during circumstances requiring immediate aid or action that are within the course of his or her official duties.[350]

As explained in Chapter 6, a "locked container" does not include a vehicle's "utility or glove compartment," even if it is locked.[351] So, you cannot store an "unsafe handgun" in the utility or glove compartment when leaving your vehicle unattended.

Failing to properly store an "unsafe handgun" in an unattended vehicle as explained above is an infraction, punishable by a fine not exceeding a thousand dollars.[352]

---

[344] The applicable law enforcement entities are: A) The Department of Parks and Recreation; (B) The Department of Alcoholic Beverage Control; (C) The Division of Investigation of the Department of Consumer Affairs; (D) The Department of Motor Vehicles; (E) The Fraud Division of the Department of Insurance; (F) The State Department of State Hospitals; (G) The Department of Fish and Wildlife; (H) The State Department of Developmental Services; (I) The Department of Forestry and Fire Protection; (J) A county probation department; (K) The Los Angeles World Airports, as defined in Section 830.15; (L) A K-12 public school district for use by a school police officer, as described in Section 830.32; (M) A municipal water district for use by a park ranger, as described in Section 830.34; (N) A county for use by a welfare fraud investigator or inspector, as described in Section 830.35; (O) A county for use by the coroner or the deputy coroner, as described in Section 830.35; (P) The Supreme Court and the courts of appeal for use by marshals of the Supreme Court and bailiffs of the courts of appeal, and coordinators of security for the judicial branch, as described in Section 830.36; (Q) A fire department or fire protection agency of a county, city, city and county, district, or the state for use by either (i) A member of an arson-investigating unit, regularly paid and employed in that capacity pursuant to Section 830.37 or (ii) A member other than a member of an arson-investigating unit, regularly paid and employed in that capacity pursuant to Section 830.37; (R) The University of California Police Department, or the California State University Police Departments, as described in Section 830.2; and (S) A California Community College police department, as described in Section 830.32. P.C. § 32000(b)(6).

[345] P.C. § 32000(b)(6).

[346] A vehicle is considered to be "'unattended' when a person who is lawfully carrying or transporting a handgun in the vehicle is not within close proximity to the vehicle to reasonably prevent unauthorized access to the vehicle or its contents." P.C. § 32000(c)(2)(C)(ii) .

[347] A "'vehicle' is a device by which any person or property may be propelled, moved, or drawn upon a highway, excepting a device moved exclusively by human power or used exclusively upon stationary rails or tracks." CAL. VEH. CODE § 670; P.C. § 32000(c)(2)(C)(i).

[348] The term "locked container" is defined in Chapter 6.

[349] P.C. § 32000(c)(2).

[350] P.C. § 32000(c)(2)(E) .

[351] P.C. § 25610(a)(1).

[352] P.C. § 32000(c)(2)(B).

F. Local Storage Laws

Along with the state's restrictions on firearm storage, a number of cities, including Los Angeles,[353] Oakland,[354] San Francisco,[355] Santa Cruz,[356] Palm Springs,[357] Sunnyvale,[358] and Tiburon[359] have also passed their own local ordinance that regulate how gun owners must store firearms inside their homes. In general, these ordinances prohibit individuals from keeping their handguns and/or long guns inside their homes unless they are stored in a locked containers or disabled with a trigger lock.

As explained in the introduction of this book, we will not go into detail local restrictions for the purpose of this book. Still, it is always important to check your local laws to make sure that you are lawfully storing your firearm inside your home.

G. Civil Penalties for Community Care Facilities, Residential Care Facilities, Residential Care Facilities for the Elderly, Family Care Homes, and Day Care Centers

Under California law, the California Department of Social Services must issue a civil penalty of $150 per day to any "community care facility,"[360] "residential care facility,"[361] "residential care facility for the elderly",[362] "family day care home,"[363] or "day care center"[364] that has firearms or ammunition accessible.[365]

---

[353] LA., CAL. MUN. CODE § 55.21.

[354] OAKLAND, CAL. MUN. CODE § 9.39.040.

[355] S.F., CA. MUN. CODE § 4512.

[356] SANTA CRUZ, CA. MUN. CODE § 9.29.020.

[357] PALM SPRINGS, CA. MUN. CODE § 11.16.045.

[358] SUNNYVALE, CA. MUN. CODE § 9.44.040.

[359] TIBURON, CA. MUN. CODE § 32-30.

[360] A "community care facility" is defined as "any facility, place, or building that is maintained and operated to provide nonmedical residential care, day treatment, adult day care, or foster family agency services for children, adults, or children and adults, including, but not limited to, the physically handicapped, mentally impaired, incompetent persons, and abused or neglected children, and includes" "residential facilities," "adult day pro-grams," "therapeutic day services facilities," "foster family agencies;" "small family homes;" "social rehabilitation facilities;" and "community treatment facilities." CAL. HEALTH & SAF. CODE § 1502.

[361] A "residential care facility" is "a residential care facility for persons with chronic, life-threatening illness who are 18 year of age or older or are emancipated minors, and for family units." CAL. HEALTH & SAF. CODE § 1568.01.

[362] A "residential care facility for the elderly" is "a housing arrangement chosen voluntarily by persons 60 years of age or over, or their authorized representative, where varying levels and intensities of care and supervision, protective supervision, or personal care are provided, based upon their varying needs, as determined in order to be admitted and to remain in the facility." CAL. HEALTH & SAF. CODE § 1569.2.

[363] A "family day care home" is "a home that regularly provides care, protection, and supervision for 14 or fewer children, in the provider's own home, for periods of less than 24 hours per day, while the parents or guardians are away, and is either a large family day care home or a small family day care home." CAL. HEALTH & SAF. CODE § 1596.78.

[364] A "day care center" is "any child day care facility other than a family day care home, and includes infant centers, preschools, extended day care facilities, and school age child care centers." CAL. HEALTH & SAF. CODE § 1596.76.

[365] CAL. HEALTH & SAF. CODE §§ 1548(c)(5) ("community care facilities"), 1568.0822(c)(5) ("residential care facilities"), 1569.49(c)(5) ("residential care facilities for the elderly"), 1596.99(c)(5) ("day care centers"), 1597.58(c)(5) ("family day care homes).

As of July 1, 2017, the fine will be increased from $150 per day to $500 per violation and $100 for each day the violation continues after the citation.[366]

Table 4.10

CALIFORNIA'S FIREARM STORAGE LAWS	
STORAGE OF A HANDGUN AND ANY FIREARM (P.C. § 25200)	
You may be guilty of a misdemeanor punishable by imprisonment in county jail not exceeding one year, by a fine not exceeding $1,000, or by both if: (1) You keep *a handgun*, loaded or unloaded, within any premises under your custody or control; *and* (2) You know or reasonably should know that a child is likely to gain access to the handgun without the permission of the child's parent or legal guardian, or that a prohibited person is likely to gain access to it; *and* (3) The child or prohibited person obtains access to the handgun and carries it off-premises.	You may be guilty of a misdemeanor punishable by imprisonment in a county jail not exceeding one year, by fine not exceeding $5,000, or by both if: (1) You keep *any firearm* within any premises under your custody or control; *and* (2) You know or reasonably should know that a child is likely to gain access to the firearm without the permission of the child's parent or legal guardian, or that a prohibited person is likely to gain access to it; *and* (3) The child or prohibited person carries the firearm off-premises to any public or private school, elementary school, middle school, high school, or to any school-sponsored event, activity, or performance, whether occurring on school grounds or elsewhere.

---

[366] *See* CAL. HEALTH & SAF. CODE § 1548(c).

CALIFORNIA'S FIREARM STORAGE LAWS

CRIMINAL STORAGE FOR LOADED FIREARMS (P.C. § 25100)

CRIMINAL STORAGE OF A FIREARM IN THE 1ST DEGREE	CRIMINAL STORAGE OF A FIREARM IN THE 2ND DEGREE	CRIMINAL STORAGE OF A FIREARM IN THE 3RD DEGREE
You may be guilty of criminal storage of a firearm in the 1st degree if: (1) You keep a *loaded firearm* within any premises that are under your custody or control; *and* (2) You know or reasonably should know that a child is likely to access the firearm without the permission of the child's parent or legal guardian, or that a person prohibited from possessing a firearm or deadly weapon is likely to gain access to the firearm; *and* (3) The child or prohibited person gains access to the firearm or deadly weapon and causes death or great bodily injury to themselves or any other person.	You may be guilty of criminal storage of a firearm in the 2nd degree if: (1) You keep any *loaded firearm* within any premises that are under your custody and control; *and* (2) You know or reasonably should know that a child is likely to gain access to the firearm without the permission of the child's parent or legal guardian, or that a person prohibited from possessing a firearm or deadly weapon is likely to gain access to the firearm; *and* (3) The child or prohibited person obtains access to the firearm and causes injury, other than great bodily injury, to themselves or any other person, or carries the firearm to a public place in violation of P.C. section 417.	You may be guilty of criminal storage of a firearm in the 3rd degree if: (1) You keep any *loaded firearm* within any premises that are under your custody or control; *and* (2) Negligently store or leave a *loaded firearm* in a location where the person knows, or reasonably should know, that a child is likely to gain access to the firearm without the permission of the child's parent or legal guardian, unless you take reasonable action to secure the firearm against access by the child.

STORAGE OF A FIREARM WHILE RESIDING WITH A PROHIBITED PERSON (P.C. § 25135)

If you live with a person prohibited from possessing, receiving, owning, or purchasing firearms under state or federal law, you cannot keep a firearm in the residence unless the firearm is either:

(1) Kept within a locked container, locked gun safe, or locked trunk, or it is locked with a locking device; *or*
(2) Disabled by a firearm safety device; *or*
(3) Carried on you or is so close in proximity to you that you can easily obtain and use it as if it were actually carried on you.

Though not restricted in section 25135 , remember that the prohibited person cannot have access to both firearms *and ammunition*. And "ammunition" includes clips, magazines , and speed loaders as well, as discussed in Chapter 2.

XI. FALSE REPORTS OF LOST OR STOLEN FIREARMS

Beginning January 1, 2017, it will be a misdemeanor under California law to report to any peace officer listed in P.C. sections 830-832.9 or an employee who is assigned to accept reports from citizens, either directly or by telephone, and who is employed by a state or local law enforcement agency which is designated in P.C. section 830.1, 830.2, 8303(e), 830.31, 830.32, 830.33, 830.34, 830.35, 830.36, 830.37, or 830.4 that a firearm has been lost or stolen, knowing that the report is false.[367]

Oddly, Proposition 63 (Prop. 63) also makes it a crime as of November 9, 2016, to report to a local law enforcement agency that a firearm has been lost or stolen, knowing that the report was false.[368] Filing a false report is an infraction, punishable by a fine of $250 for the first offense, and by a fine of $1,000 for a second or subsequent offense.[369]

But filling a false police report has always been illegal pursuant to Penal Code section 148.5, which states that it is a misdemeanor. Therefore, Prop. 63 actually made it less of a violation to falsely report a stolen firearm.

XII. Reporting Lost or Stolen Firearms

Beginning July 1, 2017, any person who discovers that they lost a firearm, or found out that their firearm was stolen, must report the theft or loss to a local law enforcement in the jurisdiction where the theft or loss occurred within five days of the time that he or she knew, or reasonably should have known, that the firearm was lost or stolen.[370]

Despite this general requirement, certain people, organizations, and firearms are exempt from the reporting requirement. Specifically, the following people, organizations, and firearms are exempt:

(1) Antique firearms;[371] and

(2) Any law enforcement agency or peace officer acting within the scope of his or her employment or official duties if he or she reports the loss or theft to his or her employing agency; and

(3) Any United States marshal or member of the Armed Forces of the United States or the National Guard, while engaged in his or her official duties; and

---

[367] P.C. § 148.5(f).

[368] P.C. § 25275, OFFICE OF THE ATTORNEY GENERAL, FULL TEXT OF PROPOSITION 63, *available at* https://www.oag.ca.gov/system/files/initiatives/pdfs/15-0098%20(Firearms)_0.pdf (last visited July 11, 2017).

[369] P.C. § 25275.

[370] P.C. § 25250.

[371] As defined in P.C. §16170. See Chapter 2.

(4) Any person who is licensed under 18 U.S.C. sections 921-931 (i.e., a federally licensed manufacturer, importer, or dealer) and the regulations issued pursuant thereto, and who reports the theft or loss in accordance with 18 U.S.C. section 923(g)(6) (i.e., loss reporting requirement that states that the theft or loss must be reported to the Attorney General and to the appropriate local authorities within 48 hours after the theft or loss is discovered), or its successor provision, and the applicable regulations issued thereto; *and*

(5) Any person whose firearm was lost or stolen prior to July 1, 2017.[372]

Any person who fails to report a lost or stolen firearm is guilty of an infraction, punishable by fine of $100.[373] Subsequent violations of this general restriction can be punished more severely, as a second violation can be punishable with a fine of $1,000 and the third can be punishable by imprisonment in a county jail for up to six months and/or a $1,000 fine.[374]

When reporting a firearm lost or stolen, you must report the make, model, and serial number of the firearm, if known, and provide "any additional relevant information required by the local law enforcement agency taking the report."[375] It is unclear what "any additional relevant information" law enforcement agencies may require. But, there may be serious Fifth Amendment concerns if they request information that may subject you to criminal liability for failing to properly report a lost or stolen firearm under this new law.

If you fail to report that your firearm is lost or has been stolen before the end of the five day window, contact an attorney who is experienced in firearms law immediately to discuss your options.

XIII. ACQUIRING AMMUNITION

It is generally unlawful to acquire "armor-piercing," "explosive," and "incendiary" rounds in California.[376] Prior to 2016, there were very few restrictions on acquiring ammunition or ammunition components. The main restrictions at the time only prevented prohibited persons from receiving ammunition.[377]

This all changed with the passage Senate Bill (SB) 1235 and Prop. 63. Over the coming years, there will be new restrictions on ammunition sales and transfers in California. These new restrictions and their effective dates are explained in further detail below.

---

[372] P.C. §§ 25250(c), 25255.

[373] P.C. § 25265.

[374] P.C. § 25265.

[375] P.C. § 25270.

[376] 18 U.S.C. § 921(a)(1)(4)(A), (17)(A)-(B); P.C. § 16520. These are discussed in Chapter 9.

[377] See Chapter 3 for more on individuals restricted from possessing ammunition.

Note, as explained in Chapter 2, as used in the sections below, the term "ammunition" does not include the components of ammunition like the projectile, primer, case, or powder. Therefore, the restrictions outlined below to not apply to reloaded ammunition.

A. Assembly Bill 962 and Similar Ammunition Regulation Efforts

Before the passage of SB 1235, anti-gun legislators made numerous attempts to regulate ammunition sales and transfers in California. Dating back to 2009, Senator Kevin de León authored a bill (AB 962) that would have imposed burdensome and ill-conceived restrictions on the sale of ammunition within and into California. This bill would have required "handgun ammunition" to be stored out of customers' reach and transferred in a "face-to-face" transaction, thereby making mail-order sales illegal. It would have also required vendors to collect sales information, including the ammunition purchaser's thumbprints.

Fortunately, even though AB 962 was signed into law, its main provisions were found unconstitutionally vague in *Parker v. State of California* because its definition of "handgun ammunition" was unclear. The government appealed the court's decision in *Parker* to the California Supreme Court. While on appeal, however, AB 962 was superseded by the passage of SB 1235 and Prop. 63 because these new laws repealed all references to "handgun ammunition" and replaced it with the term "ammunition." As of the date of publication, it seems likely that the court will dismiss *Parker* as moot. To keep up to date on the current status of this case, subscribe to or check www.crpa.org.

Several cities and counties also regulate ammunition transactions similar to AB 926. But instead of regulating "handgun ammunition" in isolation, they regulate the sale of all ammunition. Los Angeles, Sacramento, San Francisco, Inglewood, Santa Ana, Beverly Hills, and Contra Costa County are examples. Consult your local municipal code to confirm whether ordinances like these exist in your city or county.

In 2013, Senator de León introduced another bill (SB 53) to regulate the sale of ammunition in California.[378] As proposed, this bill would have required ammunition purchasers to register with the DOJ prior to purchasing any ammunition, which would have required people to submit fingerprints, a background check, and pay processing fees.[379] Moreover, this bill would have required the collection and reporting of personal consumer information and thumb printing for all ammuni-

---

[378] SB 53, 2013-2014, Leg. Counsel's Digest (Cal. 2014), *availible at* https://leginfo.legislature.ca.gov/faces/billNavClient.xhtml?bill_id=201320140SB53# (last visited July 11, 2017).

[379] SB 53, 2013-2014, Leg. Counsel's Digest (Cal. 2014), *availible at* https://leginfo.legislature.ca.gov/faces/billNavClient.xhtml?bill_id=201320140SB53# (last visited July 11, 2017).

tion purchases in California, thereby making online and mail-order sales of all ammunition illegal.[380]

Fortunately, this bill failed to garner the necessary votes to pass out of the Legislature. But, the restrictions contained in both AB 962 and SB 53 were ultimately enacted by the passage of both SB 1235 and Prop. 63.

B. Ammunition Sales & Transfers

1. Requirement that Ammunition Sales Must Be Conducted Through a Licensed Ammunition Vendor

Beginning January 1, 2018, "ammunition"[381] sales must be conducted by or processed through a licensed "ammunition vendor" (California-licensed firearms dealers are automatically considered "ammunition vendors").[382] This includes when ammunition is sold between two private parties, neither of whom is a licensed ammunition vendor.[383] And anyone selling more than 500 rounds of ammunition in 30 days needs to obtain an ammunition vendor license.[384]

Like PPTs of firearms (see above), anytime a non-licensed individual sells ammunition to another non-licensed party, they will need to first take that ammunition to a licensed vendor, who will then process the transaction in accordance with the law and deliver it to the purchaser. If the ammunition vendor cannot deliver the ammunition to the purchaser because he or she is prohibited from owning and/or possessing ammunition, the ammunition vendor must return the ammunition back to the seller.[385]

In addition to charging any other applicable fees allowed by California law, an ammunition vendor can charge the individual purchasing the ammunition an administrative fee to process the ammunition sale.[386] The administrative fee is supposed to be set by the DOJ. Yet, as of the time of publication, the DOJ has failed to implement any regulations setting the fee.[387] In fact, the DOJ has failed to imple-

---

[380] SB 53, 2013-2014, Leg. Counsel's Digest (Cal. 2014), *availible at* https://leginfo.legislature.ca.gov/faces/billNav-Client.xhtml?bill_id=201320140SB53# (last visited July 11, 2017).

[381] The term "ammunition" is defined in Chapter 2.

[382] P.C. § 30312(a)(1). A licensed "ammunition vendor" is defined as either "a firearms dealer licensed pursuant to Sections 26700 to 26915, inclusive" or "any person, firm, corporation, or other business enterprise that holds a current ammunition vendor license issued pursuant to [Penal Code section] 30385." P.C. § 16151.

[383] P.C. § 30312(a)(2).

[384] P.C. § 30342.

[385] P.C. § 30312(a)(2).

[386] P.C. § 30312(a)(2).

[387] DOJ has proposed regulations to set this administrative fee, however. DOJ proposes that the fee shall not exceed $5 if the purchaser will be present for immediate delivery of the ammunition. If the purchaser will not be present for immediate delivery of the ammunition, the vendor may charge an additional storage fee as agreed upon with the purchaser prior to the vendor receiving the ammunition. CAL. CODE. REGS., tit. 11 § 4263 (proposed). The problem with this section lies with the requirement that the storage fee be agreed upon prior to the vendor receiving the ammunition. What remains unclear is what must be done if no agreement is made prior to the ammunition being sent to and received by the vendor. Penal Code section 30312 appears to require ammunition vendors to "promptly and properly" process an ammunition transaction. But proposed section 4263 appears to allow an

ment any regulations regarding ammunition vendors, even though the DOJ was required to have regulations in place before July 1, 2017.

Between January 1, 2018 and June 30, 2019 the requirement that all ammunition sales must be conducted by or processed through a licensed ammunition vendor is merely a formality for those conducting private party sales of ammunition because the ammunition vendor does nothing for purposes of the sale until July 1, 2019. In other words, during this time period, the ammunition vendor will merely act as a middle man who will take the ammunition from the seller and literally hand it to the purchaser.

Failing to conduct an ammunition sale through a licensed ammunition vendor is punishable as a misdemeanor.[388]

2. Face-to-Face Transaction Requirement

Beginning January 1, 2018, ammunitions sales, deliveries, and transfers of ownership must occur in a face-to-face transaction with the seller, deliverer or transferor.[389] That means that anytime you plan on selling or transferring ammunition to another private party, you must actually be physically in front of the other party when conducting the transfer or sale. You cannot mail or otherwise send ammunition to another person.

California law still allows individuals to purchase ammunition over the internet or by other means of remote ordering.[390] The law specifies that "ammunition may be purchased or acquired over the Internet or through other means of remote ordering if a licensed ammunition vendor":

(1) Initially receives the ammunition and

(2) Processes the transaction in compliance with

 (a) P.C. section 30312 [law requiring ammunition sales to be conducted by and through licensed ammunition vendors] and

 (b) *P.C. sections 30342 through 30369 [i.e., California's background check and record-keeping requirements].*[391]

California's background check and record-keeping requirements do not go into effect until July 1, 2019.[392] And DOJ is nowhere close to publishing the regulations and forms needed for these background checks and record-keeping requirements.

---

ammunition vendor to refuse shipment of ammunition when it is sent to the vendor for processing (pursuant to Penal Code section 30312) but the customer does not agree to the transfer fees prior to the vendor receiving the ammunition.

[388] P.C. § 30312(d).

[389] P.C. § 30312(b).

[390] P.C. § 30312(b).

[391] P.C. § 30312(b) (emphasis added).

[392] P.C. § 30352.

Therefore, from January 1, 2018 to July 1, 2019, an ammunition vendor cannot process an Internet or remote order transaction "in compliance with . . . [P.C. sections 30342 through 30369]."[393] As such, the law as written makes no sense ,and it remains to be seen how the government will reconcile the paradox within it.

Selling, delivering, or transferring ammunition in violation of the above requirements is punishable as a misdemeanor.

3. Exceptions to the Requirement that Ammunition Sales Must Be Conducted Through a Licensed Ammunition Vendor and Face-to-Face Requirement

Both the requirement that ammunition sales must be conducted by or through a licensed firearms dealer and the requirement that any ammunition sold, delivered, or transferred to another party must be conducted in a face-to-face transaction do not apply to the following individuals:

NEW LAW

Table 4.11

PENAL CODE SECTION	EXEMPTION
P.C. § 30312(c)(1)	An authorized law enforcement representative of a city, county, city and county, or state or federal government, if the sale, delivery, or transfer is for exclusive use by the government agency and, prior to the sale, delivery, or transfer of the ammunition, written authorization from the head of the agency employing the purchaser or transferee is obtained, identifying the employee as an individual authorized to conduct the transaction, and authorizing the transaction for the exclusive use of the agency employing the individual
P.C. § 30312(c)(2)	A sworn peace officer, as defined in P.C. sections 830-832.9, or sworn federal law enforcement officer, who is authorized to carry a firearm in the course and scope of the officer's duties
P.C. § 30312(c)(3)	An importer or manufacturer of ammunition or firearms who is licensed to engage in business under 18 U.S.C. sections 921-931 and the regulations issued pursuant thereto
P.C. § 30312(c)(4)	A person who is on the centralized list of exempted federal firearms licensees maintained by the DOJ under P.C. sections 28450-28490
P.C. § 30312(c)(5)	A person whose licensed premises are outside this state and who is licensed as a dealer or collector of firearms under 18 U.S.C. sections 921-931

---

[393] P.C. § 30312(b).

PENAL CODE SECTION	EXEMPTION
P.C. § 30312(c)(6)	A person who is licensed as a collector of firearms under 18 U.S.C. sections 921-931 and the regulations issued pursuant thereto, whose licensed premises are within the state and who has a current COE
P.C. § 30312(c)(7)	An ammunition vendor
P.C. § 30312(c)(8)	A consultant-evaluator
P.C. § 30312(c)(9)	A person who purchases or receives ammunition at a target facility holding a business or other regulatory license, provided that the ammunition is at all times kept within the facility's premises
P.C. § 30312(c)(10)	A person who purchases or receives ammunition from a spouse, registered domestic partner, or "immediate family member"[340]
P.C. § 30312(c)(11) (*effective Jan. 1, 2018*)	A person enrolled in the basic training academy for peace officers or any other course certified by the Commission on Peace Officer Standards and Training, an instructor of the academy or course, or a staff member of the academy or entity providing the course, who is purchasing the ammunition for the purpose of participation or use in the course

4. Recording of Ammunition Purchaser or Transferee Information

Beginning July 1, 2019, ammunition vendors cannot sell or transfer ownership of any ammunition without, at the time of delivering the ammunition to the purchaser or transferee, first recording and submitting the following information to the DOJ:

(1) The date of the sale or other transfer; *and*

(2) The purchaser's or transferee's driver's license or other identification number and the state in which it was issued; *and*

(3) The brand, type, and amount of ammunition sold or otherwise transferred; *and*

(4) The purchaser's or transferee's full name and signature; *and*

(5) The name of the salesperson who processed the sale or other transaction; *and*

(6) The purchaser's or transferee's full residential address and telephone number;[395] *and*

(7) The purchaser's or transferee's date of birth.[396]

---

[394] An 'immediate family member" means either of the following relationships: (1) parent and child, or (2) grandparent grandchild. P.C. § 16720.

[395] It is unclear whether a telephone number will be required to purchase ammunition, or whether the dealer can put simply put "n/a" in instances where the purchaser does not actually have a telephone number.

[396] P.C. § 30352.

According to P.C. section 30355, these records shall be kept at the vendor's licensed premises for no less than five years.

5. Authorization to Purchase Ammunition

Until July 1, 2019, ammunition vendors can transfer ammunition to anyone of age who is not known, or should not be known, to be prohibited from possessing ammunition.[397] After July 1, 2019, unless the person falls within one of the exceptions outlined below, ammunition vendors can only transfer or sell ammunition to a person if the DOJ verifies that he or she is authorized to purchase ammunition.[398] Only the following people are authorized to purchase ammunition:

(1) A purchaser or transferee whose information matches an enter in the AFS and who is eligible to possess ammunition;[399] *and*

(2) A purchaser or transferee who has a current COE issued by the department under P.C. section 26710; *and*

(3) A person who was approved by the DOJ to receive a firearm from the ammunition vendor under P.C. section 28220, if the ammunition vendor is a licensed firearms dealer, and the ammunition is delivered to the person in the same transaction as the firearm.[400]

To recover the administrative fees for processing each ammunition transaction, ammunition purchasers and transferees will be charged a fee of one dollar per transaction.[401] These funds received from each firearm transaction will be placed in the Ammunition Safety and Enforcement Special Fund.[402]

Although generally only the people listed above are permitted to purchase ammunition, a purchaser or transferee who does not fit any of the categories above and is not prohibited from purchasing or possessing ammunition can still apply to make a single ammunition transaction or purchase.[403] But, as of the date of publi-

---

[397] P.C. § 30306.

[398] P.C. § 30352(c)-(d).

[399] To determine whether a person is eligible to purchase ammunition, the DOJ will first cross-reference the ammunition purchaser's or transferee's information with the information maintained in the AFS. P.C. § 30370(b). If the purchaser's or transferee's information does not match an entry, then the person is not eligible to purchase ammunition and the transaction will be denied. P.C. § 30370(b).But, if the person is denied because they do not have a firearm listed to them in the AFS and is not prohibited from purchasing and possessing ammunition, they may be able to get approved for a single ammunition transaction purchase using a process that has yet to be developed by the DOJ. P.C. § 30357. If the DOJ does confirm that the purchaser's or transferee's information matches an entry in the AFS, then the DOJ must determine whether the person is prohibited from owning or possessing ammunition by cross-referencing the individual's information with Armed Prohibited Person File. P.C. § 30370(b). If the purchaser or transferee is prohibited, the transaction will be denied. P.C. § 30370(b).

[400] P.C. § 30352(c).

[401] This fee can be increased at a rate not to exceed any increases in the California Consumer Price Index as compiled and reported by the Department of Industrial Relations, not to exceed the reasonably regulatory and enforcement costs. P.C. § 30370(e).

[402] P.C. § 30370(f).

[403] P.C. § 30357.

cations, the DOJ has yet to develop the procedure by which people can request a single ammunition transaction or purchase.

There are exceptions to this general restriction on ammunition purchases. Specifically, the restriction outlined above does not apply to the sale or other transfers of ownership of ammunition by an ammunition vendor to any of the following, if they are properly identified:

Table 4.12

PENAL CODE SECTION	EXEMPTION
P.C. § 30532(e)(1)	An ammunition vendor
P.C. § 30532(e)(2)	A person who is on the centralized list of exempted federal firearms licensees maintained by the DOJ under P.C. sections 28450-28490
P.C. § 30532(e)(3)	A person who purchases or receives ammunition at a target facility holding a business or other regulatory license, provided that the ammunition is kept within the facility's premises
P.C. § 30532(e)(4)	A gunsmith
P.C. § 30532(e)(5)	A wholesaler
P.C. § 30532(e)(6)	A manufacturer or importer of firearms or ammunition licensed under 18 U.S.C. sections 921-931 and the regulations issued thereto
P.C. § 30532(e)(7)	An authorized law enforcement representative of a city, county, city and county, or state or federal government, if the sale or other transfer of ownership is for exclusive use by that government agency, and, prior to the sale, delivery, or transfer of the handgun ammunition, "written authorization" from the head of the agency authorizing the transaction is presented to the person from whom the purchase, delivery, or transfer is being made. "Proper written authorization is defined as verifiable written certification from the head of the agency by which the purchaser, transferee, or person otherwise acquiring ownership is employed, identifying the employee as an individual authorized to conduct the transaction, and authorizing the transaction for the exclusive use of the agency by which the individual is employed."

PENAL CODE SECTION	EXEMPTION
P.C. § 30532(e)(8)	A properly identified sworn "peace officer"[404] or "properly identified"[405] sworn federal officer, who is authorized to carry a firearm in the course and scope of his or her duties

Note that when Prop. 63 was passed, only certain sections of SB 1235 went into effect. These sections *did not* include any of the exceptions that would have exempted a number of individuals and organizations, such as hunting clubs, shooting clubs, nonprofit mutual and public benefit corporations organized for recreational shooting and lawful hunting activities, and persons participating in a shooting or hunting events from the restrictions on ammunition purchases.[406] Had Prop. 63 not passed on November 8, 2016, these organizations would have been exempted from these restrictions. But unfortunately, these organizations were left behind by Lt. Gov. Newsom's Prop. 63.

Some individuals have expressed concern over whether they can purchase different calibers of ammunition from the firearms that are currently registered to them in the AFS. Logically, it would not make sense for the DOJ to restrict ammunition purchases to only those firearms that are registered to a person in the AFS because in most cases a person may informally own a firearm that is not required to be registered in the AFS. For example, long gun transfers were not required to be recorded in the AFS before January 1, 2014, so there is no "registration" information in the AFS for most long guns that were transferred or sold prior to January 1, 2014 (with the exception of "assault weapons," .50 BMG rifles, or long guns that were voluntarily registered). So, as a practical matter, a person can and should be able to purchase ammunition in a caliber that is different from the firearm that is currently listed in the AFS because they may own a firearm that is not required to be registered. But, as of the date of publication, we are uncertain how the DOJ will enforce these restrictions or whether they will try and limit what calibers of ammunition a person can purchase.

Keep in mind that the requirements and exemptions outlined above were enacted by SB 1235. These provisions essentially replaced the various ammunition purchase requirements contained in Prop. 63. Of particular importance is Prop. 63's ammunition permitting requirement. Under this requirement, an individual would have to obtain a four-year permit from the DOJ before he or she could law-

---

[404] As defined in P.C. section 830-832.9.

[405] "'Proper identification' is defined as verifiable written certification from the head of the agency by which the purchaser or transferee is employed, identifying the purchaser or transferee as a full-time paid peace officer who is authorized to carry a firearm in the course and scope of the officer's duties." P.C. § 30352(e)(8)(B). This certification must be delivered to the ammunition vendor at the time of the purchase or transfer, and the purchaser or transferee must provide bona fide evidence of identity to verify that he or she I the person authorized in the certification. P.C. § 30352(e)(8)(B)(ii).

[406] *See* SB 1235, 2015-2016 Leg., Reg. Sess. (2016), *availible at* https://leginfo.legislature.ca.gov/faces/billNavClient.xhtml?bill_id=201520160SB1235 (last visited July 11, 2017).

fully purchase ammunition.[407] Had this permitting requirement gone into effect, individuals who are eighteen-years-old or older could have begun to apply for an ammunition purchase authorization permit on January 1, 2019.[408]

Prop. 63 required the DOJ to issue an ammunition purchase authorization if all the following conditions were met:

(1) The applicant was at least eighteen-years-old; *and*

(2) The applicant was not prohibited from acquiring or possessing ammunition under P.C. section 30305 (persons who are prohibited from owning and possessing ammunition under P.C. sections 29800-29830, 29900-29905, or Cal. Welf. & Inst. Code sections 8100 or 8103) or under federal law (see Chapter 3); *and*

(3) The applicant paid the requisite fee established by the DOJ.[409]

Prop. 63 allowed the DOJ to set a reasonable fee not to exceed $50 per person for the issuance of the ammunition purchase authorization or the renewal.[410] The DOJ could not set the fees any higher than necessary to recover the reasonable estimated costs to fund the ammunition authorization program.[411] All the funds obtained from this system would have been deposited in a fund known as the "Ammunition Safety and Enforcement Special Fund."[412]

After receiving an application, the DOJ was required to examine its records, and the records it is authorized to request from the State Department of State Hospitals under Cal. Welf. & Inst. Code section 8104, and if authorized, the National Instant Criminal Background Check (NICS) system in order to determine if the applicant was prohibited from possessing or acquiring ammunition under P.C. section 30305 or federal law.[413]

The DOJ was required to either approve or deny an application for an ammunition purchase authorization within 30 days of receiving the application, meaning that individuals who wanted to purchase ammunition would have had to wait potentially thirty days before they could do so. If the DOJ denied the application, it would have been required to provide a reason for the denial.[414] But, if the DOJ determined that the person met the requirements above or was unable to ascertain the final disposition of the applicant within thirty-days, then it was required to issue the ammunition purchase authorization.[415]

---

[407] P.C. § 30370(a)(3).
[408] P.C. § 30370(a)(1).
[409] P.C. § 30370(d).
[410] P.C. § 30370(g).
[411] P.C. § 30370(g).
[412] P.C. § 30370(h).
[413] P.C. § 30370(e)(1).
[414] P.C. § 30370(e)(2).
[415] P.C. § 30370(e)(3).

The ammunition purchase authorization would have lasted four years, unless it was revoked by the DOJ, and could have been renewed for another four years anytime before its expiration if the DOJ determined that the person was not prohibited from owning or possessing firearms under California or federal law and the applicant paid the renewal fee.[416]

Fortunately, this arcane permitting process will not likely go into effect. As outlined above, instead of requiring individuals to obtain a permit using the processes above to purchase ammunition, SB 1235 requires dealers to check with the DOJ that the individual seeking to buy ammunition is not a prohibited person at the time of the purchase.

It is still unclear whether the changes made by SB 1235 trump the provisions in Prop. 63, and the legislature can amend these laws before they go into effect on July 1, 2019. You can keep up-to-date on the current status of these laws by subscribing to our eBULLETins at www.CalGunLawsBook.com.

C. Restriction on California Resident's Bringing or Transporting Ammunition Into California

Beginning January 1, 2018, California residents will be generally prohibited from brining or transporting any ammunition into this state that was purchased or otherwise obtained from outside of the state unless the ammunition is delivered to an ammunition vendor in California.[417] A violation of this provisions is a misdemeanor.[418]

There are some exceptions to this general prohibition. Specifically, the following individuals can bring or transport ammunition into the state that was purchased or otherwise obtained outside of California without having to go through an ammunition vendor:

---

[416] P.C. § 30370(a)(3), (a)(4), (f).

[417] P.C. § 30314.

[418] P.C. § 30314(c).

Table 4.13

PENAL CODE SECTION	EXEMPTION
P.C. § 30314(b)(1)	An ammunition vendor
P.C. § 30314(b)(2)	A sworn peace officer, as defined in P.C. sections 830-832.9, or sworn federal law enforcement officer, who is authorized to carry a firearm in the course and scope of the officer's duties
P.C. § 30314(b)(3)	An importer or manufacturer of ammunition or firearms who is licensed to engage in business under 18 U.S.C. sections 921-931 and the regulations issued pursuant thereto
P.C. § 30314(b)(4)	A person who is on the centralized list of exempted federal firearms licensees maintained by the DOJ under P.C. sections 28450-28490
P.C. § 30314(b)(5)	A person who is licensed as a collector of firearms under 18 U.S.C. sections 921-931 and the regulations issued thereto, whose licensed premises are within this state, and who has a current certificate of eligibility issued by the DOJ under P.C. section 26710
P.C. § 30314(b)(6)	A person who acquired the ammunition from a spouse, registered domestic partner, or "immediate family member"[419]

---

[419] An "immediate family member" refers to a parent-child relationship and a grandparent-grandchild relationship. P.C. § 16720.

CHAPTER 5

CARRYING FIREARMS OPENLY, CONCEALED, AND/OR LOADED

Violations involving the illegal transportation or possession of firearms are the most common firearm-related criminal offenses. Thousands of people are prosecuted for these violations each year in California. Knowing the restrictions on carrying firearms (discussed in this chapter), the exceptions to these restrictions (discussed in Chapter 6), and places where the possession of firearms is illegal (discussed in Chapter 7) will provide you with a good understanding of the common legal pitfalls involved with firearm ownership. Together the laws that prohibit carrying firearms openly, concealed, and/or loaded, and their exemptions, create the general framework of California's regulation of firearms outside of the house.

California law generally restricts carrying of concealed "handguns"[1] and the carrying of loaded firearms in most populated areas. And it likewise restricts the open carry of handguns and non-handguns in most populated areas.

To understand when the prohibitions apply, you first need to know how the terms used in the statutes are interpreted and defined. That is the focus of this chapter.[2]

I. WHAT DOES "CARRY" MEAN?

As discussed later in this chapter, the California Penal Code (P.C.) generally prohibits you from carrying firearms "on your person" and "in vehicles" under your control. But what exactly does it mean to "carry" a firearm?

---

[1] "Handgun" means "any pistol, revolver, or firearm capable of being concealed upon the person." P.C. § 16640(a). "Firearm capable of being concealed upon the person," "pistol," and "revolver" include "any device designed to be used as a weapon, from which is expelled a projectile by the force of any explosion, or other form of combustion, and that has a barrel less than 16 inches in length" or that "has a barrel 16 inches or more in length which is designed to be interchanged with a barrel less than 16 inches in length." P.C. § 16530(a).

[2] Note that this chapter assumes that the person possessing the firearm may legally do so and that the firearm itself is legal in California. For exceptions to carrying firearms openly, concealed, or loaded, refer to Chapter 6. For firearms that may be generally prohibited, refer to Chapters 8 and 9.

Although the Penal Code does not provide a specific definition for the term "carry", courts have provided some guidance as to what it means to "carry" a firearm. Specifically, the California Court of Appeal has explained that "[s]peaking generally in the context of statutes concerned with firearms, 'carry' or 'carrying' has been said to be used in the sense of holding or bearing arms."[3]

Moreover, the term "carry" has been construed as to not require actual locomotion, *i.e.*, movement from one place to another.[4] Rather, to be considered "carried" according to the few cases that have discussed the issue, the firearm only needs to be connected with the person or vehicle in such a way that would allow the person or vehicle to carry the firearm if it was in actual locomotion.[5] So, a firearm stowed under the seat of a parked car or on a person sitting in or on a parked car would still be considered "carried," even if the car was not actually moving.

II. WHAT DOES "IN A VEHICLE," "ON," OR "UPON THE PERSON" MEAN?

For purposes of vehicle, courts have held that a person can "carry" a firearm "in a vehicle" even if the firearm is not actually in contact with them. For example, a firearm under the seat of a vehicle is being "carried" by the person controlling the car, even though it may not be in their exclusive possession or control.[6]

Similarly, courts have held that firearms can be "carried on the person" even when they are not physically attached to the person's body, such as when a person is carrying a firearm inside a suitcase.[7] One court appears to expressly disagrees with that view, however.[8]

Specifically, in *People v. Pellecer*, the defendant was leaning on a closed backpack that contained a dagger.[9] The court held that this was not considered "carried upon the person" because "upon the person" means just that, and if the legislature intended that term to include items beyond the body, it could have said so.[10] It

---

[3] *People v. Overturf*, 64 Cal. App. 3d Supp. 1, 6 (1976) (citing *In re Bergen*, 61 Cal. App. 226, 228 (1923)); *see People v. Smith*, 72 Cal. App. 2d Supp. 875, 878 (1946).

[4] *See United States v. Parker*, 919 F. Supp. 2d 1072, 1087 n.6 (2013); *People v. Smith*, 72 Cal. App. 2d Supp. 875, 879 (1946).

[5] *See United States v. Parker*, 919 F. Supp. 2d 1072, 1087 n.6 (2013); *People v. Smith*, 72 Cal. App. 2d Supp. 875, 879 (1946).

[6] *See People v. Davis*, 157 Cal. App. 2d 33, 36 (1958) (defendant found to be "carrying" a concealed revolver under the driver's seat; exclusive possession was not required because the vehicle was under the control and/or direction of the defendant).

[7] *People v. Dunn*, 61 Cal. App. 3d Supp. 12, 14 (1976) (defendant found to be "carrying" a concealed handgun in his locked suitcase when the locked suitcase passed through an airport x-ray machine). It should be noted that this case was from the Appellate Department of the Los Angeles County Superior Court. *Pellecer* was decided by the California Court of Appeal, Second District, Division 1, a higher court located in the same jurisdiction as the *Dunn* court.

[8] *People v. Pellecer*, 215 Cal. App. 4th 508 (2013).

[9] *People v. Pellecer*, 215 Cal. App. 4th 508, 511 (2013).

[10] *People v. Pellecer*, 215 Cal. App. 4th 508, 517 (2013).

should also be noted that although the *Pellecer* court distinguished the phrase "on or about the person" from "on the person," it uses the words "upon" and "on" interchangeably. This could mean two things. First, this could be an oversight by the court, and it meant "upon" when it said "on." But given the frequency it used "on" in place of "upon," that is probably unlikely. The other, and more possible, option is the court meant that the two words ("upon" and "on") are interchangeable.

Laws for the four different types of restricted carry, discussed below, use the same language when they discuss a person carrying a firearm illegally. The restriction for carrying concealed says "upon the person,"[11] the restriction for carrying a loaded firearm says "on the person,"[12] and the restriction for open carry of a handgun says "upon his or her person" while the person is outside a vehicle, and that it doesn't matter "whether or not [the handgun is] on his or her person" while the person is inside or on a vehicle.[13] Moreover, the restriction for carrying a firearm that is not a handgun in public says "upon his or her person."[14]

In 2015, the California Court of Appeal chose to not follow the decision in *Pellecer* when it ruled in *People v. Wade* that a person wearing a backpack with a loaded firearm inside is still carrying a firearm "on their person" for purposes of restrictions on carrying loaded firearms.[15] Because this case caused a split between the courts, the California Supreme Court granted review. And on May 9, 2016, the California Supreme Court upheld the decision of the lower court's decision.[16] As the court explained, "[t]he backpack was on his person and, accordingly, anything inside that backpack was also on his person."[17]

III. CONCEALED CARRY LAW

A. Carrying "Concealed"

Unless an exemption applies, you can be found guilty of carrying a concealed *handgun*[18] if you knowingly do any of the following:

(1) Carry any concealed handgun in any vehicle under your control or direction; *or*

(2) Carry any concealed handgun on your person; *or*

---

[11] P.C. § 25400(a)(2).

[12] P.C. § 25850(a).

[13] P.C. § 26350(a)(1)-(2).

[14] P.C. § 26400(a).

[15] *People v. Wade*, 183 Cal. Rptr. 3d 714, 715 (2015), *superseded by* 63 Cal. 4th 137 (2016).

[16] *People v. Wade*, 63 Cal. 4th 137 (2016).

[17] *People v. Wade*, 63 Cal. 4th 137, 140 (2016).

[18] The term "handgun" in this section includes "rocket[s], rocket propelled projectile launcher[s], or similar device[s] containing any explosive or incendiary material." *See* P.C. §§ 16520(c)(3), 25400.

(3) Cause a handgun to be carried concealed in a vehicle where you are an occupant.[19]

Note that the concealed carry law only applies to handguns, and it applies whether or not the handgun is loaded or unloaded. This means that, under California law, a long gun (meaning a shotgun or rifle) is never considered to be "carried concealed." The concealed carry law applies any time a handgun is hidden from view, possibly even if partially hidden.

Carrying concealed is generally charged as a misdemeanor,[20] unless:

(1) You are not in "lawful possession" of the handgun[21] or are generally prohibited from possessing firearms under California law (discussed in Chapter 3);[22] or

(2) You have been convicted of a felony or certain firearm-related crimes;[23] or

(3) The handgun is stolen and you knew or had reason to believe it was stolen;[24] or

(4) You are an active participant in a criminal street gang;[25] or

(5) You have been convicted of a crime against person or property or of a narcotic or dangerous drug violation.[26]

In those cases, the charge is either a "wobbler" (meaning that it can be charged as a misdemeanor or felony) or a straight felony offense.[27]

Also, if you are unlawfully carrying a concealed handgun that is not registered to you and that handgun is either loaded (definition explained below) or unexpended ammunition for that handgun is in your immediate possession or readily accessible, you can be charged with a felony.[28] If you didn't obtain the handgun through a Federal Firearms Licensee (FFL) or register it with the California Department of Justice (DOJ) yourself, it is probably not registered to you and could be registered to someone else.[29]

---

[19] P.C. § 25400(a).

[20] P.C. § 25400(c)(7).

[21] "Lawful possession" means the person possessing the firearm either lawfully owns it or has permission from the lawful owner or a person who otherwise has apparent authority to possess it. P.C. § 16750(a).

[22] P.C. § 25400(c)(4).

[23] P.C. § 25400(c)(1). The list of firearm-related crimes is in P.C. section 16580.

[24] P.C. § 25400(c)(2).

[25] P.C. § 25400(c)(3). Whether a person is an active participant in a criminal street gang is discussed in subdivision (a) of P.C. section 186.22, under the Street Terrorism Enforcement and Prevention Act (Chapter 11 (commencing with Section 186.20) of Title 7 of Part 1).

[26] P.C. § 25400(c)(5).

[27] P.C. § 25400(c).

[28] P.C. § 25400(c)(6).

[29] If you want to find out which firearms are registered in your name, you can submit an Automated Firearms System (AFS) Request for Firearm Records to the DOJ. You can access this form at: http://oag.ca.gov/sites/all/files/pdfs/firearms/forms/AFSPrivateCitizen.pdf (last visited July 11, 2017). See Chapter 4.

B. What Does "Concealed" Mean?

The Penal Code does not define "concealed," other than to say a firearm carried openly in a belt-holster is *not* "concealed."[30] Case law provides some guidance in figuring out the definition, however.

At least one court has suggested that a semiautomatic handgun is considered legally "concealed" just by ejecting its magazine and placing the magazine in a nearby location where it is not visible, even if the firearm itself is visible.[31] In *People v. Hale*, the defendant's handgun was on the passenger seat of his car in plain view, and the handgun's magazine, full of ammunition, was underneath the ashtray in the center console.[32] The court concluded that concealing a vital part of a visible weapon in a way that "make[s] the weapon *readily available for use as a firearm*" threatens public order just like concealing the entire firearm would.[33]

It is unclear what other "vital parts" of a visible firearm – aside from a magazine containing ammunition – would render, if concealed, the entire firearm "concealed" for purposes of the concealed restriction. It is also unclear whether a concealed magazine must have ammunition in it to make a visible handgun "readily available for use as a firearm" and thus considered "concealed" under the reasoning of *Hale*. Unless you want to be a test case, you should assume that concealing even an *empty* magazine is prohibited if you are also "carrying" the handgun that uses it. To be safe, you should assume concealing any part of a handgun is prohibited.

The exact definition of "concealed" is not entirely clear. Beyond a few gray areas, like where one's shirt or jacket covers part of a holstered handgun, it is generally obvious whether a firearm is "concealed" as that term is commonly understood, *i.e.*, kept secret, hidden, or out of sight.[34]

---

[30] P.C. § 25400(b).

[31] *People v. Hale*, 43 Cal. App. 3d 353, 356 (1974).

[32] *People v. Hale*, 43 Cal. App. 3d 353, 355 (1974).

[33] *People v. Hale*, 43 Cal. App. 3d 353, 356 (1974) (emphasis added). It should be noted that this case does not specifically deal with California's concealed carry laws but provides an analysis of them that a court may find persuasive.

[34] A concealed weapon is "[a] weapon that is carried by a person but that is not visible by ordinary observation." BLACK'S LAW DICTIONARY 1624 (8th ed. 2009).

Table 5.1

CARRYING CONCEALED HANDGUNS[35]
(P.C. § 24000)

Restriction: You may be guilty of carrying a concealed handgun if you knowingly:

(1) Carry any concealed handgun in any vehicle under your control or direction; *or*

(2) Carry any concealed handgun on your person; *or*

(3) Cause a handgun to be carried concealed in a vehicle where you are an occupant.

Penalty: Carrying a concealed handgun is a misdemeanor, but may be charged as a "wobbler," or even a straight felony, under certain circumstances.

Things to Remember: These restrictions apply regardless of whether the handgun is concealed *on your person*, or *in a vehicle*; or is *loaded or unloaded*; or *where you are* carrying the concealed handgun. Remember, these restrictions apply *everywhere*, unless you are subject to an exemption (discussed in Chapter 6).

IV. LOADED CARRY LAW

A. Loaded Firearm Restrictions

You can be charged with the crime of carrying a loaded firearm if you carry it on your person or in a vehicle "while in any public place or on any public street in an incorporated city or in any public place or on any public street in a prohibited area[36] of unincorporated territory."[37] Even *inoperable* firearms may violate loaded carry laws.[38]

You can be prosecuted for carrying a loaded firearm even if you didn't know that the firearm was loaded. The prosecuting attorney does not have to prove that you knew the firearm was loaded, just that you knew you were carrying a firearm.[39] In the case of *People v. Dillard*, Mr. Dillard was stopped while riding his bicycle and carrying a rifle in its case.[40] The officer examined the rifle and found a round in the chamber and six more in the "cylinder." Mr. Dillard testified that the firearm was his, that he just picked the firearm up from his stepfather's house, and he didn't examine the firearm. The court determined that, in light of the "legislative

---

[35] All of the tables within this book are paraphrases of the law and are not a complete summary of each subject area. Please review the corresponding Sections within this Chapter for a more in-depth discussion of each topic and for the applicable statutes and/or case law that is paraphrased within the tables.

[36] As used in this code section, a "prohibited area" is "any place where it is unlawful to discharge a weapon." P.C. § 17030.

[37] P.C. § 25850(a). This includes "rockets" and related devices. P.C. § 16520(c)(4). Pay particular attention to this "prohibited area of an unincorporated territory" language. Even if the area is unincorporated and is not a place where you may lawfully discharge a firearm, carrying a loaded firearm there can be a crime.

[38] *See People v. Taylor*, 151 Cal. App. 3d 432, 437 (1984) (holding that "operability is not an element of possession of a loaded firearm in a public place"). See also Chapter 2 (defining "firearm").

[39] CALCRIM No. 2530.

[40] *People v. Dillard*, 154 Cal. App. 3d 261, 263 (1984).

concern for the public safety as against the presence of armed individuals in public places," the restriction against possessing a loaded firearm in public is a "quintessential public welfare statute" and no actual knowledge that the firearm was loaded must be proven.[41]

California law also authorizes peace officers to examine any firearm carried in any "public place" where the loaded restriction applies to determine whether it is loaded. A refusal of such an inspection is grounds for arrest.[42]

It is also a misdemeanor to permit someone to carry a loaded firearm inside your vehicle in violation of P.C. section 25850(a) or California Fish & Game Code (Cal. Fish & Game Code) section 2006. But, there is a split among the California Courts of Appeal as to whether a person can be prosecuted for allowing another person to carry a loaded firearm in their vehicle if they did not know that the firearm was loaded.[43]

On one hand, the California Court of Appeal, First District held that the prosecution does not need to prove that a person knew that the firearm was loaded.[44] Instead, the prosecutor just needs to show that the person knew that a passenger inside the vehicle was carrying a firearm.[45] As the court explained, if the prosecution was required to show that the defendant knew that the passenger was carrying a loaded firearm, then it would defeat the statute's objective of deterring drive-by shootings and making owners and drivers responsible for the presence of loaded guns in their vehicles.[46]

On the other hand, the California Court of Appeal, Sixth District has expressly rejected the First District's holding, and has instead ruled that the prosecution must prove that the person actually knew that the passenger inside their car was carrying a loaded firearm.[47] In rejecting the First District's holding, the Sixth District explained that the First District relied too heavily upon committee reports about unrelated bills in drawing out the Legislature's intent.[48] Instead, the court reasoned that the Legislature intended on limiting the restriction to only those drivers who knew that a passenger was carrying a loaded firearm in a vehicle, as it is not illegal to allow a passenger to carry an unloaded firearm in the vehicle.[49]

Because of this split in opinion, it is always a good idea to be cautious when you know that passengers inside your vehicle are carrying firearms and ensure that their firearms are not loaded.

---

41 *People v. Dillard*, 154 Cal. App. 3d 261, 266 (1984).

42 *See* P.C. § 25850(b).

43 *Compare People v. Gonzales*, 232 Cal. App. 4th 1449 (2015), with *In re. Ramon A.*, 40 Cal. App. 4th 935 (1995) and *People v. Dillard*, 154 Cal. App. 3d 261 (1984).

44 *In re. Ramon A.*, 40 Cal. App. 4th 935, 941-42 (1995)

45 *In re. Ramon A.*, 40 Cal. App. 4th 935, 941-42 (1995)

46 *In re. Ramon A.*, 40 Cal. App. 4th 935, 941 (1995)

47 *People v. Gonzales*, 232 Cal. App. 3d 1449, 1463 (2015).

48 *People v. Gonzales*, 232 Cal. App. 3d 1449, 1462 (2015).

49 *People v. Gonzales*, 232 Cal. App. 3d 1449, 1462 (2015).

Like carrying a concealed handgun unlawfully, possessing a loaded firearm in a restricted public place unlawfully is also generally a misdemeanor,[50] unless:

(1) You are not in "lawful possession" of the firearm;[51] or

(2) You are generally prohibited from possessing firearms under California law (discussed in Chapter 3);[52] or

(3) You have been convicted of a felony and certain firearm-related crimes;[53] or

(4) The firearm is stolen and you knew or had reason to believe it was stolen;[54] or

(5) You are an active participant in a criminal street gang;[55] or

(6) You have been convicted of a crime against person or property or of a narcotic or dangerous drug violation.[56]

In those cases, the charge is either a "wobbler" or a straight felony.[57] Also, if it is a "loaded" *handgun*, carrying it "concealed" can be charged as a separate (possibly felony) offense.[58]

Table 5.2

CARRYING LOADED FIREARMS (P.C. § 25850)
Restrictions: You may be guilty of carrying a loaded firearm if you carry a loaded firearm (openly or concealed) on your person or in a vehicle while you are in or on: (1) A public place or public street in an *incorporated* city; *or*   (2) A public place or public street in a *prohibited area* of *unincorporated* territory.
Penalty: Carrying a loaded firearm is a misdemeanor, but may be charged as a "wobbler," or even a straight felony, under certain circumstances.
Things to Remember: You should always be cautious when carrying firearms in any "public place" or on any public street. Peace officers may examine any of your firearms to determine if they are loaded if you are carrying them in a "public place" or on a public street, listed above.

---

[50] P.C. § 25850(c)(7).

[51] As defined in P.C. section 16750(b), "lawful possession of the firearm" "means that the person who has possession or custody of the firearm either lawfully acquired and lawfully owns the firearm or has the permission of the lawful owner or person who otherwise has apparent authority to possess or have custody of the firearm. A person who takes a firearm without the permission of the lawful owner or without the permission of a person who has lawful custody of the firearm does not have lawful possession of the firearm."

[52] P.C. § 25850(c)(4). Although juveniles are generally prohibited from possessing firearm under California law (see Chapter 3), they are not automatically subject to felony punishment under P.C. section 25850(c)(4). *See In re. D.D.*, 234 Cal. App. 4th 824, 833 (2015).

[53] P.C. § 25850(c)(1) (crimes made punishable by a provision listed in section 16580).

[54] P.C. § 25850(c)(2).

[55] P.C. § 25850(c)(3). Whether a person is an active participant in a criminal street gang is discussed in P.C. section 186.22(a), under the Street Terrorism Enforcement and Prevention Act (Chapter 11 (commencing with Section 186.20) of Title 7 of Part 1).

[56] P.C. § 25850(c)(5).

[57] P.C. § 25850(c).

[58] *See* P.C. §§ 25400, 25850

B. What Does "Loaded" Mean?

There are different definitions of "loaded" in the Penal Code. Even the California Fish & Game Code has its own definition of "loaded" that applies to shotguns and rifles transported while hunting. So it isn't surprising that people, even law enforcement, get confused about whether a firearm is legally considered "loaded."

Table 5.3

THE DIFFERENT WAYS "LOADED" IS DEFINED IN CALIFORNIA
THE GENERAL DEFINITION OF "LOADED" (P.C. § 16840(b)(1))
Generally, a firearm is loaded when it has "an unexpended cartridge or shell consisting of a case that holds a charge of powder and a bullet or shot, in, or attached to, the firearm, including, but not limited to, in the firing chamber, magazine, or clip attached in any manner to the firearm." In *People v. Clark*, though, the court held that a shotgun is not "loaded" under this definition if the ammunition is not yet in the firing position, and stored elsewhere.
THE DEFINITION OF "LOADED" WHILE COMMITTING A FELONY OR IN "SENSITIVE PLACES" (P.C. § 25800(a))
A person possesses a "loaded" firearm if the person simultaneously possesses *both* the firearm and the ammunition to fire it.
THE DEFINITION OF "LOADED" UNDER THE CALIFORNIA FISH & GAME CODE (CAL. FISH & GAME CODE § 2006)
A rifle or shotgun (but not a handgun) is "loaded" if there is a live round, *i.e.,* an unexpended cartridge or shell, *in the firing chamber.*

1. General Definition of "Loaded"

Generally, a firearm is "loaded" when it has "an unexpended cartridge or shell consisting of a case that holds a charge of powder and a bullet or shot, in, or attached in any manner to, the firearm, including, but not limited to, in the firing chamber, magazine, or clip thereof attached to the firearm."[59] This general definition of "loaded" also applies to "any rocket, rocket propelled projectile launcher, or similar device containing any explosive or incendiary material."[60] A muzzle-loader firearm is considered "loaded" "when it is capped or primed and has a powder charge and ball or shot in the barrel or cylinder."[61]

Under the general definition, a firearm must have ammunition in a position from where it can be fired or be "ready for firing." A clear example of when a firearm would be considered "loaded" is where ammunition is placed in the chamber

---

[59] P.C. § 16840(b)(1).

[60] P.C. § 16520(c).

[61] P.C. § 16840(b)(2). A muzzle-loading firearm is typically a firearm that uses black powder as a propellant, which along with the bullet (ball or shot) is inserted through the muzzle.

or cylinder. The ammunition is "attached" and is in a position from where it can be fired.[62] But not all scenarios are so clear.

In the case of *People v. Clark*, the police seized a shotgun that didn't have a shell in the firing chamber.[63] Three shells, however, were located in a covered compartment at the rear of the shotgun's stock. The shells could not be fired from their position but would have to be manually inserted into the shotgun's chamber.[64] Mr. Clark was convicted of possession of methamphetamine while armed with a "loaded," operable firearm, but the conviction was reversed on appeal because the shotgun was not "loaded" within the term's "commonly understood meaning."[65] The Court of Appeal reasoned that the phrase "attached to the firearm" applies when "the [ammunition] is placed in a position from which it can be fired" or if it is "ready for firing."[66] Additionally, the court interpreted the statute's legislative intent to *not* "indicate a clear intent to deem a gun 'loaded' when the ammunition . . . is in a storage compartment which is not equivalent to either a magazine or clip *and from which the ammunition cannot be fired*."[67]

Clark's reasoning for why the shotgun was not "loaded" is not necessarily applicable to determining whether a firearm is "loaded" when its uninserted magazine or clip (or speed loader) contains ammunition. The court expressly distinguished a permissible separate storage compartment "from which [ammunition] cannot be fired" from "a magazine or clip" (which likely includes a speed loader).[68] Of course, this language was intended to explain what does *not* constitute "loaded." It is possible – even likely – that such language does *not* mean that a firearm is "loaded" if you have ammunition in a magazine or clip that is ejected from the firearm.

 And the fact that a shotgun with ammunition inside its stock, as was the case in *Clark*, is not considered "loaded" further supports the view that a firearm that has neither a round in the chamber nor a magazine inserted into its magazine well is probably not considered "loaded" under this general definition. This likely remains true even if you have a magazine full of ammunition near the firearm, such as in the same locked container, since both scenarios allow the firearm to accept and discharge a round with similar speed. Of course, you should be cautious because this issue remains undecided, and law enforcement could see it another way.

A semiautomatic firearm without a round in the chamber but having a magazine containing ammunition inserted in the magazine well may be (and in practice usually is) considered "loaded" even though the firearm is not completely "ready for firing" until a round is cycled into the chamber.

---

[62] *People v. Clark*, 45 Cal. App. 4th 1147, 1154 (1996).

[63] *People v. Clark*, 45 Cal. App. 4th 1147, 1152 (1996).

[64] *People v. Clark*, 45 Cal. App. 4th 1147, 1152 (1996).

[65] *People v. Clark*, 45 Cal. App. 4th 1147, 1153 (1996).

[66] *People v. Clark*, 45 Cal. App. 4th 1147, 1154 (1996).

[67] *People v. Clark*, 45 Cal. App. 4th 1147, 1154 (1996) (emphasis added).

[68] *People v. Clark*, 45 Cal. App. 4th 1147, 1154 (1996).

Because of the different definitions of "loaded," you should consider transporting ammunition in a way that it cannot contact the firearm to avoid problems with law enforcement, even though it may not be required by law.

2. "Loaded" While Committing a Felony or in Sensitive Places

The general definition of "loaded" (described above) does not apply when someone is charged with "armed criminal action." "Armed criminal action" occurs when someone "carries" a "loaded" firearm and intends to commit a felony.[69] Here, a firearm is considered "loaded" if the person simultaneously possesses *both* the firearm and the ammunition to fire it.[70] The ammunition does not need to be physically touching the firearm.

An almost identical definition of "loaded" applies to carrying firearms in certain sensitive places like those listed in P.C. sections 171c and 171d, including the California State Capitol building and legislative offices.[71]

3. Fish and Game's Definition of "Loaded"

Under Cal. Fish & Game Code section 2006, a *rifle* or *shotgun*[72] (but not a handgun) is loaded if it has a live round (*i.e.*, an unexpended cartridge or shell) *in the firing chamber*.[73] This means that even if the rifle or shotgun has ammunition in it, like in a magazine, it is still not "loaded" under this definition, unless it has a round in the chamber.

This definition applies to the restriction on loaded rifles and shotguns while "in any vehicle or conveyance or its attachments, which is standing on, along, or is being driven on or along any public highway *or other way open to the public*."[74]

Careful, this does not mean you are exempt from the general prohibition on loaded firearms in public as long as you have a rifle or shotgun and you are in a vehicle on a public highway. For one, you might actually be carrying on a "public street," thereby triggering the general prohibition according to the Attorney General's opinion, as discussed at the end of the Chapter Secondly, while it is not entirely clear, it appears this section is intended to apply where the general restriction does not. Specifically, it seems to be aimed at hunters who are in or near areas where it is legal to have a loaded firearm and may be using vehicles to track or transport game. In other words, it is a reminder to eject the round from the chamber when leaving a hunting field or moving to a new one. If you are in a prohibited area, you can still

[69] P.C. § 25800(a).

[70] P.C. § 16840(a).

[71] *See, e.g.*, P.C. § 171e. See Chapter 7 for other examples.

[72] See Chapters 2 and 9 for definitions of "rifle" and "shotgun."

[73] *See* CAL. FISH & GAME CODE § 2006(b).

[74] *See* CAL. FISH & GAME CODE § 2006(a) (emphasis added). Note that this section has been interpreted as authorizing law enforcement to inspect rifles and shotguns to determine whether they are "loaded." *See People v. Perez*, 51 Cal. App. 4th 1168 (1996); *People v. Johnson*, 108 Cal. App. 3d 175 (1980).

be charged under the general loaded restriction instead, which does not require that a round be chambered to be in violation. But, if the general restriction does not apply, you can still have a loaded handgun without running afoul of Cal. Fish & Game Code section 2006.

V. OPEN CARRY OF HANDGUNS RESTRICTION[75]

You may be guilty of a misdemeanor if you openly[76] carry an unloaded[77] handgun[78] on your person, or inside or on a vehicle, while you are in or on any of the following:

(1) A public place or public street in an incorporated city or city and county; *or*

(2) A public street in a prohibited area of an unincorporated area of a county or city and county; *or*

(3) A public place in a prohibited area of a county or city and county.[79]

Violating these restrictions is a misdemeanor, generally punishable by up to six months in county jail and/or a maximum $1,000 fine.[80] But you can be sentenced to up to one year in county jail, a maximum $1,000 fine, or both, if you openly carry an unloaded handgun:

(1) Outside of a vehicle; *and*

(2) In a public place or public street in an incorporated city or city and county *or* a public street in a prohibited area of an unincorporated area of a county or city and county; *and*

(3) Have ammunition that can be used with the handgun in your immediate possession; *and*

(4) You are not in lawful possession[81] of the handgun.[82]

---

[75] In response to people protesting California's restrictive firearms laws by publicly carrying unloaded handguns in holsters, the California legislature passed AB 144 amending the Penal Code to make that practice a crime. Prior to January 1, 2012, it was generally legal to publicly carry an unloaded handgun if it was not concealed.

[76] The Penal Code provides that a handgun is carried "openly" when it is not being "carried concealed within the meaning of section 25400." P.C. § 16950. But, as explained above, P.C. section 25400 itself does not define "concealed," other than to say a firearm carried in a belt-holster is *not* "concealed." P.C. § 25400(b). So what "openly" means, just as with the definition of "concealed," is not entirely clear.

[77] A handgun is "unloaded" if it is not "loaded" within the meaning of P.C. section 16840(b). P.C. § 17295. See discussion above for determining whether a firearm is "loaded."

[78] For this restriction, "rockets" and related devices are *not* covered.

[79] P.C. § 26350(a).

[80] P.C. § 26350(b)(1).

[81] "Lawful possession" means that the person who has possession of the firearm either lawfully acquired and lawfully owns the firearm or has the permission of the lawful owner (or someone who has apparent authority to possess or have custody of the firearm). P.C. § 16750(b). In other words, if you acquired the firearm by stealing it, borrowing it without permission, exceeding California's time limits for a lawful loan, or without going through an FFL (unless acquired prior to that requirement becoming law or you meet an exception thereto), you are *not* in "lawful possession" of the firearm per P.C. section 26350(b)(2).

[82] P.C. § 26350(b)(2).

Each handgun carried in violation of P.C. section 26350(a) is chargeable as a separate offense. For example, if you are openly carrying two unloaded handguns unlawfully at the same time, you can be charged with two separate misdemeanors.

If you are the driver or owner of a motor vehicle and knowingly allow another person "to carry into or bring into" your vehicle (or the vehicle you are driving) a handgun openly carried in violation of P.C. section 26350(a), you are guilty of a misdemeanor.[83] Since the punishment for this violation is not specified, the Penal Code limits the possible punishment to "imprisonment in the county jail not exceeding six months, or by fine not exceeding one thousand dollars ($1,000), or by both."[84]

Note that the question of whether a firearm being openly carried in a "public place" as described in P.C. section 26350(a)(1)(A)-(C) is "loaded" or not is generally only important with respect to what Penal Code statute is being violated. If it is "loaded," you will be charged with violating section 25850(a) (carrying a loaded firearm). If it is "unloaded," you will be charged with violating P.C. section 26350(a) (openly carrying an unloaded handgun). Either activity is generally a criminal act. But, as explained above, the penalties for unlawfully carrying a "loaded" firearm are potentially much more severe than those for unlawfully openly carrying an unloaded handgun.

Table 5.4

OPENLY CARRYING UNLOADED HANDGUNS (P.C. § 26350)
Restrictions: You may be guilty of openly carrying an unloaded handgun if you carry on your person an exposed and unloaded handgun outside of a vehicle or inside or on a vehicle (whether or not the handgun is on your person) while you are in or on any of the following: (1) A public place or public street in an *incorporated* city or city and county; *or* (2) A public street in a *prohibited area* of an *unincorporated* area of a county or city and county; *or* (3) A public place in a *prohibited area* of a county or city and county.
Penalty: Openly carrying an unloaded handgun is a misdemeanor. But you can be sentenced to up to one year in county jail, a maximum $1,000 fine, or both, if the handgun and unexpended ammunition capable of being discharged from that handgun are in your immediate possession and you are not in lawful possession of that handgun. Each handgun carried in violation of this restriction can be charged as a separate offense.
Things to Remember: If you are the driver or owner of a vehicle and you knowingly allow another person to carry or bring into your vehicle (or a vehicle you're driving) a handgun openly carried in violation of the above restrictions, you may be guilty of a misdemeanor.

---

[83] P.C. § 17512.
[84] P.C. § 19.

VI. RESTRICTION ON CARRYING FIREARMS OTHER THAN HANDGUNS

When the ban on the open carry of handguns (Assembly Bill (AB) 144) became law in 2011, a number of individuals protested by carrying their rifles and shotguns in public. Not content to leave the laws alone, and likely upon realizing that the handgun ban didn't include long guns, the California Legislature passed AB 1527 in 2012.

AB 1527 prohibits you from carrying an unloaded "firearm that is not a handgun" when you are outside of a vehicle in an incorporated city, or city and county, unless an exception applies.[85] While almost identical to its handgun-restriction counterpart, there are at least two significant differences in the scope of AB 1527.

First, AB 1527 doesn't apply within a vehicle. So, unlike handguns, which generally must be transported in a locked container while in a vehicle and generally cannot be transported openly in a vehicle, there is no requirement that non-handguns be locked up under California law; therefore, non-handguns can be left open and unlocked within a vehicle.[86] Nevertheless, consider transporting your long gun the same way you do your handgun in order to avoid potential problems with law enforcement.

AB 1527 didn't apply to *unincorporated* areas.

But in 2017, the Legislature passed AB 7, extending the reach of AB 1527 to unincorporated areas, i.e., a public place or a public street in a prohibited area of a county's unincorporated area.[87] This new restriction comes into effect on January 1, 2018.

A. "Firearm That Is Not a Handgun"

P.C. section 26400 specifically applies to "firearms that are not handguns." Since the term is phrased in the negative (firearm that is *not* a handgun[88]), it is necessary to look at the definition of "handgun" and work back. Any firearm that doesn't fit under any of the definitions of "handgun" in Chapter 2 will be subject to P.C. section 26400. Generally, such firearms include rifles, shotguns, carbines, and those firearms that fit neither the handgun nor traditional long-gun definitions.

According to P.C. section 16520, an "antique" firearm is not considered a "firearm" for purposes of P.C. section 26400's non-handgun carry restriction. "Antique

---

[85] P.C. § 26400.

[86] Note, California generally requires handguns, "assault weapons," and .50 BMG rifles to be transported in a locked container at all times, and federal law additionally requires that all firearms (including long guns) be in a locked container or a locked firearms rack that is in a motor vehicle when in a "school zone." 18 U.S.C. § 922(q)(2)(B). See Chapter 7 for more on school zones.

[87] AB 7, 2017-2018 Leg. Council's Digest (2017), *available at* https://leginfo.legislature.ca.gov/faces/billCompareClient.xhtml?bill_id=201720180AB7 (last visited Sept. 20, 2017); *see* P.C. § 26400 (effective Jan. 1, 2018).

[88] I discuss the definitions of "firearm" and "handgun" in Chapter 2.

firearms" are also discussed in Chapter 2, but briefly put, non-handguns made in or before 1898, certain but not all replicas thereof, or certain muzzle-loading firearms using black powder that are incapable of using fixed ammunition are antiques and thus not prohibited from being publicly carried under P.C. section 26400.

B. Penalties for Unlawful Carry of Non-Handguns

Under P.C. section 26400, if you carry an unloaded "firearm that is not a handgun" on your person outside of a vehicle in an incorporated city, or city and county, you are guilty of a misdemeanor. And starting in 2018, you would also be guilty of a misdemeanor under P.C. section 26400 if you carry an unloaded "firearm that is not a handgun" on your person outside of a vehicle in a "public place or a public street in a prohibited area of an unincorporated area of a county."[89] These misdemeanors are punishable by up to six months in county jail, a maximum $1,000 fine, or both, unless you meet one of the applicable exceptions discussed in Chapter 6. You can be sentenced to one year in county jail, a maximum $1,000 fine, or both, if the unloaded "firearm that is not a handgun" and the ammunition for that firearm are in your immediate possession and you are not lawfully in possession of the firearm.[90]

Each non-handgun carried unlawfully is chargeable as a separate offense. For example, if you are carrying two unloaded non-handguns unlawfully at the same time, you can be charged with two separate misdemeanors.[91]

---

[89] P.C. § 26400(a) (effective Jan. 1, 2018).
[90] P.C. § 26400(a), (b) (effective Jan. 1, 2018).
[91] P.C. § 26400(d) (effective Jan. 1, 2018).

Table 5.5

CARRYING "FIREARMS THAT ARE NOT HANDGUNS" (P.C. § 26400)
Restrictions: You may be guilty of carrying an unloaded "firearm that is not a handgun" if you carry upon your person an unloaded "firearm that is not a handgun" outside of a vehicle while in an incorporated city or city and county *or* (starting in 2018) while in a public place or a public street in a prohibited area of a county's unincorporated area.
Penalty: Openly carrying an unloaded "firearm that is not a handgun" is a misdemeanor. But you can be sentenced to up to one year in county jail, a maximum $1,000 fine, or both, if the unloaded "firearm that is not a handgun" and ammunition for that firearm are in your immediate possession and you are not lawfully in possession of the firearm. Each non-handgun carried unlawfully is chargeable as a separate offense.
Things to Remember: Make sure you understand what a "firearm that is not a handgun" is. This generally includes such firearms as: rifles, shotguns, carbines, and those firearms that fit neither the handgun nor traditional long-gun definitions. But, this may be tricky when you are dealing with "antique firearms" (read Chapter 2 for more detail). Moreover, these provisions do not apply when you are carrying a "firearm that is not a handgun" in your vehicle. Other restrictions may apply, however.

VII. PLACES WHERE CARRY RESTRICTIONS APPLY

As explained above, California has numerous restrictions on carrying firearms, each of which has a slightly different description of where the restriction applies. Some of these distinctions are trivial while others are quite significant.

The concealed carry restriction applies to *handguns* inside vehicles and on your person, regardless of where you are, unless one of the exceptions discussed in Chapter 6 applies. The long-gun carry restriction applies only when outside of a vehicle while in an incorporated city or (starting in 2018) while in a public place or public street of a prohibited area within a county's unincorporated area.[92] The difference between an unincorporated area and an incorporated area is that an unincorporated area is not an official city, but is land that is generally governed by the county in which it lies.[93]

 While written somewhat differently, the restriction on carrying a loaded firearm and the one on carrying an unloaded handgun openly apply in the same places, *i.e.*, in any public place or on any public street in an incorporated city or in a "prohibited area" of unincorporated territory.[94] A "prohibited area" is "any place where it is unlawful to discharge a weapon."[95] This means that neither restriction applies

---

[92] For a list of incorporated cities within each county, visit: http://www.csac.counties.org/cities-within-each-county (last visited July 11, 2017). This list is subject to change.

[93] This distinction is noteworthy, as demonstrated by the case of *People v. Knight*, 121 Cal. App. 4th 1568, 1573 (2004). In *Knight* the prosecution failed to establish that the place where the defendant possessed a loaded firearm was in an incorporated city or prohibited area of unincorporated territory.

[94] *See* P.C. §§ 25850(a), 26350(a).

[95] P.C. § 17030.

in any part of an unincorporated territory where discharging a firearm is lawful. It is not always easy to determine what these areas are. When in doubt, assume it is a prohibited area to stay out of trouble. The same goes for determining what a "public place" and "public street" are for the purposes of these restrictions.

A. What Does "Public Place" Mean?

Although the Penal Code makes clear that it is generally illegal to carry a firearm, whether loaded or unloaded, in a "public place," it does not provide a definition of a "public place." Consequently, we must look elsewhere for an interpretation of what is considered a "public place." Many sources and laws define "public place" differently. For example, *Black's Law Dictionary*, a dictionary that lawyers use, defines "public place" as "[a]ny location that the local, state, or national government maintains for the use of the public, such as a highway, park, or public building."[96] A California Government Code section governing litter receptacles defines "public place" as "any area that is used or held out for the use of the public," whether publicly or privately owned or operated, not including indoor areas (*i.e.*, enclosed areas covered with a roof and protected from weather).[97]

P.C. section 653.20 (governing prostitution loitering), defines a "public place" as an area "open to the public, or an alley, plaza, park, driveway, or parking lot, or an automobile, whether moving or not, or a building open to the general public, including one which serves food or drink, or provides entertainment, or the doorways and entrances to a building or dwelling, or the grounds enclosing a building or dwelling."[98] P.C. section 647(f) (prohibiting public intoxication), includes an "area outside a home in which a stranger is able to walk without challenge" in its definition of a "public place."[99]

The closest thing to a definition for "public place" with respect to firearms is the one given for "*imitation* firearms," which is any "area open to the public" including streets, sidewalks, bridges, alleys, plazas, parks, driveways, front yards, parking lots, automobiles – whether moving or not – and buildings open to the general public, including those that serve food or drink, or provide entertainment, and the doorways and entrances to buildings or dwellings, including public schools and colleges or universities.[100] Nonetheless, because this definition was provided for "imitation firearms" and not for real firearms, courts do not have to use this definition.

California courts also attempted to define the term "public place" with mixed results. Ultimately, "[w]hether a particular location is a 'public place' depends upon

---

[96] BLACK'S LAW DICTIONARY 1267 (8th ed. 2004).

[97] CAL. GOV'T CODE § 68055.1(a).

[98] *See* CAL. HEALTH & SAF. CODE § 11530(b) (governing drug activity loitering).

[99] *People v. Cruz*, 44 Cal. 4th 636, 674 (2008); *see People v. Olson*, 18 Cal. App. 3d 592, 598 (1971) (finding that the term "public" refers to areas that are "[c]ommon to all or many; general; open to common use" and "[o]pen to common, or general use, participation, [and] enjoyment.").

[100] P.C. § 20170(b).

the facts of the individual case."[101] For example, market parking lots,[102] hospital parking lots,[103] barbershops,[104] and apartment complex driveways[105] can be "public places" due to their open access to the public.

And, as shown at the end of the Chapter, it is still a little uncertain whether every "public road" is a "public place" for purposes of applying California's restrictions on carrying loaded firearms.

But what is known for sure is that an area is *not* a "public place" just because it is exposed to public view. This means that your front yard is not necessarily a public place if it is not "open to common use"[106] or if you exclude the public. This would not be the case, though, with a privately-owned sidewalk where the public has an easement; or with walkways and driveways without fences, gates, etc.,[107] making them easily accessible to anyone, or if the public can access them "without challenge."[108]

In other words, even though your front yard, for instance, might be private property, it is likely a "public place" if the general public can walk across it to gain access to your front door.[109] It would be *unlikely*, however, for that same front yard to be considered a "public place" if it were blocked off by a 3½ foot fence with three dogs in the yard (or some other similar deterrent), as this would then be considered a "challenge to public access," even if the gate were unlocked.[110]

---

[101] See *People v. White*, 227 Cal. App. 3d 886, 890-92 (1991) (in determining whether the defendant was in a "public place," the court took into account the fact that he was in his own front yard, the yard was surrounded by a three-and-a-half-foot-tall fence with a gate that could be locked, and the defendant had released his three dogs into the yard).

[102] See *People v. Vega*, 18 Cal. App. 3d 954, 958 (1971) (defendant unlawfully carried a loaded firearm in a "public place" by having a firearm in his vehicle, which was in the parking lot of a market. A "parking lot of a market, being accessible to members of the public having business with the market, is a public place.").

[103] See *People v. Green*, 15 Cal. App. 3d 766, 771 (1971) (providing that "[t]he [hospital] parking lot, being accessible to members of the public having business with the hospital, was a public place").

[104] *In re Zorn*, 59 Cal. 2d 650, 652 (1963) (defendant found to be in public while in a barbershop because "'public' has been defined as '[c]ommon to all or many; general; open to common use,' and '[o]pen to common, or general use, participation, enjoyment, etc.; as, a *public* place, tax, or meeting.'").

[105] See generally *People v. Overturf*, 64 Cal. App. 3d Supp. 1 (1976) (apartment complex manager was properly subject to criminal conviction for "carrying" a firearm onto his driveway).

[106] See *People v. White*, 227 Cal. App. 3d 886, 891-92 (1991) (appellant was *not* in a "public place" when found in his own front yard surrounded by a three-and-a-half-foot-tall fence with a closed but unlocked gate with three dogs in the yard; fence, closed gate, and dogs all provided challenge to public access, and the area was thus not "open to common use").

[107] *People v. Tapia*, 129 Cal. App. 4th 1153, 1160 (2005) (defendant was in a "public place" by standing on a sidewalk in front of his house, though the defendant argued his father owned the property in front of his house up to the curb including the sidewalk; the court held that "a sidewalk on an easement of way which has been granted to a public entity is not private property.").

[108] *People v. Krohn*, 149 Cal. App. 4th 1294, 1298-99 (2007) (defendant was *not* in a "public place" in the courtyard of his apartment complex because the complex was guarded by a fence and an automatically locked gate; the complex's rear parking lot was also guarded by an electric gate, thereby impeding public access to that area).

[109] See, e.g., *People v. Yarbrough*, 169 Cal. App. 4th 303, 318-19 (2008) (upholding a conviction for carrying a loaded firearm in the driveway of a private residence because it was "reasonably accessible to the public without a barrier").

[110] See, e.g., *People v. White*, 227 Cal. App. 3d 886, 892 (1991).

B. What Does "Public Street" Mean?

Note that the Penal Code specifically uses the phrase "public street," as opposed to the term "public road" or "public highway," when restricting where you may carry a firearm.[111] And, as explained further below, some authorities, like the California Attorney General, thinks that this makes a significant difference.

But, as with the term "public place," the Penal Code does not define the term "public street." So, again, we must look elsewhere for an interpretation of what is considered a "public street." Many sources conflate streets, roads, and highways, but it appears that some sources agree that a "street" is a thoroughfare in a more urban setting whereas a "road" is a thoroughfare in a more rural setting. For example, *Black's Law Dictionary* defines "street" as "[a] *road* or public thoroughfare used for travel in an urban area, including the pavement, shoulders, gutters, curbs, and other areas within the street lines."[112] The same source also appears to characterize "roads" as a kind of street outside of an urban setting. Therefore, a "street" is sometimes understood to be something within a city or municipality, while a "road" is to be found mainly outside of cities or towns:

> Strictly speaking, a 'street' is a public thoroughfare in an urban community such as a city, town, or village, and the term is not ordinarily applicable to roads and highways outside of municipalities. Although a street, in common parlance, is equivalent to a highway, it is usually specifically denominated by its own proper appellation.[113]

Merriam-Webster Dictionary similarly defines "street" as "a thoroughfare *especially in a city, town, or village* that is wider than an alley or lane and that usually includes sidewalk"[114] while it defines "road" as "an open way for vehicles, persons, and animals; *especially one lying outside of an urban district.*"[115]

Despite this distinction, some people may be confused by how the Penal Code states that "public streets" may be found in both incorporated and unincorporated areas. Remember, though, that the difference between an incorporated area and an unincorporated area is that an unincorporated area is not an official city, but is land that is generally governed by the county in which it lies.[116] So, the incorporated versus unincorporated distinction does not necessarily conflict with the general

---

[111] For instance, see the Sections above discussing loaded firearm restrictions under P.C. section 25850, the restriction against carrying an unloaded "firearm that is not a handgun" under P.C. section 26400 (effective January 1, 2018), and the open carry of an unloaded handgun under P.C. section 26350.

[112] *Street,* BLACK'S LAW DICTIONARY (10th ed. 2014) (emphasis added).

[113] *Street,* BLACK'S LAW DICTIONARY (10th ed. 2014) (citing 39 Am. Jur. 2d Highways, Streets, and Bridges § 8, at 588–89 (1999)).

[114] *Street,* MERRIAM-WEBSTER ONLINE DICTIONARY, https://www.merriam-webster.com/dictionary/street (last visited Oct. 30, 2017) (emphasis added).

[115] *Road,* MERRIAM-WEBSTER ONLINE DICTIONARY, https://www.merriam-webster.com/dictionary/road (last visited Oct. 30, 2017) (emphasis added).

[116] *See People v. Knight,* 121 Cal. App. 4th 1568, 1573 (2004).

distinction between "public street" versus "public road," though it may certainly heighten people's confusion.

The issue of whether you are on a "public street" becomes significant if you are carrying a loaded firearm and want to determine whether you are on a "public street" or "public road." This is because the California Attorney General's Office concluded that California's restrictions on carrying a loaded firearm applies to those on a "public street" but not a "public road" in unincorporated territory that is not otherwise a "prohibited area."[117] The Attorney General's Office argues that because the prohibition on carrying firearms in unincorporated areas is "modified by the. . . concept, 'prohibited area,' mak[ing] 'public streets' synonymous with 'public roads and highways' would leave little meaningful difference between incorporated and unincorporated areas."[118] In reaching its decision, the Attorney General's Office appears to have applied the same reasoning as the above dictionaries.

The main difficulty for consumers and firearms owners is that it is not always easy to tell whether a thoroughfare is a street or a road, or where an incorporated street ends and an unincorporated road begins. Given this uncertainty, it may be better for you to assume that you are indeed in a place where California's restrictions on carrying a loaded firearm applies to you. For one thing, although California Attorney General opinions are afforded great weight, they are not binding on the courts.[119] In other words, a judge might still find that you are prohibited from carrying a loaded firearm even though you are indeed on a "public road." And secondly, the California Attorney General's opinion doesn't say whether or not a "public road or highway" is in fact a "public place" that triggers California's restriction against carrying a loaded firearm. Meanwhile, many California courts have held that "public streets, highways, and sidewalks" are in fact "public places" that trigger these restrictions.[120] This means that courts might be inclined to find that the "public road or highway" you are on is a "public place" that triggers the restrictions on carrying a loaded firearm.

In the end, it is very difficult to determine whether you are in an area that triggers California's restrictions on carrying a loaded firearm. Even prosecutors and law enforcement officers are confused by where exactly these restrictions apply.[121] When in doubt, you might want to assume that you are in an area triggering these restrictions.

---

[117] Opinion No. 68-175, 51 Ops. Cal. Atty. Gen. 197 (1968).

[118] Opinion No. 68-175, 51 Ops. Cal. Atty. Gen. 197 (1968).

[119] See, e.g., Moore v. Panish, 32 Cal.3d 535 (1982) (finding Attorney General interpretation of statutory provision at issue not persuasive).

[120] People v. Strider, 177 Cal. App. 4th 1393, 1401-02 (2009) (emphasis added) (citing People v. Belanger, 243 Cal. App.2d 654, 657-659 (1966)).

[121] See, e.g., People v. Knight, 121 Cal.App.4th 1568, 1575-77 (2004) (overturning defendant's conviction for violating California's restriction on carrying loaded firearm after it was determined prosecutor failed to produce any evidence that defendant was carrying in an incorporated city or a prohibited area of an unincorporated territory).

CHAPTER 6:
FIREARM CARRY RESTRICTION EXEMPTIONS AND TRANSPORTING FIREARMS

As discussed in Chapter 5, California law generally prohibits carrying a concealed *handgun* anywhere, whether or not it is loaded,[1] and generally prohibits in most "public places": (1) openly carrying *unloaded* handguns;[2] (2) carrying *unloaded* "firearms that are not handguns" (long guns);[3] and (3) carrying loaded *firearms*.[4] This chapter explains each of the exemptions to these general restrictions.

I. HOW TO USE THIS SECTION

First, determine the type of conduct you would like to engage in. Would you like to carry a concealed handgun or a loaded firearm? How about openly carrying a handgun or "firearm that is not a handgun?" Maybe you would even like to engage in a combination of these activities, such as carrying a concealed and loaded handgun.

Next, determine whether that conduct is restricted under California law, and if so, whether there are any applicable exemptions. For example, you are restricted from carrying an unloaded "firearm that is not a handgun" (*e.g.*, a rifle) outside of a vehicle in an *incorporated* city or in a public place or a public street in a prohibited area of an unincorporated area of a county. If you wish to carry your rifle in an *unincorporated* area where you can discharge firearms, this restriction is not applicable, and therefore you do not need to meet an exemption. But, if the conduct you

---

[1] P.C. § 25400.

[2] P.C. § 26350.

[3] P.C. § 26400.

[4] P.C. § 25850(a). As explained in Chapter 5, the restrictions on carrying "concealed" handguns or "loaded" firearms also apply to "rockets" and related devices, including signal flares. Although the "loaded" carry exceptions discussed in this chapter generally apply to such devices, the "concealed" exceptions do not. It is unlawful to carry a concealed "rocket" or related device, even though such devices are not "firearms." But, if a rocket-launching device is unloaded, you can carry it openly.

wish to engage in is restricted – for example, if you want to carry your rifle openly in an *incorporated* city – then read below for any applicable exemptions.

If you want to engage in a combination of restricted activities, then each activity must meet an exemption. For example, if you are engaging in two kinds of "carrying" (*e.g.*, carrying concealed while carrying loaded) both activities must be covered by an exemption. Some of the most common exemptions are listed in the beginning of this chapter (*e.g.*, carrying in your residence, place of business, when you are in grave danger, and while camping and hunting). The other exemptions are arranged according to the respective carrying activity to which they apply. Carry licenses and special exemptions for current and retired law enforcement are also covered in this chapter.

As you read this chapter, keep in mind that you may still be subject to other restrictions depending on your location even though your conduct may fall under one of the carrying exemptions. For example, even if your conduct fits within one of the carry exemptions below, you may still be restricted from carrying a firearm in a government building (discussed in Chapter 7).

For your convenience, there is a table at the end of this chapter that boils down the varying exemptions to the carry restrictions that are discussed below. This table will help you sift through these exemptions, and hopefully provide you with a simple framework to determine the circumstances in which you may lawfully carry your firearm.

II. EXEMPTIONS TO THE GENERAL CARRY RESTRICTIONS IN NON-PUBLIC PLACES: RESIDENCES, PRIVATE PROPERTY, AND PRIVATE PLACES OF BUSINESS

A. Exemptions for Carrying Loaded Firearms and Openly Carrying Unloaded Handguns

Recall from Chapter 5 that California's restrictions on carrying loaded firearms and openly carrying unloaded handguns only apply in certain "*public places*." Therefore, you may lawfully carry loaded firearms or openly carry unloaded handguns when you are not in a "public place."[5] In other words, if you are in or on a "non-public" place (*i.e.*, a place that does not fit the definition of "public place" as defined in Chapter 5), you are exempt from the restrictions on carrying loaded firearms

---

[5] Keep in mind, when you are in a place generally accessible by the public, it doesn't necessarily mean that you are illegally carrying a firearm in a "public place" as it is used in the statute. For example, if you are in an unincorporated territory, the restrictions will only apply if you are in a *prohibited area* (see Chapter 5). P.C. §§ 25850, 26350. Therefore, you can carry a loaded firearm or openly carry an unloaded handgun in a public place that is in an unincorporated territory and is not a "prohibited area."

or openly carrying unloaded handguns. These places can include your residence, certain private property, and certain private business locations.

But, if your private property or private business, or portions of your private property or private business, is located in a *"public place,"* then the carry restrictions will apply to these public places and your conduct must fall under one of the exemptions before you can lawfully carry a firearm in or on that private property or private business (discussed further below).

B. Exemptions for Carrying a Concealed Handgun

Unlike the restrictions discussed above, the restrictions on carrying *concealed* handguns are not limited to "public places." These restrictions apply in both "public" and "non-public places." In order to lawfully carry a concealed handgun, you must first meet an exemption.

One exemption to the general concealed carry restriction (and to the open carry of handgun restriction as well) is if you are carrying your concealed handgun in your residence, private property, or private place of business.[6] To meet the requirements of this exemption, you must first be able to establish that you have a "proprietary, possessory, or substantial ownership interest" in the residence, private property, or private place of business in which you wish to carry a concealed firearm or handgun.[7] To have a "possessory interest" in the property you must show two things:

(1) You have the right to exclude others from using it; *and*

(2) You control activities that occur on it.[8]

If the residence, private property, or private business in which you wish to carry a concealed handgun meets this test and you are over the age of 18, a lawful U.S. citizen or resident, and are not otherwise prohibited by law from possessing firearms,[9] you may lawfully carry a concealed handgun in that place. And if your residence, private property, or private business is located in a "non-public place" then you may also carry the concealed handgun loaded (see above).

C. Exemptions for Carrying "Firearms That Are Not Handguns"

As with the restriction on carrying a concealed handgun, the restriction on carrying "firearms that are not handguns" applies in incorporated areas regardless of whether you are in or on a "public" or "non-public place." It also restricts the car-

---

[6] P.C. § 25605.

[7] *People v. Barela*, 234 Cal. App. 3d Supp. 15, 19-20 (1991).

[8] *People v. Barela*, 234 Cal. App. 3d Supp. 15, 20 (1991) (citing 1989 Cal. Legis. Serv. 2988-89 (West)).

[9] See Chapter 3 for prohibited persons.

rying of non-handguns in public places and public streets in a prohibited area of an unincorporated area of a county. But, there is an exemption to these restrictions when you are carrying such firearms in your residence, private property, or private business.[10] To meet this exemption you must have a "possessory interest" in the property, you must be over the age of 18 and a lawful U.S. citizen or resident, and you must not otherwise be prohibited from possessing firearms.[11]

You may also carry a "firearm that is not a handgun" in or on another person's residence, private property, or private place of business if you have the other person's permission.[12] Keep in mind, though, that the person giving permission must be able to meet the exemption themselves (*i.e.*, they must have a "possessory interest" in the property, be over the age of 18, etc.) in order to give you valid permission to carry your firearm on their property.

III. EXEMPTIONS TO THE GENERAL CARRY RESTRICTIONS IN PUBLIC PLACES

A. Temporary Residences and Campsites

"Temporary residences" and "campsites" in public places are treated differently than permanent residences. California law provides that you may *have* a loaded firearm, if otherwise lawful, while in or on a "temporary residence" or "campsite."[13] Although the law does not define either term, presumably this provision exempts people from the loaded restriction when lawfully residing in non-permanent shelters that are in a "public place" since people can generally *have* a loaded firearm in a non-public place.

But, it is unclear whether you can *carry* a loaded firearm in or on a "temporary residence" or "campsite" without a Carry License (discussed in Section VI) because case law currently distinguishes the terms "carry" and "have."[14] Remember, California law only provides that you may *have* a loaded firearm while you are in or on a "temporary residence" or "campsite", it does not say that you may *carry* one.

---

[10] P.C. § 26405(a).

[11] P.C. §§ 26405(a), 25605.

[12] P.C. § 26405(b).

[13] P.C. § 26055.

[14] *See People v. Overturf*, 64 Cal. App. 3d Supp. 1, 6 (1976) (holding where a statute only says it is lawful to "have" without mentioning "carry," then the statute does not allow "carrying" a loaded firearm). It is unlikely this distinction, to the extent it prohibits carrying a firearm in any manner within a "temporary residence," will be upheld as constitutional in the wake of *Heller* and *McDonald*. Although, it remains legally unsettled. *See* Chapter 1. The confusion surrounding this restriction is compounded when the question turns to the open carry of handguns and the carrying of "firearms that are not handguns." The exemption to the open carry of handguns restriction relevant here is P.C. section 26362, which allows for the open carrying of a handgun to the extent that person may openly *carry* a loaded handgun pursuant to Article 4 (commencing with section 26000) of Chapter 3. The above exemption for loaded carry is included in Article 4. But it appears a person cannot *carry* a loaded handgun and therefore a person couldn't carry a handgun openly. The same is true for the carrying of a "firearm that is not a handgun." P.C. § 26405(f).

It is also unclear whether you can carry a concealed firearm in either place since the exemption to the concealed carry restriction for residences does not expressly mention "temporary residences" or "campsites."[15] Of course, if the "temporary residence" is on private property that you own or lawfully possess, you can carry the firearm however you want.

But the agency or department governing the land you are camping on may have its own rules concerning firearms, so check with them before bringing your firearms on your camping trip.[16]

In 2014, a district court in Idaho held that a tent is akin to a home, meaning an individual has a Second Amendment right to carry a firearm while in his or her tent.[17] In that case, the court struck down an Army Corps of Engineers regulation[18] which barred the possession of a loaded firearm in recreation areas surrounding Corps' dams because it violated the Second Amendment.[19] The court reasoned that "[w]hile often temporary, a tent is more importantly a place – just like a home – where a person withdraws from public view, and seeks privacy and security for himself and perhaps also for his family and/or his property."[20] Therefore, the court held that because an individual has a Second Amendment right to carry a firearm in his or her home, the individual can likewise carry it in his or her tent. Moreover, the court also struck down the Corps' regulation because it prohibited individuals from carrying firearms outside their tents for self-defense purposes.[21] This case was appealed to the Ninth Circuit, but, at the request of both parties, oral arguments have been cancelled and the case has been referred to the 9th Circuit's mediation program. As a result, the Army Corps of Engineers is reconsidering its firearms policy, and will work with the plaintiffs to settle the matter outside of court. While this decision sheds some light on the issue of whether you have a right to carry a firearm in a "temporary residence" like a tent, it remains to be seen how it will be treated by California courts and whether it will impact California's carry restrictions.

B. Business or Other Privately Owned or Possessed Property Open to the Public

You may *carry* an *unloaded* firearm, concealed or openly, in your business if you are age 18 or older, you are a lawful U.S. citizen or resident, and you are not oth-

---

[15] *See* P.C. § 25605(a). There is an exemption for carrying concealed, but that relates only to transporting a firearm (in a locked container) when going to or from a lawful camping activity. P.C. § 25550 (discussed below).

[16] P.C. § 25550(b). *See also* Chapter 7.

[17] *See Morris v. U.S. Army Corps of Engineers*, 990 F. Supp. 2d 1082 (D. Id. 2014).

[18] 36 C.F.R. § 237.13.

[19] *Morris v. U.S. Army Corps of Engineers*, 990 F. Supp. 2d 1082 (D. Id. 2014).

[20] *Morris v. U.S. Army Corps of Engineers*, 990 F. Supp. 2d 1082 (D. Id. 2014).

[21] *Morris v. U.S. Army Corps of Engineers*, 990 F. Supp. 2d 1082 (D. Id. 2014).

erwise prohibited from possessing firearms.[22] But it is unclear whether you can *carry* a *loaded* firearm within your business if it is located in a "public place." This is because the exemption that allows for concealed carry at one's business does not mention the loaded restriction, which applies in "public places."

Individuals engaged in a lawful business (or nonprofit organization) operating from a "public place" where the loaded restriction applies (see Chapter 5 for examples) may nevertheless *have* (as opposed to carry) a loaded firearm in their business if it is for lawful purposes connected with that business, as may their authorized agents or employees.[23] For the reasons discussed above concerning carrying at a "temporary residence" or "campsite," this means you can lawfully *have* a loaded firearm at your business, but you cannot necessarily *carry* a loaded firearm there. The distinction between "having" and "carrying" a firearm is especially blurred if you conduct your business, or reside in, a moving vehicle or boat, as discussed below.

The same exemptions that apply to a firearm lawfully possessed within your place of business generally apply to firearms on your other privately owned or possessed property, which vary depending on whether they are located in a "public place."[24] Moreover, there is arguably stronger Second Amendment protection on private property, depending on the circumstances.

C. Vehicle or Boat as a Residence

 While being driven, motor homes are generally treated like "motor vehicles," meaning you must keep your firearm like you would in a vehicle (discussed in Section III(E) of this Chapter). While "camping" in a motor home, it *might* be treated like a "temporary residence" or "campsite," meaning you can *have* a loaded firearm in it.[25] Unfortunately, since "temporary residence" and "campsite" are undefined terms, this is another legal "gray area," so how a motor home is treated for purposes of firearm possession may depend on how you are using it at the time.[26] If you are prosecuted for having a loaded firearm in your motor home, the issue will likely be whether you were at a "temporary residence" or "campsite."

If you are at an established campground with your motor home "hooked up," it should qualify as a "temporary residence" or "campsite" and you should be able to keep your firearms like you would in your home. This means you may *have* a firearm in a motorhome while it is "hooked up." But, it is unclear whether you can *carry* them on your person, especially concealed (as discussed above). Moreover,

---

[22] P.C. §§ 26405(a), 25605(a).

[23] P.C. § 26035.

[24] P.C. §§ 25605(a), 26035.

[25] P.C. § 26055.

[26] *See Garber v. Superior Court*, 184 Cal. App. 4th 724 (2010), *modified by* No. 045632, 2010 Cal. App. LEXIS 740 (May 25, 2010) (holding at the time of violating the concealed and loaded restrictions, appellant was not using his mobile home for residential purposes, though it was parked, and thus was not entitled to a "place of residence" defense).

if you pull into a rest stop to sleep for a few hours, you may not qualify for this exemption because it may not be seen as a "temporary residence" or "campsite." Public campgrounds may also impose other firearm restrictions, so check the rules beforehand.

The law is unclear with respect to boats, but it is reasonable to assume that if the boat is designed to be lived on, like a house boat, it should be treated similarly to a motor home. This means if a boat that is designed to be lived on is moored, the same firearms laws that apply to one's residence should apply to the boat. But, if the boat is motoring through "internal waters" like a marina (see Chapter 7), firearms should be kept as if they are being transported in a vehicle (explained below). Licensed fishermen may be exempt from the concealed carry restriction (see Section IV).

Although the concealed and loaded restrictions also apply to rockets and related devices, including signal flares, it is lawful to store a rocket, rocket-propelled projectile launcher, or similar device designed primarily for emergency signaling purposes on a boat.[27]

D. Vehicle or Boat as a Place of Business

If your vehicle is also your place of business, depending on the type of business, you may have a loaded and concealed firearm in your vehicle. In one case, a taxi driver possessed a loaded pistol on the floorboard of his leased taxicab. Although he kept it in the vehicle for self-defense, he did not have a Carry License (discussed below). The court concluded that although he was in his taxi cab, he possessed the firearm in his "place of business" and therefore met an exemption to the concealed and loaded restrictions.[28] On the other hand, another court held that a bounty hunter carrying a loaded and concealed firearm in his glove compartment did *not* meet this exemption because, although he was often in a car for his work, the car itself was not his "place of business."[29]

The same rules about vehicles operating as your "place of business" also presumably apply to boats.

E. Motor Vehicles

A person who is over the age of 18 and is not prohibited from possessing firearms may carry an *unloaded*, concealed handgun inside a motor vehicle that is in a "public place" when it is in an appropriate "locked container" or while being carried *directly* to or from a motor vehicle in such a container "for any lawful purpose."[30]

---

[27] P.C. § 26060.

[28] *People v. Marotta,* 128 Cal. App. 3d Supp. 1 (1981).

[29] *People v. Wooten,* 168 Cal. App. 3d 168 (1985).

[30] P.C. § 25610(a).

1. Locked Container Requirement

Firearm owners most often get in trouble when transporting firearms inside, or to and from, their vehicles in an unlawful manner. The most common mistake that people make is not storing their handguns in a proper "locked container," which is required for the transportation exemption to the concealed carry prohibition to apply.

Example of a hard case

For purposes of this exemption, a "'locked container' means a secure container that is fully enclosed and locked by a padlock, key lock, combination lock, or similar locking device."[31] A "locked container" also includes a lockable trunk of a vehicle, but does not include a vehicle's "utility or glove compartment," even if it is locked.[32]

 The law does not define "utility compartment." Therefore, handguns should not be transported in a vehicle's center console or in the storage area behind the rear seat in most "hatchback" type automobiles because these areas may not be considered "utility compartments." Also, it is not advised to use the various storage compartments found in today's popular sport utility vehicles. Further, while most of us would consider a cross-bed toolbox in a pickup truck to be the functional equivalent to a vehicle's trunk, particularly if there is no access to the cab of the pickup, it too might be considered a "utility compartment" where a firearm could not be legally stored. To be safe, carry the gun in a locked container inside the tool box because this is still a "gray area."

Even if your vehicle has a trunk, you should still use an appropriate "locked container" (*i.e.*, fully enclosed and locked by a padlock, key lock, combination lock, or similar locking device) that is solely for transporting your handgun. Otherwise, if you need to open the trunk or unlock the container to retrieve a separate item from it, the container could then be considered "unlocked" – arguably violating the concealed and/or open carry restrictions.[33]

Example of a lock to a hard case

Whether you have a handgun in a vehicle, or are carrying one directly to or from a vehicle, hard cases that can be locked, when used correctly, are the best way to be sure you are complying with California law. The law does not specifically require the container to be hard-sided, but you will be more likely to avoid questions or concerns from law enforcement if it is.

For example, you may be able to comply with California law if you transport your handgun inside of a TITAN Gun Vault. A TITAN Gun Vault is a handgun safe that can be installed in the center counsel of a vehicle or under the driver's seat.[34]

---

[31] P.C. § 16850.

[32] P.C. § 25610(a)(1).

[33] P.C. §§ 25400, 26350.

[34] *See* Titan Security Product, Inc. Titan Gun Safe/Vault (2006), http://ethostactical.com/wp-content/up-loads/2017/02/Titan_Gun_Safe_Owners_Manual_Revised_JUL_2016.pdf (last visited July 11, 2017).

This safe utilizes a combination locking mechanism that requires users to push a sequence of buttons in order to open the safe.[35] Given that the TITAN Gun vault is a fully enclosed safe that uses a combination lock, it meets the definition of a "locked container" for purposes of California law. Therefore, a person could comply with the "locked container" requirement if they transported their handgun inside a TITAN Gun Vault, as long as the handgun is kept unloaded.[36]

2. "Lawful Purpose" Requirement

It is unclear what is considered a "lawful purpose" for carrying an unloaded, concealed handgun in a "locked container" inside, and to and from, a motor vehicle. Possibly the term is referring *exclusively* to the locations and activities listed in P.C. sections 25510-25595. For the unloaded-and-locked-transportation exemption to apply, "the course of travel shall include only those deviations between authorized locations as are reasonably necessary under the circumstances."[37] The only "locations" that seem to be "authorized" are those listed in P.C. sections 25510-25595. This means that when you are outside of a vehicle, you are likely only exempt from the concealed carry restriction when transporting an unloaded handgun in a locked container *directly* to or from one of those locations.

To qualify for the exemption to have a concealed handgun when you are *inside* your vehicle, there is some debate over whether you must be directly transporting it to or from one of the locations or activities listed in P.C. sections 25510-25595. But the exemption's plain language supports the interpretation that you *can* keep an *unloaded* handgun in a locked container in a vehicle *at all times*, regardless of your destination.[38] This means you do not need to be on the way to the shooting range, hunting, or any other firearm-related "lawful purpose." You are allowed to leave your *unloaded* handgun in a "locked container" in your vehicle at all times as long as you are not in a prohibited area. This includes when you leave the vehicle "unattended" (see Chapter 4). Although this interpretation appears accurate, this practice is risky because law enforcement officers may be unaware that it is legal, or have a different point of view of its legality.

---

[35] *See* TITAN SECURITY PRODUCT, INC. TITAN GUN SAFE/VAULT (2006), http://ethostactical.com/wp-content/uploads/2017/02/Titan_Gun_Safe_Owners_Manual_Revised_JUL_2016.pdf (last visited July 11, 2017).

[36] Some gun owners who have bought and installed TITAN Gun Vaults inside of their vehicles have also attached a TITAN Ammo Box to the gun safe. TITAN Ammo Box is a separate locked container that can be installed on the outside of the TITAN Gun Vault. This device allows you to store you unloaded handgun and magazines in separate storage containers. Because of the close proximity of the ammunition to the handgun, some law enforcement have wrongfully arrested people for carrying "loaded" handguns when magazines and ammunition were kept in the TITAN Ammo Box. Yet, as long as the handgun is kept unloaded inside the gun vault and the ammunition is kept ammo box, then the handgun is likely not considered "loaded" under California law because, when locked in the ammo box, the ammunition is not in a position where it can be fired or where it is "ready for firing." *See People v. Clark*, 45 Cal. App. 4th 1147, 1154 (1996). For more information on when a firearm is considered "loaded," see Chapter 5.

[37] P.C. § 25505.

[38] P.C. § 25610(a). **WARNING:** This is subject to a few limitations including school grounds, P.C. § 626.9, playgrounds and youth centers, P.C. § 626.95, and others (see Chapter 7). This is not an exhaustive list of limitations, however, and you should always be sure to consult local county and city laws.

3. Transporting "Assault Weapons" and .50 BMG Rifles in Motor Vehicles

Generally, a person can transport a lawfully registered "assault weapon" or .50 BMG rifle between:

(1) Their residence, place of business, or other property he or she owns, or on property owned by another with the owner's express permission; *and*

(2) A target range of a public or private club or organization organized for the purpose of practice shooting at targets; *and*

(3) A target range that holds a regulatory or business license for the purpose of practicing shooting at that target range; *and*

(4) A shooting club that is licensed pursuant to the Fish & Game Code; *and*

(5) Any exhibition, display, or educational project that is about firearms and that is sponsored by, conduct under the auspices of, or approved by a law enforcement agency or a nationally recognized entity that fosters proficiency in, or promotes education about, firearms; *and*

(6) Any licensed firearms dealer who possesses a Dangerous Weapons Permit (DWP), for servicing or repair pursuant to P.C. section 31050 (exemption to restriction on possessing "assault weapon" for service or repair by licensed firearms dealer who possesses a valid DWP).[39]

When being transported between any of the places mentioned above, "assault weapons" and .50 BMG rifles must be transported in a "locked container" or in the locked trunk of the vehicle.[40]

F. Motorcycles and Bicycles

The law is unclear about how unloaded handguns are to be transported on motorcycles or bicycles. While a motorcycle is a "motor vehicle," the exemption requires that the handgun be "within" the vehicle. Generally that is not possible with a motorcycle. While some motorcycles have lockable luggage boxes, keeping a handgun in one may be problematic. Although keeping a handgun in a lockable luggage box is arguably keeping it "within" a vehicle or in a "locked container," it could alternatively be considered a "utility compartment" because it is accessible and within the driver's reach (though not safely while operating the motorcycle), thereby taking it out of the definition of "locked container."

 Until the law is clearly interpreted, motorcyclists should be particularly careful when transporting firearms in a lockable luggage box of a motorcycle. If you chose to transport firearms while you are on a motorcycle, I suggest you have the unloaded handgun in a separate "locked container" inside the motorcycle's luggage box or a rider's backpack.

---

[39] P.C. § 30945.

[40] P.C. § 30945(g).

These issues are even more important for bicyclists because the exemptions for motor vehicle transportation do not specifically apply to bicycles.[41] Therefore, it is advised that bicyclists comply with the laws for transporting firearms on foot when riding on a bicycle. Generally, these laws require that the handgun be unloaded and in a "locked container" and that the course of travel be to or from the locations and activities listed in P.C. sections 25510-25595, with only reasonably necessary deviations.

As for transporting "firearms that are not handguns," whether on a motorcycle or a bicycle, such firearms must be unloaded and should be "encased" as explained below.

G. Boats

Although the law is unclear, as explained above, it is reasonable to assume boats are treated like motor homes. This means they will probably be treated either like a residence (see Section III(C)) or a vehicle, depending on how the boat is being used at the time.[42]

H. Being in "Grave Danger"

Despite the limitations on carrying loaded firearms in "public places," if you are considered to be in "grave danger," you may fall under an exemption to the carry restrictions.[43]

1. Protected by a Restraining Order

You may lawfully carry a *loaded* firearm *openly* or *concealed* if you reasonably believe you are "in grave danger because of circumstances forming the basis of a current restraining order" issued against someone who has been found to pose a threat to your safety.[44] This is only an affirmative defense to the crime of carrying a loaded firearm openly or concealed. It is a factual consideration for the prosecutor, judge, or jury to determine whether you really were in "grave danger" at the time you were carrying a loaded firearm. But this defense may not apply if there is a mutual restraining order in place against you.[45]

---

[41] P.C. § 25610.

[42] See Chapter 7 for more on firearm possession and use on boats. As previously explained, signal flares, though considered firearms, are exempt on boats. P.C. § 26060.

[43] P.C. § 26045.

[44] P.C. §§ 25600; 26045(b), (d); 26405(d); 26362.

[45] P.C. §§ 25600; 26045(b), (d); 26405(d); 26362.

2.   Not Protected by a Restraining Order

If no restraining order exists but you still reasonably believe you or someone else is in "immediate" "grave danger" of being attacked, you are allowed to carry a firearm, loaded or unloaded, *openly*, but *not concealed*.[46] For purposes of this exemption, "immediate" means "the brief interval before and after the local law enforcement agency, when reasonably possible, has been notified of the danger and before the arrival of its assistance."[47]

In other words, it is the brief time between law enforcement being notified of the danger and their arrival. So this is a rather limited exemption. As with the restraining order exemption, this is only an affirmative defense. And in addition to whether you were in "grave danger," the prosecutor, judge, or jury will determine whether the carrying was done while the danger was "immediate." This exemption does not expressly extend to carrying *unloaded* "firearms that are not handguns."

IV. CARRYING WHILE HUNTING OR FISHING

The laws and regulations surrounding hunting are so numerous and complex that a whole book would be necessary to completely cover this subject. This book does not go into much detail about hunting laws.[48] Nevertheless, because there are specific rules for carrying firearms in connection with hunting, they will be addressed here.

A licensed hunter while engaged in hunting or while transporting a firearm when going to, or returning from, a hunting expedition is exempt from the restrictions on carrying concealed handguns, openly carrying unloaded handguns, and carrying unloaded "firearms that are not handguns."[49] Licensed fishermen who are fishing, or going to or returning from a fishing expedition, are only exempt from the carrying concealed restrictions.[50]

A licensed hunter is exempt from the restriction on openly carrying an unloaded handgun or unloaded "firearm that is not a handgun" while he or she is training a dog for use in hunting (as long as that type of hunting is not prohibited by law) or while transporting the firearm to and from that training.[51] But licensed hunters are not exempt from the restriction carrying a concealed handgun.[52]

Remember from Chapter 5 that the concealed carry restrictions are in force everywhere unless an exemption applies. Meanwhile, restrictions on open carry,

---

[46] P.C. §§ 26045(a), 26362.

[47] P.C. § 26045(c).

[48] If you are interested in the subject, the California Department of Fish and Wildlife provides information on its website at https://www.wildlife.ca.gov/ (last visited July 11, 2017).

[49] P.C. §§ 25640, 26366, 26405(j).

[50] P.C. § 25640.

[51] P.C. §§ 26405(af), 26366.5.

[52] P.C. § 26366.5.

loaded carry, and carrying a "firearm that is not a handgun" are generally not in force where hunting – or to a lesser extent fishing – is allowed because these places are generally in unincorporated areas where it is lawful to discharge a firearm (*i.e.*, they are not restricted "public places"). Otherwise, it would not be legal to hunt there in the first place.

This is why there are no provisions generally exempting hunters from the *loaded* firearm restriction. Individuals who are lawfully hunting outside city limits are, by definition, in places where the loaded firearm restriction does not apply in the first place.[53] There is, however, a provision specifically exempting individuals who are hunting within city limits in an area where the city council has not made hunting illegal.[54] Similarly, members of shooting clubs while hunting on the premises of those clubs are exempt from the loaded firearm restriction.[55]

Also, the loaded firearm restriction does not prohibit storing a rocket, rocket-propelled projectile launcher, or similar device designed primarily for emergency signaling purposes on any vessel or aircraft, carrying one in a permitted hunting area, or while traveling to or from a hunting area with a valid California hunting license.[56]

Beware: the exemptions discussed in this section are general ones. The California Fish & Game Code, and its accompanying regulations, contains an enormous number of very specific carry restrictions in very specific areas of the state, mostly state land set aside for hunting or preservation and federal restrictions may apply. For a more detailed discussion on these restrictions, see Chapter 7.

V. ADDITIONAL EXEMPTIONS TO THE GENERAL CARRY RESTRICTIONS

The exemptions discussed above cover the most common persons, places, and activities exempt from the general carry restrictions. There are many others that address more specific scenarios.

A. Exemptions for Carrying Concealed Handguns

The law divides the exemptions for carrying concealed handguns into three categories: Conditional Exemptions,[57] "Other Exemptions" (some of which apply specifically to peace officers),[58] and Peace Officer Exemptions (discussed in Section VI).[59]

---

[53] See Chapter 5.

[54] P.C. § 26040.

[55] P.C. § 26005.

[56] P.C. § 26060.

[57] P.C. §§ 25505-25595.

[58] P.C. §§ 25600-25655.

[59] P.C. §§ 25450-25475.

1. Conditional Exemptions for Carrying Concealed Handguns

Some of the conditional exemptions involve the transportation of handguns while others discuss the transportation and possession of handguns for a specific activity. The Penal Code labels these exemptions "conditional" because they are subject to or dependent on a particular condition. As discussed above, in order to be exempt from the concealed carry restriction while transporting a handgun, it must be "unloaded and kept in a locked container, and the course of travel [should] include only those deviations between authorized locations as are reasonably necessary under the circumstances."[60]

The following are conditionally exempted activities from the concealed carry restriction:

Table 6.1

STATUTE	EXEMPTED ACTIVITY[61]
P.C. § 25510(a)	Possession of a handgun by an authorized participant in a motion picture, television, or video production, or an entertainment event, when the participant lawfully uses the firearm as part of that production or event, or while going directly to or coming directly from the production or event.
P.C. § 25510(b)	Transportation of a handgun by an authorized employee or agent of a supplier of firearms while going directly to or coming directly from a motion picture, television, video production, or entertainment event for the purpose of providing the handgun to an authorized participant to lawfully use as part of that production or event.
P.C. § 25515	Possession of a handgun in a locked container by a member of any club or organization whose purpose is lawfully collecting or displaying firearms while that member is at the organization's meetings, or while going directly to or coming directly from a meeting of the club or organization.
P.C. § 25520	Transportation of a handgun by a participant going directly to or coming directly from a recognized safety or hunter safety class or sporting event involving the handgun.
P.C. § 25525(a)	Transportation of a handgun by a citizen of the U.S. or legal resident over the age of 18 who resides in or is temporarily within California, and who is not prohibited from possessing firearms under California law, when transported directly between the individual's residence, business, or other private property he or she owns or lawfully possesses.
P.C. § 25525(b)	Transportation of a handgun by a citizen of the U.S. or legal resident over the age of 18 who resides in or is temporarily within California, and who is not prohibited from possessing firearms under California law, when going from a place where the individual lawfully received the handgun to his or her residence, business, or other private property he or she owns or lawfully possesses.
P.C. § 25530	Transportation of a handgun by an individual going directly to or coming directly from a fixed place of business or private residence for the purpose of lawfully repairing, transferring, selling, or loaning that handgun.

---

[60] P.C. § 25505.

[61] All of the tables within this book are paraphrases of the law and are not a complete summary of each subject area. Please review the corresponding Sections within this Chapter for a more in-depth discussion of each topic and for the applicable statutes and/or case law that is paraphrased within the tables.

Statute	Exempted Activity
P.C. § 25535(a)	Transportation of a handgun by an individual going directly to or coming directly from a gun show, swap meet, or similar public event where the public is invited, for the purpose of displaying that a handgun in a lawful manner.
P.C. § 25535(b)	Transportation of a handgun by an individual going directly to or coming directly from a gun show or similar event, as defined under federal law, to lawfully transfer, sell, or loan that handgun to a private party using a Federal Firearms License (FFL).
P.C. § 25540	Transportation of a handgun by an individual going directly to or coming directly from a licensed target range for practicing shooting targets with that handgun.
P.C. § 25545	Transportation of a handgun by an individual going directly to or coming directly from a licensing agency authorized to issue Carry Licenses, when done at the request of the issuing agency so that the agency can determine whether or not the license should be issued to that individual to carry that firearm.
P.C. § 25550(a)	Transportation of a handgun by an individual going directly to or coming directly from lawful camping activities for purposes of having a handgun available for lawful personal protection while at the campsite.
P.C. § 25555	Transportation of a handgun by an individual for a lawful transfer of that handgun to an immediate family member by gift, bequest, intestate succession, or by operation of law.
P.C. § 25560	Transportation of a handgun by an individual exempt from using an FFL for firearm transfers or registering firearm acquisitions, ownership, or disposal to report that to the California Department of Justice (DOJ) as it relates to the handgun being transported.
P.C. § 25565	Transportation of a handgun by an individual in order to sell, deliver or transfer that handgun to an authorized representative of a city, city and county, or state or federal government that is acquiring the handgun as part of an authorized, voluntary gun buy-back event.
P.C. § 25570	Transportation of a handgun by an individual who finds a firearm in order to deliver the found firearm to the police or restore it to its owner, and if transporting the handgun to a law enforcement agency, the individual gives prior notice to the law enforcement agency that he or she is transporting the handgun there.
P.C. § 25575	Transportation of a handgun by an individual in order to comply with the personal handgun importer requirements of P.C. section 27560 as it pertains to that firearm.
P.C. § 25580	Transportation of a lawfully obtained "curio or relic"[62] handgun into California by a federally licensed "curio or relic" collector[63] whose licensed premises are located in California.
P.C. § 25585	Transportation of a handgun by an individual for the purpose of obtaining an identification number or mark assigned to that handgun from the DOJ.
P.C. § 25590	Transportation of a handgun by an individual if done directly between any of the following: (1) A place where that individual may carry that firearm concealed pursuant to an exemption to the concealed carry restriction. (2) A place where that individual may carry that firearm loaded, either pursuant to an exemption to the loaded carry restriction or when that restriction does not apply. (3) A place where that individual may openly carry a firearm pursuant to an exemption to the open carry restriction or when that restriction does not apply.

These transportation provisions do "not prohibit or limit the otherwise lawful carrying or transportation of any handgun in accordance with the provisions listed in [P.C.] Section 16580."[64] As mentioned in Chapter 1, most of the Penal Code sections concerning firearms were renumbered in 2012. P.C. section 16580 explains which newly renumbered sections are continuations of statutes under the previous numbering system. So the statute quoted directly above referencing section 16580 is a clarification that the legislature did not intend to go beyond its express limitations on transporting firearms that were in place at the time of the renumbering.

2. "Other Exemptions" for Carrying Concealed Handguns

Some of the more commonly utilized "other exemptions," such as carrying while in a home, in a business, and on private property, are discussed above. The "other exemptions" listed below also exclude the following activities and/or persons from the restriction on carrying concealed handguns, even if the handgun is *not* in a "locked container":

Table 6.2

STATUTE	EXEMPTED ACTIVITY
P.C. § 25615	Possession or transportation of unloaded handguns as merchandise by those who are licensed to manufacture, import, wholesale, repair, or deal in firearms (or their agents) while engaged in the lawful course of business.
P.C. § 25620	U.S. military members when on duty or any members of organizations legally allowed to purchase or receive firearms from the U.S. or California.
P.C. § 25625	Military or civil organization members who possess or transport a handgun while parading or transporting to or from the meeting places of these organizations.
P.C. § 25630	Guards or messengers of common carriers, banks, and other financial institutions employed in and about the shipment, transportation, or delivery of valuable items.
P.C. § 25635	Possession and transportation of handguns by members of organizations whose purpose is to practice shooting targets with handguns at established ranges.
P.C. § 25645	Transportation of unloaded handguns by licensed common carriers or their authorized agents or employees, when transported according to federal law.
P.C. § 25655	An individual with a Carry License.

B. Exemptions for Carrying Loaded Firearms

Remember that the crime of carrying a loaded firearm requires that the carrying occur in a "public place." The following persons, places, and activities are exempt from the general loaded firearm restriction:

---

[62] As defined in 27 C.F.R. section 478.11.

[63] See 18 U.S.C. section 921 and related regulations.

[64] P.C. § 25595.

Table 6.3

STATUTE	EXEMPTIONS
P.C. § 26000	State or U.S. military members engaged in the performance of their duties.
P.C. § 26005	Individuals who are using target ranges for the purpose of practice shooting and members of shooting clubs while hunting on the club's premises.
P.C. § 26010	An individual with a Carry License.
P.C. § 26015	Armored vehicle guards, as defined by the Cal. Bus. & Prof. Code section 7582.1(d), while acting in the course and scope of their employment (1) If hired before January 1, 1977; *or* (2) If hired on or after January 1, 1977, if they have received a firearms qualification card from the Department of Consumer Affairs.
P.C. § 26020	Honorably retired federal officers or agents of any federal law enforcement agency, including but not limited to the Federal Bureau of Investigation, the United States Secret Service, the United States Customs Services, the Federal Bureau of Alcohol, Tobacco, Firearms, and Explosives, the Federal Bureau of Narcotics, the United States Drug Enforcement Administration, the United States Border Patrol, and any officer or agent of the Internal Revenue Service who was authorized to carry weapons while on duty, who was assigned to duty within the state for a period of not less than one year, or who retired from active service in the state, who have approval of the sheriff of the county in which the retiree resides.
P.C. § 26025	Any of the following who have completed a regular course in firearms training approved by the Commission on Peace Officer Standards and Training (POST): (1) Patrol special police officers appointed by the police commission of any city, county, or city and county under the express terms of its charter who also, under the express terms of the charter, are subject to suspension or dismissal after hearing on charges duly filed with the commission after a fair and impartial trial, they are between the ages of 18 and 40, they possess physical qualification proscribed by the Commission, and they are designated by the Commission as the owners of a certain beat or territory; *and* (2) Certain animal control officers or zookeepers, while acting in the course and scope of their duties; *and* (3) Persons authorized to carry weapons under California Corporations Code section 14502, while actually engaged in the performance of their duties; *and* (4) Harbor police officers designated pursuant to California Harbors and Navigation Code section 663.5.
P.C. § 26030	Certain guards, messengers of common carriers, banks, and other financial institutions, private investigators and their employees, uniformed patrol operators, uniformed security guards, and alarm company operators, listed in P.C. section 26030(a)(1)-(10), with a certificate from the Department of Consumer Affairs confirming the person successfully completed the required courses per P.C. section 26030(d). Peace officers generally do not need such a certificate to carry a firearm for off-duty employment purposes per P.C. section 26030(c).
P.C. § 26035	Having a loaded firearm in a lawful business (discussed above).
P.C. § 26040	Carrying a loaded firearm while hunting (discussed above).
P.C. § 26045	Carrying a loaded firearm while in "grave danger" (discussed above).
P.C. § 26050	Individuals making or attempting to make a lawful arrest.
P.C. § 26055	Having a loaded firearm at your place of residence, including temporary residences or campsites (discussed above).

STATUTE	EXEMPTIONS
P.C. § 26060	Storing a rocket, rocket-propelled projectile launcher, or similar device, such as a flare gun designed primarily for emergency signaling purposes on any vessel or aircraft, or possessing such a device while in a permitted hunting area or transporting to or from the area while carrying a valid California permit or license to hunt.

C. Exemptions to the Restriction on Openly Carrying Handguns in Public

There are many exemptions to the general ban on openly carrying an unloaded handgun. Some exemptions are to the entire restriction (*i.e.*, carrying both on your person and in/on a vehicle), while other exemptions only apply to carrying handguns on your person.

The following people and activities are exempt from the restriction on openly carrying handguns *in public*:

Table 6.4

STATUTE	EXEMPTION
P.C. § 26362	Individuals who meet the exemptions to carrying *loaded* handguns under P.C. sections 26000-26060 (these are exceptions for carrying a loaded firearm discussed in Table 6.3).
P.C. § 26363	Possession or transportation of handguns as merchandise by those who are licensed to manufacture, import, wholesale, repair, or deal in firearms (or their agents) while lawfully engaged in their business.
P.C. § 26364	Duly authorized military or civil organizations, or members thereof, possessing a handgun while parading or while rehearsing or practicing parading at the organization's meeting place.
P.C. § 26367	Transportation of handguns by licensed common carriers or their authorized agent or employee, when transported according to federal law.
P.C. § 26368	Members of organizations chartered by the U.S. Congress or nonprofit mutual or public benefit corporations meeting the nonprofit tax-exempt organization requirements while on official parade duty, during ceremonial occasions or while rehearsing or practicing for these events.
P.C. § 26370	Individuals in school zones as defined in P.C. section 626.9, provided that their carrying of the firearm meets an exception to the Gun-Free School Zone restriction (P.C. § 626.9). (See Chapter 7).
P.C. § 26371	Individuals acting in accordance with P.C. section 171b exemptions concerning possessing weapons in state or local public buildings/meetings (see Chapter 7).
P.C. § 26372	Individuals making or attempting to make a lawful arrest.
P.C. § 26373	When a handgun is being loaned, sold, or transferred according to California law (P.C. sections 27500-27590) or under an exception to the requirement that a firearm must be transferred through a licensed firearm dealer between private parties, as long as the handgun is on private property with the property owner's permission.
P.C. § 26374	Individuals engaged in firearm-related activities, while on business premises licensed to conduct activities related to firearm sales, manufacturing, repairs, transfers, pawning, or use/training.
P.C. § 26375	Authorized employees or agents of a firearm supplier for, or participants in, a motion picture, television, video production, or entertainment event when they lawfully use firearms as part of that production or event.

Statute	Exemption
P.C. § 26378	Individuals summoned and assisting a peace officer in making an arrest or preserving the peace.
P.C. § 26380	Individuals carrying a handgun incident to and during sworn peace officer training as part of a Peace Officer Standards and Training (POST) course.
P.C. § 26381	Individuals carrying incident to and during the training course required to obtain a Carry License (P.C. sections 26150-26225) with permission from the person authorized to issue it.
P.C. § 26382	Individuals carrying incident to and at the request of a sheriff, police chief, or other municipal police department head.
P.C. § 26385	Individuals with permission from the Chief Sergeants at Arms of the State Assembly *and* the State Senate to carry upon the premises of the State Capitol or its grounds, any legislative office, any office of the Governor or other Constitutional officer, or any hearing room in which any committee of the Senate or Assembly is conducting a hearing (pursuant to P.C. section 171c).
P.C. § 26386	Individuals exempt from the restrictions against possessing firearms in state legislative members', constitutional officers', and the Governor's homes mentioned in P.C. section 171d.
P.C. § 26387	Individuals exempt from the restriction against carrying firearms in sterile areas of public transportation facilities in P.C. section 171.7(c)(1)(F).
P.C. § 26388	Individuals lawfully carrying and possessing handguns on publicly owned land if specifically allowed by the land's managing agency.
P.C. § 26389	Individuals carrying an unloaded handgun in a locked trunk of a motor vehicle or a locked container.
P.C. § 26390	Individuals who possess a permit to possess destructive devices, "assault weapons," .50 BMG rifles, machineguns, and/or short-barreled rifles or shotguns, provided the carrying of the handgun is conducted in accordance with the terms and conditions of the permit.
P.C. § 26391	Individuals who are carrying in accordance with the provisions of section 171.5(d) (lawful carry in sterile environment of airport).

The following people are exempt from openly carrying unloaded handguns *on their person*:

Table 6.5

Statute	Exemption
P.C. § 26365	Members of organizations whose purpose is to practice shooting targets with handguns at established ranges.
P.C. § 26369	Individuals at a gun show conducted according to P.C. sections 27200-27245 and 27300-27350.
P.C. § 26376	Individuals carrying a handgun incident to obtaining a DOJ identification number or mark for the handgun according to P.C. section 23910.
P.C. § 26377	Individuals at any established range while using the handgun at the target range.

Table 6.5

STATUTE	EXEMPTION
P.C. § 26379	Individuals carrying a handgun incident to any of the following (as outlined in P.C. section 26379): (1) The requirements for registering or transferring a handgun as a personal handgun importer (P.C. section 27560) or registering "curio or relic" handguns by a collector who is bringing them into the state (P.C. section 27565). (2) Reporting handgun acquisition by those exempt from P.C. section 27545's private party transfer requirements or otherwise not required to report handgun acquisition, ownership, or disposition (P.C. section 28000). (3) Firearm transfers to authorized governmental representatives for voluntary gun buy-back programs (P.C. sections 27850, 31725). (4) Handgun transfers between immediate family members (P.C. sections 27870, 27875). (5) Operation of law transfers (P.C. sections 27915, 27920, 27925).
P.C. § 26383	An individual in a place of business, a place of residence, or on private property, if done with the permission of a person who, by virtue of P.C. section 25605(a), may carry openly an unloaded handgun within that place of business, place of residence, or on that private property that is owned or lawfully possessed by that individual.
P.C. § 26384	Individuals may openly carry an unloaded handgun if all of the following conditions apply: (1) He or she is at an auction or similar event of a nonprofit public benefit or mutual benefit corporation at which firearms are auctioned or otherwise sold to fund the corporation or its local chapters; *and* (2) The handgun is to be auctioned or otherwise sold to benefit that corporation; *and* (3) The handgun is to be delivered by an FFL.

 There is an argument that the ban against open carry is also inapplicable to antique firearms.[65] So you may be able to openly carry an unloaded, antique handgun in "public places."[66] But due to law enforcement confusion, this practice is not recommended.

D. Exemptions to Restriction on Carrying "Firearms That Are Not Handguns"

There are almost as many exemptions to the restriction on carrying "firearms that are not handguns" as there are for carrying handguns openly in public.[67] Remember from Chapter 5 that the restriction on carrying "firearms that are not hand-

---

[65] P.C. § 16520(d). According to P.C. section 16170(b), "antique firearm" has the same meaning as in 18 U.S.C. section 921(a)(16). See Chapter 2.

[66] Pursuant to P.C. section 16520(d)(5), an antique firearm (discussed in Chapter 2) is not a "firearm" for purposes of the sections relating to carrying a handgun openly (Chapter 6 (commencing with P.C. section 26350) of Division 5 of Title 4 of the Penal Code). It would appear that, by including the open carry exemptions, this exception to the definition of "firearm" for antique firearms would allow for the open carry of antique handguns.

[67] All of these exemptions (with some cross-references) are listed in P.C. section 26405.

guns" only applies outside of a vehicle, so this restriction does not affect how you may transport your "firearm that is not a handgun" while *inside* a vehicle.[68] The following explains the exemptions to this restriction.

1. "Locked Container" or "Encased"

The most commonly used exemption for the ban on carrying "firearms that are not handguns" is the "locked container" or "encased" exemption. A person may carry an unloaded "firearm that is not a handgun" if it is either:

(1) In a "locked container" (as defined in Section (III)(E)(1));[69] *or*

(2) "Encased";

   AND

(3) "It is being transported directly between places where a person is not prohibited from possessing that firearm and the course of travel" and only includes "those deviations between authorized locations as are reasonably necessary under the circumstances."[70]

A firearm is "encased" "when that firearm is enclosed in a case that is expressly made for the purpose of containing a firearm and that is completely zipped, snapped, buckled, tied, or otherwise fastened with no part of that firearm exposed."[71]

The term "encased" poses a huge problem. Its definition, "expressly made for the purpose of containing a firearm," is not as straightforward as it sounds, and there is no clear understanding of what this would be. Is it sufficient that the manufacturer names a box a "firearm case?" Or must a case be approved or recognizable by law enforcement? There are a number of gun cases available that are expressly made for the purposes of containing a firearm, but do not readily appear to be capable of containing a firearm. Would the case require a certain type of material to be used? Could a gun sock suffice? These questions have not been addressed by the courts.

2. Other Exemptions to the Restriction on Carrying "Firearms That Are Not Handguns"

The restriction on carrying "firearms that are not handguns" does not apply to, or affect, the carrying of an unloaded "firearm that is not a handgun" in the following situations or by the following individuals:

---

[68] Note, however, that California generally requires "assault weapons" and .50 BMG rifles to be transported in a locked container at all times. P.C. § 30945(g). Federal law additionally requires that all firearms (including long guns) be in a locked container or a locked firearm rack that is on a motor vehicle when in a "school zone." 18 U.S.C. § 922(q)(2)(B) (see Chapter 7 for more on school zones). And almost all transportation should be done with the firearm unloaded unless you meet an exception to the loaded restriction.

[69] P.C. § 16850.

[70] P.C. § 26405(c).

[71] P.C. § 16505.

Table 6.6

STATUTE	EXEMPTION
P.C. § 26405(a)	An Individual within a place of business, a place of residence, or on private real property, if done by a citizen of the U.S. or legal resident over the age of 18 who resides in or is temporarily within California, and who is not prohibited from possessing firearms under California law, may carry a firearm within that place of business, place of residence, or on that private real property owned or lawfully occupied by that individual.
P.C. § 26405(b)	Individuals within a place of business, a place of residence, or on private real property, if done with the permission of a person who is a citizen of the U.S. or legal resident over the age of 18 who resides in or is temporarily within California, and who is not prohibited from possessing firearms under California law, may carry a firearm within that place of residence or on that private real property owned or lawfully occupied by that person.
P.C. § 26405(c)	When the firearm is either in a locked container or encased (discussed above) and it is being transported directly between places where the individual is not prohibited from possessing that firearm, and the course of travel includes only those deviations between authorized locations as are reasonably necessary under the circumstances.
P.C. § 26405(d)	Individuals carrying a "firearm that is not a handgun" while in "grave danger" (discussed above).
P.C. § 26405(e)	A peace officer or an honorably retired peace officer if that officer may carry a concealed firearm pursuant to Article 2 (commencing with P.C. section 25450) of Chapter 2, or a loaded firearm pursuant to Article 3 (commencing with P.C. section 25900) of Chapter 3.
P.C. § 26405(f)	An individual may carry a "firearm that is not a handgun" to the extent that individual may openly carry a loaded "firearm that is not a handgun" pursuant to Article 4 (commencing with P.C. section 26000-26060) of Chapter 3 (exceptions to carrying loaded handguns discussed above).
P.C. § 26405(g)	Merchandise firearms carried by an individual who is engaged in the business of manufacturing, importing, wholesaling, repairing, or dealing in firearms and who is licensed to engage in that business, or the authorized representative or authorized agent of that individual, while engaged in the lawful course of the business.
P.C. § 26405(h)	A duly authorized military or civil organization, or the members thereof, while parading or while rehearsing or practicing parading, when at the meeting place of the organization.
P.C. § 26405(i)	A member of a club or organization organized for the purpose of practicing shooting at targets upon established target ranges, whether public or private, while the members are using "firearms that are not handguns" upon the target ranges or incident to the use of a firearm that is not a handgun at that target range.
P.C. § 26405(j)	A licensed hunter while engaged in hunting or while transporting the firearm when going to or returning from a hunting expedition.
P.C. § 26405(k)	Carrying incident to transporting a handgun[72] by an individual operating a licensed common carrier, or by an authorized agent or employee thereof, when transported in conformance with applicable federal law.

---

[72] Notice that this statute only provides that a person licensed to operate a common carrier is exempt when they are transporting "handguns." The legislature likely meant that the person operating the common carrier is exempt when transporting "firearms that are not handguns."

STATUTE	EXEMPTION
P.C. § 26405(l)	A member of an organization chartered by the Congress of the U.S. or a nonprofit mutual or public benefit corporation organized and recognized as a nonprofit tax-exempt organization by the Internal Revenue Service while on official parade duty or ceremonial occasions of that organization or while rehearsing or practicing for official parade duty or ceremonial occasions.
P.C. § 26405(m)	Individuals within a gun show conducted pursuant to Article 1 (commencing with P.C. section 27200) and Article 2 (commencing with P.C. section 27300) of Chapter 3 of Division 6.
P.C. § 26405(N)	Individuals within a school zone, as defined in P.C. section 626.9, if their carrying of the firearm meets an exception to the Gun-Free School Zone restriction (P.C. § 626.9). (See Chapter 7)
P.C. § 26405(o)	Firearms carried in accordance with the provisions of P.C. section 171b (exemption for carrying a firearm in a state or local public building or public meeting as provided in that section).
P.C. § 26405(p)	Individuals engaged in the act of making or attempting to make a lawful arrest.
P.C. § 26405(q)	Individuals engaged in firearms-related activities while on the premises of a fixed place of business that is licensed to conduct and conducts, as a regular course of its business, activities related to the sale, making, repair, transfer, pawn, or use of firearms, or related to firearms training.
P.C. § 26405(r)	An authorized participant in, or an authorized employee or agent of a supplier of firearms for a motion picture, television, or video production or entertainment event, when the participant lawfully uses that firearm as part of that production or event, as part of rehearsing or practicing for participation in that production or event, or while the participant or authorized employee or agent is at that production or event, or rehearsal or practice for that production or event.
P.C. § 26405(s)	Individuals carrying incident to obtaining an identification number or mark assigned for that firearm from the DOJ pursuant to P.C. section 23910.
P.C. § 26405(t)	Individuals using the firearm upon an established public target range.
P.C. § 26405(u)	An individual summoned by a peace officer to assist in making arrests or preserving the peace, while the individual is actually engaged in assisting that officer.
P.C. § 26405(v)	An individual carrying incident to any of the following: (1) Complying with P.C. sections 27560 or 27565, as it pertains to that firearm (personal firearm importer and collector bringing curio or relic firearm into California, and registration requirements); *or* (2) P.C. section 28000, as it pertains to that firearm (transfer of firearms by persons not required to use a licensed firearm dealer); *or* (3) P.C. sections 27850 or 31725, as it pertains to that firearm (sale, delivery, or transfer of firearm to government entity as part of an authorized program, and firearm buy-back programs); *or* (4) Complying with P.C. sections 27870 or 27875, as it pertains to that firearm (transfers by immediate family members); *or* (5) Complying with P.C. sections 27915, 27920, or 27925, as it pertains to that firearm (taking title or possession of firearm by operation of law).

Table 6.6

STATUTE	EXEMPTION
P.C. § 26405(w)	Individuals carrying incident to, and in the course and scope of, training of, or by an individual to become a sworn peace officer as part of a course of study approved by the Commission on POST.
P.C. § 26405(x)	Individuals carrying incident to, and in the course and scope of, training of or by an individual to become licensed pursuant to Chapter 4 (commencing with P.C. section 26150) (license to carry concealed) as part of a course of study necessary or authorized by the person authorized to issue the license pursuant to that chapter.
P.C. § 26405(y)	Individuals carrying incident to and at the request of a sheriff, chief, or other head of a municipal police department.
P.C. § 26405(z)	If all of the following conditions are satisfied: (1) The open carrying occurs at an auction or similar event of a nonprofit public benefit or mutual benefit corporation at which firearms are auctioned or otherwise sold to fund the activities of that corporation or the local chapters of that corporation; *and* (2) The unloaded firearm that is not a handgun is to be auctioned or otherwise sold for that nonprofit public benefit or mutual benefit corporation; *and* (3) The unloaded firearm that is not a handgun is to be delivered by a person licensed pursuant to, and operating in accordance with, P.C. sections 26700 to 26915, inclusive.
P.C. § 26405(aa)	Individuals with permission from the Chief Sergeants at Arms of the State Assembly *and* the State Senate to carry upon the premises of the State Capitol or its grounds, any legislative office, any office of the Governor or other Constitutional officer, or any hearing room in which any committee of the Senate or Assembly is conducting a hearing (pursuant to P.C. section 171c).
P.C. § 26405(ab)	Individuals carrying pursuant to P.C. section 171d (exemption for carrying loaded firearm in certain state and federal government buildings).
P.C. § 26405(ac)	Individuals carrying pursuant to P.C. section 171.7(c)(1)(F) (exemption from possessing firearm in sterile area of public transit facility).
P.C. § 26405(ad)	Individuals on publicly owned land, if the possession and use of an unloaded "firearm that is not a handgun" is specifically permitted by the managing agency of the land and the person carrying that firearm is in lawful possession of that firearm.

STATUTE	EXEMPTION
P.C. § 26405(ae)	Individuals carrying in any of the following ways: (1) The carrying of an unloaded firearm that is not a handgun that is regulated pursuant to Chapter 1 (commencing with P.C. section 18710) of Division 5 of Title 2 (a destructive device) by an individual who holds a permit issued pursuant to Article 3 (commencing with P.C. section 18900) of that chapter, if the carrying of that firearm is conducted in accordance with the terms and conditions of the permit; *or* (2) The carrying of an unloaded firearm that is not a handgun that is regulated pursuant to Chapter 2 (commencing with Section 30500) of Division 10 ("assault weapon" and .50 BMG rifle) by an individual who holds a permit issued pursuant to P.C. section 31005, if the carrying of that firearm is conducted in accordance with the terms and conditions of the permit; *or* (3) The carrying of an unloaded firearm that is not a handgun that is regulated pursuant to Chapter 6 (commencing with P.C. section 32610) of Division 10 (machinegun) by an individual who holds a permit issued pursuant to P.C. section 32650, if the carrying of that firearm is conducted in accordance with the terms and conditions of the permit; *or* (4) The carrying of an unloaded firearm that is not a handgun that is regulated pursuant to Article 2 (commencing with P.C. section 33300) of Chapter 8 of Division 10 (short-barreled shotguns and rifles) by an individual who holds a permit issued pursuant to P.C. section 33300, if the carrying of that firearm is conducted in accordance with the terms and conditions of the permit.
P.C. § 26405(af)	A licensed hunter while engaged in training a dog for the purpose of using the dog in hunting that is not prohibited by law, or while transporting the firearm while going to or returning from that training.
P.C. § 26405(ag)	Individuals carrying pursuant to the provisions of P.C. section 171.5(d) (the exemption from the restriction against possessing firearm in sterile airport environments).
P.C. § 26405(ah)	An individual engaged in the business of manufacturing ammunition and who is licensed to engage in that business, or the authorized representative or authorized agent of that individual, while the firearm is being used in the lawful course and scope of the licensee's activities as an individual licensed pursuant to Chapter 44 (commencing with P.C. section 921) of Title 18 of the United States Code and regulations issued pursuant thereto.
P.C. § 26405(ai)	When on the navigable waters of this state that are held in public trust, if the possession and use of an unloaded "firearm that is not a handgun" is not prohibited by the managing agency thereof, and the person carrying the firearm is in lawful possession of that firearm.

VI. LICENSES TO CARRY A LOADED HANDGUN

The average person must obtain a Carry License to be generally exempt from the loaded and concealed (and in some cases open) carry restrictions in public.[73] These

---

[73] A Carry License is also widely known as a "CCW" (carry concealed weapon). *See* P.C. § 16360. But the trend is to move away from that term because of the negative connotation associated with the phrase "concealed weapon," and because not all licenses are for carrying "concealed" firearms – as some are for *open* carry.

licenses may only be issued to you by the police chief or the sheriff in your city or county of residence, although a *sheriff* may issue a temporary Carry License to non-residents if their principal place of employment or business is in that county and they spend a substantial amount of time there.

If you live in an unincorporated county territory, you can only apply for a Carry License with the sheriff of your county. If you live in an incorporated city, you can apply with either your local police department (if you have one) or with your county sheriff. Issuing authorities are required to accept and process all Carry License applications.[74] Chiefs of police have the option to cede their issuing authority to the sheriff of the county, in which case the police chief *must* reject *all* Carry License applications.[75] If that is the case with your city police department, you will have to apply with the sheriff of your county.[76]

In 2015, Governor Brown signed AB 1134 into law, expressly giving county sheriffs the authority to enter into an agreement with a local police chief or other head of municipal police departments to process all applications for licenses, renewals of licenses, or amendments to Carry Licenses.[77] This bill was passed in response to the California Court of Appeal's unpublished decision in *Lu v. County of Los Angeles.* In that case, the court held that Los Angeles County Sheriff's Department did not violate Equal Protection when it delegated its authority to process Carry License applications for residents who live in incorporated cities that are not policed by the Sheriff's Department to the Chief of Police in those cities. As the court explained, Equal Protection was not violated because applicants could still apply for review or reconsideration with the Sheriff if their application was denied.[78]

But note that under AB 1134, it is unclear as to whether the sheriff can still review or reconsider an application for a Carry License if a Chief of Police or other head denies the application. Nonetheless, when applying for a Carry License, you should check with the sheriff of your county to determine whom you will have to send your Carry License application to (*i.e.*, the county sheriff, local chief of police, or other head of a municipal police department).

The most common type of Carry License (excluding those for law enforcement) only allows you to carry a *concealed* handgun and is valid statewide, unless otherwise specifically limited by the issuing authority.[79] In counties of less than 200,000 residents, the sheriff or police chief may issue you a license to *openly* carry

---

[74] *Salute v. Pitchess*, 61 Cal. App. 3d 557 (1976).

[75] P.C. §§ 26150, 26155.

[76] Some issuing authorities have adopted the policy of requiring applicants to first apply with the other issuing authority. This is likely an unlawful practice and at least one court has ruled it such. *See Lu v. Baca*, No. BC480493 (Ca. Sup. Ct. Jan. 13, 2014), *available at* http://michellawyers.com/wp-content/uploads/2012/08/Ruling-Re-Motion-for-Summary-Judgment.pdf (last visited July 11, 2017).

[77] *See* P.C. § 26450.

[78] *See Vargas v. Cnty. of Los Angeles*, No. B257371, 2015 WL 5786608 (Oct. 5, 2015). Keep in mind, though, that this decisions is unpublished, meaning that it is not binding authority on the courts.

[79] A Carry License exempts you from most loaded carry restrictions. P.C. § 26010.

a handgun, but *only* while within that county.[80] A Carry License is typically valid for two years.[81] Temporary Carry Licenses issued by a sheriff to non-residents based on their employment or business in that specific county are valid for 90 days and only within the county where issued.[82]

State law generally allows Carry License holders to take a handgun into normally prohibited places such as state courts, schools, and the state Capitol. There are still places, though, where it is unlawful to possess a firearm even with a Carry License.[83] You are responsible for knowing the restrictions for the area where you travel. The sheriff or police chief who issued your Carry License may restrict you from entering additional places as well.

A. Criteria for Issuance

An issuing authority may only issue you a Carry License if you demonstrate the following:

(1) "Good cause" exists for issuance of the license; *and*

(2) You are of "good moral character"; *and*

(3) You are a "resident" of that city or county (or, if you are applying to a sheriff, your principal place of business is in the county and you spend substantial time there); *and*

(4) You have completed the course of training that the issuing authority requires.[84]

The law does not specify the age a Carry License applicant must be, but presumably the minimum age is 18 years since a minor cannot generally possess a handgun. Nonetheless, most issuing authorities will only issue to persons 21 years of age and over.

Even if you meet all these requirements, an issuing authority may still refuse to issue you a Carry License because the law is currently understood as granting the issuing authorities broad discretion to decide whether to issue one.[85] It is quite

---

[80] P.C. §§ 26150(b)(2), 26155(b)(2). Sheriffs or police chiefs may also issue a Carry License to anyone they deputize or appoint as a peace officer. P.C. § 26170. These types of Carry Licenses are generally exempt from the training and fee requirements for such licenses.

[81] P.C. § 26220(a). Certain Carry Licenses for judges, commissioners, and magistrates are valid for up to three years. P.C. § 26220(c). Carry Licenses for custodial officers working for a sheriff or peace officers, per P.C. section 830.6, can be valid for up to four years. P.C. § 26220(d)-(e).

[82] P.C. § 26220(b).

[83] See Chapter 7 for a discussion on such places.

[84] P.C. §§ 26150(a), 26155(a).

[85] *See Gifford v. City of Los Angeles*, 88 Cal. App. 4th 801, 805 (2001). Note that this case was decided before *Heller*, where the U.S. Supreme Court recognized an individual Second Amendment right. The constitutionality of this standard is thus dubious and is still being litigated. *See* Chapter 1. In contrast to *Gifford*, there are the more promising results from *Wrenn v. District of Columbia*, 864 F.3d 650 (D.C. Cir. 2017). On July 25, the D.C. Circuit issued its decision for *Wrenn*, declaring Washington D.C.'s "good reason" requirement for the issuance of a CCW as a violation of the Second Amendment. The Court also issued a permanent injunction prohibiting D.C. from

common for issuing authorities to set their standards so high that most people cannot meet them. Also, issuing authorities may require psychological testing of any initial applicant (but not of renewal applicants unless there is compelling evidence that such testing is necessary), and can deny Carry Licenses to applicants who fail such testing.[86]

1. "Good Cause"

The ability to obtain a Carry License in any given jurisdiction almost always depends on the respective issuing authority's interpretation of what constitutes "good cause." Different jurisdictional interpretations of what constitutes "good cause" have led to wide disparity in whether Carry Licenses are issued in any given jurisdiction.[87] Some issuing agencies simply require the assertion of a desire for self-defense to establish "good cause," while others refuse to issue any licenses at all, no matter what evidence of "good cause" an applicant provides. For policy reasons, these issuing agencies simply do not want civilians to have Carry Licenses.

2. "Good Moral Character"

While issuing authorities conceivably have the same authority to determine whether an applicant is of "good moral character" as they do to determine one's "good cause," this standard has, practically speaking, been of little consequence. This is likely because issuing authorities that do not want to issue many licenses will simply rely on the "good cause" standard to bar an applicant and never reach this standard. Moreover, those with a more liberal "good cause" standard are likely much less prone to reject an applicant based on lack of "good moral character" unless there is a legitimate concern.

Nevertheless, some jurisdictions have denied applicants a Carry License if they have an arrest on their record. If you have an arrest, or a criminal conviction, on

---

enforcing the requirement. On September 28, the D.C. Circuit denied Washington D.C.'s request for rehearing. In response, the Attorney General for the District of Columbia said that he would not petition the case to the United States Supreme Court. So Washington D.C. should soon amend its policies to accept "self-defense" as sufficient "good reason" for the issuance of a CCW.

[86] P.C. § 26190(f).

[87] On June 9, 2016, an en banc panel of the Ninth Circuit Court of Appeals held in *Peruta v. County of San Diego* "that there is no Second Amendment right for members of the general public to carry concealed firearms in public." *Peruta v. Cnty. of San Diego*, No. 10-56971 3 (9th Cir. June 9, 2016). As such, the court upheld the constitutionality of the "good cause" requirement under P.C. section 26150 and 26155, which requires citizens to establish some special need in order to obtain a carry license. This decision overturned a previous decision in which a three judge panel of the Ninth Circuit ruled that the Second Amendment prohibited cities and counties from requiring some special need in order for an applicant for a Carry License to establish "good cause," *see Peruta v. Cnty. of San Diego*, 10-56971, 742 F.3d 1144 (9th Cir. 2014), and that California Attorney General Kamala Harris could not intervene into the case because her petition was untimely and the decision itself did not implicate the constitutionality of any state statute, *see Peruta v. Cnty. of San Diego*, 771 F.3d 570 (9th Cir. 2014). Shortly after the en banc panel's decision, the plaintiff's petitioned the United States Supreme Court for certiorari. On June 26, the Supreme Court issued an order declining to hear the case, but not without a strong dissenting opinion from newly appointed Justice Gorsuch and Justice Thomas, highlighting how the en banc panel improperly declined to answer the core question of the case.

your record, you may be denied based on that reason alone. Although, as explained above, it is more likely that you would be denied under the "good cause" standard.

3. Residency

What constitutes "residency" for the purposes of qualifying for a Carry License is not very clear. You are obviously a resident of the city and county in which you own or rent a residence that is your exclusive dwelling, meaning you do not spend substantial amounts of time elsewhere. Nevertheless, some issuing authorities reject applicants for lack of residency who are "part-time" residents or who have only resided in the area for a short period of time. The legality of such restrictive residency definitions is unclear and will eventually need to be litigated. If you are denied for lack of residency, you may want to contact an attorney experienced in firearms law to determine what your options are.[88]

4. Training Course

First-time Carry License applicants are required to complete a training course chosen by the sheriff or police chief. The course cannot last more than 16 hours and must include instruction on firearm safety and the laws about permissible firearm uses.[89] Renewal applicants are also required to complete a minimum four-hour training course and may also become certified trainers, in which case they would be exempt from the training requirement altogether.[90]

Alternatively, sheriffs or police chiefs may require first-time Carry License applicants to pass a community college course of up to 24 hours that is certified by

---

[88] In 2013, a U.S. district court ruled on a summary judgment motion in which it interpreted the term "residency" as used within P.C. section 26160 to "mean a status akin to 'domiciliary' under California law." *Raulinaitis v. Ventura Cnty. Sheriffs Dept.*, No. 2:13-cv-02605-MAN (C.D. Cal. Filed Dec. 31, 2013) (order denying motion for summary judgment). In other words, under the court's interpretation of the word "residency," county sheriffs may grant Carry Licenses "only to those persons who are physically present within their respective counties to an extent consistent with the concept of 'domicile.'" *Raulinaitis v. Ventura Cnty. Sheriffs Dept.*, No. 2:13-cv-02605-MAN (C.D. Cal. Filed Dec. 31, 2013) (order denying motion for summary judgment). A person's "domicile" under California law is "the one location with which for legal purposes to have the most settled and permanent connection, the place where he intends to remain and to which, whenever he is absent, he has the intention of returning, but which the law may also assign to him constructively . . . ." *Raulinaitis v. Ventura Cnty. Sheriffs Dept.*, No. 2:13-cv-02605-MAN (C.D. Cal. Filed Dec. 31, 2013) (order denying motion for summary judgment) (citing Smith v. Smith, 45 Cal. 2d 235, 239 (1955)). Although this opinion is well written, it is merely persuasive and not binding authority. This interpretation of "residence" is also subject to a Second Amendment challenge. The plaintiff appealed the decision in *Raulinaitis* to the Ninth Circuit. On November 7, 2016, the Ninth Circuit affirmed the district court's summary judgment ruling, holding that the Los Angeles County Sheriff's Department's policies do not violate the Second Amendment "for the same reasons" that the San Diego and Yolo County Sheriff's Department policies at issue in *Peruta* survived a Second Amendment challenge (i.e., that a member of the general public does not have a right under the Second Amendment to carry a concealed firearm in public and a state may impose restrictions, including a showing of good cause, on concealed carry). *Raulinaitis v. Los Angeles County Sheriff's Dept.*, 670 Fed. Appx. 569 (9th Cir. 2016.)

[89] P.C. § 26165(a).

[90] P.C. § 26165(c).

the Commission on POST,[91] but only if this is required of *all* initial applicants.[92] Requiring this type of course for renewal applicants does not appear to be allowed.

B. Issuing Authorities' Mandatory Written Policy

Issuing authorities *must* publish an official written policy explaining the circumstances under which they consider an applicant to:

(1) Have "good cause" for a Carry License; *and*

(2) Be of "good moral character"; *and*

(3) Be a "resident" of the respective county or city (or, for sheriffs only, to qualify for a non-resident license based on business activity in the county).

Additionally this official written policy must explain exactly what firearm training is required by the issuing authority per P.C. section 26165.[93]

A copy of your respective issuing authority's official written policy should be available online or upon request to that agency.

C. Application Process and Fees

Carry License applications must be on a form prescribed by the Attorney General (AG) and must be the same throughout the state.[94] The issuing authority cannot require any additional information beyond what is necessary to complete the standard DOJ application form, except when it is necessary to clarify any information that was provided on the application.[95] Any false statement made on the application is at least a misdemeanor and may be a felony if the false statement is about any of the following:

(1) The denial or revocation of a license, or the denial of an amendment to a license; *or*

(2) A criminal conviction; *or*

(3) A finding of not guilty by reason of insanity; *or*

(4) The use of a controlled substance; *or*

(5) A dishonorable discharge from military service; *or*

---

[91] CAL. COMM'N ON PEACE OFFICER STANDARDS AND TRAINING, http://www.post.ca.gov/ (last visited July 11, 2017).

[92] P.C. § 26165(b).

[93] P.C. § 26160 (formerly P.C. § 12050.2). This requirement was the result of an NRA and CRPA sponsored bill, Senate Bill (SB) 610 (2011).

[94] As of publication, the required form is located online. *See Standard Initial and Renewal Application for License to Carry a Concealed Weapon*, CAL. DEPT. OF JUSTICE, BUREAU OF FIREARMS, https://www.sjpd.org/PDF_Forms/BOF_4012_CCWapplication_112012.pdf (last visited July 11, 2017). No doubt there will be revisions to the form in the future. Make sure your law enforcement agency is using the current form.

[95] P.C. § 26175.

(6) A commitment to a mental institution; *or*

(7) A renunciation of U.S. citizenship.[96]

Generally, along with the standard application, you must also provide two copies of your fingerprints and the DOJ's requisite fee ($95), all of which is forwarded to the DOJ to conduct your background check.[97]

In addition to the background check fee, you may also be charged a fee for the sheriff or police chief's costs to process the application. This additional fee cannot exceed $100. The first 20% of the fee (maximum of $20) may be collected up front.[98] For a renewal application, you may be charged up to $25 total.[99] If psychological testing is required, the issuing authority may charge an additional fee of up to $150.[100]

It is against the law for the issuing authority to charge a fee relating to the Carry License application process unless it is expressly authorized by P.C. section 26190, as are any conditions requiring the applicant to pay additional money.[101] And requiring liability insurance for a Carry License is specifically prohibited.[102]

Once you complete and submit your initial or renewal Carry License application, you must be given written notice about whether your application is granted or not. This should occur within 90 days of your application being received or 30 days after the sheriff or police chief receives your background check from the DOJ, whichever is later.[103] But except substantial delays during this process.

P.C. section 26202 also requires issuing authorities to provide Carry License applicants *written* notice that either:

(1) "Good cause" exists and the applicant should continue with any training required pursuant to P.C. section 26165; *or*

(2) The Carry License is denied for lack of "good cause," stating the specific reason why the applicant lacks "good cause" under the issuing authority's written policy (as required by P.C. section 26160).[104]

You cannot be required to pay for any required training course until you have received this written notice.[105] If you are denied a Carry License for something *other than* "good cause," the issuing authority must explain in writing what requirement

---

[96] P.C. § 26180.

[97] P.C. § 26185.

[98] P.C. § 26190(b), (c).

[99] P.C. § 26190(c).

[100] P.C. § 26190(f).

[101] P.C. § 26190(g).

[102] P.C. § 26190(g). This restriction was created by SB 610 (2011).

[103] P.C. § 26205.

[104] The specific reason should come from the issuing authority's published policy required under P.C. section 26160. This notice requirement was also part of SB 610 (2011).

[105] P.C. § 26165(d).

you did not satisfy, but they do not need to explain the specific reason(s) for the denial. But, nothing precludes such an explanation.

D. License Revocation and Moving Out of the Jurisdiction

The universe of circumstances allowing sheriffs or police chiefs to revoke currently valid Carry Licenses is unclear. But it is clear that they can revoke a Carry License if the license holder becomes a prohibited person.[106] Many issuing authorities will have their revocation policies in writing.

If you change addresses, you must notify the sheriff or police chief of this within 10 days. An address change cannot be the basis for *revoking* the Carry License, even if you move outside of the county in which it was issued. But, if your residence was the basis for the issuance of the license, it will *expire* 90 days after you move from the county of issuance. And if your license is for loaded and exposed carry, it will expire immediately upon your change of residence to another county.[107]

E. License Restrictions

Any type of Carry License may have "reasonable restrictions or conditions" placed on it by the sheriff or police chief including, but not limited to, time, place, manner, and circumstance restrictions. Any such restriction(s) must be indicated on the license itself.[108]

 Check with the authorities who have jurisdiction over the place(s) you want to go with your firearm. You should be aware that bringing a firearm to certain places may be a sensitive matter, even if it is legal to carry it there. For example, state court judges regularly prohibit Carry License holders from possessing firearms in their courtrooms even though state law allows it. Be especially careful on federal property where it generally will *not* be legal.

F. Form of Physical License

California law requires an issued Carry License to be laminated and have the license holder's name, occupation, residence and business address, age, height, weight, color of eyes and hair, the reason for desiring the license (*i.e.*, "good cause"), and a description of any handgun carried pursuant to the license with the manufacturer's name, the serial number, and the caliber.[109]

---

[106] P.C. § 26195. See Chapter 4.
[107] P.C. § 26210.
[108] P.C. § 26200.
[109] P.C. § 26175(i).

In 2016, Governor Brown signed AB 2510 into law.[110] This bill requires the California Attorney General to develop a uniform Carry License, with uniform information and criteria, that can be used throughout the state.[111]

G. License Amendments

A Carry License holder may request the issuing agency to amend the license in the following ways:

(1) Add or delete a handgun that is allowed to be carried pursuant to the license; *or*

(2) Change permission to carry the handgun from openly to concealed, or from concealed to openly (if allowed in that particular county); *or*

(3) Change any restrictions or conditions placed on the license by the issuing authority.[112]

If the issuing authority amends the license, a new physical license reflecting such amendment(s) will be issued to the license holder.[113] The new physical license does not change the original license's expiration date, meaning the license will still need to be renewed upon expiration as it would if no amendment was made.[114]

Some states honor Carry Licenses issued in another state, but this varies between states. For example, California does not recognize Carry Licenses issued in any other state, even though some states recognize California licenses. But, as discussed below, federal law requires California to allow certain active and retired law enforcement officers to carry within California as long as the requirements outlined in the Law Enforcement Office Safety Act (LEOSA). For more information on Carry License issues, visit www.CalGunLawsBook.com.

---

[110] AB 2510, 2015-2016 Leg. Council's Digest (2016), *available at* http://leginfo.legislature.ca.gov/faces/billTextClient.xhtml?bill_id=201520160AB2510 (last visited July 11, 2017).

[111] P.C. § 26175.

[112] P.C. § 26215(a).

[113] P.C. § 26215(b).

[114] P.C. § 26215(c).

VII. EXEMPTIONS FOR ACTIVE & RETIRED PEACE OFFICERS

A. Concealed and Loaded Restrictions

1. Current Law Enforcement Officers

a. California Peace Officers

Current California peace officers are exempt from both the concealed handgun and loaded firearm restrictions.[115] Whether you are considered a "peace officer" for purposes of these exemptions is usually straightforward, but there are cases that are not so clear. This is because the Penal Code sections are oddly worded, providing "[a]ny peace officer, listed in Section 830.1 or 830.2, or subdivision (a) of Section 830.33, whether active or honorably retired" is exempt from the restrictions on carrying concealed or loaded.[116] But the same sections go on to say that "[a]ny other duly appointed peace officer" is also exempt.[117] Based on this wording, it *appears* that *any* person falling under the definition of a "peace officer" is exempt from the restrictions for carrying a firearm concealed and/or loaded.[118]

But the Penal Code treats some "peace officers" differently. For example, persons employed by the Division of Investigation of the Department of Consumer Affairs may carry firearms only if authorized and under the terms and conditions as specified by their employing agency.[119] Despite the fact that a person can be a "peace officer" and be denied by his or her employer the ability to carry a firearm while on-duty, generally a "peace officer's" employer cannot restrict or deny the officer's ability to carry a firearm either loaded or concealed while off-duty.[120] Although, this too is not without limitations. For example, parole officers of the Juvenile Parole Board must receive special permission from the chairperson of the board.[121]

If you do not know whether you fall under this exemption, you should determine whether you are considered a "peace officer" under the Penal Code and if there are any limits on your ability to carry firearms. Members of law enforcement

---

[115] P.C. §§ 25450(a)-(b), 25900(a)-(b). These exceptions can generally be found in P.C. sections 25450-25475 (for carrying concealed) and 25900-29525 (for carrying loaded). While these sections are practically identical there are some minor differences. If you are a peace officer and interested in carrying concealed and/or loaded you should check both sections to confirm you are in compliance.

[116] P.C. §§ 25450(a), 25900(a). The additional requirements for retired officers are below.

[117] P.C. §§ 25450(b), 25900(b).

[118] "Peace officers" are defined in P.C. sections 830-832.9.

[119] *See* P.C. § 830.3.

[120] *See Orange Cnty. Employees Ass'n v. Cnty. of Orange*, 14 Cal. App. 4th 575 (1993). The AG's office has also issued a number of opinions concerning these issues. *See* Opinion No. 94-1106, 78 Cal. Ops. Atty. Gen. 209 (1995); Opinion No. 89-505, 72 Cal. Ops. Atty. Gen. 167 (1989); Opinion No. 79-1207, 63 Cal. Ops. Atty. Gen. 385 (1980).

[121] P.C. § 830.5.

in states neighboring California and members of the National Guard are considered "peace officers" in certain limited contexts and may be able to carry firearms in those limited contexts.[122]

b. Current Reserve Peace Officers

While it seems that active reserve peace officers enjoy these same exemptions,[123] it is unclear if this is the case in practice. Many agencies take the view that reserve officers must obtain a Carry License pursuant to P.C. section 26170 in order to be exempt.

c. Other Current Officers

The following individuals are exempt from the general laws against carrying loaded firearms in public as long as they complete a regular firearms training course approved by the POST Commission:

(1) "Patrol special police officers" appointed by the city or county police who meet the criteria set forth in P.C. section 26025(a)(1)-(4); *and*

(2) Authorized animal control officers and zookeepers compensated by the government in the scope of their duty when authorized by a local ordinance or resolution; *and*

(3) Persons authorized to carry the weapons listed in California Corporations Code section 14502 while actually engaged in duties per that section; *and*

(4) Harbor police officers.[124]

While these individuals are exempt from the general laws against carrying loaded firearms in public, this does *not* mean they are exempt from prohibitions on *concealed* carry.

d. Current Federal and Out-of-State Officers

California law exempts out-of-state and federal peace officers who are "full-time paid" and "carrying out official duties while in California"[125] from the restrictions on carrying concealed and loaded firearms. But virtually all law enforcement officers that satisfy these criteria enjoy these exemptions under *federal* law regardless of whether they meet California's preconditions, as discussed below.

---

[122] P.C. §§ 830.39, 830.4.

[123] *See* P.C. §§ 830, 830.6 (declaring reserve officers "peace officers" provided they meet specified criteria set forth in P.C. section 832.6).

[124] P.C. § 26025.

[125] P.C. §§ 25450(e), 25900(e). Full-time salaried federal law enforcement officers who are Department of Defense police officers at the Los Angeles Air Force Base may be "exempt from the state law prohibition against carrying concealed, loaded firearms even when they are not on duty." *See* Opinion No. 01-1005, 85 Ops. Cal. Atty. Gen. 68 (2002).

Federal officers meet the definition of a "peace officer" only in a limited capacity, but active officers are exempt from the restrictions on carrying concealed and loaded firearms by statute. California law explicitly states that "[f]ederal criminal investigators and law enforcement officers are *not* California peace officers" but may exercise the powers of arrest of a peace officer in certain situations.[126] As unambiguous as this language is, ambiguities abound because the statute further states "[d]uly authorized federal employees who comply with training requirements set forth in Section 832 *are* peace officers when they are engaged in enforcing applicable state or local laws on property owned or possessed by the United States government, or on any street, sidewalk, or property adjacent thereto, and with the written consent of the sheriff or the chief of police, respectively, in whose jurisdiction the property is situated."[127] Presumably, when a federal criminal investigator or law enforcement officer meets the definition of a "peace officer" as defined above, he or she would be permitted to carry concealed or loaded under the general "peace officer" exemption.

But of course, this being California law, there is an exception to the exemption because national park rangers are *not* peace officers despite having the power to arrest and the powers *of* a peace officer in certain situations and under certain criteria.[128]

2. Retired Law Enforcement

"Honorably retired" California peace officers are also generally exempt from both the concealed handgun and loaded firearm restrictions, but they must meet some preconditions that current officers do not. An "honorably retired" peace officer includes any peace officer who has qualified for and accepted "a service or disability retirement," but does not include "an officer who has agreed to a service retirement in lieu of termination."[129]

a. Retired California Peace Officers

Any honorably retired peace officer who was authorized to, and did, carry a firearm on the job, or whose position is listed in P.C. section 830.5(c), is generally entitled to be issued an identification certificate by the agency from which the officer retired.[130] In most cases the issuing agency is also required to endorse such certificates for peace officers who honorably retired after January 1, 1981, stating that the

---

[126] P.C. § 830.8(a) (emphasis added). Federal investigators and law enforcement officers are also required to have been certified by their agency heads as having satisfied the training requirements of P.C. section 832 or the equivalent thereof. Bureau of Land Management (BLM) and U.S. Forest Service officers do not have the power to arrest unless they have written consent of the sheriff or chief of police in whose jurisdiction they are assigned. P.C. § 830.8(a).

[127] P.C. § 830.8(b) (emphasis added).

[128] P.C. § 830.8(c). This exception to the exemption also applies to "Washoe tribal law enforcement officers" under certain circumstances. P.C. § 830.8(e)(1)-(b)(4).

[129] P.C. § 16690.

[130] P.C. §§ 25455(a), 25905(a); *see also* P.C. §§ 25450(c)-(d), 25900(c)-(d). The required format of the certificate is provided in P.C. section 25460. The issuing agency may charge a fee necessary to cover its reasonable expenses

retired officer is approved to lawfully carry a concealed and loaded firearm.[131] An unendorsed certificate is generally sufficient authorization for a peace officer who honorably retired prior to 1981 to lawfully carry a concealed and loaded firearm, unless it has been stamped "No CCW privilege" by the agency that issued it after a showing of "good cause" for denying the person's ability to carry.[132]

Current peace officers and those honorably retired peace officers with endorsed identification certificates issued by the agency they retired from are also exempt from both the restrictions on openly carrying unloaded handguns and "firearms that are not handguns" in "public places."[133] Generally, honorably retired peace officers must petition to renew their Carry License certificate every five years with the agency they retired from.[134] Peace officer positions listed in P.C. section 830.5(c), however, must qualify every year to maintain a valid Carry License certificate.[135]

The agency the officer retired from may only deny or revoke a Carry License certificate for "good cause."[136] Although it is unspecified what constitutes "good cause" for denial or revocation, California law provides the following:

(1) Psychological disability; *or*

(2) "[V]iolating any departmental rule, or state or federal law that, if violated by an officer on active duty, would result in that officer's arrest, suspension, or removal from the agency"; *or*

(3) Conduct that compromises public safety.[137]

An officer whose Carry License certificate is denied or revoked has 15 days after receiving proper notice of revocation to request a hearing.[138] Failing to request a hearing within that time frame forfeits the officer's right to one.[139]

Any honorably retired peace officer[140] must be issued an identification certificate by the law enforcement agency from which he or she retired.[141] "If the agency from which the officer has retired is no longer providing law enforcement services or the relevant government body is dissolved, the agency that subsequently pro-

---

incurred by issuing the certificate. P.C. § 25455(b). P.C. section 26300 was recently amended by AB 703 (2013) to also allow retired level I reserve officers to obtain a certificate equivalent to a carry license.

[131] P.C. § 26300(b)-(c); *see also* P.C. § 25455(c). This applies to those officers listed in P.C. sections 830.1, 830.2, or 830.5(c), as well as those officers who were authorized to, and did, carry a firearm during the course and scope of their appointment as peace officers.

[132] P.C. § 26300(a); *see also* P.C. § 25455(d). This applies only to those officers listed in P.C. sections 830.1, 830.2, or 830.5(c).

[133] P.C. §§ 26361, 26405.

[134] P.C. §§ 25465, 25915.

[135] P.C. §§ 25475(a), 25925(a). These are certain officers and employees of the Department of Corrections and Rehabilitation, including some in that department's Division of Juvenile Justice.

[136] P.C. §§ 25470(a), 25920(a), 26305(d).

[137] P.C. § 26305(a)-(c).

[138] P.C. § 26312. This notice must be personally served. The hearing is governed by P.C. section 26320.

[139] P.C. §§ 26310, 26312, 26315.

[140] Defined in P.C. section 25900.

[141] P.C. § 25905(a)(1).

vides law enforcement services for that jurisdiction shall issue the identification certificate" to that retired peace officer if all the following conditions are met[142]:

(1) The successor agency is in possession of the retired officer's complete personnel records or can otherwise verify the retired officer's honorably retired status; *and*

(2) The retired officer is in compliance with all the requirements of the successor agency for the issuance of a retirement identification card and concealed weapon endorsement; *and*

(3) The issuing agency may charge a fee necessary to cover any reasonable expenses incurred by the agency in issuing certificates pursuant to P.C. sections 25900, 25910, 25925, and 25905; *and*

(4) Any officer, except an officer listed in P.C. sections 830.1, 830.2, 830.33(a), or 830.5(c) who retired prior to January 1, 1981, shall have an endorsement on the identification certificate stating that the issuing agency approves the officer's carrying of a loaded firearm; *and*

(5) An honorably retired peace officer listed in P.C. sections 830.1, 830.2, 830.33(a), or 830.5(c) who retired prior to January 1, 1981, shall not be required to obtain an endorsement from the issuing agency to carry a loaded firearm.[143]

b. Retired Reserve California Peace Officers

Like retired full-time peace officers, any honorably retired reserve peace officer who was authorized to, and did, carry a firearm during the course and scope of his or her appointment as a peace officer is generally entitled to an identification certificate with an endorsement from the agency the officer retired from stating that the officer is approved to carry a concealed and loaded firearm, but only if the officer:

(1) Was a level I reserve officer;[144] *and*

(2) Served in aggregate the minimum amount of time as specified by the officer's agency's policy as a level I reserve officer, provided that the policy shall not set an aggregate term requirement.

The limitation on which reserve officers are entitled to carry permits was created in 2013 when the California Legislature passed Assembly Bill (AB) 703.[145] It appears that when the California Legislature amended this Penal Code section, it made a whole segment of retired reserve officers who were formerly able to carry under this provision ineligible. But, there is still some ambiguity since the law

---

[142] P.C. § 25905(a)(2).

[143] P.C. § 25905(a)(2).

[144] Described in P.C. section 832.6(a)(1).

[145] *See* AB 703, 2013-2014, Cal. Leg. Counsel's Digest (Cal. 2014), *available at* http://leginfo.legislature.ca.gov/faces/billNavClient.xhtml?bill_id=201320140AB703 (last visited July 11, 2017).

exempts retired "peace officers" from carry restrictions, and reserve officers meet this definition (see the preceding section). Nonetheless, this section seems to bode badly for reserve officers who want to carry but do not meet the above criteria.

A law enforcement agency has the same discretion to revoke or deny an endorsement issued to such a retired reserve peace officer for "good cause," as it does for a current full-time officer as discussed above.[146]

c. Retired Federal Peace Officers

Unlike retired state peace officers who are generally entitled to a certification exempting them from all the restrictions on carrying handguns in public, honorably retired federal officers or agents are not exempt under California law. Rather, under California law these officers might be able to carry if they apply to the sheriff of the county where they reside for a permit. The sheriff may, but is not required to, issue this permit to a retired federal officer or agent who:

(1) Was authorized to carry weapons while on duty; *or*

(2) Was assigned to duty within California for a period of not less than one year; *or*

(3) Is retired from active service in California.[147]

These officers and agents must give the sheriff a certification from the agency from which they retired certifying their service in the state that states the nature of their retirement and indicates the agency's agreement that they should be allowed to carry a loaded firearm.[148]

This permit is valid for a period not exceeding five years and must be carried by the retired federal officer or agent at all times while carrying a loaded firearm. The permit may be revoked for "good cause."[149]

Even if a retired federal officer or agent cannot obtain such a permit, he or she may still be able to carry under federal law (under the Law Enforcement Officers Safety Act (LEOSA, explained immediately below), albeit in a somewhat more limited fashion than what they would be able to with a permit from their sheriff.

B. Law Enforcement Officers Safety Act (LEOSA/H.R. 218)

LEOSA[150] amended the federal Gun Control Act (GCA) to exempt qualified law enforcement officers (QLEO) and qualified retired law enforcement officers (QRLEO) from most state and local laws prohibiting the carrying of concealed firearms as long as they have the proper photo ID (and certification if needed for QRLEOs)

---

[146] P.C. §§ 26300(c), 26305.

[147] P.C. §§ 26020(a), 25650(a).

[148] P.C. §§ 26020(b), 25650(b).

[149] P.C. §§ 26020(c), 25650(d).

[150] Also known as "H.R. 218," found at 18 U.S.C. sections 926B, 926C.

from the law enforcement agency they are currently employed by or separated from. But, LEOSA places limits on the types of firearms[151] a QLEO and QRLEO may carry and on the locations where the exemption applies.

1. QLEO Definition and ID Requirements

An employee of a governmental agency is a QLEO under LEOSA if he or she meets all of the following criteria:

(1) Is authorized by law to engage in or supervise the prevention, detection, investigation, prosecution, or the incarceration of any person for, any violation of law, and has statutory powers of arrest or apprehension;[152] *and*

(2) Is authorized by the agency to carry a firearm; *and*

(3) Is not the subject of any disciplinary action by the agency which could result in suspension or loss of police powers; *and*

(4) Meets standards, if any, established by the agency which require the employee to regularly qualify in the use of a firearm; *and*

(5) Is not under the influence of alcohol or another intoxicating or hallucinatory drug or substance; *and*

(6) Is not prohibited by federal law from receiving a firearm.[153]

Additionally, QLEOs must carry the proper identification; specifically, "photographic identification issued by the governmental agency for which the individual is employed that identifies the employee as a police officer or law enforcement officer of the agency."[154]

2. QRLEO Definition and ID Requirements

A QRLEO is an individual who:

(1) Is separated in good standing from service with a public agency as a law enforcement officer;[155] *and*

---

[151] Machine guns, silencers, and destructive devices are not found under LEOSA. 18 U.S.C. §§ 926B(e), 926C(e). Beyond those limitations, however, "firearm" is not defined.

[152] The apprehension powers must be granted under 10 U.S.C. section 807. "[A] law enforcement officer of the Amtrak Police Department, a law enforcement officer of the Federal Reserve, or a law enforcement or police officer of the executive branch of the Federal Government qualifies as an employee of a governmental agency who is authorized by law to engage in or supervise the prevention, detection, investigation, or prosecution of, or the incarceration of any person for, any violation of law, and has statutory powers of arrest or apprehension . . . ." 18 U.S.C. § 926B(f).

[153] 18 U.S.C. § 926B(c).

[154] 18 U.S.C. § 926B(d).

[155] "[T]he term 'service with a public agency as a law enforcement officer' includes service as a law enforcement officer of the Amtrak Police Department, service as a law enforcement officer of the Federal Reserve, or service as a law enforcement or police officer of the executive branch of the Federal Government." 18 U.S.C. § 926C(e) (2).

(2) Before such separation, was authorized by law to engage in or supervise the prevention, detection, investigation, prosecution, or the incarceration of any person for, any violation of law, and had statutory powers of arrest or apprehension;[156] *and*

(3) Either:

    (a) Before such separation, served as a law enforcement officer for an aggregate of 10 years or more; *or*

    (b) Separated from service with such agency after completing any applicable probationary period of such service due to a service-connected disability, as determined by such agency;

    AND

(4) During the most recent 12-month period has met, at the expense of the individual, the standards for qualification in firearms training for active law enforcement officers, as determined by:

    (a) The individual's former agency, *or*

    (b) The State in which the individual resides, *or*

    (c) If the State has not established such standards, either (1) a law enforcement agency within the State in which the individual resides; *or* (2) the standards used by a certified firearms instructor that is qualified to conduct a firearms qualification test for active duty officers within that State;

    AND

(5) Either:

    (a) Has not been officially found by a qualified medical professional employed by the agency to be unqualified for reasons relating to mental health and as a result of this finding will not be issued the photographic identification for LEOSA; *or*

    (b) Has not entered into an agreement with the agency from which the individual is separating from service in which the individual acknowledges he or she is not qualified under this section for reasons relating to mental health and for those reasons will not receive or accept the photographic identification for LEOSA;

    AND

(6) Is not under the influence of alcohol or another intoxicating or hallucinatory drug or substance; *and*

(7) Is not prohibited by Federal law from receiving a firearm.[157]

---

[156] The apprehension powers must be granted under 10 U.S.C. section 807(b).
[157] 18 U.S.C. § 926C(c).

The identification needed for a QRLEO to carry under LEOSA is either:

(1) A photo ID that:

    (a) Is issued by the agency that the individual worked for; *and*

    (b) Identifies the individual as having been employed as a police officer or law enforcement officer;

    AND EITHER OF THE FOLLOWING:

(2) The ID indicates that the individual has not been tested or otherwise found by the agency to meet the active duty standards for qualification in firearms training as established by the agency to carry a firearm of the same type as the concealed firearm less than one year before the date the individual is carrying the concealed firearm;[158] *or*

(3) The retired officer possesses a certification:

    (a) Issued by:

        (i) The state where the individual resides; *or*

        (ii) By a certified firearms instructor that is qualified to conduct a firearms qualification test for active duty officers within that State;

    AND

    (b) That indicates the individual has, not less recently than one year before the date the individual is carrying the concealed firearm, been tested or otherwise found by the agency to meet the active duty standards for qualification in firearms training as established by the state or a certified firearms instructor that is qualified to conduct a firearms qualification test for active duty officers within the state to have met:

        (i) The active duty standards for qualification in firearms training, as established by the state, to carry a firearm of the same type as the concealed firearm; *or*

        (ii) If the state has not established such standards, standards set by any law enforcement agency within the state to carry a firearm of the same type as the concealed firearm.[159]

If you meet the identification requirements from your pervious agency discussed directly above in (1) & (2), you do not need to meet the identification and certification requirements of (1) & (3). In a number of cases, an officer cannot qualify through that officer's former agency, or the agency will not qualify a retired officer so that the officer can meet the requirements of (1) & (2). Consequently, the retired officer will need to have the ID and certification discussed in (1) & (3). Most agencies issue the required identification, but some do not.

---

[158] 18 U.S.C. § 926C(d)(1).

[159] 18 U.S.C. § 926C(d)(2)(A)-(B).

LEOSA does not create a right to carry a concealed firearm, nor does it entitle an active or retired law enforcement officer to be issued the ID, or ID and certification, to carry a firearm under LEOSA. There is no requirement under federal law that a law enforcement agency issue the required ID for an officer to carry under LEOSA.[160] But, if an officer qualifies as an eligible officer under LEOSA and possesses the proper ID, or ID and certification, that person should be able to carry firearms under LEOSA without any further permission.

In the case that a QRLEO can obtain the required identification under (1), there is still the matter of the certification in (3). This "certification" requirement is rife with ambiguities.

The first is the uncertainty as to what form the "certification" must be in. Most states do not issue a "certification." Nevertheless, the "certification" can be issued by a "certified" firearms instructor "qualified" to conduct a firearms qualification test for active duty officers within the state. LEOSA creates some ambiguities here as well. There is no definition of what a "certified" firearm instructor is or what it means for the instructor to be "qualified." Apparently, any certified firearms instructor who conducts qualification tests for active duty officers within California will suffice.

The standards a QRLEO is required to meet is ambiguous as well. In addition to states rarely issuing certifications under LEOSA, some states (like California) do not have an established standard for qualification for active duty law enforcement. And as discussed above, if no set standard is established, the standards a QRLEO can qualify under can be from *any* law enforcement agency in the state. In other words, if the qualified instructor conducts qualification tests for an agency with exceedingly low qualification standards, the instructor can then test and certify a QRLEO using those same standards.[161]

3. LEOSA and the California Department of Justice

The DOJ apparently still thinks that retired federal law enforcement cannot carry a concealed firearm without a California Carry License. This opinion appears to be based in part on the fact that California has no state standard for "active duty law enforcement." According to the DOJ's website:

> Both "qualified law enforcement officers" and "qualified retired law enforcement officers" are required to meet the state's standards for the "training and qualification for active law enforcement officers to carry firearms" under the LEOSA. Penal Code Section 832.3 sets forth the initial and continuing training and testing requirements for peace officers in California. The specific curriculum for the training of peace officers is established by the California Commission on Peace Officer Standards and Training

---

[160] *Johnson v. New York State Dept. of Correctional Servs.*, 709 F. Supp. 2d 178 (N.D.N.Y. 2010).

[161] Frequently asked LEOSA questions can be found on the NRA's website at: http://le.nra.org/leosa/frequently-asked-questions.aspx (last visited July 11, 2017).

(P.O.S.T.). However, current California law does not set a statewide standard for the training and qualification of active law enforcement officers after graduation from the academy. Standards are established by individual law enforcement agencies for both active and retired officers in those agencies.[162]

A close reading of the DOJ's website and synopsis of LEOSA reveals the probable cause for confusion. The version of LEOSA that the DOJ has on its website is the version of LEOSA from when it was introduced in 2004. At that time, both QLEOs and QRLEOs had to comply with state standards for active law enforcement. But LEOSA has changed since 2004 to include the current language allowing for any state law enforcement standards. Therefore, the DOJ's written position is nine years old and inaccurate. Nevertheless, this is the DOJ's stated position on its website, and it's the position the DOJ takes when asked by representatives of retired federal law enforcement agencies.

 This position is likely also incorrect under the current LEOSA. If the DOJ changes its position, or its website is updated with additional information, it will be available on www.crpa.org.

4. Limits on LEOSA and the Types of Firearms One May Carry

Although they are exempt from *general* prohibitions on concealed carry, QLEOs and QRLEOs are still subject to state laws restricting firearm possession on state or local government property, installations, buildings, bases, or parks (this restriction would arguably cover places like schools and state courthouse as discussed in Chapter 7), as well as federal laws restricting firearm possession (*e.g.*, in airports, federal courts, and post offices). LEOSA specifies that it does not protect a person in areas a *state* restricts.[163] Consequently, it appears that a person carrying pursuant to LEOSA is exempt from *local* restrictions. You should therefore be familiar with the laws of places you intend to travel with a concealed firearm if you are carrying under LEOSA. LEOSA also doesn't supersede or limit a state's laws that allow private persons or entities to prohibit or restrict the possession of concealed firearms on their property.[164]

When LEOSA uses the term "firearm" it means "firearm" as defined in 18 U.S.C. section 921 (discussed in Chapter 2).[165] The term "firearm" also includes ammunition not expressly prohibited by federal law (like armor piercing handgun ammunition) or subject to provisions of the National Firearms Act (NFA) (like destructive

---

[162] CAL. DEPT. OF JUSTICE, OFFICE OF THE ATTORNEY GENERAL, SUMMARY OF THE LAW ENFORCEMENT OFFICERS SAFETY ACT (LEOSA) OF 2004, *available at* https://oag.ca.gov/sites/all/files/agweb/pdfs/firearms/forms/leosasummary.pdf (last visited Oct. 20, 2017).

[163] 18 U.S.C. § 926B(b).

[164] 18 U.S.C. §§ 926B(b), 926C(b).

[165] 18 U.S.C. § 926B(e)(1).

devices).[166] The term "firearm" also does not include "machinegun" (as defined in the NFA) or silencers and destructive devices (as defined in the GCA).[167]

This is a rather odd distinction because states often ban other types of firearms (for instance, "assault weapons"). Still, it would appear that in setting limits to only these types of firearms and devices, Congress intended to allow QLEOs and QR-LEOs to carry other types of firearms that are potentially prohibited by state laws. But I would strongly suggest not attempting to push this apparent hole in the law. You should wait for either clarification by Congress or a court decision. Do not make yourself a test case.

Another area of concern relates to restrictions that certain states have (like California) regarding "large-capacity magazines" (discussed in chapter 9). There appears to be no allowance for magazines in LEOSA. Consequently, restrictions on magazines would apply unless the officer meets an exemption to those restrictions pursuant to that state's laws. Because of this ambiguity, I suggest an officer wishing to carry pursuant to LEOSA familiarize himself or herself with California's restrictions to "large capacity magazines" and "large capacity magazine conversion kits" (and exemptions thereto) before bringing and possessing the magazines in California.[168]

5. LEOSA and Reserve Officers (Active and Retired)

Despite the restrictions on carrying firearms, exemptions, and special exemptions for law enforcement under California law, if a person meets the requirements for LEOSA and possesses the proper ID, or ID and certification, a person may carry a firearm in California although he or she may not be able to under an express provision of California law. With the exemptions to the restrictions under state law concerning where a person can carry and restrictions imposed by federal law, an individual who qualifies under LEOSA, and is carrying pursuant to LEOSA is protected against most violations of California law and all local laws.[169]

The ability for reserve officers to carry under LEOSA has created a point of contention between some officers and their agencies. Some reserve officers are not receiving the required ID and, thus, are unable to carry under LEOSA. Others are being told they may not carry despite the fact they meet the criteria and ID requirements. As of the publication of this book, this issue is still in contention.

---

[166] 18 U.S.C. § 926B(e)(2).

[167] 18 U.S.C. § 926B(e)(3).

[168] See Chapter 9.

[169] *See* 18 U.S.C. §§ 926A, 926B.

VIII. TRANSPORTATION OF FIREARMS IN PUBLIC TRANSPORTATION OR ACROSS STATE LINES

A. Transporting Firearms on Airplanes

If you plan to transport firearms on an airplane, you must use the ticket counter check-in process and notify the airline that you are transporting a firearm or ammunition. The firearm must be unloaded and transported as *checked* baggage in a locked, hard-sided container that only you have the key or combination to (not even law enforcement should have it). You can and should open the container for them if they request it.[170] The hard-sided, locked container may either be separate from your suitcase or inside it unless the airline tells you otherwise.

These requirements apply equally to disassembled firearms. If you have a frame or receiver, you have a "firearm."

Also, remember that when you are transporting your firearm to the airport and to and from the terminal, you must comply with all of California's transportation laws.

Ammunition[171] must also be transported as *checked* baggage, securely packed in boxes[172] or other packaging specifically designed to carry small amounts of ammunition (*e.g.*, the manufacturer's packaging). You can only transport ammunition for personal use, and the specific amount of ammunition is set by the airlines. Airline policies typically limit you to 11 pounds of ammunition,[173] so if you have a significant amount, you should call the airline and confirm the acceptable amount and weight of ammunition before arriving at the airport.

Magazines and clips must also be securely boxed.[174] The Transportation Security Administration (TSA) requires ammunition, magazines, and clips be transported in a hard-sided, locked case, even if together with an unloaded firearm, as long as properly packaged.[175] To be allowed on an airplane, the ammunition cannot be designed to shoot from firearms of a caliber larger than 19.1 mm (.75 inches) unless they are shotgun cartridges, in which case *any* gauge is permitted.[176] Addi-

---

[170] 49 C.F.R. § 1540.111(c). *See also Firearms and Ammunition,* Transp. Sec. Admin., http://www.tsa.gov/traveler-information/firearms-and-ammunition (last visited July 11, 2017); *Guide to the Interstate Transportation of Firearms,* NRA-ILA, http://www.nraila.org/gun-laws/articles/2010/guide-to-the-interstate-transportation.aspx (last visited July 11, 2017).

[171] For transporting by plane, "ammunition" means: "[a]mmunition consisting of a cartridge case fitted with a center or rim fire primer and containing both a propelling charge and solid projectile(s)." 49 C.F.R. § 173.59.

[172] The TSA recommends the box be made of a fiber (such as cardboard), wood, or metal. *See Firearms and Ammunition,* Transportation Security Administration, https://www.tsa.gov/travel/transporting-firearms-and-ammunition (last visited July 11, 2017).

[173] *See Firearms and Ammunition,* American Airlines, http://www.aa.com/i18n/travelInformation/baggage/firearms.jsp (last visited July 11, 2017).

[174] 49 C.F.R. § 175.10(a)(8).

[175] *Firearms and Ammunition,* Transportation Security Administration, https://www.tsa.gov/travel/transporting-firearms-and-ammunition (last visited July 11, 2017).

[176] 49 C.F.R. § 173.59.

tionally, black powder is not considered ammunition but rather an explosive[177] and therefore cannot be transported on a plane.

This means firearms and ammunition must be checked in and out of your possession before you go through the airport's metal detectors (and into a "sterile area" as explained in Chapter 7). All firearms and ammunition are subject to law enforcement inspection within the airport. Because the law does not specify how airlines must transport firearms and ammunition, airline policies may differ as to what containers or locks (or number of locks) are acceptable, how many firearms you may transport at once, or how much ammunition you may transport in a single flight. So it is best to call the airline in advance to ask about its policy for transporting firearms and ammunition.

The fees airlines may charge for transporting firearms also vary. It is a good idea to print out the airline's written policy from its website, confirm your compliance with it, and bring it with you to the airport in case your compliance is questioned. The TSA warns that failing to follow the proper transport regulations will preclude you from traveling with firearms, ammunition, or firearm parts.

If you are flying to another state, and especially to other countries, know the other state's and/or country's laws about transporting firearms and ammunition, as well as whether your particular firearm or ammunition is legal there. That way you will be in compliance with those laws as soon as you leave the airport.

Although federal law generally protects you from being prosecuted under state laws when transporting an unloaded firearm across state lines between places where it is legal for you to have the firearm, as long as neither the firearm nor any ammunition is "readily accessible" (*e.g.,* in a locked case),[178] people have nevertheless been arrested and prosecuted while doing so. One famous case is that of a man who was traveling by plane from Utah to Pennsylvania. His flight included a layover in New Jersey, a state that requires a state-issued permit to possess a firearm and prohibits possessing hollow-point ammunition in public. The man missed his connecting flight, which caused him to have to take a bus. But he missed the bus when he realized his luggage was not on it. The next day after finding his luggage with his firearm, as required by federal law, he told the airline that he had a firearm in his luggage and that it was unloaded and locked. He was then arrested for possessing a firearm without a New Jersey permit and for possessing hollow-point ammunition.

Even though criminal charges were eventually dropped, he spent four days in jail and did not get his firearm or related items back until two years later. He sued the New Jersey officials over the incident, but lost. The court held that the general federal immunity for transporting firearms ended once he took possession of his luggage in New Jersey because the firearm was then "readily accessible."[179] The moral of the story is that transporting firearms by plane can be risky, and you should

---

[177] 49 C.F.R. § 173.59. *See also* 27 C.F.R. section 555.11, excluding black powder from the definition of "ammunition."
[178] 18 U.S.C. § 926A.
[179] *Revell v. Port Auth. of New York, New Jersey,* 598 F.3d 128 (3d Cir. 2010), *cert. denied,* 131 S. Ct. 995 (2011).

protect yourself by knowing whether a situation like this could potentially arise in your connecting or destination state(s).

The gentleman in New Jersey would not have violated the law had he not taken possession of his luggage, but it is unclear what he should have done instead. The court suggested people in this situation request law enforcement or airport personnel keep their luggage overnight but failed to provide further guidance if law enforcement refuses to do so.

Along with Newark, LaGuardia Airport in New York also reportedly arrests and prosecutes unwitting and blameless "violators" of firearm transport laws, some of whom are not technically committing crimes.

B. Transporting on a Bus or Other Public Transportation

Assuming there is no restriction on having firearms on a specific type of public transportation, the same laws that apply when going directly to or from your vehicle "for any lawful purpose" likely also apply to public transportation. California law does not otherwise expressly address how to lawfully transport firearms on public transportation. But it does regulate where you can possess firearms and ammunition inside public transit facilities (see Chapter 7).

C. Transporting Firearms Across State Lines

Despite state or local laws to the contrary, federal law allows you to transport firearms "for any lawful purpose" by motor vehicle between any states where you may legally possess a firearm. The firearm must be unloaded, and neither the firearm nor any ammunition can be easily or directly accessible from within the vehicle's passenger compartment. If your vehicle does not have a compartment separate from the passenger compartment, the firearm or ammunition must be in a separate locked container other than a "glove compartment or console."[180]

The NRA's "Guide to the Interstate Transportation of Firearms"[181] lists numerous places with special rules about transporting firearms. Be careful because, like California, some restrict what types of weapons you can possess within the state, have specific laws on how to transport firearms, and may even require you to obtain a license/permit before carrying within the state. So before transporting a firearm through another state, check the state's laws to make sure that you comply with them.[182]

---

[180] 18 U.S.C. § 926A (part of the Firearm Owners' Protection Act (FOPA)).

[181] *See Guide to the Interstate Transportation of Firearms*, NRA-ILA, http://www.nraila.org/gun-laws/articles/2010/guide-to-the-interstate-transportation.aspx (last visited July 11, 2017).

[182] Discussed further in Chapter 8. Under FOPA you will be protected from prosecution if you are merely traveling through a state that prohibits the possession of "assault weapons" and if your firearm meets all the transportation requirements outlined in the law. *See* 18 U.S.C. 926A. But if your destination is a state that prohibits "assault weapons," or you stop in such a state, you will not be protected under the provisions the law. Out of an abundance of caution, however, you should be careful when transporting firearms across state lines.

Table 6.7

QUICK TIPS FOR TRANSPORTING YOUR FIREARMS USING PUBLIC AND PRIVATE TRANSPORTATION

AIRPLANES

If you plan on transporting firearms or ammunition on an airplane, you should keep these tips in mind:

✓ You must use the ticket counter check-in process and inform the check-in agent that you are transporting a firearm or ammunition. This requirement also applies to disassembled firearms.

✓ The firearm must be unloaded and transported as *checked* baggage in a locked, hard-sided container that only you have the key to, but keep in mind that, if law enforcement at the airport asks you to open the container, you should comply immediately.

✓ Any ammunition should be securely packed in boxes or other packaging specifically designed to carry small amounts of ammunition (*e.g.*, the manufacturer's packaging).

✓ You should also check the airline's website or call them before the flight to confirm any additional rules they may have with respect to transporting firearms. This is especially important when it comes to the amount of ammunition that you may transport on an airline as each airline differs in this respect. The typical limit, however, is 11 pounds of ammunition.

✓ You should also know the laws of any other state (or states if your flight has a layover) so you will be in compliance with them as soon as the airplane lands. Also, make sure that you transport your firearms to and from the airport in accordance with state laws.

AMTRAK TRAINS

If you are traveling on Amtrak (see Chapter 7) you should:

✓ Declare to Amtrak your intent to transport a firearm at the time the reservation is made (online reservations for checking firearms are not accepted), or at least 24 hours before departure.

✓ Unload and transport your firearm in a locked, hard-sided container in checked baggage.

MOTOR VEHICLES

If you are traveling in a motor vehicle and plan on transporting a handgun in it, you should follow these tips:

✓ The handgun must be *unloaded* and in an *appropriate container*. For specifics on what is an *appropriate container*, see Section II above, which outlines the container requirements for concealed handguns.

BUSES OR OTHER PUBLIC TRANSPORTATION

If you plan on transporting a firearm or ammunition on a bus or other public transportation system, you should keep the following in mind:

✓ You should check to see if there any restrictions on having firearms or ammunition on that specific type of public transportation system.

✓ If there are no special rules, the laws that apply to the transporting of firearms when going to or from your vehicle "for any lawful purpose" will apply. See Section II above for more details. Also, keep in mind that once inside the bus terminal (see Chapter 7).

✓ If you plan on traveling on a Greyhound Bus with your firearms, think again. Greyhound does not allow firearms or ammunition to be transported on their buses (see Chapter 7).

QUICK TIPS FOR TRANSPORTING YOUR FIREARMS USING PUBLIC AND PRIVATE TRANSPORTATION

MOTORCYCLES

If you are planning on transporting an unloaded handgun or "firearm that is not a handgun" while you are on a motorcycle, you should make sure the firearm is:

✓ Unloaded.

✓ If it is a handgun, it should be in an appropriate locked container. If it is a "firearm that is not a handgun," it must be "encased."

✓ The definition of a "locked container" here, however, is unclear, as a lockable luggage box on the side of the motorcycle may or may not be considered a "utility compartment." To be safe, you should transport the unloaded handgun in a separate "locked container" inside the motorcycle's luggage box or a rider's backpack.

BICYCLES

If you are planning on transporting your firearm while you are riding a bike, you should make sure the firearm is:

✓ Unloaded.

✓ If it is a handgun, it should be in an appropriate locked container. If it is a "firearm that is not a handgun," it must be "encased."

MOTOR HOMES

If you are transporting a firearm in a motor home, you should keep the following in mind:

✓ If the motor home is in motion, it will generally be treated the same as a motor vehicle. See the tips for transporting firearms in motor vehicles in this table.

✓ If you are "camping" in the motor home, it may be treated like a residence. But this is unclear.

✓ Always check the rules posted by public campgrounds beforehand.

BOATS

If you are transporting a firearm in a boat, you should keep the following in mind:

✓ If a boat is designed to be lived on, it is likely that it will be treated similarly to a motor home. Meaning it will be treated either as a residence or a vehicle depending on how it is used.

✓ If the boat is moving, the firearm should be kept as if it were being transported via a motor vehicle. See the section above in this table for tips for transporting firearms in motor vehicles.

IX. SUGGESTIONS ON HOW TO CARRY FIREARMS IN COMPLIANCE WITH CALIFORNIA FIREARMS LAWS

People often ask how a person should carry firearms in compliance with California's firearms laws. A lot of different considerations come into play for each situation, such as the reasons for carrying firearms, the person's destination, whether the person has a Carry License, and what areas the person is traveling through, to name a few. Nevertheless, some suggestions are universal, and some of these suggestions go beyond what California law requires. I've had more than my fair share of people who have called while facing serious criminal charges because they transported firearms under a "gray area" of California law, or law enforcement was unaware they were carrying the firearm lawfully because the way the firearm was transported was unusual or appeared to violate California law.

First of all, firearms should be transported unloaded. ALWAYS check (and double check) to see if your firearm is unloaded before packing the firearm in a case to transport it, packing it to take away from a range, etc. Especially if the handgun is the firearm you use for home defense. This being said, not only should the firearm not hold any ammunition, but there should be no ammunition in magazines, clips, speed loaders, etc. Ammunition should be transported in the box it came in (preferably) and in a separate bag or container from the firearm. The magazine should be transported with, but not in, the firearm, and no ammunition should be in the magazine.

All firearms should be transported in a gun case or container. Long guns should be locked up for reasons discussed in Chapter 7 relating to federal gun-free school zone restrictions. Handguns should be in a secure, fully enclosed case (preferably hard-sided) and locked within the case. Lawfully registered "assault weapons" or .50 BMG rifles should likewise be transported in a "locked container" or locked in the trunk of the vehicle.

If you want to put a gun lock or trigger lock on your firearm, that would be even better. Is one required? No, not if you are transporting your firearm lawfully. But it could potentially show law enforcement officers that you did everything, and even more than what's required, to transport your firearms.

The packing of firearms and ammunition should be done in your residence. Then the firearms should be taken to your vehicle for transportation. If you have a vehicle with a trunk, the firearms and ammunition should be transported in the trunk. In vehicles where the entire interior is accessible from the passenger compartment (*e.g.*, hatchback cars, SUVs, trucks), the firearms should be stored as far away as possible from the driver or anyone else occupying the vehicle. Again, this goes beyond the legal requirements for transporting firearms, but the purpose is to go beyond what is required to ease law enforcement's concerns if they happen to come across the firearms.

The course you take to your intended destination (*e.g.*, hunting area, range, dealer/gunsmith) should have as few deviations as possible (*e.g.* stopping for gas or restroom breaks). This means you should not stop to go to work, to go shopping at a mall, or to eat a big meal at a restaurant. If stops are required, make certain that the firearm and containers are not visible or recognizable from outside of the vehicle. And you should certainly make no stops at places where firearm possession is illegal or restricted, *e.g.*, schools and federal buildings (see Chapter 7 for other examples). You must also store any handguns in a "locked container" or locked in the trunk of your vehicle when leaving them in your vehicle unattended (see Chapter 4).

Once you arrive at your intended destination, keep your firearms and ammunition in the containers until you are inside the location and/or until they are needed to be used. Only load your firearms when they are ready to be discharged.

When returning to your place of residence, the above tips apply all over again: make sure the firearms are unloaded; placed in their locked containers, and placed in the vehicle; with no stops, except necessary ones, along the way; and keep the firearms in their cases until inside your residence. If you have to stop make sure that you store your handguns in a "locked container" or in the locked trunk of your care when leaving your vehicle unattended, and that all other firearms and containers are kept out of sight so that they are not visible from outside of the car.

Obviously, each person's individual needs and situations are different. Hopefully, this book sheds some light on California and federal laws, exceptions, and requirements for transporting firearms.

X. CARRY EXEMPTIONS TABLE

After reading this chapter, you probably realized there are numerous – and often convoluted – exemptions to the carry restrictions, which make it difficult to determine when, where, and how you may carry a firearm (*i.e.*, concealed, open, loaded). The following table organizes and consolidates these exemptions to assist you with the difficult chore of determining if any exemptions apply to you.

Before turning to the table, you must first determine the type of conduct you wish to engage in, and whether that conduct is restricted under California law (see Chapter 5). If that conduct is not restricted, you do not need to review this table. But, if that conduct *is* restricted, review the table to see if you fall under any applicable exemptions.

The table is broken down into three main sections: (1) exemptions based on *who* you are; (2) exemptions based on *where* you are; and (3) exemptions based on the *activity* you are engaged in. After determining that the conduct you wish to engage in is restricted, review these sections to see if there is an applicable exemption to your specific situation. Exemptions that apply to certain people because of their occupation, club affiliations, or because they possess certain licenses and/or permits, can be found in the first section entitled, "Exemptions Based on *Who* You Are." Exemptions that apply to certain locations, such as your residence or private place of business, can be found in the second section entitled, "Exemptions Based on *Where* You Are." Exemptions that apply while you engage in or travel to specific activities, such as hunting or target shooting, can be found in the third and final section entitled, "Exemptions Based on The *Activity* You Engage In."

 Once you determine the relevant section, locate your specific status or circumstance in the left-hand column of the table. From there, you should follow the row to the right to see if your status or circumstance allows you to carry an unloaded handgun concealed, an unloaded handgun openly, an unloaded "firearm that is not a handgun," and/or a loaded firearm. Beware, some exemptions have additional, important information in the "Notes and Comments" column that you should be aware of and follow to lawfully carry your firearm. These specific exemptions are marked with one or more asterisk (*) that correspond to the information in the "Notes and Comments." Information in the "Notes and Comments" column that is *not* marked with an asterisk applies to each exemption with a "yes."

Remember, if you wish to engage in a combination of restricted activities (*e.g.*, carrying concealed and loaded), each activity must be covered by an exemption. Keep in mind that even though your conduct may fall under an exemption, you can still be subject to other restrictions depending on your location (see Chapter 7). For example, you may still be restricted from carrying a firearm in a government building despite the fact that you would otherwise fall under an exemption.

Finally, although most of the exemptions to the carry restrictions appear in this table, you may not be able to find every circumstance or situation that you are involved in. Also, I make no claims, promises, or guarantees as to the completeness or accuracy of the information in this table, nor do I guarantee that adhering to this table will keep you from being arrested and/or convicted of a crime. This table is solely a guide, and you should refer to the applicable Penal Code sections before carrying a firearm while engaging in any of these activities. If you have any questions or concerns as to whether you can lawfully carry a firearm in a certain situation, you should contact an attorney experienced in firearms law.

Table 6.8

EXEMPTIONS BASED ON WHO YOU ARE

Who Are You?	Description	Can You Carry An Unloaded Handgun Concealed?	Can You Carry An Unloaded Handgun Openly?	Can You Carry An Unloaded "Firearm That Is Not A Handgun"?[168]	Can You Carry A Loaded Firearm?	Notes and Comments
Carry License Holders	Do you have a valid carry license?	Yes* P.C. § 25655	Yes** P.C. § 26150(b)(2)	No	Yes* P.C. § 26010	*The exemption to the carry concealed restriction is firearm specific, meaning the code section allows you to carry a handgun only if you are licensed to carry that specific handgun. Oddly, the exemption to the loaded restriction allows you to carry "any handgun" so long as you have a valid carry license. **This exemption applies only if you are issued a license under P.C. § 26150(b)(2), i.e., a license to carry a handgun loaded and exposed. But, a sheriff can only issue this license when the population of the county in which you live is less than 200,000 persons according to the most recent federal decennial census, and the license is only effective in the county it was issued in.
Special Permit Holders	Do you have a valid permit to possess destructive devices, "assault weapons," .50 BMG rifles, machineguns, or short-barreled rifles or shotguns, and are you carrying pursuant to the terms and conditions of your permit?	No	Yes P.C. § 26390	Yes P.C. § 26405(ae)	No	These exemptions apply only if the type of firearm (handgun or long gun) you are carrying is a destructive device, assault weapon, .50 BMG rifle, machinegun, or short-barreled rifle. See Chapter 8 & 9 for the definitions of these items.
Active Peace Officers	Are you an active peace officer listed in P.C. §§ 830.1, 830.2, 830.33(a) or any other duly appointed peace officers?	Yes P.C. § 25450(a)-(b)	Yes P.C. § 26361	Yes P.C. § 26405(e)	Yes P.C. § 25900(a)-(b)	You may also be exempted under LEOSA (discussed in Chapter 6, Section (VII)(B)).

[168] For purposes of this category, we are assuming that you are carrying the firearm outside of your vehicle. Remember, the restriction on carrying unloaded "firearms that are not handguns" does not apply when you are carrying the firearm inside of a vehicle.

Category	Question					Notes
Retired Peace Officers	Are you an honorably retired peace officer listed in P.C. §§ 830.5(c), 830.1, 830.2, 830.33(a) or were you authorized to carry a firearm while employed as a peace officer, and in fact did?	Yes P.C. § 25450(a), (c)-(d)	Yes P.C. § 26361	Yes P.C. § 26405(e)	Yes P.C. § 25900(a), (c)-(d)	You may also be exempted under LEOSA (discussed in Chapter 6, Section (VII)(B)).
Active Peace Officers From Another State	Are you a full-time, paid peace officer from another state carrying out official duties in California?	Yes P.C. § 25450(e)	Yes P.C. § 26361	Yes P.C. § 26405(e)	Yes P.C. § 25900(e)	You may also be exempted under LEOSA (discussed in Chapter 6, Section (VII)(B)).
Persons Assisting in an Arrest	Have you been summoned by any of the officers discussed in the three proceeding rows of this table to assist in making an arrest or preserving the peace?	Yes P.C. § 25450(f)	Yes* P.C. § 26378	Yes* P.C. § 26405(u)	Yes P.C. § 25900(f)	All of these exemptions apply only *while* you are assisting the officer. *These exemptions apply to any "peace officer" who requests your assistance, not just to the ones discussed in the preceding rows.
Federal Agents	Are you a full-time paid peace officer of the federal government carrying out official duties in California?	Yes P.C. § 25450(e)	Yes P.C. § 26361	Yes P.C. § 26405(e)	Yes P.C. § 25900(e)	You may also be exempted under LEOSA (discussed in Chapter 6, Section (VII)(B)).
Retired Federal Agents	Are you an honorably retired federal officer or agent who was authorized to carry weapons while on duty, who was assigned to duty within California for a period of not less than one year, or who was retired from active service in California and possess a permit from your local sheriff?	Yes P.C. § 25650	Yes P.C. § 26362	Yes P.C. § 26405(f)	Yes P.C. § 26020	You may also be exempted under LEOSA (discussed in Chapter 6, Section (VII)(B)).

EXEMPTIONS BASED ON WHO ARE YOU

WHO ARE YOU?	DESCRIPTION	CAN YOU CARRY AN UNLOADED HANDGUN CONCEALED?	CAN YOU CARRY AN UNLOADED HANDGUN OPENLY?	CAN YOU CARRY AN UNLOADED "FIREARM THAT IS NOT A HANDGUN"?	CAN YOU CARRY A LOADED FIREARM?	NOTES AND COMMENTS
Guards of Common Carriers or Financial Institutions	Are you a guard or messenger of a common carrier, bank, or other financial institution who is employed to transport money, treasure, bullion, bonds, or other things of value?	Yes P.C. § 25630	Yes* P.C. § 26362	Yes* P.C. § 26405(f)	Yes* P.C. § 26030(a)(1)	In order for any of these exemptions to apply, you must actually be employed and shipping, transporting, or delivering the money, treasure, bullion, bonds or other things of value. *In order to meet these three exemptions, you must be certified by the Department of Consumer Affairs (*i.e.,* complete a course in carrying and using firearms, and the powers of arrest). Peace officers specified in P.C. § 26030(c) do not need the certificate.
Armored Vehicle Guards	Are you an armored vehicle guard employed by an armored contract carrier who, during the course and scope of your employment, carries a deadly weapon (*see* Cal. Bus. & Prof. Code § 7581.1)?	No	Yes P.C. § 26362	Yes P.C. § 26405(f)	Yes P.C. §§ 26015, 26030(a)(2)-(3)	If you were hired **on or after** January 1, 1977, you must have received a firearms qualification card in order to qualify for these exemptions. You must also be acting within the scope of your employment for these exemptions to apply. Peace officers specified in P.C. § 26030(c) do not need the certificate.
Private Investigators	Are you a person who is licensed under the Private Investigators Act or a uniformed employee of a private investigator?	No	Yes P.C. § 26362	Yes P.C. § 26405(f)	Yes P.C. § 26030(a) (4)-(5)	In order to meet any of these exemptions, you must be certified (*i.e.,* complete a course in carrying and using firearms, and the powers of arrest), and you must be acting in the scope of your employment. Peace officers specified in P.C. § 26030(c) do not need the certificate.

Private Patrol Officers	Are you a licensed private patrol officer or a uniformed employee of a private patrol officer?	No	Yes P.C. § 26362	Yes P.C. § 26405(f)	Yes P.C. § 26030(a)(6)-(7)	In order to meet any these exemptions, you must be certified (*i.e.*, complete a course in carrying and using firearms, and the powers of arrest), and you must be acting in the scope of your employment. Peace officers specified in P.C. § 26030(c) do not need the certificate.
Alarm Company Operators/ Agents	Are you a licensed alarm company operator or uniformed alarm company agent?	No	Yes P.C. § 26362	Yes P.C. § 26405(f)	Yes P.C. § 26030(a)(8), (10)	Alarm company operators must be certified (*i.e.*, complete a course in carrying and using firearms, the powers of arrest and possess an exposed firearm permit), and acting in the scope of employment to meet any these exemptions. Peace officers specified in P.C. § 26030(c) do not need the certificate. Uniformed alarm company agents must also be certified (*i.e.*, complete a course in carrying and using firearms, the powers of arrest and possess an exposed firearm permit), and must actually be engaged in preserving the property of their employers, or on duty or en route to or from their residence, place of employment, or a target range to meet these exemptions. Peace officers specified in P.C. § 26030(c) do not need the certificate.

Exemptions Based on Who You Are

Who Are You?	Description	Can You Carry an Unloaded Handgun Concealed?	Can You Carry an Unloaded Handgun Openly?	Can You Carry an Unloaded "Firearm that Is Not a Handgun"?	Can You Carry a Loaded Firearm?	Notes and Comments
Uniformed Security Guards/Night Watch Persons	Are you a night watch person employed by a public agency, a uniformed security guard employed by a public agency, or employed by a lawful business to act as a security guard?	No	Yes P.C. § 26362	Yes P.C. § 26405(f)	Yes P.C. § 26030(a)(9)-(10)	Uniformed security guards and night watch persons employed by *a public agency* must be certified (*i.e.*, complete a course in carrying and using firearms, the powers of arrest and be acting within the scope of employment permit) and be acting within the scope of employment to meet any these exemptions. Peace officers specified in P.C. § 26030(c) do not need the certificate. Uniformed security guards employed by *a lawful business* must be certified (*i.e.*, complete a course in carrying and using firearms, the powers of arrest and possess an exposed firearm permit), and must actually be engaged in preserving the property of their employers, or on duty or en route to or from their residence, place of employment, or a target range to meet these exemptions. Peace officers specified in P.C. § 26030(c) do not need the certificate.
Patrol Special Officers	Are you a patrol special officer appointed by the police commissioner who has completed a course in firearms training approved by POST?	No	Yes P.C. § 26362	Yes P.C. § 26405(f)	Yes P.C. § 26025(a)	In order to meet any of these exemptions, the patrol special officer must: (1) be subject to suspension or dismissal after a hearing on charges duly filed with POST after a fair and impartial trial; (2) not be less than 18 years old or more than 40 years old; (3) possess physical qualities prescribed by POST; and (4) have a designated beat or territory.
Animal Control Officers or Zookeepers	Are you an animal control officer or zookeeper who works for a government agency?	No	Yes P.C. § 26362	Yes P.C. § 26405(f)	Yes P.C. § 26025(b)	You can only carry these firearms when acting in the course and scope of your employment, and it must be designated by local ordinance or resolution that you may carry these firearms.
Humane Officers	Are you a humane officer?	No	Yes P.C. § 26362	Yes P.C. § 26405(f)	Yes P.C. § 26025(c)	You can only carry under these exemptions if you are actually engaged in the performance of your duties under Cal. Corp. Code § 14502.

Category	Question					Notes
Harbor Police Officers	Are you a harbor police officer designated under Cal. Harbors & Navigation Code § 663.5?	No	Yes P.C. § 26362	Yes P.C. § 26405(f)	Yes P.C. § 26025(d)	N/A
Common Carriers	Are you a person operating a licensed common carrier or an authorized agent or employee of a common carrier transporting a firearm?	Yes P.C. § 25645	Yes P.C. § 26367	Yes* P.C. § 26405(k)	No	In order to meet these exemptions, you must transport the firearm in conformance with applicable federal law. *This exemption states that you are exempted from transporting "handguns." But, the legislature likely meant "firearms that are not handguns."
Lawful Firearms Businesses	Are you a person licensed to engaged in the business of manufacturing, importing, wholesaling, repairing, or dealing in firearms, or an agent or employee of that person?	Yes P.C. § 25615	Yes P.C. § 26363	Yes P.C. § 26405(g)	No	In order to meet any of these exemptions, the firearm must be carried as "merchandise" while you are engaged in the lawful course of business.
Ammunition Manufacturers	Are you engaged in the business of manufacturing ammunition, or an authorized representative or agent of a person who is?	No	No	Yes P.C. § 26405(ah)	No	In order to meet this exemption, you must be licensed to manufacture ammunition under Chapter 44 of Title 18 of the United States Code or employed by such a person. This exemption only applies while you are using the firearm in the lawful course and scope of activities related to the manufacturing of ammunition.
Military Members	Are you a member of the Army, Navy, Air Force, Coast Guard, or Marine Corps of the United States, or National Guard?	Yes* P.C. § 25620	Yes P.C. § 26362	Yes P.C. § 26405(f)	Yes P.C. § 26000	*This exemption specifically requires you to be "on duty" to meet, while the other exemptions only require you to be performing your duties as a military member.

Exemptions Based on Who You Are

Who Are You?	Description	Can You Carry an Unloaded Handgun Concealed?	Can You Carry an Unloaded Handgun Openly?	Can You Carry an Unloaded "Firearm hat Is Not a Handgun"?	Can you Carry a Loaded Firearm?	Notes and Comments
Organizations Acquiring Firearms from the Government	Are you an organization that is authorized by law to purchase or receive firearms from the United States or California?	Yes P.C. § 25620	No	No	No	N/A
Members of Organizations or Clubs	Are you a member of an organization or club organized for the purpose of shooting targets and are practicing shooting at targets on an established target range?	Yes* P.C. § 25635	Yes** P.C. § 26365	Yes P.C. § 26405(f), (i)	Yes*** P.C. § 26005(a)	*The concealed carry exemption also allows you to transport an unloaded handgun directly to and from an established target range. **This exemption only applies when you are outside of a vehicle. ***While the other exemptions in this section are specific to members of clubs or organizations, the exemption to the loaded restriction is not. This exemption applies to all persons who are using target ranges for the purpose of practice shooting, regardless of whether they are members of a club or organization.

EXEMPTIONS BASED ON WHERE YOU ARE

WHERE ARE YOU?	DESCRIPTION	CAN YOU CARRY AN UNLOADED HANDGUN CONCEALED?	CAN YOU CARRY AN UNLOADED HANDGUN OPENLY?	CAN YOU CARRY AN UNLOADED "FIREARM THAT IS NOT A HANDGUN"?	CAN YOU CARRY A LOADED FIREARM?	NOTES AND COMMENTS
Your Residence	Are you at your residence?	Yes* P.C. § 25605(a)	Yes P.C. § 25605	Yes P.C. § 26405(a)	Yes** P.C. § 26055	*You may also transport an unloaded handgun in a locked container directly between your place of residence, place of business, or other privately owned property. P.C. §§ 25525, 25505. **This exemption provides that you may *have* a loaded firearm at your residence; it does not say that you may *carry* a loaded firearm there.
Your Other Private Property	Are you on your private property that you own or lawfully possess?	Yes* P.C. § 25605(a)	Yes P.C. §§ 25605(a),	Yes P.C. § 26405(a)	Yes** P.C. § 26035	*You may also transport a handgun unloaded in a locked container directly between your place of residence, place of business, or other privately owned property. P.C. §§ 25525, 25505. **This exemption provides that you may *have* a loaded firearm while you are on property you lawfully possess; it does not say that you may *carry* a loaded firearm there.
Home or Privately Held Property of Another	Are you at someone else's private business, home, or private property that is lawfully owned or possessed by that person?	No	Yes* P.C. § 26383	Yes P.C. § 26405(b)	No	In order to meet any of these exemptions, if you have permission to carry the firearm from the property owner or person who lawfully possesses the property. In order for the permission to be valid, the property owner must be able to lawfully carry on his or her property under P.C. § 26605. *This exemption applies only when you are outside of a vehicle. But you may be able to carry the handgun openly in your vehicle if you meet another exemption.

EXEMPTIONS BASED ON WHERE YOU ARE

Where Are You?	Description	Can You Carry an Unloaded Handgun Concealed?	Can You Carry an Unloaded Handgun Openly?	Can You Carry an Unloaded "Firearm That Is Not a Handgun"?	Can You Carry a Loaded Firearm?	Notes and Comments
Your Private Business	Are you in your place of business?	Yes* P.C. § 25605(a)	Yes P.C. § 25605	Yes P.C. §§ 25605(a), 26405(a)	Yes** P.C. § 26035	*You may also transport a handgun unloaded and in a locked container directly between your place of residence, place of business, or other privately held property that you own. P.C. § 25525, 25505. **It is unclear whether you can *carry* a loaded firearm within your business if it located in a "public place." This exemption only provides that you may *have a* loaded firearm in your business if you have it for a lawful purpose connected with your business.
Private Business of Another	Are you in someone else's private business, residence, or privately owned property?	No	Yes* P.C. § 26383	Yes P.C. § 26405(b)	No	In order to meet any of these exemptions, you must have permission from the property owner to carry on their property. But, in order for the permission to be valid, the property owner must themselves be able to lawfully carry on their property. *This exemption only applies when you are outside of a vehicle. But, you may be able to carry the handgun openly in your vehicle if you meet another exemption.

Campsites or Temporary Residences	Are you at a campsite or temporary residence?	No* P.C. § 25515	No	No	Maybe** P.C. § 26055	*You may transport an unloaded handgun in a locked container when going to or from your campsite, if you are taking the handgun for the purpose of self-defense. P.C. § 25550(a). But keep in mind that you are still subject to any other restrictions or rules made by other governmental agencies that regulate the transportation or possession of firearms on parks or campgrounds. P.C. § 25550(b). **This exemption only provides that you may *have* a loaded firearm at your temporary residence or campsite; it does not say that you may *carry* a loaded firearm there. Therefore, it is unclear whether or not you can carry a loaded firearm in a temporary residence or campsite without a Carry License.
Club or Organization Meetings	Are you at a meeting of a club or organization, organized for the purpose of lawfully collecting and displaying handguns or other firearms?	Yes P.C. § 25515	No	No	No	In order to meet this exemption, you must actually be a member of the club or organization and the firearm must be unloaded and in a locked container while you are at the meeting of the club or organization. You may also transport the handgun when going directly to or from a meeting of the club or organization if it is unloaded and in a locked container. P.C. § 25505.
School Zones	Are you in a school zone (defined in Chapter 7)?	No	Yes P.C. § 26370	Yes P.C. § 26405(n)	No	In order to meet any of these exemptions, your carrying of the firearm must not be prohibited by the Gun-Free School Zone restriction (P.C. § 626.9). (See Chapter 7).

EXEMPTIONS BASED ON WHERE YOU ARE

WHERE ARE YOU?	DESCRIPTION	CAN YOU CARRY AN UNLOADED HANDGUN CONCEALED?	CAN YOU CARRY AN UNLOADED HANDGUN OPENLY?	CAN YOU CARRY AN UNLOADED "FIREARM THAT IS NOT A HANDGUN"?	CAN YOU CARRY A LOADED FIREARM?	NOTES AND COMMENTS
Gun Shows	Are you at a gun show, swap meet, or similar event where the public is invited, for the purpose of displaying your firearm?	Yes* P.C. § 25535	Yes** P.C. § 26369	Yes** P.C. § 26405(m)	No	*This exemption applies only to transporting an unloaded handgun to and from the event in a locked container. P.C. § 25505. This exemption also applies to any gun shows or events as defined by Section 478.100 of Title 27 of the Code of Federal Regulations for transferring the firearm via lawful private party transfer. **These exemptions apply to gun shows conducted pursuant to Article 1 (commencing with Section 27200) and Article 2 (commencing with Section 27300) of Chapter 3 of Division 6 of the Penal Code. The exemption to the open carry restriction applies only when you are carrying outside of a vehicle.
Nonprofit Auctions or Similar Events	Are you at an auction or similar event of a nonprofit public benefit or mutual benefit corporation?	No	Yes P.C. § 26384	Yes P.C. § 26405(z)	No	In order to meet any of these exemptions, the firearm must be: (1) a firearm that is going to be auctioned or otherwise sold for the benefit of the nonprofit or a firearm that you bought at the auction; and (2) it must be delivered by a firearms dealer.
State or Local Public Buildings	Are you at a place protected by P.C. § 171b (i.e., any state or local public building or at a meeting place required to be open to the public)?	No	Yes P.C. § 26371	Yes P.C. § 26405(o)	No	In order to meet any of these exemptions, you must be one of the persons listed in P.C. § 171b(b).

Location	Question					Notes
State Capital or Legislative Offices	Are you in a place protected by P.C. § 171c (*i.e.*, the State Capital or its grounds, any legislative office, any office of the Governor or other constitutional officer, or any hearing room in which a committee of the Senate or Assembly is conducting a hearing)?	No	Yes P.C. § 26385	Yes P.C. § 26405(aa)	No	In order to meet any of these exemptions, you must have permission to carry the firearm from the Chief Sergeants at Arms of the State Assembly *and* the State Senate.
Governor's Mansion or Other Constitutional Officers' Residences	Are you in, or on a place protected by P.C. § 171d (*i.e.*, the grounds of the Governor's Mansion, or any other residence of the Governor, constitutional officer, or Member of the Legislature)?	No	Yes P.C. § 26386	Yes P.C. § 26405(ab)	No	In order to meet any of these exemptions, you must be one of the persons listed in P.C. § 171d.
Airports or Passenger Vessel Terminals	Are you in an airport or passenger vessel terminal (see Chapter 7)?	No	Yes P.C. § 26391	Yes P.C. § 26405(ag)	No	In order to meet any of these exemptions, you must be one of the persons listed in P.C. § 171.5(d).
Sterile Areas of Public Transit Facilities	Are you in an area protected by P.C. § 171.7 (*i.e.*, a sterile area of a public transit facility) (see Chapter 7)?	No	Yes P.C. § 26387	Yes P.C. § 26405(ac)	No	In order to meet any of these exemptions, you must be responsible for the security of the public transit system and authorized in writing by the public transit authority's security coordinator to possess the firearm.
Publicly Owned Land	Are you on publicly owned land?	No	Yes P.C. § 26388	Yes P.C. § 26405(ad)	No	In order to meet any of these exemptions, your possession and use of the firearm must be specifically permitted by the managing agency of that land. You must also be in lawful possession of the firearm.
Navigable Waters of California	Are you on navigable waters held in public trust of California?	No	No	Yes P.C. § 26405(ai)	No	In order to meet this exemption, your possession and use of the firearm must be specifically permitted by the managing agency of the navigable waters. You must also be in lawful possession of the firearm.

EXEMPTIONS BASED ON THE ACTIVITY YOU ENGAGE IN

WHAT ARE YOU DOING?	DESCRIPTION	CAN YOU CARRY AN UNLOADED HANDGUN CONCEALED?	CAN YOU CARRY AN UNLOADED HANDGUN OPENLY?	CAN YOU CARRY AN UNLOADED "FIREARM THAT IS NOT A HANDGUN"?	CAN YOU CARRY A LOADED FIREARM?	NOTES AND COMMENTS
Shooting at a Target Range	Are you at an established target range for the purpose of practice shooting with a firearm?	No*	Yes** P.C. § 26377	Yes*** P.C. § 26405(f), (t)	Yes**** P.C. § 26005(a)	*But you may transport a handgun for the purpose of practice shooting directly to or from a target range that has a regulatory or business license. But, the handgun must be unloaded and kept in a locked container while it is being transported. P.C. § 25540, 25505. **This exemption applies only while you are using the handgun at an *established public or private* target range. ***This exemption applies only when you are using a firearm at an *established public* target range. ****This exemption applies only when you are using a target range for the purpose of practice shooting with the firearm.
Hunting at the Shooting Club	Are you a member of a shooting club and hunting on the club's premises?	Yes* P.C. § 25640	Yes* P.C. § 26366	Yes* P.C. § 26405(j)	Yes P.C. § 26005(b)	*Note that you would be exempted under these restrictions regardless of whether you are a member of a shooting club or are shooting on club premises because you would be exempted under the much broader exemptions listed in the "hunting" section above (unless you are hunting in a city that has a local law that requires membership in the club to hunt). There are no specific exemptions for the concealed, open, or "firearm that is not a handgun" restrictions that apply only to members of shooting clubs.

Hunting	Are you a licensed hunter and out hunting?	Yes* P.C. § 25640	Yes* P.C. § 26366	Yes* P.C. § 26405(j)	Yes** P.C. § 26040
Training Your Dog for Hunting	Are you a licensed hunter training your dog for the purpose of using the dog for hunting not prohibited by law?	No	Yes* P.C. § 26366.5	Yes* P.C. § 26405(af)	No

*These exemptions only allow you to carry firearms when you are actually engaged in hunting. You may also transport your firearm to and from your hunting expedition.

**The loaded restriction is not in force in areas where you are allowed to hunt because these places are generally in unincorporated areas where it is lawful to discharge a firearm. But, where the restriction does apply, you are exempted if you are actually engaged in hunting, you are in an area within an incorporated city, and *you are hunting at a place and time that is not prohibited by the city council. Note:* You may also carry a loaded or unloaded rocket, rocket propelled projectile launcher, or similar device designed primarily for emergency or distress signaling purposes while in a permitted hunting area or traveling to or from a permitted hunting area and carrying a valid California permit or license to hunt. P.C. §§ 26060, 26362, 26405(f).

*These exemptions also allow you to transport the firearm when you are going to and from the place you are training your dog.

EXEMPTIONS BASED ON THE ACTIVITY YOU ENGAGE IN

WHAT ARE YOU DOING?	DESCRIPTION	CAN YOU CARRY AN UNLOADED HANDGUN CONCEALED?	CAN YOU CARRY AN UNLOADED HANDGUN OPENLY?	CAN YOU CARRY AN UNLOADED "FIREARM THAT IS NOT A HANDGUN"?	CAN YOU CARRY A LOADED FIREARM?	NOTES AND COMMENTS
Fishing	Are you a licensed fisherman on a fishing expedition?	Yes* P.C. § 25640	No**	No**	No**	*This exemption allows you to carry the firearm when you are going to or returning from your fishing expedition. **Keep in mind that the restrictions on carrying unloaded handguns openly, "firearms that are not handguns," and loaded firearms do not apply to unincorporated areas where it is lawful to discharge a firearm. This is likely why there aren't any exemptions to these restrictions for fishing as fishing often takes place in such areas.
Camping	Are you camping?	No*	No	No	Maybe** P.C. §26055	*You may also transport an unloaded handgun in a locked container when going to or from your campsite if you are taking the handgun for the purpose of self-defense while at the lawful campsite. P.C. § 25550(a). But, you are still subject to any other restrictions or rules made by governmental agencies that may regulate the transportation or possession of firearms on parks or campgrounds. P.C. § 25550(b). **This exemption only provides that you may have a loaded firearm at your temporary residence or campsite; it does not say that you may carry a loaded firearm there. Therefore, it is unclear whether or not you may carry a loaded firearm in a temporary residence or campsite without a Carry License.

	Question					Notes
Parading with Military or Civil Org.	Are you parading with a military or civil organization?	Yes* P.C. § 25625	Yes** P.C. § 26364	Yes** P.C. § 26405(h)	No	In order to meet any of these exemptions, you must be a duly authorized member of the military or civil organization you are parading with. *This exemption applies only when you are going to and from the place where you are meeting your military or civil organization to parade. **These exemptions apply when you are at the meeting place of your military or civil organization, while parading, or while you are rehearsing or practicing for the parade.
Parading with Non-Profit or Tax Exempt Org.	Are you on official parade duty or at a ceremonial occasion of an organization chartered by the Congress of the United States or a nonprofit mutual or public benefit corporation recognized by the IRS as such?	No	Yes P.C. § 26368	Yes P.C. § 26405(l)	No	In order to meet any of these exemptions, you must be a member of the organization, nonprofit, or public benefit corporation.
Taking Your Firearm to Sell, Repair, Loan, or Transfer	Are you transporting your firearm to a business or private residence to sell, loan, or transfer that firearm or to have it lawfully repaired?	Yes* P.C. § 25530	No	No	No	*In order to for this exemption to apply, you must transport the handgun unloaded and in a locked container, and your course of travel should only include necessary deviations. P.C. § 25505.
Engaging in Firearm Related Activities at a Business	Are you at a fixed place of business and (1) engaging in activities that are related to the selling, making, repairing, transferring, pawning of a firearm; (2) using a firearm; or (3) engaging in firearms training?	No	Yes* P.C. § 26374	Yes* P.C. § 26405(q)	No	*In order to meet these exemptions, you must be at a fixed place of business licensed to conduct, and does in fact conduct, as a regular course of business, activities related to selling, making, repairing, transferring, pawning, or using the firearm, or firearms training.

EXEMPTIONS BASED ON THE ACTIVITY YOU ENGAGE IN

WHAT ARE YOU DOING?	DESCRIPTION	CAN YOU CARRY AN UNLOADED HANDGUN CONCEALED?	CAN YOU CARRY AN UNLOADED HANDGUN OPENLY?	CAN YOU CARRY AN UNLOADED "FIREARM THAT IS NOT A HANDGUN"?	CAN YOU CARRY A LOADED FIREARM?	NOTES AND COMMENTS
Buying, Renting, or Receiving a Firearm	Are you participating in a transaction to buy/sell, loan, or transfer/receive a firearm?	No	Yes* P.C. § 26373	No	No	*This exemption applies only if the handgun is possessed on private property, and you must have permission of the owner or lessee of that private property to carry and possesses that handgun.
Taking a Found Firearm to Law Enforcement	Did you find a firearm and now want to transport it to a law enforcement agency to comply with your duties as a finder under the law (see Cal. Civ. Code § 2080.1(a))?	Yes* P.C. § 25570	No	No	No	* In order to for this exemption to apply, you must transport the handgun unloaded and in a locked container, and your course of travel should only include necessary deviations. P.C. § 25505. Also, before transporting the handgun to the law enforcement agency, you must give them notice that you will be transporting the firearm there.
Taking a Firearm to Report Information	Are you taking a firearm to report information regarding the acquisition, ownership, destruction, or disposal of that firearm?	Yes* P.C. § 25560	Yes** P.C. § 26379(b)	Yes*** P.C. § 26405(v)(2)	No	In order to meet any of these exemptions, the firearm must be the firearm that you are reporting to the DOJ. * In order to for this exemption to apply, you must transport the handgun unloaded and in a locked container, and your course of travel should only include necessary deviations. P.C. § 25505 **This exemption applies only when you are outside of a vehicle incident to taking the firearm to report the information. But, you may be able to carry the handgun openly in your vehicle if you meet another exemption. ***This exemption only applies incident to taking the firearm to report the information.

	Question				
Delivering Your Firearm to a "Gun Buyback"	Are you selling, delivering, or transferring a firearm to a government entity as part of a voluntary program in which the government is buying weapons from private individuals (*i.e.*, a "gun buy-back" event)?	Yes* P.C. § 25565	Yes** P.C. § 26379(c)	Yes P.C. § 26405(v)(3)	No
Taking Your Firearm to Report it After Brining it into the State	Are you a personal firearm importer transporting your firearm in order to comply with the personal firearm importer requirements (see Chapter 4)?	Yes* P.C. § 25575	Yes** P.C. § 26379(a)	Yes*** P.C. § 26405(v)(1)	No

Keep in mind that these exemptions only apply to the specific firearm that you are selling in the "gun buyback" event.

*This exemption only allows you to transport a handgun to the "gun buyback" event. The handgun must be unloaded and in a locked container while it is being transported and your course of travel should only include necessary deviations. P.C. § 25505.

**This exemption applies only when you are outside of a vehicle. But, you may be able to carry the handgun openly in your vehicle if you meet another exemption.

*This exemption only allows you to transport a handgun to be reported/transferred/turned in under the personal firearm importer requirements. The handgun must be unloaded and in a locked container while it is being transported and your course of travel should only include necessary deviations. P.C. § 25505.

**This exemption applies only when you are outside of a vehicle and incident to an activity associated with the requirements of a personal firearm importer. But, you may be able to carry the handgun openly in your vehicle if you meet another exemption.

***This exemption applies incident to complying with the requirements of a personal firearm importer.

EXEMPTIONS BASED ON THE ACTIVITY YOU ENGAGE IN

What Are You Doing?	Description	Can You Carry An Unloaded Handgun Concealed?	Can You Carry An Unloaded Handgun Openly?	Can You Carry An Unloaded "Firearm That Is Not A Handgun"?	Can You Carry A Loaded Firearm?	Notes and Comments
Transporting Your "Curio or Relic" to Comply with the Registration Requirement	Are you a licensed collector (see Chapter 2) who acquired a "curio or relic" from outside of California and are taking it to comply with the requirements of P.C. § 27565 (having to do with licensed collectors bringing "curio and relic" firearms into the state)?	Yes* P.C. § 25580	Yes** P.C. § 26379(a)	Yes*** P.C. § 26405(v)(1)	No	*This exemption only allows you to transport a handgun to be reported as required by P.C. § 27565. The handgun must be unloaded and in a locked container while it is being transported and your course of travel should only include necessary deviations. P.C. § 25505. **This exemption applies only when you are outside of a vehicle incident to reporting the handgun per P.C. § 27565. But, you may be able to carry the handgun openly in your vehicle if you meet another exemption. ***This exemption applies only to situations incident to the reporting requirement.
Taking A Firearm You Obtained by Operation of Law to Report it	Are you a person complying with the requirements of an intra-familial or operation of law transfer?	Yes* P.C. § 25555	Yes** P.C. § 26379(d),(e)	Yes*** P.C. § 26405(v)(4), (5)	No	*This exemption only allows you to transport a handgun to comply with the requirements of the transfer. The handgun must be unloaded and in a locked container while it is being transported and your course of travel should only include necessary deviations. P.C. § 25505. **This exemption applies only when you are outside of a vehicle and incident to the transfer. But, you may be able to carry the handgun openly in your vehicle if you meet another exemption. ***This exemption applies only to situations incident to the transfer of the firearm.

Category	Question					Notes
Taking Your Firearm to Obtain an Identification Number	Are you transporting your firearm to get an identification number assigned to that firearm (under P.C. § 23910)?	Yes* P.C. § 25585	Yes** P.C. § 26376	Yes*** P.C. § 26405(s)	No	*This exemption only allows you to transport a handgun for the purpose of obtaining an identification number or mark. The handgun must be unloaded and in a locked container while it is being transported and your course of travel should only include necessary deviations. P.C. § 25505. **This exemption applies only when you are outside of a vehicle and incident to obtaining an identification number or mark. But, you may be able to carry the handgun openly in your vehicle if you meet another exemption. ***This exemption applies only to situations incident getting the identification mark.
Storing an Emergency Signaling Device on a Fishing Vessel or Aircraft	Are you making or attempting to make a lawful arrest?	No	Yes* P.C. § 26362	Yes* P.C. § 26405(f)	Yes* P.C. §26060	*These exemptions only allow you to store a loaded or unloaded rocket, rocket propelled projectile launcher, or similar device designed primarily for emergency or distress signaling purposes on a fishing vessel or aircraft.
Carrying at the Request of a Sheriff or Chief	Did a sheriff, chief of police, or other head of a municipal police department request that you carry a firearm?	No	Yes P.C. § 26382	Yes P.C. § 26405(y)	No	N/A
Acting in Self Defense When There is a Restraining Order	Are you in "grave danger" from a person against whom you have a restraining order?	Yes P.C. § 25600	Yes P.C. § 26362	Yes P.C. § 26405(d), (f)	Yes P.C. § 26045(b)	In order to meet any of these exemptions, the court must have issued the restraining order after finding that the person posed a threat to your life or safety. Keep in mind that these exemptions may not apply where there is a *mutual* restraining order. Also, the belief that you are in "grave danger" must be reasonable.

		EXEMPTIONS BASED ON THE ACTIVITY YOU ENGAGE IN				
WHAT ARE YOU DOING?	DESCRIPTION	CAN YOU CARRY AN UNLOADED HANDGUN CONCEALED?	CAN YOU CARRY AN UNLOADED HANDGUN OPENLY?	CAN YOU CARRY AN UNLOADED "FIREARM THAT IS NOT A HANDGUN"?	CAN YOU CARRY A LOADED FIREARM?	NOTES AND COMMENTS
Acting in Self Defense, Absent a Restraining Order	Are you, another person, or your or another person's property in immediate, "grave danger"?	No	Yes P.C. § 26362	Yes P.C. § 26405(f)	Yes P.C. § 26045(a)	In order to meet any of these exemptions, you or another person must be in "immediate grave danger." "Immediate" in this circumstance means the brief interval before and after law enforcement has been notified of the danger and before they arrive.
Taking a Safety or Hunter Safety Class	Are you going to, or coming from a recognized safety or hunter safety class in which you are a participant?	Yes* P.C. §25520	No	No	No	*This exemption only allows you to transport a handgun directly to or from a recognized safety or hunter safety class. The handgun must be unloaded and in a locked container while it is being transported and your course of travel should only include necessary deviations. P.C. § 25505.
Training to Become a Sworn Officer	Are you training to become a sworn peace officer?	No	Yes* P.C. § 26380	Yes* P.C. § 26405(w)	No	*These exemptions apply only when you are carrying the firearm incident to, and during the course and scope of, your training to become a sworn peace officer as part of a study approved by the Commission on POST.
Training for a Carry License	Are you training to obtain a Carry License?	No	Yes* P.C. § 26381	Yes* P.C. § 26405(x)	No	*These exemptions apply only when you are carrying the firearm incident to, and during the course and scope of, a course of study necessary to obtain your license or authorized by a person who may legally to issue the license under Chapter 4 (commencing with P.C. § 26150).

Category	Question				Notes
Taking Your Firearm to a Licensing Agency	Are you transporting your firearm to a place where Carry Licenses are issued for the purpose of determining whether or not you will be issued the license?	Yes* P.C. § 25545	No	No	*This exemption allows you to transport your firearm directly to and from a place designated to issue licenses under P.C. §§ 26150, 26155, 26170, or 26215. Also, this exemption applies only when the issuing agency requests that you bring the firearm to them so they can determine whether or not to issue you a license. Keep in mind, the handgun must be unloaded and in a locked container while it is being transported and your course of travel should only include necessary deviations. P.C. § 25505.
Participating in a Motion Picture	Are you an authorized participant in a motion picture, television, or video production, or entertainment event?	Yes* P.C. § 25510(a)	Yes** P.C. § 26375	Yes** P.C. § 26405(r)	In order to meet any of these three exemptions, you must be lawfully using the firearm as part of the entertainment production or event. *This exemption also allows you to transport the handgun unloaded and in a locked container when going to or from the entertainment production or event. **Not only do these exemptions apply while you are making the motion picture, but also while you are rehearsing or practicing for that production or event.
Supplying Firearms to a Motion Picture	Are you an authorized employee or agent of a supplier of firearms that is supplying firearms to a motion picture, television or video production, or entertainment event?	Yes* P.C. § 25510(b)	Yes** P.C. § 26375	Yes** P.C. § 26405(r)	*The concealed carry exemption also allows you to transport the handgun unloaded and in a locked container when going directly to and from the entertainment production or event. **Not only do these exemptions apply while you are making the motion picture, but also while you are rehearsing or practicing for that production or event.
Participating in a Sporting Event	Are you going to or from a recognized sporting event involving a firearm in which you are a participant?	Yes* P.C. §25520	No	No	*This exemption only allows you to transport a handgun directly to or from a recognized safety or hunter safety class. The handgun must be unloaded and in a locked container while it is being transported and your course of travel should only include necessary deviations. P.C. § 25505.

Exemptions Based on The Activity You Engage In

What Are You Doing?	Description	Can You Carry An Unloaded Handgun Concealed?	Can You Carry An Unloaded Handgun Openly?	Can You Carry An Unloaded "Firearm That Is Not A Handgun"?	Can You Carry A Loaded Firearm?	Notes and Comments
Making a Lawful Arrest	Are you making or attempting to make a lawful arrest?	No	Yes* P.C. § 26372	Yes* P.C. § 26405(p)	Yes* P.C. § 26050	*Beware, these exemptions only apply when you are actually making or attempting to make a *lawful* arrest.
Transporting Your Firearm for Any Lawful Purpose	Are you transporting your firearm for a lawful purpose (Chapter 6, Section (III)(E)(2))?	Yes* P.C. § 25610	Yes** P.C. § 26389	Yes*** P.C. § 26405(c)	No	

*In order for this exemption to apply, you must be over the age of 18 and not prohibited from possessing firearms. If you are transporting a handgun in a vehicle, it must be locked in the vehicle's trunk or in a locked container. But, if you are transporting a handgun outside of a car, this exemption only applies if you are carrying it directly to or from a motor vehicle in a locked container. Keep in mind, you may also transport a handgun between any place you may lawfully carry the handgun concealed, open, or loaded so long it is unloaded and in a locked container. P.C. § 25590.

**This exemption is applicable only when you are transporting the unloaded handgun in a vehicle. Moreover, the handgun must be unloaded and carried in either the trunk of the vehicle or a locked container.

***You may transport your long gun inside your vehicle in any manner as long as it is unloaded, unless you are in certain areas, such as a gun free school zone (see Chapter 7). If you are transporting the firearm outside of the vehicle, the firearm must be in a locked container or "encased," as discussed in Chapter 6, Section (V). Moreover, your course of travel should only include necessary deviations, unless you must meet another exemption to this restriction.

CHAPTER 7:
PLACES WHERE FIREARM POSSESSION IS PROHIBITED AND FIREARM USE IS RESTRICTED

As explained in previous chapters, the regulation of firearm possession in California is primarily based on whether the firearm is in a "private" or "public" place, "carried" or "possessed," "loaded" or "unloaded," and/or "concealed."

In addition to these categorical restrictions, both California and federal law completely prohibit firearms in specific places, or, if firearms are allowed at all, restrict who may possess them and in what manner they may be possessed. Sometimes the scope of these restrictions is not as clear as it should be. California and federal laws impose different, and sometimes overlapping, restrictions. You need to know where and what these areas are so you don't violate the law.

The following Sections discuss when and where you can, or more appropriately, when and where you *cannot* possess a firearm.

While this book covers mostly federal and state laws, keep in mind that cities and counties can pass certain laws about where and how you may possess firearms. For example, the Los Angeles Municipal Code regulates the possession of firearm parts (*e.g.*, a frame, receiver, or firearm barrel) and ammunition at the Los Angeles International Airport.[1]

Many local municipal codes also prohibit discharging firearms.[2] In Los Angeles County, for example, there are a large number of "districts" where discharging a firearm is prohibited.[3] The most common local restrictions prohibit or regulate firearm possession in city or county public parks.[4]

---

[1] L.A., CAL., MUN. CODE § 55.17. "Ammunition" is defined in Penal Code (P.C.) section 16150.

[2] The California state legislature has provided in California Government Code (Cal. Gov't Code) section 25840 that a county "board of supervisors may prohibit and prevent the unnecessary firing and discharge of firearms on or into the highways and other public places and may pass all necessary ordinances regulating or forbidding such acts." *See, e.g.*, L.A. CNTY. CODE §§ 17.04.620, 19.12.1420(p).

[3] Descriptions of these districts can be very specific and in some cases border on the absurd. *See* L.A. CNTY. CODE §§ 13.66.130, 17.04.620, 19.12.1420(o).

[4] *See Calguns Foundation, Inc. v. Cnty. of San Mateo*, 218 Cal. App. 4th 661 (2013) (upholding such an ordinance in the face of a preemption challenge).

If you plan on possessing a firearm in public, familiarize yourself with both your city's and county's applicable regulations and the state and federal restrictions discussed below. Though local governments are somewhat limited in the types of firearm restrictions they can have, knowing these additional local rules may save hours of your life and thousands of dollars in attorneys' fees if you must prove you were acting lawfully.

I. FIREARM POSSESSION IN GOVERNMENT BUILDINGS

A. Federal Law

Under federal law, it is generally illegal to knowingly possess or bring a firearm or other dangerous weapon[5] into a federal facility. A "federal facility" is any building or part thereof owned or leased by the federal government where federal employees regularly report for work.[6] Exceptions to this rule exist for officers, agents, and state or U.S. employees performing their official law enforcement duties; federal officials and military members, if authorized by law to possess a firearm; or those carrying firearms for hunting or other lawful purposes.[7]

Anyone who "knowingly possesses or causes to be present a firearm or other dangerous weapon in a federal facility (other than a federal court facility), or attempts to do so, shall be fined . . . or imprisoned not more than 1 year, or both."[8] Anyone knowingly possessing a firearm or other dangerous weapon in a federal *court* facility, or even attempting to do so, can be fined and/or imprisoned for up to two years.[9] Anyone using, or attempting to use, a firearm to commit a crime in a federal facility can be fined and/or imprisoned for up to five years.[10] You cannot, however, be convicted of bringing a firearm into a federal facility unless the facility is clearly labeled or you had actual notice of this restriction.[11]

B. California Law

It is illegal to bring a loaded firearm into, or possess "a loaded firearm within, the State Capitol, any legislative office, any office of the Governor or other constitutional officer, or any hearing room in which any committee of the Senate or Assembly is

---

[5] A "'dangerous weapon' means a weapon, device, instrument, material, or substance, animate or inanimate, that is used for, or is readily capable of, causing death or serious bodily injury . . . ." It does not include pocket knives with a blade less than 2 ½ inches long. 18 U.S.C. § 930(g)(2).

[6] 18 U.S.C. § 930(g)(1).

[7] 18 U.S.C. § 930(d). This "other lawful purpose" exception does not apply to federal courts and is unclear as to what activities it does apply. 18 U.S.C. § 930(e)(2).

[8] 18 U.S.C. § 930(a).

[9] 18 U.S.C. § 930(e).

[10] 18 U.S.C. § 930(b).

[11] 18 U.S.C. § 930(h).

conducting a hearing, or upon the grounds of the State Capitol, which is bounded by 10th, L, 15th, and N Streets in the City of Sacramento . . . ."[12]

It is also illegal to possess or bring a loaded firearm onto the grounds of or within the Governor's Mansion or any other residence of the Governor, a constitutional officer, or any member of the Legislature.[13] These offenses are "wobblers," punishable as either felonies or misdemeanors.[14]

California peace officers may examine any firearm in any place where possessing a loaded firearm is prohibited by California Penal Code (P.C.) sections 171c or 171d. Refusing to allow a peace officer to inspect your firearm in such a place or, as explained in Chapter 5, while in most "public places," is grounds for arrest.[15]

Both the prohibition on loaded firearms in the State Capitol and related offices, and in the Governor's mansion and on its grounds have exceptions for certain authorized peace officers, those summoned by law enforcement to assist in making an arrest or preserving the peace, and holders of a valid Carry License[16] (see Chapter 6).[17] The prohibition on loaded firearms in the State Capitol and related offices also has an exception for those with permission from the Chief Sergeants at Arms of both the State Assembly and Senate.[18] And the prohibition on loaded firearms in the Governor's mansion and on its grounds or any other residence of the Governor, other constitutional officer, or member of the legislature also has exceptions for military members performing their duties and other persons authorized by the occupants of the specified residences.[19]

Anyone who possesses firearms, knives with a blade longer than four inches that is either fixed or capable of being fixed in an unguarded position, switchblade knives,[20] generally prohibited weapons,[21] tasers, stun guns, or anything that expels a metallic projectile such as a BB or pellet through air or CO_2 pressure or spring action, or any spot marker or paint gun in any state or local public building or public meeting, violates California law.[22]

---

[12] P.C. § 171c.

[13] P.C. § 171d.

[14] P.C. §§ 171c, 171d. Although the definition of "loaded" is discussed thoroughly in Chapter 5, for purposes of P.C. sections 171c and 171d, "loaded" means whenever both the firearm and unexpended ammunition are immediately possessed by the same person. See P.C. § 171e. This means the ammunition does not have to be in the firearm to be "loaded" in this context.

[15] P.C. §§ 171e, 25850(b).

[16] A Carry License is also widely known as a "CCW" (carry concealed weapon). See P.C. § 16360.

[17] P.C. § 171c(b). Notably absent from those exempt are military personnel while performing their duties.

[18] But, only a peace officer acting within the scope of his or her employment may carry a firearm on the floor of the Assembly or in a committee room when the Assembly is in session or during a meeting of a committee or subcommittee. CAL. H.R. RES. 1 § 117.7A (2015-2016).

[19] P.C. § 171d.

[20] As described in P.C. section 17235.

[21] Listed in P.C. section 16590. See Chapter 9 for further information.

[22] P.C. section 171b provides a definition for "state or local public building," which includes any buildings, or part of a building, the state or local government owns or leases where government employees regularly go to perform their official duties. It includes courthouses, but not government employees' residences. See also CAL. GOV'T CODE §§ 11120, 54950 (discussing which places are intended for public business).

This prohibition does not apply to:

(1) Those possessing or transporting weapons into court for evidence as long as they are not a party to the action;[23] *or*

(2) Authorized peace officers,[24] retired peace officers with authorization to carry concealed weapons,[25] full-time paid peace officers of another state or the federal government who are carrying out official duties while in California, or those summoned by a peace officer to assist with an arrest or preserving the peace;[26] *or*

(3) Those with a valid Carry License;[27] *or*

(4) Those with written permission from an authorized official in charge of state or local government building security;[28] *or*

(5) Those who lawfully reside in, own, or possess those portions of the building that are not owned or leased by the state or local government;[29] *or*

(6) Those hired by the building's owner or manager who have permission to possess firearms in those areas they lawfully reside in, own, or lawfully possess that the state or local government does not own or lease;[30] *or*

(7) Those who lawfully bring a weapon to a gun show for sale or trade.[31]

II. FIREARM POSSESSION IN "SCHOOL ZONES"

Though exceptions exist, it is generally unlawful under both California and federal law to possess a firearm – whether loaded or unloaded – in an area you know, or reasonably should know, is a "school zone."[32] There are both California and federal laws covering gun possession in school zones. Because California and federal laws exist independently of each other, it is important to remember that you may be prosecuted for violating either state and/or federal law. So you must comply with both.

---

[23] P.C. § 171b(b)(2)(B).

[24] As defined in P.C. sections 830-832.9.

[25] As described in P.C. sections 25450-25475.

[26] P.C. § 171b(b)(2)(A).

[27] P.C. § 171b(b)(3). Although no law prohibits the carrying of firearms into a state courthouse with a valid Carry License, most state court policies prohibit carrying firearms into a courthouse by anyone other than law enforcement.

[28] P.C. § 171b(b)(4).

[29] P.C. § 171b(b)(5).

[30] P.C. 171b(b)(6). This exemption only applies to those who are "licensed or registered in accordance with, and acting within the course and scope of" their duties as private investigators and/or alarm company operators. *See* CAL. BUS. & PROF. CODE §§ 7512-7514, 7590-7590.5.

[31] P.C. § 171b(b)(7)(B).

[32] P.C. § 626.9(b); *see* 18 U.S.C. § 922(q)(2)(A).

A. Federal Law

Federal law defines a "school zone" as an area that is "in, or on the grounds of, a public, parochial or private school; or within a distance of 1,000 feet from the ground of a public, parochial or private school."[33] But, note that unlike California law (see below), federal law does not restrict firearms on college campuses or universities.

Although it is generally illegal to possess a firearm in a "school zone" under federal law,[34] there are some exceptions to this restriction. Specifically, the following people and situations are exempt from the federal firearm restriction in a "school zone":

(1) Individuals who are on private property that is not part of school grounds; *or*

(2) Certain state-licensed individuals;[35] *or*

(3) When the firearm is unloaded and in a locked container or locked firearm rack on a motor vehicle; *or*

(4) Individuals who are in a school-approved program; *or*

(5) Individuals who have contracted with a school to possess a firearm; *or*

(6) Law enforcement officers acting in their official capacity; *or*

(7) Individuals carrying unloaded while going over school premises to gain access to lawful hunting lands if the school authorizes the entry.[36]

Note that while California's exception, explained below, requires handguns be in a locked container and long guns to be transported according to California law[37] when in a "school zone," federal law additionally requires that long guns also be in locked containers.[38] Because federal law places stricter restrictions on all types of firearms, you should follow the federal restrictions regarding transportation in order to comply with both state and federal law.

---

[33] 18 U.S.C. § 921(a)(25)-(26).

[34] 18 U.S.C. § 922(q)(2)(A). The federal "school zone" restriction, however, only applies to a firearm that "has moved in or otherwise affects interstate or foreign commerce." The restriction likely still applies to nearly all firearms because even "homemade" firearms contain parts that have "moved in" or "affect" interstate commerce.

[35] For this exception to apply, federal law requires "the individual possessing the firearm [be] licensed to do so by the State in which the school zone is located or a political subdivision of the State, and the law of the State or political subdivision requires that, before an individual obtains such a license, the law enforcement authorities of the State or political subdivision verify that the individual is qualified under law to receive the license." 18 U.S.C. § 922(q)(2)(B)(ii).

[36] 18 U.S.C. § 922(q)(2)(B).

[37] As discussed in Chapter 5, long guns (unless they are "assault weapons") do not need to be in a locked container when transported in a vehicle.

[38] *See* 18 U.S.C. § 922(q)(2)(B).

B. California Law

California's Gun-Free School Zone Act defines "school zone" as "an area in, or on the grounds of, a public or private school providing instruction in kindergarten or grades 1 to 12, inclusive, or within a distance of 1,000 feet from the grounds of the public or private school."[39] Though this law is somewhat unclear, to be on the safe side you should measure the 1,000 feet starting from the school's *perimeter*, not its center-point. This advice is especially warranted since violating a "school zone" law may be a felony with mandatory jail time.

Curiously, California does not require "school zones" to be marked,[40] so the 1,000-foot "school zone" border is often difficult to determine. Whether you know, or reasonably should know, you are in a "school zone" will be a question of fact for a jury to decide if you are prosecuted – which is an expensive process – so be careful around schools!

The California Gun-Free School Zone Act (but not federal law) also generally prohibits possessing firearms, whether loaded or unloaded, at university or college campuses and their buildings for student housing, teaching, research, or administration.[41] Either offense is a felony, but possessing a "loaded"[42] firearm on university or college property where possession is prohibited has a steeper sentence.[43]

Until January 1, 2018, the following people are exempted from California's "school zone" (*i.e.*, the grounds of the school and 1,000 feet from the school grounds) and university/college campus firearm prohibitions:

(1) An individual who has written permission from the school superintendent or the university or college president, respectively, or their equivalent authority (P.C. § 626.9(b), (h), (i)); *or*

(2) While an individual is on an existing shooting range at a school, university, or college campus (P.C. § 626.9(n)); *or*

(3) An individual who is a duly appointed California peace officer,[44] either a federal officer or one from another state carrying out official duties, an

---

[39] P.C. § 626.9(e)(1).

[40] P.C. § 626.9(k).

[41] Unlike "school zones," which need not be marked as such, universities and colleges must "post a prominent notice at primary entrances on noncontiguous property [*i.e.*, property not connected to the campus] stating that firearms are prohibited on that property." P.C. § 626.9(h)-(i).

[42] The term "loaded" in this context "when there is an unexpended cartridge or shell, consisting of a case that holds a charge of powder and a bullet or shot, in, or attached in any manner to, the firearm, including, but not limited to, in the firing chamber, magazine, or clip thereof attached to the firearm." P.C. § 626.9(j). A muzzle-loading firearm is considered to be "loaded" in this context "when it is capped or primed and has a powder charge and ball or shot in the barrel or cylinder." P.C. § 626.9(j).

[43] P.C. § 626.9(h)-(i). This general prohibition is notwithstanding P.C. section 25605's general exception to the firearm restriction in one's residence. *See People v. Anaim*, 47 Cal. App. 4th 401 (1996) (depublished) (defendant violated the Gun-Free School Zone Act because he possessed a loaded firearm on university property even though the university-owned apartment complex was his residence). Post-*Heller* (see Chapter 1), this may change. But until it does, you cannot lawfully have a firearm in your residence if your residence is part of university property and marked as such.

[44] As defined in P.C. section 830.

individual summoned by any of those officers to make an arrest or keep the peace, or any military members performing their duties (P.C. § 626.9(l)); *or*

(4) An armored vehicle guard[45] performing his or her duties (P.C. § 626.9(l)); *or*

(5) A security guard authorized to carry loaded firearms (P.C. § 626.9(m));[46] *or*

(6) An honorably retired peace officer authorized to carry concealed or loaded firearms (P.C. § 626.9(o)); *or*

(7) A peace officer[47] who is authorized to carry a firearm by the appointing agency.[48]

In 2017, the California Legislature sought to remove item (1) above, i.e., the exemption based on obtaining written permission from the school superintendent, the university or college president, or their equivalent authority.[49] They did this by drafting and passing Assembly Bill ("AB") 424. On October 14, 2017, Governor Brown signed AB 424 into law. So, beginning on January 1, 2018, California will effectively remove the ability of school administrators to decide whether individuals, including those with Carry Licenses, can bring firearms onto school zones.[50] So item (1) in the list above will be deleted starting on January 1, 2018 (the other six exemptions will still apply). AB 424 did add two additional exemptions to the list above, however. Therefore, starting on January 1, 2018, the following circumstances are also exempted from California's "school zone" (and university/college campus firearm prohibitions:

(1) While an individual is participating in a program involving shooting sports or activities (including, but not limited to, trap shooting, skeet shooting, sporting clays, and pistol shooting) that is sanctioned by a school, school district, college, university, or other governing body of the institution, and that occurs on the grounds of a public or private school or university or college campus; *or*

(2) While an individual is participating in a state-certified hunter education program pursuant to Fish and Game Code section 3051, as long as he or she does not possess live ammunition in a school building.[51]

Under current California law, "school zones" (*i.e.*, the grounds of the school and 1,000 feet from the school grounds) have additional exceptions including:

---

[45] As defined in Cal. Bus. & Prof. Code section 7582.1(d).

[46] P.C. §§ 26000-26060.

[47] Appointed under P.C. section 830.6.

[48] P.C. §§ 25450, 25650, 25900-25910, 26020 , 26300(c)(2).

[49] AB 424, 2017-2018 Leg. Council's Digest (2017), *available at* https://leginfo.legislature.ca.gov/faces/billNavClient.xhtml?bill_id=201720180AB424 (last visited Oct. 20, 2017) (amends P.C. § 626.9(a) and related statutes by removing the following language: "unless it is with the written permission of the school district superintendent, his or her designee, or equivalent school authority").

[50] P.C. §§ 626.9, 26370, 26405 (all effective Jan. 1, 2018).

[51] P.C. § 626.9(q) (effective Jan. 1, 2018).

(1) When the firearm is lawfully possessed in a residence, place of business, or on private property *as long as* such places are not part of the school *grounds* (*i.e.*, on campus)[52] (P.C. § 626.9(c)(1)); *or*

(2) Any handgun being lawfully transported (meaning handguns that are unloaded and *either* in a "locked container"[53] or in the locked trunk of a car) (P.C. § 626.9(c)(2)); *or*

(3) When you reasonably believe you are in "grave danger because of circumstances forming the basis of a current restraining order issued by a court against another person or persons who has or have been found to pose a threat to . . . [your] life or safety" (P.C. § 626.9(c)(3));[54] *or*

(4) When the firearm is possessed by individuals exempt from the general concealed firearm prohibition per specific Penal Code provisions (P.C. § 626.9(c)(4));[55] *or*

(5) Any long gun being lawfully transported in accordance with California law.[56]

California law also provides an exemption that allows Carry License[57] holders to carry a firearm within the 1,000 feet "school zone" border.[58] But this exemption does not allow Carry License holders to carry a firearm on "school grounds."

C. California and Federal Discharge Restrictions

California and federal "school zone" laws also prohibit knowingly or recklessly *discharging*, or attempting to discharge, a firearm in a "school zone."[59] They both exempt discharging a firearm on private property, though.[60] Federal law further exempts discharging a firearm if the activity is part of a school-approved program,

---

[52] Public streets are considered to be easements, and are therefore not considered to be "private property." *See People v. Tapia*, 129 Cal. App. 4th 1153 (2005). That means if you live within 1,000 feet of the grounds of a public or private school, the public street and sidewalk in front of your house would not be considered "private property" for purposes of this exemption and would likely still be considered part of the "school zone."

[53] *See* Chapter 6 for a definition of "locked container" and how to lawfully transport firearms.

[54] This exception may not include mutual restraining order circumstances and does not include the general exception to the carrying loaded restriction for "carrying of any loaded firearm under circumstances where it would otherwise be lawful, by a person who reasonably believes that any person or the property of any person is in immediate, grave danger and that the carrying of the weapon is necessary for the preservation of that person or property." P.C. § 26045.

[55] The Penal Code sections listing these exemptions are: P.C. sections 25615 (transporting unloaded handguns by a licensed person who manufactures, imports, wholesales, repairs, or deals with firearms in their business); 25625 (authorized military or civil organizations carrying firearms while parading or going to and from their organization); 25630 (guards, financial institution employees, or common carriers while working); and 25645 (operating a licensed common carrier to transport unloaded firearms per federal law). *See also* Chapter 6.

[56] P.C. § 626.9(c)(5).

[57] Issued under Chapter 4 (commencing with P.C. section 26150) of Division 5 of Title 4 of Part 6.

[58] P.C. § 626.9(c).

[59] P.C. § 626.9(d); 18 U.S.C. § 922(q)(3)(A). As with the possession restriction, for the federal discharge prohibition to apply, the firearm must have moved in, or affected, interstate or foreign commerce, *and* the person must have *known* it was a "school zone."

[60] P.C. § 626.9(d); 18 U.S.C. § 922(q)(3)(B)(i). But beware of local discharge restrictions.

in accordance with a school contract, or by law enforcement officers acting in their official capacity.[61]

Be careful differentiating between California and federal "school zone" exemptions. You can be prosecuted for violating *either* federal or California law. An exception to one will not necessarily exempt you from prosecution under the other.

III. AMMUNITION & WEAPON POSSESSION ON "SCHOOL GROUNDS"

Federal law does not generally regulate the possession of ammunition on "school grounds." But, California law prohibits the carrying of ammunition, reloaded ammunition, and weapons[62] on "school grounds."[63] Unlike the restriction on possessing firearms on school grounds, which discusses and defines what a school (or "school zone") is, it is not entirely clear what is meant by "school grounds" for the ammunition restriction. Is this limited to elementary schools or does it also apply to high schools and/or universities? The legislature did not provide any guidance concerning this restriction.

Sworn law enforcement officers acting within the scope of their duties and persons exempt under P.C. section 25450 (*i.e.*, law enforcement officers exempt from the carrying concealed restriction discussed in Chapter 6) may carry ammunition onto school grounds.[64]

The ammunition restriction also does *not* apply to:

(1) A duly appointed peace officer as defined in Chapter 4.5 (commencing with P.C. section 830) of Title 3 of Part 2; *or*

(2) A full-time paid peace officer of another state or the federal government who is carrying out official duties while in California; *or*

(3) Any person summoned by any of these officers to assist in making an arrest or preserving the peace while that person is actually engaged in assisting the officer; *or*

(4) A member of the military forces of this state or of the U.S. who is engaged in the performance of his or her duties; *or*

---

[61] 18 U.S.C. § 922(q)(3)(B)(ii)-(iv).

[62] Under California law, a person can also be prosecuted for a misdemeanor or a felony for bringing or possessing any dirk; dagger; ice pick; knife having a blade longer than two and a half inches; folding knife with a blade that locks into place; razor with an unregulated blade; taser; stun gun; instrument that expels a metallic projectile, such as a BB or a pellet, through the force of air pressure, CO_2 pressure, or spring action; or spot marker gun on the grounds of, or within, any public or private school providing instruction in kindergarten or any of grades 1 to 12. P.C. § 626.10(a)(1). It is also a misdemeanor to bring or possess a razor blade or box cutter onto "school grounds." P.C. § 626.10(a)(2). In addition, a person can be prosecuted for a misdemeanor or a felony for brining or possessing a dirk; dagger; ice pick; or knife having a fixed blade longer than two and a half inches on the grounds of, or within, any private university, the University of California, the California State University, or the California Community Colleges. P.C. § 626.10(b).

[63] P.C. §§ 626.91, 30310.

[64] P.C. § 30310(a).

(5) An armored vehicle guard, who is engaged in the performance of his or her duties, as defined in subdivision (d) of Section 7582.1 of the California Business and Professions Code; *or*

(6) Any peace officer listed in P.C. sections 830.1, 830.2, or 830.33(a), whether active or honorably retired; *or*

(7) Any other duly appointed peace officer; *or*

(8) Any honorably retired peace officer listed in P.C. section 830.5(c); *or*

(9) Any other honorably retired peace officer who during the course and scope of his or her appointment as a peace officer was authorized to, and did, carry a firearm; *or*

(10) A person carrying ammunition or reloaded ammunition onto school grounds that is in a motor vehicle at all times and is within a "locked container"[65] or within the locked trunk of the vehicle.[66]

Notice, however, that there is no longer an exception to the ammunition restriction for Carry License holders.

IV. FIREARM POSSESSION IN AIRPORTS, ON AIRPLANES, AND ON COMMON CARRIERS

A. Possession in Airport "Sterile Areas"

1. Federal Law

Under federal law, you can be imprisoned for up to ten years if you have a concealed "dangerous weapon" that would be accessible to you while on, or trying to get on, most commercial flights.[67] This restriction does not apply to government law enforcement officers authorized to carry firearms in their official capacity, those authorized by the Federal Aviation Administration (FAA) or the Secretary of Transportation, or those transporting "unloaded" firearms in baggage not accessible to them during flight as long as the air carrier is notified about every firearm.[68]

---

[65] A "locked container" is "a secure container that is fully enclosed and locked by a padlock, keylock, combination lock, or similar locking device." P.C. § 16850. But the term "does not include the utility or glove compartment of a motor vehicle." P.C. § 16850.

[66] P.C. § 30310(b).

[67] 49 U.S.C. § 46505(b)(1). This statute only applies to aircraft operating in "air transportation" or "intrastate air transportation." "Air transportation" is defined to include international transportation, transportation between states, and transportation of mail by aircraft; and "intrastate air transportation" is defined as transportation by a common carrier of passengers entirely in the same state, by turbojet-powered aircraft capable of carrying at least 30 passengers. 49 U.S.C. § 40102(a)(5), (a)(27). But, if you are flying on a plane that is not covered by this statute, there are other federal and state laws that may otherwise prohibit you from bringing a firearm on a plane. *See, e.g.,* 14 C.F.R. § 135.119. Be sure to check with the aircraft operator before even arriving at the airport with a firearm.

[68] 49 U.S.C. § 46505(d).

Note that there is no exception to these restrictions for holders of a valid Carry License. These licensees can be charged just like anyone else for possessing firearms in a "sterile area" of an airport or for attempting to bring a firearm onto a plane.

The federal Transportation Safety Authority (TSA) can also separately fine you up to $3,000 (or up to $7,500 if the firearm is loaded).[69] If this happens, the TSA will normally send you a letter informing you of the violation and your options, which include paying a civil fine, submitting evidence that the violation did not occur, submitting information to reduce the fine, or requesting an informal conference or a formal hearing. If you get a letter like this, hiring an attorney experienced in firearms law to respond is strongly advised.

2. California Law

Under California law, it is generally illegal to knowingly possess firearms, frames, receivers, barrels, firearm magazines, BB devices, imitation firearms, tasers or stun guns,[70] or ammunition, in a "sterile area"[71] of an airport.[72] A "passenger vessel terminal" is "a harbor or port facility . . . regularly serv[ing] scheduled commuter or passenger operations."[73] Exceptions to this restriction include:

(1) Authorized peace officers and those summoned to assist them; *and*

(2) Retired peace officers with Carry Licenses issued pursuant to P.C. section 25450; *and*

(3) Individuals with written authorization from an airport security coordinator; *and*

(4) Individuals responsible for passenger vessel terminal security who have written authorization pursuant to an approved U.S. Coast Guard facility security plan.[74]

Laws regulating firearms or ammunition in airports are most commonly violated by people who simply forget they have a firearm or ammunition in their carry-on bags. This may seem unbelievable to those who do not regularly use firearms, but in fact people sometimes use the same bags to carry other personal items as they use to carry firearms. Depending on the weight of the firearm and the type of bag, this is a common mistake.

Although California laws prohibiting possession at airports generally have a "knowing" requirement – meaning you may not be found guilty of the offense if you legitimately forgot the firearm was in your bag – prosecutors are typically skeptical. Adding to the difficulty, people usually see their bag being removed from the

---

[69] *See* Transportation Security Administration, Enforcement Sanction Guidance Policy, available at https://www.tsa.gov/sites/default/files/enforcement_sanction_guidance_policy.pdf (last visited July 12, 2017).

[70] As defined in P.C. section 244.5.

[71] "Sterile area" is defined in P.C. section 171.5(a)(3).

[72] P.C. § 171.5(b).

[73] P.C. § 171.5(a)(2).

[74] P.C. § 171.5(d).

x-ray conveyor belt and wonder why. At that point they usually remember the fire-arm in their bag and say something along the lines of, "That's my bag. There's a gun in there." This "admission" becomes very difficult to disprove or explain.

 Don't let this mistake happen to you. Take any firearm out of the bag when you get home from the range or other lawful activity. As a general rule never use your range bag as a carry-on! No matter how thorough you are in cleaning it out, one round of ammunition is enough to cause problems.

Also, to be clear, barring any local ordinance to the contrary, you may lawfully possess firearms and ammunition in places outside airport "sterile areas" as long as you are complying with other applicable laws like those that apply generally in public places. You can also lawfully transport unloaded firearms on planes in *checked* lug-gage.[75]

B. Possession on Commercial Airplanes

Federal law generally prohibits having firearms and ammunition accessible on commercial or charter aircraft, and even private aircraft over a certain passenger or payload capacity.[76] Law enforcement officers authorized to carry firearms on duty who have completed the "Law Enforcement Officers Flying Armed" training pro-gram, and whose employer has determined a need exists to carry the firearm while on the aircraft, are allowed to carry firearms on airplanes as long as they declare the firearm to the aircraft operator, keep it concealed – but never in the overhead compartment – and on their person if in uniform, and notify the pilot and crew members of its location. If the flight does *not* require screening, those officers are not required to have special approval from their agency as long as they comply with all other requirements.[77]

This law enforcement exception does not apply to any officer who has been drinking alcohol, nor may officers drink alcohol while on the aircraft if carrying a firearm.[78]

C. Possession on Amtrak Trains

As of December 15, 2010, stations that accept checked baggage allow passengers to transport unloaded firearms in checked baggage under specific conditions. Among the requirements are:

---

[75] P.C. § 171.5(g). See Chapter 6 for how to lawfully transport unloaded firearms in checked luggage and for prob-lems that may arise in airports like New Jersey or New York City.

[76] *See* 49 C.F.R. §§ 1544.201(d), 1544.1(a)(1); *see also* 14 C.F.R. §§ 119.1(a), 135.119.

[77] *See* 49 C.F.R. §§ 1544.201(d), 1544.219, 1544.221. Air marshals are covered by a different set of laws. *See* 49 C.F.R. § 1544.223.

[78] *See* 49 C.F.R. § 1544.219(c).

(1) Passengers must declare to Amtrak their intent to transport a firearm at the time the reservation is made (online reservations for checking firearms are not accepted), or at least 24 hours before departure; *and*

(2) The firearm must be unloaded and in their checked baggage; *and*

(3) Transportation of the firearm must comply with other carriage regulations (*i.e.*, unloaded, hard-sided locked container, etc.).[79]

Check www.amtrak.com for further information about taking firearms on Amtrak trains. Even though you may be able to lawfully transport firearms on Amtrak trains, you must still follow any other applicable regulations when transporting the firearm to the train. For example, if you plan to board an Amtrak train at a "public transportation facility," you might have problems getting the firearm to the train as you cannot knowingly possess firearms in the "sterile area" of the facility (see below).

D. Possession on Greyhound Buses

Greyhound Lines, Inc. prohibits transporting firearms and ammunition on their buses.[80] Though this is their rule, not a law, you could still be prosecuted for trespassing or for a similar violation if you break this rule.

E. Possession on All Other Common Carriers

If you cross state lines with a common carrier, even if the carrier allows firearm possession, federal law requires you to declare and surrender the firearm to the carrier operator for the duration of the trip.[81]

Also, federal law only protects you from state prosecution for violating a state's firearms laws if your firearm is not immediately accessible.[82] This means, if you enter a state on a carrier where it is illegal to possess a firearm without a permit (*e.g.*, New Jersey) and you do not have that permit, federal law does *not* protect you from prosecution under that state's laws if a firearm is in your carry-on bag and not stored away in a place where you cannot readily access it.[83]

F. Possession in Harbors & Ports

Under California law, it is generally illegal to knowingly possess firearms, frames, receivers, barrels, firearm magazines, BB devices, imitation firearms, tasers or stun

---

[79] *See Firearms in Checked Baggage*, AMTRAK, http://www.amtrak.com/servlet/ContentServer?c=Page&pagename=am%2FLayout&cid=1248542758975 (last visited July 12, 2017).

[80] *Baggage Information*, GREYHOUND, http://extranet.greyhound.com/revsup/pfsm/baggage.html (last visited July 12, 2017).

[81] 18 U.S.C. § 922(e).

[82] 18 U.S.C. § 926A (part of FOPA).

[83] See Chapter 6 for properly transporting firearms across state lines and consequences for not doing so properly.

guns,[84] or ammunition, in a "sterile area"[85] of a passenger vessel terminal.[86] A "passenger vessel terminal" is "a harbor or port facility . . . regularly serv[ing] scheduled commuter or passenger operations."[87] Exceptions to this restriction include:

(1) Authorized peace officers and those summoned to assist them; *and*

(2) Retired peace officers with Carry Licenses issued pursuant to P.C. section 25450; *and*

(3) Individuals with written authorization from an airport security coordinator; *and*

(4) Individuals responsible for passenger vessel terminal security who have written authorization pursuant to an approved U.S. Coast Guard facility security plan.[88]

G. Possession in "Sterile Area" of Public Transportation Facility

Under California law, it is generally illegal for a person to knowingly possess any firearm[89] within the "sterile area" of a public transportation facility, if the "sterile area"[90] is posted with a statement providing reasonable notice that prosecution may result from possession of these items.[91]

A "public transportation facility" is any land, building, or equipment that has as its primary purpose the operation of a public transit system or that provides services to the passengers of a public transportation system.[92] This includes any vehicles in the public transportation system that transport people for hire, such as "motor vehicles, street cars, trackless trolleys, buses, light rail systems, rapid transit systems, subways, trains, [and] jitneys."[93]

The following people are exempt from this restriction:

(1) Authorized peace officers and those summoned to assist them; *and*

(2) Retired peace officers with Carry Licenses issued pursuant to P.C. section 25450; *and*

---

[84] As defined in P.C. section 244.5.

[85] "Sterile area" is defined in P.C. section 171.5(a)(3).

[86] P.C. § 171.5(2).

[87] P.C. § 171.5(a)(2).

[88] P.C. § 171.5(d).

[89] This restriction includes any imitation firearm as defined in P.C. section 417.4; instrument that expels a metallic projectile, such as a BB or pellet, through the force of air pressure, CO_2 pressure, or spring action; spot marker or paint gun; metal military practice hand grenade; metal or plastic replica hand grenade; unauthorized tear case weapon, or undetectable knife as described in P.C. section 17290.

[90] For purposes of this restriction, a "sterile area" is "any portion of a public transit facility that is generally controlled in a manner consisted with the public transit authority's security plan." P.C. § 171.7(a)(2).

[91] P.C. § 171.7(b).

[92] P.C. § 171.7(a)(1).

[93] P.C. § 171.7(a)(1).

(3) A person responsible for the security of the public transportation system and who has been authorized by the public transit authority's security coordinator, in writing, to possess a weapon specified in P.C. section 171(b); *and*

(4) A person who is exempt from the prohibition against carrying concealed handguns, if they are carrying the handgun in accordance with the terms and conditions of an exemption specified in Article 2 (commencing with P.C. section 25450) of Chapter 2 of Division 5 of Title 4 of Part 6 of the Penal Code, or P.C. sections 25615 to 25655, inclusive;[94] *and*

(5) Any person who possess a tear gas weapon if the possession is permitted by Division 11 (commencing with P.C. section 22810) of Title 3 of Part 6 of the Penal Code.[95]

V. FIREARM POSSESSION IN PARKS, FORESTS, AND REFUGES

A. Federal Lands

1. National Parks and Wildlife Refuges

Federal law allows firearm possession on National Park land and within National Wildlife Refuge Systems as long as you are not otherwise prohibited from possession,[96] and you comply with the state law where the National Park System or National Wildlife Refuge System is located.[97]

---

[94] This exemption is somewhat redundant given that P.C. section 171.7(c) already provides exemptions for most of the people listed in these code sections. For example, P.C. section 171.7 already provides an exemption for authorized peace officers and honorably retired peace officers with Carry Licenses under P.C. section 25450. *See* P.C. § 171.7(c)(1)(B). But,this exemption also exempts peace officers and retired peace officers with Carry Licenses under P.C. section 25450. P.C. § 171.7(c)(2). Additionally, this code section also provides that persons carrying in accordance with the following code sections are also exempt from California's restriction on possessing firearms in "sterile area" of a "public transportation facility": P.C. sections 25615 (Concealed carry exemption for possession or transportation of unloaded firearms in lawful course of business), 25620 (Concealed carry exemptions for members of the Army, Navy, Air Force, Coast Guard, Marine Corps, or National Guard); 25625 (Concealed carry exemption for authorized military or civil organization members in relation to parading) 25630 (Concealed carry exemption for guards or messengers of common carriers, banks, or financial institutions when shipping things of value); 25636 (Concealed carry exemption for use or transport of firearms for use at target ranges); 25640 (Concealed carry exemption for licensed hunters or fisherman); 25645 (Concealed carry exemptions the transportation of firearms by common carriers); 25650 (Concealed carry exemption for honorably retired federal officers or agents); 25655 (Concealed carry exemption for people with valid Carry Licenses). But, note that anyone meeting these restrictions is still prohibited from possessing any imitation firearm as defined in P.C. section 417.4; instrument that expels a metallic projectile, such as a BB or pellet, through the force of air pressure, CO_2 pressure, or spring action; spot marker or paint gun; metal military practice hand grenade; metal or plastic replica hand grenade; unauthorized tear case weapon, or undetectable knife as described in P.C. section 17290 while in the "sterile area" of the airport.

[95] P.C. § 171.7(c).

[96] 16 U.S.C. § 1a-7b. *See* Chapter 3 for who is prohibited from possessing firearms.

[97] H.R. 627, § 512(b) (2009) (codified as 16 U.S.C. § 1a-7b). Prior to this law changing, *United States v. Masciandaro*, 638 F.3d 458 (4th Cir. 2011), was decided. In this case, the petitioner fell asleep in his car on National Park property. A federal park ranger woke him and found a loaded handgun in a backpack in his trunk. Unfortunately, this

This means, while federal law allows for firearm possession in National Parks and Wildlife Refuges, California's carry restrictions still apply, as do their exceptions, which include lawfully transporting a firearm to an activity where carrying a firearm is permitted, such as hunting, camping, target shooting, etc., or if discharging firearms is allowed in that area.[98]

Though federal law allows *possessing* firearms in National Park land and within National Wildlife Refuge Systems, as long as you comply with the state law where the park or refuge is located, *discharging* firearms is a different story. Discharging firearms on National Wildlife Refuges is federally prohibited unless specifically authorized.[99] National Parks and Refuges, or specified areas within those parks and refuges, in California may be open for hunting as outlined in 36 Code of Federal Regulations (C.F.R.) Part 7 and 50 C.F.R. section 32.24, but are still subject to California laws and requirements.

2. National Forests

National Forests are not to be confused with National Parks. These are two separate types of lands regulated by different portions of the federal code and government (the Department of Agriculture and the Department of the Interior, respectively).

Within the National Forest System it is unlawful to discharge "a firearm or any other implement capable of taking human life, causing injury, or damaging property":

(1) In or within 150 yards of a residence, building, campsite, developed recreation site or occupied area; *or*

(2) Across or on a National Forest System road or a body of water adjacent thereto, or in any manner or place whereby any person or property is exposed to injury or damage as a result of such discharge; *or*

(3) Into or within any cave.[100]

The use of tracer bullets and incendiary ammunition is also prohibited in the National Forest System.[101] The Department of Agriculture Forest Service also has discretion to close or restrict those areas where discharging firearms is lawful.[102]

---

incident occurred before firearms were allowed in National Park land. The Fourth Circuit upheld Masciandaro's conviction. Additionally, it noted that Second Amendment rights outside the home, and the appropriate standards for if and how those rights can be regulated by the government, is still uncertain. So make sure you comply with state laws in National Parks.

[98] See Chapter 6 for the specific restrictions and exceptions.

[99] 50 C.F.R. § 27.41.

[100] 36 C.F.R. § 261.10(d).

[101] 36 C.F.R. § 261.5(b). Tracers are also illegal "destructive devices" under California law. See Chapter 9.

[102] 36 C.F.R. § 261.58(m).

3. Bureau of Land Management (BLM) and Other Federally Protected Areas

The Bureau of Land Management's (BLM) California policy is to allow the use of firearms on public lands,[103] as provided for in state law, and to cooperate with state authorities in the enforcement of firearms regulations.[104] It is still unlawful, however, to discharge or use firearms on developed recreation sites and areas[105] unless authorized.[106] The BLM can also limit hunting and discharging firearms to protect certain locations. Before you head to BLM land to use your firearms, contact the local BLM office for information on where they think you can lawfully shoot.

4. United States Army Corps of Engineers (USACE) Managed Land

The USACE manages almost 12 million acres of land and water.[107] The law is currently unclear about whether firearms may be lawfully possessed on USACE land. But, the USACE has taken the position that laws permitting firearms in National Parks and Wildlife refuges do not apply to USACE managed land. Congressional attempts to specifically amend the law to permit firearms on this land have thus far failed.[108] But, there have been some legal challenges to the USACE's firearms prohibitions.[109] At the time of the writing of this book, it appears that the new USACE administration may be cooperating in lifting this ban. Still, in the meantime, given that USACE's position has not been finalized, it is still advisable to refrain from possessing firearms on USACE land, or to confirm the current policy with the USACE before entering these areas with a firearm.

---

[103] Maps of BLM land are available at: https://www.blm.gov/maps (last visited July 12, 2017).

[104] *See California Recreational Shooting*, U.S. DEPT. OF THE INTERIOR, BUREAU OF LAND MANAGEMENT, https://www.blm.gov/programs/recreation-programs/recreational-shooting/california (last updated July 12, 2017).

[105] "Developed recreation sites and areas means sites and areas that contain structures or capital improvements primarily used by the public for recreation purposes. Such sites or areas may include such features as: Delineated spaces for parking, camping or boat launching; sanitary facilities; potable water; grills or fire rings; tables; or controlled access." 43 C.F.R. § 8360.0-5.

[106] 43 C.F.R. § 8365.2-5.

[107] *Environmental Stewardship Program Statistics*, U.S. ARMY CORPS OF ENGINEERS, http://www.usace.army.mil/Media/FactSheets/FactSheetArticleView/tabid/219/Article/173/environmental-stewardship-program-statistics.aspx (last visited July 12, 2017).

[108] Kevin Freking, *Senate rejects firearms on Army Corps of Engineers lands, boosting gun control supporters*, FOX NEWS (May 8, 2013), http://www.foxnews.com/us/2013/05/08/senate-rejects-firearms-on-army-corps-engineers-lands-boosting-gun-control/ (last visited July 12, 2017). But, in 2015, Republican lawmakers in both the House and the Senate introduced two companion bills (H.R. 578 and S. 263) to amend this law. *See* Chris Eger, *Bill Filed to Lift Army Corps of Engineers' Ban on Guns*, GUNS.COM (Feb. 2, 2015), *available at* http://www.guns.com/2015/02/02/bills-filed-to-lift-army-corps-of-engineers-ban-on-guns/ (last visited July 12, 2017). As of the date of publication, these bills have not been passed.

[109] *See Morris v. U.S. Army Corps of Engineers*, 990 F. Supp. 2d 1082 (D. Idaho 2014); see also Chapter 6. As of the date of publication, the district court in Morris has granted a preliminary injunction, prohibiting the USACE from enforcing 36 C.F.R. section 327.13 as to law-abiding citizens possessing functional firearms on Corps-administered public lands for the purpose of self-defense. This decision has been appealed to the Ninth Circuit and is not final. Recently, USACE has requested the case to be moved into mediation because it is reconsidering its firearm policy.

B. California State Lands

Firearms are generally prohibited in the state park system[110] and are only permitted in areas (including state marine recreational management areas) that are developed for the use of firearms.[111] There are some exceptions to this general restriction. Specifically, a person can possess a firearm in:

(1) Underwater parks or designated archery ranges where the Department of Parks and Recreation finds that it is in its best interest; *and*

(2) Lands open to lawful hunting; *and*

(3) Unloaded firearms that are inoperable or stored to prevent their ready use within either a temporary lodging or a mechanical mode of conveyance (*e.g.*, car, bike, RV, boat, etc., but not a horse).[112]

The restrictions listed above are separate from those in "state wildlife areas." Firearms are generally prohibited from possessing, discharging, and using any firearms in "state wildlife areas," except:

(1) Where the Department of Fish and Wildlife has designated a hunting area or shooting site; *or*

(2) When the person has been issued a permit by the Department of Fish and Wildlife; *or*

(3) As authorized for dog training in a designated area; *or*

(4) When fishing with bow and arrow tackle as defined in Cal. Code Regs. title 14, section 550(b)(9) and allowed in Cal. Code Regs. title 14, section 550(h); *or*

(5) When dispatching a trapped animal as provided in Cal. Code Regs. title 14, section 465.5(g)(1) and 550(ee).[113]

Nonetheless, even in state wildlife areas where a person may be exempted from the general restriction, the use and discharge of firearms can be limited (as to the type/quantity of ammunition, type of firearm, and when the firearm may be used) and in some cases outright banned.[114]

California also designates "State Game Refuges." Unless you have a permit or specific authorization, it is illegal to possess or discharge a firearm (or BB device or bow and arrow) in a game refuge, with few exceptions.[115] Firearms *can* be transported through a game refuge, but only if they are taken apart or encased and un-

---

[110] The Department of Parks and Recreation controls the state park system (*i.e.*, California state parks, park property, recreation areas, natural reserves, etc.). CAL. CODE REGS. tit. 14, §§ 4300, 4313. This restriction includes "any weapon, firearm, spear, bow and arrow, trap, net, or device capable of injuring, or killing any person or animal, or capturing any animal, or damaging any public or private property." CAL. CODE REGS. tit. 14, § 4313(a).

[111] *See* CAL. CODE REGS. tit. 14, § 4501 (allowing hunting in specific state park lands).

[112] CAL. CODE REGS. tit. 14, § 4313.

[113] CAL. CODE REGS. tit.14, §§ 550(cc).

[114] CAL. CODE REGS. tit.14, §§ 550, 551, 552.

[115] CAL. FISH & GAME CODE § 10500.

loaded.[116] Also, when traveling on something other than a public highway, public thoroughfare, or right of way within a State Game Refuge, you have to give the Department of Fish and Game at least 24 hours' notice that you will be transporting a firearm. You have to give your name and address, the name of the refuge, the approximate route, and the approximate time when you intend to travel through the refuge.[117]

The state has also created "ecological reserves"[118] where possessing and discharging firearms is generally prohibited except by law enforcement and in areas that allow hunting.[119] The California Fish and Game Code (Cal. Fish & Game Code) and its companion regulations are full of intricate and specific prohibitions on all sorts of activity involving firearms. Before you enter state-owned lands, you should contact the state entity in charge of the land and ask what the law, regulations, or policies are with respect to firearms. Respectfully request such information in writing. If they are unable to do so, you should speak with an attorney experienced in firearms law before entering state land with a firearm.

1. Other Parks

Be aware that city, county, state, and national parks may be run by different government agencies that have different rules and regulations. As discussed at the beginning of this chapter, local ordinances also often restrict possessing firearms in city or county public parks. If you plan on visiting one of these parks, call ahead, check the park's website, and familiarize yourself with the rules regarding firearms *before* you go.

VI. FIREARM POSSESSION IN UNITED STATES AND INTERNATIONAL WATERS

Federal, state, local and/or another country's laws may apply depending on where your boat is in the water. Federal, state, and local firearms laws apply in waters within California's baseline boundary (coastline),[120] called its "internal waters."[121] To lawfully possess firearms on your boat while in "internal waters," you need to

---

[116] Cal. Fish & Game Code § 10506.

[117] Cal. Fish & Game Code § 10506.

[118] These areas are outlined in Cal. Code Regs. title 14, section 630.

[119] *See* Cal. Code Regs. tit. 14, §§ 550(cc)(4)(B), 630.

[120] Except where otherwise provided, the baseline boundary is the low-water line along the coast. *See* United Nations Convention on the Law of the Sea, (hereinafter, "UNCLOS") 27, art. 5, *available at* http://www.un.org/depts/los/convention_agreements/texts/unclos/unclos_e.pdf (last visited July 12, 2017). Note that the U.S. has never ratified UNCLOS in its entirety but has selected a few sections for adoption via presidential proclamation. It is therefore not controlling law, but its descriptions of the various maritime zones are generally accurate.

[121] "Internal waters" includes rivers, bays, and harbors. *See* Scott Jasper, Securing Freedom in the Global Commons 52 (2010).

know how your boat is classified because "internal waters" are likely "public places" where general firearm restrictions apply.[122]

Three nautical miles[123] from the state's coastline is the state's "seaward boundary." All waters within this three mile stretch are subject to federal and California firearms laws. Local laws do not apply.[124] You may therefore possess firearms in these waters as long as you comply with state and federal law. But this is no easy task, as knowing *how* you are supposed to lawfully possess a fircarm depends on whether you are in a restricted "public place." If you are not, then there are generally no restrictions on possessing firearms. But if you are in such a place, then how you possess firearms depends on whether your boat is considered a residence, vehicle, or place of business.[125] You may also be a licensed fisherman who is exempt from the concealed carry laws.[126]

Since there are no express California restrictions on discharging firearms in this area, the legality of doing so depends on whether it is a restricted "public place," which is sometimes unclear. Whether it is such a "public place" may depend on how close you are to land and other vessels at the time. What is clear, however, is that California does ban discharging a firearm in certain other areas. For example, the discharge ban also includes the "sea otter translocation zone" surrounding San Nicolas Island (except for government employees performing their duties).[127] Possessing and discharging firearms in certain marine areas and ecological reserves is also prohibited.[128]

From the "seaward boundary" to the 12-mile mark is the U.S.'s "territorial waters," where only federal firearms laws apply.[129] There are no real restrictions on possessing a "regular" firearm within this twelve mile zone because federal law does not generally regulate where and how a non-prohibited person can *possess* firearms.[130]

From the baseline out to 200 miles from the coastline is the "exclusive economic zone" (EEZ).[131] From the end of the EEZ to 350 miles from the coastline (or to the end of subsurface land, whichever is shorter) is the "continental shelf."[132] The U.S. has generally asserted authority over natural resources in the continental shelf

---

[122] See Chapters 5 & 6.

[123] All "miles" in this section refer to nautical miles unless otherwise specified (1 "nautical mile" is approximately 1.15 statute miles).

[124] *See People v. Weeren*, 26 Cal. 3d 654, 661-63, 665 (1980); *see also* 43 U.S.C. §§ 1301(b), 1312.

[125] *See* Chapter 6.

[126] P.C. § 25640. See also Chapter 6.

[127] CAL. FISH & GAME CODE § 8664.2. See this section for the coordinates of the areas around San Nicolas Island.

[128] See Cal. Code Regs. title 14, sections 630 and 632 for a list of areas and specific restrictions.

[129] *See* UNCLOS 27, arts. 3-4, *available at* http://www.un.org/depts/los/convention_agreements/texts/unclos/unclos_e.pdf (last visited July 12, 2017). The U.S. accepted this portion of UNCLOS via Presidential Proclamation in 1988. *See* Proclamation No. 5928, 54 Fed. Reg. 777 (Dec. 27, 1988).

[130] Unless it is an National Firearms (NFA) firearm as discussed in Chapters 2 and 9.

[131] *See* UNCLOS 43-44, arts. 55-57, *available at* http://www.un.org/depts/los/convention_agreements/texts/unclos/unclos_e.pdf (last visited July 12, 2017).

[132] *See* UNCLOS 53-54, art. 76, *available at* http://www.un.org/depts/los/convention_agreements/texts/unclos/unclos_e.pdf (last visited July 12, 2017).

region beyond the EEZ. Because firearms are not natural resources, the federal government likely does not assert jurisdiction over them in that region.

Past the "continental shelf" you will either be in international waters or waters belonging to another country. It appears U.S. firearms laws generally do not apply in the EEZ or on the "continental shelf." But, the first twelve miles of the EEZ is called the "contiguous zone."[133] In this zone, federal pollution, taxation, customs, and immigration laws, and possibly international laws, may apply.[134] Though it is unclear what, if any, firearm or ammunition possession restrictions apply, if you are boating in the "contiguous zone," be sure to check the laws concerning pollution, as expended bullets, shot, and casings may bring you under the purview of pollution laws.

Again, even if federal firearms laws apply beyond U.S. "territorial waters" (*i.e.*, past the 12-mile mark) – perhaps under a "flag of the state" theory, where the law of the state (country) a boat originally embarks from is controlling – federal law has very few restrictions on firearm possession, aside from possessing NFA firearms and certain individuals prohibited from possessing firearms under the Gun Control Act (GCA).

Finally, if you will be boating in Canadian, Mexican, or another country's waters, you should learn that country's firearms law and act accordingly. Also, check with the ATF and Customs and Border Protection, as you may have to get a permit and/or fulfill other requirements in order to enter another country's waters or re-enter U.S. waters with firearms.

This is a simplified overview of the laws concerning firearms on boats. Specific questions concerning your boating activities with firearms should be directed to a maritime attorney.

VII. FIREARM POSSESSION AT PROTEST EVENTS

California law prohibits carrying concealed, loaded, or deadly weapons while picketing or engaging in other informational activities in public that relate to a concerted refusal to work.[135] Violating this is a misdemeanor that results in a 10-year firearm prohibition under P.C. section 29805, and there is no exception for those with a valid Carry License.[136]

---

[133] *See* UNCLOS 35, art. 33, *available at* http://www.un.org/depts/los/convention_agreements/texts/unclos/unclos_e.pdf (last visited July 12, 2017). To be clear, the first 24 miles past the "seaward boundary" is considered the "contiguous zone." The U.S. accepted this portion of UNCLOS via Presidential Proclamation in 1999. *See* Proclamation No. 7219, 64 Fed. Reg. 48, 701 (Aug. 2, 1999).

[134] *See* UNCLOS 35, art. 33, *available at* http://www.un.org/depts/los/convention_agreements/texts/unclos/unclos_e.pdf (last visited July 12, 2017).

[135] P.C. § 17510.

[136] P.C. § 17510.

VIII. FIREARM POSSESSION AND POLITICIANS

Under federal law, Congress has directed and authorized the U.S. Secret Service to protect the President of the United States as well as other presidential personnel and their family members, where it is warranted. So, although federal possession laws do not expressly mention the President, the Secret Service can protect the President from private party firearm possession if it threatens the President.

Law enforcement personnel are thus not authorized to arrest or charge peaceful demonstrators who do not pose a threat to the President and who are not violating any laws. But whether the Secret Service considers someone a threat is left to its discretion.

IX. OTHER RESTRICTED PLACES UNDER CALIFORNIA LAW

A. Gun Shows

You must be at least age 18 to go to gun shows or events, unless you are accompanied by a parent, grandparent, or legal guardian.[137] Except for sworn peace officers, show/event security, and vendors, any firearm you bring to the gun show or event must be checked, cleared of any ammunition, and secured to prevent it from being operated. Before you will be allowed to enter the show, an identification tag or sticker must also be attached to it identifying the owner[138] and explaining that sales must go through an FFL.[139] Except for sworn peace officers, security, and vendors, you cannot possess a firearm with ammunition designed to be fired in that firearm at the same time as you are attending a gun show.[140]

B. Polling Places

Any person possessing a firearm at a polling place without city or county written authorization can be prosecuted with a felony or a misdemeanor.[141] Unless a peace officer, security guard, or security personnel meets an exception discussed below, they are in violation of this section as well. This restriction does not apply to:

(1) An unarmed uniformed guard or security personnel who is at the polling place to cast his or her vote; *or*

(2) A peace officer conducting official business or who is at the polling place to cast a vote; *or*

---

[137] P.C. § 27335.
[138] Including the owner's signature, printed name, and government-issued identification.
[139] P.C. § 27340.
[140] P.C. § 27330.
[141] CAL. ELECTIONS CODE § 18544(a).

(3) A private guard or security personnel hired or arranged for by an elections official; *or*

(4) A private guard or security personnel hired or arranged for by the owner or manager of the polling place, as long as not hired solely for Election Day.[142]

In addition, a person can be prosecuted with a felony or misdemeanor if they hire or arrange for a person in possession of firearm or a uniformed peace officer, private guard, security guard, or any person wearing a uniform of a peace officer, guard, or security personnel to be stationed in the immediate vicinity of, or posted at, a polling place without written authorization.[143] Note that, just like "sterile areas" in airports, there is *no* exception to the above restrictions for valid Carry License holders. They can be charged just like anyone else for possessing firearms at a polling place.

C. Playgrounds and Youth Centers

If you unlawfully draw a firearm in a rude, angry, or threatening manner while you are knowingly on, or within, the grounds of certain child care facilities, or carry a firearm in violation of the concealed and/or loaded firearm restriction in public while on or around a playground or youth center when it is open for business, classes, or school-related programs, or whenever minors are using it, you can be prosecuted with a felony or misdemeanor.[144] Those who brandish or carry concealed and/or loaded lawfully should not be in violation of this law.

A "playground" is "any park or recreational area specifically designed to be used by children that has play equipment installed, including public grounds designed for athletic activities such as baseball, football, soccer, or basketball, or any similar facility located on public or private school grounds, or on city or county parks."[145] A "youth center" is "any public or private facility that is used to host recreational or social activities for minors while minors are present."[146]

X. RESTRICTING FIREARM POSSESSION BY PRIVATE BUSINESSES

After a number of gun owners began carrying firearms inside grocery stores, shopping centers, and restaurants in protest of carry restrictions, private businesses and restaurants began adopting policies prohibiting people from bringing firearms into their establishments. For example, some national businesses, such as Buffalo Wild

---

[142] CAL. ELECTIONS CODE § 18544(b).

[143] CAL. ELECTIONS CODE § 18545. But, this restriction does not apply to the owner or manager of the facility or property in which the polling place is located if the private security guard or security personnel is not hired or arranged solely for the day on which the election is held. CAL. ELECTIONS CODE § 18545.

[144] P.C. §§ 417(a)-(b), 25400, 25850, 626.95(a).

[145] P.C. § 626.95(c)(1).

[146] P.C. § 626.95(c)(2).

Wings, Costco, Whole Foods Market, Target, and Starbucks have either prohibited firearms inside their stores[147] or have requested that patrons not carry firearms inside their stores.[148] Some have even gone as far as checking patron's bags and purses for weapons before they enter the establishment. But are these store policies legal in California? And can stores enforce them?

The simple answer to this question is, yes. Although private business cannot arbitrarily exclude customers from their property based on things like race, ethnicity, gender, religion, sexual orientation, medical condition, disability, genetic information, or martial status,[149] California law does not regulate or prohibit private business owners from establishing policies that prohibit firearms inside their stores, restaurants, or businesses.

These policies generally do not carry the weight of the law, meaning that if you lawfully carry a firearm inside a store that has a "no gun" policy in place, you have not committed a criminal act. But, if someone inside the store asks you to leave the premises because you are carrying a firearm in violation of a store policy, then you can be arrested and charged with trespassing[150] if you refuse to leave the store.

Note that although the practice of openly carrying a firearm might be considered a form of protected speech under the First Amendment, private business owners are not government entities and therefore do not violate your right to free speech by prohibiting firearms inside their stores or asking patrons who are carrying firearms to leave the premises.

XI. GENERAL FIREARM DISCHARGE RESTRICTIONS

Outside of specific areas like state parks and refuges owned by the state, California does not generally regulate non-negligent[151] or non-felonious discharge of firearms, leaving it to local entities or those that manage public lands to regulate instead. You should therefore generally look to local laws to determine where it is lawful to discharge firearms.

---

[147] See *Personal Firearms/Guns in Costco Stores*, Costco.com, *available at* https://customerservice.costco.com/app/answers/detail/a_id/709/kw/guns (last visited July 12, 2017); *see also 8 Companies That Have Actually Banned Guns*, The Huffington Post (Sep. 18, 2013), *available at* http://www.huffingtonpost.com/2013/09/18/company-gun-bans_n_3948309.html (last visited July 12, 2017).

[148] See *Target Addresses Firearms in Stores*, Target (July 2, 2014), *available at* https://corporate.target.com/article/2014/07/target-addresses-firearms-in-stores (last visited Oct. 20, 2017); *see also* Open letter from Howard Schultz, CEO of Starbucks Coffee (Sep. 17, 2013), *available at* https://news.starbucks.com/views/open-letter-from- (last visited Oct. 20, 2017).

[149] See 42 U.S.C § 2000a; Cal. Civ. Code § 51.

[150] See P.C. § 602.

[151] See P.C. § 246.3(a)-(b) (making a willful discharge of a firearm in such a *grossly negligent* manner is a possible felony, and a misdemeanor if done so with a BB device).

That being said, California makes it unlawful for you to discharge a firearm at an *unoccupied* motor vehicle or *uninhabited* building or dwelling house *without the owner's permission.*[152]

California also makes it unlawful to discharge "any firearm or other deadly weapon within 150 yards of any occupied dwelling house, residence, or other building or any barn or other outbuilding" related to it, without being the owner or person possessing the premises, or without having the owner or lawful possessor's permission.[153] It is also illegal to shoot a firearm from or onto a public road or highway[154] or to "intentionally discharge a firearm or release an arrow or crossbow bolt over or across a public road or other established way open to the public, in an unsafe and reckless manner."[155] It is also unlawful to "willfully and maliciously" shoot a firearm at an *unoccupied* aircraft.[156] Likewise, you cannot "discharge any firearm within 500 feet of any magazine or any explosive manufacturing plant."[157]

If permitted in the first place, the discharge of firearms in any of the five California state forests is prohibited in the vicinity of camps or within 150 yards of designated camping areas, "residence sites, recreation grounds and areas, and over lakes or other bodies of water adjacent to or within such areas, whereby any person is exposed to injury as a result of such discharge."[158] The California Fish & Game Code also prohibits *discharging* firearms in certain specified refuges.[159]

If you enter private lands, be wary of trespassing. "It is unlawful to enter land for the purpose of discharging a firearm or taking or destroying a mammal or bird, including waterfowl, on that land without having first obtained written permission from the owner, or the owner's agent, or the person in lawful possession of that land, if either of the following is true":

(1) The land belongs to or is occupied by another person and is either under cultivation or enclosed by a fence; *or*

(2) There are signs of any size and wording forbidding trespass or hunting or both displayed along all exterior boundaries of the land, at intervals not less than three to the mile, and at all roads and trails entering the land, including land temporarily inundated by water flowing outside the established banks of a river, stream, slough, or other waterway, which fairly advise a person about to enter the land that the use of the land is so restricted.[160]

---

[152] P.C. § 247(b).

[153] CAL. FISH & GAME CODE § 3004(a).

[154] P.C. § 374c.

[155] CAL. FISH & GAME CODE § 3004(b).

[156] P.C. § 247(a).

[157] CAL. HEALTH & SAF. CODE § 12084.

[158] CAL. CODE REGS. tit. 14, § 1413.

[159] CAL. FISH & GAME CODE § 10662. For example, certain areas of California Fish & Game District 4D in Riverside County are outlined in Cal. Fish & Game Code section 10837.

[160] CAL. FISH & GAME CODE § 2016. See also P.C. § 602(l).

Also, except for lawful self-defense, aiming or pointing a laser scope[161] or laser pointer[162] at anyone in a threatening manner to cause them fear of bodily harm is a misdemeanor.[163]

"[W]illfully and maliciously discharg[ing] a laser at an aircraft,"[164] whether it is moving or not, is also a crime.[165] This rule does not apply to laser development activity by, or on behalf of, the U.S. Armed Forces.[166]

XII. SHOOTING RANGE USE RESTRICTIONS

A well-established range can provide an environment where you can discharge your firearm without fear of criminal prosecution.[167] For the first-time shooter going to the range, make sure you contact the range ahead of time and get information on the kinds of firearms they allow (some ranges are handguns or rifles or shotguns only). If you are bringing ammunition to the range, inquire into what kinds of ammunition you can bring (some ranges do not allow you to shoot steel-jacketed, steel-core, or semi-jacketed ammunition, etc.), what kind of eye/ear wear they require, and whether they provide such protection. If you plan on renting firearms, ask whether the range has firearms for rent and, if so, what the requirements are to rent (ID, age restrictions, number of persons, etc.).

XIII. SUGGESTIONS FOR SHOOTING IN PUBLIC

If you have found a place where you may lawfully shoot, here are some tips:

(1) Since areas where you can discharge your firearm may be closed or restricted, contact the respective state and/or national authorities in these areas *before* shooting. They will be your best authority as to where you can lawfully shoot in these areas. When possible, get the name of the person you spoke with and get their permission in writing beforehand.

(2) Know your surroundings. Even if you find a place to lawfully shoot, you may be near an area where the sound of firearms being fired is not appreciated. Contact law enforcement to let them know where you plan to shoot and ask for suggestions to avoid complaints.

---

[161] A "laser scope" is "a portable battery-powered device capable of being attached to a firearm and capable of projecting a laser light on objects at a distance." The "laser scope" does not need to be attached to a firearm to be a crime. P.C. § 417.25(a)-(b).

[162] A "laser pointer" is "any hand held laser beam device or demonstration laser product that emits a single point of light amplified by the stimulated emission of radiation that is visible to the human eye." P.C. § 417.25(c).

[163] P.C. § 417.25(a).

[164] "Aircraft" means any contrivance intended for and capable of transporting persons through the airspace. P.C. § 247.5.

[165] P.C. § 247.5.

[166] P.C. § 247.5.

[167] Keep in mind that law enforcement members frequent firearm ranges for firearm qualification and training. Make certain the firearms you possess and your activities are lawful.

(3) Shoot only at retrievable, freestanding targets and do not attach targets to living plants or against rocks, plants or solid objects. Under federal law it is illegal to deface/destroy trees, signs, or other objects on federal land that are for the public's enjoyment.[168]

(4) Watch the area behind your intended target. Make certain no one can enter into the area where you are shooting without you seeing them first. Try to choose a place with a natural backstop or berm. Never shoot where you don't know where your rounds will land.

(5) Leave the area as you found it. Pick up your trash, spent casings, targets, etc. If you are using clays or any other launch targets, do not launch them into areas where you cannot go and retrieve pieces later, such as cliffs, steep hillsides, or water.

(6) Discharging firearms directly into the air on the Fourth of July, New Year's Eve, or really *anytime*, is a horrible idea and may subject you to criminal and/or civil liability.

For more information on where to shoot and how to shoot safely, visit the websites of the NRA (http://home.nra.org/), CRPA (http://www.crpa.org/), and the National Shooting Sports Foundation (NSSF) (http://www.nssf.org/).

---

[168] 43 C.F.R. § 8365.1-5(a)(1).

CHAPTER 8:
REGULATION OF "ASSAULT WEAPONS" AND .50 BMG RIFLES

Technically, the term "assault weapon" is meaningless. In firearm technical parlance, an "assault rifle" is military jargon believed to have originally been coined by the Nazis for a rifle that could fire sub- or mid-caliber rounds and allowed choosing either a semiautomatic or fully-automatic (*i.e.*, a "machinegun") fire mode – a unique feature at the time.[1]

The term "assault rifle" fell out of use until it was revived by anti-gun publicists who twisted the term into the politically charged phrase, "assault weapon." This phrase was developed by the anti-gun lobby as a political tactic meant to confuse the general public and underhandedly expand the scope of the term "so as to allow an attack on as many additional firearms as possible on the basis of undefined 'evil' characteristics."[2]

Today, the firearms that California law considers to be "assault weapons" are civilian semiautomatics that are incapable of fully-automatic fire, despite their external appearance. They are legally defined as "assault weapons" for political reasons, based on appearance, name, or cosmetic characteristics, and *not* because they function differently or have more stopping power than other popular semiautomatic firearms. In fact, various firearms legally available in California are practically identical to some that are considered "assault weapons," having only minor modifications and different names. Why some civilian semiautomatics are defined as "assault weapons" and others are not is beyond the scope of this book, and in most cases defies logic.

For a while federal law prohibited creating new firearms with certain characteristics, classifying them as "assault weapons." That federal restriction ended in 2004 and is no longer enforceable. Confusion still exists, however, about the differences

---

[1] The assault rifle first appeared as "the Sturmgewehr 44, a lighter, rapid fire military small arm [that] fired a projectile smaller (and logistically lighter and cheaper) than . . . the standard battle rifle." JOSEPH P. TARTARO, THE GREAT ASSAULT WEAPON HOAX 3 (The Second Amendment Found., 1993).

[2] Bruce H. Kobayashi & Joseph E. Olson, *In Re 101 California Street: A Legal and Economic Analysis of Strict Liability for the Manufacture and Sale of "Assault Weapons,"* 8 STAN. L. & POL'Y REV. 41, 43 (1997).

and overlap between California law and federal law "assault weapon" restrictions. It is common for people to think that certain federal "assault weapon" provisions apply under California law too. For example, one of the federally prohibited features on an "assault weapon" was a bayonet mount.[3] Bayonet mounts are not regulated under California's "assault weapons" law.

To help clear up the confusion surrounding the term "assault weapon" and to understand California's restrictions, it is necessary to understand some of California's "assault weapon" history, the reasoning behind those laws, and how they have changed over the years to create California's current "assault weapon" ban(s).

I. ROBERTI-ROOS ASSAULT WEAPONS CONTROL ACT (AWCA) OF 1989[4]

A. Passing the "Assault Weapon" Ban

Following a tragic school shooting in Stockton, California, on February 13, 1989, the California State Assembly met as a "Committee of the Whole" to discuss implementing a state-wide "assault weapon" ban.[5] At the time the firearms used in the shooting were characterized by the California Legislature as "semi-automatic military assault rifles."[6] Attorney General (AG) John Van de Kamp testified to the "Committee of the Whole" that the number of semiautomatic firearms seized by law enforcement and used in crimes had doubled in the preceding two years, and those used in shootings had gone up nearly 300%. He concluded: "Clearly, we are seeing an escalation in the arms race, and law enforcement is losing."[7]

The debate surrounding the regulation of "assault weapons" can be summarized as follows:

> Originally, both Senate Bill No. 292 (1989–1990 Reg. Sess.) (Senate Bill 292), introduced by Senator Roberti, and Assembly Bill No. 357 (1989–1990 Reg. Sess.) (Assembly Bill 357), introduced by Assemblyman Roos, defined assault weapons generically. As amended in the Senate on January 31, 1989, Senate Bill 292 defined "assault weapons" to include, for example, "[a]ll semiautomatic action, centerfire rifles that accept detachable magazines with a capacity of 20 rounds or more." The parallel provision of Assembly Bill 357, as amended in the Assembly on February 27, 1989, was identical. Although a majority in the Senate favored the approach of defining assault weapons generically, that approach was not acceptable to a

---

[3] 18 U.S.C. § 921(a)(30)(B)(iii) (1994).

[4] P.C. §§ 30500-31115.

[5] 1 Cal. Assem. J. (1989-1990 Reg. Sess.) pp. 436-37; *see also Kasler v. Lockyer*, 23 Cal. 4th 472, 482 (2000).

[6] 1 Cal. Assem. J. (1989-1990 Reg. Sess.) pp. 436-37; *see also Kasler v. Lockyer*, 23 Cal. 4th 472, 482 (2000).

[7] *Kasler v. Lockyer*, 23 Cal. 4th 472, 484 (2000) (citing SB 292, 1989-1990, Leg., Reg. Sess., (Cal. 1989)).

majority of the Assembly .... Assemblyman Charles W. Quackenbush ... was quoted as saying, "As it stands right now, I am against [the legislation]. There would have to be major changes for me to support it." According to the Los Angeles Times, "Quackenbush and other opponents say the bills would ban some legitimate hunting rifles as well as assault weapons and say they could support a measure that contained a more exact definition of assault weapons."[8]

SB 292 passed the Senate on March 9, 1989.[9] This bill ultimately followed the generic definition approach and banned firearms based upon their features, a restriction similar to the Category 3 definition of "assault weapons" (discussed below). Governor George Deukmejian, however, disapproved of the generic definition approach used in the senate bill and preferred the "make and model" approach that was later adopted by the Assembly in AB 357.[10] In contrast to the generic definition approach, the Assembly chose to list the firearms by name, manufacturer, and model instead of describing the firearms with an ambiguous definition. Nearly a month after the Assembly passed AB 357, the Assembly Public Safety Committee amended SB 292 to replace the generic definition of "assault weapons" with the much "more sensible" list approach.[11]

On May 15, 1989, a Senate Assembly conference committee added a provision to rid the marketplace of "facsimile assault arms that are so close to being the real thing that they constitute an assault weapon."[12] This provision also allowed firearms to be added to the list of "assault weapons." In order to do this, however, the AG had to persuade a Superior Court judge that the firearm was a "facsimile" of one already on the banned list.[13]

On May 24, 1989, Governor Deukmejian signed the "Assault Weapon Control Act" (AWCA). But, before he signed the measures, he claimed:

> It's well known that some drug dealers and violent gang members are using assault-type weapons .... In the face of such firepower, our state's courageous law enforcement officers need all the help that we can give them as they seek to preserve our public safety ....[14]

---

[8] *Kasler v. Lockyer*, 23 Cal. 4th 472, 485 (2000) (citing Ingram, *State Anti–Gun Measures Facing an Uncertain Fate*, L.A. TIMES, Feb. 24, 1989, at. I32, cols. 3–4). Ironically, Assemblyman Quackenbush is pointed to as the key vote that resulted in the passing of the "assault weapon" ban.

[9] *Kasler v. Lockyer*, 23 Cal. 4th 472, 486 (2000).

[10] *Kasler v. Lockyer*, 23 Cal. 4th 472, 486 (2000).

[11] *Kasler v. Lockyer*, 23 Cal. 4th 472, 486 (2000).

[12] *Kasler v. Lockyer*, 23 Cal. 4th 472, 486 (2000).

[13] *Kasler v. Lockyer*, 23 Cal. 4th 472, 486 (2000) (citing Ingram, *Panel Votes Compromise on Assault Weapons Ban*, L.A. TIMES, May 16, 1989, at I3, col. 5; *see also* Sample, *Conferees Approve Gun-Ban Compromise*, SACRAMENTO BEE, May 16, 1989, p. A3).

[14] *Kasler v. Lockyer*, 23 Cal. 4th 472, 486-87 (2000) (citing Sample, *Duke Signs into Law Ban on Most Assault Arms*, SACRAMENTO BEE, May 25, 1989, p. A1).

As enacted, the AWCA began with the Legislature's findings and declarations[15]:

The Legislature hereby finds and declares that the proliferation and use of assault weapons poses a threat to the health, safety, and security of all citizens of this state. The Legislature has restricted the assault weapons specified in [California Penal Code (P.C.)] Section 12276 based upon finding that each firearm has such a high rate of fire and capacity for firepower that its function as a legitimate sports or recreational firearm is substantially outweighed by the danger that it can be used to kill and injure human beings. It is the intent of the Legislature in enacting this chapter to place restrictions on the use of assault weapons and to establish a registration and permit procedure for their lawful sale and possession. It is not, however, the intent of the Legislature by this chapter to place restrictions on the use of those weapons which are primarily designed and intended for hunting, target practice, or other legitimate sports or recreational activities.[16]

Keeping in mind the AWCA's stated goal of banning firearms for their supposed "high rate of fire" and their "capacity for firepower" versus the actual facts concerning how few "assault weapons" are actually used in crimes and how they function, the banning of these firearms and turning their possession into felony violations of California law was not logically justified for several reasons.

First, in early 1989 the Bureau of Justice Information Service's "assault rifle" survey results showed less than 1,000 annual so-called "assault rifle use in crime" incidents in each of the preceding three years.[17] As a result, AG John Van de Kamp decided not to support "assault weapon" legislation without hard data.[18] After the Stockton shooting, sponsors of the AWCA decided that "'certain weapons probably had too large a constituency to ever be worth the [political] risk of including' and that '[i]nformation on assault weapons would not be sought from forensic laboratories as it was unlikely to support'" the mantra the legislation was based on, *i.e.*, drug-trafficking organizations and violent criminals preferred "assault weapons."[19] Had the "hard data" been revealed, the Bureau of Forensic Services and Bureau of Narcotics Enforcement records would have shown a very low number of "assault weapons" that were used in connection with serious crimes.[20] Officials confirmed

---

[15] These findings were used, in part, as a basis for a court to declare that unlawful possession of an "assault weapon" was a crime of moral turpitude. *People v. Gabriel*, 206 Cal. App. 4th 450, 456-58 (2012).

[16] P.C. § 30505(a).

[17] Bruce H. Kobayashi & Joseph E. Olson, *In Re 101 California Street: A Legal and Economic Analysis of Strict Liability for the Manufacture and Sale of "Assault Weapons,"* 8 STAN. L. & POL'Y REV. 41, 44 (1997) (citing Memorandum from Robert W. Drake, Chief, Bureau of Justice Information Services, California Department of Justice, to Carolyn McIntyre, Supervising Special Agent, Legislative Unit, California Department of Justice 1 (Jan. 10, 1989)).

[18] Bruce H. Kobayashi & Joseph E. Olson, *In Re 101 California Street: A Legal and Economic Analysis of Strict Liability for the Manufacture and Sale of "Assault Weapons,"* 8 STAN. L. & POL'Y REV. 41, 44 (1997).

[19] Bruce H. Kobayashi & Joseph E. Olson, *In Re 101 California Street: A Legal and Economic Analysis of Strict Liability for the Manufacture and Sale of "Assault Weapons,"* 8 STAN. L. & POL'Y REV. 41, 44 (1997).

[20] The statistics showed that only 1.8-2.9% of serious crimes involved an "assault weapon." Bruce H. Kobayashi & Joseph E. Olson, *In Re 101 California Street: A Legal and Economic Analysis of Strict Liability for the Manufacture and Sale of "Assault Weapons,"* 8 STAN. L. & POL'Y REV. 41, 44 (1997) (citing Memorandum from S.C. Helsley,

that, at least in 1989 and thereafter, violent criminals, gangs, and drug dealers[21] did not typically choose "assault weapons" to commit serious crimes.

When the legislature determined which firearms to ban and how to ban them, it did not base its decisions on what firearms were actually used to commit crimes, but instead it focused on the appearance of the weapons. As a result, the Legislature's final list of good/bad guns resulted in "an odd collection of firearms which range[d] from the long out of production, to exorbitantly expensive."[22] As a California Department of Justice (DOJ) official noted, the efforts to draw rational distinctions between what should and should not be regulated "were hampered by: (1) the absence of a specifically defined problem; (2) artificial distinctions made between semiautomatic weapons, such as targeting the semiautomatic AK look-alike but exempting the functionally-identical Ruger Mini-30"; (3) the legislation's drafters not having firearm knowledge; and (4) that most of the listed weapons constituted "no conceivable threat."[23] Nonetheless, the AG later claimed the "weapons listed in [P.C.] section 12276 are 'highly dangerous offensive weapons which are unambiguously hazardous.'"[24]

Interestingly, the Norinco model 56S rifle used in the Stockton school shooting, the rifle that prompted the introduction of the "assault weapon" ban in the first place, was not included in the original list of banned "assault weapons."[25]

The legislature's reasons for creating the AWCA are nonsensical. As originally enacted, the legislature cited two main concerns for implementing the AWCA within former P.C. section 12275.5: "assault weapons" have a "high rate of fire" and a "capacity for firepower."[26]

Assistant Director, Investigation and Enforcement Branch, California Department of Justice, to G.W. Clemons, Director, Division of Law Enforcement, California Department of Justice 1 (Feb. 13, 1991)).

[21] Bruce H. Kobayashi & Joseph E. Olson, *In Re 101 California Street: A Legal and Economic Analysis of Strict Liability for the Manufacture and Sale of "Assault Weapons,"* 8 STAN. L. & POL'Y REV. 41, 44 (1997) (citing David Freed, *Assault Rifles Are Not Heavily Used in Crimes,* L.A. TIMES, May 20, 1992, at A18; David Kopel, *Rational Basis Analysis of "Assault Weapon" Prohibition,* 20 J. CONTEMP. L. 381, 406-10 (1994) (reviewing data from numerous jurisdictions); Eric C. Morgan, *Assault Rifle Legislation: Unwise and Unconstitutional,* 17 AM. J. CRIM. L. 143, 151-52 (1990); Gary Kleck, *Assault Weapons Aren't the Problem,* N.Y. TIMES, Sept. 1, 1992, at A1 ("Assault Weapons" are used in less than one-half of one percent of violent crimes); *What Is An Assault Weapon?,* WALL ST. J., Aug. 25, 1994, at A12 (0.14% of violent crimes in Florida and 0.026% in New Jersey involve "assault weapons")).

[22] NEAL KNOX, THE GUN RIGHTS WAR 269 (2009) (citing S.C. Helsley, Assistant Director, Investigation and Enforcement Branch, California Department of Justice, to Patrick Kenady, Assistant Attorney General, California Department of Justice (Feb. 14, 1991)).

[23] Bruce H. Kobayashi & Joseph E. Olson, *In Re 101 California Street: A Legal and Economic Analysis of Strict Liability for the Manufacture and Sale of "Assault Weapons,"* 8 STAN. L. & POL'Y REV. 41, 44 (1997) (citing Memorandum from S.C. Helsley, Acting Assistant Director, Investigation and Enforcement Branch, California Department of Justice, to Patrick Kenady, Assistant Attorney General, California Department of Justice 3-4 (Feb. 14, 1991)).

[24] *In re Jorge M.,* 23 Cal. 4th 866, 882 (2000).

[25] Bruce H. Kobayashi & Joseph E. Olson, *In Re 101 California Street: A Legal and Economic Analysis of Strict Liability for the Manufacture and Sale of "Assault Weapons,"* 8 STAN. L. & POL'Y REV. 41, 44 (1997) (citing Letter from Thomas R. Heuer, Deputy Legislative Counsel of California, to Hon. Richard L. Mountjoy, Member of California State Assembly 4-5 (May 31, 1989)).

[26] P.C. § 12275.5(a) (1989) (currently codified at P.C. § 30505(a)).

As discussed above, and again in Chapter 9, a big difference exists between semiautomatic and fully-automatic firearms. All of the AWCA's firearms are semiautomatic, meaning they fire one round per one trigger pull. These firearms do not have a "rate of fire" significantly different than any other semiautomatic used for hunting or sport, either then or now. None of the firearms listed as "assault weapons" fire fully automatic. If they were fully automatic, they would be classified as "machineguns," which arc already heavily regulated under California and federal law and were already banned at the time the AWCA was enacted.

The legislature also claimed it was concerned about an "assault weapon's" "capacity for firepower," but did not explain what that means. If the legislature was implying that the cartridges used in the listed "assault weapons" are more powerful than those used for sporting or hunting, they were wrong. There are thousands of firearms (handguns, shotguns, and rifles) that use more powerful cartridges than the firearms banned on the "assault weapon" list with more "capacity for firepower."[27] For example, a Colt AR-15 generally uses a .223 caliber cartridge.[28] Compare that to the M1 Garand, which is also semiautomatic. The M1 Garand typically fires a much larger, and more powerful, .30-06 round. The Colt AR-15 is a prohibited firearm under California law, while the M1 Garand may be purchased through the mail under federal law, without even using a Federal Firearms Licensee (FFL), from the federal Civilian Marksmanship Program.[29]

None of the reasons for passing the AWCA hold up under scrutiny. And sadly, thousands of Californians have been prosecuted for possessing, transporting, or making firearms that are lawful to possess throughout most of the country and are virtually identical to firearms available to 18-year-olds in California stores because they were unaware their firearms fell under the "assault weapon" law. The legacy of the AWCA is one of inadvertent violations, accidental felons, and injustice.

II. THE "ASSAULT WEAPON" BAN'S EVOLUTION

A. The Original 1989 AWCA Ban

The original AWCA restricted over 55 semiautomatic firearms by name.[30] At the time, this list included the "Avtomat Kalashnikovs (AK) series," "Colt AR-15 and CAR-15 series" rifles,[31] the "SKS with detachable magazine," and any firearm de-

---

[27] The ban on .50 BMG rifles, which use some of the largest commercially available cartridges, occurred almost 15 years *after* the AWCA ban.

[28] Depending on how the firearm is configured, the AR-15 can chamber several calibers; .223 is probably the most common.

[29] See the Civilian Marksmanship Program for details on how to acquire M1 Garands, carbines and other firearms from the federal government at: http://www.thecmp.com/. This website also depicts several firearms matching the description of California "assault weapons" being used at national shooting events.

[30] *See* P.C. § 12275 (1989) (currently codified at P.C. § 30500-30530); *see also Kasler v. Lockyer*, 23 Cal. 4th 472, 477 (2000).

[31] 1989 Cal. Stat. 60-70.

clared an "assault weapon" by a court under former P.C. section 12276.5[32] (a.k.a. "the add-on provision"). Under the add-on provision, the AG could petition courts in counties with populations greater than 1,000,000 to temporarily suspend the manufacture, sale, distribution, transportation, importation, or the giving or lending of a firearm alleged to be an "assault weapon" under former P.C. section 12276 if the firearm was either:

(1) Another model by the same manufacturer or a copy by another manufacturer of an "assault weapon" and listed in subdivision (a), (b), or (c) of former P.C. section 12276 which is identical to one listed therein except for slight modifications or enhancements including, but not limited to: a folding or retractable stock; adjustable sight; case deflector for left-handed shooters; shorter barrel; wooden, plastic or metal stock; larger magazine size; different caliber; or bayonet mount; *or*

(2) First manufactured or sold to the California general public after June 1, 1989, and has been redesigned, renamed, or renumbered from one of the firearms listed in subdivision (a), (b), or (c) of former P.C. section 12276, or that another company manufactured or sold under a licensing agreement to manufacture or sell one of the firearms listed in subdivision (a), (b), or (c) of former P.C. section 12276, regardless of the production or distribution company, or the country of origin.[33]

Once a court temporarily suspended a firearm, the DOJ had to notify the public. The court who suspended it would then schedule a hearing to determine whether to permanently declare the firearm an "assault weapon."[34]

The law required California citizens who lawfully possessed an "assault weapon" before June 1, 1989, to register their firearm(s) with the state by January 1, 1991.[35] Transferring a listed "assault weapon" was generally prohibited on and after January 1, 1990.[36]

B. 1991 Amendment

In 1991, firearms were added to the AWCA list including the following: "Made in China AK, AKM, AKS, AK47, AK47S, 56, 56S, 84S, and 86S."[37] The language about the "Avtomat Kalashnikovs (AK) series" and "CAR-15 series" was removed, while the subsection banning "Colt AR-15 series" remained. And "[a]ll AK series" were added to the list.

---

[32] 1989 Cal. Stat. 60-70.

[33] P.C. § 12276.5 (1990).

[34] P.C. § 12276.5 (1990).

[35] *See* P.C. § 12285(a)(1) (1990) (currently codified at P.C. § 30900(a)).

[36] P.C. § 12285 (1990).

[37] *See* P.C. § 12276 (1992) (currently codified at P.C. § 30510). The firearm used in the Stockton shooting was also finally added to the list of prohibited weapons; the "Norinco 56S."

Two additional subsections of former P.C. section 12276 would come back to haunt California firearm owners: subsections (e) and (f). Subsection (e) stated "[t]he term 'series' includes all other models that are only variations, with minor differences, of those models listed in subdivision (a), regardless of manufacturer."[38] The legislature also added subsection (f) to supposedly make it clear that they intended to: (1) ban the listed firearms, (2) ban those added by the add-on procedure, and (3) ban "any other models which are only variations of those weapons with minor differences, regardless of the manufacturer."[39] The Legislature explained that it had "defined assault weapons as the types, series, and models listed in this section because it was the most effective way to identify and restrict a specific class of semiautomatic weapons."[40]

Finally, former P.C. section 12276.5 was amended to allow the DOJ to add firearms to the list deemed "assault weapons" by the add-on procedure or by the DOJ itself.

The rationale for these changes was later explained by the California Supreme Court in *Harrott v. County of Kings*:

> When the AWCA was originally enacted, the Legislature clearly intended to reach all series assault weapons. In amending section 12276 to add subdivision (e), the Legislature articulated the standard under which the Attorney General was to *administratively* identify the semiautomatic firearms considered to be series assault weapons.[41]

The registration cut-off date was extended too. The new registration date was extended 90 days after the bill's enactment, and the additional subsections became effective March 31, 1992.[42]

The reason for this extension is also discussed in *Harrott*:

> [C]onsidering the fact that the great majority of gun owners are law abiding citizens, regardless of their opinion of a particular law, it is unlikely that a 90% rate of noncompliance can [be] explained as a concerted political statement. Far more likely is the possibility that owners of assault weapons were simply unaware of the deadline, *or unaware that their particular weapons were included on the list of proscribed firearms.* The low rate of compliance evident at the time of the registration deadline led the Attorney General to suggest an extension permitting lawful compliance, on the grounds that *no public interest is served by punishing a large class of individuals for failure to perform due to insufficient disclosure of the law. Certainly, respect for the law is not served by the punishment of individuals*

---

[38] P.C. § 12276(e) (1992).
[39] P.C. § 12276(f) (1992).
[40] P.C. § 12276(f) (1992).
[41] *Harrott v. Cnty. of Kings*, 25 Cal. 4th 1138, 1150 (2001) (emphasis in original).
[42] *See* P.C. § 12285(f) (1992).

lacking an opportunity to know its terms and conditions. Thus, some additional opportunity for compliance, accompanied by a genuine education effort, seems reasonable.[43]

At the same time, former P.C. section 12289[44] was added to the AWCA, allowing for "assault weapon" registration education and notification programs. Despite the legislature's mandate that the DOJ create an education and notification program, California's confusing "assault weapon" laws have not become clear even though it has been over 25 years since the AWCA passed. Law-abiding citizens with no criminal history are still being prosecuted today for possessing firearms they did not know met the "assault weapon" definition.

During the registration period and subsequent extension, the DOJ admitted that so much confusion existed as to what firearms need to be registered that as many as 25-30% of the total registrations filed might have been unnecessary.[45]

For a while, the DOJ allowed "late" firearm registration, but then invalidated those registrations to settle litigation brought by the gun control lobby. That move invalidated 16,000 registered firearms, making them illegally possessed unregistered "assault weapons" overnight. Notices then went out to those people who owned late-registered firearms stating that their firearms had to be surrendered. That is, registration led to confiscation. Fortunately, attorneys representing the NRA stopped this confiscation process, but gun owners were left with few options and they had to destroy the guns or move them out of state[46]

The "assault weapons" make and model list was again modified in 1992 and 1993 and then remained unchanged until 1999. During this time, semiautomatic firearms could be designated "assault weapons" by being listed by make and/or model by the legislature, by being similar to certain models listed in former P.C. section 12276[47] (a.k.a. "series") models, or by being declared an "assault weapon" by the DOJ through the add-on process.[48]

C. SKS With Detachable Magazine

The "SKS with detachable magazine" caused the most confusion on the early "assault weapon" list. As discussed above, the legislature intended to ban certain fire-

---

[43] *Harrott v. Cnty. of Kings*, 25 Cal. 4th 1138, 1150-51(2001) (emphasis in original, citations omitted).

[44] Currently codified at P.C. section 31115.

[45] Bruce H. Kobayashi & Joseph E. Olson, *In Re 101 California Street: A Legal and Economic Analysis of Strict Liability for the Manufacture and Sale of "Assault Weapons,"* 8 Stan. L. & Pol'y Rev. 41, 44 (1997) (citing Memorandum from S.C. Helsley, Acting Assistant Director, Investigation and Enforcement Branch, California Department of Justice, to Randy Rossi, Chief, BOCCI (July 29, 1991)).

[46] *See HCI v. Lungren*, No. A083872 (Cal. Ct. App. Dec. 15, 1997). AG Lockyer ultimately reached a "settlement" with HCI in this case, and the confiscation process was stopped. HCI is the abbreviation for Handgun Control, Inc. – the (not so subtly named) precursor to the Brady Campaign.

[47] P.C. § 12276 (1992) (currently codified at P.C. § 30510). "'[B]ecause it was the most effective way to identify and restrict a specific class of semiautomatic weapons.'" *Kasler v. Lockyer*, 23 Cal. 4th 472, 488 (2000) (citing P.C. § 12276(f) (1992)).

[48] "The Legislature was mindful of the fact that the section 12276 list was not, and could not be, complete. In its uncodified findings and declarations, the Legislature explained that the add-on provision was intended to compensate for the inherent limitations of the list approach." *Kasler v. Lockyer*, 23 Cal. 4th 472, 488 (2000).

arms as "assault weapons" because of their make/model designation. But the SKS was banned under the phrase "SKS with detachable magazine." This term is not a make and model designation, and was undefined by statute or regulation at the time.

The legal issues surrounding this firearm culminated in the case of *People v. Dingman.*[49] In that case, Mr. Dingman was prosecuted for possessing an unregis-

tered SKS rifle with a supposedly "de-tachable" magazine. Experts pointed out that Mr. Dingman's rifle, a type 56, was originally manufactured with a "fixed" magazine.[50] A different SKS, type 84, was manufactured with a "detachable" magazine. The problem with this case was that the AG had

Example of a SKS with detachable magazine

concluded that only the type 84 was banned, even if the type 56 was retrofitted with an aftermarket detachable magazine. Moreover, the AG had previously allowed thousands of California citizens to purchase SKS type 56s and convert them from fixed magazines into a firearm with a detachable magazine after the original "as-sault weapon" ban.

Example of a SKS without detchable magazine

The California Court of Appeal ruled it did not matter whether the firearm was originally manufactured with a fixed or a detachable magazine, but simply that the SKS was contra-band if it had a detachable magazine.[51] Mr. Dingman appealed this decision to the California Supreme Court. In an unprecedented move the AG's office wrote to the high court in support of Mr. Dingman and his request for review. The review was granted and the Court of Appeal decision was vacated. But, due to a number of articles in the *Los Angeles Times* that strongly criticized AG Dan Lundgren for sup-porting Mr. Dingman, the AG's office withdrew its prior support, and the Califor-nia Supreme Court reversed the grant of review (without even hearing the case). The case was then sent back to the Court of Appeal and remains de-published.

Given the confusion and problems surrounding the SKS[52] rifle, the California legislature enacted former P.C. section 12281,[53] which created immunity for those who manufactured, distributed, transported, imported, possessed, possessed for sale, offered for sale, or transferred SKS rifles for commercial purposes between

---

[49] *People v. Dingman,* 55 Cal. Rptr. 2d 211(1996), *superseded by* 924 P.2d 97 (Cal. 1996).

[50] *People v. Dingman,* 55 Cal. Rptr. 2d 211, 212-13 (1996), *superseded by* 924 P.2d 97 (Cal. 1996).

[51] *People v. Dingman,* 55 Cal. Rptr. 2d 211, 217 (1996), *superseded by* 924 P.2d 97 (Cal. 1996).

[52] The immunity also extended to all "SKS rifles" meaning "all SKS rifles commonly referred to as 'SKS Sporter' versions." P.C. § 12281(i) (1998) (currently codified at P.C. § 30710).

[53] AB 48, 1998-1999 Leg., Reg. Sess. (Cal. 1998).

January 1, 1992, and December 19, 1997.[54] These firearms were thus immune from being seized as "assault weapons" until January 1, 2000.[55] This law also required those possessing SKS rifles to relinquish them to the DOJ or law enforcement, sell them, take them out of state, or destroy them as permitted by former P.C. section 12285.[56] Note, though, that the SKS with detachable magazine is listed amongst the make/model "assault weapons," but this actually refers to the Norinco SKS with detachable magazine.

Another court case, *Kasler v. Lockyer,*[57] and 1999's SB 23 triggered the next two major changes in California "assault weapons" law.

D. *Kasler* and "Category 2 Assault Weapons"

In *Kasler,* the California Supreme Court summarized the statutory provisions governing whether a semiautomatic firearm is considered an "assault weapon." Prior to the AWCA's amendment in 1999 (SB 23), semiautomatic firearms were designated "assault weapons" by (1) being listed by type, series, and model in former P.C. section 12276, or (2) by being declared an "assault weapon" under the add-on procedure.[58]

AK or AR-15 "series" firearms could be added to the "assault weapon" list because former P.C. section 12276(e) made the term "series" include "all other models that are only variations, with minor differences, of those models listed" in former P.C. section 12276 regardless of manufacturer and former P.C. section 12276.5(g) granted the AG authority to "prepare a description for identification purposes, including a picture or diagram, of each assault weapon listed in Section 12276, and any firearm declared to be an assault weapon pursuant to this section."[59] Once added to the list, those firearms were illegal to possess in California. Immediately following the California Supreme Court's decision in *Kasler,* the DOJ did just that and added over sixty AR-15 and AK "series" firearms to the prohibited list. These new additions to the "assault weapon" list are referred to as "Category 2 assault weapons." The deadline to register them was January 23, 2001.

No real "public education" or "notification program" was ever provided for these newly added "assault weapons." Those who found out about the newly listed firearms had less than six months to register them. Many firearm owners never heard about this change to the law. Those who failed to register their firearms became criminal possessors of "assault weapons" overnight – again, often unknowingly.

---

[54] P.C. § 12281 (1998) (currently codified at P.C. § 30715).

[55] P.C. § 12281 (1998) (currently codified at P.C. § 30715).

[56] P.C. § 12281 (1998) (currently codified at P.C. § 30720).

[57] *Kasler v. Lockyer,* 23 Cal. 4th 472 (2000).

[58] *Harrott v. Cnty. of Kings,* 25 Cal. 4th 1138, 1141 (2000); *see* P.C. § 12276.5 (1998) (currently codified at P.C. § 30505).

[59] P.C. § 12276.5(g) (1998).

E. SB 23: Old Definition of "Category 3 Assault Weapons"[60]

In 1999, the Legislature again amended the AWCA to define "assault weapons" a third way, this time generically by a firearm's characteristics.[61] The 1999 amendments did not, however, replace either the list method of designating "assault weapons" in former P.C. section 12276 or the add-on provision of former P.C. section 12276.5.[62] This meant that those amendments created a new category of "assault weapons" known as "Category 3."

In fact, SB 23, which added former P.C. section 12276.1, specifically emphasized "assault weapon" characteristics, as opposed to the make or model, because of "copycat" firearms. The Assembly Committee on Appropriations analysis stated:

> According to the author, copycat weapons have circumvented the Roberti-Roos Assault Weapons Control Act of 1989. This bill attempts to create a definition that treats owners *of identical weapons equally under the law and addresses legal concerns related to the current* definitions. SB 23 takes weapons that are made, then modified, named and re-named off the market. *It fixes the loophole in current law that bans guns by name, not by capability, by providing a generic definition of the weapons.*[63]

Again, this meant that those with firearms meeting the old Category 3 "assault weapon" definition had only one year to register their firearms with the DOJ once SB 23 became effective (*i.e.*, December 31, 2000). Those prosecuted for possessing a Category 3 "assault weapon" during the ban's first year may have received an infraction if it was their first violation of the ban on "assault weapon" possession and if they met other criteria (see below).[64] Now, this offense is almost always prosecuted as a felony.

F. SB 23: Expanding Peace Officer Exceptions

Along with the addition of a new definition of "assault weapons," the 1999 amendments also added two additional provisions relating to peace officers. As originally enacted, the AWCA allowed specified law enforcement agencies to purchase and possess "assault weapons," and allowed officers of those agencies to purchase, possess, and use "assault weapons" during the course of their official duties.[65] The

---

[60] We refer to the "old" Category 3 definition of "assault weapons" or "the pre-2017 'assault weapon' law"—and correspondingly, the "new" Category 3 definition of "assault weapons" or "post-2017 'assault weapon' law"—instead of "Category 3" and "Category 4," respectively, as we did in the last edition of the book. This is because the Code section covering both is the same. Ultimately, we are talking about "assault weapons" based on their features.

[61] Described in former section 12276.1(a), currently codified at P.C. section 30515.

[62] *Kasler v. Lockyer*, 23 Cal. 4th 472, 478 (2000).

[63] Bill Analysis: Hearing on SB 23 Before the Assemb. Comm. on Appropriations, at 4 (July 12, 1999), *available at* http://leginfo.legislature.ca.gov/faces/billAnalysisClient.xhtml?bill_id=199920000SB23# (last visited July 12, 2017) (emphasis added).

[64] P.C. § 12280(c) (2000) (currently codified at P.C. § 30610).

[65] *See* P.C. § 12280(f) (2000) (currently codified at P.C. § 30630).

amendments revised this exception to the "assault weapons" ban, essentially allowing peace officers to possess and use "assault weapons," regardless of whether the officer was on or off duty.[66]

The 1999 amendments also added a new exception for retired peace officers. This new provision allowed certain law enforcement agencies to sell or transfer "assault weapons" to any peace officer who retired from that specific agency.[67] In addition, the provision provided that a retired peace officer who received an "assault weapon" upon retirement from a law enforcement agency was exempt from the general restrictions on possession and use of an assault weapon under the AWCA.

In short, the 1999 amendments created a ban on the possession of "assault weapons" by private individual citizens while arbitrarily allowing retired peace officers – who were no differently situated than private individuals – the right to obtain and possess an "assault weapon" from their employer at the time of their retirement.

G. *Silveira*: Assault Weapons and "Equal Protection"

One month after the enactment of the 1999 amendments, the AWCA was challenged in *Silveira v. Lockyer* by a group of individuals who were either required to register their firearms, or were barred from purchasing firearms that fell under the new amended definition of "assault weapon."[68] The parties contended, among other things, that the amended AWCA unconstitutionally infringed upon their right to "bear arms" under the Second Amendment.[69] Significantly, the parties also argued that the off-duty and retired peace officer exceptions that were added to the AWCA violated the Equal Protection Clause of the Fourteenth Amendment.[70]

The Ninth Circuit Court of Appeals disagreed with the parties' contention that the AWCA was unconstitutional under the Second Amendment.[71] In reaching this conclusion, the court erroneously found that the Second Amendment – as interpreted through the now outdated "collective rights model"[72] – did not afford an

---

[66] *See* P.C. § 12280(g) (2000) (currently codified at P.C. § 30635).

[67] *See* P.C. § 12280(h) (2000) (currently codified at P.C. § 30645).

[68] *Silveira v. Lockyer*, 312 F.3d 1052, 1059 (9th Cir. 2002), *abrogated on other grounds by Dist. of Columbia v. Heller*, 554 U.S. 570 (2008).

[69] *Silveira v. Lockyer*, 312 F.3d 1052, 1059 (9th Cir. 2002), *abrogated on other grounds by Dist. of Columbia v. Heller*, 554 U.S. 570 (2008).

[70] *Silveira v. Lockyer*, 312 F.3d 1052, 1059 (9th Cir. 2002), *abrogated on other grounds by Dist. of Columbia v. Heller*, 554 U.S. 570 (2008).

[71] Despite the fact that the Ninth Circuit has not found the AWCA to be unconstitutional under the Second Amendment, in 2016, a district court in the Northern Mariana Islands found that the Commonwealth of the North Mariana Island's ban on "assault weapons," which was similar to the AWCA, violated the Second Amendment. *Murphy v. Guerrero*, 1:14-CV-00026 (D. N. Mar. I Sep. 28, 2016).

[72] In finding that the Second Amendment did not protect an individual's right to possess and carry a firearm, the court applied the "collective rights" model of the Second Amendment. *Silveira v. Lockyer*, 312 F.3d 1052, 1060-61 (9th Cir. 2002), *abrogated on other grounds by Dist. of Columbia v. Heller*, 554 U.S. 570 (2008). This model asserts that "the Second Amendment right to 'bear arms' guarantees the right of the people to maintain effective state militias, but does not provide any type of individual right to own or possess weapons." *Silveira v. Lockyer*, 312 F.3d

individual the right to possess and carry a firearm.[73] Therefore, the court reasoned that the California Legislature was free to enact legislation regulating or prohibiting the possession or use of firearms, including "assault weapons." As a result of the court's finding, the parties were held to not have standing to assert their Second Amendment claim and the AWCA was held to be valid law.

As for the parties' other constitutional claims, the court found that the amended exception for *off-duty* officers did not violate the Equal Protection Clause. The court stated that the exception only allowed off-duty police officers to possess and use "assault weapons" when they were used for law enforcement purposes. The court believed that there was a rational basis for allowing off-duty peace officers to carry and use "assault weapons," as "off-duty officers may find themselves compelled to perform law enforcement functions in various circumstances, and that . . . it may be necessary to have their weapons available."[74] Hence, despite the fact that private individuals are no differently situated than an off-duty peace officer, the court held that it was "manifestly rational for . . . peace officers to possess and use firearms more potent than those available to" the general public, and the off-duty officer exception was upheld.[75] This ruling was also cited by the California Attorney General's Office in 2010 when then Attorney General Jerry Brown wrote an opinion stating that the possession of "assault weapons" is not a protected Second Amendment right in California and that, therefore, allowing retired peace officers to meet the law enforcement exceptions to the AWCA would "contravene both the express language and underlying policy of the Act, and would do nothing to further law enforcement purposes."[76]

In contrast, the court concluded that the exception for *retired* peace officers was unconstitutional under the Equal Protection Clause.[77] Applying the same reasoning above, the court found that there was no rational justification as to why a retired officer should be able to "possess and use assault weapons for any purpose whatsoever."[78] Accordingly, the court held that the retired peace officer exception was an arbitrary classification, as there was no rational reason why a retiree, but not a private individual, should be permitted to carry and use "assault weapons."

1052, 1061 (9th Cir. 2002), *abrogated on other grounds by Dist. of Columbia v. Heller*, 554 U.S. 570 (2008). But, as the Supreme Court has recognized in *Heller* and *McDonald* that an individual *does* have a fundamental right to possess a firearm, this theory is no longer correct. Nonetheless, most of the *Silveira* holding still remains valid.

[73] *Silveira v. Lockyer*, 312 F.3d 1052, 1087 (9th Cir. 2002) *abrogated on other grounds by Dist. of Columbia v. Heller*, 554 U.S. 570 (2008).

[74] *Silveira v. Lockyer*, 312 F.3d 1052, 1089 (9th Cir. 2002), *abrogated on other grounds by Dist. of Columbia v. Heller*, 554 U.S. 570 (2008).

[75] *Silveira v. Lockyer*, 312 F.3d 1052, 1089 (9th Cir. 2002), *abrogated on other grounds by Dist. of Columbia v. Heller*, 554 U.S. 570 (2008).

[76] 93 Ops. Cal. Atty. Gen. 130 (Cal.A.G. Dec. 31, 2010).

[77] *Silveira v. Lockyer*, 312 F.3d 1052, 1089-90 (9th Cir. 2002) *abrogated on other grounds by Dist. of Columbia v. Heller*, 554 U.S. 570 (2008).

[78] *Silveira v. Lockyer*, 312 F.3d 1052, 1091 (9th Cir. 2002), *abrogated on other grounds by Dist. of Columbia v. Heller*, 554 U.S. 570 (2008).

As a result, the exception violated the Equal Protection Clause of the Fourteenth Amendment, and was found unconstitutional.[79]

H. *Hunt*: Clarifying Vague & Ambiguous Terms Under SB 23

Along with the many changes explained above, SB 23 also required the DOJ to adopt regulations to carry out the purpose and intent of the AWCA. The DOJ, under then Attorney General Bill Lockyer, first published notice of proposed regulations on December 20, 1999. And after multiple public comment periods, corresponding responses, and substantial revisions, the regulations were finalized on December 7, 2000 – twenty-four days before the deadline to register firearms that were newly designated as "assault weapons" under SB 23.

In an effort to aid gun owners in determining what firearms were considered "assault weapons" under the new law, the DOJ added a number of definitions to the regulations, including definitions for the terms "detachable magazine," "flash suppressor," and "threaded barrel capable of accepting a flash suppressor, forward pistol grip, or silencer." Not only were these definitions poorly drafted, but they also failed to define other very important terms that were used in SB 23 to define an "assault weapon." For example, the regulations failed to define the term "permanently alter" (as the term was used to define a device that was not considered a "large capacity magazine") or the phrase "capacity to accept" (as in "capacity to accept" a detachable magazines).[80]

Because the newly adopted regulations failed to adequately define certain terms and phrases in SB 23, gun owners found it very difficult to determine exactly what firearms were considered "assault weapons" under the new law and whether they needed to register their firearms with the DOJ or otherwise remove the features from their firearms, disable them, or remove them from the state before the January 1, 2001, registration deadline. Moreover, the lack of guidance on the meaning of certain terms caused a great deal of confusion among prosecutors and law enforcement about what was considered an "assault weapon." Many police and prosecutors, including the San Francisco District Attorney's Office, spoke out against the confusion that was created by the passage SB 23. Still, many police and prosecutors were unwilling to challenge the law in court.

Nonetheless, two California elected District Attorneys (Fresno District Attorney Ed Hunt and Mendocino District Attorney Norm Vorman) decided to challenge SB 23 in *Hunt v. Lockyer* on September 18, 2001.[81]

This lawsuit was meant to force the DOJ to clarify certain terms that were used in SB 23 so that law enforcement, prosecutors, and (most importantly) normal law-

---

[79] *Silveira v. Lockyer*, 312 F.3d 1052, 1091-92 (9th Cir. 2002), *abrogated on other grounds by Dist. of Columbia v. Heller*, 554 U.S. 570 (2008).

[80] These definitions were expanded upon in 2017 for the new Category 3 restriction (discussed later).

[81] I litigated this lawsuit on behalf of District Attorney Hunt and Vorman.

abiding citizens could determine exactly what firearms were considered "assault weapons" under this new law. Specifically, this lawsuit alleged, among other things, that the term "flash suppressor," "threaded barrel capable of accepting a flash suppressor, forward, pistol grip, or silencer," "large capacity feeding device," and "permanently alter" were so unconstitutionally vague and ambiguous that average citizens could not determine what the Legislature meant by these terms. And where the DOJ defined certain terms in the regulations, their application of those definitions were so inconsistent that it only caused more confusion.

Over the course of two years, the DOJ hotly contested this lawsuit. The lawsuit was eventually settled and dismissed to wait for a determination from the Supreme Court in *District of Columbia v. Heller.*

Nevertheless, *Hunt* served several valuable purposes for the gun rights community. The fact that some District Attorneys and law enforcement were willing to speak out and take these positions in court gave credibility to the position of gun rights activists in opposing additional firearm restrictions, commenting on administrative regulations, and defending criminal prosecutions. Moreover, during *Hunt,* the plaintiffs were able to gather thousands of pages of documents regarding the classification of "assault weapons" and "assault weapon" characteristics and depose a number of DOJ experts and employees during the discovery phase of the litigation. This information not only provided great insight into how the DOJ interpreted the definitions of certain terms used in SB 23 and the regulations, but it also proved very useful in future gun rights cases. Interestingly, "detachable magazine" was one of the terms the DOJ defined by regulation to help citizens determine what the specific characteristics of an "assault weapon" were at the time SB 23 passed, and this term was negotiated and discussed with the DOJ before the DOJ ultimately approved of the definition and codified it as:

> any ammunition feeding device that can be removed readily from the firearm with neither disassembly of the firearm action nor use of a tool being required. A bullet or ammunition cartridge is considered a tool. Ammunition feeding device includes any belted or linked ammunition, but does not include clips, en bloc clips, or stripper clips that load cartridges into magazines.[82]

Years later, the DOJ's apparent approval of this definition seemed to be forgotten when the DOJ attempted to redefine the term "detachable magazine" (see Sections II(J), III(C), and III(E) below) and when the Legislature repeatedly attempted to redefine "assault weapon" until they succeeded in 2016 (see Sections II(M), II(N), III(C), and III(E) below)

---

[82] CAL. CODE. REGS., tit. 11, § 5469 (2016).

I. *Harrott* and "Off-List Lower" Receivers

Harrott v. County of Kings[83] was another important case for self-defense advocates because it limited what firearms could be considered "assault weapons." The question presented in *Harrott* was whether the court could declare Mr. Harrott's rifle, an AK "series," an "assault weapon" per former P.C. section 12276(e),[84] which allowed the AG or certain courts to deem firearms with "minor" differences from AK or Colt AR-15 "series" firearms as "assault weapons," when they had not been identified as such in the AG's Assault Weapon Identification Guide (AWIG) or its list of "assault weapons."[85] The California Supreme Court only tolerated the lack of notice about what the government considered an "assault weapon" to a certain point. The *Harrott* court held that for a Category 1 or 2 "assault weapon," the DOJ must list the firearm, including make and model, as an "assault weapon."[86]

This meant that to have semiautomatic firearms declared "assault weapons" under former P.C. section 12276, the AG must use former P.C. section 12276.5's add-on procedure[87] so that *ordinary citizens need only consult the California Code of Regulations* (Cal. Code Regs.) in order to determine what firearms were considered "assault weapons."[88]

This means that to determine whether any firearms are within the AWCA's Category 1 or 2 type "assault weapons," you should only have to consult the list of "assault weapons" identified in the AWIG.[89] And if it is not listed, it cannot be a "Category 1 or 2 assault weapon."

But the AWIG was still problematic as noted in *Harrott*:

[W]e observe that section 12276 lists weapons primarily by manufacturer and model. Accordingly, the identification markings are the most important factor in determining if a particular firearm is an "assault weapon" within the meaning of section 12276. Yet the Identification Guide also suggests markings may vary from gun to gun: Department of Justice staff has attempted to locate examples of each of the identified "assault weapons" to identify accurately the markings on them. However, some of the identified "assault weapons" were not physically located and some which were found were not marked as specified in Section 12276. Accompanying the Identification Guide's photograph of a Valmet M78S (listed in § 12276, subd. (a)

---

[83] *Harrott v. Cnty. of Kings*, 25 Cal. 4th 1138 (2001).

[84] Currently codified at P.C. section 30510(f).

[85] *Harrott v. Cnty. of Kings*, 25 Cal. 4th 1138, 1143-44 (2001).

[86] *See Harrott v. Cnty. of Kings*, 25 Cal. 4th 1138, 1155 (2001).

[87] *Harrott v. Cnty. of Kings*, 25 Cal. 4th 1138, 1155 (2001).

[88] *Harrott v. Cnty. of Kings*, 25 Cal. 4th 1138, 1153 (2001).

[89] The DOJ's AWIG is available at: http://ag.ca.gov/firearms/forms/pdf/awguide.pdf (last visited July 12, 2017). It classifies "assault weapons" into three categories: *Category 1*: former P.C. section 12276(a), (b), and (c) (original make and model list); *Category 2*: former P.C. section 12276 (e) and (f) (regulatory make and model additions to the original make and model list) (partially repealed 2006); and *Category 3*: former P.C. section 12276.1 (SB 23 – generic characteristics/features based "assault weapons").

(16)) is the note, no firearm marked M78S has been located. However, the firearm pictured may be the M78S. A similar note accompanies the photograph of a SIG PE-57 (listed in § 12276, subd. (a)(12)). Consequently, although most firearms listed in section 12276 are likely to be readily identifiable, some instances in which the possessor of a semiautomatic firearm could reasonably be in doubt as to whether the weapon is subject to regulation under the AWCA are also likely.[90]

The DOJ was quick to correct these errors in a later version (and to date the most recent version) of the AWIG, dated November 2001, though Steyr is still misspelled (incorrectly as Steyer) in former P.C. section 12276, as noted by the AWIG.[91]

One thing *Harrott* did not do, however, was restrict the AG's ability to determine that certain semiautomatic firearms are "assault weapons" by simply identifying them as such in the list published by the AG in the California Code of Regulations, but:

> That authority applies only to the two types of firearms defined in [former P.C.] section 12276 by the use of the term series, namely, the AK47 series and the Colt AR-15 series . . . In order to have any other semiautomatic firearms declared assault weapons within the meaning of [former P.C.] section 12276, the [AG] must utilize the add-on procedure set forth in [former P.C.] section 12276.5. And, of course, the [AG's] identification of a particular firearm as a series "assault weapon" would, in an appropriate case, be subject to challenge on the ground the firearm in question did not satisfy the standard set forth in [former P.C.] section 12276 (e), namely that the variations between it and the AK47 series or the Colt AR-15 series were more than "minor."[92]

After *Kasler* and *Harrott*, the AG did not change or add to the prohibited "assault weapons" list. When people contacted the DOJ with questions about firearms not on the "assault weapons" list that did not have the SB 23 features, the DOJ almost always stated that those firearms could be added to the "assault weapons" list in the future. Instead of this having a chilling effect on acquiring AK and AR-15 type firearms, however, Californians increasingly bought the lower receivers of

---

[90] *Harrott v. Cnty. of Kings*, 25 Cal. 4th 1138, 1146 (2001) (citations and internal quotations omitted).

[91] *See* CALIFORNIA ATTORNEY GENERAL, ASSAULT WEAPONS IDENTIFICATION GUIDE 32 (2001) *available at* http://ag.ca.gov/firearms/forms/pdf/awguide.pdf (last visited July 12, 2017).

[92] *Harrott v. Cnty. of Kings*, 25 Cal. 4th 1138, 1155 (2001) (citations omitted).

firearms not listed as "assault weapons" (*i.e.*, "off-list lower receivers")[93] for fear they may not be able to purchase them in the future.[94]

J. The DOJ's Attempts to Attack "Bullet Button" Firearms

Due to the increase in "off-list lower receiver" sales, in 2007 the DOJ tried to modify the "assault weapons" list once again to cover these "off-list lower receivers" and thereby create a new category (Category 4) of impermissible "assault weapons."[95] Groups like the National Rifle Association (NRA) and California Rifle and Pistol Association (CRPA), however, quickly pointed out the problem with the DOJ's plan to add these "off-list lower receivers" to the list.

The NRA and CRPA argued that in *Harrott* the California Supreme Court determined that the AG must list a "series" weapon, *i.e.*, a firearm with similar characteristics to a named "series" model specifically listed in former P.C. section 12276 (namely AK/Colt AR-15 "series" weapons), before it could be identified as an "assault weapon." In order for the AG to add any "series" weapon to the list, the newly identified firearm had to be a *"variation, with minor differences,"* of an AK/Colt AR-15 "series" weapon regardless of the manufacturer.[96]

On the other hand, if the firearm was not an AK/Colt AR-15 "series" weapon, then it could only be added to the "assault weapons" list under the add-on provisions of former P.C. section 12276.5, meaning the firearm must be:

> Another model by the same manufacturer or a copy by another manufacturer of an assault weapon listed in subdivision (a), (b), or (c) of Section 12276 which is identical to one of the assault weapons listed in those subdivisions except for slight modifications or enhancements including, but not limited to: a folding or retractable stock; adjustable sight; case deflector for left-handed shooters; shorter barrel; wooden, plastic or metal stock; larger magazine size; different caliber provided that the caliber exceeds .22 rimfire; or bayonet mount. *The court shall strictly construe this paragraph so that a firearm which is merely similar in appearance but not a prototype or copy cannot be found to be within the meaning of this paragraph.*[97]

---

[93] As used in this chapter, "off-list" means those firearms not on the Category 1 or 2 "assault weapons" list. "Lower" is in reference to the lower receiver of AR-15 type firearms. The lower receiver is the part that is considered to be the "firearm" for transfer purposes (see Chapter 2). While the AR is probably the most common type of receiver sold, the term "off-list lower" is also used to refer to any receiver of any type of firearm that is not make/model prohibited as an "assault weapon." The receiver (or commonly just called the "lower") is the part of the firearm with the markings for determining whether it is a Category 1 or 2 "assault weapon."

[94] *See* Bill Lockyer, *Important Notice: California Department of Justice Information Regarding the Sale/Possession of Newly Identified AR-15/AK 47 "Series" Firearms, available at* http://gunwiki.net/pub/Gunwiki/HistoryOLL/AWpolicyrev4.pdf (last visited July 12, 2017).

[95] *See* Bill Lockyer, *Important Notice: California Department of Justice Information Regarding the Sale/Possession of Newly Identified AR-15/AK 47 "Series" Firearms, available at* http://gunwiki.net/pub/Gunwiki/HistoryOLL/AWpolicyrev4.pdf (last visited July 12, 2017).

[96] *See* P.C. § 12276(e) (2000) (currently codified at P.C. § 30510(f)).

[97] P.C. § 12276.5(a)(1) (2006) (currently codified at P.C. § 30510(d)-(e)) (emphasis added).

In essence, the add-on provisions allowed the DOJ to add "copycat" firearms to the "assault weapons" list if the AG went through the proper administrative and judicial procedures.

The problem with the DOJ's plan to amend the "assault weapons" list was that some of the "off-list lower receivers" were not AK/Colt AR-15 "series" weapons, and therefore the AG could only add these firearms to the list through the add-on provisions of former P.C. section 12276.5. But, using this add-on provision to add the AK/Colt AR-15 "series" firearms to the list as "copycat" firearms did not make sense given that the main purpose of SB 23[98] was to preempt the manufacture of "copycat" weapons by specifically identifying "assault weapons" by certain express characteristics that the Legislature identified as "copycat assault weapons." According to SB 23, if the firearm lacked the specific characteristics of a "copycat" firearm, then it was not considered an "assault weapon."[99]

So, it did not make sense for the AG to use the add-on provisions to add the "off-list lower receivers" to the "assault weapons" list because they lacked the specific characteristics (*i.e., capacity to accept a detachable magazine, a pistol grip, forward pistol grip, etc.*) of a "copycat assault weapon" that were defined in SB 23.

After becoming aware of these challenges, the DOJ issued another notice and changed tactics. This time the DOJ stated it would not update the list of "series" "assault weapons," but instead attacked the definition of "detachable magazine."

Because of the DOJ's definition of "detachable magazine" in 2000 (as explained above), owners of rifles whose magazines were attached to the rifle by screws or a latch and could not be released without using a tool believed their firearms did not have detachable magazines (*i.e.,* "fixed" or "non-detachable magazines") and that registering them as "assault weapons" was not required. Firearm owners generally interpreted this regulation to mean that, to be considered a non-detachable magazine, the firearm would have to automatically re-engage the screw, latch, or other mechanism when the magazine was reinserted into the magazine well. If it did not re-engage automatically, then the magazine would be "detachable" because it could be removed from its seat in the magazine well without tools whenever it was not engaged. But, if a tool had to be used to release the magazine, then it was considered "non-detachable."

In early 2005, relying on the *Harrott* decision and the DOJ's definitions, some firearm manufacturers began importing large quantities of "off-list lowers" to be assembled as firearms that did not possess any of SB 23's "assault weapon" features, specifically "detachable magazines." Firearm owners also began examining the DOJ's regulations, interpretations, and applications to determine how they could modify their receivers to avoid "assault weapon" status. It became widely understood that a receiver could be modified to render it without the "capacity to accept

---

[98] SB 23 was codified at former P.C. section 12276.1 (currently codified at P.C. section 30510(d)-(e)). For the remainder of this section, the provisions of former P.C. section 12276.1 will be referred to as "SB 23."

[99] P.C. § 12276.1 (2001) (currently codified at P.C. § 30515),

a detachable magazine," allowing characteristics otherwise prohibited under SB 23 to be lawfully attached to it. Various new devices and modifications were developed to do this.

Recognizing these complications, the DOJ issued an "Important Notice" on May 9, 2006, explaining that it would not add any more firearms to the list of "assault weapons." The DOJ decided, however, that it would clarify the definition of a "detachable magazine."[100] Specifically, the DOJ explained:

> Law enforcement officials, firearm dealers and the public should be aware that semiautomatic centerfire rifles that are modified to be temporarily incapable of accepting detachable magazines, but can be restored to accommodate detachable magazines, are assault weapons if they have any of the features listed in section 12276.1(a)(1). The Department intends to exercise its power pursuant to section 12276.5(i) to adopt regulations as necessary and proper to carry out the purposes and intent of California law to ban assault weapons in the state.

***

> Individuals who own firearms that meet the generic definition of assault weapons banned by SB 23 must do one of the following in order to comply with existing law: remove the features, sell the firearm (without the features) or permanently[101] alter the firearm so that it cannot accept a detachable magazine.[102]

On November 1, 2006, after scrapping its first set of proposed regulations, the DOJ once again revised its regulations intending to define the phrase "capacity to accept a detachable magazine" as it applied to former P.C. section 12276.1.

One proposed regulation defined this phrase as "currently able to receive a detachable magazine or readily modifiable to receive a detachable magazine."[103] Another defined "readily modifiable" as it is used above in the "capacity to accept" definition as follows:

---

[100] *Bill Lockyer, Important Notice: California Department of Justice Information Regarding the Sale/Possession of Newly Identified AR-15/AK 47 "Series" Firearms, available at* http://gunwiki.net/pub/Gunwiki/HistoryOLL/AWpolicyrev4.pdf (last visited July 12, 2017).

[101] During SB 23's second 15-day comment period, a commentator stated: *"[t]he firearm should have to be permanently modified so that it lacks the capacity to accept a detachable magazine or any of the offensive features* in order for the Department to accept a cancellation of a registration." The DOJ disagreed and responded: *"[t]he Department disagrees with this comment.* Registration cancellation is not exclusive to modification of the firearm, nor does the Department believe permanent modification is required." *Department of Justice Regulations for Assault Weapons and Large Capacity Magazines: Final Statement of Reasons,* CAL. DEPT. OF JUSTICE, Attachment B, http://oag.ca.gov/sites/all/files/pdfs/firearms/regs/fsor.pdf (last visited July 12, 2017).

[102] Bill Lockyer, *Important Notice: California Department of Justice Information Regarding the Sale/Possession of Newly Identified AR-15/AK 47 "Series" Firearms, available at* http://gunwiki.net/pub/Gunwiki/HistoryOLL/AWpolicyrev4.pdf (last visited July 12, 2017).

[103] Proposed CAL. CODE REGS. tit. 11, § 5469(f)(1) (2006).

A firearm is readily modifiable to receive a detachable magazine if it has a device that prevents the magazine from being released but allows the firearm to accept a detachable magazine when the device is removed, reversed, or disengaged, without alterations to the magazine well.[104]

Another provided examples of what is "not readily modifiable" as follows:

A firearm is not readily modifiable to receive a detachable magazine if, for example:

(1) It does not have a magazine well; *or*

(2) The magazine is fixed to the receiver by a continuous ribbon of welding around the perimeter of the magazine well, or by multiple ribbons of welding that are each at least one half inch in length; *or*

(3) The magazine is fixed to the receiver with a rivet (or other irreversible locking device) that is driven through the magazine well and fixed in place with epoxy; *or*

(4) The modification requires disassembly of the action.[105]

Many rifles whose magazines can be made non-detachable were not registered because the DOJ's previous regulations and reports led owners to believe their firearms did not need to be registered if so configured. Since thousands of Californians relied on the DOJ's statements that *temporary* modifications, including modifications involving devices that *could* be "removed, reversed, or disengaged" *were* allowed,[106] when SB 23's registration deadline passed, those who failed to register SB 23-covered rifles would have become felons and their rifles contraband if the DOJ's new regulations were implemented.

In the end, facing opposition including potential NRA lawsuits, as well as the injustice of leading people to believe their rifles were legal then changing the regulations, the DOJ did not implement the proposed regulatory changes.

K. AB 2728: Removing the Add-On Provision and Civil Compromise for "Assault Weapon" Possession

While modifying the "assault weapon" list and changing the "detachable magazine" definition were being discussed, AB 2728 passed unopposed.[107] The bill served two

---

[104] Proposed CAL. CODE REGS. tit. 11, § 5469(f)(2) (2006).

[105] Proposed CAL. CODE REGS. tit. 11, § 5469(f)(3) (2006).

[106] Before the passage of SB 23, countless letters were sent to the DOJ inquiring into whether firearms configured with temporary modifications were "assault weapons" under California law. The DOJ consistently responded to these letters stating that firearms with temporary modifications, including modifications involving devices that could be "removed, reversed, or disengaged," were not prohibited "assault weapons."

[107] Letter from Bill Lockyer, California Attorney General, to Arnold Schwarzenegger, Governor of California (Sept. 1, 2006), *available at* http://www.hoffmang.com/firearms/Lockyer%20Letter%20-%20AB%202728.pdf (last

purposes: to remove the now obsolete "add-on" procedure, and to give a prosecutor the option to make possession of an "assault weapon" a "nuisance," allowing the criminal case to be resolved as a "civil compromise" instead of a misdemeanor or felony conviction.

In a letter supporting AB 2728, AG Bill Lockyer admitted "updating the assault weapons list with new makes and models will serve no purpose other than to completely undermine California law by allowing the proliferation of registered assault weapons."[108]

Since AB 2728's passage, the DOJ has not been authorized to add to the list of prohibited "assault weapons."[109]

L. Second Amendment Challenges to "Assault Weapons" Bans Post-*Heller*

In the wake of the Supreme Court's decision in *District of Columbia v. Heller*, lower courts across the nation have been faced with an increasing number of challenges to "assault weapons" bans under the theory that these laws violate the Second Amendment. The first decision of note to address the constitutionality of California's "assault weapons" ban post-*Heller* was *People v. James*.[110] The question presented in *James* was whether former P.C. section 12280(b) and (c), which prohibited the private possession of an "assault weapon" or .50 caliber BMG rifle, violated Michael James' right to bear arms under the Second Amendment.[111] After applying its understanding of *Heller* to former P.C. section 12280(b) and (c), the California Court of Appeal held that both sections of the AWCA were constitutional because "assault weapons" and .50 caliber BMG rifles were types of weapons that were outside of the scope of protection afforded by the Second Amendment.[112]

As the court explained, under its interpretation of *Heller,* the Second Amendment does not protect an individual's right to possess a military M-16 rifle[113] because the firearm's nature made it an unusually dangerous weapon.[114] The court then analyzed the nature of an "assault weapon" and the legislative intent behind the law and offhandedly concluded that the "assault weapons" were akin to the M-16 rifle because they "are not the type of weapons that are typically possessed

---

visited July 12, 2017).

[108] Letter from Bill Lockyer, California Attorney General, to Arnold Schwarzenegger, Governor of California (Sept. 1, 2006), *available at* http://www.hoffmang.com/firearms/Lockyer%20Letter%20-%20AB%202728.pdf (last visited July 12, 2017).

[109] P.C. § 12276.5 (2006) (currently codified at P.C. § 30520).

[110] *People v. James*, 174 Cal. App. 4th 662 (2009).

[111] *People v. James*, 174 Cal. App. 4th 662, 667 (2009).

[112] *People v. James*, 174 Cal. App. 4th 662, 676 (2009).

[113] Highlighting the Court's confusion of the issue, it kept referring to an "M-16." An M-16 is a *machinegun* and highly regulated under both California and federal law. An AR-15 is semiautomatic and readily available in almost all states.

[114] *People v. James*, 174 Cal. App. 4th 662, 675-76 (2009).

by law-abiding citizens for lawful purposes such as sport hunting or self-defense; rather, these are weapons of war."[115] So, the court found that "assault weapons" fell outside of the protections that *Heller* extended to private citizens under the Second Amendment, and the California Legislature was free to prohibit them from individual use.[116]

A similar challenge to the AWCA was brought in a more recent case named *People v. Zondorak*.[117] In *Zondorak*, the California Court of Appeal was once again faced with the issue of whether former P.C. section 12280(b) of the AWCA infringed upon an individual's right to bear arms under the Second Amendment.[118] But, unlike in *James* where the claim was not firearm specific, William Zondorak specifically argued that his possession of an AK-47 was protected by the Constitution for several self-defense-based reasons.[119] Yet the court disagreed with Zondorak's assertions and upheld the ruling of *James*, *i.e.*, that "assault weapons" do not fall under the ambit of protections afforded by the Second Amendment.[120] Therefore, the court held that Zondorak did not have a constitutional right to possess or own an "assault weapon."[121]

Under the current state of California and federal law, courts have been willing to uphold the constitutionality of the AWCA and its ban on so-called "assault weapons." This could change in the future as a number of cases, such as *Heller II*[122] and *New York State Rifle and Pistol Association v. Cuomo*,[123] have continued to challenge "assault weapons" bans as being unconstitutional under the Second Amendment.

In fact, as recently as 2016, a district court in the Northern Mariana Islands found that the Commonwealth of the Northern Mariana Island's ban on "assault weapons" violated the Second Amendment.[124] Although this opinion is not final

---

[115] *People v. James*, 174 Cal. App. 4th 662, 676 (2009).

[116] *People v. James*, 174 Cal. App. 4th 662, 676-77 (2009).

[117] *People v. James*, 220 Cal. App. 4th 829 (2013).

[118] *People v. Zondorak*, 220 Cal. App. 4th 829, 831 (2013).

[119] *People v. Zondorak*, 220 Cal. App. 4th 829, 836-37 (2013).

[120] *People v. Zondorak*, 220 Cal. App. 4th 829, 836-37 (2013).

[121] *People v. Zondorak*, 220 Cal. App. 4th 829, 837-38 (2013).

[122] *Heller II* was brought in the aftermath of the landmark decision in *District Columbia v. Heller* (Heller I), after the D.C. Council enacted the Firearms Registration Amendment Act (FRA), which banned "assault weapons" and required all firearms to be registered in the District. *Heller* II argued that these restrictions violated the Second Amendment. But on October 4, 2011, the D.C. Circuit Court of Appeals upheld the ban on "assault weapons" and "large-capacity magazines" under the Second Amendment. See *Heller v. District of Columbia* (*Heller* II), 670 F.3d 1244 (D.C. Cir. 2011).

[123] *New York State Rifle and Pistol Association v. Cuomo* is a case that challenges New York's "assault weapons" ban as being unconstitutional under the Second Amendment. See *New York State Rifle and Pistol Association v. Cuomo*, 13-cv-00297-WMS (W.D.N.Y., complaint filed Mar. 21, 2013). In 2015, this case was combined with *Shew v. Malloy*, 994 F. Supp. 2d 234 (D. Conn. 2014), a case that challenged Connecticut's "assault weapons" ban as being unconstitutional under the Second Amendment, and both were heard on appeal to the United States Court of Appeals for the Second Circuit. Unfortunately, on October 19, 2015, the Second Circuit ruled that core provisions of New York and Connecticut's "assault weapon" bans were constitutional under the Second Amendment. See *New York State Rifle and Pistol Association, Inc. v. Cuomo*, --- F.3d ---, 2015 WL 61182288 (2nd Cir. 2015).

[124] *Murphy v. Guerrero*, 1:14-cv-00206 (D. N. Mar. I Sep. 28, 2016).

and may still be appealed, it does suggest that things in the future may change in terms of these restrictions.

And until things change, gun rights groups will persevere in challenging "assault weapon" restrictions under Second Amendment grounds. For instance, in August 2017, several briefs advancing such a position were filed in the *Kolbe v. Hogan* case, including briefs from the NRA and the CRPA Foundation, in support of the plaintiffs' petition to the United States Supreme Court.[125] The *Kolbe* case seeks to have the Supreme Court address whether *Heller* excludes "assault weapons" from Second Amendment protection and whether they may be banned even though they are typically possessed for lawful purposes, including self-defense in the home. Also, on April 24, 2017, I filed the *Rupp v. Becerra* case in federal court to challenge California's entire "assault weapon" regulatory scheme as a violation of the Second Amendment, due process clause, and takings clause of the United States Constitution.[126] Plaintiffs will be conducting discovery and will soon file a motion for summary judgment.

To stay updated on the status of these cases and other changes in firearms laws, visit www.crpa.org.

M. Further Attempts by the California Legislature to Classify More Firearms as "Assault Weapons"

The gun ban lobby has tried to exploit tragedies to push their agenda to ban as many guns as possible. There is no easier target than the ever-expandable class of firearms legally deemed "assault weapons." By expanding the definition of "assault weapon," politicians can condemn common, popular firearms. California is one of the prime battleground states in this fight over terminology.

In 2012, and again in 2013, State Senator Leland Yee[127] attempted to ban California-compliant firearms that possessed "magazine locks." Neither of these bills made it to Governor Brown. Senator Yee's rationale behind the attempted ban was that firearm manufacturers were exploiting a "loophole" in California law. But no "loophole" exists. When these laws were passed, politicians claimed that the problem they needed to address was the speed that a firearm could be reloaded. A magazine lock slows down the reloading process. They got what they asked for, but now it's not enough. This typifies the endless cycle of efforts at gun control. Gun

---

[125] *Kolbe v. Hogan*, 813 F.3d 160 (4th Cir. 2016), *reh'g en banc granted*, 636 Fed.Appx. 880 (4th Cir. 2016), *and on reh'g en banc*, 849 F.3d 114 (4th Cir. 2017). On February 21, 2017, an "en banc" panel of the 4th Circuit issued an opinion upholding Maryland's ban that referred to America's most popular types of rifles as "exceptionally lethal weapons of war." In response, the plaintiffs petitioned the United States Supreme Court for review.

[126] *Rupp v. Becerra*, No. 8:17-cv-00746 (C.D. Cal., Apr. 24, 2017).

[127] On March 26, 2014, former State Senator Leland Yee was arrested on charges of corruption and conspiracy to traffic firearms. *See* Alexei Koseff, *Former Sen. Leland Yee Pleads Guilty to Corruption Charge*, THE SACRAMENTO BEE (July 1, 2015), *available at* http://www.sacbee.com/news/politics-government/capitol-alert/article25986487.html (last visited July 12, 2017). On July 1, 2015, Yee cut a deal with prosecutors and plead guilty to one felony count racketeering. On February 24, 2016, Yee was sentenced to five years in federal prison.

control proponents are told the law won't work. When it doesn't, they say it's because the law doesn't go far enough. So they propose a law that goes further. Again, and again, and again.

In 2013, State Senator Darrell Steinberg jumped into the fray with SB 374, his initial attempt to ban all "semiautomatic, *rimfire*[128] or centerfire rifle[s] that do[] not have a fixed magazine with the capacity to accept no more than 10 rounds."[129] Not only was this bill awkwardly and poorly written, but it would have had a devastating effect on California's firearm community and industry. Hunting and target rifles would have been prohibited, "curio and relic" firearms (highly collectible pieces) would have been illegal, and hundreds of lawful firearm owners would have been prosecuted for illegally possessing these firearms.[130] Thankfully, this bill was vetoed by Governor Brown.

N. AB 1135 and SB 808: 2017 Change to the Definition of "Assault Weapons"

It didn't take long for gun-control advocates to renew their calls from further restrictions on so-called "assault weapon" after the mass shooting that took place in San Bernardino, California on December 2, 2015. Within days of the shooting, anti-gun legislators quickly seized the opportunity to push a number of gun-control bills through the California Legislature, including two bills (AB 1135 and SB 880) that sought to close what they deemed the "bullet button loophole" by outlawing the possession and sale of firearms with magazines locks, namely those with "bullet buttons."

As the Senate Public Safety Committee's analysis of SB 880 explained:

According to the author, "bullet button-equipped semi-automatic weapons have no legitimate use for sport hunters or competitive shooters. They are designed only to facilitate the maximum destruction of human life. Such weapons have been used in a number of recent gun attacks including the recent terrorist attack in San Bernardino . . . .

SB 880 will make our communities safer and upholds our commitment to reduce gun violence in California by closing the bullet button loophole in California's Assault Weapons Ban. This bill clarifies the definition of assault weapons and provides the DOJ the authority to bring existing regulations into conformity with the original intent of California's Assault Weapon

---

[128] "Rimfire" was later removed.

[129] SB 374, 2013-2014, Leg. Counsel's Digest (Cal. 2013) (emphasis added), *available at* http://www.leginfo.ca.gov/pub/13-14/bill/sen/sb_0351-0400/sb_374_bill_20130220_introduced.pdf (last visited July 12, 2017).

[130] There is no way to ascertain how many lawful firearm owners have been prosecuted under the current "assault weapon" ban. All I can say is my office still receives calls from people who were unaware that a firearm they acquired in the 1980s or 1990s is considered an "assault weapon." Luckily, most of these people are contacting me before facing felony criminal prosecution. Many, many more Californians aren't as lucky.

Ban. Absent this bill, the assault weapon ban is severely weakened, and these types of military-style firearms will continue to proliferate on our streets and in our neighborhoods.[131]

Even ignoring the fact that the firearms used by the San Bernardino shooters were illegally modified (the shooters removed the "bullet buttons" from the firearms) and illegally obtained through an alleged straw purchase,[132] these bills do nothing to increase public safety. But that did not stop anti-gun legislators from passing these bills on June 29, 2016.

On July 1, 2016, Governor Brown signed both AB 1135 and SB 880 into law. As explained in more detail below, these bills amend the definition of an "assault weapon" under P.C. section 30515(a) to include any semiautomatic, centerfire rifle or semiautomatic pistol that does not have a fixed magazine and is equipped with one (or more) prohibited features.[133] This expansion effectively modified the definition of Category 3 "assault weapons" so that it now also includes "assault weapons" with "bullet buttons" attached.

Firearms meeting the definition of a California "assault weapon" now fall under one (and potentially two) of three categories: Categories 1, 2, and/or 3.

III. "ASSAULT WEAPON" DEFINED

A. Category 1 "Assault Weapons"

Firearms listed in the 1989 AWCA and those added in 1991, which included: "Made in China AK, AKM, AKS, AK47, AK47S, 56, 56S, 84S, and 86S," are commonly known as Category 1 "assault weapons."[134] They are the same firearms specifically named by make and model in P.C. section 30510.[135] They had to be registered with the DOJ on or before March 31, 1992.[136] See the AWIG for representative photos of each Category 1 "assault weapon."

Today, it is no longer possible to register a Category 1 "assault weapon."

---

[131] BILL ANALYSIS: HEARING ON SB 880 BEFORE THE SENATE COMM. ON PUBLIC SAFETY at 1 (May 17, 2016), available at https://leginfo.legislature.ca.gov/faces/billAnalysisClient.xhtml?bill_id=201520160SB880# (last visited July 12, 2017).

[132] Ashby Jones & Dan Frosch, *Rifles Used in San Bernardino Shooting Illegal Under State Law*, THE WALL STREET JOURNAL (Dec. 3, 2015), *available at* http://www.wsj.com/articles/rifles-used-in-san-bernardino-shooting-illegal-under-state-law-1449201057 (last visited July 12, 2017).

[133] AB 1135, 2015-2016 Leg., Reg. Sess. (Cal. 2016), *available at* http://leginfo.legislature.ca.gov/faces/billNavClient.xhtml?bill_id=201520160AB1135 (last visited July 12, 2017); SB 880, 2015- 2016 Leg., Reg. Sess. (Cal. 2016), *available at* http://leginfo.legislature.ca.gov/faces/billNavClient.xhtml?bill_id=201520160SB880 (last visited July 12, 2017).

[134] P.C. § 30510. See the "Assault Weapon" list at the end of this chapter.

[135] P.C. § 30510 ; *see also* CAL. CODE REGS. tit. 11, § 5495.

[136] CAL. DEPT. OF JUSTICE, OFFICE OF THE ATTORNEY GENERAL, ASSAULT WEAPONS IDENTIFICATION GUIDE, (3rd ed. Nov. 2001), *available at* http://oag.ca.gov/sites/all/files/agweb/pdfs/firearms/forms/awguide.pdf (last visited July 12, 2017).

Examples of Category 1 "Assault Weapons"

Colt AR-15 Semi-Automatic Rifle

Intratec TEC-9

B. Category 2 "Assault Weapons"

As discussed above, in 2000 the California Supreme Court upheld the validity of the AWCA, including the DOJ "add-on" provision, in the face of a lawsuit challenging its constitutionality.[137]

As a result, the DOJ added over sixty Colt AR-15 and AK "series" firearms to the list of restricted "assault weapons," making those firearms illegal to possess in California if not registered by the applicable deadline. These new additions are referred to as Category 2 "assault weapons," and the deadline to register them was January 23, 2001. These added Category 2 "assault weapons" are listed in Cal. Code Regs. title 11, section 5499. The public education program advising people that these guns had been "series" designated as "assault weapons" was meager. Many people did not realize these firearms had become Category 2 "series" "assault weapons" and did not realize the firearms now needed to be registered.

If a firearm is not currently listed as an "assault weapon" in the Penal Code, California Code of Regulations, or the AWIG, it is not a Category 1 or 2 "assault weapon." If a firearm does not have the same manufacturer and model designation as the ones on the list, it also is not a Category 1 or 2 "assault weapon."

A number of manufacturers have made California-compliant firearms similar to the ones on the list with different model designations. These firearms cannot be considered "assault weapons" under Category 1 or 2. They could, however, still

---

[137] *Kasler v. Lockyer*, 23 Cal. 4th 472 (2000). The DOJ has been unable to use this provision to add to the prohibited "assault weapons" list since January 1, 2007, because it was statutorily "unsettled" – meaning it expired – by passage of AB 2728, and the list has remained fixed ever since.

meet the definition of a Category 3 or 4 "assault weapon" depending on the firearm's features, as discussed below.

The DOJ has argued, somewhat inconsistently, that Category 1 and 2 "assault weapons" are "assault weapons" at the bare receiver/frame level – regardless of any other particular characteristic. This is debatable, because frames and receivers are considered "firearms" under certain Penal Code sections,[138] but *not* under the AWCA. Under the AWCA, therefore, a frame or receiver should not be considered a "firearm." For a frame or receiver to be considered an "assault weapon," it first must be considered a "firearm" that is either a semiautomatic rifle, pistol, or shotgun.[139]

Since a bare frame or receiver alone cannot function as a firearm at all because it does not have the characteristics of a rifle, pistol, or shotgun, and particularly not in a manner to justify designating it "semiautomatic,"[140] a fully functioning "make and model" firearm should be present to be a "firearm" under the AWCA, not just a frame or a receiver.

Nevertheless, since the DOJ may disagree, it is not recommended that you possess even bare firearm frames/receivers listed by make and model as "assault weapons" unless they are registered.

Examples of Category 2 "Assault Weapons"

Norinco MAK 90

Colt Sporter

---

[138] P.C. § 16520.

[139] P.C. § 30510.

[140] A shotgun with a revolving cylinder does not need to be semiautomatic. P.C. § 30515(a)(8).

CATEGORY 1 "ASSAULT WEAPONS" RIFLES	CATEGORY 2 "ASSAULT WEAPONS" RIFLES

• Any AK series including but not limited to the following models:
  • Made in China AK, AKM, AK47, AK47S, 56, 56S, 84S, and 86S
  • Norinco 56, 56S, 84S and 86S
  • Poly Technologies AKS and AK47
  • MAAI AK47 and ARM
• Any of the following MAC types:
  • RPB Industries Inc. sM10 and sM11
  • SWD Incrporated M11
• Armalite AR-180
• Berctta AR-10
• Bushmaster Assault Rifle
• Calico M-900
• CETME Sporter
• Colt AR-15 series
• Daewoo K-1, K-2, Max 1, Max 2, AR 100, and AR 110C
• Fabrique Nationale FAL, LAR, FNC, 308 Match, and Sporter
• HK-91, HK-93, HK-94, and HK-PSG-1
• J&R ENG M-68
• MAS 223
• SKS with detachable magazine
• SIG AMT, PE 57, SG 550, and SG 551
• Springfield Armory BM59 and SAR-48
• Sterling MK-6
• UZI and Galil
• Valmet M62S, M71S, and M78S
• Weaver Arms Nighthawk
 	
• Steyr AUG
	• American Arms AK-C47, AK-F 39, AK-F 47, AK-Y 39
	• American Spirit ASA Model
	• Armalite AR 10 (all), Golden Eagle, M15 (all)
	• Arsenal SLG (all), SLR (all)
	• B-West AK-47 (all)
	• Bushmaster XM15 (all)
	• Colt AR-15 (all), Law Enforcement (6920), Match Target (all), Sporter (all)
	• Dalphon B.F.D.
	• DPMS Panther (all)
	• Eagle Arms EΛ-15 AS H-Bar, EA-15 E1, M15 (all)
	• Frankford Arsenal Ar-15 (all)
	• Hesse Arms, Model 47 (all), Wieger STG 940 Rifle, HAR 15A2 (all)
	• Inter Ordinance - Monroe, NC AK-47 (all), NC M-97, NC RPK
	• Kalashnikov USA Hunter Rifle/Saiga
	• Knights RAS (all), SR-15 (all), SR-25 (all)
	• Les Bauer Ultimate AR (all)
	• MAADI CO AK, 47, ARM, MISR (all), MISTR (all)
	• Made in China AK, AKM, AKS, AK47-, 56, 56S, 84S, 86S
	• Mitchel Arms, Inc. AK-47, AK-47 Cal .308 (all), M-76, M-90, RPK
	• Norinco 56, 56 S, 81 S (all), 84 S, 86 (all), 86 S, AK-47 (all), Hunter Rifle, MAK 90, NHM 90, 90-2, 91 Sport, RPK Rifle
	• Ohio Ordinance Works (o.o.w.) AK-74, ROMAK 991
	• Olympic Arms AR-15, Car-97, PCR (all)
	• Ordnance, Inc. AR-15
	• Palmetto SGA (all)
	• Poly Technologies AKS, AK47
	• Professional Ordinance, Inc. Carbon 15 Rifle
	• PWA All Models
	• Rock River Arms, Inc. Car A2, Car A4 Flattop, LE Tactical Carbine, NM A2-DCM Legal, Standard A-2, Standard A-4 Flattop
	• Valmet 76 S, Hunter Rifle
	• Wilson Combat AR-15
	• WUM WUM (all)

CATEGORY 1 "ASSAULT WEAPONS" PISTOLS	**CATEGORY 2 "ASSAULT WEAPONS" PISTOLS**

• UZI
• Encom MP-9 and MP-5
• The following MAC Types
   • RPB Industries Inc. sM10 and sM11
   • SWD Incorporated M-11
   • Advanced Armament Inc. M-11
   • Military Armament Corp. Ingram M-11
   • Intratec Tec-9
   • Sites Spectre
   • Sterling MK-7
   • Calico M-950
 	
   • Bushmaster Pistiol
	• MARS Pistol
	• Professional Ordnance, Inc. Carbon 15 Pistol

C. Category 3 "Assault Weapons"

In 1999, the AWCA was again amended to define "assault weapons" a third way: generically by a firearm's characteristics.[141] These Category 3 "assault weapons" are rifles, pistols, and shotguns with certain external characteristics that do not alter their "rate of fire" or "capacity for firepower." Today, these characteristics are listed in P.C. section 30515, and if present or added on a firearm in certain combinations, they can convert a lawful firearm into a Category 3 "assault weapon."[142]

On July 1, 2016, Governor Jerry Brown signed AB 1135 and SB 880 into law, which amended the original definition of Category 3 "assault weapons" that was implemented in 2000.[143] AB 1135 and SB 880 became effective on January 1, 2017, and these virtually identical[144] bills amended the definition of an "assault weapon" under P.C. section 30515 by replacing the phrase "capacity to accept a detachable magazine" with "does not have a fixed magazine." This amendment was meant to close the so-called "bullet button" loophole by expanding the definition of an "assault weapon" to cover certain semiautomatic, centerfire rifles and semiautomatic pistols that were previously legal to purchase and possess in California.

---

[141] P.C. § 30515.

[142] *See* P.C. § 30515.

[143] AB 1135, 2015-2016 Leg., Reg. Sess. (Cal. 2016), *available at* http://leginfo.legislature.ca.gov/faces/billNavClient.xhtml?bill_id=201520160AB1135 (last visited July 12, 2017); SB 880, 2015- 2016 Leg., Reg. Sess. (Cal. 2016), *available at* http://leginfo.legislature.ca.gov/faces/billNavClient.xhtml?bill_id=201520160SB880 (last visited July 12, 2017).

[144] SB 880 and AB 1135 were practically identical for all intents and purposes. Technically, they were never reconciled when they were passed, so both are current California law. As a result, there are two versions of P.C. section 30680 in existence due to a slight variation in wording between AB 1135 and SB 880. The Legislature needs to fix this for housekeeping purposes, but it does not substantively affect the analysis discussed later in detail.

1. AB 1135/SB 880 and the DOJ's Regulations for Shotguns with Ability to Accept a Detachable Magazine

The Legislature did not change the definition of "assault weapon" for shotguns when it drafted AB 1135 and SB 880. The Legislature is presumed to have intentionally revised the definition of "assault weapon" for pistols and rifles while leaving the definition of "assault weapon" for shotguns completely unchanged.[145] Therefore, semiautomatic shotguns with "bullet buttons" *should* not be considered "assault weapons" based on what is in the Penal Code. But that is not the case. The DOJ took it upon itself to change the definition of "assault weapons" for shotguns against the Legislature's intentions. The DOJ redefined the phrase "ability to accept a detachable magazine" to "mea[n] with respect to a semiautomatic shotgun, it does not have a fixed magazine."[146] This means that after July 31, 2017—the date that the DOJ's regulations were approved—semiautomatic shotguns with "bullet buttons" became "assault weapons." This requires them to be registered, modified, or removed from the state before July 1, 2018 like all the other newly-designated "assault weapons."

2. Old Category 3 – Rifles

Until January 1, 2017, a rifle was considered a Category 3 "assault weapons" if it was:

(1) Semiautomatic; *and*

(2) Centerfire; and

(3) Capable of accepting a detachable magazine; *and*

(4) Had any one, or a combination, of the following:

    (a) A pistol grip that protrudes conspicuously beneath the action of the weapon, *or*

    (b) A thumbhole stock, *or*

    (c) A folding or telescoping stock, *or*

    (d) A grenade launcher or flare launcher, *or*

    (e) A flash suppressor, *or*

    (f) A forward pistol grip.[147]

Semiautomatic centerfire rifles with *fixed* magazines capable of accepting more than 10 rounds and semiautomatic centerfire rifles with overall lengths of less than 30 inches are also Category 3 "assault weapons."[148]

---

[145] "As a general rule, when a legislature 'includes particular language in one section of a statute but omits it in another section of the same Act, it is generally presumed that [it] acts intentionally and purposely in the disparate inclusion or exclusion.'" *Gaines v. Fidelity Nat. Title Ins. Co.*, 62 Cal.4th 1081, 1113 (2016) (citing *Russello v. United States*, 464 U.S. 16, 23 (1983)).

[146] CAL. CODE. REGS, tit. 11, . § 5471(a).

[147] P.C. § 30515(a)(1).

[148] P.C. § 30515(a)(2)-(3).

Example of a Category 3 Rifle

AR 180 Semi-Automatic Rifle

3. Old Category 3 – Pistols

Until January 1, 2017, a semiautomatic pistol with the capacity to accept detachable magazine was considered an "assault weapon" if it had any of the following:

(1) A threaded barrel, capable of accepting a flash suppressor, forward handgrip, or silencer; *or*

(2) A second handgrip; *or*

(3) A shroud that is attached to, or partially or completely encircles, the barrel that allows the bearer to fire the weapon without burning the bearer's hand, except a slide that encloses the barrel; *or*

Threaded barrel from a Ruger 22.45

(4) The capacity to accept a detachable magazine at some location outside of the pistol grip.[149]

Semiautomatic pistols with *fixed* magazines capable of accepting more than 10 rounds are also considered Category 3 "assault weapons."[150]

4. Old Category 3 – Shotguns

Under both the pre-2017 and post-2017 definitions of "assault weapon," shotguns are considered "assault weapons" if they are semiautomatic and have the ability to accept a detachable magazine.[151]

As of July 31, 2017, shotguns are *also* considered "assault weapons" if they are semiautomatic and do not have a fixed magazine. In other words, "bullet buttoned" shotguns are now considered "assault weapons." As mentioned above, the term for "ability to accept a detachable magazine" was redefined by the DOJ for purposes of transforming certain semiautomatic shotguns into "assault weapons." But the

---

[149] P.C. § 30515(a)(4).

[150] P.C. § 30515(a)(5).

[151] P.C. § 30515(a)(7).

change made by the DOJ to the regulations did not go into effect until July 31, 2017. Before that, the restriction on shotguns having the "ability to accept a detachable magazine" was regulated by the *old* regulations and, specifically, the old definition of "detachable magazine." Hence, up until the day the DOJ changed the regulations for "ability to accept a detachable magazine," a shotgun with a "bullet button" was not considered to be an "assault weapon." Under the Penal Code and California regulations, "bullet buttoned" shotguns only became "assault weapons" when the DOJ changed the regulations on July 31, 2017. Therefore, semiautomatic shotguns that do not have a fixed magazine should also be considered "assault weapons" now by the DOJ's rewriting of the regulations.

The DOJ's new regulations did not affect the other definitions of "assault weapon" for shotguns in the Penal Code. Therefore, under both the pre-2017 and post-2017 definitions of "assault weapon," shotguns are still considered "assault weapons" if they are semiautomatic and have *both* of the following:

(1) A folding or telescoping stock; *and*

(2) A pistol grip that protrudes conspicuously beneath the action of the weapon, thumbhole stock, or vertical handgrip.[152]

And, under both the pre-2017 and post-2017 definitions of "assault weapon," any shotgun with a revolving cylinder is an "assault weapon."[153]

5. Old Category 3 Definitions for Pre-2017 "Assault Weapons"

Prior to July 31, 2017, the California Code of Regulations defined various characteristics of features on a firearm that pertain to a Category 3 "assault weapon" under the old definition of "assault weapon" up until July 31, 2017. The following is a list of these definitions:

(1) "'Detachable magazine' . . . [is] any ammunition feeding device that can be removed readily from the firearm with neither disassembly of the firearm action nor use of a tool being required. A bullet or ammunition cartridge is considered a tool. Ammunition feeding device includes any belted or linked ammunition, but does not include clips, en bloc clips, or stripper clips that load cartridges into the magazine."[154]

(2) "'Pistol grip that protrudes conspicuously beneath the action of the weapon' [is] a grip that allows for a pistol style grasp in which the web of the trigger hand (between the thumb and index finger) can be placed below the top of the exposed portion of the trigger while firing."[155]

---

[152] P.C. § 30515(a)(6).

[153] P.C. § 30515(a)(8).

[154] CAL. CODE REGS. tit. 11, § 5469(a) (2016).

[155] CAL. CODE REGS. tit. 11, § 5469(d) (2016).

(3) "'Thumbhole stock' [is] a stock with a hole that allows the thumb of the trigger hand to penetrate into or through the stock while firing."[156]

(4) "'Flash suppressor' [is] any device designed, intended, or that functions to perceptibly reduce or redirect muzzle flash from the shooter's field of vision."[157]

(5) "'Forward pistol grip' [is] a grip that allows for a pistol style grasp forward of the trigger."[158]

(6) "Fixed magazine" is a magazine that stays attached to the firearm while loading. Often fixed magazines are charged or loaded "from a clip (en bloc or stripper) of cartridges inserted through the open breech into the magazine."[159]

Example of a conspicuously protruding pistol grip

Example of a thumbhole stock

Example of a forward pistol grip

D. Making Category 3 "Assault Weapons" Comply With the Old Definition of "Assault Weapon"

Before the law changed on January 1, 2017, firearms owners and manufactures made their firearms California compliant by removing certain characteristics (semiautomatic, centerfire, or accepting a "detachable magazine") from their firearms so that they were no longer considered Category 3 "assault weapons." Some would convert their semiautomatic rifles or pistols too manual-cycled, or convert their centerfire rifles to rimfire. Although these conversions may still remove a firearm out of the definition of an "assault weapon" (see below), most gun owners and manufacturers did not chose to use these methods to make their firearms California complaint. Instead, most gun owners and manufacturers chose to make their "detachable magazines" "non-detachable," thereby making it so that the firearm could no longer accept a "detachable magazine." But, as explained below, some of the processes that were used to make a firearm unable to accept a "detachable magazine" will no longer make a firearm California compliant after January 1, 2017.

---

[156] CAL. CODE REGS. tit. 11, § 5469(e) (2016).

[157] CAL. CODE REGS. tit. 11, § 5469(b) (2016).

[158] CAL. CODE REGS. tit. 11, § 5469(c) (2016).

[159] CAL. DEPT. OF JUSTICE, OFFICE OF THE ATTORNEY GENERAL, ASSAULT WEAPONS IDENTIFICATION GUIDE, (3rd ed. Nov. 2001), *available at* http://oag.ca.gov/sites/all/files/agweb/pdfs/firearms/forms/awguide.pdf (last visited July 12, 2017).

In making the firearm unable to accept a "detachable magazine," firearm owners and manufacturers typically retrofitted their firearms with an aftermarket product generally called a "magazine lock." The most common kind of "magazine lock" is known as a "Bullet Button." The standard magazine release for a "detachable magazine" can usually operate with the push of a finger, so no "tool" is required to release the magazine. The typical "magazine lock" for AR type rifles, however, replaces the standard one-piece magazine release button with a two-piece assembly that cannot be operated with just the push of a finger.

The new two-piece magazine release typically has an inner and outer button. The outer button directly replaces the standard magazine release button in shape and size but without actuating the spring that allows magazine removal. The much smaller inner button sits recessed within the outer button and becomes the firearm's true magazine removal mechanism. Since the inner button is too small and recessed to be pushed by a finger; a tool is needed to push the inner button to release the magazine so it can be removed. The most common "tool" used to push the recessed button and remove the magazine is the tip of a bullet, hence the term "bullet button." Because a tool is needed to release the magazine, the firearm would no longer be said to have the capacity to accept a "detachable magazine." That means the firearm would no longer be classified as an "assault weapon" under P.C. section 30515(a)(1), even if it had one (or more) of the characteristics listed in P.C. section 30515(a)(1)(A)-(F).

But, since January 1, 2017, attaching a magazine lock, like the "bullet button," to a firearm no longer made a firearm California compliant, unless the magazine lock causes the firearm to have a "fixed magazine" (see below). Most of the "bullet buttons" that individuals used and installed onto their firearms before SB 880 and AB 1135 were passed do not cause the firearm to have a "fixed magazine" as that term is defined.

As of January 1, 2017, the term "fixed magazine" is defined as "an ammunition feeding device contained in, or permanently attached to, a firearm in such a manner that it cannot be removed without disassembly of the firearm action."[160] Because most "bullet buttons" that are used and/or have been installed onto most firearms do not make it so that the magazine is contained in, or permanently attached to, the firearm in such a way as to make it so that the magazine cannot be removed without disassembling the action of the firearm, these devices will no longer make the firearm California compliant, meaning that it is highly likely that these firearms were considered "assault weapons" starting on January 1, 2017. Individuals with these firearms will need to modify, register, or choose another option to dispose of the firearm, as discussed later in this Chapter, before July 1, 2018.

Also note that some firearms are not capable of accepting a "detachable magazine," but are still considered Category 3 "assault weapons." For example, a rifle with a fixed magazine that is capable of accepting more than ten rounds is considered a

---

[160] P.C. § 30515(b).

Category 3 "assault weapon," as is a semiautomatic centerfire rifle with an overall length of less than 30 inches.

1. Troublesome Magazine Locks – Pushing the Law Too Far

Since the birth of the "magazine lock," companies have altered its design and created other devices to use with it. While some of these improvements and devices make magazine locks easier to use, they also present new problems.

Some "magazine lock" versions have different settings. One version allows the firearm owner to use the "magazine lock" regularly on one setting, and then by a simple twist of a screw or Allen wrench, the "magazine lock" functions as a standard magazine release. Manufacturers advertised these devices for use in and outside of California, with the standard "magazine lock" setting intended for use in California and the magazine release button setting for use outside of California.

Before the change in "assault weapon" law, we cautioned people about the use of these items. This is because the settings of these devices can be easily changed from one to the other and can invite possibilities like forgetting to reset the device to the standard setting upon returning to California, device failure, and possible felony prosecution.

There are also a number of similar devices calling themselves either the "Wonder Wrench" or "Mag Magnet." While differing in design they function in similar ways. They are designed to remain inserted in or attached to the "magazine lock" while the firearm is being used. The devices cause the "magazine lock" to function like a standard magazine release. Like the magazine lock with different settings, these devices are designed to be used outside of California. We recommended against buying or using these devices. At a minimum, we advised people to never leave any device or item inserted in the "magazine lock" while in California. If the device left in allows it to function like a standard magazine release, law enforcement has argued that the firearm can still accept a "detachable magazine" and thus may constitute an illegal "assault weapon." A counter argument is that the item still functions as a tool, and should no longer be said to have the capacity to accept a "detachable magazine." But the regulations passed on July 31, 2017 addressed this issue. Through its regulations, the DOJ was able to drive home its theory that leaving something in a "bullet button" constitutes a "detachable magazine":

> An AR-15 style firearm that has a bullet-button style magazine release with a magnet left on the bullet-button constitutes a detachable magazine. An AR-15 style firearm lacking a magazine catch assembly (magazine catch, magazine catch siring and magazine release button) constitutes a detachable magazine. An AK-47 style firearm lacking a magazine catch assembly (magazine catch, spring and rivet/pin) constitutes a detachable magazine.[161]

---

[161] CAL. CODE. REGS. tit. 11, § 5471(m).

E. New Definition of Category 3 "Assault Weapons"

1. Rifles that Are Now Considered "Assault Weapons" as a Result of the New Change in Law on January 1, 2017

After January 1, 2017, a rifle is considered a Category 3 "assault weapon" if it:

(1) Is semiautomatic; *and*

(2) Is centerfire; *and*

(3) Does not have a "fixed magazine"; *and*

(4) Has any one, or a combination of, the following:

(a) A pistol grip that protrudes conspicuously beneath the action of the weapon; *or*

(b) A thumbhole stock; *or*

(c) A folding or telescoping stock; *or*

(d) A grenade launcher or flare launcher; *or*

(e) A flash suppressor; *or*

(f) A forward pistol grip.[162]

The term "fixed magazine" means "an ammunition feeding device contained in, or permanently attached to, a firearm in such a manner that the device cannot be removed without disassembly of the firearm action."[163]

Note that SB 880 and AB 1135 did not change the working of the other definitions of an "assault weapon" under P.C. section 30515 for rifles. Therefore, even if a semiautomatic, center rifle does not fall within the definition of an "assault weapon" above, it may nonetheless fall under the definition of a Category 3 "assault weapon" if it has a "fixed magazine" with the capacity to accept more than ten rounds, or if it has an overall length of less than thirty inches (see above).[164] These types of rifles were banned before 2017 and remain banned "assault weapons" today.

2. Pistols that Are Now Considered "Assault Weapons" as a Result of the Change in Law on January 1, 2017

After January 1, 2017, pistols are considered Category 3 "assault weapons" if they:

(1) Are semiautomatic; *and*

(2) Do not have a "fixed magazine"; *and*

(3) Have any one, or a combination of, the following:

(a) A threaded barrel, capable of accepting a flash suppressor, forward handgrip, or silencer; *or*

---

[162] P.C. § 30515(a)(1).

[163] P.C. § 30515(b).

[164] P.C. § 30515(a)(2), (3).

     (b) A second handgrip; *or*

     (c) A shroud that is attached to, or partially or completely encircles, the barrel that allows the bearer to fire the weapon without burning the bearer's hand, except a slid that encloses the barrel; *or*

     (d) The capacity to accept a detachable magazine at some location outside of the pistol grip.[165]

Note that even if a semiautomatic pistol doesn't meet the definition of an "assault weapon" as defined above, it may still be considered a Category 3 "assault weapon" if it is has a "fixed magazine" with the capacity to accept more than ten rounds.[166]

3. Shotguns that Are Now Considered "Assault Weapons" as a Result of the Change in Law on July 31, 2017

As mentioned repeatedly above, shotguns that have the ability to accept a detachable magazine are considered "assault weapons" because the DOJ redefined the term "ability to accept a detachable" so that it "means with respect to a semiautomatic shotgun, it does not have a fixed magazine."[167]

And note that the DOJ and Legislature's recent actions did not affect the following shotguns, which were "assault weapons" under the pre-2017 definitions and still remain "assault weapons" now:

    (1) A semiautomatic shotgun that has both of the following:

     (a) A folding or telescoping stock, *and*

     (b) A pistol grip that protrudes conspicuously beneath the action of the weapon, thumbhole stock, or vertical handgrip; *or*

    (2) Any shotgun with a revolving cylinder.[168]

4. History Behind the DOJ's New "Assault Weapon" Regulations and Analysis of Some of the Definitions Set Forth by the Regulations

a. The DOJ's Embattled Attempts to Implement Regulations for the New Category 3 "Assault Weapons"

Because AB 1135 and SB 880 converted thousands of previously-legal rifles and pistols into newly-defined "assault weapons," the Legislature wanted to carve a way to allow law-abiding owners to continue possessing these firearms after January 1, 2017. Therefore, AB 1135 and SB 880 added provisions to the Penal Code that created a registration process for these newly-defined "bullet button assault

---

[165] P.C. § 30515(a)(4).

[166] P.C. § 30515(a)(5).

[167] CAL. CODE. REGS. tit. 11, § 5471(a).

[168] P.C. § 30515(a)(6), (a)(8).

weapons."[169] The new law *required* the DOJ to adopt regulations for the purpose of implementing this registration process so that people can register their newly-defined "assault weapons" before the December 31, 2017 registration deadline.[170] The DOJ knew about this statutory duty as early as July 1, 2016, when AB 1135 and SB 880 were chaptered into law.

Yet, the DOJ essentially did nothing until the end of 2016. On December 30, 2016, a Friday immediately preceding New Year's Eve, the DOJ submitted proposed regulations to the Office of Administrative Law ("OAL"), claiming that its regulations were exempt from public comment and requesting that the regulations be published by the OAL "ASAP" with an effective date of January 1, 2017. The NRA/CRPA and other Pro-Second Amendment groups quickly sent in written oppositions to these proposed regulations. The proposed regulations went far beyond what was needed to register the new "bullet button assault weapons" and redefined a number of key terms used to define firearms as "assault weapons." Then, on February 10, 2017, the DOJ withdrew the regulations.

Meanwhile, in January 2017, the DOJ sent a "Budget Change Proposal" to the Department of Finance to request more money to cover the costs of setting up the "assault weapon" registration system and hiring new employees to process the registrations. At that time, the DOJ did not have the money or the manpower to process "assault weapons" registrations. Resultantly, the DOJ asked for approximately 2.6 million dollars to process "assault weapon" registrations. This January request for money made its way into AB 97, the Budget Act of 2017. AB 97 was signed by Governor Brown on June 26, 2017, thereby giving the DOJ the money it requested.

On May 12, 2017, the DOJ tried again to submit proposed regulations for "bullet button assault weapons" to the OAL, requesting expedited review. This time, the DOJ refused to disclose copies of these proposed regulations to members of the public who requested them. The DOJ ultimately did post the proposed regulations on its website on or about May 22, 2017, days after they were obtained from the OAL and widely distributed by the NRA/CRPA and other pro-Second Amendment groups. These proposed regulations were virtually identical to those that the DOJ previously submitted to the OAL on December 30, 2016. Accordingly, the NRA/CRPA and other pro-Second Amendment groups sent in written oppositions once again. Then, on June 26, 2017, the OAL rejected the DOJ's proposed regulations, forcing the DOJ to go back to the drawing board.

With less than half a year to go before the December 31, 2017 registration deadline due to the DOJ's delay in implementing valid registration regulations, the government realized that the original registration deadline needed to be extended. The DOJ went to the Legislature for assistance, and it was decided that the extension shall be implemented through AB 103. Originally a "Budget Bill," AB 103 was

---

[169] *See* P.C. §§ 30680, 30900(b). Note that there are two versions of P.C. section 30680 in existence due to a slight variation in wording between AB 1135 and SB 880. The Legislature needs to fix this for housekeeping purposes, but it does not substantively affect our analysis.

[170] *See* P.C. §§ 30680(c), 30900(b)(5).

rebranded into a "Public Safety Omnibus Bill." The bill's scope was huge, but it also included sections that extended the exception to be able to possess and the deadline to register newly designated "assault weapons" from December 31, 2017 to June 30, 2018.[171]

With the extension and money in place, the DOJ made a third attempt to submit its proposed regulations to the OAL on July 19, 2017. The proposed regulations were substantively unchanged from the previous two versions. But, inexplicably, the OAL approved of these proposed regulations on July 31, 2017, a month before its own deadline to make a decision. Shortly after the OAL's approval, the DOJ's online registration system went "live." The system immediately experienced outages and crashes, and it is still plagued with problems at the time of the writing of this book. The procedure to register the newly-designated "assault weapons" is explained in Section VII below.

In addition, the DOJ's new "bullet button assault weapon" regulations effectively expanded the definition of "assault weapon" that the Legislature drafted for AB 1135 and SB 880, and it changed the definitions of terms that apply to all Category 3 "assault weapons." Arguably, the DOJ exceeded its authority when doing this, and lawsuits are being prepared to be filed against the DOJ to remedy this. But, until those lawsuits have reached a resolution, the DOJ's regulations are still the law for purposes of "assault weapon" registration.

b. The New Definitions that the DOJ Added as Part of Its 2017 Regulations for "Assault Weapon" Registration and Analysis of Some of Them

The following is a list of the definitions that the DOJ published as part of the regulations that took effect in August 2017, along with some analysis and commentary that will illuminate them:

(1) "Ability to accept a detachable magazine' means with respect to a semiautomatic shotgun it does not have a fixed magazine."[172]

As discussed in detail in Section III(C) above, the DOJ's new definition of "ability to accept a detachable magazine" shoehorned semiautomatic shotguns with "bullet buttons" into the definition of "assault weapons." This is contrary to the Legislature's intentions, but it currently remains the law. So, semiautomatic shotguns with "bullet buttons" have to be registered, modified, or removed from the state before July 1, 2018.

(2) "'Action' means the working mechanism of a semiautomatic firearm, which is the combination of the receiver or frame and breech bolt together with

---

[171]*See* P.C. §§ 30680, 30900(b); *see also* AB 103 2017-2018, Leg. Counsel's Digest (Cal. 2017), *available at* https://leginfo.legislature.ca.gov/faces/billTextClient.xhtml?bill_id=201720180AB103 (last visited Sept. 29, 2017).

[172] CAL. CODE. REGS. tit. 11, § 5471(a).

the other parts of the mechanism by which a firearm is loaded fired and unloaded."[173]

(3) "'Barrel' means the tube usually metal and cylindrical through which a projectile or shot charge is fired. Barrels may have a rifled or smooth bore."[174]

(4) "'Barrel length' means the length of the barrel measured as follows: Without consideration of any extensions or protrusions rearward of the closed bolt or breech-face the approved procedure for measuring barrel length is to measure from the closed bolt (or breech-face) to the furthermost end of the barrel or permanently attached muzzle device. Permanent methods of attachment include full-fusion gas or electric steel-seam welding, high-temperature (1100°F) silver soldering, or blind pinning with the pin head welded over. Barrels are measured by inserting a dowel rod into the barrel until the rod stops against the closed bolt or breech-face. The rod is then marked at the furthermost end of the barrel or permanently attached muzzle device, withdrawn from the barrel, and measured."[175]

This definition is odd because the new law does not redefine the definition for "assault weapon" based on barrel length. This appears to be the DOJ, again through regulation, molding the law into what it thinks it should be. It will remain to be seen if law enforcement and/or the courts will attempt to use this definition for other things like "short-barreled" rifles and "short-barreled" shotguns.

(5) "'Bullet' means the projectile expelled from a gun. It is not synonymous with a cartridge. Bullets can be of many materials, shapes, weights, and constructions such as solid lead, lead with a jacket of harder metal, round-nosed, flat-nosed. hollow-pointed, et cetera."[176]

(6) "'Bullet-button' means a product requiring a tool to remove an ammunition feeding device or magazine by depressing a recessed button or lever shielded by a magazine lock. A bullet-button equipped fully functional semiautomatic firearm does not meet the fixed magazine definition under Penal Code section 30515(b)."[177]

(7) "'Bore' means the interior of a firearm's barrel excluding the chamber."[178]

(8) "'Caliber' means the nominal diameter of a projectile of a rifled firearm or the diameter between lands in a rifled barrel. In the United States, caliber is

---

[173] CAL. CODE. REGS. tit. 11, § 5471(b).
[174] CAL. CODE. REGS. tit. 11, § 5471(c).
[175] CAL. CODE. REGS. tit. 11, § 5471(d).
[176] CAL. CODE. REGS. tit. 11, § 5471(e).
[177] CAL. CODE. REGS. tit. 11, § 5471(f).
[178] CAL. CODE. REGS. tit. 11, § 5471(g).

usually expressed in hundreds of an inch; in Great Britain in thousandths of an inch; in Europe and elsewhere in millimeters."[179]

(9) "'Cartridge' means a complete round of ammunition that consists of a primer, a case, propellant powder and one or more projectiles."[180]

(10) "'Centerfire' means a cartridge with its primer located in the center of the base of the case."[181]

(11) "'Contained in' means that the magazine cannot be released from the firearm while the action is assembled. For AR-15 style firearms this means the magazine cannot be released from the firearm while the upper receiver and lower receiver are joined together."[182]

(12) "'Department' means the California Department of Justice."[183]

(13) "'Detachable magazine' means any ammunition feeding device that can be removed readily from the firearm without disassembly of the firearm action or use of a tool. A bullet or ammunition cartridge is considered a tool. An ammunition feeding device includes any belted or linked ammunition, but does not include clips, en bloc clips, or stripper clips that load cartridges into the magazine. [ ] An AR-15 style firearm that has a bullet-button style magazine release with a magnet left on the bullet-button constitutes a detachable magazine. An AR-15 style firearm lacking a magazine catch assembly (magazine catch, magazine catch spring and magazine release button) constitutes a detachable magazine. An AK-47 style firearm lacking a magazine catch assembly (magazine catch, spring and rivet/pin) constitutes a detachable magazine."[184]

The second half of this definition appears to be the DOJ extending what it thinks the law should be. As mentioned before, we know the DOJ's opinion was that "bullet buttons" with magnets or other items within them constituted "detachable magazines." This position, while far from ideal, was debatable because a "tool" was still required. Through its new definition, the DOJ has effectively slammed the door on the debate.

We are aware of past instances where law enforcement has come across firearms that lack a "magazine catch assembly." Law enforcement attempted to classify firearms in this situation as capable of accepting a detachable magazine. Of course, there is a question of whether the firearms, without a magazine catch, are capable of accepting any magazine, let alone a "detachable" one.

---

[179] CAL. CODE. REGS. tit. 11, § 5471(h).

[180] CAL. CODE. REGS. tit. 11, § 5471(i).

[181] CAL. CODE. REGS. tit. 11, § 5471(j).

[182] CAL. CODE. REGS. tit. 11, § 5471(k).

[183] CAL. CODE. REGS. tit. 11, § 5471(l).

[184] CAL. CODE. REGS. tit. 11, § 5471(m).

(14) "'Disassembly of the firearm action' means the fire control assembly is detached from the action in such a way that the action has been interrupted and will not function. For example, disassembling the action on a two part receiver, like that on an AR-15 style firearm, would require [1] the rear take down pin to be removed, [2] the upper receiver lifted upwards and away from the lower receiver using the front pivot pin as the fulcrum, before the magazine may be removed."[185]

This phrase, when first used in the Penal Code to define "fixed magazine," caused a lot of confusion because the "action" of a firearm has a rather fluid meaning.[186] And the public had concerns about the amount of "disassembly" required by the Penal Code. The DOJ appears to clear some of these concerns. The DOJ also appears to lend its approval to devices that prevent the removal of the magazine unless the upper receiver of an AR-15 style firearm is tilted up. As a result, and explained in more detail later in this Chapter, certain aftermarket parts should take a firearm out of the new definition of "assault weapon" because they make it so that the magazine can only be removed by (1) releasing the takedown pin and (2) swinging the upper receiver away from the lower receiver. Hence, these aftermarket products make it so that the magazine cannot be removed without "disassembling the firearm's action" (as that term is defined by the DOJ's regulations), which means that there is a "fixed magazine" and no "assault weapon" under the new definition of "assault weapon."

(15) "'Featureless' means a semiautomatic firearm (rifle, pistol, or shotgun) lacking the characteristics associated with that weapon, as listed in Penal Code section 30515."[187]

The DOJ's definition isn't entirely clear. The DOJ references the characteristics listed in Penal Code section 30515, but it never states which characteristics it means. For example, for rifles, "semiautomatic," "centerfire," "does not have a fixed magazine," "pistol grip," "flash suppressor," etc. can all be lumped together into "characteristics." While there are some firearms that lack all of the characteristics listed in section 30515, they come nowhere near approaching the definition of an "assault weapon."

---

[185] CAL. CODE. REGS. tit. 11, § 5471(n).

[186] For example, some sources define "action" as "[t]he mechanism of a gun, usually breechloading, by which it is loaded, fired, and unloaded." John Quick, DICTIONARY OF WEAPONS & MILITARY TERMS 3 (Harold B. Crawford et al., 1973). Other sources say that "the action of a firearm is the method of firing, expelling the spent casing, and chambering a new one, as mechanically facilitated by the design of the firearm." Kevin Inouye, THE THEATRICAL FIREARMS HANDBOOK 19 (CRS Press 2014). And others think of an "action" as "[t]he part of a firearm that loads fires, and ejects a cartridge. Includes lever action, pump action, bolt action, and semi-automatic. The first three are found in weapons that fire a single shot. Firearms that can shoot multiple rounds ("repeaters") include all these types of actions, but only the semi- automatic does not require manual operation between rounds. A truly 'automatic' action is found on a machine gun." *Firearms Handout, Firearms Definitions,* TENNESSEE STATE COURTS, http://www.tncourts.gov/sites/default/files/docs/firearmshandout_1.pdf (last visited Oct. 21, 2017).

[187] CAL. CODE. REGS. tit. 11 , § 5471(o).

"Featureless" as that term is most commonly used by the public usually refers to a rifle that will have the following characteristics: semiautomatic, centerfire, and does not have a fixed magazine (or prior to 2017, may have had "the capacity to accept a detachable magazine") but didn't have any of the additional, required features that would cause the rifle to meet the definition of an "assault weapon" under P.C. section 30515(a)(1), i.e., a pistol grip that protrudes conspicuously beneath the action of the weapon, a thumbhole stock, a folding or telescoping stock, a grenade launcher or flare launcher, a flash suppressor, and a forward pistol grip).

With the above definition, it is unclear what the DOJ means by "featureless." Maybe the DOJ should have requested public comment before simply enacting the regulations.

(16) "'Fixed magazine' means an ammunition feeding device contained in, or permanently attached to, a firearm in such a manner that the device cannot be removed without disassembly of the firearm action."[188]

(17) "'Flare launcher' means a device used to launch signal flares."[189]

(18) "'Flash suppressor' means any device attached to the end of the barrel, that is designed, intended, or functions to perceptibly reduce or redirect muzzle flash from the shooter's field of vision. A hybrid device that has either advertised flash suppressing properties or functionally has flash suppressing properties would be deemed a flash suppressor. A device labeled or identified by its manufacturer as a flash hider would be deemed a flash suppressor."[190]

The original, horrible definition of "flash suppressor" remains from the original regulation. It is still unclear what or how much flash must be "perceptibly reduced" for a device to meet the definition of a "flash suppressor." But the DOJ made a bad definition worse by tacking on to the definition new second and third sentences. We know that law enforcement, in order to attempt to determine whether a device is a flash suppressor, would turn to instruction manuals for certain firearms and see what the manufacturer calls the device. Now, the DOJ has codified the practice into a regulation. Now, a device, according to the DOJ, can meet the definition of "flash suppressor" just by being called that no matter if the device reduces muzzle flash. Based on this definition, if the device increased the muzzle flash but was called a "flash hider" by its manufacturer, it would be a "flash suppressor" under California law. Good thing this theory doesn't apply to other California laws or a person could be prosecuted for possession of a destructive device for possessing a pack of "Bazooka Joe" bubble gum.

---

[188] CAL. CODE. REGS. tit. 11, § 5471(p).

[189] CAL. CODE. REGS. tit. 11, § 5471(q).

[190] CAL. CODE. REGS. tit. 11, § 5471(r).

(19) "'FMBUS' means a Firearm Manufactured By Unlicensed Subject."[191]

This on its face is just an acronym, but it lends a little guidance into the DOJ's thought process. "Unlicensed subject" is not a firearm industry term but rather a law enforcement term. A "subject" is often what law enforcement refer to when it is talking about a person who is the subject of a criminal investigation.

(20) "'Forward pistol grip' means a grip that allows for a pistol style grasp forward of the trigger."[192]

(21) "'Frame' means the receiver of a pistol."[193]

(22) "'Grenade launcher' means a device capable of launching a grenade."[194]

(23) "'Permanently attached to' means the magazine is welded, epoxied, or riveted into the magazine well A firearm with a magazine housed in a sealed magazine well and then welded, epoxied, or riveted into the sealed magazine well meets the definition of 'permanently attached to.'"[195]

(24) "'Overall length of less than 30 inches' with respect to a centerfire rifle means the rifle has been measured in the shortest possible configuration that the weapon will function/fire and the measurement is less than 30 inches. Folding and telescoping stocks shall be collapsed prior to measurement. The approved method for measuring the length of the rifle is to measure the firearm from the end of the barrel, or permanently attached muzzle device, if so equipped, to that part of the stock that is furthest from the end of the barrel, or permanently attached muzzle device. (Prior to taking a measurement the owner must also check any muzzle devices for how they are attached to the barrel.)"[196]

This definition is odd in that the "assault weapon" definition for semiautomatic centerfire rifles less than 30 inches in length was unchanged by the recent legislation. They were illegal to possess before January 1, 2017 and remained illegal thereafter. The DOJ's definition is odd unless the DOJ wanted to make a firm case for what it considered illegal to possess, as it did with its other regulations. Even odder is the fact that the "assault weapon" registration system appears to allow for the registration of rifles less than 30 inches in length, despite the Penal Code clearly not allowing for the registration of that type of firearm (discussed later).

(25) "'Pistol' means any device designed to be used as a weapon, from which a projectile is expelled by the force of any explosion, or other form of combustion, and that has a barrel less than 16 inches in length. This

---

[191] CAL. CODE. REGS. tit. 11, § 5471(s).

[192] CAL. CODE. REGS. tit. 11, § 5471(t).

[193] CAL. CODE. REGS. tit. 11, § 5471(u).

[194] CAL. CODE. REGS. tit. 11, § 5471(v).

[195] CAL. CODE. REGS. tit. 11, § 5471(w).

[196] CAL. CODE. REGS. tit. 11, § 5471(x).

definition includes AR-15 style pistols with pistol buffer tubes attached. Pistol buffer tubes typically have smooth metal with no guide on the bottom for rifle stocks to be attached, and they sometimes have a foam pad on the end of the tube farthest from the receiver."[197]

(26) "'Pistol grip that protrudes conspicuously beneath the action of the weapon' means a grip that allows for a pistol style grasp in which the web of the trigger hand (between the thumb and index finger) can be placed beneath or below the top of the exposed portion of the trigger while firing. This definition includes pistol grips on bullpup firearm designs."[198]

(27) "'Receiver' means the basic unit of a firearm which houses the firing and breech mechanisms and to which the barrel and stock are assembled."[199]

(28) "'Receiver, lower' means the lower part of a two part receiver."[200]

(29) "'Receiver, unfinished' means a precursor part to a firearm that is not yet legally a firearm. Unfinished receivers may be found in various levels of completion. As more finishing work is completed the precursor part gradually becomes a firearm. Some just have the shape of an AR-15 lower receiver for example, but are solid metal. Some have been worked on and the magazine well has been machined open. Firearms Manufactured by Unlicensed Subjects (FMBUS) began as unfinished receivers."[201]

(30) "'Receiver, upper' means the top portion of a two part receiver."[202]

(31) "'Rifle" means a weapon designed or redesigned, made or remade, and intended to be fired from the shoulder and designed or redesigned and made or remade to use the energy of the explosive in a fixed cartridge to fire only a single projectile through a rifled bore for each single pull of the trigger."[203]

(32) "'Rimfire' means a rimmed or flanged cartridge with the priming mixture located in the rim of the case."[204]

(33) "'Second handgrip' means a grip that allows the shooter to grip the pistol with their nontrigger hand. The second hand grip often has a grip texture to assist the shooter in weapon control."[205]

(34) "'Semiautomatic' means a firearm functionally able to fire a single cartridge, eject the empty case, and reload the chamber each time the trigger is pulled and released. Further, certain necessary mechanical parts that will allow

---

[197] CAL. CODE. REGS. tit. 11, § 5471(y).
[198] CAL. CODE. REGS. tit. 11, § 5471(z).
[199] CAL. CODE. REGS. tit. 11, § 5471(aa).
[200] CAL. CODE. REGS. tit. 11, § 5471(bb).
[201] CAL. CODE. REGS. tit. 11, § 5471(cc).
[202] CAL. CODE. REGS. tit. 11, § 5471(dd).
[203] CAL. CODE. REGS. tit. 11, § 5471(ee).
[204] CAL. CODE. REGS. tit. 11, § 5471(ff).
[205] CAL. CODE. REGS. tit. 11, § 5471(gg).

a firearm to function in a semiautomatic nature must be present for a weapon to be deemed semiautomatic. A weapon clearly designed to be semiautomatic but lacking a firing pin, bolt carrier, gas tube, or some other crucial part of the firearm is not semiautomatic for purposes of Penal Code sections 30515, 30600, 30605(a), and 30900.

(a) A mechanically whole semiautomatic firearm merely lacking ammunition and a proper magazine is a semiautomatic firearm.

(b) A mechanically whole semiautomatic firearm disabled by a gun lock or other firearm safety device is a semiautomatic firearm. (All necessary parts are present, once the gun lock or firearm safety device is removed, and weapon can be loaded with a magazine and proper ammunition.)

(c) With regards to an AR-15 style firearm, if a complete upper receiver and a complete lower receiver are completely detached from one another, but still in the possession or under the custody or control of the same person, the firearm is not a semiautomatic firearm.

(d) A stripped AR-15 lower receiver, when sold at a California gun store, is not a semiautomatic firearm. (The action type, among other things, is undetermined.)"[206]

As is apparent from the definition above, if the firearm is broken or missing a key component that would prevent it from functioning, the firearm cannot be considered semiautomatic and, therefore, it cannot be considered to be an "assault weapon." Only shotguns with revolving cylinders don't need to be semiautomatic in order to meet the definition of an "assault weapon." Therefore, before anyone can determine whether a firearm meets the definition of an "assault weapon," they must physically inspect the firearm or personally see the firearm function while it is in an illegal configuration. But, as discussed later, there may still be a problem if a person possesses the parts to make an illegal "assault weapon" and has the intent to put the firearm together in an illegal configuration.

(35) "'Shotgun with a revolving cylinder' means a shotgun that holds its ammunition in a cylinder that acts as a chamber much like a revolver. To meet this definition the shotgun's cylinder must mechanically revolve or rotate each time the weapon is fired. A cylinder that must be manually rotated by the shooter does not qualify as a revolving cylinder."[207]

While the regulations define "rifle," they overlook "shotgun." One would assume that "shotgun," used here and elsewhere, requires the firearm to have a smooth bore barrel.

(36) "'Shroud' means a heat shield that is attached to, or partially or completely encircles the barrel, allowing the shooter to fire the weapon with one hand

---

[206] CAL. CODE. REGS. tit. 11, § 5471(hh).
[207] CAL. CODE. REGS. tit. 11, § 5471(ii).

and grasp the firearm over the barrel with the other hand without burning the shooter's hand. A slide that encloses the barrel is not a shroud."[208]

(37) "'Spigot' means a muzzle device on some firearms that are intended to fire grenades. The spigot is what the grenade is attached to prior to the launching of a grenade."[209]

(38) "'Stock' means the part of a rifle, carbine, or shotgun to which the receiver is attached and which provides a means for holding the weapon to the shoulder. A stock may be fixed, folding, or telescoping."[210]

(39) "'Stock, fixed' means a stock that does not move, fold, or telescope."[211]

(40) "'Stock, folding' means a stock which is hinged in some fashion to the receiver to allow the stock to be folded next to the receiver to reduce the overall length of the firearm. This definition includes under folding and over folding stocks."[212]

(41) "'Stock, telescoping' means a stock which is shortened or lengthened by allowing one section to telescope into another portion. On AR-15 style firearms, the buffer tube or receiver extension acts as the fixed part of the stock on which the telescoping butt stock slides or telescopes."[213]

(42) "'Those weapons with an ammunition feeding device that can be readily removed from the firearm with the use of a tool' includes functional semiautomatic rifles, pistols, and shotguns with bullet-button style magazine releases. These weapons do not have a fixed magazine."[214]

(43) "'Thumbhole stock' means a stock with a hole that allows the thumb of the trigger hand to penetrate into or through the stock while firing."[215]

(44) "'Threaded barrel, capable of accepting a flash suppressor, forward handgrip, or silencer' means a threaded barrel able to accept a flash suppressor, forward handgrip, or silencer, and includes a threaded barrel with any one of those features already mounted on it. Some firearms have "lugs" in lieu of threads on the end of the barrel. These lugs are used to attach some versions of silencers. For purposes of this definition a lugged barrel is the same as a threaded barrel."[216]

---

[208] CAL. CODE. REGS. tit. 11, § 5471(jj).

[209] CAL. CODE. REGS. tit. 11, § 5471(kk).

[210] CAL. CODE. REGS. tit. 11, § 5471(ll).

[211] CAL. CODE. REGS. tit. 11, § 5471(mm).

[212] CAL. CODE. REGS. tit. 11, § 5471(nn).

[213] CAL. CODE. REGS. tit. 11, § 5471(oo).

[214] CAL. CODE. REGS. tit. 11, § 5471(pp).

[215] CAL. CODE. REGS. tit. 11, § 5471(qq).

[216] CAL. CODE. REGS., tit. 11 5471(rr).

Table 8.1: Category 3 "Assault Weapon" Identification Flowchart

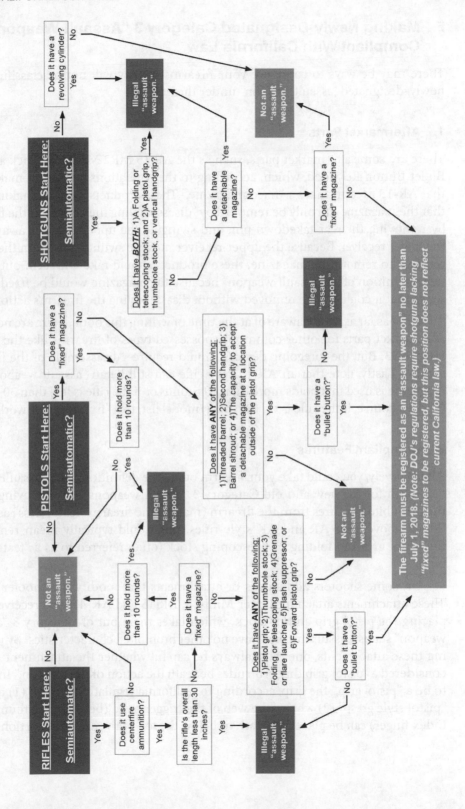

F. Making Newly-Designated Category 3 "Assault Weapons" Compliant With California Law

There may be ways to configure your firearms so they will not be classified as a newly-designated "assault weapon" under the new law.

1. Aftermarket Parts

There are some aftermarket parts, such as the AR-15 MR2 Magazine Lock and the Bullet Button Reloaded, which, according to the regulations, appear to make it so that AR-15 firearms have a "fixed magazine." These products work by making it so that the magazine can only be removed by "disassembling the action" of the firearm by removing the rear takedown pin, and swinging the upper receiver away from the lower receiver. Because the upper receiver must be swung away from the lower receiver to remove the magazine, these products should take a firearm out of the new definition of an "assault weapon" because the magazine would be fixed in the sense that it could not be removed without disassembling the firearm's action.

Only as far as we are aware of at the time of writing this book, there are no other aftermarket parts for other commonly possessed types of firearms like the AK or HK-91/93. But, the foregoing devices should require "disassembly of the firearm action." Lastly, note that an AR-15 type rifle can still be an "assault weapon" if a magazine is used that holds more than 10 rounds or if the rifle is less than 30 inches (and, of course, if the rifle is on the make/model list, this "fix" does not work).

2. Compliant Features

Alternatively, you could take your firearm out of the definition of an "assault weapon" (both for the new and old Category 3 "assault weapons") by removing all of the prohibited features from the firearm (making the firearm "featureless" as mentioned above). For AR and AK style rifles, this would typically mean removing the pistol grip and folding or telescoping stock (often referred to as a "featureless build").

Or, some shooters add stocks or attachments that modify the shooter's grip. These attachments attach to Rutger Mini-14, AR-15 and AK-47 type receivers, replacing the pistol grip and/or stock, which takes them out of Category 3 "assault weapon" status – assuming they have no other prohibited characteristics. By installing these attachments, one must always be careful whether the attachment can be considered a "pistol grip that protrudes beneath the action of the weapon." In order to be a "pistol grip," the grip, according to California regulations, must: (1) allow a "pistol style grasp" (2) where "the web of the trigger hand (between the thumb and index finger) can be placed beneath or below the top of the exposed portion of the trigger while firing."[217] Make certain that any grip or stock marketed as "California compliant" does not meet both of these criteria.

Removing or altering the pistol grip only works for rifles with "off-list lowers" that are otherwise lawful in California. Adding these items to rifles that are considered Category 1 or 2 "assault weapons," however, does *not* make those rifles lawful. In addition, keep in mind that even if you remove restricted features or use after-market features, the firearm may still meet one of the other definitions of "assault weapon" some other way.

G. Possessing the Parts of an "Assault Weapon"

If you merely possess parts that, if assembled, would make a "machinegun," you can be prosecuted for possessing a "machinegun."[218] The same is usually true if you possess parts that, if assembled, would only make a "short-barreled shotgun"[219] or "short-barreled rifle."[220] But, the same is not true for "assault weapons." Possessing unassembled parts that, if assembled, would make a firearm an "assault weapon" is *not* considered "possession" of an "assault weapon. This is because, as mentioned above in the regulations, a firearm that is disassembled is not considered to be "semiautomatic."[221] Because a firearm must be "semiautomatic" in almost all instances before it can meet the definition of an "assault weapon," a firearm in pieces (i.e., a disassembled firearm) should not be considered an "assault weapon."

 The Penal Code defines "assault weapons" as "rifles," "pistols," or "shotguns" listed by make and model, or that have certain features, not mere *parts* of a firearm.[222] Nothing prohibits having mere "assault weapon" *parts*, even if those parts can be assembled into a complete "assault weapon." In other words, a firearm, as assembled, is either an "assault weapon" or it is not. Having parts around that might turn a firearm into one does not change the analysis. But continuing to possess an unregistered receiver for a firearm listed by make and model as a California "assault weapon" is still playing with fire given law enforcement's interpretation of the law.

In 2013, a case opened the door a crack for potential criminal liability for attempted possession or manufacturing of an "assault weapon" even if you merely possess the parts of an "assault weapon."[223] The Orange County District Attorney's Office presented this novel theory in *People v. Nguyen*.[224] Nguyen, who was prohibited from possessing firearms as a result of a prior felony conviction, purchased

---

[217] CAL. CODE. REGS. tit. 11, § 5471(z).

[218] P.C. § 16880.

[219] P.C. § 17180.

[220] P.C. § 17170.

[221] CAL. CODE. REGS. tit. 11, § 5471(hh).

[222] P.C. §§ 30510, 30515.

[223] *See People v. Nguyen*, 212 Cal. App. 4th 1311 (2013).

[224] *People v. Nguyen* 212 Cal. App. 4th 1311 (2013).

all of the parts and an 80% receiver[225] and he put work into completing the receiver.[226] When law enforcement came by his auto shop during an investigation, Nguyen discussed possessing the parts with the officers, how he obtained them, and his intent to make an "AK-47."[227] At the time of the investigation, some of these parts were incomplete and he did not possess a magazine lock, which, at the time, would have made the firearm California compliant.[228] The District Attorney's office charged him with *attempted* manufacturing and *attempted* possession of an "assault weapon." He was convicted and appealed.[229]

The Court of Appeal affirmed the conviction, reasoning that Nguyen violated the laws for attempted manufacturing and possession because he admitted to having the intent to make an "AK-47," he admitted to gathering all of the parts, he had the ability to complete the firearm, and he apparently would have done so if law enforcement had not shown up.[230]

The moral to be learned from this case is, do not discuss any of your intentions with law enforcement because your statements can and will be used against you.

IV. .50 BMG RIFLES

Outside of some limited exceptions, all .50 BMG rifles must have been registered with the DOJ prior to April 30, 2006.[231] A .50 BMG[232] rifle is a centerfire rifle that is not already an "assault weapon" or a "machinegun"[233] and can fire a .50 BMG cartridge. It does not include "antique firearms" or "curios or relics."[234]

A .50 BMG cartridge is a cartridge for firing from a centerfire rifle that has the following criteria:

(1) An overall length of 5.54 inches from the base to the tip of the bullet; *and*

(2) The bullet diameter for the cartridge is from .510 to, and including, .511 inch; *and*

(3) The case base diameter for the cartridge is from .800 inch to, and including, .804 inch; *and*

---

[225] Discussed in Chapter 4.

[226] *See People v. Nguyen*, 212 Cal. App. 4th 1311, 1315-16 (2013).

[227] *People v. Nguyen*, 212 Cal. App. 4th 1311, 1316 (2013).

[228] *People v. Nguyen*, 212 Cal. App. 4th 1311, 1316 (2013).

[229] *People v. Nguyen*, 212 Cal. App. 4th 1311, 1317 (2013).

[230] *People v. Nguyen*, 212 Cal. App. 4th 1311, 1323 (2013).

[231] P.C. § 30905 (also stating that registration is only available to .50 BMG rifles that were lawfully possessed prior to January 1, 2005).

[232] "BMG" is the abbreviation for Browning Machine Gun. Keep in mind that under California law, a .50 BMG rifle is not a "machinegun." It is a rifle that can fire a .50 BMG cartridge.

[233] P.C. § 30530(a). *See also* P.C. § 16880(a) (defining a "machinegun" as "any weapon that shoots, is designed to shoot, or can readily be restored to . . . automatically [shoot] more than one shot, without manual reloading, by . . . [one] function of the trigger").

[234] P.C. § 30530(b). See Chapters 2 and 4 for "antique firearm" and "curio and relics" definitions.

(4) The cartridge case length is 3.91 inches.[235]

To be clear, just because a firearm is chambered in .50 BMG does not necessarily mean it is a .50 BMG rifle; the firearm must be a "rifle." In order to be a "rifle," the firearm should be "intended to be fired from the shoulder . . . ."[236] For example, a firearm chambered in .50 BMG, without a stock, that is fired from a mount using spade grips is not a .50 BMG rifle and thus need not be registered to be lawfully possessed in California. Since many law enforcement officers are unaware of this distinction, know that even a legal firearm chambered in .50 BMG may still cause law enforcement issues.

Example of a .50 BMG Rifle: A Barrett Model 95

V. "ASSAULT WEAPON" AND .50 BMG RIFLE USE RESTRICTIONS

With few exceptions, anyone in California who manufactures, distributes, transports, imports, sells, gives, or lends any "assault weapon" or .50 BMG rifle is guilty of a felony. And if you transfer, loan, sell, or give an "assault weapon" or .50 BMG rifle to a minor, an additional one year penalty could be added to your sentence.[237]

Mere possession of a Category 1, Category 2, and Category 3 "assault weapon" or .50 BMG rifle that is not properly registered to you may also result in a felony or misdemeanor conviction for "assault weapons" and a misdemeanor for .50 BMG rifles.[238] Category 3 "assault weapons" that meet the definition of "assault weapon" from before January 1, 2017 are, and remain, illegal to possess.[239] But firearms that became "assault weapons" on January 1, 2017 as a result of the change in law can still be possessed in their present configuration without registration until July 1, 2018 (discussed below).[240] And transporting one improperly can result in a separate felony charge (or a misdemeanor) *even if it is registered to you.*[241] You can be prosecuted for any of these violations even if you lawfully obtained the "assault weapon" or .50 BMG rifle before the law requiring their registration took effect if you did not properly register it.

---

[235] P.C. § 30525.

[236] P.C. § 17090 (defining "rifle" generally for purposes of defining "short-barreled rifle").

[237] P.C. § 30600(a)-(b).

[238] P.C. §§ 30605, 30610. Mere possession of an "assault weapon" is also considered a crime of "moral turpitude," *i.e.* the possession of such an "assault weapon" demonstrates a "general willingness to do evil." *People v. Gabriel,* 206 Cal. App. 4th 450, 458 (2012).

[239] *Cf* P.C. § 30515 (2016) with P.C. § 30515 (2017). A firearm "that has the capacity to accept a detachable magazine" is a firearm "that does not have a fixed magazine[.]" And the other pre-2017 definitions of "assault weapon" in P.C. section 30515 that do not use those terms are worded exactly the same in 2017.

[240] P.C. § 30680.

[241] P.C. §§ 30600(a), 30945.

For the first year after the window for registering "assault weapons" and .50 BMG rifles closes, the violation for possession can only be charged as an infraction in certain circumstances. For some reason, however, the same conduct that was an infraction several years ago is now a felony or misdemeanor with possible jail time and a possible lifetime ban on your right to possess a firearm. When the window closes for registering newly-defined "assault weapons" (on July 1, 2018), first time offenders of the new restrictions may also be charged as infractions in certain circumstances (see below). After that year, the same conduct that would have resulted in an infraction for the first offense will be treated as a felony or a misdemeanor.

In 1991, former P.C. section 12289 was added to the Penal Code allowing for "assault weapon" registration education and notification programs.[242] Despite the legislature's mandate that the DOJ create an education and notification program, California's confusing "assault weapon" laws have not become any clearer in the 25 years since the AWCA was passed. Law-abiding citizens with no criminal history are *still* being prosecuted today for possessing firearms they were unaware met the "assault weapon" definition even though they may have lawfully purchased them years ago.

Interestingly, when the California Legislature passed SB 880 and AB 1135, they failed to include any kind of notice provisions in these bills. As a result, there will likely be thousands of law-abiding citizens who will, once again, be unaware of the fact that their once legal to possess firearms will be considered illegal "assault weapons" after January 1, 2017.

A. Grace Period for Newly-Designated "Assault Weapons"

Those who legally acquired firearms that were legal to possess before 2017 but that were transformed into "assault weapons" because of SB 880 and AB 1135 (and apparently DOJ regulations for shotguns) will be exempt from the restrictions on possessing "assault weapons" until July 1, 2018 (the deadline to register these newly-designated "assault weapons").[243]

P.C. section 30605 allows people to possess a newly-designated "assault weapon," provided that all of the following are met:

(1) Prior to January 1, 2017, the person was eligible to register that "assault weapon" under the DOJ's registration scheme for newly-defined "assault weapons," *and*

(2) The person lawfully possessed that assault weapon prior to January 1, 2017, *and*

---

[242] P.C. § 12289 (currently codified at P.C. § 31115).
[243] *See* P.C. § 30605.

(3) The person registers the assault weapon by July 1, 2018, in accordance with the new laws and regulations for registering newly-defined "assault weapons."

In other words, you had to possess the fully functional "bullet buttoned" firearm (rifle, pistol, or shotgun) before January 1, 2017 in order to possess it legally during the "grace period" mentioned above. You *cannot* acquire the firearm after January 1, 2017, assemble a "bullet button" "assault weapon," and register it. You could be charged with felony manufacturing of an "assault weapon" and possession of an "assault weapon." And you certainly cannot attempt to register a firearm with a "detachable magazine" that met the definition of "assault weapon" before the change in the law (and you cannot currently possess it for that matter) because this firearm was not lawful for you to possess before January 1, 2017.

So, it is important to understand what firearms qualify for the "grace period" for newly-designated "assault weapons." And it is crucial that you remember the July 1, 2018 deadline. If the firearm in question meets the new definition of "assault weapon" and is not registered, modified, or taken out of the state before July 1, 2018, the owner will be considered in violation of California law.

B. Civil Compromise for Illegally Possessing an "Assault Weapon" or .50 BMG Rifle

P.C. section 30800 allows government attorneys to settle criminal cases involving "assault weapon" and/or .50 BMG rifle *possession* with a civil compromise instead of criminal charges. This rule offers those charged with possession of these firearms a way to resolve their case without the consequences of a criminal conviction.[244] In this instance, you will not be convicted of a criminal offense, but you will almost certainly have to surrender the firearm to law enforcement permanently and pay a fine. The availability of this option, however, is subject to the sole discretion of the prosecuting agency.

C. Infraction for First Violation of Possessing an "Assault Weapon"

As explained above, any person who possesses an unregistered "assault weapon" can generally be convicted of a misdemeanor or a felony. But, first time offenses are generally treated as infractions if the person was found in possession of no more than two or more firearms in compliance with P.C. section 30945[245] and all the person meets all the following conditions:

---

[244] P.C. § 30800.

[245] Meaning a registered "assault weapon."

(1) The person proves that he or she lawfully possessed the "assault weapon" prior to the date it was defined as an "assault weapon"; *and*

(2) The person has not previously been convicted of a violation of P.C. sections 30600-30675 (an unlawful act relating to an "assault weapons" or .50 BMG rifle); *and*

(3) The person was found to be in possession of the "assault weapon" within one year following the end of the one-year registration period established under P.C. section 30900 (discussed later); *and*

(4) The person relinquished the firearm to law enforcement under P.C. section 31100 (transportation of "assault weapon" or .50 BMG rifle to police or sheriffs office for relinquishment).[246]

Generally, any person who is found to be in possession of an unregistered Category 1 or Category 2 "assault weapon," or a Category 3 "assault weapon" that was not affected by the new "assault weapon" law in 2017, would fall under this provision because their one-year registration periods for these firearms have long passed. But, any person found to be in possession of an unregistered newly-defined Category 3 "assault weapons" may be able to receive an infraction from July 1, 2018 to June 30, 2019, provided that he or she meets all of the other conditions listed above. Still, it is best not to get caught with an unregistered "assault weapon" after July 1, 2018, as it may cost thousands of dollars in attorney's fees to convince a prosecutor to reduce your charges from a felony to an infraction.

VI. EXCEPTIONS TO "ASSAULT WEAPON" AND .50 BMG RIFLE LAWS

A. Law Enforcement and Other Government Agencies

The general "assault weapon" and .50 BMG rifle possession restrictions do not apply to their sale, purchase, import, or possession "by the [DOJ], police departments, sheriffs' offices, marshals' offices, the Department of Corrections and Rehabilitation, the Department of the California Highway Patrol, district attorneys' offices, the Department of Fish and Wildlife, the Department of Parks and Recreation, or

---

[246] P.C. § 30605.

the military or naval forces of this state or of the United States, or any federal law enforcement agency for use in the discharge of their official duties."[247]

Sworn peace officers who are members of the aforementioned agencies may also possess and use "assault weapons or . . . 50 BMG rifle[s] . . . for law enforcement purposes, *whether on or off duty*."[248]

B. Peace Officers and Federal Law Enforcement Acquiring "Assault Weapons" and .50 BMG Rifles

Sworn peace officers may also acquire, register, and possess "assault weapons" or .50 BMG rifles if authorized in writing by the head of their agency.[249] They must also register their "assault weapon" with the DOJ within 90 days of receiving it (or one year for .50 BMG rifles) and include a copy of the required authorization with their registration.[250] This is the only exception that allows *registering* a newly acquired "assault weapon" and/or .50 BMG rifle.

Unlike the "law enforcement purposes" exception for *agency*-owned "assault weapons," this exception does *not* limit an officer's "assault weapon" or .50 BMG rifle use. This means that an officer obtaining an "assault weapon" or .50 BMG rifle under this exception is not limited to only using it for "law enforcement purposes."[251]

Federal law enforcement members may also purchase, receive, and possess "assault weapons" or .50 BMG rifles as long as they are authorized by their employer to possess the firearm.[252]

And, due to a lawsuit I filed in August 2016, the Los Angeles Superior Court ruled in September 2017 that reserve peace officers are also entitled to the peace officer exemptions for the acquisition, possession, and use of "assault weapons," so long as they are authorized by their department.[253] Whether the California Attorney General and the Department of Justice appeal this decision remains to be seen.

---

[247] P.C. § 30625.

[248] P.C. § 30630(a) (emphasis added).

[249] P.C. § 30630(b)(1).

[250] P.C. § 30630(b)(1)-(3).

[251] An AG opinion states that any peace officer who legally purchased and registered an "assault weapon" or .50 BMG rifle under this exception cannot continue to possess it after retiring. Opinion No. 09-901, 93 Ops. Cal. Atty. Gen. 130 (2010), *available at* http://ag.ca.gov/cms_attachments/opinions/pdfs/o564_09-901.pdf (last visited July 12, 2017). This opinion is still disputed and not binding law, but may be persuasive to courts interpreting the law.

[252] P.C. § 30630(c).

[253] *Llanos v. Harris*, Case BS163796 (L.A. Sup. Ct. Sept. 2017). The court also issued an injunction preventing the DOJ from refusing to register an "assault weapon" acquired by any California sworn reserve peace officer who is eligible and authorized by the head of the officer's agency to possess and use this firearm for law enforcement purposes in compliance with Penal Code Section 30630(b)

C. Carrying "Assault Weapons" Under the Law Enforcement Officer Safety Act (LEOSA)

As explained in Chapter 6, the exemption provided by the Law Enforcement Officer Safety Act (LEOSA) allows qualified law enforcement officers (QLEOs) and qualified retired law enforcement officers (QRLEOs) to possess and carry concealed any firearm that meets the definition of a "firearm" under 18 U.S.C. section 921(a)(2). 18 U.S.C. section 921(a)(2) defines the term "firearm" as:

(1) Any weapon (including a starter gun) which will or is designed to or may readily be converted to expel a projectile by the action of an explosive; or

(2) Any firearm muffler or firearm silencer; or

(3) Any destructive device.[254]

The term "firearm" also includes ammunition not expressly prohibited by federal law (like armor piercing handgun ammunition) or subject to provisions of the National Firearms Act (NFA) (like destructive devices and machineguns).[255]

The term "firearm" under LEOSA, however, does not include any "machinegun" (as defined in 26 U.S.C. section 5848),[256] "silencer" (as defined under 18 U.S.C. 921),[257] or "destructive device" (as the term is defined under 18 U.S.C. 921).[258]

Interestingly, while a QLEO or QRLEO could not possess or carry a "machinegun," "silencer," or "destructive device" under, they may be able to possess "assault weapons" even though state law prohibits them from doing so because "assault weapons" are considered to "firearms" for purposes of this exemption. Although this is a rather odd distinction because some states, such as California, generally ban these types of firearm, this language suggests that Congress intended to allow QLEOs and QRLEOs to carry firearms that may potentially be prohibited by state laws.

But, despite the fact that the law seems to allow QLEOs and QRLEOs to possess and carry "assault weapons," I strongly suggest not attempting to push this apparent loophole in the law until Congress or a court clarifies the exception.

D. Estate Executor and Inheritance

An executor or administrator of an estate cannot be prosecuted for possessing or transporting an "assault weapon" or .50 BMG rifle properly registered (or lawfully possessed by a sworn peace officer pursuant to P.C. section 30630(a)) if it is being lawfully disposed of as authorized by a probate court.[259]

---

[254] 18 U.S.C. § 921(a)(3). See also Chapter 2.

[255] 18 U.S.C. § 926B(e)(2).

[256] 18 U.S.C. §§ 926B(e)(3)(A), 926C(e)(1)(C)(i).

[257] 18 U.S.C. §§ 926B(e)(3)(B), 926C(e)(1)(C)(ii).

[258] 18 U.S.C. §§ 926B(e)(3)(C), 926C(e)(1)(C)(iii).

[259] P.C. § 30655.

If you inherit title to a properly registered "assault weapon," you must make it permanently inoperable, sell it to an FFL with an "assault weapon" permit, obtain a Dangerous Weapons Permit from the DOJ, or remove it from California within 90 days (180 days for .50 BMG rifles) of receiving it.[260]

E. Loaning and Returning an "Assault Weapon" or .50 BMG Rifle

If you lawfully possess an "assault weapon" or .50 BMG rifle, you may lend it to someone else as long as the person you lend it to is at least age 18[261] and is not otherwise prohibited from possessing, receiving, owning, or purchasing a firearm, *the registered owner remains in the presence of the "assault weapon" or .50 BMG rifle,* and the "assault weapon" or .50 BMG rifle is possessed at any of the places it is permissible to use an "assault weapon" listed in Section IX.[262]

 Parents often run into problems at ranges when they allow their children to shoot their registered "assault weapon." Remember the age restriction for the loan of an "assault weapon" is 18 years and older. I know of parents who have been thrown off ranges when they allow their son or daughter to shoot their "assault weapons." Thankfully I am aware of no arrests or criminal prosecutions for this innocuous practice.

F. Nonresident Possession at Match or Competition

Subject to the transportation requirements,[263] California non-residents over age 18 who are not otherwise prohibited from possessing firearms may possess and import "assault weapons" or .50 BMG rifles in California if they are "going directly to or coming directly from an organized competitive match or league competition that involves the use of an assault weapon or a .50 BMG rifle."[264] For this exception to apply, the competition or match must take place at a "target range that holds a regulatory or business license for the purpose of practice shooting at that target range" or a "target range of a public or private club or origination that is organized for the purpose of practice shooting at targets."[265] In addition, "[t]he match or competition . . . [must be] sponsored by, conducted under the auspices of, or approved by, a law enforcement agency or a nationally or state recognized entity that fosters proficiency in, or promotes education about, firearms."[266] Because the law says you must be going directly to or from the approved locations, detours are risky.

---

[260] P.C. §§ 30915, 30935.

[261] Anyone under age 18 cannot even *touch* an "assault weapon." No exceptions. *See* P.C. § 30660.

[262] P.C. § 30660.

[263] "Assault weapons" and .50 BMG rifles must be transported according to P.C. section 25610 or 25505.

[264] P.C. § 30665(a).

[265] P.C. § 30665(b).

[266] P.C. § 30665(c).

G. California Department of Justice Permits

Today anyone other than certain peace officers can, *in theory*, acquire an "assault weapon" or .50 BMG rifle in California if they first obtain a Dangerous Weapons Permit.[267] The permit process involves filling out a six-page form with references, fingerprints, and a statement of "good cause," and it is the same process used to acquire a "machinegun" license and a "destructive device" permit in California.[268]

For "good cause" you must give "clear and convincing evidence that there is a bona fide market or public necessity for the issuance of a dangerous weapons license or permit and that . . . [you will not] endanger[] public safety."[269] "Good cause" includes the following:

(1) Sales to and/or manufacture for sales to law enforcement, military and/or other Dangerous Weapon Permit holders; *or*

(2) Training, research and development; and/or manufacturing pursuant to government contract; *or*

(3) Use and/or manufacture of dangerous weapons as props in commercial motion picture, television production, or other commercial entertainment events; *or*

(4) Possession for the purpose of maintaining a collection of destructive devices as defined in P.C. section 16460 but such possession shall not be allowed for short-barreled shotguns, short-barreled rifles, machineguns or "*assault weapons*"; *or*

(5) Repair and maintenance of dangerous weapons lawfully possessed by others; *or*

(6) Use of dangerous weapons in activities sanctioned by government military agencies by members of those agencies; *or*

(7) The sale of assault weapons and/or the manufacture of assault weapons for the sale to, purchase by, or possession of assault weapons by: the agencies listed in P.C. section 30625 and the officers described in P.C. section 30630; entities and persons who have been issued assault weapon permits; entities outside the state who have, in effect, a federal firearms dealer's license solely for the purpose of distribution to an entity listed within this paragraph; federal law enforcement and military agencies; law enforcement and military agencies of other states; and foreign governments and agencies approved by the United States State Department; *or*

---

[267] P.C. §§ 31000, 32650; CAL. CODE REGS. tit. 11, § 4128. For the Dangerous Weapons License/Permit Application, see *Dangerous Weapons License/Permit(s) Application*, CAL. DEPT. OF JUSTICE, http://ag.ca.gov/firearms/forms/pdf/FD030DWApp.pdf (last visited July 12, 2017).

[268] Out-of-state residents who have lawfully acquired an "assault weapon" or a .50 BMG rifle before moving to California cannot simply register their firearms; they have to get a Dangerous Weapons Permit first. P.C. §§ 30925, 30940.

[269] CAL. CODE REGS. tit. 11, § 4128(c).

(8) Use of dangerous weapons for the design, manufacture, demonstration, and sales of dangerous weapons accessories to law enforcement, military and/or other Dangerous Weapon Permit Holders.[270]

In the highly unlikely event that the DOJ gives you a Dangerous Weapons Permit, you are required to *annually* renew it along with paying a renewal and inspection fee of up to $1,500, keep an inventory of all "dangerous weapons," and store them in a safe place.[271] If you have less than five devices that require the permit, only one inspection every five years is required.[272]

H. "Licensed Gun Dealer" Exceptions

For purposes of "assault weapons" and .50 BMG rifles, "licensed gun dealers" are those who not only possess a standard license to sell firearms (as discussed in Chapter 4),[273] but who *also* possess Dangerous Weapons Permit for "assault weapons" and/or .50 BMG rifles.[274]

1. Service or Repair

"Licensed gun dealers" can take possession of "assault weapons" or .50 BMG rifles to service or repair them from a lawfully registered owner or Dangerous Weapons Permit holder. The "licensed gun dealer" may also give possession of them to a gunsmith to help with the service or repair as long as the gunsmith is employed by, or has a contract with, the dealer for gunsmithing[275] services.[276]

Despite being able to take possession of an "assault weapon" for service or repair, the DOJ has taken the position that these FFLs cannot convert an "assault weapon" into a California compliant firearm for the purposes of sales.[277] This kind of action may be considered "manufacturing," which is not usually covered by a Dangerous Weapons Permit.

---

[270] CAL. CODE REGS. tit. 11, § 4128. *See also* P.C. § 31005 (giving the DOJ authority to issue "assault weapons" permits upon a finding of "good cause").

[271] CAL. CODE REGS. tit. 11, §§ 4129, 4130, 4145.

[272] CAL. CODE REGS. tit. 11, § 4145(b).

[273] Having the "standard license to sell firearms" means that you are a California-licensed firearms dealer (i.e., someone licensed per P.C. sections 26700 to 26915, inclusive).

[274] P.C. § 16790.

[275] For this exception the gunsmith must have an FFL of his or her own and a business license required by a state or local governmental agency. P.C. § 31050(c).

[276] P.C. § 31050.

[277] *Important Notice Re: Dangerous Weapons*, CALIFORNIA DEPARTMENT OF JUSTICE, BUREAU OF FIREARMS (on file with author).

2. Other Special Allowances

These "licensed gun dealers" may also transport an "assault weapon" or .50 BMG rifle between dealers or to out-of-state dealers per the NFA,[278] display firearms at licensed state or local government gun shows, sell them to out-of-state residents, or sell them to someone with a Dangerous Weapons Permit.[279]

VII. ACQUIRING NEW "ASSAULT WEAPONS" OR .50 BMG RIFLES

A. Registration

As mentioned above, registration periods for 50 BMG rifles, Category 1 and Category 2 "assault weapons," and firearms meeting the old definition of Category 3 "assault weapons" have long passed.[280] With the exception of peace officers, the DOJ no longer accepts registration applications for these firearms.

In the past, a lot of folks believe that their firearms were registered as "assault weapons" when they originally purchased their firearm from the dealer. But in order to have properly registered a firearm as an "assault weapon" or .50 BMG rifle, you must have submitted an application to the DOJ that required you to provide the firearms description and all unique identification marks, your full name and address, date of birth, thumbprint, and other pieces of information, and you were required to pay the requisite fee to process the application ($20 for an "assault weapon," and $25 for a .50 BMG rifle).[281]

If you properly sent in your registration for an "assault weapon" or .50 BMG rifle within the specified time period and all of the information was accurately provided, the registration should have been entered into the DOJ's Automated Firearm System (AFS) database, and you should have received a confirmation notice. If you have a firearm that should have been registered as an "assault weapon" but was not, there will be no record in the AFS for the firearm as an "assault weapon." In other words, if your "assault weapon" is not registered to you as an "assault weapon" in the AFS, you may be possessing it illegally.

There have been reports of the DOJ inadvertently omitting "assault weapon" registrations for an "assault weapons" from the AFS, and in the past an ex-DOJ official testified to the unreliability of the AFS system for keeping accurate firearm

---

[278] NFA firearms are discussed in Chapter 2. Almost all "assault weapons" and .50 BMG rifles are not "firearms" under the NFA, showing that the legislature did not know what it was doing when writing these laws. Also remember that transporting "assault weapons" has specific requirements discussed in Section IX(A) of this Chapter and in Chapter 6.

[279] P.C. § 31055.

[280] All of the deadlines for registering Category 1, Category 2, and Category 3 "assault weapons" have passed. April 30, 2006, was the most recent deadline applying to the registration of .50 BMG rifles. P.C. § 30905.

[281] P.C. §§ 30900(c)-(d) ("assault weapons"), 30905(b)-(c) (.50 BMG rifles).

disposition records (not just "assault weapon" records). It is therefore wise to keep the confirmation notice of your "assault weapon" registration in a safe place, along with copies saved in paper and electronic format. Some "assault weapon" owners keep a copy of their registration in the hollow of their "assault weapons" pistol grip or buttstock in case law enforcement asks them about it. That's smart.

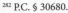

Although you can no longer register Category 1 and Category 2 "assault weapons," and firearms meeting the pre-2017 definition of Category 3 "assault weapons," you will be able to register firearms that fall under the new, post-2017 definition of a Category 3 "assault weapon." Under SB 880 and AB 1135, any person *who lawfully possessed a newly-designated "assault weapon" before January 1, 2017* (the date the new definition became effective) may continue to possess the firearm if it is registered before July 1, 2018.[282]

These bills also require the DOJ to create an electronic registration system and regulations so that individuals can register these firearms. But, as stated in detail in Section III(E)(4) above, the DOJ delayed in drafting and implementing the necessary regulations required by law. So, AB 103 extended this registration deadline to June 30, 2018 due to the DOJ's problems in implementing regulations for registration. And, as further shown in Section III(E) above, the regulations that the DOJ ultimately implemented in August 2017 are problematic. The discussion below goes into detail about the DOJ's regulations and explains how you can register a newly-designated "assault weapon."

Again, those who are planning on registering their firearms as "assault weapons" will have until June 30, 2018 to do so.

Table 8.2

QUICK REVIEW OF REGISTRATION DEADLINES FOR ASSAULT WEAPONS AND .50 BMG RIFLES[283]		
FIREARM	**DESCRIPTION OF FIREARM**	**REGISTRATION DATE**[284]
Category 1 "Assault Weapons"	Firearms listed in the 1989 Assault Weapons Control Act and those added later to the Penal Code are considered Category 1 assault weapons. These firearms are specifically named in P.C. § 30510.	Category 1 "assault weapons" must have been registered with the DOJ before March 31, 1992.
Category 2 "Assault Weapons"	AR-15 and AK "series" firearms that were added through the "add on procedure" are considered Category 2 "assault weapons." These firearms are listed in Cal. Code Regs. tit. 11, § 5499.	Category 2 "assault weapons" must have been registered with the DOJ before January 23, 2001.
Pre-2017 Category 3 "Assault Weapons"	Firearms with certain features that are listed in P.C. § 30515 are considered Category 3 "assault weapons."	Category 3 "assault weapons" must have been registered with the DOJ before December 31, 2000.
.50 BMG Rifles	A .50 BMG rifle is a centerfire rifle that is not already an "assault weapon" or a "machinegun" and can fire a .50 BMG cartridge. See Section IV for a complete discussion of what kind of rifle is considered a .50 BMG rifle.	Must have been registered before April 30, 2006.[285]
Category 3 "Assault Weapons" Added After January 1, 2017	Semiautomatic, centerfire rifles and semiautomatic handguns that do not have a "fixed magazine," and contain one (or more) of the features listed in P.C. § 30515 are now considered Category 3 "assault weapons."	Firearms newly-classified as Category 3 "assault weapons" after January 1, 2017 must be registered with the DOJ before July 1, 2018. Semiautomatic shotguns with "bullet buttons" attached must also be registered before July 1, 2018

---

[283] All of the tables within this book are paraphrases of the law and are not a complete summary of each subject area. Please review the corresponding sections within this Chapter for a more in-depth discussion of each topic and for the applicable statutes and/or case law that is paraphrased within the tables.

[284] The registration dates for all three categories of "assault weapons" can be found in the AWIG. *See* CAL. DEPT. OF JUSTICE, OFFICE OF THE ATTORNEY GENERAL, ASSAULT WEAPONS IDENTIFICATION GUIDE, (3rd ed. Nov. 2001), *available at* http://oag.ca.gov/sites/all/files/agweb/pdfs/firearms/forms/awguide.pdf (last visited July 12, 2017).

[285] P.C. § 30905.

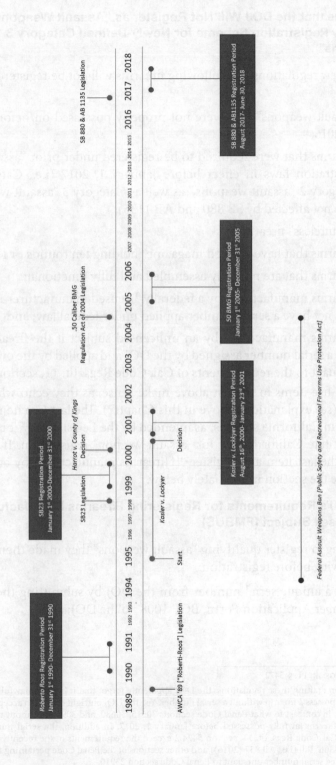

California "Assault Weapon" Registration Period Historical Timeline

1. **Firearms that the DOJ Will Not Register as "Assault Weapons" Under the New Registration Scheme for Newly-Defined Category 3 "Assault Weapons"**

Under the new regulations, the following firearms will not be registered as "assault weapons":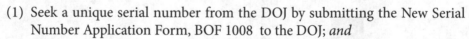

(1) "Assault weapons" that were not properly possessed on/before December 31, 2016;

(2) Firearms that were required to be registered under prior "assault weapon" registration laws in effect before January 1, 2017 (i.e., Category 1 and Category 2 "assault weapons," as well as Category 3 "assault weapons" that were not affected by SB 880 and AB 1135);

(3) "Featureless" firearms;

(4) Firearms that have a "fixed magazine" holding ten rounds or less;

(5) Firearms that are not fully assembled and fully functional;

(6) Firearms manufactured by a federally-licensed manufacturer if the firearm does not have a serial number applied under federal law; and

(7) Firearms manufactured by an unlicensed subject if the firearm does not have a serial number assigned by the DOJ and applied by the owner or agent pursuant to the requirements of Cal. Code Regs. tit. 11, section 5474.2.[286]

The first five items in the list above make sense, as they echo what the Penal Code states (see explanations above in this Chapter). The last two items do not reflect what is in California statutes, as intended by the Legislature,[287] but they nonetheless constitute California law for "assault weapon" registration. If you want to get around the last item and register "[f]irearms manufactured by an unlicensed subject[,]"see the section immediately below.

2. **The DOJ's Requirements for Registering Firearms Manufactured by an Unlicensed Subject (FMBUS)**

Those seeking to register qualifying "assault weapons" they made themselves must do the following before registration:

(1) Seek a unique serial number from the DOJ by submitting the New Serial Number Application Form, BOF 1008 to the DOJ; *and*

---

[286] Cal. Code Regs. tit. 11, § 5472.

[287] For instance, in drafting these regulations, the DOJ apparently forgot that it is not unlawful under federal or California law to possess a firearm without a serial number. Yet, the DOJ outright refuses to accept the registration of these firearms, in contrast to what Penal Code sections 30515, 30680, and 30900 say about registration being allowed for any firearm lawfully-possessed before January 1, 2017. In addition, the serial number application requirements of Cal. Code Regs. tit. 11, section 5474.2 exceed the requirements of the recently-enacted sections from the "Ghost Gun" Bill (i.e., AB 857 (2016)) and other sections of the Penal Code pertaining to the application for a DOJ-provided serial number pursuant to Penal Code section 23910.

(2) Have the serial number placed on the firearm pursuant to federal specifications;[288] *and*

(3) Have additional information placed onto the firearm pursuant to the requirements of Cal. Code Regs. tit. 11, section 5474.2.[289]

When it comes to the second item (having the serial number placed on the firearm), you should stay with the firearm while it is being engraved. The DOJ's regulations say that you can either (1) contact a Federal Firearms Licensed Manufacturer (type 7) to place the serial number on the firearm for you or (2) provided that you do not leave the firearm unattended, have a non-licensed party apply the serial number for you.[290] This is not entirely correct. For one, the DOJ forgets to mention that, under federal law, a federally licensed gunsmith/dealer (commonly referred to as an "01") can also engrave serial numbers onto firearms.[291] More importantly, the DOJ forgets to tell you that California law requires the person doing the engraving to have a "Dangerous Weapon" Permit because the firearms in question are "assault weapons."[292] Without such a permit, the firearms cannot be lawfully taken to or left with a firearm manufacturer/dealer/gunsmith. Doing so would cause the firearm owner and licensee to violate the restrictions on transferring and possessing "assault weapons."

When it comes to placing the required information onto the firearm pursuant to section 5474.2, the DOJ is requiring more information to be engraved, casted, or otherwise placed on the firearm than California statutory law, which just requires the serial number. Presumably, the DOJ borrowed this heightened engraving/stamping standard from federal law (for licensed firearm manufacturers and importers who have the machinery and capability to comply with these requirements). Regardless, the fact remains that the following information must be placed on the frame, barrel, or receiver in order to register an "FMBUS":

(1) The model of the firearm, if such designation has been made; *and*

(2) The caliber or gauge of the firearm; *and*

(3) The manufacturer's first and last name as provided to the DOJ for registration purposes, when applicable; *and*

(4) The city and state (or recognized abbreviation thereof) where the manufacturer made the firearm.[293]

---

[288] The engraving, casting, stamping (impressing), or otherwise placing of the serial number must be to a minimum depth of .003 inch and in a print size no smaller than 1/16 inch. CAL. CODE REGS., tit. 11, § 5474.2(a)(3). And proof of the serial number being applied to the firearm must be given to the DOJ in the form of one or more digital photographs of the newly serialized firearm being submitted in accordance with the photo requirement described later in this Chapter. CAL. CODE REGS., tit. 11, § 5474.2(a)(2).

[289] CAL. CODE REGS. tit. 11, § 5474.2.

[290] CAL. CODE REGS. tit. 11, § 5474.2(a)(2).

[291] *See* ATF Rul. 2009-1.

[292] P.C. §§ 16790, 31000, 31050; CAL. CODE REGS. tit. 11, § 4128.

[293] CAL. CODE REGS. tit. 11, § 5474.2(a)(3).

Lastly, those seeking serial numbers for firearms they made themselves, and who are attempting to register such firearms as "assault weapons," should always answer "N/A" in response to questions on the DOJ's registration website asking who they acquired the firearm from, where it was acquired, etc. This is because the regulations specify that registration is available *only* for firearms made by non-licensees[294]; if you purchased an unmarked firearm from an individual who made or completed the firearm for you and who is not a licensed dealer, you need to consult with an attorney before filling out the DOJ's form. Likewise, if you purchased a firearm without serial numbers that was made prior to the federal requirement for a manufacturing license and marking requirements, when you were not required to go through a firearm dealer, you should also consult with an attorney.

3. Age Requirement to Register and Possess "Assault Weapons"

Under California law, those under the age of eighteen are prohibited from registering and possessing "assault weapons."[295] And the DOJ states that a registrant must turn 18 on or before June 30, 2018.[296] Therefore, individuals failing to meet this age requirement cannot register an "assault weapon" using the new registration procedures.

4. The Requirement to Create a California Firearms Application Reporting System ("CFARS") Account and Enter Your Personal Information

All "assault weapon" registrations must be filed electronically through the DOJ's California Firearms Application Reporting System (CFARS). This website can be accessed at https://cfars.doj.ca.gov/login.do. In order to register an "assault weapon," you will be required to make a CFARS account. In doing so, you will need to agree to a number of waivers. In addition, the following information must be provided in order to create a CFARS account: your full name, e-mail address, three security questions and answers, and a password.[297]

Once you have created a CFARS account, you must provide the following information to register your firearm as an "assault weapon":

(1) Your full name (first name and last name are required fields); *and*

(2) Address (residence is required, as is mailing address if different); *and*

(3) E-mail address (this is required by the DOJ even though it's not in the Penal Code); *and*

(4) Telephone number (CFARS instructions say one number is required and includes home, business, and/or mobile); *and*

(5) Date of birth (required); *and*

---

[294] *See* CAL. CODE REGS. tit. 11, § 5474.2.

[295] *See* P.C. § 30950.

[296] *See* CAL. CODE REGS. tit. 11, § 5474.1(b).

[297] CAL. CODE REGS. tit. 11, § 5473.

(6) Sex (required, but the pull-down menu does not include California's new recognition of the "non-binary" gender option); *and*

(7) Height (required); *and*

(8) Weight (required); *and*

(9) Race (not a required field); *and*

(10) Eye color (required); *and*

(11) Hair color (required); *and*

(12) ID type and number (the Penal Code only allows for "California DL" and "California ID" as the type of ID you can use, but, oddly, the DOJ has the following ID types to choose from: "California DL," "California ID," "Dept. of Defense ID," and "Military ID"); *and*

(13) Whether or not you are a U.S. citizen (required); *and*

(14) Place of birth (required, asking you to specify state or county of birth); *and*

(15) Country of citizenship (if applicable); *and*

(16) Alien registration number or I-94, if applicable (required).[298]

The last four items on the list above are probably added by the DOJ for purposes of running NICS background checks on registrants; the previous required fields (except for e-mail address and certain military options for ID types) are required by the Penal Code for registration.[299] So items like the military ID number, U.S. citizen status, place of birth, country of citizenship, and alien registration number or I-94 number are required by the DOJ's regulations, not by the Penal Code.

5. Joint Registration of Newly-Designated Category 3 "Assault Weapons"

Under California law, individuals can jointly register an "assault weapon" if it is "owned by family members over 18 years old residing in the same household."[300] Families are strongly advised to avail themselves of this joint registration process, as failing to do so could lead to problems in the future.

For example, say an "assault weapon" is registered to one person in the home, in this case a husband, and that husband leaves the "assault weapon" in a gun safe at home. If the husband's wife knew the combination or had access to the key to the gun safe and knew the "assault weapon" was in the safe, then she would be violating California law because she was technically in "possession" of an "assault weapon" that was not registered to her.

To minimize these problems, we recommend that you register Category 3 "assault weapons" to every family member who lives in your household that is over the age of eighteen. This will help avoid any legal issues later on down the road.

---

[298] *See* Cal. Code Regs. tit. 11, § 5474(a), (b).

[299] *See* P.C. § 30900(b)(3).

[300] P.C. § 30955.

If you would like to jointly register a firearm as an "assault weapon," you will be required to identify one family member as the primary registrant and provide the name and relationship of each joint registrant. All joint registrants must be 18 years of age by June 30, 2018 and reside in the same "household," and only individuals who fit within the following family relationships can jointly register a firearm:

(1) Spouses,

(2) Parent to Child,

(3) Child to Parent,

(4) Grandparent to Grandchild,

(5) Grandchild to Grandparent,

(6) Domestic Partners, *or*

(7) Siblings.[301]

Each joint registrant must be named, and their relationship must be specified. The form has room for one person but mentions that other joint registrants must be described in the comments field.

Furthermore, the DOJ is requiring "joint registrants" to complete individual registration forms in addition to the primary registrant's application. Joint registrants also need to provide the primary registrant's CRIS number for that "assault weapon's" registration. And each joint registrant must provide proof of address at the time they submit the application. Acceptable forms of proof of address are:

(1) Carry Concealed Weapon (CCW)Permit; *or*

(2) Curio and Relic (C & R) federal firearm license with name and address; *or*

(3) Utility bill, cable, electricity, garbage, gas, pipeline, propane, alarm/security, or water bill with purchaser's name on it and dated within three months of application for registration; *or*

(4) Military permanent duty station orders indicating assignment within California (active duty military spouse ID is not acceptable); *or*

(5) Property deed: valid deed or deed of trust for the individual's property or a certificate of title; *or*

(6) Resident Hunting License; *or*

(7) Signed and dated rental agreement/contract or residential lease; *or*

(8) Trailer certification of title; *or*

(9) DMV Vehicle Registration; *or*

(10) Certificate of Eligibility for firearms.[302]

---

[301] CAL. CODE REGS. tit. 11, § 5474.1(b).

[302] CAL. CODE REGS. tit. 11, § 5474.1(c).

6. Firearm Information and Photographs That Need to be Submitted for Registration

As a preliminary matter, know that early reports from individuals attempting to register suggest that the DOJ's online system is allowing people to submit registrations for firearms previously classified as an "assault weapon" or firearms otherwise prohibited in California. Therefore, it is important that you confirm that the firearm you are registering is an "assault weapon" as a result of the recent change in California law. Do not attempt to register make/model "assault weapons" or firearms that were considered "assault weapons" prior to 2017. Should you seek to register a firearm, you should ensure that doing so will not expose you to liability for being in possession of an "assault weapon" that was previously required to be registered. Likewise, do not attempt to register any other highly-restricted firearm, such as a short-barreled rifle or shotgun or a .50 BMG rifle.

That being said, know that the Penal Code requires you to give "a description of the firearm that identifies it uniquely, including all identification marks, the date the firearm was acquired, the name and address of the individual from whom, or business from which, the firearm was acquired[.]"[303] Meanwhile, the DOJ is requiring you to enter information like "firearm type, make, model, caliber, firearm color, barrel length, serial number, all identification marks, firearm country of origin manufacturer, the date the firearm was acquired, the name and address of the individual from whom, or business from which, the firearm was acquired."[304] If the caliber you want to enter is not listed in the DOJ's pull-down menus, choose the next closest caliber and enter the actual description in the comments.

Interestingly, during past "assault weapon" and .50 BMG rifle registrations, "individual from which or business from which, the firearm was acquired" was an optional field. But now, it is required. So, remember California firearm transfer requirements (discussed in Chapter 4) when you fill out this field. If you did not acquire the firearm lawfully, contact an attorney before filling out this field.

The DOJ's website requires you to specify the "type" of firearm to be registered (pistol, rifle, or shotgun).[305] Once you make your selection, you may be confronted with boxes to check as to what features your firearm has. For shotguns, there will be no additional boxes because there are no other shoguns, besides a semiautomatic shotgun that does not have a fixed magazine, that is being considered an "assault weapon" for this registration period. But the DOJ requires you to specify the features for rifles and pistols. Surprisingly and potentially disturbing is the fact that, for rifles, one of the characteristics you can choose is "Semi-automatic, Centerfire, and Overall Length of Less than 30 Inches [measured whiled the rifle is in

---

[303] P.C. § 30900(b)(3).

[304] CAL. CODE REGS. tit. 11, § 5474(b).

[305] *See CFARS Assault Weapons Reg. Process,* STATE OF CALIFORNIA DEPARTMENT OF JUSTICE, https://oag.ca.gov/sites/all/files/agweb/pdfs/firearms/regs/cfars-awr-process.pdf (last visited Oct 27, 2017).

the shortest possible configuration in which it will fire]." This is disturbing because semiautomatic, centerfire rifles less than 30 inches in length were "assault weapons" before the 2017 change in law and are certainly "assault weapons" thereafter. According to the Penal Code, this is not a type of rifle you can register as a result in the change in the law or through the DOJ's regulations. Why is this here, then? We don't know. This could be another of a string of DOJ errors when it comes to the "assault weapon" registration and regulation process. It could be the DOJ attempting to "bait" registration of a firearm that cannot be lawfully possessed and registered (though this is unlikely). Or, because the DOJ defined "overall length of less than 30 inches" in the new "assault weapon" regulations (discussed above), the DOJ feels it needs to allow people to register this type of "assault weapon." There is no clear answer here. And we strongly caution anyone who wants to register such a rifle with these characteristics. They should talk to an attorney before submitting the registration.

In addition, the DOJ requires you to submit four "clear" digital photos of the firearms you are attempting to register:

(1) One photo must depict the bullet-button style magazine release installed on the firearm.

(2) One photo must depict the firearm from the end of the barrel to the end of the stock if it is a long gun or the point furthest from the end of the barrel if it is a pistol.

(3) The other two photos must show the left side of the receiver/frame and right side of the receiver/frame (this is usually where the manufacturer marks the firearm).[306]

The DOJ has the discretion to allow you to substitute the last two photos for photos of identification markings at some other locations on the firearm.[307]

For the photographs, the DOJ accepts pdf, gif, jpg, or png files. The maximum size is 10 MB. But there are still a lot of unanswered questions regarding the digital photos. For instance, do they need to be a specific resolution? What about the backdrop? So Californians are advised to err on the side of caution in taking clear photographs of their firearms.

7. Fees Required for Registration

The fee to register an "assault weapon" is $15 per person, per transaction.[308] There is no limit to the number of "assault weapons" a person can register in a single transaction.[309]

---

[306] CAL. CODE REGS. tit. 11, § 5474(c).
[307] CAL. CODE REGS. tit. 11, § 5474(c).
[308] CAL. CODE REGS. tit. 11, § 5475(a).
[309] CAL. CODE REGS. tit. 11, § 5475(a).

The fee must be paid by credit or debit card at the time the electronic registration is submitted, at which point it will be deposited in the Dealer's Record of Sale Special Account.[310]

In addition, a $5 fee is required to obtain a copy of the original registration letter.[311] There is no restriction on making copies, so registrants are advised to make a lot of copies.

8. Processing of Applications

According to the regulations, applications must be received between January 1, 2017 and June 30, 2018, and will be processed in the order in which they are received.[312] Once the registration has been submitted and the fees have been paid, the DOJ will inform you (via e-mail) that your application:

1) Has been received and accepted for processing; *or*

(2) Is being returned as incomplete (and specifying what further information is required); *or*

(3) Has been rejected.[313]

If the DOJ deems your application incomplete, you must provide the requested information or documentation to the DOJ within 30 days. For instance, we have heard of the DOJ requesting additional and/or clearer pictures of certain parts. If the DOJ does not receive the information within that time, your application will be rejected and your fee will not be refunded.[314] If you can't get the information to the DOJ within the 30 day window, you can still complete a new application before June 30, 2018. But you will have to pay a new registration fee.[315]

Once the DOJ has determined that all the necessary information has been received and the firearm qualifies for registration, the firearms eligibility check will begin.[316] If you think you may be prohibited, run your own background first using the Personal Firearms Eligibility Check form before attempting to register an "assault weapon." If the eligibility check is successful, the registrant will receive an "assault weapon" registration disposition letter in the mail.[317]

9. Post-Registration Modification of "Bullet Buttons" of Registered Assault Weapons Is Prohibited

The DOJ has declared that you are prohibited from changing the release mechanism for the ammunition feeding device on any "assault weapon" registered under

---

[310] Cal. Code Regs. tit. 11, § 5475(b).

[311] Cal. Code Regs. tit. 11, § 5475(c).

[312] Cal. Code Regs. tit. 11, § 5476(a).

[313] Cal. Code Regs. tit. 11, § 5476(b).

[314] Cal. Code Regs. tit. 11, § 5476(c).

[315] Cal. Code Regs. tit. 11, § 5476(c).

[316] Cal. Code Regs. tit. 11, § 5476(d).

[317] Cal. Code Regs. tit. 11, § 5476(e).

the new regulations.[318] But this restriction does not apply to: (1) the repair or like-kind replacement of the mechanism, or (2) firearm undergoing the deregistration process.[319]

According to the DOJ, this is because "[a]ny alteration to the release mechanism converts the assault weapon into a different weapon from the one that was registered."[320] So, you cannot modify or remove the "bullet button" on your firearm.

Yet, the DOJ doesn't specify that other modifications are prohibited. Hence, you should be able to change other parts of the firearms (e.g., stocks, muzzle attachments, forward grips, etc.), so long as you don't make anything illegal, i.e., a short-barreled rifle or shotgun, machinegun, destructive device, or "any other weapon."

10. Voluntary Deregistration

You can voluntarily deregister your firearm as an "assault weapon" if:

(1) You no longer possess the "assault weapon," *or*

(2) The firearm has been modified or reconfigured to no longer meet the definition of an "assault weapon."[321]

If the firearm is deregistered, the DOJ will delete the "assault weapon" registration for the specified firearm(s).[322] Once deregistered, the firearm cannot be possessed in the state in its "assault weapon" configuration, unless another exception to the "assault weapon" restrictions applies.

B. Alternatives to Registration

Those who own newly-designated Category 3 "assault weapons" and who do not want to register them may have some other options to avoid the requirements of the law. These include:

(1) Removing the firearm from California; *and*

(2) Lawfully selling or transferring the firearm; *and*

(3) Surrendering the firearm to law enforcement; *and*

(4) Rendering the firearm permanently inoperable; *and*

(5) Properly configuring the firearm so that it is no longer classified as an "assault weapon."

---

[318] CAL. CODE REGS. tit. 11, § 5477(a).
[319] CAL. CODE REGS. tit. 11, § 5477(b), (c).
[320] CAL. CODE REGS. tit. 11, § 5477(a).
[321] CAL. CODE REGS. tit. 11, § 5478.
[322] CAL. CODE REGS. tit. 11, § 5478(b).

VIII. MOVING INTO CALIFORNIA WITH AN "ASSAULT WEAPON" OR .50 BMG RIFLE

If you plan on moving to California and bringing an "assault weapon" or .50 BMG rifle, you must get a Dangerous Weapons Permit from the DOJ *before* you can bring your firearm into California. Alternatively, you can have the firearm sent to an FFL who has a Dangerous Weapons Permit in California, and once you get a Dangerous Weapons Permit, *then* the FFL will redeliver the firearm to you.[323] If the FFL is prohibited from delivering the firearm to you, either because you did not obtain the DOJ permit or because you are prohibited from owning firearms in general (see Chapter 3), the FFL will keep possession or lawfully dispose of it according to California law.[324] There is little chance the DOJ will issue this permit to you.

You always have the option to render your "assault weapon" California compliant before bringing it into the state. This means modifying your non-make/model prohibited "assault weapon" into a configuration that does not meet the definition of an "assault weapon" (discussed throughout this chapter). You will still have to meet the requirements of a "personal firearm importer" (discussed in Chapter 4) if you are moving to the state with the firearm.

IX. LAWFULLY USING "ASSAULT WEAPONS" AND .50 BMG RIFLES

Unless the DOJ issues you a permit for additional uses, you may only possess an "assault weapon" or .50 BMG rifle *registered to you*:

(1) At your residence, place of business, or other property you own or on the property of another with their express permission; *or*

(2) While on the premises of a target range of a public or private club or organization organized for the purpose of practicing shooting at targets; *or*

(3) While on a target range that holds a regulatory or business license for the purpose of practicing shooting at that target range; *or*

(4) While on the premises of a shooting club licensed pursuant to the California Fish and Game Code; *or*

(5) While attending any exhibition, display, or educational project that is about firearms and that is sponsored by, conducted under the auspices of, or approved by a law enforcement agency or a nationally or state recognized entity that fosters proficiency in, or promotes education about, firearms; *or*

(6) While on publicly owned land, if the possession and use of an "assault weapon" is specifically permitted by the managing agency of the land; *or*

---

[323] P.C. §§ 30925, 30940.

[324] *See* P.C. §§ 30925 ("assault weapons"), 30940 (.50 BMG rifles).

(7) While transporting the assault weapon or .50 BMG rifle between any of the places mentioned here, or to any FFL (who also has a dangerous weapons permit) for service or repair.[325]

If you want to use an "assault weapon" or .50 BMG rifle for something other than the things above, you have to get a Dangerous Weapons Permit from the DOJ first.[326]

A. Transporting Registered "Assault Weapons" and .50 BMG Rifles

Firearms meeting the definition of an "assault weapon" must be transported like handguns, even if they are non-handguns, meaning that they must be transported unloaded and in a "locked container."[327] Only the registered owner of the "assault weapon" may lawfully transport it and only between the places and activities where you can lawfully use your "assault weapons," which are listed above.

X. WHAT TO DO IF YOU THINK YOU HAVE AN "ASSAULT WEAPON" OR .50 BMG RIFLE THAT YOU AREN'T SURE IS LEGAL

A. Determine if It *Is* an "Assault Weapon" or .50 BMG Rifle

Using the above information, determine if your firearm meets the definition of an "assault weapon" or .50 BMG rifle. As discussed above, some of the laws prohibiting "assault weapons" were passed with little fanfare. No doubt thousands of California residents are unknowingly "in possession" of unregistered "assault weapons." If you have any doubts about your firearm, ask an attorney familiar with California firearms law.

B. Determine if Your "Assault Weapon" or .50 BMG Rifle Was Registered or Can be Registered

If you do not know or *think* that you registered your "assault weapon" or .50 BMG rifle, you may request a list of all firearms of which you are the registered owner by submitting an Automated Firearms System Record Request to the DOJ. This form can be found at http://ag.ca.gov/firearms/forms/pdf/AFSPrivateCitizen.pdf.

---

[325] P.C. § 30945.

[326] P.C. § 31000(a).

[327] P.C. § 30945(g).

If you know or believe you registered your "assault weapon" or .50 BMG rifle but no registration record appears in the DOJ's system, you should contact an attorney experienced in firearms law immediately for possible options.

Often people are confused and believe that filling out the Form 4473 and DROS form (discussed in Chapter 4) registers their firearm as an "assault weapon." They are incorrect. A separate form needs to be filled out and sent to DOJ registering their firearm as an "assault weapon." If you did not do this or don't remember doing this, there is a strong chance you firearm is not registered as an "assault weapon."

Lastly, if your firearm is now considered an "assault weapon" as a result of the change in the law on January 1, 2017, and was legally obtained before January 1, 2017, you still have until July 1, 2018 to register it.

C. If Your "Assault Weapon" or .50 BMG Rifle Is Unregistered

If you possess an unregistered "assault weapon" or .50 BMG rifle and do not meet any of the above exceptions, you are violating California law. Unfortunately, there is no way for you to register a Category 1, Category 2, or pre-2017 Category 3 "assault weapon" or .50 BMG rifle now. But, for firearms now considered to be "assault weapons" as a result of the change in California law in 2017 (and DOJ regulations for shotguns), you can register it as explained above. If you possess an unregistered Category 1, 2, or 3 "assault weapon" or .50 BMG rifle, you should contact an attorney with experience in California firearms law immediately to determine what to do with it.

X. "ASSAULT WEAPONS" LISTED BY NAME[328]

A. Combined Listing of Category 1 and Category 2 "Assault Weapons"

Table 8.2 on the following page lists Category 1 and Category 2 "Assault Weapons." Italicized models are Category 1 "assault weapons" and were required to be registered on or before March 31, 1992. Non-italicized models are Category 2 "assault weapons" and were required to be registered with the Department of Justice on or before January 23, 2001. Category 3 and 4 "assault weapons" are not included in this table.

---

[328] This list is from the AWIG. *See* CALIFORNIA ATTORNEY GENERAL, CALIFORNIA ASSAULT WEAPONS IDENTIFICATION GUIDE 82-84 (3d ed., 2001), *available at* http://ag.ca.gov/firearms/forms/pdf/awguide.pdf (last visited July 12, 2017).

Table 8.3

RIFLES		
American Arms	**American Spirit**	**Armalite**
AK-C 47	ASA Model	AR 10 (all)
AK-F 39		*AR-180*
AK-F 47		Golden Eagle
AK-Y 39		M15 (all)
Arsenal	**Beretta**	**Bushmaster**
SLG (all)	*AR-70*	*Assault Rifle*
SLR (all)		XM15 (all)
B-West	**Calico**	**Colt**
AK-47 (all)	*M-900*	*AR-15 (all)*
		Law Enforcement (6920)
		Match Target (all)
		Sporter (all)
Daewoo	**Dalphon**	**DPMS**
AR100, AR110C	B.F.D.	Panther (all)
K-1, K-2		
Max 1, Max 2		
Eagle Arms	**Fabrique Nationale**	**Frankford Arsenal**
EA-15 A2 H-BAR	*308 Match, Sporter*	AR-15 (all)
EA-15 E1	*FAL, LAR, FNC*	
M15 (all)		
Hesse Arms	**HK**	**IMI**
HAR 15A2 (all)	*91, 94, PSG-1*	*Galil*
Model 47 (all)	*93*	*Uzi*
Wieger STG 940 Rifle		
Inter Ordnance - Monroe, NC	**J&R ENG**	**Kalashnikov USA**
AK-47 (all)	*M-68*	Hunter Rifle / Saiga
M-97		
RPK		

RIFLES		
Knights	**Les Baer**	**MAADI CO**
RAS (all)	Ultimate AR (all)	*AK 47*
SR-15 (all)		*ARM*
SR-25 (all)		MISR (all)
		MISTR (all)
Made in China	**Made in Spain**	**MAS**
56	*CETME Sporter*	*223*
56S		
84S		
86S		
AK		
AK47		
AKM		
AKS		
Mitchell Arms, Inc.	**Norinco**	**Ohio Ordnance Works (O.O.W.)**
AK-47 (all)	*56*	AK-74
AK-47 Cal .308 (all)	*56 S*	ROMAK 991
M-76	81 S (all)	
M-90	*84 S*	
RPK	86 (all)	
	86 S	
	AK-47 (all)	
	Hunter Rifle	
	MAK 90	
	NHM 90, 90-2, 91 Sport	
	RPK Rifle	
	SKS w/ detachable magazine	
Olympic Arms	**Ordnance, Inc.**	**Palmetto**
AR-15	AR-15	SGA (all)
Car-97		
PCR (all)		
Poly Technologies	**Professional Ordnance, Inc.**	**PWA**
AK47	Carbon 15 Rifle	All Models
AKS		

RIFLES		
Rock River Arms, Inc. Car A2 Car A4 Flattop LE Tactical Carbine NM A2 - DCM Legal Standard A-2 Standard A-4 Flattop	**RPB Industries, Inc.** *sM10, sM11*	**SIG** *AMT, PE-57* *SG 550, SG 551*
Springfield Armory *BM59, SAR-48*	**Sterling** *MK-6*	**Steyr** *AUG*
SWD Incorporated *M11*	**Valmet** 76 S Hunter Rifle *M62S, M71S, M78S*	**Weaver Arms** *Nighthawk*
Wilson Combat AR-15	**WUM** WUM (all)	

PISTOLS		
Advance Armament Inc. *M11*	**Bushmaster** *Pistol*	**Calico** *M-950*
Encom *MP-9* *MP-45*	**IMI** *UZI*	**Intratec** *TEC-9*
MARS Pistol	**Military Armament Corp.** *M-11*	**RPB Industries Inc.** *sM10, sM11*
Sites *Spectre*	**Sterling** *MK-7*	**SWD Incorporated** *M11*

SHOTGUNS		
Cobray	**Franchi**	
Streetsweeper	*SPAS 12*	
S/S Inc.	*LAW 12*	
SS/12		
Striker 12		

CHAPTER 9

OTHER HEAVILY REGULATED FIREARMS AND DEVICES

As discussed throughout this book, California and federal laws often differ and overlap. To comply with laws about heavily regulated firearms and devices, you must comply with both state and federal requirements.

Unlike California law, federal law does not have many restrictions on what types of firearms a person may possess. But there is one notable exception: the National Firearms Act (NFA). Items meeting the NFA's unusual definition of "firearm"[1] have a separate set of federal requirements you must meet before you can lawfully possess them. These requirements are discussed briefly at the end of this chapter.

If you want to possess any of the items described below, believe you already possess them, and/or have questions on whether your possession of them is legal, you should contact an attorney experienced in firearms law immediately.

I. "MACHINEGUNS"

Under both California and federal law, a "machinegun" is "any weapon which shoots, is designed to shoot, or can be [easily] restored to . . . automatically [shoot,] more than one shot, without manual reloading, by a single function of the trigger."[2] A "machinegun" "also include[s] the frame or receiver[,] . . . any part designed solely and exclusively, or combination of parts designed and intended, for use in converting a weapon into a machinegun, . . . [any weapon the Bureau of Alcohol, Tobacco, Firearms, and Explosives (ATF) consid-

Example of a "machinegun":
A Saco Defense Systems
Division M60 E3 Light Machinegun

---

[1] See Chapter 2 for "firearm" definitions.

[2] 26 U.S.C. § 5845(b); P.C. § 16880.

ers easily convertible to a 'machinegun,'[3] or] any combination of parts from which a machinegun can be assembled if" they were under the same person's possession or control.[4]

These parts vary in size and description. For some firearms you only need a specially shaped metal piece that will allow a firearm to fire fully automatic (a.k.a. an auto or conversion sear). So this one single part could be considered a "machinegun." For other firearms, small mechanisms that attach to the firearm or replace internal parts are all you need. These metal parts and pieces can be considered "machineguns" by themselves even if you do not possess the actual firearm they are designed to be used with.

An auto sear, a part of a "machinegun," is specifically addressed under the law. The ATF has interpreted the NFA to include auto sears in the definition of a "machinegun."[5] Therefore, you may not possess an auto sear unless it is properly registered under the NFA.[6]

 Another way a firearm may be considered a "machinegun" is if its parts wear out over time, causing the firearm to fire two shots per trigger pull. Although this is incorrect because a firearm with worn parts isn't *designed* to shoot fully automatic, under these circumstances, law enforcement might believe you have created or modified your firearm into a "machinegun." If this happens to you, take your firearm apart and to a gunsmith as soon as possible.

The term "automatic" firearm is used and abused a lot. An "automatic" firearm is simply one that "automatically" loads another round into the chamber after a round is discharged. The term can include "semiautomatic," meaning one shot per trigger pull, and "fully automatic," meaning rounds will continue to fire as long as the trigger is pressed down or until the firearm runs out of ammunition. The media often uses the phrases "automatic weapon" or "automatic firearms." Because the term "automatic" can include many firearm types – ranging from semiautomatic pistols to tank-mounted "machineguns" – pay attention to how the word is used. The next time you come across an "automatic" firearm in a news story, consider whether the word is being used incorrectly, or whether it is being used to elicit a certain public reaction.

People often think of Gatling guns as "machineguns" because of their relatively rapid fire potential. But, because they have no trigger and instead are crank-operated, they cannot meet the "machinegun" definition. Their ammunition feeding de-

---

[3] 26 U.S.C. § 5845(b); P.C. § 16880.

[4] 26 U.S.C. § 5845(b); P.C. § 16880. The ATF's position is that a shoestring attached to a semiautomatic rifle that causes the firearm to fire more than one round per trigger pull is, when attached to the firearm, a "machinegun." Letter from Richard Vasquez, Acting Chief, Firearms Technology Branch, U.S. Department of Justice, to Brian Blakely (Jun. 25, 2007), *available at* http://www.everydaynodaysoff.com/2010/01/25/shoestring-machine-gun/ (last visited July 12, 2017). This position is a modification of a previous ATF opinion which stated a shoestring, by itself, could be a "machinegun."

[5] ATF Rul. 81-4 (1981), *available at* http://www.atf.gov/file/55331/download (last visited July 12, 2017); 27 C.F.R. § 479.11.

[6] *United States v. Dodson*, 519 Fed. App'x. 344 (6th Cir. 2013).

vices, however, likely constitute "large-capacity magazines" and are thus regulated as such, as discussed below.

A. Prohibitions

Under federal law, it can be legal to acquire a "machinegun" that was lawfully possessed before May 19, 1986, as long as you comply with the strict requirements for transferring and possessing NFA firearms discussed in Section XII of this Chapter. But even if you meet the federal NFA requirements to lawfully possess a "machinegun," you must also meet one of the exceptions to California's general ban on possessing them (explained below).[7]

It is generally illegal for anyone to knowingly possess, transport, manufacture, sell, or convert an existing firearm into a "machinegun" under both California and federal law.[8] Severe penalties exist for violating this prohibition, including potentially years in prison following a California felony conviction,[9] and up to 10 years and/or a fine of no more than $10,000 for violating federal law.[10]

Given the stiff penalties for violating California and federal "machinegun" laws, you should be sure to take certain precautions if you inadvertently come into possession of one of these firearms. For example, you may discover that granddad's WWII souvenir from Italy is actually a "machinegun." Alternatively, a deceased family member could leave you such a firearm in their will. If you come into possession of an unregistered NFA firearm, the ATF suggests that you contact your nearest ATF office.[11] But, given the sensitivity of this issue and the potential criminal liability for possessing such an item, you should first consult an attorney experienced in firearms law to understand your full range of options.

B. California Exceptions to "Machinegun" Restrictions

California law provides for a few narrow exceptions to the restrictions on possessing "machineguns." These exceptions, discussed below, are limited to certain law enforcement agencies and military forces, and those possessing certain permits.

---

[7] 26 U.S.C. § 5812(a). "Applications [for NFA firearms] shall be denied if the transfer, receipt, or possession of the firearm would place the transferee in violation of law." 26 U.S.C. § 5812(a).

[8] P.C. § 32625; 18 U.S.C. § 922(o); 26 U.S.C. § 5861, *declared unconstitutional as applied to law enforcement officers by U.S. v. Vest*, 448 F. Supp. 3d 1002 (S.D. Ill. 2006).

[9] P.C. § 32625.

[10] 26 U.S.C. § 5871.

[11] *Firearms- Frequently Asked Questions- National Firearms Act (NFA)*, U.S. DEPT. OF JUSTICE, BUREAU OF ALCOHOL, TOBACCO, FIREARMS AND EXPLOSIVES, http://www.atf.gov/qa-category/national-firearms-act-nfa#unregistered-possession (last visited July 12, 2017).

1. Law Enforcement and Military

Certain law enforcement agencies and military forces may receive and possess "machineguns," including ones made after 1986.[12] Though such agencies and military forces are exempt from the NFA tax[13] (discussed below), they still must register the "machineguns."[14]

2. Permits to Possess, Manufacture, and Transport

Upon satisfactorily showing that "good cause" exists, the California Department of Justice (DOJ) may issue you a permit to possess, manufacture, or transport "machineguns."[15] These permits must be renewed annually.[16] Unless you are involved with law enforcement, the military, a business that supports, advises, trains, or supervises these organizations, or the entertainment industry, it is unlikely you will be able to establish the "good cause" required to obtain this permit.[17]

If you are able to obtain the permit, it must be kept on you or with the "machinegun" and must be made available for law enforcement inspection.[18] The DOJ will also annually inspect the license holder for proper security and safe storage of any "machinegun," and to confirm the "machinegun" inventory.[19]

The DOJ may revoke the permit at any time if it determines that your need for the "machinegun" has ceased, the "machinegun" was used for an unauthorized purpose, or you failed to exercise great care in retaining custody of any firearm possessed under the permit.[20]

Federal law does not require a separate permit to lawfully *possess* "machineguns."[21] But it does require that you get California's "machinegun" permit, or otherwise be exempt from the "machinegun" restriction. Without a permit or exemption, the ATF will deny the transfer. And since it is almost impossible for common people to obtain such a permit from the DOJ (and most people do not fall under an exemp-

---

[12] The federal exception to the ban on "machineguns" made after 1986 includes "a transfer to or by, or possession by or under the authority of, the United States or any department or agency thereof or a State, or a department, agency, or political subdivision thereof." 18 U.S.C. § 922(o)(2)(A). Under California law these entities' personnel may possess "machineguns" too, but only while acting within the scope of their duties. P.C. § 32610(a).

[13] 26 U.S.C. §§ 5852, 5853; 27 C.F.R. §§ 479.89-479.90.

[14] Unless the firearms are possessed or under the control of the U.S., the "machineguns" must be registered in the National Firearms Registration and Transfer Record. 26 U.S.C. § 5841. Federal law also allows certain government entities to acquire and register NFA firearms (including "machineguns") for official use when the firearm has been abandoned or forfeited. 27 C.F.R. § 479.104.

[15] P.C. § 32650.

[16] P.C. § 32655(d).

[17] *See* CAL. CODE REGS. tit. 11, § 4128(c)(1)-(7). See Chapter 8 for examples.

[18] P.C. § 32660.

[19] P.C. § 32670. If a permittee has fewer than five "machineguns," however, the inspection is only once every five years, unless the DOJ determines additional inspections are necessary. P.C. § 32670(b).

[20] P.C. § 32665.

[21] Remember, federal law still requires registration and importer, dealer, and manufacturing licenses.

tion), the fact that you can theoretically own a "machinegun" in California under federal law is practically irrelevant.

C. Licenses to Sell "Machineguns"

The ATF may grant licenses to engage in the business of selling "machineguns."[22] But, for the license to be valid in California, you must get a separate license from the DOJ, renew it annually, and comply with numerous regulations.[23]

D. "Bump Stocks" in the Context of Machinegun Restrictions

Also known as "bump-fire stocks," bump stocks were catapulted into the spotlight recently due to their apparent usage by the gunman in the 2017 Las Vegas mass shooting. Bump stocks allow people to "bump fire" semiautomatic firearms. Simply put, "bump fire" is the act of using a semiautomatic firearm's recoil in part to discharge the firearm. Further analyses and descriptions of bump stocks are located under Section III(F) of this Chapter, which discusses multiburst trigger activators.

1. Bump Stocks Under Federal Law

Because a bump stock has no automatically functioning parts or springs, and because the shooter's finger is still technically causing compression of the trigger for each round fired (i.e., the bump stock is not performing a full automatic mechanical function when installed), the bump stock is not banned under federal law. For instance, the Bureau of Alcohol, Tobacco, Firearms, and Explosives has issued advisory letters stating that bump stocks are not "machineguns" or any device regulated under the Gun Control Act or the National Firearms Act.[24]

Therefore, federal law still considers (otherwise lawful) semiautomatic firearms with bump stocks attached to be legal semiautomatic firearms. But that could change soon. Senator Dianne Feinstein (D-Calif.) and a number of Democrats introduced the Automatic Gun Fire Prevention Act on October 4, 2017, a bill that intends to ban the sale, transfer, importation, manufacture, and possession of bump stocks, trigger cranks, and similar accessories that accelerate a semi-automatic rifle's rate of fire.[25]

---

[22] 18 U.S.C. § 923(a); 26 U.S.C. § 5802; 27 C.F.R. § 478.44.

[23] *See* P.C. §§ 32700-32720.

[24] *See, e.g.,* Letter from John R. Spencer, Chief of the Firearms Technology Branch of the Bureau of Alcohol, Tobacco, Firearms and Explosives (June 7, 2010), *available at* https://www.slidefire.com/downloads/BATFE.pdf (last visited Oct. 25, 2017).

[25] Automatic Gun Fire Prevention Act, H.R., 3947 115th Cong. (2017).

2. Bump Stocks Under California Law

As stated above, the commonly understood definition of a "machinegun" under California law is any firearm that shoots more than one round per operation of the trigger.[26] And California law regulates any part designed and intended solely and exclusively for use in converting a weapon into a machinegun.[27]

Given this definition, bump stocks do not convert a firearm into a "machinegun." And a bump stock, by itself, cannot be considered a "machinegun." A firearm equipped with a bump stock requires a separate operation of the trigger to discharge each separate round from the firearm; the firearm does not shoot more than one round per operation of the trigger. The firearm is pulled into the shooter's trigger finger, and one round is discharged. The firearm recoils, the trigger is reset, and the act of pulling the firearm forward causes the trigger to be engaged again, and so on. Hence, bump stocks do not violate California's restrictions on machineguns. We discuss bump stocks further below in the section on multiburst trigger activators.

II. "DESTRUCTIVE DEVICES"

"Destructive device" definitions vary between California and federal law. Under federal law a "destructive device" is any of the following weapons:

(1) Any explosive, incendiary, or poison gas:

A grenade is considered a "destructive device" under both California and federal law

    (a) bomb, *or*

    (b) grenade, *or*

    (c) rocket having a propellant charge of more than four ounces, *or*

    (d) missile having an explosive or incendiary charge of more than one-quarter ounce, *or*

    (e) mine, *or*

    (f) similar device; *or*

(2) Any type of weapon by whatever name known which will, or which may be readily converted to, expel a projectile by the action of an explosive or other propellant, the barrel or barrels of which have a bore of more than one-half inch in diameter, except a shotgun or shotgun shell which the Secretary of the Treasury[28] finds is generally recognized as particularly suitable for sporting purposes; *or*

---

[26] P.C. § 16880(a).

[27] P.C. § 16880(a).

[28] The NFA is part of the Internal Revenue Code, which is typically under the Secretary of the Treasury. After the events of September 11, 2001, the ATF was placed under the supervision of the U.S. Attorney General (AG). So, while the NFA refers to the Secretary of the Treasury, these references now actually mean the U.S. AG.

(3) Any combination of parts either designed or intended for use in converting any device into a destructive device as defined in subparagraphs (1) and (2) and from which a destructive device may be readily assembled.[29]

Under federal law the term "destructive device" does not include:

(1) Any device which is neither designed nor redesigned for use as a weapon;[30] *or*

(2) Any device, although originally designed for use as a weapon, which is redesigned for use as a signaling, pyrotechnic, line throwing, safety, or similar device; *or*

(3) Surplus ordnance sold, loaned, or given by the Secretary of the Army pursuant to federal codes; *or*

(4) Any other device which the Secretary finds is not likely to be used as a weapon, or is an antique or a rifle that the owner intends to use solely for sporting purposes.[31]

Much like they do with "machineguns," the ATF strictly regulates transferring "destructive devices." A "destructive device" is an NFA "firearm" and, if it is regulated under California law, it *can only be* lawfully acquired and possessed if, in addition to meeting the strict federal requirements discussed in Section XII of this Chapter, your possession falls within one of California's exceptions.

Under California law, a "destructive device" is any of the following *weapons*:

(1) Any projectile containing any explosive or incendiary material or any other chemical substance, including, but not limited to, that which is commonly known as tracer or incendiary ammunition, except tracer ammunition manufactured for use in shotguns; *or*

(2) Any bomb,[32] grenade, explosive missile, or similar device or any launching device therefor; *or*

(3) Any weapon of a caliber greater than 0.60 caliber which fires fixed ammunition, or any ammunition therefor, other than:

    (a) a shotgun (smooth or rifled bore) conforming to the definition of a "destructive device" found in 27 C.F.R. section 479.11(b), *or*

    (b) shotgun ammunition (single projectile or shot), *or*

    (c) an antique rifle,[33] *or*

---

[29] 26 U.S.C. § 5845(f). The definition of "destructive device" under the Gun Control Act (GCA) is phrased slightly different than the NFA definition. *See* 18 U.S.C. § 921(a)(4).

[30] It is important to note that in order to be a "destructive device" under state and federal law the device must be a weapon. What constitutes a "weapon" under California law is discussed in Chapter 2.

[31] 26 U.S.C. § 5845(f).

[32] A California court defined the term "bomb" as "a device carrying an explosive charge fused to blow up or detonate under certain conditions." *People v. Morse*, 2 Cal. App. 4th 620, 647 n. 8 (1992); CALCRIM No. 2570.

[33] The term "antique rifle" means a firearm conforming to the definition of an "antique firearm" in 27 C.F.R. section 479.11. P.C. § 16180.

(d) an antique cannon;[34] *or*

(4) Any rocket, rocket-propelled projectile, or similar device of a diameter greater than 0.60 inch, or any launching device therefor, and any rocket, rocket-propelled projectile, or similar device containing any explosive or incendiary material or any other chemical substance, other than the propellant for that device, except those devices as are designed primarily for emergency or distress signaling purposes; *or*

(5) Any breakable container that contains a flammable liquid with a flash point of 150 degrees Fahrenheit or less and has a wick or similar device capable of being ignited (*i.e.*, devices like a Molotov cocktail), other than a device which is commercially manufactured primarily for the purpose of illumination (*i.e.*, tiki torches); *or*

(6) Any sealed device with dry ice (CO_2) (*i.e.*, a dry ice bomb) or other chemically reactive substances assembled for the purpose of causing an explosion by a chemical reaction.[35]

Under California law it is generally illegal for any person or entity to possess,[36] sell, offer for sale, knowingly transport,[37] make or intend to make,[38] import, export, manufacture, or use in business any "destructive device" in the state without a valid permit.[39] Federal law likewise restricts activities like importing, manufacturing, dealing, transporting, and possessing "destructive devices."[40]

Under California law, unlawful possession of a "destructive device" can be punished as a misdemeanor or a felony.[41] Possession of a "destructive device" is punishable as a felony if your possession is reckless or malicious and you possess the "destructive device":

(1) On a public street or highway; *or*

(2) In or near any:

(a) Theater, *or*

(b) Hall, *or*

---

[34] For this section, the term "antique cannon" "means any cannon manufactured before January 1, 1899, which has been [made] incapable of firing or for which ammunition is no longer manufactured in the [U.S.] and is not readily available in the ordinary channels of commercial trade." P.C. § 16160. With the internet, what "ordinary channels of commercial trade" means may change in coming years. Please see www.CalGunLawsBook.com for a more detailed discussion on this topic.

[35] P.C. § 16460(a)(1)-(6). "A bullet containing or carrying an explosive agent is not a destructive device . . . ." P.C. § 16460(b). But it may be considered ammunition "containing . . . an explosive agent[]" as discussed in P.C. section 30210(b).

[36] P.C. § 18710.

[37] P.C. § 18730.

[38] P.C. § 18720.

[39] P.C. § 18900.

[40] 18 U.S.C. § 923; 26 U.S.C. § 5871. The federal definition of "destructive device" is slightly different from California's. *See* 26 U.S.C. § 5845 (defining "destructive device").

[41] P.C. § 18710.

    (c) School, *or*

    (d) College, *or*

    (e) Church, *or*

    (f) Hotel, *or*

    (g) Other public building, *or*

    (h) Private habitation; *or*

  (3) In, on, or near any:

    (a) Aircraft, *or*

    (b) Railway passenger train, *or*

    (c) Car, *or*

    (d) Cable road, *or*

    (e) Cable car, *or*

    (f) Vessel engaged in carrying passengers for hire, *or*

    (g) Other public place ordinarily passed by human beings.[42]

The unlawful sale, offer for sale, or knowing transportation of a "destructive device" is a felony punishable by up to four years in prison.[43] It is also a felony to possess any substance, material, or combination of substances or materials, intending to make a destructive device or explosive without the proper permit.[44] If, however, the "destructive device" that is unlawfully possessed, sold, offered for sale, or transported is fixed ammunition greater than .60 caliber, the first offense is only a misdemeanor.[45] Any offenses committed after that can be a misdemeanor or a felony.[46]

Regardless of whether it is a misdemeanor or a felony offense, under California law any conviction involving a "destructive device" is ineligible for probation or a suspended sentence, meaning jail or prison time will almost certainly be imposed.[47]

A. Permits

If you are a dealer, manufacturer, importer, or exporter of "destructive devices" or if you use a "destructive device" in a motion picture or television studio, you must first get a special permit from the DOJ and renew it annually.[48] Likewise, if you or your firm or corporation does not fall into any of these categories and you wish to possess or transport a "destructive device," you must obtain a permit from the

---

[42] P.C. § 18715.

[43] P.C. § 18730.

[44] P.C. § 18720.

[45] P.C. § 18735.

[46] P.C. § 18735.

[47] P.C. § 18780.

[48] P.C. §§ 18900(a), 18905(b).

DOJ and meet specific criteria.[49] Similar to "machinegun" inspections, the DOJ may inspect places where "destructive devices" are kept.[50] Such inspections are held annually. If the permit holder has less than five "destructive devices," the DOJ will only inspect every five years, unless they determine additional inspections are necessary.[51]

B. Exceptions for Peace Officers, Firefighters, and Military

Certain peace officers,[52] including those in the DOJ authorized by the California Attorney General (AG), military personnel, and national guardsmen, may purchase, possess, transport, store, or use a "destructive device" "while on duty and acting within the scope and course of employment."[53]

Exceptions also apply to any equipment considered a "destructive device" that is used by a fire department or fire protection or firefighting agency in the course of fire suppression by "any person who is a regularly employed and paid officer, employee, or member of a fire department or fire protection or firefighting agency of the . . . state, [local or federal government,] while on duty and acting within the scope and course of employment."[54]

C. 37mm Flare Launchers v. Grenade Launchers and 22mm Grenade Launchers v. Flash Suppressors/Muzzle Brakes

Some firearm enthusiasts possess 37mm *flare* launchers. These devices are typically stand-alone launchers or attach under the barrel of a rifle.[55] Because flare launchers closely resemble 40mm *grenade* launchers, law enforcement often mistakes them for "destructive devices." But they are not. You should make sure that any launcher you have is the 37mm variety, not the 40mm version.

As mentioned above, in order to be a "destructive device" under state and federal law, a 37mm *flare* launcher must be considered a weapon. The ATF has issued a ruling saying that 37mm flare guns are not destructive devices so long as they are not possessed with "anti-personnel" ammunition.[56] The same rule should apply for California law; however, there is no case law telling us so and no opinion from the DOJ confirming it.

---

[49] P.C. § 18900(b).

[50] P.C. § 18910.

[51] P.C. § 18910(b).

[52] Those listed in P.C. sections 830.1 and 830.2.

[53] P.C. § 18800(a).

[54] P.C. § 18800(b).

[55] Note that when a flare or grenade launcher is attached to a semiautomatic centerfire rifle that does not have a "fixed magazine," the rifle meets the restricted "assault weapon" definition in California (see Chapter 8).

[56] ATF Rul. 95-3 (1995), *available at* http://www.atf.gov/file/55446/download (last visited July 12, 2017). *See* Chapter 2.

Also, even though 37mm launchers are available nationwide, some California law enforcement agencies still classify them as "destructive devices," claiming that a 37mm grenade exists *somewhere* that can launch from the device. You should therefore carefully consider whether you want to possess one and what your local law enforcement agency's position is.

A similar attempt has been made by certain law enforcement agencies to say that any muzzle attachments are "grenade launchers." Under this theory muzzle devices (flash suppressors and/or muzzle brakes) measuring 22mm in diameter (a common dimension) are alleged to be "grenade launchers." These law enforcement agencies theorize that there are devices that can attach to a 22mm flash suppressor/muzzle brake, making these devices capable of holding a grenade. When a blank cartridge is inserted into the rifle and discharged, the grenade then shoots off the end of the device. There are also 22mm grenades that fit on the ends of rifle muzzles that either catch a discharged bullet or use the force of a discharged blank to launch. Often it is only the law enforcement agency that is aware of this process, and the firearm owner does not possess the grenade, device that attaches to the flash suppressor or muzzle brake, or blank cartridge. Much like the 37mm flare launchers, typical flash suppressors and muzzle brakes are not considered "weapons" by themselves.

There are other devices that do attach to rifle muzzles designed solely for the purpose of launching a grenade. These devices are also 22mm in diameter but are specifically designed to launch grenades. Usually the manufacturer will explicitly list these devices as "grenade launchers" in the firearm's packaging material or manual. The DOJ has information concerning one type of these devices on their website.[57] If you possess a device described by the manufacturer as a "grenade launcher," you should contact an attorney experienced in firearms law immediately.

D. Cannons

Cannons represent an interesting question with respect to their legality under both state and federal law. Remember first that in order to be a "destructive device" the cannon must be a "weapon." If the cannon is solely decorative or designed solely for signaling purposes, it should not fall under the definition of a "destructive device." Under California law, "antique rifles" and "antique cannons" are exempt from the definition of "destructive devices" as are "antiques" under federal law.

Oddly, the definition of "antique rifle" under California law means "a firearm conforming to the definition of an 'antique firearm' in Section 479.11 of Title 27 of the Code of Federal Regulations [(C.F.R.)]."[58] "An antique firearm" under the Code of Federal Regulations is "[a]ny firearm not designed or redesigned for using rim

---

[57] *See Public Notice - Zastava SKS Carbines*, Cal. Dept. of Justice, Office of the Attorney General, http://oag.ca.gov/firearms/zastava (last visited July 12, 2017).
[58] P.C. § 16180.

fire or conventional center fire ignition with fixed ammunition and manufactured in or before 1898 (including any matchlock, flintlock, percussion cap, or similar type of ignition system or replica thereof, whether actually manufactured before or after the year 1898) and also any firearm using fixed ammunition manufactured in or before 1898, for which ammunition is no longer manufactured in the United States and is not readily available in the ordinary channels of commercial trade."[59]

While there are a number of ways a cannon can be exempt from California and federal restrictions on "destructive devices," one should take precautions not to violate California's restriction on "zip guns" (discussed in Section III(H) of this Chapter).

III. "GENERALLY PROHIBITED WEAPONS"

Former P.C. section 12020 was an extremely long statutory provision that generally prohibited the manufacturing, importing, selling, gifting, loaning, or possessing of an odd array of weapons and related equipment. That provision had numerous exceptions, some of which related to all the listed weapons, while others only related to one specific type. This means that people interested in a particular weapon's legality had to read a lot of irrelevant material before finding the portion of former P.C. section 12020 relevant to them.[60]

To ease confusion and eliminate this problem, the Penal Code was revised to separate former P.C. section 12020 and its subdivisions out. As a result of this revision, the prohibited items were separated out in new sections according to the specific firearm, equipment, or device to which they pertain. For example, the restriction on "cane guns" can now be found in a separate section specifically concerning "cane guns." Some of these items are "firearms" and some are not.

Former P.C. section 12020 also discussed of the following exotic items:

(1) Wallet guns

(2) Undetectable firearms

(3) Firearms not immediately recognizable as firearms

(4) Camouflaging firearm containers

(5) Ammunition containing or consisting of flechette darts

(6) Bullets containing or carrying an explosive agent

(7) Ballistic knives

(8) Multiburst trigger activators

(9) Nunchakus

---

[59] 27 C.F.R. § 479.11.

[60] *Nonsubstantive Reorganization of Deadly Weapon Statutes Recommendation*, 38 CAL. L. REVISION COMM'N REPORTS 217, 245 (2009).

(10) Short-barreled shotguns

(11) Short-barreled rifles

(12) Metal knuckles

(13) Belt buckle knives

(14) Leaded canes

(15) Zip guns

(16) Shurikens

(17) Unconventional pistols

(18) Lipstick case knives

(19) Can swords

(20) Shobi-zues

(21) Air gauge knives

(22) Writing pen knives

(23) Metal military practice hand grenades

(24) Metal replica hand grenades

(25) Instruments/weapons of the kind commonly known as a blackjack, slungshot, bill, sandclub, sap or sandbag

(26) "Large-capacity magazines"

(27) Carrying concealed explosive substances other than fixed ammunition

(28) Dirks

(29) Daggers

For most of these items, manufacturing, importing, keeping for sale, offering or exposing for sale, giving, lending, and possessing are illegal.[61] All of these weapons are now listed as "generally prohibited weapons" under P.C. section 16590, and each is defined in its own additional code section.

Certain items like dirks, and daggers may be legal to possess, but other restrictions on them exist and "large-capacity magazines" are discussed below.

There are restrictions on "large-capacity magazine conversion kits" (discussed below). But, these items were not added to the list of "generally prohibited weapons," although they would have more than likely ended up in former P.C. section 12020. As discussed below, the exceptions for "generally prohibited weapons" apply to "large-capacity magazine conversion kits."

If you are concerned that you possess any of the above-listed non-firearm items or if you have questions about them, you should refer directly to the Penal Code

---

[61] P.C. section 16590 contains a list of the "generally prohibited weapons" and the code sections restricting them.

and the sections defining these items. And, as always, when in doubt consult an attorney knowledgeable in California weapons laws.

A. "Cane Gun"

"Cane guns"[62] are "any firearm mounted or enclosed in a stick, staff, rod, crutch, or similar device, designed to be, or capable of being used as, an aid in walking, if the firearm may be fired while mounted or enclosed therein."[63] "Cane guns" were popular in the mid-1850s and served not only as a walking accessory, but also for self-defense.[64]

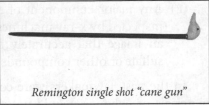
Remington single shot "cane gun"

B. "Wallet Gun"

"'[W]allet gun'[65] means any firearm mounted or enclosed in a case, resembling a wallet, designed to be or capable of being carried in a pocket or purse, if the firearm may be fired while mounted or enclosed in the case."[66] Because of its shape and size, a "wallet gun" can look and feel like an actual wallet. These devices are also problematic under the federal law's "any other weapon" definition.[67]

Example of a wallet gun

Interestingly enough, the "wallet" is not illegal under California law by itself, nor is the "gun" necessarily illegal by itself. Once the "gun" is mounted or enclosed in the "wallet," however, it becomes illegal. This means you could lawfully possess either the "wallet" or the "gun" by themselves or both, as long as the "gun" is not "mounted or enclosed" or you did not intend to mount or enclose[68] it in the "wallet." But I suggest that you don't possess both, even if the "gun" is not "mounted or enclosed" in the "wallet."

The device also may not need to be a conventional wallet. Certain holsters come dangerously close to a "wallet gun" by allowing you to shoot them while they are mounted or enclosed in them, and could fall under the definition.

---

[62] Prohibited via P.C. section 24410.

[63] P.C. § 16330.

[64] *Remington Cane Guns*, THE REMINGTON SOCIETY OF AMERICA, http://www.remingtonsociety.org/remington-cane-guns/ (last visited July 12, 2017).

[65] Contraband pursuant to P.C. section 24710.

[66] P.C. § 17330.

[67] 26 U.S.C. § 5845(e).

[68] As discussed in Chapter 8, according to the *Nguyen* case, the possession of the parts of an illegal weapon can be problematic if you have the intent to make an illegal weapon with these parts.

C. "Undetectable Firearm"

An "undetectable firearm"[69] is any weapon that satisfies either of the following:

(1) After removal of grips, stocks, and magazines, the weapon is not as detectable as the Security Exemplar by a walk-through metal detector calibrated and operated to detect the Security Exemplar; *or*

(2) Any major component of the weapon defined by federal law that, when inspected by x-ray machines commonly used at airports, does not generate an image that accurately depicts the shape of the component. Barium sulfate or other compounds may be used to make the component.[70]

In the past, lawmakers were concerned that firearms made out of composite materials or polymers would not show up in metal detectors or x-ray machines. These concerns proved baseless. These firearms, such as most Glock models (high-tech polymer based, corrosion resistant, 86% lighter,[71] and tougher than steel), still have enough metal to be easily detected by metal detectors and x-ray machines, especially when loaded.

Note that if you plan to make your own plastic or polymer 3D printed firearm, you must incorporate some kind of metal into the design in order to make the firearm detectable. For example, Defense Distributed, the group that created the first fully 3D printed handgun, incorporated a six ounce chuck of steel into the body of the firearm in order to make the firearm detectable by a walk-through metal detector.[72]

D. Firearms Not "Immediately Recognizable" as Firearms

The Penal Code does not specifically define "immediately recognizable" or a "firearm that is not immediately recognizable." Nevertheless, it is illegal under P.C. section 24510. So, exactly what is prohibited by this California statute is unclear. Obvious examples are firearms disguised as cell phones and the "Braverman Stinger."[73] The "Palm Pistol"[74] is also arguably covered.

Example of a palm pistol: a Chicago Firearms Co. Protector Palm Pistol

---

[69] P.C. section 24610 prohibits "undetectable firearms."

[70] P.C. § 17280. See 18 U.S.C. section 922(p) for a comparison to federal law.

[71] *See Glock "Safe Action" Pistol*, GLOCK.COM, https://us.glock.com/technology/safe-action (last visited July 28, 2016).

[72] To learn more about 3D printed firearms, see Chapter 4.

[73] *See Stinger Penguns*, PENGUN.COM, http://pengun.com/ (last visited July 28, 2016).

[74] *See* John B. Snow, *Strange Guns: Palm Pistol*, OUTDOOR LIFE (Apr. 13, 2011), http://www.outdoorlife.com/blogs/gun-shots/2011/04/strange-guns-palm-pistol (last visited July 12, 2017).

Painting a firearm to resemble a BB device or an imitation firearm by adding a fluorescent orange tip or other painting is highly risky. It is also likely illegal because it might be considered disguising a real firearm as an imitation firearm and thus not "immediately recognizable" as a firearm.

E. "Camouflaging Firearm Container"

A "camouflaging firearm container"[75] is a container that meets the following criteria:

(1) It is designed and intended to enclose a firearm; *and*

(2) It is designed and intended to allow the firing of the enclosed firearm by external controls while the firearm is in the container; *and*

(3) It is not readily recognizable as containing a firearm.[76]

A common "camouflaging firearm container" is the briefcase for a "briefcase gun" where the firearm is mounted inside of a normal-looking briefcase. The case has an internal mechanism that allows the operator to discharge the firearm by either pulling a trigger on the briefcase handle or by pushing a secret button somewhere on the case.

F. "Multiburst Trigger Activator"

A "multiburst trigger activator"[77] means one of the following:

(1) A device designed or redesigned to be attached to a semiautomatic firearm, which allows the firearm to discharge two or more shots in a burst by activating the device; *or*

(2) A manual or power-driven trigger-activating device constructed and designed so that when attached to a semiautomatic firearm it increases the rate of fire of that firearm.[78]

Examples of these devices are the "Hell-Fire" or "Hellstorm 2000." While these devices differ in design, they function using the same principle. When a shooter attaches the device to a semiautomatic rifle and the rifle is fired from the shoulder, the shooter holds the firearm to allow the rifle to move forward and backward against the shooter's shoulder, causing the trigger to be rapidly pulled by the shooter's finger – a shooting technique commonly referred to as "bump fire." These devices reset the trigger quickly with some resistance and, combined with "bump firing," allow the operator to fire rapidly.

---

[75] Illegal under P.C. section 24310.

[76] P.C. § 16320(a). "'Camouflaging firearm container' does not include any camouflaging covering used while . . . lawful[ly] hunting or while going to or returning from a lawful hunting expedition." P.C. § 16320(b).

[77] Considered contraband under P.C. section 32900.

[78] P.C. § 16930.

Another design of a "multiburst trigger activator" may be attached to the trigger guard and has a crank-like device that sticks out of the side of the firearm. The operator holds the firearm with his or her non-trigger hand like normal. The shooter's trigger hand is then used to turn the crank. When the crank is turned, the device pulls the trigger. The rate at which the trigger is pulled coincides with the speed the crank is turned. Some devices can pull the trigger four times per rotation. By this method, 20 or 30-round magazines and 50-round drums can be emptied in seconds. These devices likely meet the "multiburst trigger activator" definition. There are no published opinions, and the DOJ has refused to opine on what is or is not a "multiburst trigger activator."

If you are out in public or at a range shooting ammunition at high rates of speed, you may alert law enforcement to investigate whether you are firing a fully automatic firearm or not.

1. Bump Stocks Should Not be Considered "Multiburst Trigger Activators" Under California Law

While models of bump stocks differ in design, they function using the same principle in "bump firing." A shooter attaches the bump stock to the receiver of a semiautomatic rifle where the pistol grip usually is. To discharge the firearm using a bump stock in "bump-fire" mode, the shooter places his or her trigger finger on a rest on the pistol grip built into the bump stock. The trigger is not pulled by the shooter squeezing his/her trigger finger. Rather, the shooter's finger remains on the rest platform located in front of the trigger, while the butt end of the stock rests against the shooter's shoulder. Because the firearm can slide back and forth at the bump stock attachment, the shooter's non-trigger hand pulls the barrel and receiver portions of the firearm, and consequently the trigger, forward. The act by the shooter of pulling the firearm forward causes the trigger to collide with the shooter's trigger finger. The recoil force from the discharge of the firearm causes the firearm to slide backwards again, and the trigger resets. If the shooter continues to pull the firearm forward with the non-trigger hand, the trigger and the rest of the firearm will again be pulled forward into the shooter's static trigger finger. With some practice, a shooter can regulate the operation of the trigger, and the number of times the trigger is engaged to shoot one, two, three, or numerous rounds. Hence, the "bump-fire" action is generated by the shooter's own movements, the firearm's recoil, and the trigger being bumped against the shooter's own finger.

Based on the analysis below (as well as the analysis in Section I(D) of this Chapter discussing machinegun law), bump stocks should be considered legal devices under federal and California law and, for the most part, should not be found to convert an otherwise legal semiautomatic rifle into an illegal firearm in California. Nonetheless, it must be kept in mind that there are no published California court opinions providing guidance on the legality of bump stocks. In addition, the California Attorney General issued a press release recently claiming that these stocks are illegal.[79] Given the California Attorney General's position, the current political climate, the widespread media attention given to bump stocks, and probable federal and state bills banning possession of bump stocks next year, one can expect to get prosecuted for possessing a bump stock. To defend against such charges would cost thousands of dollars in attorney fees. So, the downside of getting caught with one (i.e., arrest, prosecution, and possibly a judge or jury not adopting the correct legal analysis) is way too consequential to justify current possession.

That being said, remember that there are two ways that a device can meet the definition of a "multiburst trigger activator": either as a "burst fire" device or a trigger activating device.[80] Bump stocks meet neither definition.

For one, bump stocks are not "burst fire devices," which the Penal Code defines as "[a] device designed or redesigned to be attached to a semiautomatic firearm, which *allows the firearm to discharge two or more shots in a burst* by activating the device."[81] This is because bump stocks do not "allow the firearm to discharge two or more shots in a burst." As discussed above, the bump stock requires the trigger to be engaged once for each round that is discharged. The stock does not allow or convert a firearm to shoot more than one round per operation of the trigger.

Second, bump stocks are not trigger activating devices, which the Penal Code defines as "[a] manual or power-driven *trigger activating* device constructed and designed so that when attached to a semiautomatic firearm it *increases the rate of fire* of that firearm."[82] This definition requires an attachable device that activates the trigger. Bump stocks do not "activate" a firearm's trigger. Bump stocks do not attach to, or touch, a firearm's trigger. The shooter's own finger engages the trigger each and every time a round is fired. In addition, the definition above requires the device to increase the firearm's "rate of fire." Technically, bump stocks do not increase the firearm's "rate of fire." A semiautomatic firearm's rate of fire is one round per operation of the trigger. The firearm's rate of fire is limited by, among other things, how fast the shooter can pull the trigger. A semiautomatic rifle can reach discharge speeds near full automatic if the shooter pulls the trigger very quickly; no additional attachments or parts are required. With bump stocks, the "rate of fire" of the semi-automatic firearm is never increased. Like all semi-automatic firearms, it will fire as fast as a finger engages its trigger.

Therefore, a reasonable reading of the Penal Code shows that bump stocks are not "multiburst trigger activators" under California law. And other, secondary mechanisms used by courts and lawyers to interpret the law, such as a review of

---

[79] *See California Department of Justice Issues Advisory Reminding Gun Retailers That Bump Stocks Are Illegal,* State of California Department of Justice, Office of the Attorney General (Oct. 19, 2017), https://oag.ca.gov/news/press-releases/california-department-justice-issues-advisory-reminding-gun-retailers-bump (last visited Oct. 30, 2017).

[80] P.C. § 16930.

[81] P.C. § 16930(a) (emphasis added).

[82] P.C. § 16930(a) (emphasis added).

legislative history and the application of the Rule of Lenity,[83] further support this conclusion.

G. "Short-Barreled Shotguns" and "Short-Barreled Rifles"

Both California and federal law restrict possessing and transferring shotguns and rifles if they are under a certain length.[84]

1. "Short-Barreled Shotguns"

Two separate definitions exist under federal law for restricted shotguns of certain lengths. The Gun Control Act (GCA) has one, and the National Firearms Act (NFA) does too.

Under the GCA, "[t]he term 'short-barreled shotgun' means a shotgun having one or more barrels less than eighteen inches in length and any weapon made from a shotgun (whether by alteration, modification or otherwise) if such a weapon as modified has an overall length of less than twenty-six inches."[85] The GCA defines "shotgun" as "a weapon designed or redesigned, made or remade, and intended to be fired from the shoulder and designed or redesigned and made or remade to use the energy of an explosive to fire through a smooth bore either a number of ball shot or a single projectile for each single pull of the trigger."[86]

The GCA restricts transferring and transporting firearms meeting this definition but does not generally restrict possessing them.[87] The GCA does, however, add additional penalties if these firearms are possessed while committing a crime.[88]

In contrast to the GCA, the NFA does *not* refer to shotguns of prohibited lengths as "short-barreled shotguns," but instead describes them by their physical dimensions. The NFA specifically restricts "shotguns" with one or more barrels less than 18 inches long and weapons made from "shotguns" with overall lengths of less than 26 inches or that have one or more barrels that are less than 18 inches long.[89]

---

[83] The Rule of Lenity generally provides: "[W]hen a statute defining a crime or punishment is susceptible of two reasonable interpretations, the appellate court should ordinarily adopt that interpretation more favorable to the defendant. [Citation]. This rule has constitutional underpinnings. The defendant is entitled to the benefit of every reasonable doubt, whether it arise out of a question of fact, or as to the true interpretation of words or the construction of language used in a statute.' [Citations.]" [Citation]. Indeed, it is "the policy of California [citation] to construe and apply penal statutes as favorably to the defendant as the language of the statute and the circumstances of its application may reasonably permit." *Chessman v. Superior Court,* 50 Cal.2d 835, 843 (1958).

[84] P.C. § 33215; 18 U.S.C. § 922; 26 U.S.C. § 5861.

[85] 18 U.S.C. § 921(a)(6).

[86] 18 U.S.C. § 921(a)(5).

[87] 18 U.S.C. § 922(a)(4), (b)(4).

[88] 18 U.S.C. § 924(c)(1)(B).

[89] Note that the NFA has an additional category of restricted short-barreled shotguns that the GCA does not, *i.e.*, weapons made from a "shotgun" that have one or more barrels less than 18 inches long. This means that a firearm no longer meeting the "shotgun" definition (*e.g.*, one not intended to be fired from the shoulder) but made from a "shotgun" is restricted under the NFA but not necessarily under the GCA. The NFA also restricts "weapons with combination shotgun and rifle barrels 12 inches or more, less than 18 inches in length, from which only a single

The NFA defines the term "shotgun" the same way as the GCA, but additionally includes "any such weapon which may be readily restored to fire a *fixed shotgun shell*."[90]

Like all NFA firearms, "shotguns" restricted based on length can be lawfully acquired, possessed, and transferred under federal law *as long as* you meet all of the NFA requirements discussed in Section XII of this Chapter. As noted below, however, the possession of most NFA firearms is strictly prohibited under California law, even if they can be lawfully possessed under federal law.

Under both the GCA and the NFA, a firearm has to actually be a "shotgun" – meaning it must be "intended to be fired from the shoulder" – or made from a "shotgun" to be federally restricted as a "short-barreled shotgun." This may sound obvious based on the name, but as mentioned below, California law considers any "firearm" with certain dimensions that fires fixed shotgun shells, even handguns, to be "short-barreled shotguns." Because this is not the case under federal law, firearms like the Taurus Judge and Smith & Wesson Governor (handguns designed to shoot .410 shotgun shells) are legal under federal law but not under California law.[91]

Example of a short-barreled shotgun

California's "short-barreled shotgun" definition is different from the federal definitions for "shotguns" that are restricted based on their length. Under California law a "short-barreled shotgun" means any of the following:

(1) A *firearm* that is designed or redesigned to fire a fixed shotgun shell and has a barrel or barrels of less than 18 inches in length; *or*

(2) A *firearm* that has an overall length of less than 26 inches and that is designed or redesigned to fire a fixed shotgun shell; *or*

(3) Any weapon made from a shotgun (whether by alteration, modification, or otherwise) if that weapon, as modified, has an overall length of less than 26 inches or a barrel or barrels of less than 18 inches in length; *or*

(4) Any device that may be readily restored to fire a fixed shotgun shell and, when so restored, is a device defined in subdivisions (1) to (3), inclusive; *or*

(5) Any part, or combination of parts, designed and intended to convert a device into a device defined in subdivisions (1) to (3), inclusive, or any combination of parts from which a device defined in subdivisions (1) to (3), inclusive, can be readily assembled if those parts are in the possession or under the control of the same person.[92]

discharge can be made from either barrel without manual reloading, and shall include any such weapon which may be readily restored to fire." Those are discussed in the "any other weapon" section. 27 C.F.R. § 479.11.

[90] 26 U.S.C. § 5845(d) (emphasis added).

[91] C. D. Michel, *Judging the Judges – Illegal Firearms in California?*, CALGUNLAWS.COM (June 13, 2011), http://www.CalGunLaws.com/wp-content/uploads/2012/09/Judging-the-Judges-Illegal-Firearms-in-California.pdf (last visited July 12, 2017).

[92] P.C. § 17180.

Know that the California "short-barreled shotgun" definition above does not require the firearm to actually *be* a "shotgun."[93] Any *firearm* "designed or redesigned" to shoot fixed shotgun ammunition can be a "short-barreled shotgun" if it fails to meet the length requirements. In fact, even a handgun can be considered one.[94]

"Short-barreled shotguns" are generally restricted under California law the same way as all "generally prohibited weapons" listed in P.C. section 16590.

2. "Short-Barreled Rifles"

As with shotguns, two separate federal definitions exist under the GCA and the NFA for restricted "rifles" of certain lengths.

Under the GCA a "short-barreled rifle" "means a rifle having one or more barrels less than sixteen inches in length and any weapon made from a rifle (whether by alteration, modification, or otherwise) if such weapon, as modified, has an overall length of less than twenty-six inches."[95] The GCA defines the term "rifle" as "a weapon designed or redesigned, made or remade, and intended to be fired from the shoulder and designed or redesigned and made or remade to use the energy of an explosive to fire only a single projectile through a rifled bore for each single pull of the trigger."[96] The GCA restricts these rifles the same way it does "short-barreled shotguns" as described above.

Example of a short-barreled rifle

As with shotguns, the NFA also does *not* refer to rifles with prohibited lengths as "short-barreled," but instead describes them by their physical dimensions. It specifically restricts "rifles" with one or more barrels less than 16 inches long and weapons made from a "rifle" with an overall length of less than 26 inches or that have one or more barrels that are less than 16 inches long.[97] The NFA also defines "rifle" the same way the GCA does, but additionally includes "any such weapon which may be readily restored to fire a fixed cartridge."[98]

Under the NFA, "short-barreled rifles" are restricted the same way shotguns are restricted as described above.

---

[93] *See* P.C. § 17190 (defining "shotgun" for purposes of defining "short-barreled shotgun" as "a weapon designed or redesigned, made or remade, and intended to be fired from the shoulder and designed or redesigned and made or remade to use the energy of the explosive in a fixed shotgun shell to fire through a smooth bore either a number of projectiles (ball shot) or a single projectile for each pull of the trigger.") *See also* Chapter 2.

[94] P.C. §§ 16530(b), 16640(b).

[95] 18 U.S.C. § 921(a)(8).

[96] 18 U.S.C. § 921(a)(7).

[97] 26 U.S.C. § 5845(a)(3)-(4). Note that, as with shotguns, the NFA has an additional restricted "short-barreled rifle" category not found in the GCA, *i.e.*, weapons made from a "rifle" that have one or more barrels less than 16 inches long. 26 U.S.C. § 5845(a)(3). The same implications apply as for shotguns discussed above.

[98] 26 U.S.C. § 5845(c).

"Short-barreled rifles are illegal simply because they are short, which makes them 'suitable for unlawful purposes because of their concealability and ease of handling.'"[99] This is also the case with "short-barreled shotguns." This can be a problem because the prosecution can use circumstantial evidence to show that you knew a firearm was unusually short and could be classified as a "short-barreled shotgun/rifle."[100]

Under California law, a "short-barreled rifle" is any of the following:

(1) A rifle[101] having a barrel or barrels of less than 16 inches in length; *or*

(2) A rifle with an overall length of less than 26 inches; *or*

(3) Any weapon made from a rifle (whether by alteration, modification, or otherwise) if that weapon, as modified, has an overall length of less than 26 inches or a barrel or barrels of less than 16 inches in length; *or*

(4) Any device which may be readily restored to fire a fixed cartridge which, when so restored, is a device defined in subdivisions (1) to (3), inclusive;[102] *or*

(5) Any part, or combination of parts, designed and intended to convert a device into a device defined in subdivisions (1) to (3), inclusive, or any combination of parts from which a device defined in subdivisions (1) to (3), inclusive, may be readily assembled if those parts are in the possession or under the control of the same person.[103]

"Short-barreled rifles" are generally subject to the same restrictions under California law as all "generally prohibited weapons" listed in P.C. section 16590.

While the Penal Code does not specify how a rifle or shotgun's "overall length" is determined, law enforcement will measure any "short-barreled shotgun/rifle" with the firearm in its shortest configuration (*e.g.*, with its stock folded).[104] Unlike California law, to determine whether the firearm is either a "short-barreled shotgun/rifle," federal law measures firearms in their lengthiest configuration (*e.g.*, with a folding stock extended).[105]

---

[99] *People v. King*, 38 Cal. 4th 617, 627 (2006) (citing *People v. Rooney*, 17 Cal. App. 4th 1207, 1211 (1993)); *see also People v. Stinson*, 8 Cal. App. 3d 497, 500 (1970).

[100] *People v. King*, 38 Cal. 4th 617, 627-28 (2006).

[101] See P.C. section 17090 for the California definition of "rifle." *See also* Chapter 2.

[102] Note that under both California law and the federal NFA, a firearm must fire a "fixed cartridge" to be a "rifle," but to be a restricted "short-barreled rifle" it only needs to be *readily able to be restored* to fire a "fixed cartridge," so be careful. Interestingly, if the firearm does not meet either of these definitions (*i.e.,* it does not and cannot be readily made to fire a "fixed cartridge"), it cannot be a "short-barreled rifle" under California law or the federal NFA. This means that you could lawfully possess a muzzle-loading firearm that would otherwise be considered a restricted "short-barreled rifle" based on its length without violating California law or the federal NFA. Such a firearm *would*, however, still be subject to the federal GCA limitations on transfers explained above.

[103] P.C. § 17170.

[104] *People v. Rooney*, 17 Cal. App. 4th 1207, 1211-13 (1993).

[105] 27 C.F.R. § 479.11 (stating in pertinent part: "The overall length of a weapon made from a shotgun or rifle is the distance between the extreme ends of the weapon measured along a line parallel to the center line of the bore").

Though not expressly adopted by California, the proper way to measure barrel length, as explained by the ATF, is by inserting a rod down the barrel from the muzzle through the chamber to the back of the breach.[106] This should be standard practice but is often overlooked by California law enforcement who incorrectly exclude the chamber in measuring overall barrel length.

3. Possession of Parts Constituting "Short-Barreled Shotguns/Rifles"

Note that, under both California and federal law, mere parts can be considered a "short-barreled shotgun/rifle" if, when combined, they could readily be made into one.[107] In *United States v. Thompson/Center Arms Co.*, the U.S. Supreme Court explained that pistol parts and carbine kits – parts that can be assembled to create either a handgun or a rifle – are not necessarily a "short-barreled rifle" under federal law if the parts could possibly be assembled in a way that would *not* constitute a "short-barreled rifle." The court clarified, however, that if the parts, when assembled, could *only* create a "short-barreled rifle," or are so assembled, then the parts would themselves be considered a restricted "short-barreled rifle."[108] The Ninth Circuit Court of Appeals (the controlling Court of Appeals for California) further explained that "an aggregation of weapons parts may not constitute [an NFA] firearm if the parts have an apparent legal purpose other than the creation of such a firearm" (*e.g.*, a "short-barreled rifle" under federal law).[109]

Although there is no California case law on this subject, presumably this same analysis would apply in determining whether parts would constitute a "short-barreled shotgun" or "short-barreled rifle" under California law.

Parts kits that are used to make firearms into pistols or rifles like those considered by the U.S. Supreme Court in the *Thompson* case – with a receiver that you can attach both the parts for a pistol (a short barrel and pistol grip) and the parts for a rifle (a long barrel and shoulder stock) – have caused a lot of confusion. Because of *Thompson* and its progeny, case law has explained that such kits are legal unless the parts can *only* be, or *are*, configured in a way to create a "short-barreled rifle" (this is not such a problem with shotguns). But people run into problems when they attach

---

[106] *See* U.S. Dept. of Justice, Bureau of Alcohol, Tobacco, Firearms, and Explosives, ATF National Firearms Act Handbook 6 (2009), *available at* https://www.atf.gov/firearms/docs/guide/atf-national-firearms-act-handbook-atf-p-53208/download (last visited July 12, 2017) ("The ATF procedure for measuring barrel length is to measure from the closed bolt (or breech-face) to the furthermost end of the barrel or permanently attached muzzle device. Permanent methods of attachment include full-fusion gas or electric steel-seam welding, high-temperature (1100°F) silver soldering, or blind pinning with the pin head welded over. Barrels are measured by inserting a dowel rod into the barrel until the rod stops against the bolt or breech-face. The rod is then marked at the furthermost end of the barrel or permanently attached muzzle device, withdrawn from the barrel, and measured.").

[107] P.C. §§ 17170(d)-(e) (rifles), 17180(d)-(e) (shotguns).

[108] *United States v. Thompson/Center Arms Co.*, 504 U.S. 505, 511-12 (1992) (plurality opinion).

[109] *United States v. Kwan*, 300 Fed. App'x. 485 (9th Cir. 2008) (citing *United States v. Thompson/Center Arms Co.*, 504 U.S. 505, 512-13 (1992)); *see also United States v. Kent*, 175 F.3d 870 (11th Cir. 1999). For more in-depth analysis of this and other federal firearms law related topics, see Stephen P. Halbrook, Firearms Law Deskbook (West 2011-2012 ed. 2011).

their pistol barrel and shoulder stock to the receiver. This kind of firearm is one designed to be fired from the shoulder with a rifled barrel, but the barrel (and usually the overall length of the firearm) is too short under both California and federal law, thereby creating a "short-barreled rifle." Having the wrong parts attached at the wrong time can subject you to serious criminal charges.

4. Pistol Stabilizing Braces

Attaching a pistol stabilizing brace (*e.g.,* a Sig Sauer SB15 Pistol Stabilizing Brace) to a buffer tube equipped pistol does not convert it into a "short-barreled rifle" under California or federal law. But it may be considered a "short-barreled rifle" depending on how the shooter *uses or modifies* the forearm brace.

A pistol stabilizing brace is a device that is meant to aid shooters – especially with those who have limited strength or mobility due to a handicap – in operating rifle-caliber or large caliber pistols. These devices look like short stocks on the end of the pistol and attach to the shooter's forearm by a Velcro strap, which allows the weight the firearm to be distributed evenly in order to improve accuracy and reduce the recoil felt by the shooter.

Generally, attaching a pistol stabilizing brace to a buffer tube equipped pistol and using it as it is intended to be used (*i.e.,* as a forearm brace) does not convert the firearm into a "short-barreled rifle" because the resulting firearm is still a pistol, meaning it is not intended to be fired from the shoulder – a requirement that must be met before a firearm can be a "short-barreled rifle" under both California and federal law.[110]

The ATF's position on pistol-stabilizing braces has repeatedly changed over the years. On March 5, 2014, the ATF originally decided that using a pistol-stabilizing brace as a shoulder stock does not change the classification of the weapon or transform the pistol into a "short-barreled rifle."[111]

Then, in a series of letters between November 2014 and January 2015, the ATF changed course and said that using an arm brace as a shoulder stock on a pistol "redesigned" the firearm into an NFA "short-barreled rifle." On November 10, 2014, the ATF explained (in response to an inquiry about the Sig Sauer SB15 Arm Brace) that attaching a stabilizing brace to the pistol alone does not change the pistol into a "short-barreled rifle" under federal law. But, if the brace stabilizer was used as a shoulder stock, it would then be classified as a "rifle" and therefore considered a "short-barreled rifle" under federal law.[112] On December 15, 2014, the ATF issued

---

[110] As with California law, before a firearm can be considered a "short-barreled rifle" under federal law, it must first be a "rifle," meaning that it must be intended to be fired from the shoulder. 26 U.S.C. § 5845(a), (c).

[111] Letter from Earl Griffith, Chief, Firearms Technology Branch to Sergeant Joe Bradley, Greenwood Police Department (Mar. 5, 2014), *available at* http://www.gunsandammo.com/files/2014/04/S72-LEGAL-B1404030900021.jpg (last visited July 28, 2017).

[112] Letter from Max M. Kingery, Acting Chief, Firearms Technology Industry Services Branch to Anonymous (Nov. 10, 2014), *available at* https://princelaw.files.wordpress.com/2014/12/sig-brace-nov-2014.pdf (last visited July 28, 2017).

another letter supporting this decision, finding that attaching a Shockwave Blade AR Pistol Stabilizer to a pistol does not convert the weapon into a "short-barreled rifle" for purposes of federal law as long as it is used as originally designed and not used as a shoulder stock.[113] Later, in an open letter released on January 16, 2015, the ATF stated that any person who intends to use or uses a pistol stabilizing brace as a shoulder stock converts the firearm into a "short-barreled rifle" under the NFA.[114]

The reasoning outlined in these letters raises an obvious question: how does merely shifting the firearm from the arm to the shoulder "convert" or "redesign" the firearm into a rifle? On March 21, 2017, the ATF attempted to clarify this issue by stating that one may use an arm brace as a shoulder stock in an "incidental", "situational" or "sporadic" manner.[115] But, attaching a stabilizing brace that is not in its "original approved condition" to a pistol may convert it into a "short-barreled rifle" under the NFA.[116] As explained earlier in this chapter, the NFA defines a "rifle" as any "weapon, designed or redesigned, made or remade, and intended to be fired from the shoulder."

Although neither the NFA nor GCA define the term "redesign," in the ATF's opinion, any affirmative steps" to configure the device as a shoulder stock constitute a "redesign" of the firearm into a "rifle."[117] Examples of some affirmative steps include, but are not limited to: (1) "configuring the brace so as to permanently affix it to the end of a buffer tube, (thereby creating a length that has no other purpose than to facilitate its use as a stock); (2) removing the arm-strap; or (3) otherwise undermining its ability to be used as a brace."[118] So any person who consistently uses a pistol stabilizing brace as a shoulder stock regardless of the situation, or at any time connects a pistol stabilizing brace that is not in its "original approved condition" to a pistol with a rifled barrel under 16 inches as a shoulder stock has "redesigned" the firearm into a "short-barreled rifle" for purposes of the NFA.[119]

---

[113] Letter from Michael R. Curtis, Acting Chief, Firearms Technology Industry Services Brach to Martin Ewer, Owner, Shockwave Technologies (Dec. 15, 2014), *available at* http://shockwavetechnologies.com/site/?p=2114 (last visited July 28, 2017).

[114] Open Letter on the Redesign of "Stabilizing Braces" from Max M. Kingery, Acting Chief, Firearms Technology Criminal Branch, Firearms and Ammunition Technology Division, Bureau of Alcohol, Tobacco, Firearms, and Explosives (Jan. 16, 2015), *available at* https://www.atf.gov/file/11816/download (last visited July 12, 2017).

[115] Letter from Marvin G. Richardson, Assistant Director of Enforcement Programs and Services, Bureau of Alcohol, Tobacco, Firearms and Explosives (Mar. 21, 2017), *available at* https://www.sigsauer.com/wp-content/uploads/2017/04/atf-letter-march-21-2017.pdf (last visited Oct. 20, 2017).

[116] Letter from Marvin G Richardson, Assistant Director of Enforcement Programs and Services, Bureau of Alcohol, Tobacco, Firearms and Explosives (Mar. 21, 2017), *available at* https://www.sigsauer.com/wp-content/uploads/2017/04/atf-letter-march-21-2017.pdf (last visited Oct. 20, 2017).

[117] 26 U.S.C. § 5845(a).

[118] Letter from Marvin G Richardson, Assistant Director of Enforcement Programs and Services, Bureau of Alcohol, Tobacco, Firearms and Explosives (Mar. 21, 2017), *available at* https://www.sigsauer.com/wp-content/uploads/2017/04/atf-letter-march-21-2017.pdf (last visited Oct. 20, 2017).

[119] Note that because almost all buffer tube equipped pistols are based on the AR15 platform and have rifled barrels. Therefore, even if a stabilizing brace is attached to an AR pistol, it would not fall under the definition of "any other weapon" under the NFA because it is designed to be gripped by one hand (see Section XII(A) of this Chapter).

Despite the fact that the ATF has repeatedly changed its position on this issue, the letter that was issued on March 21, 2017, reflects the most recent decisions by the ATF and should be followed.

Moreover, even though there is no case law on the matter in California, presumably law enforcement would likely apply the same analysis in determining whether a buffer tube equipped pistol is an illegal "short-barreled rifle" under California law if a person attaches a stabilizing brace to the pistol with the intent of using it as, or actually uses it as, a shoulder stock.

 Therefore, if you plan on attaching and using a stabilizer brace on a buffer tube attached pistol in California, we still suggest you use it as intended (i.e., as a forearm brace).

H. "Zip Gun"

Under California law, a "zip gun"[120] is any weapon or device that meets all of the following:

(1) It was not imported as a firearm by a licensed importer;[121] *and*

(2) It was not originally designed to be a firearm by a licensed manufacturer;[122] *and*

(3) No tax was paid on the weapon or device, nor was it exempt from a tax;[123] *and*

(4) It is made or altered to expel a projectile by the force of an explosion or other form of combustion.[124]

"Zip guns" are typically small homemade firearms. They are usually destroyed once fired. This does not mean, however, that a larger, sturdier item could not be considered a "zip gun." In the past some law enforcement agencies have claimed that *all* firearms made from raw materials are "zip guns."[125] But that is incorrect. It is not necessarily illegal for people to assemble or build firearms for their own personal use (see Chapter 4).

Example of a "zip gun": this one was made in prison with metal parts

Firearms made to expel projectiles by combustive force, but that have been made from raw materials, have clearly not been imported as a firearm, nor would

---

[120] Illegal under P.C. section 33600.

[121] Licensed pursuant to 18 U.S.C. section 923.

[122] Licensed pursuant to 18 U.S.C. section 923.

[123] This exemption is granted under 26 U.S.C. sections 4181, 4216-4227 and the regulations issued pursuant thereto.

[124] P.C. § 17360.

[125] If the "zip gun" is created from a receiver acquired from an FFL, a tax would have been paid.

taxes be paid on them.[126] The issue, then, is about the firearm's *design*. If you make a brand new firearm from an original design (*i.e.*, not based on an existing firearm design), you have arguably created a "zip gun" unless you are a licensed firearm manufacturer (see Chapter 4). This means that, if you create a firearm based on a licensed firearm manufacturer's design, it should *not* be considered a "zip gun" under the above criteria.

I. "Unconventional Pistol"

Under California law, an "unconventional pistol"[127] is a firearm: (1) without a rifled bore, and (2) that "has a barrel or barrels of less than 18 inches in length or has an overall length of less than 26 inches."[128]

J. "Large-Capacity Magazine" and "Large-Capacity Magazine Conversion Kits"

1. Definition

Under California law, a "large-capacity magazine" is "any ammunition feeding device with the capacity to accept more than 10 rounds," but it does *not* include:

(1) A feeding device that has been permanently altered so that it cannot accommodate more than 10 rounds; *or*

(2) A .22 caliber tube ammunition feeding device; *or*

(3) A tubular magazine that is contained in a lever-action firearm.[129]

California law does not explain further what a "large-capacity magazine" is, but in the definition of "detachable magazine," an "ammunition feeding device" includes "any belted or linked ammunition" but not "clips, en bloc clips, or stripper clips that load cartridges into the magazine."[130]

Ammunition feeding devices of any size and capacity may be permanently[131] altered to make them unable to accept more than ten rounds. If this happens, they lose their "large-capacity magazine" status and thus are not restricted.

---

[126] There is an argument to be made that if the "zip gun" was manufactured for personal use, no tax was due, and therefore the gun was exempt from the tax requirement. But the ins and outs of federal tax law far exceed the scope of this book.

[127] Contraband under P.C. section 31500.

[128] P.C. § 17270.

[129] P.C. § 16740.

[130] Cal. Code Regs. tit. 11, § 5471(m).

[131] Whether an alteration is "permanent" can affect the magazine's legal status and is not always clear. In fact, the DOJ attempted to define "permanently altered" in the California Code of Regulations but deleted the definition. *See Notice of Modification to Text of Proposed Regulations*, California Dept. of Justice, Office of the Attorney General, http://oag.ca.gov/sites/all/files/agweb/pdfs/firearms/regs/sb23rev.pdf (last visited July 12, 2017).

Some law enforcement agencies have tried to cram an eleventh round into magazines designed, sold, and used as ones with a ten-round maximum capacity. Some magazines' springs will allow this and still function, even though they are not designed to accept that eleventh round. Though this scenario is unlikely and uncommon, it is worth trying to force an eleventh round into a magazine to see if it is considered a "large-capacity magazine" (explained below).

The DOJ attempted to define the phrase "permanently altered" in the proposed emergency regulations for "large-capacity magazines" that it submitted to the Office of Administrative Law on December 23, 2016. Specifically, the DOJ's proposed regulations stated that individuals must do the following to "permanently alte[r] the magazine's feeding device" in order to keep the magazine after the July 1, 2017 ban on "large-capacity magazines" was supposed to go into effect:

(1) A large-capacity magazine that is a box type can have its capacity permanently reduced by using both of the following methods

(a) Inserting a rigid magazine capacity reduction device, also known as a magazine block, into the magazine body and then affixing the floor plate of the magazine to the body of the magazine with permanent epoxy. Metal magazines with metal floor plates have the option of being either welded closed or permanently epoxied closed once the magazine block(s) have been inserted. Due to magazine manufacturing variations (such as drum magazines or tubular magazines) it may be necessary to insert multiple magazine blocks in order to reduce the capacity to 10 rounds; and

(b) Once the capacity of the magazine has been reduced by inserting a rigid magazine block into the magazine, it shall be riveted in place through either the floor plate or side wall of the magazine body.

(2) A large-capacity magazine that is a drum or tubular style can be permanently reduced by using any of the following methods:

(a) Drum magazines generally come in two styles: those that are fed from the neck of the magazine (neck fed drum magazines, and those that open from the side and are loaded once a lid or cover is opened up (clam shell drum magazines)

(i) A neck fed drum magazine needs a specific number of "dummy rounds" inserted into the neck fed magazine drum and then the "dummy rounds" needs to be epoxied in place in an attempt at reducing the capacity of the neck fed drum magazine. The actual numbers of dummy rounds vary per neck fed drum magazine depending on its original capacity. For example, a 50 round neck fed drum magazine needs 40 dummy rounds epoxied in placed so that no more than 10 rounds could be loaded. Once these dummy rounds are permanently epoxied into place the lid shall be closed and also permanently epoxied closed. Due to the internal moving parts of these magazines, a rivet securing the lid or cover is not possible in most cases. Armatac AR-15 style magazines are one example of this type of magazine.

(ii.) Clam shell drum magazines are fed by opening the cover or lid and then loading the magazine. This magazine type cannot be loaded via the neck because of its design. Examples of this type are the AK-47 style Suomi, PPSH 41 and Thompson "Tommy Gun" drum magazines. If the capacity is reduced down to 10 rounds or less, (as described above), and the cover or lid is epoxied closed, the magazine could never be reloaded once the 10 rounds are fired. This magazine type is not a good candidate for reduction to 10 rounds or less and shall be disposed by other means if not permanently altered as described in this section.

(b) A tubular magazine that has more than a 10 round capacity shall have its capacity permanently reduced by insertion of a magazine block and use of permanent epoxy to hold the block in place. Then, a rivet shall secure the block in place by penetrating the tubular magazine and the magazine block.[132]

In these same regulations, the DOJ also attempted to define "large-capacity magazine" for dual tube shotguns. According to the withdrawn regulations, "[o]ne or more magazines each having a 10 round or less capacity, that are then attached to each other with tape, a plastic or metal coupler, or welded together would not be deemed a large-capacity magazine unless one of the following circumstances exist:

(1) The internal magazines of a firearm are part of a design function in which the combined ammunition capacity exceeds 10 rounds, and can be fired by the shooter without manipulating the magazine selector switch. An example of this type of firearm is the Standard Manufacturing DP-12 pump shotgun. If the tubular magazines are permanently altered to reduce their capacity to 10 rounds or less as described in this section, then this firearm would not be deemed a large-capacity magazine.

(2) The internal magazines of a firearm are part of a design function in which the combined ammunition capacity exceeds 10 rounds and the firearm has a selector switch that allows the shooter to alternatingly use ammunition from more than one tubular magazine without having to manually switch the ammunition feeding process. An example of this type of firearm is the UTAS MAKINE LTD., MODEL: UTS-15, pump shotgun which has two seven-round tubular magazines. If the tubular magazines are permanently altered to reduce their capacity to 10 rounds or less as described in this section, then this firearm would not be deemed a large-capacity magazine. Alternatively, if the UTS-15 magazine selector switch was modified so that the shooter had to manually switch the ammunition feed from one tube to another, then this firearm would not be deemed a large-capacity magazine.

---

[132] Proposed CAL. CODE. REGS. tit. 11 § 5491(b)(1), (b)(2) (2016).

[] If a firearm with multiple tubular magazines, each having a 10 round or less capacity, must be manually switched from one tube to the other tube to us each group of ammunition, this type of firearm would not be deemed a large-capacity magazine. An example of this type of firearm is the KEL TEC, KSG shotgun which has two seven-round tubular magazines. While the tubes can collectively hold 14 rounds, the shooter must manually switch magazines. Another example of this type of firearm is the SRM-1216 semi automatic shotgun which has four four-round tubular magazines welded together. After firing the first four rounds the shooter must manually rotate the quad magazine clockwise to enable firing of the next group of four rounds. If a version of this firearm was manufactured that mechanically rotated the quad ammunition tubes it would be deemed a large-capacity magazine.[133]

Because these regulations were withdrawn, following opposition to them by the NRA and CRPA and other pro-Second Amendment advocates, they never became law. Nevertheless, they are a good indication of DOJ's position on the requirements.

2. Restricted Activity for "Large-Capacity Magazines"

Like most of the items discussed in this chapter, under California law it is generally illegal to manufacture or cause to be manufactured, import, keep for sale, offer or expose for sale, give, lend, buy, or receive a "large-capacity magazine."[134]

Prior to the passage of Senate Bill (SB) 1446 and Proposition 63 (Prop. 63), it was not generally illegal to possess a "large-capacity magazine" under California law.[135] Beginning July 1, 2017, unless you meet one of the exceptions outlined below, it would have been illegal to possess "large-capacity magazines" throughout California. But due to the efforts of our office in the U.S. District Court in San Diego for the *Duncan v. Becerra* case, the enforcement of the ban on "large-capacity magazine" has been enjoined for the time being.[136] At the time of this book's writing, we do not know how long this enjoinment will last and where the law and our case will end up. You should monitor the status of the *Duncan v. Becerra* case to make certain you are compliant.

Meanwhile, note that violations of this general restriction are treated differently under SB 1446 and Prop. 63. Under SB 1446, any person who possess a "large-capacity magazine" in California is guilty of an infraction, punishable by a fine not to exceed $100 for the first offense, $250 for the second offense, and $500 for any sub-

---

[133] Proposed CAL. CODE. REGS. tit. 11 § 5491(b)(4), (b)(5) (2016).

[134] P.C. § 32310(a).

[135] Although it was not generally unlawful to possess a "large-capacity magazine" under California law, some cities, such as San Francisco and Los Angeles, had passed ordinances that made it illegal to possess "large-capacity magazines" within their respective city limits (see below).

[136] *Duncan v. Becerra*, 2017 WL 2813727(S.D. Cal., June 29, 2017, No. 3:17-CV-1017-BEN).

sequent offenses.[137] On the other hand, a violation of this restriction under Prop. 63 is treated as an infraction, punishable by a fine not to exceed $100 per magazine; or a misdemeanor, punishable by a fine not to exceed $100, imprisonment in a county jail not to exceed one year, or by both fine and imprisonment.[138]

Prop. 63 appears to trump SB 1446, so any person who violates this general restriction on the possession of "large-capacity magazines" may be charged with an infraction or misdemeanor.

If the restriction on the possession of "large-capacity magazines" had not been stayed by the *Duncan* case, you would have had to do one of the following under SB 1446 before July 1, 2017:

(1) Remove the "large-capacity magazine" from the state; *or*

(2) Sell the "large-capacity magazine" to a licensed firearms dealer; *or*

(3) Destroy the "large-capacity magazine"; *or*

(4) Surrender the "large-capacity magazine" to a law enforcement agency for destruction.[139]

In contrast, Prop. 63 only provides three different methods for disposing of your "large-capacity magazine":

(1) Remove the "large-capacity magazine" from the state; *or*

(2) Sell the "large-capacity magazine" to a licensed firearms dealer; *or*

(4) Surrender the "large-capacity magazine" to a law enforcement agency for destruction.[140]

Once again, Prop. 63 appears to trump SB 1446 in this case.

Although it is not included within the new law, an individual could theoretically also lawfully dispose of their "large-capacity magazine" by converting it to a magazine that holds ten rounds or less before July 1, 2017. At this point, the magazine would no longer fit within the definition of a "large-capacity magazine" because the magazine would no longer be able to hold more than ten rounds. Therefore, the magazine would no longer fall under any of the restrictions above. As further discussed above, DOJ's proposed (and withdrawn) regulations appeared to have attempted to address this. But, again, the regulations never became law and

[137] *See* SB 1446, 2015-2016 Leg., Reg. Sess. (Cal. 2016), *available at* http://leginfo.legislature.ca.gov/faces/billNav-Client.xhtml?bill_id=201520160SB1446 (last visited July 12, 2017).

[138] *See* OFFICE OF THE ATTORNEY GENERAL, FULL TEXT OF PROPOSITION 63, *available at* http://www.oag.ca.gov/system/files/initiatives/pdfs/15-0098%20%28Firearms%29_0.pdf (last visited July 12, 2017); P.C. § 32310(c).

[139] *See* SB 1446, 2015-2016 Leg., Reg. Sess. (Cal. 2016), *available at* http://leginfo.legislature.ca.gov/faces/billNav-Client.xhtml?bill_id=201520160SB1446 (last visited July 12, 2017); OFFICE OF THE ATTORNEY GENERAL, FULL TEXT OF PROPOSITION 63, *available at* http://www.oag.ca.gov/system/files/initiatives/pdfs/15-0098%20%28Fire-arms%29_0.pdf (last visited July 12, 2017).

[140] *See* SB 1446, 2015-2016 Leg., Reg. Sess. (Cal. 2016), *available at* http://leginfo.legislature.ca.gov/faces/billNav-Client.xhtml?bill_id=201520160SB1446 (last visited July 12, 2017); P.C. § 32310(d).

the possession restriction was enjoined. How this matter will be resolved remains to be seen as of the time of the writing of this book.

3. Restricted Activity for "Large-Capacity Magazine Conversion Kits"

Along with the restrictions on "large-capacity magazines," it is also unlawful under California law to manufacture, cause to be manufactured, import into the state, keep for sale, offer or expose for sale, give, lend, buy, or receive any "large-capacity magazine conversion kit."[141] Notice that unlike with "large-capacity magazines," the Legislature and Lt. Governor Newsom did not attempt to ban the possession of "large-capacity magazine conversion kits." Therefore, possession of a "large-capacity magazine conversion kit" in California is still allowed regardless of our lawsuit.

A "conversion kit" is defined as "a device or combination of parts of a fully functioning large capacity magazine, including, but not limited to, the body, spring, follower, and floor plate or end plate, capable of converting an ammunition feeding device into a large capacity magazine."[142]

 Due to the problematic definition of "conversion kit," there is still a great deal of confusion over what magazine parts and/or accessories are restricted by this section. Magazine extenders that are capable of converting an ammunition feeding device into a "large-capacity magazine" are likely to be treated as prohibited "conversion kit" devices under this section. In fact, DOJ's defunct regulations attempted to say as much.[143]

It is also unknown at this time what items will be considered a "combination of parts" of a fully functioning large-capacity magazine capable of converting an ammunition feeding device into a large-capacity magazine. Because "large-capacity magazine" rebuild kits do not really "convert" an existing magazine into a "large-capacity magazine," a plain reading of the law suggests that rebuild kits, *i.e.* parts kits, are not prohibited.

 According to the author's statements about the intent of the law, the law was intended to ban the sale of these rebuild kits. The confusion seems to have arisen based on the author's misunderstanding of how a rebuild kits can be used to assemble a "large-capacity magazine," rather than to "convert" an existing magazine into a "large-capacity magazine." If a court finds the definition of a conversion kit is not clear on its face, it may turn to the bill's legislative history for clarification. And while the author's comments alone may not be enough to convince a court that the law applies to rebuild kits, for the time being there is risk of criminal prosecution for transferring them.[144]

---

[141] P.C. § 32311.

[142] P.C. § 32311.

[143] Proposed Cal. Code. Regs. tit. 11, § 5492(a) (2016).

[144] In 2013, the San Francisco City Attorney's Office filed a lawsuit alleging unfair business practices against three online vendors and a gun show company for selling "large-capacity magazine" rebuild kits. The City Attorney alleged that the disassembled parts kits are still unlawful "large-capacity magazines," and that the sellers knowingly

Neither the language of AB 48 or its legislative history suggest that magazines that are not "large-capacity magazines," or their parts, were intended to be restricted as "conversion kits." Due to the ambiguous nature of the law, however, it is difficult to predict how law enforcement agencies and prosecutors will interpret and enforce this section. Nothing in this book is intended to suggest that the law prohibits the sale of any individual part(s), whether interchangeable with a "low-capacity" magazine or not.

It is *not* illegal to merely possess a "conversion kit." This means that those who possessed a "large-capacity magazine conversion kit" prior to P.C. section 32311 taking effect on January 1, 2014, may continue to possess them so long as they are not assembled into, or used to assemble, a "large-capacity magazine." Again, be careful. This does not mean law enforcement agencies cannot prosecute you for a "large-capacity magazine conversion kit" found in your possession if they can prove you imported, manufactured, bought, received, or sold it after January 1, 2014.

If you lawfully possess a "large-capacity magazine" that requires repair, the Penal Code expressly authorizes transfers of "large-capacity magazines" to a licensed firearms dealer for repairs.[145] And owners of lawfully obtained "large-capacity magazines" who have parts kits acquired prior to January 1, 2014, are not prohibited from making the repairs themselves.

And note that DOJ's also gives an opinion about "large-capacity magazine conversion kits" in the proposed and withdrawn regulations. For instance, DOJ stated that disassembled "large-capacity magazines" that may be "readily assembled" and that "is in the possession of or under the control of the same person is a large -capacity magazine conversion kit."[146] DOJ also states that a grip extension whose sole purpose is to increase grip space on the magazine is not a "large-capacity magazine conversion kit."[147] And DOJ wanted to continue to allow those in lawful possession of "large-capacity magazines" to disassemble the magazines for cleaning, maintenance, or other lawful purpose without running afoul of the restrictions on "large-capacity magazine conversion kits."[148] It bears repeating, though, that these proposed regulations are *not* California law. Rather, they may be used as insight to what DOJ thinks the law should be.

---

assisted in the unlawful manufacture of "large-capacity magazines." Ultimately, this case was settled outside of court, with the vendors agreeing to pay $15,000 and discontinuing the sales of "large-capacity magazines" to California customers.

[145] P.C. § 32425.

[146] Proposed CAL. CODE. REGS. tit. 11, § 5492(b) (2016).

[147] Proposed CAL. CODE. REGS. tit. 11, § 5492(c) (2016).

[148] Proposed CAL. CODE. REGS. tit. 11, § 5492(d) (2016).

4. Local Restrictions on "Large-Capacity Magazines"

Currently, two cities in California – the City of San Francisco and Sunnyvale– have enacted laws that make it illegal to possess "large-capacity magazines,"[149] regardless of whether the magazines are assembled or disassembled.[150] The city of Los Angeles used to have such laws,[151] but it repealed its ordinances in response to the NRA and CRPA's pre-litigation demands in the *Bosenko v. City of Los Angeles* case. [152]Because of this repeal, and because *Duncan v. Becerra* enjoined the state-wide ban on "large-capacity magazine" possession, there is currently no law prohibiting the possession of "large-capacity magazines" in the City of Los Angeles at the time of the book's publication. This may change, though, depending on the outcome of the *Duncan v. Becerra* case.

Meanwhile, the restrictions from San Francisco and Sunnyvale still apply, regardless of the state-wide enjoinment. There are some exceptions to these general restrictions, however. Specifically, the following people and entities are exempt from San Francisco's ban on the possession of "large-capacity magazines":

(1) Any government officer, agent, or employee, member of the armed forces of the United States, or peace officer, to the extent that such person is otherwise authorized to possess a "large-capacity magazine" in connection with his or her official duties; *and*

(2) A licensed firearms dealer; *and*

(3) A gunsmith for the purposes of maintenance, repair, or modification of the "large-capacity magazine"; *and*

(4) Any entity that operates an armored vehicle business under the laws of the state, and an authorized employee of such entity, while in the course and scope of his or her employment for purposes that pertain to the entity's armored vehicle business; *and*

(5) Any person, corporation, or other entity that manufactures "large-capacity magazines" for a government officer, agent, or employee, member of the armed forces of the United States, or peace officer; *and*

(6) Any person using the "large-capacity magazine" solely as a prop for motion picture, television, or video production, or entertainment event; *and*

---

[149] San Francisco and Sunnyvale both define the term "large capacity magazine" as "any detachable feeding device with the capacity to accept more than" ten rounds, but does not have an exception for a feeding device that has been permanently altered so that it cannot accommodate more than ten rounds, a .22 caliber tubular ammunition feeding device, or a tubular magazine that is contained in a level-action firearm as allowed by the California Penal Code. S.F., CAL., POLICE CODE § 619; SUNNYVALE, CAL., MUN. CODE § 9.44.050(a)(1)-(3).

[150] S.F., CAL., POLICE CODE § 619; Sunnyvale, CAL., MUN. CODE § 9.44.050.

[151] A ban similar to Los Angeles's ban on "large-capacity" magazines was found to be constitutional under the Second Amendment by the United States Court of Appeals for the Second Circuit in *New York State Rifle & Pistol Association v. Cuomo*, 804 F.3d 242 (2d Cir. 2015), *cert. denied sub nom. Shew v. Malloy*, 136 S.Ct. 2486 (2016).

[152] *Bosenko v. City of Los Angeles*, BS158682, (LA Sup. Ct. 2015).

(7) Any holder of a special weapon's permit issued under P.C. section 33300 (permit for "short-barreled rifle" or "short-barreled shotgun"), 32650 (permit for possession, manufacture, or transportation of machineguns), 32700 (license to sell machineguns), 31000 ("assault weapons" and .50 BMG permit), or 18900 (permit to conduct business using, or to possess or transport "destructive devices"); *and*

(8) Any person issued a permit under P.C. section 32315 by the DOJ upon a showing of "good cause" for the possession, transportation, or sale of "large-capacity magazines" between a person licensed under P.C. sections 26700 to 26915 and an out-of-state client, when those activities are in accordance with the terms and conditions of that permit; *and*

(9) Any federal, state, or local historical society, museum or institutional collection which is open to the public, provided that the large-capacity magazine" is properly housed, secured form unauthorized handling and unloaded; *and*

(10) Any person who finds a "large-capacity magazine," if the person is not prohibited form possessing firearm or ammunition under federal or California law, and the person possess the "large-capacity magazine" no longer than is necessary to deliver or transport the same to a law enforcement agency for that agency's disposition according to law; *and*

(11) A forensic laboratory or any authorized agent or employee thereof in the course and scope of his or her authorized activities; *and*

(12) Any person in the business of selling or transferring "large-capacity magazines" in accordance with P.C. section 32310 who is in possession of a "large-capacity magazine" solely for the purpose of doing so; *and*

(13) Any person lawfully in possession of a firearm that the person has obtained prior to January 1, 2000, if no magazine that holds ten or less rounds of ammunition is compatible with that firearm and the person possess the "large-capacity magazine" solely for use with that firearm.[153]

Unlike San Francisco, Sunnyvale only exempts the following people and entities from its ban on "large capacity magazines":

(1) Any federal, state, county, or city agencies that are charged with the enforcement of any law, or use by agency employees in the discharge of their official duties; *and*

(2) Any government officer, agent or employee, member of the armed forces of the United States, or peace officer, to the extent that such person is otherwise authorized to possess a "large-capacity magazine" and does so while acting within the course and scope of his or her duties; *and*

---

[153] S.F., CAL., POLICE CODE § 619.

(3) A forensic laboratory or any authorized agent or employee thereof in the course and scope of his or her duties; *and*

(4) Any entity that operates an armored vehicle business pursuant to the laws of the state, and an authorized employee of such entity, while the course and scope of his or her employment for purposes that pertain to the entity's armored vehicle business; *and*

(5) Any person who has been issued a license or permit by the California Department of Justice pursuant to Penal Code Sections 18900, 26500-26915, 31000, 32315, 32650, 32700-32720, or 33300, when the possession of a "large-capacity magazine" is in accordance with that license or permit; *and*

(6) A licensed gunsmith for purposes of maintenance, repair or modification of the "large-capacity magazine"; *and*

(7) Any person who finds a "large-capacity magazine," if the person is not prohibited from possessing firearms or ammunition pursuant to federal or state law, and the person possesses the "large-capacity magazine" no longer than is reasonably necessary to deliver or transport the same to a law enforcement agency; *and*

(8) Any person lawfully in possession of a firearm that the person obtained prior to January 1, 2000, if no magazine that holds fewer than 10 rounds of ammunition is compatible with the firearm and the person possesses the large-capacity magazine solely for use with that firearm; *and*

(9) Any retired peace officer holding a valid Carry License.[154]

Under Sunnyvale and San Francisco's restrictions, persons who possessed "large-capacity magazines" when these laws went into effect were given a grace period during which they were required to surrender their "large-capacity magazines" to law enforcement, remove them from the city, or sell or transfer them to a dealer with a dangerous weapons permit.[155] But these grace periods have ended.

 Moreover, note that San Francisco and Sunnyvale *do not* exempt visitors or people passing through the state from the restrictions on "large-capacity magazines," even if the magazines are in a locked container or the trunk of a car. Therefore, you should be cautious when you are traveling through California with "large-capacity magazines" because although they may be legal in the city you currently live in, you can be held criminally liable for possessing them if you pass into the city limits of San Francisco or Sunnyvale.

---

[154] SUNNYVALE, CAL., MUN. CODE § 9.44.050(c). Note that currently only Sunnyvale exempts retired peace officers from the restriction on "large-capacity magazines."

[155] S.F., CAL., POLICE CODE § 619; SUNNYVALE, CAL., MUN. CODE § 9.44.050.

Again, these local laws are not currently affected by the injunction on the state-wide possession ban. Depending on how *Duncan v. Becerra* plays out, though, these local laws may be affected in the future.

IV. EXCEPTIONS TO CALIFORNIA LAW FOR "GENERALLY PROHIBITED WEAPONS," "LARGE-CAPACITY MAGAZINE CONVERSION KITS," AND THE BAN ON "LARGE-CAPACITY MAGAZINE" POSSESSION

Former P.C. section 12020(b) combined all 32 exceptions to the "generally pro-hibited weapons" restrictions into one large list. Those exceptions are now laid out as one exception per section number. Unless otherwise indicated, the following exceptions apply to each of the above firearms, weapons, devices, and ammunition that are considered "generally prohibited weapons" and listed in P.C. section 16590.

As discussed above, when the law was changed on January 1, 2014, to include restrictions on "large-capacity magazine conversion kits," these items were not added to the list of "generally prohibited weapons." Regardless of this obvious over-sight, all of the exceptions to the restrictions for "generally prohibited weapons" extend to "large-capacity magazine conversion kits."[156]

It is also important to note that the following exemptions also apply to the gen-eral prohibition on the possession of "large-capacity magazines," which would have gone into effect on July 1, 2017 (see above).

A. "Antique Firearms"

An item is not considered a "generally prohibited weapon" if it is an "antique firearm."[157] See Chapter 2 for the definition of "antique firearm" applicable to "gen-erally prohibited weapons."[158]

B. "Curios or Relics"

Certain firearms and ammunition are not prohibited if they are lawfully possessed "curios or relics" under federal law.[159] "Curios or relics" are of special interest to col-lectors for "some quality other than [those] associated with firearms intended for

---

[156] P.C. § 32311.

[157] P.C. § 17700.

[158] P.C. § 16170(c).

[159] P.C. § 17705. For example, someone not prohibited from possessing firearms under 18 U.S.C section 922.

sporting use or as offensive or defensive weapons."[160] See Chapter 2 for the definition of "curios or relics."

C. "Any Other Weapons"

A "generally prohibited weapon" meeting the NFA definition of "any other weapon" (defined below) is legal to possess if you are not otherwise generally prohibited from possessing these firearms under the GCA.[161]

D. Historical Society, Museum, or Institutional Collection

The "generally prohibited weapons" restrictions "do not apply to any instrument or device that is possessed by a federal, state, or local historical society, museum, or institutional collection that is open to the public," as long as they are "properly housed," "secured from unauthorized handling," and, "if the instrument or device is a firearm, it is unloaded."[162]

In addition, the version of P.C. section 32406 implemented by SB 1446 states that the ban on "large-capacity magazine" possession does not apply to these entities (i.e., "[a] federal, state, or local historical society, museum or institutional society, or museum or institutional collection, that is open to the public"), "provided that the "large-capacity magazine is unloaded, properly housed within secured premises, and secured from unauthorized handling."[163]

E. Media or Entertainment Events

The "generally prohibited weapons" restrictions (other than those for "short-barreled shotguns/rifles") do not apply when they are "possessed or used during the course of a motion picture, television, or video production or entertainment event by an authorized participant therein in the course of making that production or event or by an authorized employee or agent of the entity producing that production or event."[164]

---

[160] 27 C.F.R. § 478.11.

[161] P.C. § 17710. Oddly, it is the NFA, not the GCA, that strictly regulates "any other weapons." It is unclear why the California legislature said GCA instead of NFA, or if it was a mistake. While the GCA regulates who may lawfully possess firearms under federal law (i.e., prohibited persons), "any other weapons," like other NFA firearms, are highly regulated.

[162] P.C. § 17715.

[163] P.C. § 32406(b).

[164] P.C. § 17720.

F. People Who Sell Items to Historical Societies, Museums, Institutional Collections, or Entertainment Events

The "generally prohibited weapons" restrictions (other than those for "short-barreled shotguns/rifles") do not apply when they are "sold by, manufactured by, exposed or kept for sale by, possessed by, imported by, or lent by" those whose business it is to sell instruments or devices to historical societies, museums or institutional collections, or entertainment events while "engaging in transactions with those entities."[165]

G. Law Enforcement Firearm Purchases and Those Who Sell to Law Enforcement

The "generally prohibited weapons" restrictions (other than those for "short-barreled shotguns/rifles") do not apply to selling, possessing, or purchasing "any weapon, device, or ammunition" (other than "short-barreled shotguns/rifles") that is used by any law enforcement agency in discharging their official duties. Nor does it restrict their possession by any federal, state, or local peace officers when on duty and authorized by the agency and when the possession is "within the course and scope of the[ir] . . . duties."[166] The "generally prohibited weapons" restrictions also do not apply (other than those for "short-barreled shotguns/rifles") when "sold by, manufactured by, exposed or kept for sale by, possessed by, imported by, or lent by" anyone whose business it is to sell these items to law enforcement agencies "when engaging in transactions with those entities."[167]

H. Transporting Most "Generally Prohibited Weapons" to Law Enforcement

The "generally prohibited weapons" restrictions do not apply to the *non-firearm devices* listed therein when possessed by someone who is allowed to possess firearms or ammunition (see Chapter 3) if the non-firearm device is possessed no longer than necessary to transport it to a law enforcement agency to turn it in.[168]

The "generally prohibited weapons" restrictions (other than those for "short-barreled shotguns/rifles") do not apply to the *firearms* listed therein when possessed by someone allowed to possess firearms or ammunition, as long as they are possessed no longer than necessary to transport them, in a locked container,[169] to

---

[165] P.C. § 17725.
[166] P.C. § 17730(a)-(b).
[167] P.C. § 17730(c).
[168] P.C. § 17735.
[169] As defined in P.C. section 16850.

a law enforcement agency.[170] Such persons must also give prior notice that they are transporting the firearms for disposition.[171]

I. Forensic Laboratory

The "generally prohibited weapons" restrictions (other than those for "short-barreled shotguns/rifles") do not apply to a forensic laboratory's possession of "any weapon, device, or ammunition," including possession by its authorized agents or employees, as long as in the course of authorized activities.[172]

In addition, the version of P.C. section 32406 implemented by SB 1446 states that the ban on "large-capacity magazine" possession also does not apply to "[a] forensic laboratory, or an authorized agent or employee thereof in the course and scope of his or her authorized activities."[173]

V. ADDITIONAL CALIFORNIA LAW EXCEPTIONS FOR "LARGE-CAPACITY MAGAZINE" AND "LARGE-CAPACITY MAGAZINE CONVERSION KIT" RESTRICTIONS

Recall that since January 1, 2000, it has been generally illegal for anyone to manufacture, import, sell, or give any "large-capacity magazine." And recall that the restrictions on the possession of "large-capacity magazines" in California should have gone into place on July 1, 2017.

In addition to the exceptions for "generally prohibited weapons" discussed above, which include "large-capacity magazines," there are a number of exceptions that only apply to "large-capacity magazines." These exceptions are discussed in further detail below.

When California law was changed in 2014 to add the restrictions on "large-capacity magazine conversion kits," the California legislature did not amend certain code sections to specifically include the phrase "large-capacity magazine conversion kits" and many of the exceptions do not even reference "large-capacity magazine conversion kits." Nevertheless, many of the following exceptions apply to "large-capacity conversion kits." The Penal Code section restricting "large-capacity magazine conversion kits" specifically references the following exceptions for "large-capacity magazines" to include "large-capacity magazine conversion kits."[174]

---

[170] P.C. § 17740.

[171] P.C. § 17740(d).

[172] P.C. § 17745.

[173] P.C., § 32406(d).

[174] P.C. § 32311(a).

Consequently, the following exceptions to the restrictions on "large-capacity magazines" extend to "large-capacity magazine conversion kits" as well.

A. Law Enforcement Agencies

The general "large-capacity magazine" and "large-capacity magazine conversion kit" restrictions do not apply to selling, giving, lending, importing, purchasing, or the possession of any "large-capacity magazine" to or by any government agency charged with enforcing any law for use in "discharg[ing] . . . their official duties, whether on or off duty, and where the use is authorized by the agency and is within the course and scope of their duties."[175]

B. Use During a Basic Training Course Prescribed by the Commission on Peace Officer Standards and Training

In 2017, the California Legislature added section 32455 to the law to, among other things, provide peace officer cadets with an exception to "large-capacity magazine" restrictions.[176] Consequently, starting on January 1, 2018, the general "large-capacity magazine" and "large-capacity magazine conversion kit" restrictions do not apply to:

(1) The sale, gift, or loan of a "large-capacity magazine" to a person enrolled in the course of basic training prescribed by the Commission on Peace Officer Standards and Training, or any other course certified by the Commission; *or*

(2) The possession of, or purchase by, that enrolled person.[177]

But, the sale, gift, loan, possession, or purchase of the "large-capacity magazine" must only be for purposes of participating in the course during the period of enrollment.[178]

Also, upon completion of the course, the "large-capacity magazine" must be removed from the state, sold to a licensed firearms dealer, or surrendered to a law enforcement agency, unless an exemption applies.[179] There is a question of how this new law will play out in the context the injunction on the possession of "large-capacity magazines." We know that there is no ban on possession of "large-capacity magazines" as of the writing of this book, and that the injunction is likely to last into the beginning of 2018. It would appear that in order to still meet the exceptions to the restrictions on acquiring "large-capacity magazines," the magazines would

---

[175] P.C. § 32400.

[176] *See* AB 693, 2017-2018 Leg., Reg. Sess. (Cal. 2017), *available at* https://leginfo.legislature.ca.gov/faces/billCompareClient.xhtml?bill_id=201720180AB693 (last visited Oct. 27, 2017).

[177] P.C. § 32455 (effective Jan. 1, 2018).

[178] P.C. § 32455 (effective Jan. 1, 2018).

[179] P.C. § 32455 (effective Jan. 1, 2018).

likely need to be transferred. It is also likely that the other exceptions to P.C. section 32310 (i.e., the prohibition on manufacture, import, sale, gift, loan, purchase, receipt, or possession of "large-capacity magazines") mentioned in P.C. section 32455 (*i.e.,* the new law discussed in this section) is in reference to the exception carved out for law enforcement (discussed immediately below). Therefore, if a person does not meet an exception to the restrictions on acquiring "large-capacity magazines" after his or her training is over, he or she may want to strongly consider getting rid of the "large-capacity magazine" at that time.

C. Peace Officers

The general "large-capacity magazine" and "large-capacity magazine conversion kit" restrictions do not apply to selling to, lending to, transferring to, purchasing, receiving, possessing, or importing into this state a "large-capacity magazine" "by a sworn peace officer[180] . . . authorized to carry a firearm in the course and scope of that officer's duties."[181]

1. Federal Law Enforcement

Prior to the passage of SB 1446 and Prop. 63, federal law enforcement officers were not allowed to purchase or receive "large-capacity magazines" because they were not defined as "peace officers" under California law. [182] For years, the DOJ allowed federal law enforcement to purchase "large-capacity magazines," even though they were not exempted from the general restriction. But, after the DOJ noticed that federal law enforcement were not included in the general peace officer exemption (see above) a couple of years ago, they stopped allowing these purchases.

Then, SB 1446 and Prop. 63 amended the "peace officer" exception in P.C. section 32405 to include sworn federal law enforcement officers. Now, sworn federal law enforcement officers who are authorized to carry a firearm in the course and scope of their duties may also purchase, receive, and possess "large-capacity magazines."[183]

2. Honorably Retired Sworn Peace Officers & Federal Law Enforcement Officers

The general restriction on the possession of "large-capacity magazines" "does not apply to any honorably retired sworn peace officer[184] . . . or any honorably retired

---

[180] As defined in P.C. sections 830-832.9.

[181] P.C. § 32405.

[182] *See* P.C. §§ 830-832.9.

[183] P.C. § 32405.

[184] As defined in P.C. sections 830-832.9

sworn federal law enforcement officer, who was authorized to carry a firearm in the course and scope of the officer's duties."[185]

The term "'honorably retired' includes any peace officer who has qualified for, and has accepted, a service or disability retirement. . . . [it] does not include an officer who has agreed to a service retirement in lieu of termination."[186]

This exception expressed in P.C. section 32406 was added by both Prop. 63 and SB 1446 to California's body of law. But, Prop. 63 and SB 1446 added different versions of P.C. section 32406.

Under the section 32406 added by Prop. 63, only authorized honorably retired peace officers and honorably retired federal law enforcement officers are exempt from the restriction on possession of "large-capacity magazines." The section added by SB 1446 also prohibited , honorably retired peace officers and honorably retired federal law enforcement officers.[187] Currently, *both* versions of P.C. section 32406 are in existence, and both of them are California law. Despite having the same section number in the Penal Code and saying different things, both delineate the exceptions to the general restriction on the possession of "large-capacity magazines" and need to be understood.

D. Dealer Acquisition

The general "large-capacity magazine" and "large-capacity magazine conversion kit" restrictions do "not apply to the possession, sale, or purchase of any large-capacity magazine to or by a" licensed firearms dealer.[188]

E. Loans Between Individuals

The general "large-capacity magazine" and "large-capacity magazine conversion kit" restrictions do not apply to loaning a lawfully possessed "large-capacity magazine" to any individual who is not otherwise prohibited from possessing firearms (see Chapter 3), as long as the exchange occurs at a location where "large-capacity magazines" are lawful. The lender must also stay in the recipient's "accessible vicinity."[189]

Given that this exemption only applies if the exchange occurs at a location where "large-capacity magazines" are lawful, there is an argument to be made that individuals can no longer use this exemption because technically it is not illegal to possess "large-capacity magazines" anywhere in the state. But, given that this ex-

---

[185] P.C. § 32406.

[186] P.C. §§ 16990, 32406.

[187] *See* SB 1446, 2015-2016 Leg., Reg Sess. (Cal. 2016), *available at* http://leginfo.legislature.ca.gov/faces/billNavClient.xhtml?bill_id=201520160SB1446 (last visited July 12, 2017).

[188] P.C. § 32410. *See also* P.C. §§ 26700-26915.

[189] P.C. § 32415.

emption was created far before the passage of SB 1446 and Prop. 63, it is likely that when this exemption refers to a "location," it is referring to localities, such as San Francisco or Sunnyvale, where the possession of "large-capacity magazines" was already outlawed. Because of this ambiguity, it may be best to play it safe and not loan any lawfully possessed "large-capacity magazines" to another person.

F. Dealer or Gunsmith Loan for Maintenance/Repair

The general "large-capacity magazine" and "large-capacity magazine conversion kit" restrictions do not apply to lending or giving a "large-capacity magazine" to, or possession of that magazine by, a Federal Firearms Licensee (FFL)[190] or gunsmith for maintenance, repair, or modification. It also does not apply to an FFL or gunsmith returning it to the lawful possessor.[191]

G. Importing or Selling Between Out-of-State Clients With a Permit

The general "large-capacity magazine" and "large-capacity magazine conversion kit" restrictions do not apply to those FFLs issued a permit to import, possess, transport, or sell "large-capacity magazines"[192] between themselves and out-of-state clients.[193] The terms and conditions for these permits can be found on the permit application at the DOJ website.[194] Once the magazine is in-state, in order to be transferred lawfully, another exception to the general restriction must be used (*i.e.*, sell to law enforcement or the entertainment industry).

H. Entities Operating An Armored Vehicle Business

The general "large-capacity magazine" and "large-capacity magazine conversion kit" restrictions do not apply to the selling, giving, lending, possession, importing, or purchasing of "large-capacity magazines" to or by entities lawfully operating armored vehicle businesses.[195]

The general "large-capacity magazine" restrictions do not apply to those entities lending "large-capacity magazines" to their "authorized employees, while in the course and scope of employment for purposes that pertain to the entity's armored

---

[190] P.C. §§ 26700-26915.

[191] P.C. § 32425.

[192] P.C. § 32315.

[193] P.C. § 32430.

[194] *Application for Large-Capacity Magazine Permit*, CALIFORNIA DEPT. OF JUSTICE, BUREAU OF FIREARMS, http://ag.ca.gov/firearms/forms/pdf/CLlcmpapp.pdf (last visited July 12, 2017).

[195] P.C. § 32435(a).

vehicle business," or those employees returning them to the business," or to the possession of those "large-capacity magazines" by those authorized employees.[196]

I. Manufacturing "Large-Capacity Magazines" by Law Enforcement

The general "large-capacity magazine" and "large-capacity magazine conversion kit" restrictions do not apply to manufacturing "large-capacity magazines":

(1) By any law enforcement agency for use by their employees in the discharge of their official duties, whether on or off duty, and where the use is authorized by the agency and is within the course and scope of their duties; *or*

(2) For use by sworn officers[197] authorized to carry a firearm in the course and scope of their duties; *or*

(3) For export or for sale to government agencies or the military per federal regulations.[198]

J. Entertainment Industry Props

The general "large-capacity magazine" and "large-capacity magazine conversion kit" restrictions do not apply when a "large-capacity magazine" is loaned "solely as a prop for a motion picture, television, or video production."[199]

K. Purchase by Special Weapons Permit Holder

The general "large-capacity magazine" and "large-capacity magazine conversion kit" restrictions do not apply when a special weapons permit[200] holder purchases or possesses a "large-capacity magazine" to:

(1) Use solely as a prop for a motion picture, television, or video production; *or*

(2) Export pursuant to federal regulations; *or*

(3) Resell it "to law enforcement agencies, government agencies, or the military, pursuant to applicable federal regulations."[201]

---

[196] P.C. § 32435(b)-(c).

[197] Defined in P.C. sections 830-832.9.

[198] P.C. § 32440.

[199] P.C. § 32445.

[200] Special weapons permits are issued per P.C. sections 31000 ("assault weapons" permit), 32650 (permit to possess, manufacture, or transport machineguns), 33300 (permit for "short-barreled rifle" or "short-barreled shotgun"), 18900-18910 (permit to conduct business using, or to possess or transport "destructive devices"), 32700-32720 (license to sell machineguns).

[201] P.C. § 32450.

L. Receipt or Disposition by Trustees, Executors, or Administrators

According to the version of P.C. section 32406 implemented by SB 1446, the ban on the possession of "large-capacity magazines" does not apply to the receipt or disposition of a "large-capacity magazine" by:

(1) A trustee of a trust that includes a "large-capacity magazine," *or*

(2) An executor or administrator of an estate, including an estate that is subject to probate, that includes a large-capacity magazine.[202]

M. Finding and Delivering "Large-Capacity Magazines" to Law Enforcement

According to the version of P.C. section 32406 implemented by SB 1446, the ban on the possession of "large-capacity magazines" does not apply to a person who finds a "large-capacity magazine," if:

(1) The person is not prohibited from possessing firearms or ammunition, *and*

(2) The person possessed the "large-capacity magazine" no longer than necessary to deliver or transport it to the nearest law enforcement agency.[203]

N. Possessing the "Large-Capacity Magazine" Solely for Use with a Firearm that Is Lawfully-Obtained Prior to 2000 that Is Incompatible with Magazines Holding 10 or Fewer Rounds

According to the version of P.C. section 32406 implemented by SB 1446, the ban on the possession of "large-capacity magazines" does not apply to a person:

(1) (Who is lawfully in possession of a firearm that he or she obtained prior to January 1, 2000, if no magazine that holds 10 or fewer rounds of ammunition is compatible with that firearm; *and*

(2) Who possesses the "large-capacity magazine" solely for use with that firearm.[204]

 We strongly advise you to use this exception with caution. If the ban on the possession of "large-capacity magazines" ever becomes enforceable, law enforcement will likely be suspicious of any "large-capacity magazine" they encounter. Therefore, you may likely be cited and/or arrested for possessing a "large-capacity magazine," and you or your attorney will have to explain this exception to a prosecutor, judge, or jury.

---

[202] P.C. § 32406(e).
[203] P.C. § 32406(c).
[204] P.C. § 32406(f).

VI. ADDITIONAL EXCEPTIONS TO CALIFORNIA LAW FOR RESTRICTIONS ON "SHORT-BARRELED SHOTGUNS/RIFLES"

There are two additional exceptions to the general ban on possessing "short-barreled shotguns/rifles." Both exceptions, however, are conditioned on you also meeting the requirements to lawfully possess or make an NFA firearm.

A. Law Enforcement Agencies

The "short-barreled rifle" and "short-barreled shotgun" restrictions do not apply to sales to, purchases by, or possession by a "police department, sheriff's office, marshal's office, the California Highway Patrol, the Department of Justice, the Department of Corrections and Rehabilitation, or the military or naval forces . . . for use in the discharge of their official duties."[205] Peace officers who are "members of a police department, sheriff's office, marshal's office, the California Highway Patrol, the Department of Justice, or the Department of Corrections and Rehabilitation" may also possess "short-barreled rifles" and/or "short-barreled shotguns" "when on duty and the use is authorized by the agency and is within the course and scope of their duties, and the officers have completed a training course in the use of these weapons certified by the Commission on Peace Officer Standards and Training."[206] Though law enforcement agencies are exempt from the NFA tax, they must comply with the other requirements, including registration.

B. Permit Authorization

"Short-barreled rifle" and "short-barreled shotgun" restrictions do not apply when the DOJ authorizes the manufacture, possession, transportation, or sale of "short-barreled shotguns" or "short-barreled rifles" by issuing a permit.[207]

A Dangerous Weapons Permit can be obtained from the DOJ by submitting an application to the DOJ's Bureau of Firearms.[208]

One must have "good cause" for this permit, including showing the DOJ that issuing the permit does not endanger public safety. "Good cause" for obtaining a permit relating to "short-barreled shotguns" or "short-barreled rifles" *only* exists when:

(1) The permit is sought for the manufacture, possession, or use with blank cartridges of a "short-barreled rifle" or "short-barreled shotgun," solely as a

---

[205] P.C. § 33220.

[206] P.C. § 33220.

[207] P.C. § 33225 (issued per P.C. sections 33300-33320 and in compliance with federal law).

[208] *Dangerous Weapons License/Permit(s) Application*, CALIFORNIA DEPT. OF JUSTICE, BUREAU OF FIREARMS, http://ag.ca.gov/firearms/forms/pdf/FD030DWApp.pdf (last visited July 12, 2017).

prop for a motion picture, television, or video production or entertainment event; *or*

(2) The permit is sought for the manufacture of, exposing for sale, keeping for sale, sale of, importation or lending of "short-barreled rifles" or "short-barreled shotguns" to certain law enforcement entities by persons who are licensed as dealers or manufacturers under the NFA.[209]

VII. "SILENCERS"/"SOUND SUPPRESSORS"

The NFA regulates "silencers" (which are considered "firearms" under the NFA), but does not provide a definition. Instead, the NFA refers to the GCA's definition.[210]

Cutaway of a silencer

Under the GCA, a "firearm silencer" and "firearm muffler" "mean any device for silencing, muffling, or diminishing the report of a portable firearm, including any combination of parts, designed or redesigned, and intended for use in assembling or fabricating a firearm silencer or firearm muffler, and any part intended only for use in such assembly or fabrication."[211]

Certain silencers, and the rifles they attach to, received a lot of attention in the media in late 2017 as being exempt from federal restriction. These silencers attach to muzzle-loading rifles and, as a result, are not regulated under federal law. This is because most muzzle-loading rifles meet the definition of "antique firearms" under the GCA and NFA[212] and, thus, are not considered "firearms" under the GCA and NFA. In turn, this means that the silencers that attach to "antique" muzzle-loading rifles are not "any device for silencing, muffling, or diminishing the report of a portable *firearm*." Hence, silencers that attach to "antique" muzzle-loading rifles are not prohibited by federal law.[213] This is not the case under California law, though, because California's definition of an "antique firearm" is not as generous as the federal definition.

"Silencers" are generally prohibited in California. The Penal Code defines "silencer" as follows:

---

[209] P.C. § 33300. *See also* P.C. § 33220 (providing the approved law enforcement entities for whom "short-barreled shotguns" and "short-barreled rifles" may be manufactured).

[210] 26 U.S.C. § 5845(a) (defining a "silencer" as that in 18 U.S.C. section 921).

[211] 18 U.S.C. § 921(a)(24) (emphasis added).

[212] As stated in Chapter 2, muzzle-loading rifles that use black powder and cannot use fixed ammunition are expressly included in the GCA's definition of "antique firearm" and appear to fall within the NFA's definition of "antique firearm."

[213] *See* Letter from Michael R. Curtis, Chief of the Firearms Technology Industry Services Branch of the Bureau of Alcohol, Tobacco, Firearms and Explosives, to Stephen P. Halbrook (Jan. 23, 2017), *available at* https://silencerco.com/wp-content/themes/silencerco/documents/maxim50/full-atf-letter.pdf (last visited Oct. 18, 2017).

[A]ny device or attachment of any kind designed, used, or intended for use in silencing, diminishing, or muffling the report of a firearm. The term "silencer" also includes any combination of parts, designed or redesigned, and intended for use in assembling or fabricating a silencer [including] any part intended only for use in assembly or fabrication of a silencer.[214]

Unlawfully possessing a "silencer" is a felony.[215]

In California, "the sale to, purchase by, or possession of silencers by" certain law enforcement agencies[216] or state or U.S. military forces for "use in the discharge of their official duties" is lawful.[217] Members of these law enforcement agencies (provided they are regular, salaried, full-time peace officers) and members of the military may possess "silencers" "when [they are] on duty and when the use of silencers is authorized by the agency and is within the course and scope of their duties."[218]

Also, FFLs and manufacturers (who are also licensed under the NFA) may manufacture, possess, transport, sell, or transfer "silencers" to any of the entities listed above.[219]

Unlike highly regulated firearms and devices (*i.e.*, machineguns, "assault weapons," destructive devices), there is no special permit required under California law to deal in or possess "silencers." You simply have to meet one of the above criteria. As mentioned above, silencers for muzzle-loading firearms are likely to be considered "silencers" under California law. As mentioned in Chapter 2, California law exempts "antique firearms" from a certain list of California Penal Code sections.[220] If a Penal Code section is mentioned on this list, then the section's corresponding restrictions on "firearms" do not apply to "antiques" (because "antique firearms" are not considered to be "firearms" for purposes of these sections). On the other hand, if a Penal Code section corresponding to a restriction on "firearms" is *not* mentioned in that list, then the restriction will apply to all firearms ("antique" or otherwise). And the definition of "silencer" and the restrictions on these devices are not on that list. Therefore, silencers are still considered "silencers" under California law, even when they are made only for "antique firearms."

The practice of attaching homemade devices to the end of a firearm to make it look "cooler" is risky because the device could be considered by law enforcement to be a "silencer." The ATF has reportedly considered simple homemade items, such as copper pot scrubbers used with fiberglass insulation, oil filters, and solvent traps, to be "silencers" when people use them as silencers, which means that they would be subject to the NFA "firearm" requirements. Also beware that some law enforce-

---

[214] P.C. § 17210.

[215] P.C. § 33410.

[216] These law enforcement agencies are specified in P.C. section 830.1.

[217] P.C. § 33415(a).

[218] P.C. § 33415(b).

[219] P.C. § 33415(c).

[220] *See* P.C. § 16170.

ment agencies confuse "silencers" with barrel extensions and devices that look like "silencers" (but are not). It is not uncommon for law enforcement to discover a long

pipe-like item that might fit on the end of a firearm and incorrectly believe it to be a "silencer." Certain firearms come with or have the ability to install items that have the same outward appearance as a "silencer."

 I strongly suggest you reconsider keeping items like these. If law enforcement stumbles across them, your attorney will have some explain-

Example of a homemade silencer

ing to do, usually in the context of a felony criminal case where you are the defendant.

VIII. OBLITERATED OR COVERED SERIAL NUMBERS

Under federal law, "[i]t shall be unlawful for any person knowingly to [1] transport, ship, or receive, in interstate or foreign commerce, any firearm which has had the importer's or manufacturer's serial number removed, obliterated, or altered or [2] to possess or receive any firearm which has had the importer's or manufacturer's serial number removed, obliterated, or altered and has, at any time, been shipped or transported in interstate or foreign commerce."[221]

Contrary to the federal restriction on obliterating *serial numbers*, California's rule is much more restrictive. Under California law it is a felony to change, alter, remove, or obliterate either the name of a firearm maker, its model, the manufacturer's number, or other identification mark on any firearm without first receiving written permission from the DOJ.[222] There are no exceptions. This means that if you enjoy modifying and refurbishing firearms, you have to be very careful not to remove the manufacturer's or model's name, and certainly not the serial number.

Even if you are not the one who actually altered the firearm's *identifying marks*, it is a misdemeanor under California law to possess, receive, transfer, or offer for sale any firearm, knowing that the name of the maker, model, manufacturer's number, or other identification mark has been changed, altered, removed, or obliterated.[223] This restriction does not apply to such a firearm being acquired or possessed by any:

(1) State or U.S. military members while on duty and acting within the scope of their employment; *or*

---

[221] 18 U.S.C. § 922(k).

[222] P.C. § 23900.

[223] P.C. § 23920. At least one court has upheld a conviction for possessing a firearm with an obliterated serial number over a Second Amendment challenge. *United States v. Marzzarella*, 614 F.3d 85 (3d Cir. 2010). Though not a California case, the result here would almost certainly be the same – California's prohibition and your conviction will probably be upheld.

(2) Peace officers while on duty acting within the scope of their employment;[224] *or*

(3) Forensic laboratory employees while on duty and acting within the scope of their employment.[225]

Nor do they apply to firearm possession and disposition by someone who:

(1) Is not prohibited by state or federal law from possessing, receiving, purchasing, or owning a firearm (see Chapter 3); *and*

(2) Possessed the firearm no longer than necessary to deliver it to law enforcement for lawful disposition; *and*

(3) Gave prior notice to law enforcement, then transported the firearm in a locked container (as defined in P.C. section 16850) and in accordance with the law to law enforcement for its lawful disposition.[226]

Currently, it is generally lawful to possess a firearm *without* identifying marks because, as explained in Chapter 4, not all firearms must have identifying marks in the first place, *e.g.*, lawfully home-built firearms.[227] Problems arises when already existing identifying marks are altered. But, be mindful of the new regulations on "assault weapons" made by unlicensed persons (discussed in Chapter 8) and the new laws on "ghost guns," which require individuals to obtain a serial number or identification mark for any homemade firearms that they currently own or plan to create after July 1, 2018 (see Chapter 4).

Possessing a firearm with its serial number or identification number covered from view seems clearly illegal under P.C. section 537e. But, since P.C. section 23920 says it is only unlawful if the marks are "changed, altered, removed, or obliterated," it is unclear whether it is legal to *temporarily* cover a firearm's otherwise valid and intact identification marks (*e.g.*, with tape). According to P.C. section 537e:

> Any person who knowingly . . . has in his or her possession any personal property from which the manufacturer's serial number, identification number, electronic serial number, or any other distinguishing number or identification mark has been removed, defaced, *covered*, altered, or destroyed, is guilty of a public offense. . . .[228]

P.C. sections 23920 and 537e seem to conflict because P.C. section 537e covers almost all of the prohibited activity in P.C. section 23920, making P.C. section 23920 somewhat redundant.

---

[224] These officers are described in the Penal Code commencing with section 830.

[225] P.C. § 23925(a)-(c).

[226] P.C. § 23925(d).

[227] If requested, the DOJ "may assign a distinguishing number or identification mark to any firearm" if it lacks one or if the previous one was destroyed or obliterated. P.C. § 23910.

[228] P.C. § 537e (emphasis added).

When statutes are inconsistent with each other, or when a specific statute covers almost the same things as a more general law does, the more specific law usually applies.[229] This means that since P.C. section 23920 is more specific, it should be followed with respect to firearm identifying marks.

IX. "UNSAFE" HANDGUNS

The DOJ maintains the Roster of Handguns Certified for Sale in California.[230] With certain exceptions, California residents cannot buy handguns not appearing on the Roster *from FFLs*. Those not listed on the Roster are legally referred to as "unsafe" handguns, though this description is not factually accurate.[231]

It is illegal for "any person in this state who manufactures or causes to be manufactured, imports into the state for sale, keeps for sale, offers or exposes for sale, gives, or lends"[232] an "unsafe handgun," subject to the limited exceptions discussed below. Simple possession of a handgun not on the Roster is legal. Handguns that you've possessed before the "unsafe" handgun law took effect, handguns you acquired through PPTs that were not on the Roster, and handguns that might have fallen off the Roster are all still lawful for you to possess, provided they are not illegal for some other reason (like meeting the definition of an "assault weapon").

Depending on the handgun type (whether a revolver or a pistol), handguns must meet certain "safety" criteria before they can be placed on the Roster.[233] Firearm manufacturers must have their handguns tested and pay a fee before their handguns can be put on the Roster, and must also pay an annual renewal fee.[234] The annual fee is due before January 1 of each year. Every year, we have people contact us in a panic because of all the handguns they see dropping off the Roster as of the first of the year. Don't panic. January 1 is just the renewal date. Nothing requires a manufacturer to renew the handgun on the Roster. It is entirely up to the manufacturer to renew the handgun or not.

Typically, if a handgun is not on the Roster, the manufacturer has not submitted it for DOJ testing or has allowed it to drop off the list by not paying the annual fee, or the firearm cannot meet California's so called "safety" requirements because of its design.

---

[229] *People v. Vessell*, 36 Cal. App. 4th 285, 289 (1995); *People v. Jenkins*, 28 Cal. 3d 494, 505-06 (1980); *People v. Gilbert*, 1 Cal. 3d 475, 481 (1969).

[230] The DOJ's Roster can be searched by a handgun's make, model, type, barrel length, or caliber, or when the handgun is scheduled to be removed from the Roster. *See Roster of Handguns Certified for Sale*, CALIFORNIA DEPT. OF JUSTICE, BUREAU OF FIREARMS, *available at* http://certguns.doj.ca.gov/ (last visited July 12, 2017).

[231] In 2015, a district court held that the limitations imposed under the Unsafe Handgun Act do not violate Second Amendment. *Peña v. Lindley*, 2:09-CV-01185-KJM-CKD (E.D. Cal. Feb. 25, 2015), *available at* http://michellawyers.com/wp-content/uploads/2012/06/February-25-2015-Order.pdf (last visited July 28, 2016). But this decision is not final and is currently being appealed to the Ninth Circuit Court of Appeals. Check www.CalGunLaws.com for more updates about this case.

[232] P.C. § 32000.

[233] P.C. § 31910. See also P.C. sections 31905, 31900, 32010 for the requirements.

[234] P.C. § 32015.

In order to be available for sale the handgun must not be unsafe. As backwards as that sounds, that is how California law is written.

A handgun is considered unsafe under P.C. section 31910 if:

For a revolver:

(1) It does not have a safety device that, either automatically in the case of a double-action firing mechanism, or by manual operation in the case of a single-action firing mechanism, causes the hammer to retract to a point where the firing pin does not rest upon the primer of the cartridge; *or*

(2) It does not meet the firing requirement for handguns; *or*

(3) It does not meet the drop safety requirement for handguns.[235]

For pistols and semiautomatic pistols:

(1) It does not have a positive manually operated safety device, as determined by standards relating to imported guns issued by the ATF; *or*

(2) It does not meet the firing requirement for handguns; *or*

(3) It does not meet the drop safety requirement for handguns.[236]

For semiautomatic pistols:

(1) Commencing January 1, 2006, for a center fire semiautomatic pistol that is not already listed on the Roster pursuant to P.C. section 32015, it does not have either a chamber load indicator, or a magazine disconnect mechanism; *or*

(2) Commencing January 1, 2007, for all center fire semiautomatic pistols that are not already listed on the Roster pursuant to P.C. section 32015, it does not have both a chamber load indicator and if it has a detachable magazine, a magazine disconnect mechanism; *or*

(3) Commencing January 1, 2006, for all rimfire semiautomatic pistols that are not already listed on the Roster pursuant to P.C. section 32015, it does not have a magazine disconnect mechanism, if it has a detachable magazine; *or*

(4) Commencing January 1, 2010, for all semiautomatic pistols that are not already listen on the Roster pursuant to P.C. section 32015, it is not designed and equipped with microstamping technology, provided that the DOJ certifies that the technology used to create the imprint is available to more than one manufacturer unencumbered by any patent restrictions.[237]

---

[235] P.C. § 31910.

[236] P.C. § 31910.

[237] P.C. § 31910. "The [AG] may also approve a method of equal or greater reliability and effectiveness [than microstamping] in identifying the specific serial number of a firearm from spent cartridge casings discharged by that firearm than that which is set forth in this paragraph, to be thereafter required as otherwise set forth by this paragraph where the [AG] certifies that this new method is also unencumbered by any patent restrictions. Approval

A. "Microstamping"

The concept of "microstamping" ammunition gained recognition a number of years ago. In theory "microstamping" is the process of laser-engraving a pistol's make, model, and serial number on parts of a firearm, typically including its firing pin, so that the information is stamped on the cartridge casing or primer upon discharging the pistol. This means that when the casing is ejected from the pistol after being shot, you can examine it under a microscope and theoretically know what pistol it was shot from. Let's be clear: the addition of microstamping does not make the handgun "safer." This is not a "safety" feature. It is a law enforcement one. Microstamping does not help to prevent the negligent discharge of a firearm.

As of January 1, 2010, all semiautomatic pistols not already listed on the DOJ's Roster had to be "designed and equipped" with "microstamping" technology or they were considered "unsafe." But that requirement only applied if and when the California AG certified that the technology was *not* encumbered by a patent and was thus available to more than one manufacturer.[238]

Until May of 2013 there was no movement on the part of the California AG regarding the certification. On May 17, 2013, former California AG Kamala Harris certified that microstamping was available unencumbered by patent and available to more than one firearm manufacturer.[239] Consequently, no semiautomatic pistols, barring limited exceptions, can be added to the Roster unless they have microstamping.

The firearms already on the Roster, submitted for testing as of May 2013, or later submitted as "similar" to firearms already on the Roster, do not need to have microstamping. But any new semiautomatic pistol that manufacturers seek to add to the Roster must have microstamping in addition to all the other requirements. As of the time of publication, only one obscure manufacturer (discussed below) has implemented microstamping. So the handful of other pistols added to the Roster as of May 17, 2013, are those that were already submitted for testing prior to May 17, 2013, or "similar" semiautomatic pistols. Because of this restriction, more and more pistols fall off the Roster with no new pistols replacing them.

The certification of "microstamping" creates a new problem. Because California's law is so poorly written, whenever a manufacturer makes a non-cosmetic change to their firearm, it is viewed by the DOJ as a "new" firearm. Under the current interpretation of the "unsafe" handgun law, this "new" handgun must be retested in order for it to be sold in California. Because of microstamping these "new" handguns cannot be resubmitted for testing and consequently cannot be

---

by the [AG] shall include notice of that fact via regulations adopted by the [AG] for purposes of implementing that method for purposes of this paragraph." P.C. § 31910(b)(7)(B).

[238] P.C. § 31910(b)(7)(A)-(B).

[239] Information Bulletin from DOJ to California Licensed Firearms Dealers, California Department of Justice Certified Laboratories, Firearms Manufacturers with Firearms listed on the Roster of Handguns Certified for Sale in California, and all Other Interested Persons/Entities (May 17, 2013), *available at* http://oag.ca.gov/sites/all/files/agweb/pdfs/firearms/infobuls/2013-BOF-03.pdf (last visited July 12, 2017).

sold in California. Ironically, newer, safer, state-of-the-art pistols cannot be sold in California because of California's "unsafe" handgun laws.

The problems with microstamping are well documented. First, the technology itself was determined to be unreliable by a University of California, Davis, study.[240] Because microstamping is laser engraved on firearm parts, it takes little effort to remove or render impressions illegible. The parts of the pistol microstamping is placed on can be easily replaced with parts that do not possess microstamping. Microstamping was alleged to be a fantastic crime-fighting tool, and proponents of the technology claim that the additional costs of microstamping will only add a few dollars to the cost of firearms. They seem to forget that parts, individually stamped and intended for certain firearms, must be tracked and installed in the specific serialized firearm they are intended for. This type of tracking and matching is time consuming and expensive, especially when you consider that most manufactures obtain different parts of firearms from different manufacturers. Proponents also fail to take into account the problem that, if the microstamped part proves faulty, a replacement must be found (with the same microscopic number) before the firearm can be sent to California.

Proponents of the technology didn't bother to take into account the hobby of reloading ammunition and how casings might be stamped with multiple numbers before they are considered unusable. Hopefully, law enforcement agents realize that the casing they have at a murder scene only matches your firearm because you used (and left) that casing at a range a year before. Lastly, this technology does not prevent a criminal from "seeding" a crime scene with casings from rounds they picked up at a firearm range the day before.

As of the publication of this book, no firearms with microstamping technology have been added to the Roster since this requirement took effect.[241]

1. "Smart Gun" Technology

Another topic that has received attention recently is "smart gun" technology, which is technology that is intended to limit firearm operability to the owner of the gun through different types of mechanisms.[242] This is unproven technology that car-

---

[240] David Howitt, Frederic A. Tulleners & Michael T. Beddow, *What Micro Serialized Firing Pins Can Add to Firearm Identification in Forensic Science: How Viable are Micro-Marked Firing Pin Impressions as Evidence?*, FORENSIC SCIENCE GRADUATE GROUP, UNIV. OF CAL., DAVIS, *available at* http://www.firearmsid.com/pdfs/microserialnumber.pdf (last visited July 12, 2017).

[241] As of the date of publication, two separate court cases have been brought challenging the microstamping law. One case lost at the state appellate court level, but the California Supreme Court granted review of it *See National Shooting Sports Foundation v. State of California*, 6 Cal.App.5th 298 (2016), *reh'g denied* (Dec. 15, 2016); *National Shooting Sports Foundation v. State of California*, 215 Cal.Rptr.3d 1 (Cal. 2017). The other case lost at the federal district court level and is currently being appealed. *Pena v. Lindley*, No. 2:09-CV-011185-KJM-CKD (E.D. Cal. Feb. 25, 2015), *available at* http://michellawyers.com/wp-content/uploads/2012/06/February-25-2015-Order.pdf (last visited July 12, 2017). While these cases are being appealed, microstamping is here for the foreseeable future.

[242] *Debate Over Futuristic 'Smart Gun' Technology Resumes as Gun Control Issue Takes Center State in National Politics*, N.Y. DAILY NEWS (Jan. 28, 2013, 10:53 AM), http://www.nydailynews.com/news/national/futuristic-

ries large risks since most of the "smart gun" solutions include electrical and/or battery-powered mechanisms of questionable reliability, which could prevent the operability of a firearm.

During the 2013 legislative session, Senator Mark DeSaulnier introduced Senate Bill (SB) 293, which would have required that any new firearm added to the DOJ Roster contain "smart gun" technology two years after the date when there were two firearms on the Roster with "smart gun" technology. This recent effort failed; however, there may be renewed attempts to require this type of technology in future firearms.

If the ill-conceived "smart gun" bill had passed, this would have been the first of the two required handguns on the Roster that could have resulted in the requirement that all handguns added to the Roster possess "smart gun" technology.

B. Exceptions to the "Unsafe" Handgun Roster Requirement

Under certain circumstances you may be able to acquire firearms that are not on the Roster. See below for a list of these exceptions and circumstances where such a transfer may be permitted.

1. Law Enforcement and Military

The restriction on "unsafe handguns" does not apply if the handgun is sold to, or purchased by, the DOJ, a police department, a sheriff's official, a marshal's office, the Department of Corrections and Rehabilitation, the California Highway Patrol, any district attorney's office, any federal law enforcement agency, or the military or naval forces of this state or of the United States for use in the discharge of their official duties.[243] The restriction on "unsafe handguns" also does not apply to the sale to, or purchase by, sworn members of these agencies.[244]

Before January 1, 2014, federal law enforcement was not included in this exemption. Nevertheless, for years the DOJ allowed federal law enforcement to purchase non-Roster handguns. That changed in 2013 when the DOJ presumably "discovered" federal law enforcement was not included in the exception. Following the uproar from federal law enforcement officers, the Legislature quickly changed the law and included them in this list of exempt individuals.[245]

---

smart-gun-technology-gun-control-solution-threat-2nd-amendment-article-1.1249466 (last visited July 12, 2017).

[243] P.C. § 32000(b)(4). While this exemption provides for the sale and purchase of "unsafe handguns" to law enforcement and the military, it does not actually say how those firearms are supposed to be imported into the state so that they can actually be sold and purchased. Nonetheless, the DOJ has stated that it is implied from this exemption that "unsafe handguns" can be imported into the state in order to be sold to, or purchased by, law enforcement or military.

[244] P.C. § 32000(b)(4).

[245] See AB 169, 2013-2014 Leg., Reg. Sess. (Cal. 2013) (creating the new exception for federal officers at P.C. section 32000(b)(4)).

2. Purchase of a State-Issued Handgun to Spouse or Domestic Partner of a Peace Officer Who Died in the Line of Duty

The restrictions on "unsafe handguns" do not apply to the sale, purchase, or delivery of a state-issued handgun to a spouse or domestic partner of a peace officer[246] who was employed by the State of California and died in the line of duty.[247] But, these transfers must still be processed through an FFL (when an FFL is required).[248]

3. Private Party, Spousal, Operation of Law, Etc. Transfers

The restriction on "unsafe handgun" transfers does not apply to Private Party Transfers (PPT) (as further discussed below), pawn or consignment sales, intra-family transfers, operation of law transfers, or other specifically described transfers.[249] These transfers, however, must still go through an FFL (when an FFL is required), as was discussed in detail in Chapter 4. The return of handguns in these situations is also exempted from the "unsafe" handgun restriction.

4. Certain Peace Officers from Specified Agencies/Departments

The restrictions on the sale and purchase of "unsafe handguns" does not apply to the following entities or sworn members of the following entities who have completed the firearms portion of a training course prescribed by the Commission on Peace Officer Standards and Training (POST) under P.C. section 832:

(1) The Department of Parks and Recreation; *and*

(2) The Department of Alcoholic Beverage Control; *and*

(3) The Division of Investigation of the Department of Consumer Affairs; *and*

(4) The Department of Motor Vehicles; *and*

(5) The Fraud Division of the Department of Insurance; *and*

(6) The State Department of State Hospitals; *and*

(7) The Department of Fish and Wildlife; *and*

(8) The State Department of Developmental Services; *and*

(9) The Department of Forestry and Fire Protection; *and*

(10) A county probation department; *and*

(11) The Los Angeles World Airports, as defined in P.C. section 830.15; *and*

(12) A K-12 public school district for use by a school police officer, as defined in P.C. section 830.32; *and*

---

[246] As defined in Chapter 4.5 (commencing with P.C. section 830) of Title 3 of Part 2 of the Penal Code.

[247] P.C. § 32000; Cal. Pub. Contract Code § 10334(d).

[248] P.C. § 10334(d).

[249] P.C. § 32110.

(13) A municipal water district for use by a park ranger, as described in P.C. section 830.34; *and*

(14) A county for use by a welfare fraud investigator or inspector, as described in P.C. section 830.35; *and*

(15) A county for use by the coroner or the deputy coroner, as described in P.C. section 830.35; *and*

(16) The Supreme Court and the courts of appeal for use by marshals of the Supreme Court and bailiffs of the courts of appeal, and coordinators of security for the judicial branch, as described in P.C. section 830.36; *and*

(17) A fire department or fire protection agency of a county, city, city and county, district, or the state for use by either of the following:

(a) A member of an arson-investigating unit, regularly paid and employed in that capacity under P.C. section 830.37; *or*

(b) A member other than a member of an arson-investigating unit, regularly paid and employed in that capacity under P.C. section 830.37; *and*

(18) The University of California Police Department, or the California State University Police Departments, as described in P.C. section 830.2; *and*

(19) A California Community College police department, as described in P.C. section 830.32.[250]

Interestingly, under P.C. section 32000 firearms dealers are expressly prohibited from "processing the sale or transfer of an unsafe handgun between a person who has obtained an unsafe handgun pursuant to [the exemption above] and a person who is not exempt from the *requirements* of [P.C. section 32000].[251] The language used in this restriction is somewhat odd. It seems like the Legislature was attempting to restrict to whom a person could transfer an "unsafe handgun," namely to individuals who fall under an exemption listed in P.C. section 32000.

But, there seem to be multiple issues with the way this restriction is phrased. First, the restriction does not state that a person who has acquired an "unsafe handgun" under the exemptions above cannot transfer an "unsafe handgun" to a person who is not exempt from the requirements of P.C. section 32000 at all. Instead, it states that a *dealer* cannot process these transactions. Therefore, it appears that if the transaction does not need to be processed through a dealer, such as an intrafamilial transfer or operation of law transfer as discussed in Chapter 4, then the transaction would not be prohibited under California law. In other words, individuals who obtain an "unsafe handgun" under the exemption above can freely transfer the "unsafe handgun" through operation of law of law or intra-familial transfer.

---

[250] P.C. § 32000(b)(6) (effective Jan. 1, 2017).
[251] P.C. § 32000(c)(1) (effective Jan. 1, 2017).

In addition, it appears that the Legislature may have overlooked that fact that there are numerous other exemptions to the *requirements* of P.C. section 32000.[252] For example, as explained above, PPTs, pawn or consignment sales, and other specifically described transfers are all exempt from the requirements of P.C. section 32000.[253] Therefore, it would appear that a firearms dealer would not be restricted from processing a PPT of an "unsafe handgun", regardless of whether the individual receiving the firearm falls under an exemption listed in P.C. section 32000 because the transaction itself is exempt from the requirements of P.C. section 32000.

Any person who obtains an "unsafe handgun" under this exception must, when leaving their handgun unattended[254] in a vehicle,[255] adhere to the storage requirements stated in P.C. section 32000 (which we explain in Chapter 4).

5. Testing and Prototypes

Firearms sent into the state for testing and employees or agents of entities sending their firearms into the state for testing are also exempt.[256]

6. "Curios or Relics"

Firearms listed as "curios or relics," as defined in 27 C.F.R. section 478.11, are exempt.[257]

7. Repairs

The Penal Code allows for a handgun to be delivered to a California-licensed firearms dealer for purposes of repair. The return of the handgun is also exempt.[258]

8. Pistols Used as Props and Loans to Consultant-Evaluators

Oddly, only semiautomatic pistols are exempt from the "unsafe handgun" restrictions when they are sold, loaned, or transferred to use "solely as a prop during the course of a motion picture, television, or video production by an authorized participant therein in the course of making that production or event or by an authorized

---

[252] *See* P.C. §§ 32100-32110.

[253] P.C. § 32110 (effective Jan. 1, 2017).

[254] A vehicle is considered to be "'unattended' when a person who is lawfully carrying or transporting a handgun in the vehicle is not within close proximity to the vehicle to reasonably prevent unauthorized access to the vehicle or its contents." P.C. § 32000(c)(2)(C)(ii) (effective Jan. 1, 2017).

[255] A "'vehicle' is a device by which any person or property may be propelled, moved, or drawn upon a highway, excepting a device moved exclusively by human power or used exclusively upon stationary rails or tracks." CAL. VEH. CODE § 670; P.C. § 32000(c)(2)(C)(i).

[256] P.C. § 32000(b)(1)-(2).

[257] P.C. §§ 32000(b)(3); 32110(c), (g). "Curios or relics" are also discussed in Chapter 2.

[258] P.C. § 32110(d)-(e).

employee or agent of the entity producing that production or event."[259] It appears that, according to the California legislature, movies and television productions using revolvers are out of luck.

The loaning and the return of handguns to a "consultant-evaluator"[260] are also exempt from the Roster requirements.[261]

9. Certain Handguns Exempt From the Roster Requirement

Certain handguns are exempt from the Roster requirement. All "curios or relics," as defined in 27 C.F.R. section 478.11, are exempt.[262] Single-action revolvers with at least a five-cartridge capacity and barrel lengths of at least three inches are also exempt if the firearm meets any of the following specifications:

(1) It was originally manufactured prior to 1900 and is a "curio or relic," as defined in 27 C.F.R. section 478.11; *or*

(2) It has an overall length measured parallel to the barrel of at least 7½ inches when the handle, frame or receiver, and barrel are assembled; *or*

(3) It has an overall length measured parallel to the barrel of at least 7½ inches when the handle, frame or receiver, and barrel are assembled and is currently lawful to import into the U.S. per 18 U.S.C. section 925(d)(3).[263]

Certain pistols designed expressly for Olympic target shooting events are also exempt.[264]

In the summer of 2014, the California Legislature passed AB 1964, which limited the amount of pistols exempt from the "unsafe handgun" restriction.[265] As of January 1, 2015, the Roster requirement does not apply to single-shot pistols with a break top or bolt action, a barrel length of six inches or more, and "an overall length of at least 10½ inches when the handle, frame or receiver, and barrel are assembled."[266] But, even if a single-shot pistol meets these requirements, it will still be subject to Roster requirements if it is a semiautomatic pistol that has been temporarily or permanently altered so that it will not fire in a semiautomatic mode.[267]

---

[259] P.C. § 32110(h).

[260] "'[C]onsultant-evaluator' means a consultant or evaluator who, in the course of that person's profession is loaned firearms from a person licensed pursuant to Chapter 44 (commencing with Section 921) of Title 18 of the United States Code and the regulations issued pursuant thereto, for research or evaluation, and has a current certificate of eligibility issued pursuant to Section 26710." P.C. § 16410.

[261] P.C. § 32110(e), (i), (j), (k).

[262] P.C. § 32000(b)(3); *see* Chapter 2.

[263] P.C. § 32100(a).

[264] *See* P.C. § 32105; CAL. CODE REGS. tit. 11, § 5455 (listing exempt Olympic pistols).

[265] *See* AB 1964, 2013-2014, Leg. Counsel's Digest (Cal. 2014), *available at* http://leginfo.legislature.ca.gov/faces/billNavClient.xhtml?bill_id=201320140AB1964 (last visited July 12, 2017).

[266] P.C. § 32100(b).

[267] P.C. § 32100(b).

Prior to January 1, 2015, any semiautomatic pistols with a barrel length of not less than six inches and that had an overall length of at least 10 ½ inches when the handle frame or receiver, and barrel were assembled that had been temporarily or permanently altered so that they could not fire in semiautomatic mode fell under this exception. As a result, people could purchase semiautomatic handguns that had been converted into single-shot pistols. Typically, this was done buying the pistol from an out-of-state FFL. That FFL (if he or she has a manufacturer's license) or another FFL (with a manufacturer's license) would then install a longer barrel so that the pistol meets the length requirements for the exception to apply and insert a mechanism to make the handgun a single-shot pistol. This modified single-shot pistol would then be sent to an FFL in California. The California FFL would then note in the Dealer's Record of Sale (DROS) form that the handgun is exempt from these Roster requirements because of its dimensions and because it is single-shot, and the transfer would be conducted like any other handgun transaction.

AB 1964 closed this so-called "loophole" that some Californians used to buy certain pistols not on the approved Roster. As a result, now only single shot pistols (*i.e.*, handguns that have not been altered to be single-shot) can fall under the "single-shot" exemption.[268]

As a practical matter, the DOJ's Roster has greatly limited the number of handguns available for purchase in California, such as through its microstamping requirement that took effect in May 2013. As a result of the microstamping requirement, the DOJ's Newly Added Firearms list has not seen much activity since May 2013, as the microstamping requirement cannot be met by manufacturers of certain pistols. Meanwhile, hundreds of firearms fell of the list since May 2013 and can no longer be sold by retailers in California.

A way for manufacturers to get firearms on the Roster is for the firearm to be "similar" to one already on the Roster.[269] Firearms determined to be "similar" to handguns already on the roster can be added to the Roster without testing. Generally, the changes must be purely cosmetic.

X. AMMUNITION RESTRICTIONS

There are several different types of prohibited ammunition under California and federal law.

---

[268] For example, in 2015, the DOJ determined that the Franklin Armory model SE-SSP was a semi-automatic pistol that had been temporarily altered so that it will not fire in a semiautomatic mode. Therefore, the single-shot pistol exemption did not apply to the firearm, despite the fact that the firearm was not semiautomatic to begin with.

[269] P.C. § 32030.

A. Ammunition With "Flechette Darts" and "Explosive Agents"

Under California law it is illegal to manufacture, cause to be manufactured, import into the state, offer or expose for sale, give, lend, or possess ammunition with a "flechette dart" or "[a]ny bullet containing or carrying an explosive agent."[270]

A "flechette dart" is a dart that can be "fired from a firearm, that measures approximately one inch in length, with tail fins that take up approximately five-sixteenths of an inch of the body."[271]

The Penal Code does not say what constitutes a "bullet containing or carrying an explosive agent," only that tracer ammunition manufactured for shotguns does not qualify.[272] One case, however, found a defendant guilty of possessing ammunition with an explosive agent when he possessed a hollow point bullet[273] with a primer[274] wedged into the hollow portion of the bullet and held in place by paraffin wax.[275]

Hence, although undefined in the Penal Code, any ammunition with an additional explosive agent designed to explode after being fired, or once the bullet strikes its target, may violate California law.

Both ammunition with "flechette darts" and ammunition with an explosive agent are listed among the "generally prohibited weapons." The exceptions for those weapons and devices would therefore apply to these two kinds of ammunition, where applicable, as well.

B. Armor-Piercing Handgun Ammunition

Both California and federal law have restrictions on "armor-piercing ammunition." Under the GCA, "armor-piercing ammunition" is:

(1) A projectile or projectile core which may be used in a handgun and which is constructed entirely (excluding the presence of traces of other substances) from one or a combination of tungsten alloys, steel, iron, brass, bronze, beryllium copper, or depleted uranium; or

---

[270] P.C. § 30210.

[271] P.C. § 16570.

[272] P.C. § 30215.

[273] A "hollow point bullet" is a "bullet with a cavity in the nose, exposing the lead core, to facilitate expansion upon impact. Hollow point cartridges are used for hunting, self-defense, police use and other situations to avoid over-penetration." NATIONAL SHOOTING SPORTS FOUNDATION INC., THE WRITER'S GUIDE TO FIREARMS & AMMUNITION 9 (2012).

[274] "Primer" is defined as an "ignition component consisting of a brass or gilding metal cup, priming mixture, anvil and foiling disc. It creates a spark when hit by a firing pin, igniting the propellant powder." NATIONAL SHOOTING SPORTS FOUNDATION INC., THE WRITER'S GUIDE TO FIREARMS & AMMUNITION 15 (2012).

[275] *People v. Lanham*, 230 Cal. App. 3d 1396 (1991).

(2) A full jacketed projectile larger than .22 caliber designed and intended for use in a handgun and whose jacket has a weight of more than 25 percent of the total weight of the projectile.[276]

The phrase "'armor-piercing ammunition' does not include shotgun shot required by Federal or State environmental or game regulations for hunting purposes, a frangible projectile designed for target shooting, a projectile which the [U.S. AG] finds is primarily intended to be used for sporting purposes, or any other projectile or projectile core which the [U.S. AG] finds is intended to be used for industrial purposes, including a charge used in an oil and gas well perforating device."[277]

Federal law restricts manufacturing and importing "armor-piercing ammunition," unless it is manufactured for:

(1) The use of the U.S., any department or agency of the U.S., any State, or any department, agency, or political subdivision of a State; *or*

(2) The purpose of exportation; *or*

(3) AG-authorized testing or experimentation. This exception also applies to importation.[278]

Further, those who manufacture or import "armor-piercing ammunition" may not sell or deliver it unless the sale or delivery is also for:

(1) The use by the U.S., any department or agency of the U.S., any State, or any department, agency, or political subdivision of a State; *or*

(2) Exportation; *or*

(3) U.S. AG-authorized testing or experimentation.[279]

It is also illegal for any federally licensed firearm importer, manufacturer, dealer, or collector to sell or deliver "armor-piercing ammunition" to another person without recording that person's information[280] into the FFL's records.[281]

Under California law, it is illegal for a person or entity to knowingly possess, manufacture, import, sell, or transport "handgun ammunition" primarily designed to penetrate metal or armor.[282] This includes "any ammunition, except a shotgun shell or ammunition primarily designed for use in a rifle, that is designed primarily to penetrate a body vest or body shield, and has either of the following characteristics":

---

[276] 18 U.S.C. § 921(a)(17)(B).

[277] 18 U.S.C. § 921(a)(17)(C).

[278] 18 U.S.C. § 922(a)(7).

[279] 18 U.S.C. § 922(a)(8).

[280] 18 U.S.C. § 922(b)(5) ("name, age, and place of residence of such person if the person is an individual, or the identity and principal and local places of business of such person if the person is a corporation or other business entity").

[281] The records are those required to be kept pursuant to 18 U.S.C. section 923. 18 U.S.C. § 922(b)(5).

[282] P.C. §§ 30315, 30320.

(1) A projectile or projectile core constructed entirely, excluding the presence of traces of other substances, from one or a combination of tungsten alloys, steel, iron, brass, beryllium copper, or depleted uranium, or any equivalent material of similar density or hardness; *or*

(2) The ammunition is primarily manufactured or designed, by virtue of its shape, cross-sectional density, or any coating applied thereto, including but not limited to, ammunition commonly known as "KTW ammunition," to breach or penetrate a body vest or body shield when fired from a handgun.[283]

Military personnel, police agencies, persons with permits, and other persons listed in P.C. sections 30325 and 30330 are exempt from this prohibition.

1. The Attempt to Ban "Green Tip" Ammunition

In 2015, the ATF attempted to ban M855 and SS109 "green tip" rifle ammunition in 5.56 and .233 calibers when it quietly released a proposal to adopt a new regulatory framework for determining whether certain types of ammunition were "primarily intended for sporting purposes" and therefore exempt from the federal restrictions on "armor piercing ammunition."[284]

"Green tip" ammunition has been considered exempt from the federal restriction since 1986, when the ATF held that 5.56mm ammunition fell under the "sporting purposes" exemption because of its well-documented use during target shooting with rifles. Yet, under the proposed framework, "green tip" ammunition would no longer be exempt from the federal restriction because when a 5.56mm bullet is "loaded into M855 or SS109 cartridges," it can be used in AR-platform handguns, which were very popular among firearm enthusiasts.[285] Under the ATF's proposed regulations, "green tip" ammunition would no longer fall under the "sporting purposes" exemption because it could be used in a handgun that was not "single-shot."[286]

Barely a week after issuing its proposal, the ATF began to pull back from its controversial decision to change the regulatory framework and its decision to ban "green tip" ammunition after it has received over 80,000 comments from the public—most of which were very critical of the ATF's decision.[287] Moreover, 299 mem-

---

[283] P.C. § 16660.

[284] *ATF Framework For Determining Whether Certain Projectiles Are "Primarily Intended For Sporting Purposes" Within the Meaning of 18 U.S.C. 921(a)(17)(C)*, BUREAU OF ALCOHOL, TOBACCO, FIREARMS, AND EXPLOSIVES, *available at* https://www.atf.gov/file/11266/download (last visited July 12, 2017).

[285] *ATF Framework For Determining Whether Certain Projectiles Are "Primarily Intended For Sporting Purposes" Within the Meaning of 18 U.S.C. 921(a)(17)(C)*, BUREAU OF ALCOHOL, TOBACCO, FIREARMS, AND EXPLOSIVES, *available at* https://www.atf.gov/file/11266/download (last visited July 12, 2017).

[286] For purposes of the ATF's proposed regulations, a "single shot handgun" was defined as "a break-open or bolt action handgun that can accept only a single cartridge manually, and does not accept or use a magazine or other ammunition feeding device. The term does not include a pocket pistol or derringer-type firearm." *ATF Framework For Determining Whether Certain Projectiles Are "Primarily Intended For Sporting Purposes" Within the Meaning of 18 U.S.C. 921(a)(17)(C)*, BUREAU OF ALCOHOL, TOBACCO, FIREARMS, AND EXPLOSIVES, *available at* https://www. atf.gov/file/11266/download (last visited July 12, 2017).

[287] *See Special Advisory: Notice to Those Commenting on the Armor Piercing Ammunition Exemption Framework*, BUREAU OF ALCOHOL, TOBACCO, FIREARMS, AND EXPLOSIVES (Mar. 10, 2015), *available at* https://www.atf.gov/

bers of Congress (241 in the House[288] and 58 in the Senate) signed on to letters to the former ATF Director B. Todd Jones urging him to rescind the proposal.[289] Given this opposition, the ATF did not issue a final framework and moved away from their decision to ban "green tip" ammunition.[290]

Although the ATF backed off their decision to ban "green tip" ammunition, gun owners should keep in mind that they are not safe yet and the government may still try to ban this type of ammunition in the future. In retrospect, it seems clear that the ban itself was a backdoor attempt to limit the public's access to AR style firearms and restrict gun ownership.

C. Tracer Ammunition

As mentioned above, any projectile with an explosive or incendiary material or other chemical substance like tracer ammunition (except tracer ammunition made for shotgun use) is illegal to possess in California without proper permits and/or licensing, as it meets one of the state's definitions of a "destructive device."[291] Specific military members, peace officers, firefighters, permit holders, and other groups listed in P.C. sections 18800 and 18900 may possess and use "destructive devices," including tracer ammunition.

For some reason tracer ammunition is lumped in with "destructive devices" and consequently carries that stigma in California. In fact, tracer ammunition is generally available in most states and can be purchased over the Internet. Firearm enthusiasts, often with no criminal record, unknowingly violate California's law when they are discovered with tracer ammunition they lawfully purchased in another state. Because this ammunition is readily available in other states, it is common for people to not know that they cannot possess it in California.

---

news/pr/notice-those-commenting-armor-piercing-ammunition-exemption-framework (last visited July 12, 2017).

[288] *See Congress Halts ATF Attempt to Ban 'Green Tip' Bullets*, NBC29.COM (Mar. 24, 2015), *available at* http://www.nbc29.com/story/28356908/congress-halts-atf-attempt-to-ban-green-tip-bullets (last visited July 12, 2017).

[289] Letter to B. Todd Jones, Director, Bureau of Alcohol, Tobacco, Firearms, and Explosives from United States Senate (Mar. 9, 2015), *available at* http://judiciary.house.gov/wp-content/uploads/2016/02/030415_ATF-Letter.pdf (last visited July 12, 2017).

[290] *See Special Advisory: Notice to Those Commenting on the Armor Piercing Ammunition Exemption Framework*, Bureau of Alcohol, Tobacco, Firearms, and Explosives (Mar. 10, 2015), *available at* https://www.atf.gov/news/pr/notice-those-commenting-armor-piercing-ammunition-exemption-framework (last visited July 12, 2017).

[291] P.C. §§ 16460(a) (defining "destructive device"), 18720, 18900 (permit requirement).

D. Lead-Based Ammunition Used in Certain Hunting Applications

Federal law limits the types of ammunition that can be used to hunt certain animals. For example, federal law prohibits using lead shot when hunting waterfowl.[292] In addition, California currently prohibits using projectiles with more than 1% lead when hunting big game (deer, black bear, wild pig, elk, pronghorn antelope, and bighorn sheep),[293] non-game birds, or non-game mammals[294] in designated California condor range areas.[295] In California condor range areas, it is also illegal for hunters to possess the combination of:

(1) Lead-based ammunition; *and*

(2) A firearm capable of firing that lead-based ammunition, even if the lead-based ammunition is not being used for hunting.[296]

Different states have different regulations related to the use of lead-based ammunition, but the limitations on lead-based ammunition across the country are generally related to migratory bird hunting or other forms of hunting occurring near some type of water source (*e.g.*, river, pond, lake).[297]

By the end of this decade, it will be illegal to hunt in California using traditional lead-based ammunition. In 2013, California Governor Jerry Brown signed a bill into law (AB 711) which required that the California Fish & Game Commission (referred to in this section as the Commission) to enact regulations to make it illegal for anyone in California to take any game or non-game animal with lead-based ammunition.[298] Although these regulations are not required to be in complete effect until July 1, 2019,[299] the Commission adopted regulations (as it was required to do by law) shortly after AB 711 passed. These regulations create a three-phase implementation process by which more and more restrictions on lead based ammunition will take effect each year, starting with January 1, 2015, until the complete ban takes effect on January 1, 2019.

 Beware: the restriction on lead based ammunition and the regulations passed by the Commission do not replace or eliminate the preexisting lead ammunition restrictions for hunting certain species within designated California condor range

---

[292] 50 C.F.R. §§ 20.21(j), 20.108.

[293] CAL. FISH & GAME CODE § 3004.5; CAL. CODE REGS. tit. 14, §§ 350, 353(h).

[294] CAL. CODE REGS. tit. 14, § 475(f).

[295] CAL. FISH & GAME CODE § 3004.5(a). For the California Condor range, *see Ridley-Tree Condor Preservation Act*, CAL. DEPT. OF FISH & GAME, https://nrm.dfg.ca.gov/FileHandler.ashx?DocumentID=82802 (last visited July 12, 2017).

[296] CAL. CODE REGS. tit. 14, §§ 353(h), 475(f).

[297] *State Regulations*, HUNTFORTRUTH.ORG, http://www.huntfortruth.org/legal/state-regulations/ (last visited July 12, 2017).

[298] CAL. FISH & GAME CODE § 3004.5(i); Letter from Edmund G. Brown, Governor of California, to the Members of the California State Assembly (Oct. 11, 2013), *available at* http://gov.ca.gov/docs/AB_711_2013_Signing_Message.pdf (last visited July 12, 2017).

[299] CAL. FISH & GAME CODE § 3004.5(i).

areas. Therefore, even if you meet an exception to AB 711 (see below), it will not apply to any ammunition use that is currently illegal under the 2008 Condor Zone ban. But, note that the California condor range restrictions will be repealed on July 1, 2019, the date when the restriction on lead based ammunition and the regulations passed by the Commission go into complete effect.[300]

1. The Push to Ban Hunters' Use of Lead-Based Ammunition

The first major attempts to limit lead-based ammunition used by hunters in the United States occurred in the 1970s. The International Association of Game, Fish and Conservation Commissioners passed a resolution in 1970 calling upon the United States Fish & Wildlife Service (referred to in this section as the Service) to begin a transition from "toxic" (*i.e.*, lead) to "nontoxic" (*e.g.*, steel) shot for waterfowl hunting.[301] In 1976, the Service implemented a limited "nontoxic shot program" intended to "alleviate the lead poisoning problem in waterfowl."[302]

As described by the Service,

[l]ead poisoning occurs in migratory waterfowl when spent lead pellets are ingested by ducks, geese, swans and other birds while feeding. The ingested pellets are retained in the gizzard and are both dissolved and worn away by the action of the gizzard. This results in soluable [sic] lead passing into the body system, causing sublethal effects and death.[303]

During the 1980s the Service and others expanded the scope of harm being linked to waterfowl hunters' use of lead-based ammunition. The National Wildlife Federation petitioned the Service in 1984 to "immediately designate nontoxic shot zones for six counties located in five States . . . [and] that an additional 89 counties in 30 States be proposed as nontoxic shot zones for 1985-86 hunting season."[304] In 1986, the Service stated that:

examinations of dead bald eagles have demonstrated that they are dying from lead poisoning also. The major source of this lead exposure is believed to be lead pellets embedded in or ingested by hunter-crippled or -killed waterfowl. To date, 119 lead-poisoned bald eagles have been diagnosed as dying from lead poisoning by the FWS National Wildlife Health

---

[300] CAL. CODE. REGS., tit. 11, § 250.1(e).

[301] *Nat'l Rifle Ass'n v. Kleppe*, 425 F. Supp. 1101, 1105 (D.D.C. 1976).

[302] Migratory Bird Hunting; Criteria and Schedule for Implementing Nontoxic Shot Zones for 1987-88 and Subsequent Waterfowl Hunting Seasons, 51 Fed. Reg. 23444-01, 23445 (proposed June 27, 1986) (to be codified at 50 C.F.R. pt. 20).

[303] *Nat'l Rifle Ass'n v. Kleppe*, 425 F. Supp. 1101, 1104 (D.D.C. 1976) (citing the Environmental Impact Statement the Service created as part of the adoption of regulations prohibiting the use of lead shot when hunting waterfowl in certain locations).

[304] Migratory Bird Hunting Zones in Which Nontoxic Shot Will Be Required for Waterfowl Hunting In the 1985-86 Hunting Season, 50 Fed. Reg. 6017-01, 6018 (proposed Feb. 13, 1985) (to be codified at 50 C.F.R. pt. 20).

Laboratory; lead shot is considered to be the most probable source of the lead.[305]

The Service's position was far from undisputed; the Commission and the National Rifle Association of America (NRA) made it clear that they did not agree with the Service's decision to impose "nontoxic shot zones," though legal challenges against the Service on this point were unsuccessful.[306] By September 1, 1991, a nationwide ban on lead shot applied to hunters taking waterfowl.[307] The ban was supported by many advocacy groups, including the Humane Society of the United States (HSUS).[308]

Though "indirect" or "secondary" poisoning claims (*e.g.*, lead poisoning of scavengers or predators via ingestion of animals shot with lead-based ammunition) certainly did not disappear during the mid- to late- 1990s, the issue was somewhat dormant until the 2000s. In 2004, a relatively new, litigation-based, and self-proclaimed radical environmental group, the Center for Biological Diversity (CBD), entered the lead-based ammunition discussion by filing a petition requesting that the Commission "revise rules governing hunting to require the use of non-lead ammunition for all hunting within the State of California . . . [and] immediate[ly take] emergency action to require non-lead ammunition for hunting in the habitat of the California condor."[309] The CBD's co-petitioners were the Natural Resources Defense Council and the Public Employees for Environmental Responsibility, in addition to less well-known organizations and advocates.[310] Though that particular petition was rejected by the Commission, the CBD has used aggressive litigation and lobbying tactics for the past ten years to push its agenda, although they have seen mixed results.

---

[305] Migratory Bird Hunting; Criteria and Schedule for Implementing Nontoxic Shot Zones for 1987-88 and Subsequent Waterfowl Hunting Seasons, 51 Fed. Reg. 23444-01, 23445 (proposed June 27, 1986) (to be codified at 50 C.F.R. pt. 20).

[306] Migratory Bird Hunting: Nationwide Requirement to Use Nontoxic Shot for the Taking of Waterfowl, Coots, and Certain Other Species Beginning in the 1991-92 Hunting Season, 56 Fed. Reg. 22100-01, 22101 (May 13, 1991) (to be codified at 50 C.F.R. pt. 20).

[307] 50 C.F.R. § 20.108. Technically, the ban applies to the use of lead-based ammunition when "hunting waterfowl, coots and certain other species. 'Certain other species' refers to those species, other than waterfowl or coots, that are affected by reason of being included in aggregate bags and concurrent seasons." 50 C.F.R. § 20.108.

[308] Migratory Bird Hunting: Nationwide Requirement to Use Nontoxic Shot for the Taking of Waterfowl, Coots, and Certain Other Species Beginning in the 1991-92 Hunting Season, 56 Fed. Reg. 22100-01, 22102 (May 13, 1991) (to be codified at 50 C.F.R. pt. 20).

[309] Petition for Rulemaking under the Administrative Procedure Act: Petition for Rulemaking to Address Lead Poisoning from Toxic Ammunition in California at 1 (filed Dec. 16, 2004), *available at* http://www.biologicaldiversity.org/species/birds/California_condor/pdfs/lead_petition.pdf (last visited July 12, 2017).

[310] Petition for Rulemaking under the Administrative Procedure Act: Petition for Rulemaking to Address Lead Poisoning from Toxic Ammunition in California at 1 (filed Dec. 16, 2004), *available at* http://www.biologicaldiversity.org/species/birds/California_condor/pdfs/lead_petition.pdf (last visited July 12, 2017).

2. The Future of the Lead-Based Ammunition Debate

The debate over hunters' use of lead-based ammunition is likely to continue for the foreseeable future, especially as to one hotly contested aspect of the debate: the contention that humans consuming animals taken with lead-based ammunition are ingesting detrimental amounts of lead. David Bellinger, an environmental health researcher at the Harvard School of Public Health in Massachusetts, recently commented that "[t]he ban in California could encourage other states to pass similar laws . . . . 'If history is a reliable judge, we expect to see a domino effect.'"[311] Hunters and firearms-advocates, however, hope to prove the passage of AB 711 was an aberration, founded on scare tactics, or as one member of the Commission termed it, "psuedo-science."[312]

Groups like the NRA, the National Shooting Sports Foundation (NSSF), and HuntForTruth.org have countered anti-lead arguments, noting that banning hunters' use of lead-based ammunition would likely result in ammunition prices skyrocketing because roughly 95% of ammunition used for hunting and recreation includes some portion of lead.[313] Traditional ammunition advocates also question some of the studies and research that are being used by opponents of lead-based ammunition, citing data omissions and data secrecy practices that are claimed to not only prevent full scientific review, but to suggest an unwillingness to admit that the relevant research results are not as clear-cut as lead-based ammunition opponents contend.[314]

There are relevant state and federal statutes and regulations not mentioned in this section that address hunting with lead ammunition. Those laws, however, are beyond the scope of this book. So, if you have specific questions, you should consult an attorney who specializes in the relevant area of law.

3. Phased-in Lead Ammunition Restrictions

a. Phase 1: Wildlife Areas and Ecological Reserves; and Nelson Bighorn Sheep

Since July 1, 2015, it has been unlawful to use ammunition that has not been certified as lead free, or to possess said ammunition in combination with any firearm capable of firing it, when taking:

---

[311] Sandeep Ravindran, *Banning Lead Ammunition Could Give Condors a Chance*, NATIONAL GEOGRAPHIC, Oct. 14, 2013, *available at* http://news.nationalgeographic.com/news/2013/10/131014-lead-ammunition-ban-condor-california-science/ (last visited July 12, 2017).

[312] Cal-Span, *Meeting of Aug. 6, 2009*, CAL-SPAN.ORG (Aug. 6, 2009), http://www.cal-span.org/cgi-bin/archive_old.php?owner=CFG&date=2009-08-06&player=silverlight (last visited July 12, 2017).

[313] Letter from Lawrence G. Keane, National Shooting Sports Foundation, to the Honorable Jack Kingston (July 31, 2013), *available at* http://www.nssf.org/share/pdf/NSSF%20%28Keane%29%20ltr%20to%20Rep%20Kingston%20Re%20Support%20Interior%20Approps%20EPA-TSCA%20Admt_2013-07-31.pdf (last visited July 12, 2017).

[314] *See, e.g. Science and Advocacy: The Balance Between Principle & Objectivity*, HUNTFORTRUTH.ORG (Aug. 6, 2013), http://www.huntfortruth.org/scientists-as-partisan-activists-the-science-behind-lead-ammo-ban-advocacy/ (last visited July 12, 2017).

(1) Nelson bighorn sheep anywhere in California; *or*

(2) Any species of wildlife on any "wildlife area"[315] or "ecological reserve"[316] anywhere in the state.[317]

Since there are over 260 "wildlife areas" and "ecological reserves" within California, it is important to familiarize yourself with the boundaries of these areas, especially if there are any near a location where you plan on taking any wildlife species with lead ammunition. A list of California's "wildlife areas" and "ecological reserves" can be found in sections 551, 553, and 630 of title 14 of the California Code of Regulations. A partial list can also be found on the California Department of Fish and Wildlife's website at: https://www.wildlife.ca.gov/Lands/Places-to-Visit.[318]

b. Phase 2: Additional Restrictions on Shotgun Shells

Since July 1, 2016, it has been "unlawful to use, or possess with any *shotgun* capable of firing, any projectiles certified as non-lead[319] . . . when taking":

(1) Resident upland game birds, except dove, quail, and snipe;[320] *or*

(2) Resident small game mammals;[321] *or*

(3) Fur-bearing mammals;[322] *or*

(4) Nongame mammals;[323] *or*

---

[315] A "wildlife area" is an area that the Commission has designated a "wildlife area." CAL. CODE REGS. tit. 14, § 551(a)

[316] An "ecological reserve" is an area that the commission has designated as such. CAL. CODE REGS. tit. 14, § 630(a).

[317] CAL. CODE REGS. tit. 14, § 250.1(d)(1).

[318] Legal descriptions of the boundaries of each "wildlife area" and "ecological reserve" should also be on file at the California Department of Fish and Wildlife's headquarters. *See* CAL. CODE REGS. tit. 14, §§ 551, 630.

[319] "Non-lead ammunition" is "any centerfire, shotgun, muzzleloading, or rimfire ammunition containing projectiles certified pursuant to" the Commissions "Non-lead Projectile and ammunition Certification Process." It also includes any "[s]hotgun ammunition containing pellets composed of materials approved as nontoxic by the U.S. Fish and Wildlife Service." CAL. CODE REGS. tit. 14, §§ 250.1(b)(2), (3); *see also* CAL. CODE REGS. tit. 14, § 507.1 (explaining that these materials include "bismuth-tin, steel, copper-plated steel, nickel-plated steel, tin-plated steel, zinc-plated steel, zinc chloride-plated steel, zinc chromate-plated steel, iron-tungsten, iron-tungsten-nickel, tungsten-bronze, tungsten-iron-copper-nickel, tungsten-matrix, tungsten-polymer, tungsten-tin-iron, tungsten-tin-bismuth, and tungsten-tin-iron-nickel or other nontoxic shot approved by the U.S. Fish and Wildlife Service . . .").

[320] Upland game bird species include: (1) sooty or blue grouse; (2) ruffed grouse; (3) sage hens or sage grouse; (4) white-tailed ptarmigan; (5) Hungarian partridges; (6) red-legged partridges, including the chukar and other varieties; (7) ring-necked pheasants and varieties thereof; and (8) band-tailed pigeons. CAL. FISH & GAME CODE § 3683(a).

[321] Resident small game mammals include: (1) jackrabbits and varying hares (genus Lepus); (2) cottontail rabbits; (3) brush rabbits; (4) pigmy rabbits (genus Sylvilagus); and (5) tree squirrels (genus Sciurus and Tamiasciurus). CAL. CODE REGS. tit. 14, § 257.

[322] Fur bearing mammals include: (1) pine marten; (2) fisher; (3) mink; (4) river otter; (5) gray fox; (6) red fox; (7) kit fox; (8) raccoon; (9) beaver; (10) badger; and (11) muskrat. CAL. FISH & GAME CODE § 4000.

[323] Nongame mammals are "[a]ll mammals occurring naturally in California which are not game mammals, fully protected mammals, or fur-bearing mammals." CAL. FISH & GAME CODE § 4150. Accordingly, nongame mammals include all mammals except for: (a) all of the following game mammals: (1) deer (genus Odocoileus); (2) elk (genus Cervus); (3) prong-horned antelope (genus Antilocapra); (4) wild pigs, including feral pigs and European wild boars (genus Sus); (5) black and brown or cinnamon bears (genus Euarctos); (6) mountain lions (genus Felis); (7) jackrabbits and varying hares (genus Lepus); (8) cottontails; (9) brush rabbits; (10) pigmy rabbits (genus Sylvilagus); (11) tree squirrels (genus Sciurus and Tamiasciurus); and (12) nelson bighorn sheep (subspecies Ovis

(5) Nongame birds;[324] *or*

(6) Any wildlife for depredation purposes, regardless of whether the take is authorized by a permit.[325]

It is important to note that the distinction between Phase 1 and Phase 2 is that Phase 2's prohibition only applies to shotgun shells. That means that, assuming that it is otherwise legal to do so, you may be able to use lead ammunition to hunt the species outlined in the list above or for depredation purposes until July 1, 2019, if you use a rifle or a handgun, and are not in a "state wildlife area," "ecological reserve," or (if you are hunting nongame birds or mammals) a California condor range area.

Phase 2's restriction also does not apply when hunting on a "licensed game bird club."[326] As a result, lead ammunition can be used for taking any game birds,[327] other than waterfowl, when on land under the authority of a licensed game bird club until the complete ban takes effect on July 1, 2019. Since California does not provide a specific definition for "licensed game bird clubs," you should confirm in

---

canadensis nelsoni) for the purposes of sport hunting (CAL. FISH & GAME CODE § 4902(b)); (b) all of the following fully protected mammals: (1) Morro Bay kangaroo rat (Dipodomys heermanni morroensis); (2) bighorn sheep (Ovis canadensis), except nelson bighorn sheep (subspecies Ovis canadensis nelsoni) as provided by section 4902(b); (3) northern elephant seal (Mirounga angustirostris); (4) guadalupe fur seal (Arctocephalus townsendi); (5) ring-tailed cat (genus Bassariscus); (6) pacific right whale (Eubalaena sieboldi); (7) salt-marsh harvest mouse (Reithrodontomys raviventris); (8) southern sea otter (Enhydra lutris nereis); and (9) wolverine (Gulo luscus); and (c) all of the following fur-bearing mammals: (1) pine marten; (2) fisher; (3) mink; (4) river otter; (5) gray fox; (6) red fox; (7) kit fox; (8) raccoon; (9) beaver; (10) badger; and (11) muskrat. *See* CAL. FISH & GAME CODE §§ 3950, 4700(b), 4000.

[324] Nongame birds are "[a]ll birds occurring naturally in California that are not resident game birds, migratory game birds, or fully protected birds." CAL. FISH & GAME CODE § 3800(a). Accordingly, nongame birds include all birds except for: (a) all of the following resident game birds: (1) doves of the genus Streptopelia, including, but not limited to, spotted doves, ringed turtledoves, and Eurasian collared-doves; (2) California quail and varieties thereof; (3) gambel's or desert quail; (4) mountain quail and varieties thereof; (5) sooty or blue grouse and varieties thereof; (6) ruffed grouse; (7) sage hens or sage grouse; (8) Hungarian partridges; (9) red-legged partridges including the chukar and other varieties; (10) ring-necked pheasants and varieties thereof; and (11) wild turkeys of the order Galliformes; (b) all of the following migratory game birds: (1) ducks and geese; (2) coots and gallinules; (3) jacksnipe; (4) western mourning doves; (5) white-winged doves; and (6) band-tailed pigeons; and (c) all of the following fully protected birds: (1) American peregrine falcon (Falco peregrinus anatum); (2) brown pelican; (3) California black rail (Laterallus jamaicensis coturniculus); (4) California clapper rail (Rallus longirostris obsoletus); (5) California condor (Gymnogyps californianus); (6) California least tern (Sterna albifrons browni); (7) golden eagle; (8) greater sandhill crane (Grus canadensis tabida); (9) light-footed clapper rail (Rallus longirostris levipes); (10) southern bald eagle (Haliaeetus leucocephalus leucocephalus); (11) trumpeter swan (Cygnus buccinator); (12) white-tailed kite (Elanus leucurus); and (13) yuma clapper rail (Rallus longirostris yumanensis). CAL. FISH & GAME CODE §§ 3500(a), 3500(b), 3511(b).

[325] CAL. CODE REGS. tit. 14, § 250.1(d)(2).

[326] CAL. CODE REGS. tit. 14, § 250.1(d)(2)(A).

[327] Game Birds include both resident game birds and migratory game birds. CAL. FISH & GAME CODE § 3500(c). Game bird species include: (a) all of the following resident game birds: (1) doves of the genus Streptopelia, including, but not limited to, spotted doves, ringed turtledoves, and eurasian collared-doves; (2) California quail and varieties thereof; (3) gambel's or desert quail; (4) mountain quail and varieties thereof; (5) sooty or blue grouse and varieties thereof; (6) ruffed grouse; (7) sage hens or sage grouse; (8) hungarian partridges; (9) red-legged partridges including the chukar and other varieties; (10) ring-necked pheasants and varieties thereof; and (11) wild turkeys of the order Galliformes; and (b) all of the following migratory game birds: (1) ducks and geese; (2) coots and gallinules; (3) jacksnipe; (4) western mourning doves; (5) white-winged doves; and (6) band-tailed pigeons. CAL. FISH & GAME CODE § 3500(a), (b). The restriction on lead ammo for the migratory game birds like water fowl remain in effect.

writing with the California Department of Fish and Wildlife and the owner of any place you intend to hunt as to whether the club is, in fact, a licensed game bird club.

c. Phase 3: Statewide Lead Ammunition Ban for All Species

Effective July 1, 2019, it will be "unlawful to use, or possess with any firearm capable of firing, any projectile(s) not certified as non-lead when taking any wildlife for any purpose in the state."[328] With the few exceptions listed below, when Phase 3 takes effect on July 1, 2019, there will be a total ban on the "use" or "possession with any firearm capable of firing" it, any ammunition that has not been certified as lead-free when taking any and all wildlife species anywhere within the state of California.

d. General Exceptions to the Lead Ammunition Restrictions

i. Possession of Handguns for Self-Defense

The lead ammunition restrictions are "[not] intended to prohibit the possession of [handguns] containing lead ammunition, provided that the firearm is possessed for personal protection and is not used to take or assist in the take of wildlife."[329] In other words, you may carry a handgun that contains lead ammunition while hunting, provided that you are only carrying the handgun for personal protection and it is not used to take, or assist in taking, any wildlife.

This exception does not apply within California condor range areas until after July 1, 2019.[330] Therefore, individuals hunting inside of a California condor range area should not be in possession of a handgun containing non-certified ammunition, even if it is intended to be used solely for purposes of personal protection, until July 1, 2019. But, you may be able to possess a handgun with non-certified ammunition if you are hunting the following species outside of any "state wildlife area" or "ecological reserve":

(1) Small game mammals or fur-bearing mammals (and only with a non-shotgun after July 1, 2016); *or*

(2) Game birds (until July 1, 2016, unless on a licensed game bird club or the target is a dove, quail, or snipe).[331]

Note that this self-defense handgun exception does not apply when taking any wildlife with a shotgun (even those mentioned above) within a California condor range area for depredation purposes after July 1, 2016.

---

[328] CAL. CODE REGS. tit. 14, § 250.1(d)(3).
[329] CAL. CODE REGS. tit. 14, § 250.1(c)(3).
[330] CAL. CODE REGS.. tit. 14, § 250.1(e).
[331] *See* CAL. CODE REGS. tit. 14, §§ 250.1(d), 353, 475.

ii. Temporary Exception for "Calibers" that Are Commercially Unavailable in Non-lead Due to Federal "Armor Piercing Ammunition" Restrictions

The lead ammunition restrictions "shall be temporarily suspended for a specific hunting season and caliber upon a finding by the [California Department of Fish and Wildlife] director that non-lead ammunition of a specific caliber is not commercially available from any manufacturer because of federal prohibitions relating to armor-piercing ammunition . . . ."[332]

This exception attempts to account for the potential unavailability of some "non-lead ammunition" because of the federal restrictions on "armor piercing ammunition" (explained above). As the federal government can declare that a given projectile meets the definition of "armor piercing ammunition" at any time, if a particular "caliber"[333] of certified ammunition is not commercially available because of federal law, this exception requires that the director of the California Department of Fish and Wildlife temporarily suspend California's ban and allow the use of non-certified ammunition in that "caliber."

Note that this exception does not apply "when taking big game mammals, nongame birds, or nongame mammals in" any California condor range area. This means that this exception will only apply in California Condor range areas when hunting small game. And unlike the exception for self-defense handguns (explained above), this distinction will not expire on July 1, 2019.

iii. Law Enforcement Engaged in Official Duties Exception

Law enforcement and other government official are exempt from the restriction on lead ammunition, but only if they are "carrying out a statutory duty required by law."[334] This means that law enforcement officers engaging in recreational hunting are not exempt from the lead ammunition restrictions.

---

[332] Cal. Fish & Game Code § 3004.5(b),(j)(1).

[333] Unfortunately, the term "caliber" is not defined for purposes of this exception and there isn't really much guidance on what projectiles would even be included. Many bullets of the same caliber can be loaded in different size cartridges. For example, the same .30 caliber bullet can be loaded into a .300 Savage, .308 Winchester, .30-06 Springfield, .300 Remington Short Action Ultra Magnum, .300 Winchester Short Magnum, .300 H&H Magnum, .308 Norma Magnum, 300 Winchester Magnum, 300 Weatherby Magnum, 300 Remington Ultra Magnum, and 30-378 Weatherby Magnum, all of which are distinct cartridges that serve a specific purpose with their unique performance characteristics. *See ATF Framework For Determining Whether Certain Projectiles Are "Primarily Intended For Sporting Purposes" Within the Meaning of 18 U.SC. 921(a)(17)(C)*, Bureau of Alcohol, Tobacco, Firearms, and Explosives, *available at* https://www.atf.gov/file/11266/download (last visited July 12, 2017).

[334] Cal. Fish & Game Code § 3004.5(h).

e. Penalties for Violating Restriction on Lead Ammunition

Except when waterfowl are involved,[335] anyone who violates the restrictions on the use of lead ammunition can be punished with a fine of $500, and if it is their second offense, a fine between $1,000 to $5,000.[336]

XI. OTHER REGULATED DEVICES

A. BB Guns

California law does not use the term "BB gun" but rather "BB device." A "BB device" is anything "that expels a projectile, such as a BB or a pellet, through . . . air pressure, gas pressure, or spring action, or any spot marker gun."[337] This means that any spot marker gun or device expelling any projectile through air pressure, gas pressure, or spring action will be considered a "BB device."[338] Devices that meet the definition of "BB device" are not "firearms."[339]

It's illegal to sell "BB devices" to minors, and no one may loan or give a "BB device" to a minor without permission from that minor's parent or legal guardian.[340]

Despite generally being considered a non-lethal weapon, a BB gun used while committing a robbery is a "dangerous weapon," according to a decision by the California Court of Appeal.[341] Under California law, a person who uses a deadly or "dangerous weapon" in the commission of a felony can receive an additional jail sentence on top of the jail sentence they receive for a felony conviction. These are referred to as sentence enhancements.[342] So don't think you won't face serious charges just because you use a BB gun to commit a crime and not a real firearm.

Example of a "BB gun"

---

[335] Violations of the federal regulations governing waterfowl can result in a misdemeanor, which can carry a fine up to $15,000 and imprisonment for up to six months, 16 U.S.C. § 707(a), as well as civil penalties and seizure of property, see 50 C.F.R. §§ 11.1, 12.1. In addition to the federal regulations, violations of state regulations can result in an infraction punishable as a fine between $100 and $1,000, or a misdemeanor. CAL. FISH & GAME CODE § 12000.

[336] CAL. FISH & GAME CODE § 3004.5(g).

[337] P.C. § 16250.

[338] P.C. § 16250(a). This is due to SB 199, which was signed into law in September 2014. *See* SB 199, 2013-2014, Leg. Counsel's Digest (Cal. 2014), *available at* https://leginfo.legislature.ca.gov/faces/billNavClient.xhtml?bill_id=201320140SB199 (last visited July 12, 2017).

339 Remember that in order to be a "firearm," there must be combustion. P.C. § 16250. "Firearms" are discussed and defined in Chapter 2.

[340] P.C. §§ 19910, 19915.

[341] *In re Bartholomew D.*, 131 Cal. App. 4th 317, 322-26 (2005).

[342] P.C. § 12022(b).

B. Toy Guns a.k.a. "Imitation Firearms"

When discussing "imitation firearms," it is best to start with federal law and work back to California law. Under federal law, it is illegal for anyone "to manufacture, enter into commerce, ship, transport, or receive any toy, look-alike, or imitation firearm unless such firearm contains, or has affixed to it, a marking approved by the Secretary of Commerce . . . ."[343]

Unless there is an exception or the Secretary of Commerce has provided for an alternate marking or device,[344] "each toy, look-alike, or imitation firearm shall have as an integral part, permanently affixed, a blaze orange plug inserted in the barrel of such toy, look-alike, or imitation firearm. Such plug shall be recessed no more than 6 millimeters from the muzzle end of the barrel of such firearm."[345]

A "'look-alike firearm' means any imitation of any original firearm which was manufactured, designed, and produced since 1898, including and limited to toy guns, water guns, replica nonguns, and airsoft guns firing nonmetallic projectiles."[346] A "look-alike firearm" does not include "any look-alike, nonfiring, collector replica of an antique firearm developed prior to 1898, or traditional BB, paint-ball, or pellet-firing air guns that expel a projectile through the force of air pressure."[347] That is why certain airsoft guns need the orange tips while BB guns that fire metallic pellets do not, despite looking in all other respects identical.

Example of a Toy Gun

Going back to California law, an "imitation firearm" is "any BB device, toy gun, replica of a firearm, or other device [including "a protective case for a cellular telephone"] that is so substantially similar" in color and overall appearance to an existing firearm that a reasonable person would think it is a firearm.[348]

Anyone who modifies an "imitation firearm" to look more like a firearm is guilty of a misdemeanor.[349] This does not apply to manufacturers, importers, or imitation firearm distributors or those who lawfully use imitation firearms for theatrical, film, or television productions.[350] Manufacturers, importers, or distributors of imitation firearms who fail to comply with federal law or regulations relating to

---

[343] 15 U.S.C. § 5001(a).

[344] The Secretary of Commerce has promulgated a number of regulations concerning alternate markings and identifies how to request a waiver from the marking requirement if you seek to use an imitation firearm in the entertainment industry. *See* 15 U.S.C. § 50001(b)(2);15 C.F.R. §§ 272.1-272.5.

[345] 15 U.S.C. § 5001(b)(1).

[346] 15 U.S.C. § 5001(c).

[347] 15 U.S.C. § 5001(c).

[348] P.C. § 16700(a)(1), (a)(2).

[349] P.C. § 20150(a).

[350] P.C. § 20150(b)-(c).

the markings of "a toy, look-alike, or imitation firearm, as defined by federal law or regulation," (discussed above) can be prosecuted criminally under California law.[351]

California puts additional burdens on those who purchase, sell, manufacture, ship, transport, distribute, or receive (by mail order or in any other manner) "imitation firearms" for commercial purposes, unless the firearm is:

(1) Only for "export" (interstate or internationally) in commerce; *or*

(2) Only "for lawful use in theatrical productions, including motion picture, television, and stage productions"; *or*

(3) For "a certified or regulated sporting event or competition"; *or*

(4) For "military or civil defense activities, or ceremonial activities"; *or*

(5) For public displays authorized by public or private schools.[352]

But, these restrictions (relating to the purchase, sale, manufacture, shipping, transporting, distribution, or receipt of "imitation firearms" in P.C. section 20165) do not include: non-firing collector's replicas that are "historically significant and offered for sale in conjunction with a wall plaque or presentation case"; a "*BB device*"; or a "device where the entire exterior surface of the device is white, bright red, bright orange, bright yellow, bright green, bright blue, bright pink, or bright purple, either" by itself or predominantly "with other colors in any pattern, as provided by federal regulations governing imitation firearms, or where the entire device is constructed of transparent or translucent materials which permits unmistakable observation of the device's complete contents, as provided by federal regulations governing imitation firearms."[353]

Yet, only the following types of BB devices will be exempt from the restrictions on the purchase, sale, manufacture, shipment, transportation, distribution, or receipt (by mail order or in any other manner) of "imitation firearms" for commercial purposes under P.C. section 20165:

(1) A BB device that expels a projectile that is neither 6mm nor 8mm caliber; *or*

(2) A BB device that is an airsoft gun expelling a 6mm or 8 mm caliber projectile, only if it has the blaze orange ring on the barrel required by federal law, a trigger guard entirely covered in fluorescent colors, *or*

(3) If it is configured as a handgun, a two centimeter wide adhesive band[354] around the circumference of a fluorescently-colored protruding pistol grip; *or*

---

[351] P.C. § 20155.

[352] P.C. § 20165.

[353] P.C. § 16700(b).

[354] This adhesive band needs to be in place before the BB device is sold to a customer and must be applied in a manner where it is not intended for removal. P.C. § 16700(c).

(4) If it is configured as a rifle or long gun, a two centimeter wide adhesive band[355] around the circumference of any two of the following: the protruding pistol grip, the buttstock, or a protruding ammunition magazine or clip.[356]

Also as of January 1, 2016, spot marker guns that expel a projectile greater than 10 mm caliber will be exempt from these restrictions, as they too will not be considered to be "imitation firearms for purposes of P.C. section 20165."[357] As will "a nonfiring collector's replica that is historically significant, and is offered for sale in conjunction with a wall plaque or presentation case."[358]

While we may think we know what an "airsoft gun" is, the Legislature did not do the California public and retailers any favors in defining the term. It is still not yet known what items the Legislature meant to regulate as "airsoft guns" and what items are covered under this restriction. This is yet another example of the legislators in Sacramento, and particularly Senator de León (again), drafting legislation that does not provide a clear indication of what is legal or illegal in California.

Finally, a person cannot openly display or expose an "imitation firearm" in a "public place"[359] unless it is:

(1) Packaged or concealed so it is not subject to public viewing; *or*

(2) Displayed or exposed for commerce, including commercial film or video productions, or for service, repair, or restoration; *or*

(3) Used for a theatrical, movie, video, television, or stage production; *or*

(4) Used in conjunction with a certified or regulated sporting event or competition; *or*

(5) Used in conjunction with lawful hunting or pest-control activities; *or*

(6) Used or possessed at a certified or regulated shooting range; *or*

(7) Used at a fair, exhibition, exposition, or other similar activity for which the proper permits have been obtained; *or*

(8) Used in military, civil defense, or civic activities, including flag ceremonies, color guards, parades, award presentations, historical reenactments, and memorials; *or*

(9) Used for public displays authorized by any school or museum; *or*

---

[355] This adhesive band needs to be in place before the BB device is sold to a customer and must be applied in a manner where it is not intended for removal. P.C. § 16700(c).

[356] P.C. § 16700(b)(3), (4), (d) (effective January 1, 2016). This is due to the passing of SB 199. *See* SB 199, 2013-2014, Leg. Counsel's Digest (Cal. 2014) *available at* https://leginfo.legislature.ca.gov/faces/billNavClient.xhtml?bill_id=201320140SB199 (last visited July 12, 2017).

[357] P.C. § 16700(b)(2), (d).

[358] P.C. § 16700(b)(1), (d).

[359] A "public place" is any "area open to the public" including streets; sidewalks; bridges; alleys; plazas; parks; driveways; front yards; parking lots; automobiles, whether moving or not; buildings open to the general public, including those that serve food or drink or provide entertainment; and the doorways and entrances to buildings or dwellings, including public schools and colleges or universities. P.C. § 20170(b).

(10) Used in a parade, ceremony, or other similar activity for which proper permits have been obtained; *or*

(11) Displayed on a wall plaque or in a presentation case; *or*

(12) Used where discharging a firearm is lawful; *or*

(13) "The entire exterior surface of the imitation firearm is white, bright red, bright orange, bright yellow, bright green, bright blue, bright pink, or bright purple," either by itself or mainly with other colors, or "the entire device is constructed of transparent or translucent material that permits unmistakable observation of the device's complete contents." Merely having an orange tip is not enough. "The entire surface must be colored or transparent or translucent."[360]

Also, even if you meet one of the above "displaying" exceptions, you may still be prosecuted for possessing the device[361] at a state or local public building or meeting,[362] in an airport,[363] or on school grounds.[364]

C. "Tear Gas," "Less Lethal Weapons," and "Stun Guns"

1. "Tear Gas," Pepper Spray, and Mace

"Tear gas" is a catch-all term in California that "includes any liquid, gaseous or solid substance intended to produce temporary physical discomfort or permanent injury through being vaporized or otherwise dispersed in the air."[365] Obviously, "tear gas" includes items like mace and pepper spray.

A "tear gas weapon" is:

(1) Any shell, cartridge, or bomb capable of being discharged or exploded, when the discharge or explosion will cause or permit the release or emission of tear gas; *or*

(2) Any revolver, pistol, fountain pen gun, billy, or other form of device, portable or fixed, intended for the projection or release of tear gas, except those regularly manufactured and sold for use with firearm ammunition.[366]

Most people may purchase and use "tear gas" and "tear gas weapons" (the devices must only expel the "tear gas" by aerosol spray and have no more than two

---

[360] P.C. § 20175.

[361] *See* P.C. § 20180(c) ("[n]othing in Section 20170, 20175, or this section shall be construed to preclude prosecution for a violation of Section 171b, 171.5, or 626.10").

[362] P.C. § 171b.

[363] P.C. § 171.5.

[364] P.C. § 626.10.

[365] P.C. § 17240(a). "Tear gas" does not include substances such as an "economic poison," as listed in the Food and Agricultural Code sections 12751-13192, "provided that the substance is not intended to be used to produce discomfort or injury to human beings." P.C. § 17240(b).

[366] P.C. § 17250.

and a half ounces net weight of aerosol spray)[367] if they use them for self-defense purposes. Using "tear gas" or a "tear gas weapon" for a purpose other than self-defense is a crime.[368] The following people, however, are prohibited from purchasing, possessing, or using "tear gas" or "tear gas weapons":

Example of pepper spray

(1) Persons convicted of a felony or any crime involving an assault; *or*

(2) Those convicted of misusing tear gas; *or*

(3) Persons addicted to any narcotic drug.[369]

It is further unlawful for minors to possess a "tear gas weapon" and for people to sell or give "tear gas" or a "tear gas weapon" to a minor unless the minor is at least age 16 and is accompanied by, or has written consent from, a parent or guardian.[370] Parents or legal guardians who allow their minor over age 16 to possess "tear gas" may, however, be civilly liable if the minor misuses it.[371]

Many "tear gas" devices on the market store their contents in a form other than aerosol spray. It is questionable whether these devices are legal for ordinary citizens to possess in California.

Specified peace officers, custodial officers, military personnel, and private investigators/patrol guards are exempt from "tear gas" and "tear gas weapon" restrictions.[372]

For additional laws about permissible "tear gas" amounts that may be possessed, warning label and instruction requirements, and permits for using "tear gas" for anything other than self-defense, see P.C. sections 22810-23025.

2. "Less Lethal Weapons"

A "less lethal weapon" is any device "designed to or that has been converted to expel or propel less lethal ammunition[373] by any action, mechanism, or process for the purpose of incapacitating, immobilizing, or stunning a human being through the infliction of any less than lethal impairment of physical condition, function, or

---

[367] P.C. § 22810(e)(1).

[368] P.C. § 22810(g).

[369] P.C. § 22810(a)-(b).

[370] P.C. §§ 22810(c)-(d), 22815(a)-(b).

[371] P.C. § 22815(c).

[372] P.C. §§ 22820, 22825, 22830, 22835.

[373] "Less lethal ammunition" is any ammunition "designed to be used in any less than lethal weapon or any other kind of weapon (including . . . any firearm, pistol, revolver, shotgun, rifle, or spring, compressed air, or compressed gas weapon)" and, "[w]hen used in . . . [any] weapon, it is designed to immobilize, incapacitate, or stun a human being through the infliction of any less than lethal impairment of physical condition, function, or senses, including physical pain or discomfort." P.C. § 16770.

senses, including physical pain or discomfort.[374] It is unnecessary for the weapon to "leave any lasting or permanent incapacitation, discomfort, pain, or other injury or disability to be a less lethal weapon."[375]

A "less lethal weapon" includes the weapon's frame or receiver "but does not include any of the following unless the part or weapon has been converted" as described in the previous paragraph:

(1) A pistol, revolver, or firearm; *or*

(2) A machinegun; *or*

(3) A rifle or shotgun using fixed ammunition consisting of standard primer and powder and not capable of being concealed upon the person; *or*

(4) A pistol, rifle, or shotgun that is a firearm having a barrel less than 0.18 inches in diameter and that is designed to expel a projectile by any mechanical means or by compressed air or gas; *or*

(5) When used as designed or intended by the manufacturer, any weapon that is commonly regarded as a toy gun, and that as a toy gun is incapable of inflicting any impairment of physical condition, function, or senses; *or*

(6) A "destructive device"; *or*

(7) A "tear gas weapon"; *or*

(8) A bow or crossbow designed to shoot arrows; *or*

(9) A device commonly known as a slingshot; *or*

(10) A device designed for the firing of stud cartridges, explosive rivets, or similar industrial ammunition; *or*

(11) A device designed for signaling, illumination, or safety; *or*

(12) An "assault weapon."[376]

Selling a "less lethal weapon" to anyone under the age of 18 years is a misdemeanor.[377]

3. "Stun Guns"

A "stun gun" is "any item except a less lethal weapon used or intended to be used as either an offensive or defensive weapon that is capable of temporarily immobilizing

---

[374] P.C. § 16780(a).

[375] P.C. § 16780(a).

[376] P.C. § 16780(b).

[377] P.C. § 19405.

a person by the infliction of an electrical charge."[378] A "stun gun" is not a "less lethal weapon."

As with "tear gas weapons," most people may purchase, possess, and use a "stun gun." But, the following people cannot:

Example of a stun gun

(1) Those convicted of a felony, misusing a stun gun, or any crime involving an assault; *or*

(2) Those addicted to narcotic drugs; *or*

(3) Minors (it is illegal for you to sell or furnish a "stun gun" to a minor and it is illegal for a minor to possess a "stun gun" unless the minor is age 16 or older and has written parental or legal guardian consent).[379]

D. "Blowguns"

A "blowgun" is a hollow tube through which a dart is propelled by force of breath.[380] "Blowgun ammunition" is the "dart designed and intended for use in [the] blowgun."[381]

Unless an individual falls under an exception,[382] manufacturing, selling, offering for sale, possessing, or using a "blowgun" or "blowgun ammunition" is unlawful in California.[383]

E. 3D-Printed Guns

3D-printed firearms, as discussed in Chapter 4, may also have restrictions under California and federal law based on their design and how they are made. You should exercise caution in making, obtaining, or possessing these types of firearms since their specifications could make them subject to some of the prohibitions and restrictions discussed in this chapter.

First, they may be subject to the "undetectable firearms" laws depending on the material they are made of. Both California and federal law contain provisions requiring firearms to be detectable in walk-through metal detectors and x-ray machines commonly used at airports.[384]

---

[378] P.C. § 17230.

[379] P.C. § 22610 (referencing P.C. section 244.5 governing stun gun misuse).

[380] P.C. § 16270.

[381] P.C. § 16280.

[382] This includes zookeepers, animal control officers, Fish and Game personnel, certain humane officers, and veterinarians "in the course and scope of their business in order to administer medicine to animals." P.C. § 20015.

[383] P.C. § 20010.

[384] *See* P.C. §§ 24610, 17280(a); 18 U.S.C. § 922(p)(1)(A) (discussed above).

Second, under California law a 3D-printed firearm also has the potential of meeting the definition of a "zip gun." See the discussion of "zip guns" in Section (III)(H) to assist in determining whether your firearm is compliant.

Third, a 3D-printed firearm could be considered an "unconventional pistol," which is a prohibited weapon under California law as discussed above. It is unclear from the information available about these firearms whether they have a rifled bore or instead have a smooth bore. Therefore, depending on the length of the 3D-print-ed firearm, it could fall under the definition of an "unconventional pistol."

In 2013, a bill was introduced in Congress that attempted to regulate these types of firearms, but the bill failed to pass out of the federal legislature.[385] But, the "Ghost Gun" bill will require these firearms to be registered and will require permission to be obtained before they are made.[386]

F. Sniperscopes (Night Vision Scopes) and Laser Scopes or Laser Pointers

It is illegal to knowingly buy, sell, receive, dispose of, conceal, or have in your pos-session a "sniperscope" under California law.[387]

Although the term "sniperscope" might sound broad, California law defines it very narrowly and not in a way that you would think. A "sniperscope" is "any attachment, device or similar contrivance designed for or adaptable to use on a firearm which, through the use of a projected infrared light source and electronic telescope, enables the operator thereof to visually determine and locate the pres-ence of objects during the nighttime."[388]

The restrictions on "sniperscopes" do not apply to "member[s] of the armed forces of the United States or [to] police officers, peace officers, or law enforcement officers authorized by the properly constituted authorities for the enforcement of

---

[385] *See* H.R. 1474, 113th Cong. (2013). *See also* H.R. 3626, 113th Cong. (2013). On December 2, 2013, the House of Representatives passed H.R. 3626, which extends the Undetectable Firearms Act of 1988 for ten more years without tightening any of the restrictions already outlined in the Act. Kasie Hunt & Carrie Dann, *Senate to Vote on Extension of Undetectable Gun Ban*, NBCNEWS.COM (Dec. 9, 2013, 11:16 PM), http://www.nbcnews.com/news/other/senate-extends-ban-undetectable-guns-nixes-tighter-restrictions-f2D11717122 (last visited July 12, 2017). The Act restricts the manufacture, sale, and possession of guns that cannot be detected by x-ray machines or metal detectors, as discussed above in Section III(C) of this Chapter. Democrats, however, have tried to tack on language to the bill that would create tighter restrictions on plastic weapons produced by 3D-printing technology because, as they argue, under the current law gun makers can easily meet the Act's requirements by simply adding an easily detachable metal piece to the firearm. Kasie Hunt & Carrie Dann, *Senate to Vote on Extension of Undetectable Gun Ban*, NBCNEWS.COM (Dec. 9, 2013, 1:16 PM), http://www.nbcnews.com/news/other/senate-extends-ban-undetectable-guns-nixes-tighter-restrictions-f2D11717122 (last visited July 12, 2017). Although the Senate will likely approve the ten year extension of the Act, it will likely not pass any new restrictions on undetectable firearms. As of the publication of this book, the Senate has yet to vote on the bill.

[386] *See* P.C. sections 29180 through 29184.

[387] P.C. § 468.

[388] P.C. § 468.

law or ordinances" when they are authorized to use or possess "sniperscopes."[389] The restriction also does not extend to the use or possession of "sniperscopes" "when used solely for scientific research or educational purposes."[390]

The language of this restriction is odd because there are a number of similar scopes that do not meet the definition of a "sniperscope." This is likely because P.C. section 468 was enacted in 1958. At that time technology like electronic scopes that project infrared light enabling a person to see objects at night was, no doubt, cutting edge technology. But there have been great strides in firearm optics since that time. There are a variety of low soluble light or nighttime rifle scopes that do not require the use of a projected infrared light to illuminate a target. Nevertheless, one should be mindful as some modern scopes do have an infrared light source and others have the ability to turn on an infrared light in low-light conditions. Additionally, some scopes come with a laser range finder. These are not an "infrared light source" and are not intended to allow the operator to "visually determine and locate the presence of objects during the nighttime." Lastly, infrared lasers are also used as sights for handguns and rifles that project a small dot on the intended target. These sights, of course, do not possess an electronic telescope or assist in nighttime vision.

Every person who aims or points a "laser scope" or "laser pointer" "at another person in a threatening manner with the specific intent to cause a reasonable person fear of bodily harm," except in self-defense, is in violation of California law.[391] In other words, the possession of these items is lawful. A person runs afoul of California law only when these items are used to threaten another person with the intent to give that person a "fear of bodily harm." The laser scope does not need to be attached to a firearm to be used illegally.

Under this law a "laser scope" is "a portable battery-powered device capable of being attached to a firearm and capable of projecting a laser light on objects at a distance."[392] And a "laser pointer" is "any hand held laser beam device or demonstration laser product that emits a single point of light amplified by the stimulated emission of radiation that is visible to the human eye."[393]

XII. NATIONAL FIREARMS ACT – FIREARM POSSESSION

Unlike California law, federal law allows those who can lawfully possess firearms to possess certain "machineguns," "destructive devices," "short-barreled shotguns/rifles," "silencers," and "any other weapons" – also known as "NFA firearms."

---

[389] P.C. § 468.

[390] P.C. § 468.

[391] P.C. § 417.25(a).

[392] P.C. § 417.25(b).

[393] P.C. § 417.25(c).

A. "Any Other Weapon" Defined

Although "machineguns," "destructive devices," "short-barreled shotguns/rifles," and "silencers" are all regulated under California law (discussed above), the "any other weapons" category is unique to the NFA. The NFA defines "any other weapon" as:

(1) Any weapon or device capable of being concealed on the person from which a shot can be discharged through the energy of an explosive; *or*

(2) A pistol or a revolver having a barrel with a smooth bore designed or redesigned to fire a fixed shotgun shell; *or*

(3) Weapons less than 18 inches in total length with combined shotgun and rifle barrels of 12 inches or more "from which only a single discharge can be made from either barrel without manual reloading"; *or*

(4) Any weapon described above that may be readily restored to fire.[394]

"Any other weapon" does not include pistols or revolvers[395] with rifled bores or weapons for firing from the shoulder "and not capable of firing fixed ammunition" (*e.g.*, a blunderbuss or musket).[396] This means these firearms cannot be considered and regulated as "any other weapons."

Be careful, handguns with forward grips may meet the definition of "any other weapon" (in addition to possibly meeting the "assault weapon" definition discussed in Chapter 8).[397] Despite the fact that these handguns meet the general definition of "pistol" and "revolver" under California law (see Chapter 2), they likely are not "pistols" or "revolvers" under the federal definition because they are no longer designed, made, or intended to fire a projectile when "held in one hand," which is a precondition to being a "pistol" or "revolver."[398] But they still fall under the definition of "any other weapon" since they *are* firearms with rifled bores that are "capable of being concealed on the person."

---

[394] 26 U.S.C. § 5845(e).

[395] According to 27 C.F.R. section 479.11, a "pistol" is "[a] weapon originally designed, made, and intended to fire a projectile (bullet) from one or more barrels when held in one hand, and having (a) a chamber(s) as an integral part(s) of, or permanently aligned with, the bore(s); and (b) a short stock designed to be gripped by one hand and at an angle to and extending below the line of the bore(s)." A "revolver" is "[a] projectile weapon, of the pistol type, having a breechloading chambered cylinder so arranged that the cocking of the hammer or movement of the trigger rotates it and brings the next cartridge in line with the barrel for firing." 27 C.F.R. § 479.11.

[396] 26 U.S.C. § 5845(e).

[397] *See* U.S. DEPT. OF JUSTICE, BUREAUS OF ALCOHOL, TOBACCO, FIREARMS, AND EXPLOSIVES, ATF NATIONAL FIREARMS ACT HANDBOOK 9 (2009).

[398] *See* U.S. DEPT. OF JUSTICE, BUREAUS OF ALCOHOL, TOBACCO, FIREARMS, AND EXPLOSIVES, ATF NATIONAL FIREARMS ACT HANDBOOK 9 (2009); *see also* 27 C.F.R. § 479.11. In order to be a "pistol" under the Code of Federal Regulations, the firearm must be designed to be "held in one hand." 27 C.F.R. § 479.11. Therefore, a pistol with a forward grip would not fit within this definition. But this distinction isn't as clear with "revolvers" that are modified to have a forward grip. In order to be a revolver under the Code of Federal Regulations, the firearm must be "of the pistol type." 27 C.F.R. § 479.11. While it is not clear what the phrase "of the pistol type" means, it is likely that a revolver with a forward grip would not fall under this definition, as "of the pistol type" most likely denotes that it must be designed to be "held in one hand."

Nail guns may also fall under the definition of "any other weapon" if they are used as weapons.[399]

Unlike other NFA firearms ("machineguns," "silencers," "short-barreled shot-guns/rifles"), most items meeting the "any other weapon" definition *can* be possessed, imported, or transferred (to persons age 21 or older) in California as long as they satisfy the respective NFA requirements.

B. Transferring NFA Firearms

To transfer an NFA firearm, you must be the registered owner of the firearm, file the proper ATF forms, and make sure the applicable transfer tax is paid.[400] The ATF must also approve the transfer,[401] and the transferee generally must notify the local chief of police, sheriff of the county, head of the state police, state or local district attorney or prosecutor, or such other authority where the transferee resides.[402] It is otherwise illegal to possess unregistered NFA firearms.[403] If you want to *build* one of these types of firearms, you must have the proper permission from the federal government and, if you are in the business of making NFA firearms, a federal license and tax stamp.[404]

Though federal law makes it much easier to lawfully obtain and own those items constituting NFA firearms, this will not help you much if you are a California resident. As mentioned above, California requires an additional permit (or exception) to possess most of these items, which is nearly impossible to obtain for "normal" people. And the ATF will not approve the transfer of an NFA firearm where state or local law would be violated by doing so.[405]

Nevertheless, people have found a way to avoid some federal restrictions and procedures associated with getting an NFA firearm by creating a legal document known as an NFA Trust or "Gun Trust." These are discussed in Chapter 4.

---

[399] *See Open Letter on the Redesign of "Stabilizing Brace,"* BUREAU OF ALCOHOL, TOBACCO, FIREARMS, AND EXPLOSIVES, https://www.atf.gov/file/11816/download (last visited July 12, 2017).

[400] The tax is $200 generally or $5 for "any other weapons." 26 U.S.C. § 5811(a).

[401] 26 U.S.C. § 5812(b); 27 C.F.R. § 479.86.

[402] 27 C.F.R. § 479.85.

[403] *United States v. Freed*, 401 U.S. 601, 607 (1971).

[404] 18 U.S.C. § 922(a)(1)(A); 26 U.S.C. §§ 5822, 5801, 5802.

[405] 26 U.S.C. § 5812(a); 27 C.F.R. § 479.85.

XIII. EXPLOSIVES

A. "Fireworks" and "Explosives"

"Fireworks" and "explosives" are wide and varying topics with special state and federal laws regulating their transportation, importation, sale, and possession.[406] "Explosives" are especially a concern for firearm enthusiasts who enjoy reloading their own ammunition.

B. Ambiguity Concerning the Amount of Black Powder a Person Can Possess

The amount of smokeless and black powder a person may legally possess can be located in Chapter 2. But there appears to be a conflict in the law concerning the actual amount of *black powder* that a person may legally possess in California.

The conflict exists between California Health and Safety Code (Cal. Health & Saf. Code) sections 12001 and Cal. Health & Saf. Code section 12101.

Cal. Health & Saf. Code sections 12000-12405 regulate the use, transportation, and possession of "explosives."[407] The term "explosives," as used and defined within this part of the California Health & Safety Code, specifically includes smokeless and black powder.[408] Yet, the sections, as provided in section 12001, do not apply to the possession of "[b]*lack powder* in quantities of 25 pounds or less in the hands of a retailer having a permit . . . and in quantities of five pounds or less in the hands of all others[,]" or to "*smokeless powder* in quantities of 20 pounds or less [when] used, possessed, stored, sold, or transported" if it is "exempted under, or authorized by, the Federal Organized Crime Control Act of 1970[409] . . . and applicable federal regulations thereunder."[410] In other words, Cal. Health & Saf. Code section 12001 essentially says that quantities of black powder of five pounds or less are not "explosives," and are therefore exempt from this entire part of the California Health & Safety Code.

In contrast, Cal. Health & Saf. Code section 12101 restricts anyone from receiving, storing, or possessing "explosives" without a *permit*. The "chapter" concerning

---

[406] *See, e.g.,* Cal. Health & Saf. Code §§ 12500-12759. *See also* Cal. Code Regs. tit. 19, §§ 979-1039; 27 C.F.R. §§ 555.221-555.224; 18 U.S.C. § 842. There may also be other relevant statutes, regulations, or local municipal codes that address fireworks and pyrotechnics. Those are beyond the scope of this book, however, so if you have specific questions, you should consult an attorney who specializes in that area of law.

[407] *See* Cal. Health & Saf. Code §§ 12000-12405.

[408] Cal. Health & Saf. Code § 12000.

[409] *See* 18 U.S.C. §§ 831-837. The Federal Organized Crime Control Act of 1970 includes exemptions for both black powder (*i.e.,* "black powder in quantities not to exceed fifty pounds . . . intended to be used solely for sporting, recreational, or cultural purposes in antique firearms as defined in section 921(a)(16) of title 18 of the United States Code") and smokeless powder (smokeless is construed by the ATF as falling under the "small arms ammunition components thereof"). 18 U.S.C. § 845(a)(4)-(5). Federal regulation 27 C.F.R. section 555.141 also contains exemptions for smokeless and black powder.

[410] Cal. Health & Saf. Code § 12001 (emphasis added).

permits (meaning Chapter 4 of the Cal. Health & Saf. Code), however, provides an exemption to the permit requirement in Cal. Health & Saf. Code section 12102. This statute exempts the possession of 20 pounds or less of smokeless powder, or *one pound or less of black sporting powder* from the permit requirement, provided that: (1) the smokeless powder is intended only for hand-loading small arms ammunition of .75 caliber or less; or (2) the black sporting powder is intended for loading of small arms or small arms ammunition of .75 caliber or less.[411] This seems to indicate that a person would need a permit to possess more than one pound of black powder.

This is clearly a conflict in the law. Cal. Health & Saf. Code section 12001 provides that quantities of black powder in five pounds or less are not considered "explosives," and are therefore exempt from the entire "explosives" part of the California Health & Safety Code. Following this understanding, a person would not need a permit to receive, store, or possess black powder in quantities of five pounds or less because it is not considered an "explosive" under the statute. Therefore, the added language of Cal. Health & Saf. Code section 12102, which seems to indicate that a permit would be needed if you are looking to possess black powder in quantities of *one* pound or more, doesn't make sense because you wouldn't need a permit to possess black powder in quantities of *five* pounds or less, as explained above.

If this was litigated, however, a court must follow the maxim that the legislature is deemed to be aware of existing laws and judicial decisions in effect at the time the legislation is enacted.[412] And when there is a conflict in the law that cannot be harmonized, the later statue enacted prevails.[413] In this case, both Cal. Health & Saf. Code sections 12001 and 12102 were added at the same time in 1967. But the subsection of Cal. Health & Saf. Code section 12001 that exempts black powder in quantities of five pounds or less from the definition of "explosive" was enacted four years after the most recent amendment to Cal. Health & Saf. Code section 12102 and therefore should trump the one pound or less language contained in Cal. Health & Saf. Code 12102. Consequently, the five pound restriction on the possession of black powder should be controlling. Still, out of an abundance of caution, you might want to carry black powder in quantities of one pound or less.

C. Binary Exploding Targets

A number of people have been arrested and prosecuted for possessing and/or using binary exploding targets (*i.e.*, products like Tannerite, White Lightning, etc.). These individuals have been charged with possession of destructive devices or explosives for possessing these targets. While the law concerning these substances is complex

---

[411] CAL. HEALTH & SAF. CODE § 12102.

[412] *Fiscal v. City and Cnty. of San Francisco*, 158 Cal. App. 4th 895, 908 (1999).

[413] *Cal. Corr. Peace Officer Assn. v. Dep't of Corr.*, 72 Cal. App. 4th 1331, 1337 (1999).

and delves into an area outside the scope of this book, I strongly advise against possessing and/or using these substances in the state of California.

XIV. IGNORANCE OF THE LAW IS NO EXCUSE

Despite California's massive amount of confusing laws about which firearms and devices are, and are not, legal, ignorance of the law is no excuse. You essentially violate California and federal law if you knowingly possess an item that is something California prohibits you from possessing.[414] It does not matter if you did not know it was illegal.[415]

In some rare instances, however, you may be able to use the "entrapment by estoppel" defense. "Entrapment by estoppel" means that a government representative has informed you that a certain act is lawful, then prosecutes you for that same act.[416] For example, if California law enforcement informs you that a certain firearm is legal in California and then you are arrested because the firearm is actually *illegal* under California law, you might be able to claim "entrapment by estoppel" to defend yourself since law enforcement previously informed you that the firearm was legal.

In general, however, the law expects you as a firearm owner to be familiar with all of the laws discussed above, and those that might not be mentioned as well.

---

[414] *See, e.g., In re Jorge M.*, 23 Cal. 4th 866, 869-70 (2000) (the state must prove defendant knew that he possessed it and knew or reasonably should have known the firearm was prohibited by make and model or its features, but need not prove defendant knew of the law banning unregistered "assault weapon" possession or that the make, model, or features caused the firearm to be classified as an "assault weapon").

[415] *People v. King*, 38 Cal. 4th 617, 627 (2006) ("[T]he prosecution must prove that the item had the necessary characteristic to fall within the statutory description. It must also prove that the defendant knew of the characteristic. That is, it must prove that a defendant charged with possession of a short-barreled rifle knew the rifle was unusually short, but the defendant need not know the rifle's actual dimensions. Similarly, a defendant charged with illegally possessing a cane sword must know that the cane contained a sword, and a defendant charged with possessing a writing pen knife must know that the pen contained a stabbing instrument. Knowledge can, of course, be proved circumstantially. Further, the prosecution need not prove that the defendant knew there was a law against possessing the item, nor that the defendant intended to break or violate the law."); *see People v. Taylor*, 4 Cal. App. 2d 220, 223 (1935) ("It is clear from a reading of the transcript herein that the sole proof on the part of the prosecution which tended to establish the crime charged was the fact of possession by defendant of the proscribed cartridges. There was no proof that he had knowledge of their character as tear gas shells, nor was there any evidence from which such knowledge could be inferred . . . . Without proof of the fact of possession by defendant of an instrumentality capable of discharging these cartridges found in his pocket, there was no sufficient evidence in this case to sustain a conviction.").

[416] *United States v. Batterjee*, 361 F.3d 1210, 1216-17 (9th Cir. 2004).

ABOUT THE AUTHOR

C.D. "Chuck" Michel is Senior Counsel and owner of Michel & Associates, P.C., a boutique law firm employing 15 attorneys located in Long Beach, California. The firm's practice focuses on litigation, both civil and criminal. Areas of practice include firearms law, constitutional law, civil rights advocacy, business litigation, land use law, employment law and environmental law. The firm's website is www.MichelLawyers.com.

Mr. Michel has been litigating civil and criminal firearms cases since 1991. His clients include the National Rifle Association (NRA), the California Rifle and Pistol Association (CRPA) Foundation, *FFLGuard*, gun manufacturers, wholesalers, retailers, and individual gun owners. He has represented thousands of individuals and companies charged with violating California's confusing firearms laws. He has been trial counsel in scores of jury trials, many of which were high profile and attracted state and national media attention. He has litigated hundreds of firearms cases involving constitutional issues, including Second Amendment challenges, in both state and federal trial and appellate courts. As an attorney for the NRA, Mr. Michel has been a stakeholder in drafting legislation to protect California gun owners and an advocate in opposing ill-conceived legislation. Since 2002, Mr. Michel and his law firm have donated over 1.5 million dollars worth of *pro bono* legal work to the NRA and the CRPA Foundation.

Among many other victories, Mr. Michel won the NRA-sponsored lawsuit that struck down Proposition H – the San Francisco law that would have banned the civilian possession of handguns in the city. He also led the successful CRPA Foundation lawsuit that struck down Assembly Bill 962, an anti-gun politician's attempt to severely restrict and require registration of all ammunition purchases. Mr. Michel filed prestigious, influential, and unprecedented *amicus* briefs on behalf of dozens of California district attorneys in both the 2008 *District of Columbia v. Heller* and the 2010 *McDonald v. Chicago* Supreme Court gun-rights cases. He has been honored with numerous awards for his legal successes, including awards for his civil rights advocacy, trial advocacy skills, writing skills, and *pro bono* work.

Mr. Michel has served as a spokesperson for the NRA, CRPA, other civil rights group clients, and individual clients. He has appeared on dozens of television and radio interviews and been quoted in thousands of newspaper articles. He publishes a monthly column, *Legal Front Lines*, and a blog at www.CalGunLaws.com. He has had articles and editorials published in the *Los Angeles Times*, the *Los Angeles Daily Journal*, and other state and national newspapers and magazines.

"Professor" Michel has also taught classes in Firearms Law and Law Practice Management as an adjunct professor at Chapman University Dale E. Fowler School of Law in Orange, California.

Mr. Michel graduated near the top of his classes from both Rutgers University in New Jersey in 1980 and from Loyola Law School in Los Angeles in 1989. He began his legal career with a coveted judicial clerkship for U.S. District Court Judge William J. Rea in Los Angeles. He worked as a criminal prosecutor for the Los Angeles County District Attorney's Office and several Southern California cities and as an advocate with the Los Angeles Federal Public Defender's office. Mr. Michel also practiced environmental and general civil litigation as an attorney at the renowned international law firm of O'Melveny & Myers, LLP. While at O'Melveny, Mr. Michel represented clients ranging from individuals to multinational corporations. Among many other cases and clients, he represented Exxon in connection with the Exxon Valdez oil spill and served as staff counsel to the "Christopher Commission" which investigated the Los Angeles Police Department after the Rodney King incident.

Mr. Michel grew up in what used to be rural New Jersey at a time when neighbors wished him luck as he walked out his back door and into the woods behind his house to go rabbit hunting before high school – these days the neighbors would call the SWAT team on a high school student with a gun. His father was a businessman who loved teaching others, including his three sons, the shooting sports as an NRA instructor. Some of Mr. Michel's fondest childhood memories are of backyard plinking contests with his entire family. He is striving to pass this firearm heritage along to his own sons and hopes that they will be able to pass it on to future generations of free Americans.

NATIONAL RIFLE ASSOCIATION
MEMBERSHIP APPLICATION

NRA RECRUITER ID#
XP025815

STEP ONE: Provide Personal Information

NAME: Mr./Mrs./Ms. _____

ADDRESS: _____

CITY/STATE/ZIP: _____

E-MAIL: _____

PHONE: _____ BIRTHDATE: _____

STEP TWO: Select Membership Type

__ 1 YEAR	$35
__ 3 YEAR	$85
__ 5 YEAR	$125
__ JUNIOR (15 years & up)	$15
__ ASSOCIATE (no magazine)	$10
__ REGULAR LIFE MEMBERSHIP	$1,000
__ JUNIOR LIFE MEMBERSHIP	$550
__ DISTINGUISHED LIFE MEMBERSHIP – Age 65+	$375
__ EASY PAY LIFE MEMBERSHIP*	$25 (minimum)

* Easy Pay for Life Membership: minimum $25 down payment,
then minimum $25 quarterly payments until total dues are paid.

__ Foreign Postage (per year: $5 Canadian – $10 other) ____

CALCULATE TOTAL AMOUNT DUE $ _____

STEP THREE: Select One Magazine

(Junior Members under age 15 receive Insights digital* magazine,
15 and older choose magazine) *E-mail address required for digital version.

AMERICAN RIFLEMAN	AMERICAN HUNTER	AMERICA'S 1ST FREEDOM
__ Digital __ Print	__ Digital __ Print	__ Digital __ Print

STEP FOUR: Provide Payment Information

__ CHECK PAYABLE TO NRA: Check # _____ enclosed

__ CHARGE TO: __ AMEX __VISA __ MC __ DISCOVER

ACCOUNT # _____

EXPIRATION DATE: _____

SIGNATURE: _____

STEP FIVE: Please Read The Following:

Contributions, gifts, or membership dues made or paid to the National Rifle Association of America are not refundable or transferable and are not deductible as charitable contributions for Federal income tax purposes.

Please allow 4 to 6 weeks for delivery of membership credentials and materials.

Call NRA at 800-672-3888 for more information about
membership programs, or visit us at **www.NRA.org.**
Manage your membership online at **www.NRAMemberServices.org**

STEP SIX: Mail this application with payment to:

National Rifle Association of America
c/o Recruiting Programs
11250 Waples Mill Road

WHY JOIN THE NRA?

800-392-VOTE • www.NRAILA.org

NRA Membership Benefits

These basic membership benefits are automatically included with your NRA Annual Membership or Life Membership, along with special members-only discounts and services.

- An official NRA Membership ID card - showing your Membership ID number and expiration date or Life Member status. You should carry this card with you at all times.
- With all regular memberships, you will get a choice of subscription to American Rifleman, American Hunter, or America's 1st Freedom.
- Junior members receive a subscription to Insights.
- Annual members receive $5,000 of Accidental Death and Dismemberment coverage at NO COST to you. The plan covers accidents at, or to and from, an NRA event; and accidents that occur during the use of firearms or hunting equipment while hunting. Insurance must be activated at time of renewal. (Does not include Junior membership.)
- Life members receive $10,000 of Accidental Death and Dismemberment coverage at NO COST to you. The plan covers accidents at, or to and from, an NRA event; and accidents that occur during the use of firearms or hunting equipment while hunting. Insurance must be activated at time of upgrade to Life member status
- Law Enforcement Officers, that are NRA members, killed in the line of duty will have $25,000 in coverage.
- $2,500 of ArmsCare coverage with your NRA membership. This plan covers insured firearms, air guns, bows and arrows against theft, accidental loss, and damage. Insurance must be activated.

  For purposes of insurance, NRA members must be current active members of the NRA whose name appears on the NRA membership list. Activation is required.

- New and Enhanced insurance coverages through the NRA Endorsed Insurance Programs. Enroll on-line for Life, Health and Accident and Individual Property and Liability insurance or call Toll free 1-877-NRA-3006 (1-877-672-3006.) New Commercial Property Liability Insurance Program for NRA Affiliated Clubs and Business Alliance Members, visit on-line or call Toll Free 1-877-487-5407.
- The most important benefit of NRA membership, however, is the defense of your Constitutional right to keep and bear arms, both nationally and in California. NRA-ILA tracks the issues and alerts members about legislation involving firearms and hunting at the federal, state and local levels of government. Successful legislative action begins with you -- the individual member. For information regarding legislative action or to become an ILA grassroots volunteer, call 1-800-392-8683.
- NRA Institute for Legislative Action representatives are your voice on Capitol Hill and in Sacramento.
- Your NRA Membership dues payment receipt allows you to immediately enter NRA registered tournaments.

For real American values, shop NRAstore.com,
where 100% of the profits go directly to support vital NRA programs
Request a catalog • 888-607-6007 • Shop online: www.NRAstore.com

Membership starts the day of processing of dues payments by NRA. Insurance benefits are subject to the conditions contained in the Master Policy on file at NRA Headquarters at the time a claim arises. There are special exclusions and limitations to such policy. Furthermore, NRA and its Insurers specifically reserve the right to alter or change any conditions in the Master Policy; including but not limited to, reductions in the amount of coverage, and the cancellation or non-renewal of such policy. Annual Junior members are not eligible for insurance benefits. Affinity card available for applicants who meet all credit criteria. The moving discount is off the Interstate Commerce Commission approved tariff rate. $3.75 of membership dues are designated for magazine subscriptions. For specific state by state disclosures, please visit www.NRA.org/NRAUniformDisclosureStatement.pdf

CALIFORNIA RIFLE & PISTOL ASSOCIATION

MEMBERSHIP APPLICATION

STRENGTH IN MEMBERS

Ways to Join:

Return this form by mail to
California Rifle & Pistol Association
271 E. Imperial Highway
Fullerton, CA 92835

Or

Become a member online at:
www.CRPA.ORG

Or

Call the office:
(800) 305-2772

2018 CRPA Memberships Levels

Membership Option	Price
1 Year Membership	$35
5 Year Membership	$150
2A Sustaining Membership	$17^{91} / Month
Life Membership	$500
	Or $135 / 4 quarterly payments
Senior Life Membership	$275
	Or $75 / 4 quarterly payments
Veteran Life Membership	$450
	Or $125 / 4 quarterly payments
Defender Life Member	$1000 + Life Membership
Activist Life Member	$2500 + Defender Membership
Patriot Life Member	$4000 + Activist Membership
Business Affiliate	$150 / Annually

Check next to membership of choice

A portion of CRPA membership dues are used for lobbying and political activities. The portion used for these purposes is 25% of the total cost of membership paid.

Name: _____ DOB: / /

Address: _____

City: _____ State: _____ Zip: _____

Home Phone: ( ) _____ Mobile Phone: ( ) _____

Email: _____

PAYMENT INFORMATION:

Credit Card #: _____ Exp. Date: /

Membership: $ _____ Additional Donation: $ _____ Total: $ _____ Check #: _____

MICHEL & ASSOCIATES, P.C.
Attorneys at Law

Helping Firearms Owners, Businesses, Ranges and Clubs Nationwide

FIREARMS | ENVIRONMENTAL | LAND USE | CIVIL RIGHTS ADVOCACY
LABOR & EMPLOYMENT | CIVIL LITIGATION | CRIMINAL DEFENSE

LEGAL *FIREPOWER*

- Civil Litigation
- Restoration of Gun Rights
- Gun Seizures & Returns
- Inventory Cataloging
- Restraining Order Removal
- Criminal Defense
- Hunter & Hunting Protection
- Regulatory Compliance Checks
- Governmental Licensing & Permits
- Range Protection & Development
- Range Environmental Issues
- Explosives & Destructive Devices
- Entertainment Industry Props
- & Much More

Michel & Associates, P.C.
180 East Ocean Boulevard, Suite 200
Long Beach, California 90802
(562) 216-4444
www.michellawyers.com

Free Gun Law Info
www.calgunlaws.com

Michel & Associates, P.C. is a full-service law firm representing businesses throughout the country. Owner C.D. "Chuck" Michel leads a team of over a dozen highly qualified and experienced attorneys with extensive experience in a variety of legal specialties. The firm has been litigating civil and criminal firearm cases since 1991.

Some law firms undermine your right to keep and bear arms by providing *pro bono* legal services to politicians who would deprive you of your Second Amendment rights. This *pro bono* work is subsidized through the legal fees paid by business clients. Since it was formed, **Michel & Associates has provided over $3 million worth of** *pro bono* **legal service to indigent gun owners, and to the non-profit associations that protect your rights. Shop for your legal service provider carefully so you don't inadvertently subsidize the gun ban lobby!**

As attorneys for the NRA, CRPA, firearm manufacturers, wholesalers, and retailers, the lawyers at Michel & Associates have litigated thousands of cases involving civil rights issues, including Second Amendment challenges, in both state and federal trial and appellate courts. They have represented many clients in high-profile cases that have garnered national media attention, and have appeared as spokespersons for the NRA and CRPA.

Mr. Michel is frequently quoted concerning Second Amendment rights by the major daily newspapers, and by television and radio stations. He is the author of *California Firearms Laws, A Guide to State and Federal Firearm Regulations* (available at CalGunLawsbook.com). Mr. Michel has been honored and profiled in recognition of his corporate and civil-rights work in multiple periodicals and by the NRA, which awarded him its prestigious *Defender of Justice* Award in 2013. Professor Michel also teaches *Firearms Law* and *Law Practice Management* at Chapman University School of Law.

MORE LAWYERS | MORE EXPERIENCE | MORE RELATIONSHIPS | MORE RESOURCES | MORE RESULTS

Coming Soon from Coldaw Publishing

*Gun Owner's Guide to Firearm Seizure,
Surrender, and Return*

Gun Owner's Guide to Restoring Your Gun Rights

*Gun Owner's Guide to the Law of Self-Defense & Use of
Force in California*

*Gun Owner's Guide to Police Encounters: Know All Your
Constitutional Rights & Avoid Becoming an Accidental
Criminal*

Notes

Notes

Notes

Notes

Notes

Notes

Notes

Notes

Notes

Notes

Notes

Notes

Notes

Notes